Understanding Schools:

The Foundations of Education

GARY K. CLABAUGH
LaSalle University

EDWARD G. ROZYCKI
The School District of Philadelphia

HARPER & ROW, PUBLISHERS, New York
Grand Rapids Philadelphia St. Louis
San Francisco London Singapore
Sydney Tokyo

1817

Photo credits appear at the back of the book on page C1, following the appendixes.

Sponsoring Editor: Alan McClare
Project Coordination: Publishing Synthesis, Ltd.
Text and Cover Design: Delgado Design, Inc.
Cover Coordinator: Kathie Vaccaro
Art Direction: Kathie Vaccaro
Photo Research: Inge King
Production: Beth Maglione

Library of Congress Cataloging-in-Publication Data
Clabaugh, Gary K.
    Understanding schooling: the foundations of education/Gary K.
Clabaugh, Edward G. Rozycki.
        p.   cm.
    Includes bibliographical references.
    ISBN 0-06-041318-2
    1. Education—Study and teaching—United States.   2. Education—
History.   3. Education—United States—History.   4. Educational
sociology.   I. Rozycki, Edward G.   II. Title.
LB17.C49   1990   89-77201
370'.973—dc20   CIP

90 91 92 93   9 8 7 6 5 4 3 2 1

Contents

Some of the most telling criticisms and evaluations of schooling's purposes and practices have come from foundations scholars. To make certain that *Understanding Schools* reflects this tradition of influential and useful scholarship, we relied heavily on recent work in the field. Our writing was also guided by the standards of the Council of Learned Societies in Education. Intended to define the nature of foundations as a field, these standards stress that foundational studies must:

- Promote analyses of the meaning, intent and effects of educational institutions, including schools.
- Encourage students to develop their own value position regarding education on the basis of critical study
- Promote critical understanding of educational thought and practice, and of the decisions and events which have shaped them, in their various contexts.
- Encourage the development of policy making perspectives and skills in searching for resolutions to educational problems and issues.

Following these standards helped us make certain that *Understanding Schools* provides students with information and techniques which, with your help, encourage an articulate point of view that looks beyond the walls of the schools, is guided by reason rather than rhetoric, and moves well beyond an unexamined personal experience of schooling.

We have also included many special features which make the book more accessible to students and handier for you. Specifically, we:

- Provide analytic techniques of broad applicability
- Place facts and events in the context of social processes, institutions and ideas
- Furnish competing accounts and explanations for school and social realities
- Incorporate unifying themes and imagistic analysis using common images of the school
- Supply over two hundred learning enhancing illustrations, tables and graphs
- Include more than one hundred interesting and provocative photos
- Furnish a powerful instructor's manual that includes, among other things, answers to the end of chapter discussion questions, lead-in questions which direct student reading, suggested learning activities, transparency masters and the customary test questions. (This manual is particularly useful for those teaching the course without formal training in the field.)

The text treats numerous topics of contemporary interest. In addition to developing the educational implications of drugs, child abuse, gangs, teenage pregnancy, sexism, racism, AIDS and the like; we also provide:

- Conflict and negotiation theory
- Organization and institutionalization theory
- Procedures for the analysis of educational policy statements
- Techniques for evaluating the feasibility of educational programs and the rationality of educational interventions
- A continuing and in-depth focus on the problems of schooling consensus in a pluralistic society

Many reviewers have contributed to the development of this book and we thank them for their conscientious criticism and helpful comments:

Morris L. Anderson, Wayne State College
William Cutler, Temple University
Joseph L. DeVitis, S.U.N.Y.— Binghamton
Michael S. Katz, San Jose State University
Christopher Lucas, University of Missouri—Columbia
C.J.B. Macmillan, Florida State University
Michael Oliker, Loyola University of Chicago
Lita L. Schwartz, Pennsylvania State University
Thomas Skrytic, University of Kansas
Timothy Smith, Hofstra University
Janice Streitmatter, University of Arizona

G. K. C.
E. G. R.

This text in the foundations of education is designed to help you gain the competence based on knowledge that is the distinctive characteristic of a learned professional. Only when you have learned to think clearly and systematically about educational issues can you act with the integrity that comes from knowing what you are doing. The alternative is to accept standard formulations from others and simply do what you are told. And that is hardly ethical when you are dealing with the lives of children and the future of our nation.

The foundations tradition offers an approach to knowledge that is very distinct from the single-discipline approach. Using the interpretative perspectives of a variety of disciplines to examine and explain the educational process, it provides three major perspectives:

- The interpretive perspective—using theories and resources developed within the humanities and the social and behavioral sciences, foundational studies promote analyses of the meaning, intent and effects of educational institutions, including schools
- The normative perspective—foundational studies encourages the development of value positions regarding education on the basis of critical study and reflection.
- The critical perspective—foundational studies promotes understanding of the inevitable presence of normative influences in educational thought and practice. It also encourages the development of policy making perspectives and skills in searching for resolutions to educational problems and issues.

You will have no difficulty in finding these perspectives throughout this text. They were the guidelines within which our writing was accomplished.

We could have offered a celebrationist approach, stressing only the wonderful things that educators can accomplish. But this would have encouraged a superficial understanding of the relationship of school and social realities while simultaneously discouraging critical inquiry. Worse, it would have promoted unrealistic expectations which ultimately interfere with effective teaching.

Foundational studies takes you beyond your own impressions and feelings about school, increases your knowledge and enlarges your arsenal of intellectual techniques. Having accomplished this you will be able to move beyond unexamined personal experience to interpret situations and determine courses of action with a subtlety and competence which will make you clearly distinguishable from the untrained layperson. In short, you will be on your way to becoming a true professional.

G. K. C.
E. G. R.

Framing the Inquiry

The "Interesting" Enterprise

. . . When we think we see with the naked eye, we are only oblivious of the particular spectacles we wear. We become conscious of our own conceptual commitments by exploring alternative ways of structuring the world. These may treat lightly things we esteem; yet to see the world organized according to a different order of importance is to discover something new about men and the possible conceptual worlds they create to inhabit and the kinds of satisfaction and fulfillment they can achieve.

— *S.I. Benn*[1]

---

[1]Stanley I. Benn, "Nature of Political Philosophy," *The Encyclopedia of Philosophy,* Vol. 6 (New York: Macmillan, 1967), p. 391.

Daily, educators are confronted with decisions that would try the wisdom of Solomon and the patience of Job. They are called on routinely to judge the future prospects, educability, and corrigibility of students. They are asked to concern themselves with social problems such as drug and child abuse, racism, and national productivity. Their very careers may depend upon influences that have little or nothing to do with their success at getting children to learn. Yet they are seldom prepared for such burdens in their professional training and rarely have the time on the job for discussion of principles upon which relevant decisions might intelligently rest.

ANCIENT AND BASIC PROBLEMS

There is an ancient Chinese curse that goes: "May you live in interesting times." What some people find interesting others find problematic as well. Education has always been interesting in this sense.

Even today, the human sciences are in their infancy. What knowledge we have that is relevant to running schools is small compared to the traditions and practices we have inherited through the millennia. Yet, there *is* knowledge and those who would pursue educational goals effectively cannot allow themselves the bliss of ignorance. A certain informed judgment is required to avoid the educational fads and fashions that are often—with the best of intentions—mistaken for educational progress.

There is knowledge, but basic questions persist. They remain the core concerns not only of academic researchers but, also of the casual conversations of practicing teachers and administrators. What can we teach people? How much do outside influences determine what they can learn? What is worthwhile learning? What is the best way to go about teaching it? Are some people uneducable? Why study this, or that? Do school routines promote or impede learning? What can we do for the handicapped, the addicted, the distracted, the uninterested? What is an education supposed to be?

In Chapter 1 we begin the framing of our inquiry with an apparent paradox. Large numbers of people agree that huge amounts of money be spent on schooling. Almost all believe that the purpose of schooling is education. But there is little, if any, agreement as to what education is.

NEEDED: PRACTICAL JUDGMENT

Educators are willy-nilly called on to exercise three often conflicting roles: moral example, technologist, and politician. As moral examples to children, they are urged to act in a manner worthy of emulation. As pedagogical technicians, they are expected to be efficient in their pursuit of student achievement. And as politicians they are called on to be skillful in exercising that unfairly maligned art of reconciling disparate ends to common means. Good intentions, love of children, faith, and dedication are not enough. Neither is intellectual brilliance or knowledge of subject enough. Insufficient also is a knack for wheeling and dealing for school resources. Educators must aspire to develop a practical judgment that incorporates ethical, technical, and political expertise.

Chapter 2 frames our inquiry with images of the school as a moral forum, a productive enterprise, and a political "marketplace": temple, factory, and town meeting. Throughout the book, the interplay of these images provides a practical understanding of what schooling is.

CONFLICTS

Conflict occurs when one course of action impedes another. Conflict cannot be avoided. The most intimate, long-term relationships are not without it. What matters is how it is handled. The problems and controversies about schools so often detailed in the daily papers are symptoms of conflict. However, conflict is not a disease and should not be considered as such. In Chapter 3 we develop an approach to dealing with conflict that substantially follows widely accepted negotiation theories. Conflicts are opportunities for negotiation. But a variety of factors influences whether they ever reach that stage.

We explain throughout the book that education is not schooling. This premise sets the stage for understanding how it is that the pursuit of various educational ideals may be in conflict with and either helped or hindered by that social structure called the school.

FRONTIERS

Educators work up against the frontiers of human knowledge. They are practitioners on the boundaries of uncertainty. It is their faith and their fear that what they do has consequences beyond the moment of classroom and school. For those who undertake to inform their practice with the best we have in research and critical educational thinking, the profession is constantly challenging and self-renewing. Burnout is but one symptom of ignorance and despair.

These first four chapters constitute a foundation for the rest of the book. We believe it is not enough to present a variety of concerns, facts, and theories. To develop needed practical judgment, an educator must have at his or her disposal a variety of approaches and conceptual frameworks. These should enable anyone interested in education and schooling to get at pertinent concerns and identify possible techniques for dealing with them. A book cannot substitute for experience. But it can provide the structure that makes that experience amenable to the development of intelligent practice.

AMERICAN SCHOOLING: REALITIES and EXPECTATIONS

Chapter 1

There was a time in American history when schools played little or no role in the life of the average citizen. Today, nearly one out of every four U.S. citizens is enrolled in the nation's schools and colleges. In 1990, the total amounted to a projected 58.6 million Americans.[1] There were millions more, not counted, who were enrolled in training programs in business, industry, government, and so forth.

Although private schools were a significant part of this picture, public schooling was far more important in terms of numbers. The following graphs compare national enrollments in public and private schooling both at the elementary/secondary level, and higher education. The importance of the public elementary and secondary level is clearly indicated in Figure 1.1.

We can see the greater importance of private education in the higher education category by comparing Figure 1.1 with Figure 1.2. The actual importance of private higher education may be even greater than is suggested by the graph because many of the nation's most prestigious colleges and universities are private.

EDUBUSINESS

School attendance of 56.6 million Americans means that schooling is one of the biggest businesses in the nation. It involves vast sums of money and generates millions of jobs.

---

[1]These figures are based on projections of the U.S. Department of Education, Center for Educational Statistics, as published in *Digest of Education Statistics, 1988.*

Figure 1.1

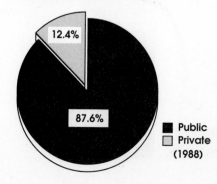

ELEMENTARY AND SECONDARY ENROLLMENT BY TYPE

Figure 1.2

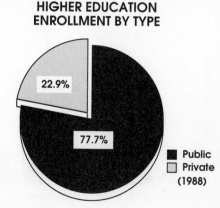

HIGHER EDUCATION ENROLLMENT BY TYPE

Source: National Center for Education Statistics

Money

Counting expenditures for all types of formal education, including the training done by business, industry, health care institutions, and the like, the 1987 total came to nearly $0.5 trillion. This makes it one of the most expensive undertakings in the nation.

The bill for public elementary and secondary schooling came to $170 billion in 1987—a figure identical to the Gross National Product of Mexico. Publicly financed colleges and universities cost an additional $57 billion. Private schooling of all types, including higher education, added $52.1 billion more.[2] Altogether, public and private elementary, secondary, and higher education cost $278.8 billion.[3] Corporate training added a remarkable $210 billion to that total.[4] (See Figure 1.3.)

The enormous size of this expenditure is difficult to comprehend. At the rate of one dollar per second, 12 hours a day, seven days a week, it would take over 15, 000 years just to count it. And we spend more every year.

Jobs

More than half of the money spent on schooling goes for salaries, and $278.8 billion generates a lot of jobs. In 1986–1987, a total of 2.8 million Americans

---

[2]The total bill for all college and university education came to $109 billion in 1987. About half of those dollars were raised by taxes. Students paid only one third of the total through fees and tuition. The remainder came from endowments and contributions.

[3]Data were obtained from the U.S. Department of Education, Office of Educational Research and Improvement.

[4]Thomas Kean, "Partners for Today and Tomorrow," *Education and Society*, Vol. 1, No. 3 (Fall 1988), p. 9.

Figure 1.3

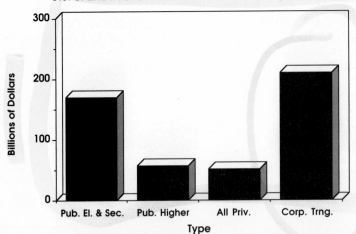

U.S. SPENDING ON FORMAL EDUCATION (ALL TYPES)

Billions of Dollars

Type

Pub. El. & Sec.   Pub. Higher   All Priv.   Corp. Trng.

Source: 1987 Data, U.S. Department of Education

were employed as preschool, elementary, and secondary school teachers. (About 85% of them worked in public schools.) Counting all employees, professional and nonprofessional, schools generated approximately 7.9 percent of all the employment in the nation (see Figure 1.4).[5]

Many other jobs are dependent on schooling and training. Employment by the $1.5 billion a year textbook industry, by manufacturers of audiovisual equipment, by firms producing instructional materials, by the fabricators of the nation's fleet of more than 400,000 school buses, and many similar ventures would not exist were it not for the nation's schools.

Many additional jobs are created by the corporate training industry.[6] Public health services, the military, law enforcement, and similar organizations create still more educational employment. All things considered, formal education of every type (training as well as schooling) is one of the biggest sources of employment in the nation. As a matter of fact, all aspects of edubusiness accounts for at least 10 percent of all the employment in the nation.[7] And, as we can see from Figure 1.5, even if we count only the jobs directly involved in the actual educational process, eliminating school bus drivers, cafeteria cooks, school custodians, and the like, we are still talking about 7.41 percent of all the jobs in the nation.

---

[5]Arthur Applegate et al., "Learning to Be Literate in America," *The National Assessment of Educational Progress, The Nation's Report Card* (Princeton, N.J.: Educational Testing Service, 1987).
[6]Because corporate training is often done on a part-time basis by employees with other responsibilities, no reliable employment figures are available. Clearly, it involves millions of persons.
[7]This estimate was produced for the authors by employees of the Bureau of Labor Statistics of the U.S. Department of Labor during an interview in April 1988.

Figure 1.4 *Figure 1.5*

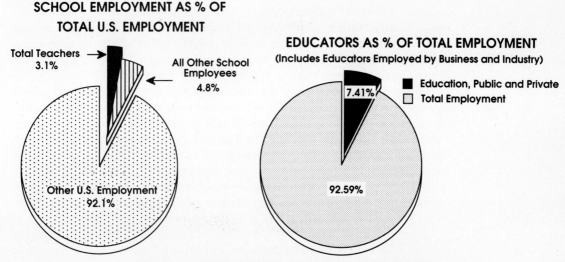

SCHOOL EMPLOYMENT AS % OF TOTAL U.S. EMPLOYMENT

Total Teachers 3.1%

All Other School Employees 4.8%

Other U.S. Employment 92.1%

EDUCATORS AS % OF TOTAL EMPLOYMENT
(Includes Educators Employed by Business and Industry)

■ Education, Public and Private
▫ Total Employment

7.41%

92.59%

Source: Unpublished 1986 Data from Bureau of Labor Statistics

Schools support other industries.

Schooling occurs in many settings.

Some Other Comparisons

We can better appreciate the true extent of the nation's edubusiness by means of some additional comparisons. For example, schooling is far and away the biggest single source of government employment. All levels of government had more than 4 million instructional employees in 1985. Governmental health and hospital employees were second, totaling 1.7 million. Civilian defense employees were third at 1.1 million. (See Figure 1.6.)

International comparisons are also revealing. When we measure school spending as a percentage of Gross National Product (GNP), the United States is exceeded by only two nations—Canada and the Netherlands. Even Japan, which lacks natural resources and capitalizes on its human resources instead, does not commit as great a percentage of its GNP to schooling as does the United States. It is informative to note, however, that Japanese teachers are paid 40 percent more than American teachers relative to national incomes. Perhaps that is why Japan has five times as many applicants as teacher openings. We shall read more on this in a later chapter.

Another way of measuring U.S. commitment to schooling is to compare government expenditures by category. In Figure 1.7 we see that government spending on schools is exceeded only by that on health care and defense.

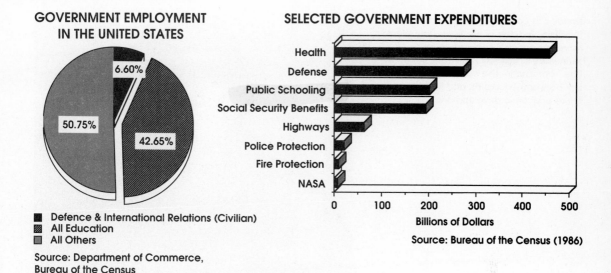

GOVERNMENT EMPLOYMENT
IN THE UNITED STATES

6.60%

50.75%

42.65%

■ Defence & International Relations (Civilian)
▨ All Education
▨ All Others

Source: Department of Commerce,
Bureau of the Census

Figure 1.6

SELECTED GOVERNMENT EXPENDITURES

Health
Defense
Public Schooling
Social Security Benefits
Highways
Police Protection
Fire Protection
NASA

0   100   200   300   400   500

Billions of Dollars

Source: Bureau of the Census (1986)

Figure 1.7

SCHOOLING AND THE ECONOMY

Important as schooling is today, the changing American economy will make it even more important in the future. Jobs requiring low skill levels are moving overseas or becoming automated. Fewer and fewer jobs are available in manufacturing. Highly technical employment, particularly in personal and business services, requires far greater skills than those required of industrial workers and promises to take their place as the mainstay of the economy. As industrial theorist Peter Drucker points out, it is no longer possible for a worker to make an upper middle class living except through knowledge.[8]

Schooling and Economic Growth

The Presidential Commission on Excellence in Education noted: "Knowledge, learning, information, and skilled intelligence are the new raw materials of international commerce and are today spreading throughout the world as vigorously as miracle drugs, synthetic fertilizer and blue jeans did earlier.... Learning is the indispensable investment for success in the 'information age' we are entering."[9]

Belatedly, under the pressure of foreign competition, many Americans are now realizing that schooling affects the overall quality and productivity of the nation's businesses and this, in turn, affects our collective standard of living

---

[8]Peter Drucker, Interview, *U. S. News & World Report,* February 2, 1987.
[9]*A Nation at Risk: The Imperative for Educational Reform* (Washington, D.C.: The National Commission on Excellence in Education, U.S. Department of Education, 1983), p. 7.

Dressed in costume to make a point about terrorism, Teacher of the Year, Terry Weeks serves as national spokesman for Tennessee's "Schools That Work, Jobs That Pay," campaign. This campaign stresses the link between education and the state's future economic development.

THIS MAN MAKES EDUCATION SERIOUS BUSINESS IN TENNESSEE.

relative to other nations.[10] Similarly, some state and local officials are beginning to understand that good schools are fundamental to prosperity.

Current demographic trends suggest that we will have to pay even more attention to this matter in the future because the nation has a shrinking talent pool from which to choose. In the first place, there just are not as many young people these days. In addition, the National Assessment of Educational Progress notes that more of that pool will be from those minority populations who traditionally have been the least successful in school.[11]

Business leaders find such a prospect alarming. One out of three major corporations must already provide new workers with basic reading, writing, and arithmetic courses at a cost of approximately $2 billion.[12] And many of those requiring remedial training are high school graduates. Business has a stake in ensuring that as many people as possible have these skills before they are hired.

---

[10]Council of Chief State School Officers, "Education and the Economy," *Position Paper and Recommendations for Action,* November 1986, Washington, D.C., p. 1.
[11]Arthur Applebee et al., "Learning to be Literate in America," *The National Assessment of Educational Progress, The Nation's Report Card* (Princeton, N.J.: Educational Testing Service, 1987).
[12]Applebee, op. cit., p. 3.

Broader Issues

There are those who question the assumption that our schools should concentrate on providing capable employees for corporations. These experts insist that there are far broader and more fundamental issues that must be dealt with.

We will learn in Chapter 7, for example, that some economists are convinced that economic development will not really improve the chances that students from lower social backgrounds will find decent jobs in the future. These experts claim that *if* we can improve educational outcomes for these students it will merely enable them to remain occupationally in the same situation as their parents, at the bottom of a segmented labor system.[13]

There are also very definite limits to economic growth. The earth's irreplaceable natural resources are being used up at a rate the planet cannot sustain, and the earth's population will likely double within the next 40 years.[14] Such considerations suggest that educators must be concerned with broader issues such as the responsible use of nonrenewable resources and preserving the delicate balance of our planet's ecosystem.

There are also matters relating to values that need to be considered. If, for example, our schools turn out the world's most capable scientists, engineers, and technicians while neglecting to address the need for moral and ethical development it might be humanity's last mistake.

A SHALLOW CONSENSUS

Given the nation's remarkable expenditures on schools, the laws that compel children to attend them, and schooling's ever increasing importance, it is easy to overlook the fact that although we agree that schooling is good, there is no end to the different opinions available regarding what it ought to amount to. There is a bewildering diversity of opinion concerning both *what* should be taught and *how* that instruction should be accomplished which reflects our nation's remarkable and exciting pluralism.

To be sure, there is some measure of common commitment to individual freedom and perhaps even equality of opportunity to which most Americans subscribe. Ultimately, however, America's enormous edubusiness is promoted and sustained by a series of delicate compromises and a frequent disregard of just how much we really disagree. In the next chapter we examine this process and see how it works.

Aristotle's View

Given the treasure and time devoted to schooling, Americans' failure to agree about the meaning and purpose of education is surprising, but not without

---

[13]Alan DeYoung, *Economics and American Education* (New York: Longman, 1989), p. 176.
[14]E. F. Schumacher, *Small Is Beautiful: Economics As If People Mattered* (New York: Harper & Row, 1973).

precedent. In fact, if we survey our Western intellectual heritage we discover a long history of disagreement regarding the nature and purpose of education and schooling that can be traced back to the ancient Greeks. Three hundred and fifty years before the birth of Christ, for example, Aristotle observed:

> That education should be regulated by law and should be an affair of state is not to be denied, but what should be the character of this public education, and how young persons should be educated, are questions which remain to be considered. As things are, there is disagreement about the subjects. For mankind are by no means agreed about the things to be taught, whether we look to virtue or the best life. Neither is it clear whether education is more concerned with intellectual or moral virtue. The existing practice is perplexing; no one knows on what principle we should proceed— should the useful in life, or should virtue, or should the higher knowledge, be the aim of our training; all three opinions have been entertained. Again, about the means, there is no agreement; for different persons, starting with different ideas about the nature of virtue, naturally disagree about the practice of it.[15]

The ancient conflicts about education noted by Aristotle included disputes about both the ends education pursues and the means necessary to achieve them. For example, should schools stress academics or morality and, once that is decided, what method of instruction should be used? But these disputes really went beyond such boundaries. Ultimately they had to do with the meaning and purpose of life itself. In Chapter 2 we will see that such disputes define the very nature of our pluralistic society.

Competing Definitions

Perhaps these conflicts explain why the history of humanity contains so many different attempts to define education. Each attempt at definition has reflected its author's underlying assumptions about the good, the true, and the beautiful.

Consider the following quotations regarding education and see if you can identify the underlying assumptions that gave them birth.

Education in virtue . . . which makes a man eagerly pursue the ideal perfection of citizenship, and teaches how to rightly rule and obey, this is the only education . . . which deserves the name.

————— *Plato (c. 427–347 B.C.), Greek philosopher and seminal thinker*

---

[15] Aristotle, *Politics,* Book VIII.

The supreme end of education is expert discernment in all things—the power to tell the good from the bad, the genuine from the counterfeit, and to prefer the good and the genuine rather than the bad and the counterfeit.

———————— *Samuel Johnson (1709–1784), English lexicographer, essayist, and critic*

moral issue

Education is the instruction of the intellect in the laws of nature.

———————— *Thomas Huxley (1825–1895), English naturalist who helped pioneer evolutionary theory*

There can be no true education which is not wholly directed to man's last end, . . . there can be no ideally perfect education which is not Christian education.

———————— *Pius XI (1857–1939), Pope of the Roman Catholic Church from 1922 to 1939*

Education proceeds by the participation of the individual in the social consciousness of the race. This process begins unconsciously at birth, and is continually shaping the individual's powers, saturating his accomplishments, forming his habits, training his ideas, and arousing his feelings and emotions. . . . The most formal and technical education in the world cannot safely depart from this general process. It can only organize it or differentiate it in some particular direction.

———————— *John Dewey (1859–1952), American philosopher and educator*

Education is the acquisition of the art of the utilization of knowledge. . . . There is only one subject-matter for education, and that is Life in all its manifestations.

———————— *Alfred North Whitehead (1861–1947), English philosopher and mathematician*

Education is a weapon whose effect depends on who holds it in his hands and who is struck with it.

———————— *Joseph Stalin (1879–1953), Soviet dictator*

The aim of education is to guide man in the evolving dynamism through which he shapes himself as a human person—armed with knowledge, strength of judgement and moral virtues—while at the same time conveying to him the spiritual heritage of the nation and the civilization in which he is involved, and preserving in this way the centuries-old achievements of generations.

———————— *Jacques Maritain (1882–1973), French philosopher and essayist*

These quotations, a small sampling of the many available, illustrate fundamental disagreements about the nature of "education." The fact that they are international in origin should not cause us to think that purely American definitions would fare much better. America is one of the most pluralistic societies on earth. As a consequence there is an amazing diversity of opinion regarding the good life that readily translates into conflicts and controversies about education and schooling.

Significant Choices Make Significant Controversies

Of course, there is widespread agreement both here and elsewhere that, whatever else a proper education turns out to be, schooling is clearly about the acquisition of basic academic skills such as reading, writing, and arithmetic. Unfortunately, the utility of this elemental agreement is limited by the fact that there is virtually no agreement regarding the ends these basic skills should serve.

The implications of all this disagreement for those who are thinking about careers in the nation's schools are fully developed elsewhere. For now it is enough to observe that no matter what choices we make regarding our schools, if they are significant choices they are likely to create significant controversies.

Hopes and Doubts

Our enormous expenditure of time, treasure, and human resources, much of it spent on unenthusiastic recipients, is not accomplished without doubts or controversy. In fact, the nation's schools are the focus of profound concerns. As the United States loses ground in international economic competition some have come to see our schools as both a cause and potential cure for this threat to national prosperity; and as the United States grapples with declining productivity, unemployment, crime, drug abuse, teenage pregnancy, poverty, and similar stubborn problems, attention also focuses on the schools. Many Americans ask what our educators are doing, or failing to do, to deal with these problems. They want to know why they still plague us when we spend well over $200 billion in taxes on public schooling every year.

The reason the public looks to our schools for solution is that many see them as the best hope for dealing with America's most critical problems. Ironically, however, our schools not only offer hope of solution, but also reflect the larger America that sustains these problems. It is for this reason that educators too are daily confronted by the subtlety and persistence of the nation's most elemental problems. For instance, while educators struggle to eradicate poverty or drug abuse, they are hindered in their work by these very same problems. Similarly, the educational consequences of teenage pregnancy, crime, and unemployment are many and troubling.

Conventional wisdom has it that more and better schooling is the key to more desirable behavior and a more abundant life; but careful scholarship reveals that it is more complicated than that. Some immigrant groups such as the Jews, Japanese, and Chinese, for example, are noted for quickly achieving relative prosperity, and it is widely believed that they used schools to achieve this advantage. But research shows that Japanese- and Chinese-American success in school has tended to come to the second generation following their parents' initial success in business. So for these groups the schools confirmed advantages more than they created them.[16]

Elsewhere we learn of the profound educational importance of family matters that are well underway before youngsters reach school and that continue daily after schooling is begun. For example, about one-third of all black children and one half of all Puerto Rican children are born to women who never reached the ninth grade.[17] Not only are these women likely to be poor, they are also likely to be ill-equipped to provide their children with the role modeling or orientation that encourages success in the essentially middle class settings of our schools. Given this consideration, it is hardly surprising to learn that in the 1984–1985 school year one-third of all blacks and Hispanics received failing grades in at least one major academic subject. Has changed 1995.

Of course, it is not only minorities who fail to accomplish all that is expected of them in school. A recent federal study concluded that most American youths write so poorly they cannot make themselves understood. The study claimed that only one out of four precollege students writes well enough to succeed in later studies or their careers.[18] Such basic deficiencies appear to be so widespread that the Presidential Commission on Excellence in Education claimed that for the first time in American history the younger generation may not be as well educated as their parents. Given the complex nature of modern life and the ever growing importance of science and technology, such a trend is troublesome.

Types of Benefits

> There is a growing national consensus that our future depends upon public education.
>
> ——————— *Dr. Ernest L. Boyer, former U.S.*
> *Commissioner of Education*

Convinced that schooling pays off in a lot of ways, many of us are concerned about the quality of American schooling because we are convinced that any serious deficiencies threaten the loss of present or future benefits. For ex-

---

[16]Thomas Sowell, *Ethnic America* (New York: Basic Books, 1981), p. 61.
[17]Thomas Sowell, *The Economics of Politics and Race* (New York: William Morrow), 1983.
[18]*The National Assessment of Educational Progress, 1984* (Princeton, N.J.: Educational Testing Service, under a grant from the Department of Education).

ample, maintaining a democratic society as well as one of the world's highest standards of living seems to most of us to be inextricably entangled with the quality of the nation's schools. In the paragraphs that follow we suggest several ways of understanding what kinds of benefits schools deliver. These will help frame the inquiry and provide students with some tools for developing more informed opinions.

Absolute and Positional Benefits

One of the most fundamental distinctions one can make with respect to school benefits is that they range along a continuum from absolute to positional.

Absolute benefits retain their value no matter how many people acquire them. For instance, hugs can be very beneficial, and their value does not diminish if a lot of people get them. Therefore, a hug can be an absolute benefit. Similarly, in a school setting, it does not matter if teachers can get ten or a thousand youngsters to be more knowledgeable. To the extent that knowledge itself is a benefit, that benefit is undiminished by the number of children who enjoy it. Likewise, if an art teacher is able to get every student in both the first and second grades in his or her school to enjoy drawing and painting, the benefit the students derive from these activities is not diminished because it is widely shared.

Positional benefits are very different. They lose their value as more people acquire them. For example, gold is valuable, in part, because it is scarce. If it were found in boulder form in every farmer's field it would be more nuisance than precious. In school "A's" are positional benefits. If everyone had them on their report cards their value would be reduced to nothing by grade inflation. Licenses to practice medicine are also positional benefits. If everyone had one they would be nearly worthless.

If this distinction between positional and absolute benefits seems far removed from practical concerns, consider this. Presently, there are many efforts to get youngsters to stay in school so that they will be able to get a job. In most states these efforts take the form of attempts at persuasion through posters, public service advertising, and the like. In some states, like West Virginia, however, laws have been codified that stipulate that if you drop out of school you lose your drivers license until you are 18.

It seems likely that there are many folks who imagine that if every youngster were to stay in school we would be well on the way to having unemployment licked. But here is where our positional-absolute benefit distinction becomes eminently practical. Paradoxically, if these efforts to reduce the dropout rate to near zero were successful, it would cancel out almost all of the job-getting advantages that having a high school diploma bestows. It is beneficial in job seeking primarily because everyone does not have one. If they did, some other way of sorting through job applicants would be found. Possibly, two years of college would become the new cutoff point.

We see, then, that a high school diploma is a positional benefit. So is a college diploma or a teachers certificate, or even money. If there were

Figure 1.8   **ABSOLUTE AND POSITIONAL BENEFITS**

an unlimited and readily obtainable supply of any of these, they would be worthless.

That teachers certificates are positional benefits should be of supreme interest to aspiring educators. The fact that the more of them there are the less they are worth is of more than theoretical interest to someone who is paying thousands of dollars and years of effort to get one. For instance, to deal with a shortage of qualified teachers 23 states have adopted "alternative," and easier, routes to certification. By increasing the availability of the certificates in this way, these programs inevitably cheapen the certificate's value. In turn, state and local authorities no longer have to pay as much to staff vacant positions and teaching, in the long run, becomes a less well-paid occupation.[19] Of course, the alternative would be to raise pay and improve working conditions sufficiently to attract more certification candidates in the first place. That too would deal with the shortage.

The distinction between absolute and positional benefits is reasonably obvious once it is pointed out (see Figure 1.8). But it is surprising how many people in positions of great responsibility seem to miss the point entirely.

Divisible and Indivisible Benefits

Benefits also occur along a continuum from the divisible to the indivisible. **Divisible benefits** are those that some people can enjoy without sharing them with others. A candy bar, a lovely house, a new Jaguar automobile, a high school diploma are all divisible benefits. **Indivisible benefits,** on the other hand, are those benefits that must be enjoyed by all if they are to be enjoyed by any.

National defense is a good example. If a "Star Wars" defense really could be devised that afforded absolute protection from nuclear missiles, if there were an attack, that benefit would extend to everyone in the United States, provided the system actually worked. It would be impractical to have it otherwise. On an even broader scale, the preservation of the earth's ozone layer

---

[19]Fred Hirsch carefully develops the absolute/positional benefit phenomena in *Social Limits to Growth* (Cambridge, Mass.: Harvard U. Press, 1976). Thomas Green uses similar considerations to detail educational benefits in *Predicting the Behavior of the Educational System* (Syracuse, N.Y.: Syracuse U. Press, 1980).

Figure 1.9

DIVISIBLE AND INDIVISIBLE BENEFITS

will benefit everyone on the planet. This makes it an even more highly indivisible benefit than national defense.

Figure 1.9 illustrates how we can arrange divisible/indivisible benefits on a continuum. Notice that we have classified equality and justice as indivisible benefits, for, if some citizens are more equal than others, we have *in*equality. Similarly, if justice is not available to all citizens, there is *in*justice. National defense is also indicated on the chart as relatively indivisible. If U.S. defense measures deter attack, this benefit extends to all Americans. National competitiveness is placed midway between divisible and indivisible. It is so listed because improved national competitiveness tends to promote greater prosperity for MOST, but not *all* Americans. Liberty is put at the divisible end of the continuum because America's own history demonstrates that some can be free while others are enslaved. (A subtle dissection of the real effects of enslaving another might reveal that it is far more costly to the freedom of the enslaver than might first be thought.) Finally, note that benefits such as high school diploma or personal knowledge are listed as clearly divisible, because one person can enjoy them while others cannot.

Schooling conveys a mixture of both divisible and indivisible benefits. On the one hand, we can easily teach some persons to read without bothering to teach everyone. Similarly, some can earn bachelors degrees while others do without them. Clearly, these sorts of school benefits are divisible. On the other hand, if the nation is better schooled it is likely to be more prosperous and better governed; and these benefits are less divisible. Finally, if, through schooling, human beings could be convinced to be more careful with our planet, the benefits that would accrue would be indivisible.

Americans disagree about which indivisible benefits educators should promote. Some favor defense, for example, while others favor social justice. Right now, the more conservative option seems to have the upper hand. But that is subject to change.

Divisible school benefits generate special concerns about fairness or equity. What schools do for one, many Americans expect, or at least hope, they will do for everyone. These expectations for a just division of school benefits places a major burden on educators: that of trying to provide equitable treatment and ensuring that divisible benefits are distributed fairly.

Making these divisible/indivisible distinctions can focus our attention on who benefits when we make decisions relative to school policy. Take, for example, *A Nation at Risk*. The chief benefit of the scholastic excellence the Presidential Commission on Excellence in Education is promoting in this report is described as, " . . . improving America's ability to compete in world markets."

At first glance this looks like an indivisible benefit. Surely all Americans would gain from improving our economic competitiveness relative to other nations. But will they? Can we be sure that the advantages will accrue equally to all Americans regardless of status? By this we do not mean benefits that supposedly "trickle down," but *direct* benefits.

Clearly, business leaders are not the only Americans who will gain if the nation's schools train more young people to read, write, compute, and reason with greater excellence. As we saw earlier in the chapter, most of us have some stake in our national capacity for meeting foreign competition. This is one reason why, though we disagree about the details, we still plan to spend even more of our resources on schools.

Unfortunately, however, because academic talent and determination to excel are distributed unevenly, the drive for academic excellence is going to benefit some while it inflicts costs on others. For example, it seems reasonable to conclude that mentally retarded youngsters will enjoy little immediate gain. Similarly, as long as the wealth of the United States is distributed as unevenly as it is, some Americans have a great deal more to gain from improved international competitiveness than do others. We will learn in Chapter 7, for example, that the top 20 percent of the population of the United States owns or controls three-quarters of all the wealth in the nation. The remaining 80 percent share the other quarter, with the bottom 20 percent having less than 0.2 percent of the wealth to divide among them.[20]

Given this distribution of wealth, it is not difficult to appreciate who is likely to benefit most from improved American competitiveness. It is also likely that a less advantaged group of Americans will pay a disproportionate share of the costs. Suppose, for example, excellence in education ultimately permits us to produce computers that are clearly superior to those of any other nation in the world. Suppose, further, that in order to sell them it still might be necessary to bargain with other nations relative to trade concessions. If we want to sell these computers in Brazil, for instance, U.S. officials might have to drop import restrictions on Brazilian-made shoes in return for their doing the same for our computers. Our computer sales would then improve, and well-educated Americans working in the computer industry would benefit. Unfortunately, less well-educated shoe factory workers would be put out of work.

The point of this little excursion into economics is to point out that the benefits from improved national competitiveness are *divisible,* not indivisible. In addition, given the present distribution of wealth, it is quite reasonable to think that when and if these benefits are realized, they will be divided very unequally. Thus our seemingly theoretical distinction between divisible and indivisible benefits permits an eminently practical insight that should at least be considered before we rush toward educational "excellence" in order to improve our international competitiveness.

---

[20]Lester Thurow, *Generating Inequality* (New York: Basic Books, 1975).

Indeed, it may well be wise to make the divisible/indivisible distinction in all educational policy debates where questions of benefit are involved. We may be thought impertinent if we do, but that is only because it is such a very powerful distinction.

The Burden of Individual Hopes

Predictably, nearly everyone is particularly interested in the divisible benefits that they think their own children need. No matter how compelling the public rhetoric about the indivisible benefits our schools should pursue, one suspects that this sort of highly divisible benefit is at the heart of why the United States has such an amazing commitment to the process of schooling.

Certainly many of us are concerned about such apparently indivisible benefits as improving our national competitiveness or promoting economic growth. But the benefits we want most turn out to be those extremely personal and highly divisible things that individual parents hope will make life kinder and gentler for their children.

Such expectations place an immense burden on the school. But we have little choice. This particular sort of divisible expectation is the measure of our love for our children. Thus, we begin to understand why, despite a basic inability to agree about what schools should do or how they should do it, Americans are generally in favor of investing still more time and treasure in the process.

TOWARD A DEEPER UNDERSTANDING OF OUR EXPECTATIONS FOR SCHOOLING

Each of us has his or her own idea of the benefits that schooling should produce. In fact, each of us has an entire constellation of expectations. But these expectations are not totally individual. Patterns can be detected that help us understand how they work to influence what goes on in schools. In what follows we develop these considerations.

At the simplest level, for example, we could look at what students want relative to what teachers want. We can readily imagine that what would satisfy one of these constituencies might dissatisfy the other. At a more complex level we could begin to make differentiations among our categories. For instance, we might divide teachers into two classes, teachers of academics and teachers who are also coaches. We then can appreciate why the former would probably applaud raising eligibility requirements for sports, while the latter might revile the move.

Students could be similarly divided. We know, for example, that children from different social classes have different systems of values. One consequence of this is that upper and middle class youngsters see schooling as a major condition of achieving what they want from life. Lower class youngsters, on the other hand, tend to want different sorts of things, and see school as less important than luck or social connections in their achievement.[21]

If we expand these considerations to include everyone in American society who has some sort of interest in our schools, it becomes readily apparent why schooling is so controversial and so interesting. In what follows we offer an exploration of various types of school-related expectations. It is intended to frame our future inquiries, to provide a basis of comparison, and to introduce a means of understanding American schooling at a fairly sophisticated level.

Competing and Noncompeting Expectations

Some expectations about schooling cannot be realized without denying others. For one thing, resources and time are often not available for both. For instance, it might be the case that if expectations related to national defense are met, expectations relative to the special needs of individual children might suffer. After all, time and resources are finite, and if we are to pursue military supremacy through academic excellence in technical subjects certain other priorities must be sacrificed.

Proposals also compete, for what is expected from one can be contrary to what is expected from another. Their criteria of success are contradictory. In many cases, this is a harder problem to deal with than just a scarcity of time or resources.

Figure 1.10 explores a few of our competing expectations with respect to schools. Read like a mileage chart in a road map, it shows how expectations can conflict with respect to:

- **time**: not everything can be fit into the available hours;
- **resources**: money goes only so far;
- **criteria**: the success of one proposal undermines another.

Note, for example, where Improve Mathematics and Improve History & Literature intersect. We list *T* and *R* as potential conflicts. *Time* is listed because there is a limited amount of it in the school day. If we devote more of it to improving students' mathematics there will be less to devote to improving their history and literature. *Resources* are similarly finite. If we devote more of the school budget to mathematics instruction, there will be less available for history and literature.

Criteria conflicts involve those situations where, as the old saying goes, "You can't have your cake and eat it too." The line labeled "Develop Job Skills" lists four conflicts of criteria: concentrating on developing job skills using a narrow performance-oriented focus undermines efforts to improve students' understanding of pure mathematics, history, or literature. It also is incompatible with developing cultural literacy and instilling liberal arts traditions of value, which are very different sorts of endeavors. Helping At-Risk Youth could well produce similar conflicts of criteria.

---

[21]Raymond Boudon, *Education, Opportunity, and Social Inequality* (New York: Wiley, 1973), pp. 22–23.

Figure 1.10

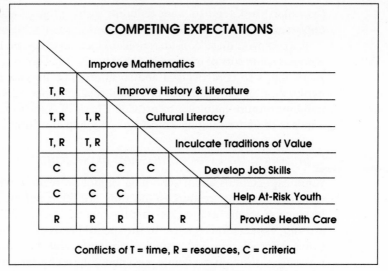

COMPETING EXPECTATIONS

	Improve Mathematics					
T, R	Improve History & Literature					
T, R	T, R	Cultural Literacy				
T, R	T, R		Inculcate Traditions of Value			
C	C	C	C	Develop Job Skills		
C	C	C			Help At-Risk Youth	
R	R	R	R	R		Provide Health Care

Conflicts of T = time, R = resources, C = criteria

Educational reformers frequently downplay or even hide these sorts of difficulties, claiming that we all can have what we want from schools. But when reforms become policy, this public posturing is replaced by hard choices. It is at this point that consensus often evaporates as various special interests try to impose their priorities to the detriment of others.

Professed and Unprofessed Expectations

If everyone were totally candid about his or her expectations for schools, the situation would still be complicated. But the fact is that candor sometimes takes second place to other considerations. For example, parents might profess that they send their child to private school because of their expectation that he or she will get a better academic education. However, their unprofessed expectation might well be that their child will not have to attend a racially integrated school. Social status, "being one up on neighbors," is another important expectation they might be reluctant to admit.

Sometimes unprofessed expectations can produce ironic, even funny educational consequences. Imagine, for example, the desperate parents of a young man who has just flunked out of his second college in as many years because he is considerably more interested in partying than in studying. Anxious to free him from such distractions the parents eagerly scan the brochures of dozens of schools before coming upon a Catholic college in rural Alabama run by a severe order of monks. In telling their friends about Junior's new school they stress how impressed they are with the beauty and solitude of the campus and with the Christian atmosphere that pervades everything. But their unexpressed expectation is that the place will be so grim and Puritanical that Junior will have little choice except to get down to work.

Of course, much to Junior's delight, it turns out that most of the young people at this school are there because of similar unprofessed parental expectations. Thus, despite the eternal vigilance of the brothers, it is a party school of extraordinary scope.

The moral of this true story is that any careful consideration of expectations relative to schools has to take unprofessed expectations into account. The fact that they are covert makes this very difficult, but it does not mean that they are unimportant. As a matter of fact, they may be the most important considerations of all.

Expectations as Expressions of Disappointment

Sometimes it is difficult for people to be aware of the full range of what they expect from schools until they find themselves disappointed over some "failure." Take, for example, the disappointment that accompanied the launching of Sputnik. Only after the Soviets were first into space did many citizens realize that one of their expectations was that our schools would provide the technical emphasis to boost supremacy in space technology.

We can imagine the bewilderment of many school authorities when they were accused of incompetence with respect to the space race. They had had no idea that such a race would even occur when, in the 1930s and 1940s, they operated the schools that were unknowingly preparing some of the nation's future space scientists. (Some, like Werner von Braun, were even educated in Germany.) After all, the experts who eventually succeeded in putting Americans on the moon were schooled when spaceflight was only a science fiction fantasy.

Educators often find expectations realized only as disappointments to be particularly unhelpful and more than a little unfair. But they do remind us of an important consideration: students will be called upon to solve problems that their teachers cannot even imagine. This consideration often escapes the attention of the general public and educational reformers alike. We hope it will no longer escape the attention of the reader.

The Costs and Benefits of Dissensus

We can hardly expect citizens of a democratic society as heterogeneous as the United States to agree about what we expect from our schools. Conflicts regarding such matters are an inevitable by-product of our freedom and diversity.

Perhaps the biggest cost of this situation is that it encourages a lack of focus and concentrated effort. For example, after completing an extensive inspection of the nation's high schools Professor Ernest Boyer observed, "After visiting high schools from coast to coast, we are left with the distinct impression that high schools lack a clear and vital mission. . . . They seem unable to put it all together."[22] Similarly, the National Commission on Excellence in Education claimed, "Secondary school curricula have been homogenized, diluted

---

[22]Ernest L. Boyer, *High School* (New York: Harper & Row, 1983), p. 64.

and diffused to the point where they no longer have a central purpose."[23]

Disagreements about which benefits schools should help us gain contributes to this situation. In attempting to meet everyone's expectations, sometimes the schools fail to satisfy anyone. For our schools to work well, Americans must carve out at least some common understandings regarding their purpose. And, because the world continually confronts us with new realities, this process must be ongoing. We can expect that these agreements will probably be temporary or, at best, durable but shallow. Our disagreements are too fundamental for anything more. Probably in most circumstances the best we can do is to agree to disagree with civility. Even this requires that we learn to balance conviction with tolerance and discretion.

Where might we gain such a skill? Thomas Jefferson offered a solution. He suggested:

> I know no safe depository of the ultimate powers of the society but the people themselves: and if we think them not enlightened enough to exercise their control with a wholesome discretion, the remedy is not to take it from them but to inform their discretion.

In other words, Jefferson's solution was to see to it that Americans were better schooled. All we have to do is come up with sufficient consensus concerning the means and ends of this schooling to ensure that it has this to offer. How do we do that? Here, Jefferson was silent.

We can see that we are no better off than were Aristotle's Athenians. We have learned that they could not agree on either the ends or the means of schooling and neither can we. What we are left with is wondering how much dissent is too much, and trying to determine how we can accomplish our goals when we often do not even agree as to what many of them should be.

Perhaps when it comes to really basic issues our disagreements are more apparent than real. For example, most of us seem to share a common commitment to individual freedom and perhaps even to equality of opportunity. Admittedly, there is not much depth to this consensus. It would be hard to get agreement on how far individual freedom should go, or how much we should do to ensure everyone equality of opportunity. But a shallow consensus may be all we really need. After all, controversy and conflict generate benefits as well as costs. By subjecting our different ideas, beliefs, and values to the fire of disagreement, for example, they are inevitably tempered and refined.

SUMMARY

1. The money and jobs involved in American edubusiness are a major factor in the nation's economy. However, the broad but shallow consensus supports

---

[23]The National Commission on Excellence in Education, *A Nation At Risk: The Imperative for Educational Reform* (Washington, D.C., Superintendent of Documents, U.S. Government Printing Office, 1985), p. 18.

the endeavor because American diversity ɪ
Schooling has become particularly vital to
possibility that broader issues, such as the
might be even more important.

2. There are competing definitions of edu
examining types of educational benefits off
ing the competing interests that are so c
various types of expectations with respect
our appreciation of the tensions and differe
school policy. In the end, however, schools carry the burden of each parent's
hopes for his or her children. This is the clearest explanation of why Americans
spend hundreds of billions of dollars on schools.

3. There are benefits, as well as the costs, to dissensus. It is sometimes overlooked that controversy and conflict can refine our truths and temper our
values.

QUESTIONS *Answer these :*

1. People in schools are not counted among the unemployed. Suppose colleges and schools turned out 50 percent of their charges onto the labor
   market. How do you think this might affect
   a. unemployment; or
   b. the demand for goods and services?
2. List industries that depend substantially on schooling for their business.
3. If public schools were replaced with private schools, how do you think
   this would affect the economy?
4. List three areas of employment for teachers other than public elementary
   or secondary schools. What percentage of total educator employment
   does each of these contribute?
5. What do you see as the advantages and disadvantages of the pursuit of
   educational excellence prescribed in *A Nation At Risk*?
6. Consider how few people work at jobs that require even algebra. Why
   then is there any need to be concerned that U.S. students do badly in
   math?
7. Speculate on what the connection between math skills and national productivity might be. Do you know of any evidence that supports your
   speculation?
8. a. Consider Figure 1.10, "Competing Expectations."
   b. List five additional things schools are expected to do.
   c. Construct a similar chart indicating whether you think these expec-
      tations will have conflicts of time, resources, or criteria.
9. List five expectations about schools that tend to remain unexpressed.
10. List five expectations about schools that tend to be expressed as disap-
    pointments.

CONSENSUS, PLURALISM, and IMAGES of the SCHOOL

Chapter 2

PREVIEW

More than $0.25 trillion is spent on schooling. Yet, schooling serves
no common, agreed upon goal. How are we to account for the size
and complexity of this enterprise, for the vast resources it consumes,
given profound dissensus about its goals?[1] We must take a careful
look at the consensus that sustains our schools. That is a major goal
of this chapter. To start, we look at a way of evaluating consensus.
Then we analyze pluralism in terms of consensus.

Because slogans are the language of consensus, they, too, are
examined. Educational problems are often posed as slogans, a form
well suited to maintaining a broad consensus. But slogans obscure a
shallowness that impedes effective action.

Finally, we examine three images of the school. These produce
different expectations about the proper functioning of the school
and the roles of the people in it. Many educational problems
and controversies can be understood as resulting from the conflict
among the three images.

CONSENSUS AND PLURALISM

What is consensus? *Consensus* is an agreement that pursues a common purpose. Its opposite is *dissensus*. We will see that consensus is a complex concept that we can evaluate in terms of its breadth and depth. If everyone agreed
on the basic values of life then conflict would be the relatively trivial dissensus
over choice of means. Once the disputes over the means were settled, we
would have a *deep and broad consensus*, a uniform *moral community*. Such
communities have existed throughout human history, but disputes that affected their consensual foundations helped to undo them. A *pluralistic* society
is one where a broad consensus may exist on means, but not on ends.

Ends and Means

Now we call that which is in itself worthy of pursuit more final than that
which is worthy of pursuit for the sake of something else.

_____ *Aristotle*[2]

---

[1]Cf. Dorothy Westby Gibson, "Unity and Diversity of our Educational Goals," Ch. 5 in *Social
Perspectives on Education* (New York: Wiley, 1965), pp. 93–111.
[2]See Richard McKeown, "Nicomachean Ethics," *Introduction to Aristotle* (New York: Modern
Library, 1947), Bk.1, Ch. 7, p. 315.

Conflict occurs when one course of action interferes with another.[3] In order to judge the seriousness of the conflict, it is useful to find out whether it concerns means or ends.

Two people may quarrel about taking a bus or train (the means) to visit a vacation spot. Or they may quarrel about which vacation spot to visit (the end). The exact nature of their quarrel may well determine how or whether they can reconcile their differences. We learned in Chapter 1 that there are many ideas as to what education is. Schools are expected to provide education as a means to a variety of ends. The conflict in expectations that schools face comes from their being seen as a common means to deeply valued and very different ends.

The distinction between means and ends is not an absolute one. Something conceived as an end at one time, for example, graduating *summa cum laude,* may be understood later as a means, e.g., a way to get into medical school. The distinction, though not hard and fast, is useful and important, nonetheless.

For example, teachers have to be careful that they don't undermine a student's motivation by treating an end as a means. Children often do things for their own sake, that is, they find activities such as reading, coloring and writing instrinsically valuable. When extrinsic rewards are introduced, for example, grades or points, what happens is that the activities become means rather than ends. Students tend to stop doing them "spontaneously." They may come to value such activities more for their extrinsic reward.[4] The teacher is now able to control student behavior more easily by controlling the reward, but the motivational structure may be seriously affected. Teachers complain all the time that students do not show much interest in their studies. Is it perhaps because they have been trained to see them only as means?

In pluralistic societies there is disagreement on ends. Agreement on common means that serve those different ends is far more likely. The schools are a good example of this. Different people see them as an instrument to different ends and so are willing to support them as a common means. For example, a large number of people support sex education in the schools as a means to address concerns about AIDS and teenage pregnancy. But there is little consensus as to the ends it is aimed at. Should sex education measure its success in terms of increased contraceptive use, or decrease in teenage sexual activity? These are controversial questions that practicing educators must face daily.

Because schools are expected to be moral communities, we will be particularly interested in using consensus to define *moral community,* any group where there exists a deep and broad consensus both on the means and the ends of life. Imagine the conflicts schoolpeople face when what they do is judged by different parents in terms of different ends. This is no small problem.

---

[3]Cf. Dean G. Pruit and Jeffry Z. Rubin, *Social Conflict: Escalation, Stalemate and Settlement* (New York: Random House, 1986), p. 4.

[4]M. R. Lepper, D. Greene, and R. E. Nisbett, "Undermining Children's Intrinsic Interest with Extrinsic Rewards: A Test of the Overjustification Hypothesis," *Journal of Personality and Social Psychology,* Vol. 28, 1973, pp. 129–137.

Evaluating Consensus

How would we distinguish between the consensus on the following two statements?

a. Schools are necessary.
b. Schools should stay open seven days a week, twelve months a year.

We would probably find that the consensus for **a** is broad; for **b**, it is narrow.[5] A broad consensus exists when a great number of people agree on something. We can compare by a mere head count different statements relative to the *breadth of consensus.*

Another dimension of consensus to be considered is its *depth.* A consensus can be *deep* or *shallow,* depending whether initial agreement leads to additional agreements as well. Consider the following:

c. Schools should be compulsory.
d. Schools should be compulsory; arithmetic should be taught in them.
e. Schools should be compulsory; arithmetic should be taught in them. Also, calculus should be taught in them.

The depth of consensus on **c** is deeper relative to **e** than to **d**, because the number of related agreements is greater.

Depth of consensus is a matter of the commitments people derive from their agreement on an issue. Figure 2.1 shows how we can evaluate consensus in two dimensions. It is not enough to know that consensus is broad. To plan effective action we have to know how deep it is. That is, we have to know if general agreement can be transformed into specific proposals that people will accept. We can find broad consensus on many issues in our society, such as the need for schools, military spending, and Social Security. But the critical point is whether there is enough depth of consensus to support concrete steps to be taken in setting policy or solving problems.

The Consensus Curve

As consensus grows broader, it gets shallower. Vague generalizations are easily agreed upon; very specific plans for action are not. This helps us understand why in the 1988 presidential race both Dukakis and Bush spoke in generalities and avoided specifics. Specificity loses votes. Consequently, we might expect that in a pluralism deep consensus exists only among relatively small groups of people. Figure 2.2 illustrates that breadth and depth of consensus are inversely related in a pluralistic society. Discussions about sex education, for example, illustrate the point that the breadth of consensus shrinks as its depth increases. A large number of people believe that children should receive sex

---

[5]Cf. "Year-Round Schooling Is Voted in Los Angeles," *New York Times,* October 14, 1987, p. 1.

Figure 2.1

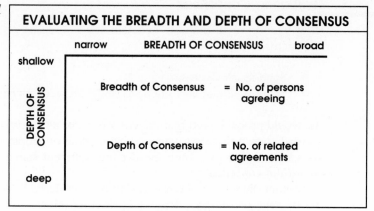

EVALUATING THE BREADTH AND DEPTH OF CONSENSUS

Figure 2.2

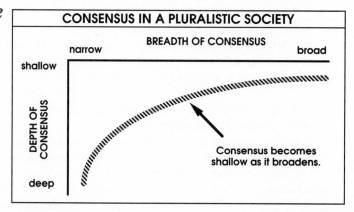

CONSENSUS IN A PLURALISTIC SOCIETY

education. A smaller constituency think this is best done by putting clinics in high schools where students may receive contraceptives or get abortion counseling.[6]

Consensus and pluralism are intimately related. But societies can be pluralistic in some ways and not in others. A state religion may coexist with an amazing variety of life styles. Or, as in this country, 50,000 different independent schoolboards may participate in a process that is amazingly uniform from ocean to ocean. Let's look at an actual case of pluralism in American society. We will see how value commitments relate to voter preferences.

AN AMERICAN PLURALISM

How pluralistic is the United States? A survey done by the Gallup Organization for the Times Mirror Corporation[7] gives us an idea. From a large number of

---

[6]E.g., Debra Viadero, "Debate Intensifies Over School-Based Health Clinics," *Education Week,* October 15, 1986, p. 9.

[7]*The People, Press & Politics* (Washington, D.C.: Times-Mirror, 1987), p. 4.

Table 2.1	NINE VALUE DISCRIMINANTS OF AMERICAN PLURALISM

- *Religious Faith:* belief in God.
- *Tolerance:* belief in freedom for those who don't share one's values.
- *Social Justice:* belief in the government's obligation to ensure social justice and social welfare.
- *Militant Anti-Communism:* belief in a strong, aggressive military defense to halt Communism.
- *Alienation:* belief that the American system does not work for oneself.
- *American Exceptionalism:* belief that there are no limits to what America can do.
- *Financial Pressure:* belief about one's financial status, i.e., feeling affluent vs. feeling pressed for money.
- *Attitudes Toward Government:* belief about the proper role and effectiveness of government.
- *Attitudes Toward Business Corporations:* belief about the goals and effectiveness of business corporations.

possible value commitments, nine value orientations were found that divide Americans into eleven distinct voter groups. The kinds of values that distinguish them are given in Table 2.1.

The extent to which people agree or not on these attitudes defines eleven groups of the American electorate. The consensus we look for to support schooling in America turns out to be severely compromised by coalitions of conflicting values. A synopsis of the eleven groups identified in the poll is given.

The Basic Coalitions

The American political pluralism identified by the Gallup poll is shown in Table 2.2.

Politics and schooling are intimately connected in America. We can expect that different groups will have different expectations for the schools. For example, some value differences that directly generate controversies about the schools are differences in religious faith, tolerance, anti-Communism and the role of government in society. Let's see how a few of these differences affect the schools:

- *Religious faith* controversies raise the question of prayer in the schools, the direct teaching of values, censorship, and sex education.
- *Tolerance* issues are found in disputes over bilingual education, student dress codes, and integration.
- *Militant anti-Communism* asserts itself in concerns about the nature of social studies education and the place of American history in the curriculum.

Table 2.2

THE BASIC AMERICAN PLURALISM

REPUBLICAN-ORIENTED GROUPS / % LIKELY ELECTORATE
- **Enterprisers / 16%:** Affluent. Well educated. Pro-business. Anti-government. Worry about deficit.
- **Moralists / 14%:** Middle income. Anti-abortion. Pro-school prayer. Pro-military.
- **Upbeats / 9%:** Young, optimistic, strongly patriotic. Pro-government. Worry about deficit.
- **Disaffecteds / 7%:** Middle-aged, alienated, pessimistic. Anti-government and anti-business. Pro-military.

****

DEMOCRAT-ORIENTED GROUPS / % LIKELY ELECTORATE
- **1960s Democrats / 11%:** Well educated. Identify with 1960 peace, environmental and civil liberties movements.
- **New Dealers / 15%:** Older, middle income. Religious. Pro-union protectionist. Pro-government.
- **Passive Poor / 6%:** Older. Religious. Patriotic. Pro-social spending. Anti-Communist.
- **Partisan Poor / 9%:** Militantly Democratic. Pro-social spending. Anti-tax hike.
- **Followers / 4%:** Young. Little faith in America or in politics. Worry about unemployment.
- **Seculars / 9%:** Middle-aged. Well educated. Nonreligious. Nonmilitant. Pro-personal freedoms.

****

NONVOTING GROUP / 0% LIKELY ELECTORATE
- **Bystanders/ 0%:** Young, poorly educated. 82% white. Many unmarried. Concerned with unemployment, threat of war.

■   *Role of government* issues are raised because federal funding for schools makes them subject to federal directives on nondiscrimination.

Figure 2.3 shows the orientation of the eleven electorate groups to these school related issues:

As you look over Figure 2.3, can you see the difficulty a politician would have trying to find a strong enough coalition of groups to support government programs to increase tolerance? Those people who show common attitudes on the tolerance issue are divided on their attitude toward the role of government. The chart also gives us some insight as to why there has been little success at introducing prayer into the public schools despite a persistent and vocal clamor for it.

Figure 2.3

AMERICAN PLURALISM: VALUES IN CONFLICT

++ = strong positive   + = positive   ( ) = probable   - = negative

AFFINITY	Republican 30/21		Democratic 41/35				Swing Vote 29/44				
% electorate / % adult population	Enterprisers	Moralists	1960's Democrats	New Dealers	Passive Poor	Partisan Poor	Upbeats	Disaffecteds	Bystanders	Followers	Seculars
Religious Faith	+	++	+	+						(-)	-
Tolerance	+	-	+	-	-						+
Anti-Communism	-	+		+	(+)			+			
Attitudes to GOVT	-	-	+		+	+	+	-			

An Example of Diminishing Consensus

A later survey done by the Gallup Organization demonstrates how breadth of consensus shrinks as depth increases.[8] Respondents were asked whether they thought that improving the quality of public education was a problem. They were additionally asked if they thought government action was required and if additional taxes should be raised to deal with it. We can identify consensus of increasing depth but decreasing breadth:

- Issue A: The quality of public education should be improved; consensus—93%
- Issue B: The quality of public education should be improved by government action; consensus—73%
- Issue C: The quality of public education should be improved by government action and new taxes; consensus—47%.

Figure 2.4 illustrates these relationships.

We can see how each additional commitment reduces the breadth of consensus even as it increases its depth.

Coalitions: Who Are the Liberals and Conservatives?

The Gallup analysis of American pluralism show that there are no consistent pro or con choices on the issues of support for public schools, federal role in

---

[8]For Times Mirror Corporation, field dates 5/13/88–5/22/88. Private correspondence with Margaret Petrella of the Gallup Organization.

Figure 2.4

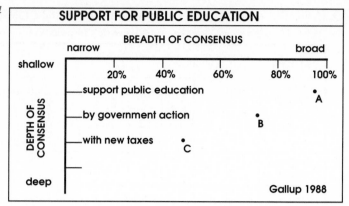

schooling, censorship, school prayer, and anti-Communism. If by the terms "liberal" and "conservative" we mean to indicate people who vote *consistently* pro or con on these issues, the polls indicate there are no such groups. If we look at issues for the *coalitions* (consensus groups) that support them, we come to realize that the terms "liberal" and "conservative" do not help us in understanding the complexities of political support for the schools. Figure 2.5 suggests some potential coalitions on different school concerns.

AMERICAN PLURALISM: POSSIBLE COALITIONS

■ indicates coalition partners

Figure 2.5

AFFINITY	Republican 30/21		Democratic 41/35				Swing Vote 29/44				
% electorate / % adult population	Enterprisers	Moralists	1960's Democrats	New Dealers	Passive Poor	Partisan Poor	Upbeats	Disaffecteds	Bystanders	Followers	Seculars
% Likely Electorate	16	14	11	15	6	9	9	7	0	4	9
% Adult Population	10	11	8	11	7	9	9	9	11	7	8
Support Public Ed.	■	■	■	■	■	■	■	■	■	■	■
Reduce Fed. Role	■	■						■			
Pro-Censorship		■		■	■						
Pro-School Prayer		■		■		■					
Anti-Communism		■		■	■			■			

If "liberals" and "conservatives" are people who vote consistently on the same opposing sides of the issues shown in Figure 2.6, then it appears there aren't many "conservatives" or "liberals" to be found in this country. The *Times Mirror* data point out that the terms "liberal" and "conservative" do not serve us well for analytical purposes. They are slogans—terms that obscure important differences among people. Simplistic political sloganeering both obscures and undermines the consensus that might support American schooling. What are these slogans? Are they no more than shallow words for shallow people? Or do they serve important purposes? We will learn that consensus and slogans are intimately related.

THE LANGUAGE OF CONSENSUS: SLOGANS

Slogans are statements that we find compelling but whose crucial terms are often too vague for practical purposes. Slogans promote consensus but often at the cost of undermining serious attempts at implementation. Negotiation researchers Susskind and Cruikshank comment:

> There are many examples ... of situations in which disparate groups of politicians and the constituents they represent have joined together in common cause but consensus has represented nothing more than a superficial commitment to a simple slogan. Many groups with fundamentally different values can identify with cries such as "Energy Independence," "Save Social Security," "Protect Our National Parks," "A Strong Defense," or "Clean Up Toxic Wastes."
>
> In some cases slogans can be very effective. More often than not, though, technical complexity, or differences over which approach to implementation would be best, thwart such calls to action and dissipate the consensus that seems to exist.[9]

Take, for example, the inspiring, "Every school, a good school!" This statement has two characteristics common to slogans:

a. *Slogans tend to preempt discussion of options.* They intimidate us to concur. The contrary sounds hardly worth saying, "Some schools will be bad schools!"
b. *Slogans obscure dissensus by vagueness.* It is not clear what "a good school" is supposed to mean. Is it one where nobody fails? Or one where a few excel in math and science? Or one where kids are happy to be? These different conditions may not be be met concurrently.

---

[9]Lawrence Susskind and Jeffry Cruikshank, *Breaking the Impasse: Consensual Approaches to Resolving Public Disputes* (New York: Basic Books, 1987), pp. 63–64.

Can we find consensus on this issue?

Slogans push for breadth of consensus and often obscure a shallowness that makes implementation difficult, if not impossible. What are often discussed in public as problems and controversies turn out, on closer inspection, to be slogans. This does not mean they have no substance, but rather that the concern they express is done in such a manner as to sacrifice practicality to advertising impact.

Slogans in Education

Education is often discussed in slogans. This is true not only in wide public debates, but commonly among teachers and administrators because slogans are embedded in the culture of the school.[10] Consider, for example, the following list of questions:

---

[10]See B. Paul Komisar, "The Language of Education," in L. C. Leighton, ed., *The Encyclopedia of Education,* Vol. 5 (New York: Macmillan, 1971).

- Should schooling pursue excellence?
- Should schools address the needs of the individual child?
- Should schools provide equal opportunity for all children?
- Should school programs be judged on their efficiency?

It would be difficult to answer No to these questions. They are formulated in such a way as to intimate assent. But it is far from clear what is meant by such terms as "excellence," "needs," "equal opportunity," "all children," and "efficiency." Indeed, we will see in the chapters to come that such questions are exactly the kind we cannot deal with both casually and intelligently.

We can locate slogans and sloganistic terms on a scale defined by the breadth and depth of consensus among the people who employ them. For example, we can identify different common uses of language in terms of the depth and breadth of consensus among communities of speakers:

- slogans: broadly and easily assented to or disagreed with, vague in meaning, for example:

    Schools must provide quality education.

    Americans love freedom.

    Educators must address individual needs.

    Prevent child abuse!

- slang, well accepted in narrow communities of speakers, vague in meaning for example:

    That's the jimson.

    He's calling Ralph on the big white telephone.

    That's kicky, dude!

    Don't mess with that jaho!

- technical language, used in small communities of consensual depth, for example:

    Ontology is not reality.

    The eighth bit toggles the overflow register.

    The sine is its own fourth derivative.

    Don't plane across the grain!

- simple everyday language, broad and wide consensus with generally great depth of consensus also.

    Ferraris are fast cars.

    August is a hot month.

    The Liberty Bell is cracked.

    Please, shut the door!

It is important to understand how language is being used so as not to overestimate either the breadth of consensus or the clarity of the ideas expressed in it. Also, it is important to understand why both simple, everyday English and technical English enjoy such a depth of consensus: *they are used in a context of well-established practice.* For example, depth of consensus is found in activities such as making a living, that is, working at some undertaking

Behavior that shows broad and deep consensus.

where theoretical problems and value decisions have long been settled and where traditions, rules of thumb, and habits make the doing relatively straightforward.

Figure 2.6 diagrams the relationships among the four uses of language in terms of breadth and depth of consensus. Unlike practical, everyday language, slogans tend not to have the kind of depth that enables long-term cooperation. Even if we think "everybody" knows what is meant by a slogan, we must remember that the consensus is likely to be shallow.

Slogans often serve as *public goals* in educational and political debates because they appeal to a wide constituency so long as they are not pressed for agreement on specifics. Often the slogan hides potential conflicts. Organization theorist Charles Perrow comments on this:

> Actual goals are discovered only when the public goal ... is factored into operational goals—those for which specific operations

Figure 2.6

SLOGANS AND CONSENSUS		
	BREADTH OF CONSENSUS	
narrow		broad
Slang		Slogans
Technical Language		Everyday Language

DEPTH OF CONSENSUS — shallow ... deep

Figure 2.7

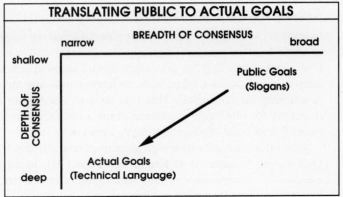

can be discovered. Once this is done, it turns out that there are several goals involved, and maximizing one will usually be at the expense of another."[11]

We illustrate the translation of public goals to actual goals in Figure 2.7.

We can see that such a translation is a move from sloganistic, public goals to the technical language of actual goal statements. For example, a statement such as

a. Every child should be provided with an education.

enjoys a broad consensus. Some of what this public goal or slogan might translate to when we get specific is any of the following:

b. Children with AIDS should be admitted to the local school.
c. Autistic children should be admitted to the local school.
d. The children of illegal aliens will be admitted to the local school.

Now, placing AIDS-affected and autistic children in local schools might be possible, but not without substantial preparation and all the controversy attendant to it. Admitting to school the children of illegal aliens, who themselves do not wish to be identified, is a real problem for educators. In any case, the breadth of consensus that **a** enjoyed will certainly evaporate if *a* is translated into *b, c,* or *d.*

Must public goals lose consensus when they are made specific? Is agreement at the level of practical action a hopeless dream? Not necessarily. But practical educators must avoid assuming that their work is done once broad consensus has been achieved. The real work of developing a coalition for action, a deeper consensus, has only just begun.

---

[11]Charles Perrow, *Complex Organizations* (Oakland, N.J.: Scott-Foresman, 1979), p. 58.

The Careful Use of Slogans

Slogans serve a variety of important purposes and we should not think of them as some kind of inferior language. (In fact, we will see in the next chapter how slogans can help us develop a model of good schooling.) But we must keep in mind that we often have to trade consensus for practicality, or even practicality for consensus. This text aims to develop in the reader the skills necessary for intelligent treatment of this conflict, and understanding both the benefits and costs of sloganeering is a necessity.

One important area in which slogans play a major role is in policy making (which will be treated at length in Chapter 9). In an important study on educational reform, Elmore and McLaughlin characterize policy in a manner that makes clear its nature as slogan:

> Policy operates on a high level of abstraction and tends to concentrate on general rules that apply to a wide variety of circumstances. For this reason alone, policy is often not useful to administrators and teachers in solving concrete problems of practice. Conflicts between policy and practice are inevitable. The question is not whether they occur, but how they are handled.[12]

A major factor undermining consensus on what school problems are and what the school should do is that different people have different expectations of the school. We can understand these expectations in terms of their having three different images of the school, the Temple image, the Factory image, and the Town Meeting image. Conflicting images generate conflicting expectations. Conflicting expectations maintain school controversies. Let's look at this interpretation more closely.

THREE IMAGES OF THE SCHOOL

The most common complaint that teachers make about students is that they lack interest in their studies.[13] But techniques of motivation have been known since antiquity. Why don't schools have torture chambers or brothels? It's immoral.

Some school districts pay certain students to attend school. This practice is often objected to as improper. But why is it done? It's effective.

A large school district threatened to discontinue football on the grounds that it was too costly per student to justify it over educational necessities such

---

[12]Richard F. Elmore and Milbrey Wallin McLaughlin, *Steady Work. Policy, Practice and the Reform of American Education,* RAND/R-3574-NIE/RC (Santa Monica, Calif: Rand Corp., 1988), p. 35.
[13]John Goodlad, *A Place Called School* (New York: McGraw-Hill, 1984), pp. 71–75.

as reading and summer school. Powerful members of the community prevailed on the superintendent to change his mind. He did, after extracting from them pledges of substantial financial support. But why not just drop football? It would have been impolitic.

What is the school that people worry about its being moral and effective and politic, often all at the same time? It is a very complex organization and it is often best to approach complexity through piecemeal simplicity. Better to ask, what is a school like? A school is like a church or temple. A school is like a factory. A school is like a town meeting, a political forum where different interests meet to trade off support on common means to ends they may not share. But the school is different from all these in being complex enough to incorporate all of them in itself. Because the school is perceived as different things by different people, their expectations are different. Because certain images of the school are preferred by some, and different ones by others, consensus on school issues can be hard to find.

The Moral Community: School as Temple

Men, if they do not learn, will never know what is proper.

_____ *Chinese Proverb*

The most ancient and still most common image of the school is as a moral community, a temple of learning.[14] In our pluralistic society this image captures for many the breadth and depth of consensus hard to find in the multiple and shifting associations of our daily lives. As a temple, the school's primary function is nurturant and formative. The principal is the moral leader, a high priest. Teachers are clergy. Students are novices being inducted into the order. What is studied is good; what is ignored is ignoble. What the teacher or principal tells you, you do. The rules of the school are sacrosanct; authority is unquestioned. Success is acceptance as a properly educated person, a kind of character formation. Infractions are moral evils, a kind of sin.

This depiction is exaggerated but captures what many parents and students expect of the school. A study of parent expectations in middle schools indicates the top five of nine in rank order are[15]:

- Children should be physically and psychologically safe.
- Each child should know an adult well enough to confide in.
- The school should be concerned that students have "constructive" friends.

---

[14]William Cutler III, "Cathedral of Culture: The Schoolhouse in American Educational Thought and Practice since 1820," *History of Education Quarterly,* Vol. 29, No. 1 (Spring 1989).
[15]James P. Garvin, "What Do Parents Expect from Middle Level Schools?" *Middle School Journal,* November 1987, pp. 3–4.

- The school should get children involved in activities.
- Children should have enough good experiences to want to return the next day.

Their next four expectations were that the middle school should prepare students for high school, it should keep parents informed, it should make parents feel welcome, and it should teach parents about adolescent behavior.

Clearly the parents conceive of the school as a "normative community" where "proper" nurturance is provided. There seems to be less concern on the parents' part for what the kids might want to do, since the school is to monitor their friendships and get them involved in activities. (Every educator encounters this demand sooner or later: "Make the kids do what I think is proper, but keep them happy in the process.")

The image of the school as moral community is reinforced in a variety of ways. Sports letters, pins, and honor codes[16] are used to bolster community. The most efficient techniques of test-score maximization are condemned as cheating. Gossip about faculty is of particular interest and can lead to their dismissal. The most effective teacher can be fired for moral turpitude[17]; indeed, it has been character, not knowledge, upon which hiring and firing faculty has traditionally been based.

The Production Unit: School as Factory

In a productive organization, the management must determine the order and sequence of all of the various processes through which the raw material or the partially developed product shall pass, in order to bring about the greatest possible effectiveness and economy.

———— *John Franklin Bobbitt*[18]

The factory model of the school, like the temple, does not permit questioning its basic authority. Its values and goals are preordained. What differs however is that where the main concern of the temple is propriety, the main concern of the factory is efficiency. Accordingly, the roles played by various participants are interpreted differently.

The principal is chief executive officer (CEO) or production manager — "instructional leader" to use a term very much in vogue. Teachers are workers

---

[16]"West Point Honor System Faces Study After Expulsion Furor," *New York Times*, June 19, 1988, p. A1.

[17]Cf."No Tie, No Job, Veteran Teacher Told," News & Trends, *American Teacher*, Vol. 3, No .7, (April 1989), p. 3.

[18]John Franklin Bobbitt, "The Supervision of City Schools: Some General Principals of Management Applied to the Problems of City School Systems," *Twelfth Yearbook of the National Society for the Study of Education, Part 1* (Bloomington, Ill.: 1913), p. 96.

Table 2.3	THE ACTUAL AND DESIRED RANK OF PRINCIPALS' DUTIES		
MORAL RANK	*PRINCIPALS' DUTIES*	*ACTUAL RANK*	*DESIRED RANK*
1	Self-evaluator	10	10
2	Disciplinarian	2	9
3	Staff selector	9	3
4	Teacher evaluator	3	5
5	Morale builder	7	6
6	PR facilitator	6	7
7	Curriculum supervisor	8	2
8	Instructional supervisor	5	1
9	Public services coordinator	4	8
10	Program administrator	1	4

or supervisors to students' being, respectively, raw material or workers. Success is judged by testing outputs. Infractions are dealt with because they impede production.

Schoolpeople tend to prefer the factory model, particularly administrators, as it ties into newer scientific traditions.[19] Five-hudred fifty-two secondary principals provided data for a survey compiled to determine whether what principals did matched what they preferred to do.[20] In Table 2.3 ten tasks are organized so that they go from practices characteristic of a moral community leader to practices of the director of a productive unit. The numbers indicate the actual rank of these activities in the principals' daily routine and the rank the principals allotted them.

[19]Cf. Raymond E. Callahan, *Education and the Cult of Efficiency* (Chicago: University of Chicago Press, 1962,) esp. Chap. 4, "American Educators Apply the Great Panacea."
[20]Robert T. Krajewski, "Secondary Principals Want to Be Instructional Leaders," *Phi Delta Kappan,* September 1978, p. 65.

Productive organizations.

From the table it seems that neither the actual nor the desired rank of the principals' daily activities corresponds clearly to that of either a moral leader or the CEO of a productive organization. Certainly, discipline is a moral task of high order. But it is not desired by the principals, even though it is an high frequency actual task. Also confusing is the fact that principals want to select teachers, but not to evaluate them. And they neither want to nor are often required to do self-evaluation. What this all likely indicates is the deep conflict and confusion that the different images create in expectation and judgment.[21]

A particularly poignant conflict between the two models arises about the problem of discipline: should it be effective or fair? Effectively changing behavior for many students may require a wide range of very different treatments, individualized to each student. But is it fair to inflict widely different consequences for the same type of offense? The moral community demands fairness and leaves one vulnerable to criticisms of ineffectiveness. The productive unit requires effectiveness, running the risk of accusations of brutality, favoritism, or overindulgence.

The expectations of the school as temple versus those of the school as factory create many conflicts.[22] Even more tension is introduced by a third aspect of schooling: the "political marketplace," or school-as-town-meeting.

The Town Meeting

If teaching or managing schools were certain, clear, and straightforward tasks, then educators could find a haven in a professional culture or technology. But education is an indeterminate enterprise. Its purposes and technologies are unclear. Its goals are diverse, diffuse and disputed among various stakeholders.[23]

It is upsetting to many people to think of the school in political terms. Our third image, however, is that of the Town Meeting (a political "marketplace," as economists understand the term). In a marketplace, morals count for little — perhaps, at best, to create confidence about promises. What really matters are knowledge, position, and power. Negotiation is the process by which concerns are dealt with. Appeals to morality or efficiency are just part of this process. Again, this is an idealization that seldom appears full-blown in the real world.

---

[21]See Joseph Berger, "New York's Principals Tell Why They 'Break the Rules,'" *New York Times*, February 21, 1989, p. B1.

[22]Cf. Stanley M. Elam, "Differences Between Educators and the Public on Questions of Education Policy," *Phi Delta Kappan,* December 1987, pp. 294–298. See also, Linda M. McNeil, "The Contradictions of Control, Part 1: Administrators and Teachers." *Phi Delta Kappan,* January 1988, pp. 333–339.

[23]Terrence Deal and Martha Stone Wiske, "Planning, Plotting and Playing in Education's Era of Decline," Ch. 23 in J. Victor Baldridge and Terrence Deal, *The Dynamics of Organizational Change in Education* (Berkeley, Calif.: McCutchan, 1983), p. 452.

But there are unmistakable signs that schools function to some extent as does a Town Meeting.

Unhappy as people may be with the image of the school as a Town Meeting, every parent, indeed, every citizen expects that school procedures and processes will be open to negotiation for their sake. Parents expect to be able to take their children with them on trips during the school year without the children suffering penalties for missing classes. They press principals to rescind suspensions or expunge disciplinary records. Community personages expect to be able to drop in for visits. Local committeepersons expect to be able to negotiate a use of school space for political purposes. Teachers see fewer of these than do principals, but it happens frequently. The expectation that the school will allow for negotiation defines the Town Meeting image of the school.

How would we understand the roles of different people under the Town Meeting image? The principal is the representative of an interest group: administration. An individual teacher represents teachers. A student, students. Each is a negotiator for the goals of his or her special interest group. Success under this model is judged by having and maintaining power: control of available resources. There are no infractions—right and wrong have no substantial meaning—only occasions for renegotiation.

David Hogan identifies four types of political issues in education:

- structural issues, e.g., differentiated vs. vocational education, unionization, professionalization;
- human capital issues, e.g., conflicts among parents for school benefits for their children;
- cultural capital issues, e.g., conflicts over curricular content or textbooks;
- displacement politics, e.g., schools becoming involved in outside conflicts.[24]

So uncomfortable are people with the political aspect of schooling that they recast the above conflicts as moral or technical problems. So it is that teachers debate the merits of vocational education and professionalization, arguing from technical considerations. Parents argue that their children have special needs that entitle them to a larger share of the school's resources. Pressure groups worry curriculum and book selection committees about the truth and morality of their decisions.

Political issues do have associated moral and technical arguments worthy of consideration. But it is not on the basis of a consensus on moral or technical agreements that these issues are decided, but rather by other processes, for example, avoiding court suits, convincing state education commissioners, and

---

[24]David Hogan, "Education and Class Formation: the Peculiarities of the Americans," in Michael W. Apple (ed.), *Cultural and Economic Reproduction in Education: Essay on Class, Ideology and the State* (Boston: Routledge & Kegan Paul, 1982), 52–53.

School politics.

securing legislation from sympathetic representatives. They are political for these reasons, rather than moral or technical ones.

The very nature of the political process poses problems for the teacher. Harry Broudy cogently captures this dilemma (emphasis by the authors of this text).

> Especially awkward for the public schools are the accounts of the civic and political process. Political action in all societies, but certainly in a democratic one, is suffused by a self-serving rhetoric. This is only to be expected because the rhetoric is intended to persuade the body politic to feel and vote in one way rather than another. Sophisticated adults understand this and discount a good deal of it, but young children may not. *The school operates on the principle that it must reinforce the ideals the community professes and not the behavior that it tolerates.* Yet it is difficult to keep up the pretense that the behavior of officials, elected and appointed, does not violate professed ideals. For one thing, the mass media are exposing the pretense daily; almost hourly. The peccadillos of politicians become media events. How much of this can the school teach as part of the social studies or social science

curriculum? How does a junior high school social studies class handle Watergate?[25]

Let's examine now the three images for contrast and comparison.

Comparing the Images

To review, we can contrast and compare the three images of the school in Chart 2.1. Let us consider how differently principal, teacher, and student might be seen as well as the bases for decision and criteria of success and wrongdoing. As we compare the three columns we can begin to understand how people with different images of the school might find it hard to agree on both ends and means in schooling. What causes even greater difficulty is that people carry around a bit of each image of the school in their heads and are not aware of the potential for conflict the differences among them produce. Consider, for example, the way discipline might be conceived of under the different images. For the Temple, infractions are a moral affront; discipline is conceived as morally uplifting. For the Factory, infractions undercut efficiency; discipline is a kind of technical correction. At the Town Meeting it is not clear what kind of behavior is critically undesirable. Such political arenas are notorious for "undisciplined" displays of behavior, sometimes barely contained within constraints of legality. (For additional comparisons and contrasts, see the Technical Appendix for Chapter 2.)

Which image is the right one for the school? It depends upon what benefits we are looking for and what costs we are willing to bear. This book will give

---

[25]Harry S. Broudy, *Truth and Credibility: The Citizen's Dilemma* (New York: Longman, 1981), p. 23

Chart 2.1

IMAGES OF THE SCHOOL			
Role/Item ╲ Image	Temple	Factory	Town Meeting
Principal	High Priest	Production Manager	Negotiator
Teacher	Clergy	Worker	Negotiator
Student	Novice	Raw Material	Negotiator
Basis for Decision	Morality	Efficiency	Power
Success	Attaining Intrinsic Goods	Achieving Output Quotas	Maintaining Power
Infraction	Immorality	Inefficiency	(inapplicable)

you the relevant information and methods of evaluation so that you can develop an informed answer to such a question.

SCHOOL IMAGES: COSTS AND BENEFITS

> Studying all of a school at once is virtually impossible. One inevitably looks at pieces and then seeks to put them together. The results are neither fully satisfying nor completely accurate. They are an approximation of reality . . .[26]
>
> —————— *John Goodlad*, A Place Called School

What is the school really? What should it be? What is important is not coming up with some general characterization about schools, but understanding the process and institution of schooling. How should we think about what goes on in schools? What gives us a handle to deal with the complexities of schooling? These are the important questions and their answers are the tools we are searching for.

Chart 2.2 depicts an array of benefits and costs we can associate with each of the models of the school. Each of the images of the schools we have seen has its attractions and its drawbacks. The tight-knit moral community of the Temple, like that of the family, offers security and a sense of belonging. But it can stifle individuality and produce pecking orders unable to be challenged. A technically skilled teacher may have little ability to relate to the concerns of his or her students. The very impersonality that the Factory celebrates may alienate students from the schooling process. The political power game of the Town Meeting is exciting, but you have to watch your back. Also, the educational nostrums proposed in the political sphere often strike both parents and teachers as frivolous. So we see that the three images compete and conflict. And it is in the pursuit of the benefits and the avoidance of the costs of each model that the dynamics of schooling are to be found.

SUMMARY

1. *Consensus and Pluralism*. Consensus is a measure of the agreement on an issue. It is not enough to know that a broad consensus exists on an issue. Practical efforts will depend upon the depth of the consensus. The breadth of consensus is determined by the number who agree on an issue; its depth, by the number of agreements believed to follow from this original agreement.

---

[26]Goodlad, op. cit., p.16.

Chart 2.2

	THREE IMAGES OF THE SCHOOL: SOME COSTS AND BENEFITS		
	Moral Community: "Temple"	Productive Organization: "Factory"	Political Marketplace: "Town Meeting"
B E N E F I T S	Clear authority Sense of community Personal contact Ends control means Role models are available Sense of unity Power can be confronted Deep consensus	Given goals, clear measures of costs and benefits Impersonality of decision Technology is applicable Means can be optimized Deep consensus	Moral equality Changeability Responsiveness Broad consensus
C O S T S	Castes develop: leaders vs. followers in-group vs. outcasts Domination Nepotism Ends undiscussible Stereotyping Suppression of dissent Suppression of variety Power can be disguised Narrow consensus	Disputability of goals Alienation Avoidance of ethical issues Roles defined: planners, doers Narrow consensus	Power tends to dominate Instability Frivolousness Shallow consensus

A moral community is defined by deep consensus on both means and ends. A pluralism is defined by a broad consensus on means but a narrow consensus on ends. In a pluralistic society, consensus tends to narrow as it deepens. Schools in the United States are broadly conceded to be a common means to a variety of narrowly or shallowly supported ends.

2. *American Pluralism.* The *Times Mirror* poll of 1987 identifies values that bear directly on educational controversies. These values determine eleven electoral groups. Their position on educationally related issues does not consistently define a "liberal" or "conservative" division. Although there is a broad consensus that supports public education, this consensus narrows substantially as questions of government action and new taxes are raised.

3. *The Language of Consensus: Slogans.* Slogans are part of a consensual language that trades ease of implementation for the sake of broad acceptance. Slogans tend to sacrifice practicality to public relations. School goal statements tend to be sloganistic. Wise implementation requires judgment that maintains consensus while pursuing effectiveness.

4. *Three Images of the School.* Schools are complex institutions that can be analyzed in terms of three images. The school as Temple is an ancient and revered image that comprehends the school as a moral community. This image generates expectations that conflict with those of the image of the school as Factory, a productive organization. The basic conflict here is between morality and efficiency. A third image—that of the Town Meeting—complicates matters even more. Here the currency is Power and the pursuit is the trade-off of values. In the interplay of these three images we will discover the dynamics of schooling in America.

QUESTIONS

1. Conflict occurs when one course of action interferes with another. Television and the movies have made much of the conflict between Nerds and Jocks. What is the nature of this conflict?
2. Give examples of means and ends in schooling. Can you give an example of an end that in another situation becomes a means?
3. Consider Figure 2.4, "Support for Public Education." Is it possible that a broader consensus might exist for reallocating revenues from other governmentally funded programs—for example, from farm supports or military spending—to education?
4. List five slogans you have heard about education. For each show how you could dispute it. (Example: If you think education costs a lot, try ignorance.)
5. What is mainstreaming? Who is the mainstream? What kind of consensus (shallow, deep) supports your conception of it?
6. Classify the following as slang, technical language, slogans, or ordinary language:
   a. Bush has to confront the Wimp Factor.
   b. Principals have managerial prerogatives.
   c. Boil for six minutes.
   d. Just say No to drugs.
   e. Quality education needs quality teachers.
   f. This school stands for excellence.
7. Make the following slogans more specific. Give different interpretations for each one. Do these different interpretations conflict?
   a. We teach all of the children.
   b. We teach children, not subjects.
   c. Develop each child to his or her full potential.
   d. We require excellence in all endeavors.

8. Can you give other examples of the conflict between effectiveness and fairness?

9. Consider the "school principle" given by Broudy. What is the consensus problem here?

10. Do different kinds of schools or grade levels tend to emphasize different images of the school? Is there any connection with school image and age of student?

CONFLICT and PROBLEMS in SCHOOLING

Chapter 3

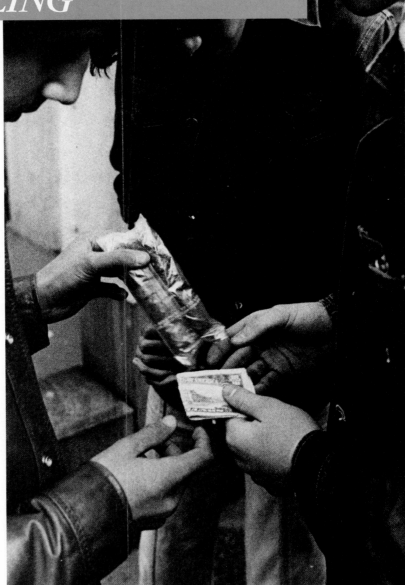

To study the strategy of conflict is to take the view that most conflict situations are essentially bargaining situations. . . . Viewing conflict behavior as a bargaining process is useful in keeping us from becoming exclusively preoccupied either with the conflict or with the common interest.[1]

Thomas C. Shelling

PREVIEW

What are educational problems? Why are there schooling controversies? What conflicts underlie them? How can we deal with them? The aim of this chapter is to develop critical thinking skills needed to handle schooling problems effectively. Rather than just surveying school problems and controversies, we will use the set of basic questions given in Chart 3.1 to help us understand and deal with educational conflict.

These Analysis Questions will help us to understand why school problems are particularly troublesome and surprisingly persistent.

PROBLEMS

Problems are human judgments about situations. Problems do not exist independent from some human being's finding some situations problematic. When someone says, "I have a problem," he or she means, "Here is something that concerns me and I want you to be concerned, too." It is an attempt to impose expectations on us in a way that is difficult for us to reject. It is often seen as unsympathetic to respond, "That is not **my** problem." But, given a scarcity of time and resources, it may be a wise thing to do.

As we discovered in the last chapter, a school is often considered a **moral community** whose members cannot easily profess lack of concern for anything that might be thought to have an impact upon children. The question "How are drugs and alcohol abuse a *school* problem?" sounds heartless and unworthy of a "real" educator. But the catch is this: schools are imagined also to be **productive organizations**, "factories" as it were, that are expected to yield substantial results. By accepting concerns on moral grounds, educators are trapped into possibly unfulfillable expectations for results.

THE SCHOOLS AND THEIR "PROBLEMS"

Everyone seems to agree that the schools have problems. Indeed, many believe that the severity of school problems has increased over the last forty years. According to a survey reported in *TIME* magazine, the 1940s schools were

---

[1]Thomas C. Schelling, *The Strategy of Conflict* (Cambridge: Harvard U. Press, 1960), p. 5.

Chart 3.1   **ANALYSIS QUESTIONS**

Q1. What is the situation?
Q2. Whom does it concern?
Q3. How do they perceive it?
Q4. Why does it concern them?
Q5. What changes, if any, do they propose?
Q6. Can and will anything be done?
Q7. Who gains and who loses from the change?

faced with "problems" that look quite minor compared to those of the 1980s. Compare the lists in Chart 3.2.

The contrast between the two lists is startling. How can we account for the difference in both the number and severity of school problems over forty years?

Four explanations come to mind:

- *Degeneracy*: Kids are worse than they've ever been.
- *Selection*: There was a 50 percent dropout rate during the 1940s compared to a 10 percent dropout rate in 1986. Perhaps "trouble-makers" are being kept in school.
- *Exposure*: Problems that were covered up in the 1940s are made public today.
- *Expansion of Responsibility*: Schools have been asked to deal with situations they formerly gave over to other agencies.[2]

Of these four explanations, only the last avoids jumping to conclusions. To talk of "degeneracy," or "troublemakers," or "problems," even, is to rush to judgment. Besides, there is no evidence that young people are more "degenerate" nowadays than they have ever been. We have to avoid getting caught

---

[2]William W. Wayson, "The Politics of Violence in School: Doublespeak and Disruptions in Public Confidence," *Phi Delta Kappan*, October 1985, pp.127–132.

Chart 3.2   **SCHOOL PROBLEMS**

In the 1940s	In the 1980s
Talking	Drug Abuse
Chewing Gum	Alcohol Abuse
Making Noise	Pregnancy
Running in Halls	Suicide
Getting out of place in line	Rape, Robbery
Improper Clothing	Assault, Burglary
Littering	Arson, Bombings

Source: TIME, *February 1, 1988.*

up too soon in judgmental language and transforming a real, but specific concern into a slogan.

In the next section we will develop a method for applying the analysis questions given above. One purpose of these analysis questions is to reduce the sloganistic quality of problem statements. This helps us get at the concerns people have about situations without forcing us to share their concerns until we decide it is wise to do so.

ANALYZING PROBLEMS

When people see that a situation conflicts with their interests, they often declare, "There is a problem here." This impersonal, "objective" manner of statement obscures their own involvement in the situation. But lacking *their specific interests*, and *their perception* that a certain *conflict* faced them, they would not talk of a "problem." "Problem" is a sloganistic term. People talk of problems in order to enlist our sympathies and particularly our resources. Wisdom requires we examine their claims before committing ourselves.

The intelligent use of limited resources requires us to carefully assess expectations before undertaking action. Recall the questions in Chart 3.1 we will use to examine possible problems.

Let's consider teenage alcohol abuse. In many countries around the world, teenagers have access to alcoholic beverages in ways that are forbidden in this country. But why is the use of alcohol by American teenagers a "school problem" of the 1980s, when it was not considered such in the 1940s? What are the underlying concerns that prompt some to consider it a **school** problem? What is the situation here and whom does it concern?

The Situation

Let's begin with a basically "distant," impersonal attitude: there are no problems, per se. There are only situations; and some people find those situations problematic. Let's look at our first Analysis Question. Each Analysis Question is simple enough, but to use it effectively we have to follow certain directions. These will be presented in each section and explained with examples.

Q1: **What is the situation?**
Describe the situation in practical terms.
Avoid or replace slogans
Reduce or replace judgmental language

To describe the situation in "practical terms" is to describe it in such a way that we can determine if that situation has changed independently of the mood or judgment of the complainant. It is important to separate the "problem"

For whom is this a problem?

from the person,[3] so that we can make out to what extent the "problem" is a very personal concern. If a person needs only cheering up, or a placebo of some sort, we need not get ourselves too worked up about "the problem." Also, we will try to "tone down" as much as possible whatever judgmental language we have to use: there may be another side to the story.

We will normally encounter two broad kinds of problems in schooling: concrete and abstract. Concrete problems are easier to understand. Let's begin with examples of these.

Concrete Problems

Imagine a teacher, Harry Smith, who complains, "Section 805 really drives me up the wall!" Let's rewrite this as a report and consider it to be the basic form of the problem:

> Harry Smith says that section 805 drives him up the wall.

---

[3]Cf. Roger Fisher and William Ury, *Getting to YES. Negotiating Agreement Without Giving In* (New York: Penguin, 1987), p. 11.

Chart 3.3	**Problem**	**Situation, Person**
	Mary Jones says her principal hates her.	Her relationship with the principal concerns Mary Jones.
	John Doe says he needs more supplies.	The amount of supplies concerns John Doe.
	Sam Smith says his students are jumpy.	Certain student behavior concerns Sam Smith.

This is hardly specific, so let's tone it down to:

Something about section 805 concerns Harry Smith.

We forgo the emotional engagement of Harry's original statement in order to dig up additional information. To get a useful characterization of the situation we may have to question Harry further: "What bothers you about 805?" Harry replies, "They never get their work done." We can recast the Problem as:

The Problem: The amount of work completed by some students in 805 concerns Harry Smith.

We have to be careful not to take too literally Harry's lumping together everybody in 805 under the term "they." Also, the "never" is suspicious. We don't know if Harry is complaining that 95 percent of his students complete 99 percent of their work or if 0 percent complete 0 percent. We should err on the side of caution: our time and resources are seldom in such abundance that we can commit them uncritically.

Chart 3.3 gives some more examples of concrete problems that have been changed into the situation, person form. In every case we must have (or imagine) a specific person claiming to have a problem. These are only first approximations. After further questioning we may end up with examples like the ones of Chart 3.4.

We may decide to push even further. How far should we continue? Until we have defined a situation *well enough to compare it with a possible im-*

Chart 3.4	**Problem**	**Situation, Person**
	Mary Jones says her principal hates her.	Her principal's not saying hello concerns Mary Jones.
	John Doe says he needs more supplies.	That he has only six cartons of paper concerns John Doe.
	Sam Smith says his students are jumpy.	Some students' calling out concerns Sam Smith.

provement without having to depend on the person involved to tell us if we have succeeded. The purpose of clarifying a problem situation is to see if a change proposal will have an effect. If we cannot identify what the problematic situation is, we cannot hope to change it for the better. But to have to rely upon the original complainant to find out if we have succeeded threatens no end of involvement—this is the reason why researchers, whenever possible, try to describe situations in terms of measurable or countable items. This is not always possible, but it is a useful approach.

Abstract Problems

Problems are abstract when it is not clear who is concerned or whether they are concerned to the same degree or for the same reason. Abstract problem statements are slogans. The problems of the 1940s and 1980s listed in Chart 3.2 are abstract ones: we find it difficult to deny they are problems, but it is far from clear who is concerned and to what depth or breadth that concern goes.

The difficulty with abstract problems is that they can be "dealt with" in the abstract without having to deal with the concrete realities that underlie them.

Is this an abstract problem?

Organizational responses to problems are very often abstract responses, for example, policy changes, reprioritizations, committee resolutions, and reorganization of departments. The plight of a man who sleeps on the streets, when televised to millions of voters, might move a city council to fund a shelter program for the homeless. But the man might still be out on the street.

Because abstract problem statements are slogans, it is particularly easy to deal with them by creating a corresponding abstract solution. What really matters, however, is whether abstract "solutions" attack the very concrete problems that specific individuals are burdened with.

We have to deal with abstract problems in a manner that does not avoid the question of who is concerned. At the same time we want to tone down the statement of the problem, deemotionalizing it into a statement of a situation that can be evaluated easily. So we can recast the problem of alcohol abuse we encountered earlier as someone's concern that **x**% of schoolchildren drink **y** ounces of alcohol daily.

In the same way, the pregnancy problem could be cast neutrally as someone's concern that x% of students get pregnant each year. What could the values of x and y be? For the moment let's overlook specific quantities. Certainly, the kinds of numbers we have for x and y will have a great bearing upon whether anyone will be concerned about the situation. Kids can get a small amount of alcohol in them by using mouthwash. Is that a concern? What numbers do we need to generate concern and in whom? Why are they concerned? Those are the questions we will consider.

We can list these abstract problems in Chart 3.5 in much the same way we did the concrete problems. We use the phrase "some people" as a variable to remind us that we have yet to determine the breadth and width of the consensus for each value of x (or y) we specify. This is a very practical consideration. One way to cool down a controversy over an abstract problem is to use the Analysis Questions of this chapter to press for specific information.

It is hard to overestimate the importance of abstract problems. They form the bulk of the substance of public discussion. Because it is unclear just exactly who is concerned and to what extent, abstract problems are well suited for ceremonial, public expressions of community concern. However, in their abstract form, problems cannot be solved.

Chart 3.5	**Problem**	**Situation, Person**
	There is an alcohol problem.	That x% of schoolchildren drink y% of alcohol daily concerns some people.
	There is a pregnancy problem.	That x% of students get pregnant each year concerns some people.
	There is a drug problem.	That x% of students use drugs concerns some people.

Whom does this concern?

The People

Our second question is:

Q2:   **Whom does it concern?**
      Identify the "Stakeholders."
         Distinguish between
         • who in fact is concerned and
         • who ought to be concerned.

Stakeholders are people who are concerned with the situation. It's important to distinguish between those who are in fact concerned and those who know of the situation but are not concerned about it, yet, we believe, should be concerned about it. The point of characterizing something as a "problem" is to involve others as stakeholders. Our counterstrategy in characterizing something as a "situation" is to avoid being brought in as stakeholders until we can see that our interests are really involved.

Varieties of Stakeholder

> The stakeholders were citizen advocate groups.... Though this loose coalition ... uniformly supported the idea of new state imposed priorities, their united front dissolved quickly in the face of a need to be specific.[4]
>
> —————— *Susskind and Cruikshank*

This quote from Susskind and Cruikshank reiterates the point made earlier that specifics create dissension. Stakeholders may share a common concern but only up to the point that their specific interests are not made obvious. Who are the stakeholders in a problem and how can we identify their interests?

For concrete problems, at least one stakeholder is obvious: the person making the complaint. What the complainant often does is to deny that there are any stakeholders in the situation whose contrary interest might be threatened by settling his or her complaint. That is why problems involving several people often become controversies.

Abstract problems require a bit more work. We have to translate the phrase "some people" into specific stakeholders. People are stakeholders in a situation because that situation threatens, maintains, or promotes something they value. They may be directly or indirectly concerned about the situation. In our everyday life we spend a good deal of energy getting people to share the burden of our problems by convincing them that they are more directly concerned than they might want to admit. Here we will reverse the process and try to keep clear how directly a stakeholder may be involved with a situation.

Who are the stakeholders for the problem

> That x% of schoolchildren drink y% of alcohol daily concerns some people.

Surely, it depends on the numbers. For purposes of exploration, let's suppose them to be big. Suppose

> **50**% of schoolchildren drink **8** ounces of alcohol daily.

This would concern a variety of people, but for possibly different reasons. For example, a list of stakeholders might look like this:

- parents of drunken children
- parents of sober children
- teachers of drunken children

---

[4]Lawrence Susskind and Jeffry Cruikshank, *Breaking the Impasse: Consensual Approaches to Resolving Public Disputes* (New York: Basic Books, 1987), p. 53.

- teachers of sober children
- drunken children
- sober children
- distributors of alcoholic beverages
- manufacturers of alcoholic beverages
- manufacturers of sports equipment

There is no reason to suppose that the different stakeholders would have common concerns. Even more important: they may have different ideas about how to attack the problem.

Parents of drunken children may be worried about their children, whereas parents of sober children may be concerned to keep their own children away from those who drink. Drunken children may worry about getting into trouble and sober children worry about their drunken friends. Distributors and manufacturers of alcoholic beverages may worry about public reaction that will affect their business. If drunken kids play few sports, manufacturers of sports equipment may be concerned to promote sobriety as a first step to athletic participation.

From this example it becomes clear that, as we analyze problems, it is important to identify stakeholders without assuming they must see eye-to-eye. This is a hard habit to cast off because in our normal everyday role as advocates for our concerns we tend to "see" common interests as a preliminary to arguing for them. Assuming common interest in schooling is particularly tempting for educators. But those of us with this particular concern would be wise to remember that everyone does not share it.

Perceptions

> Understanding the other side's thinking is not simply a useful activity that will help you solve your problem. Their thinking *is* the problem.... Ultimately ... conflict lies not in objective reality, but in people's heads. Truth is simply one more argument—perhaps a good one, perhaps not—for dealing with the difference. The difference itself exists because it exists in their thinking.... It is ultimately the reality as each side sees it that constitutes the problem in a negotiation and opens the way to a solution.[5]
>
> ——————— *Fisher and Ury*

In mulling over this quote from Fisher and Ury, we should not misunderstand what they are saying. They are not saying that truth is relative or merely a matter of personal opinion. What they are saying is that, if people disagree, then one person's presenting his or her case to the other as "the Truth" is

---

[5]Fisher and Ury, op. cit., pp. 22–23.

Chart 3.6 **Situation, Stakeholder** **Perception**

Situation, Stakeholder	Perception
That her principal didn't say hello concerns Mary Jones.	Mary Jones: My principal hates me.
Having only six cartons of paper concerns John Doe.	John Doe: I need more supplies.
Some students' calling out a lot concerns Sam Smith.	Sam Smith: My students are jumpy.

not necessarily going to bring about agreement. The disagreement will extend, most likely, to what the disputing parties will claim to be the truth. We will see below that agreements on the truth depend basically upon agreements about authority.

What people think they are talking about is critical to their coming to an agreement about how to settle a problem. Our third question is concerned with the way the various stakeholders perceive the situation.

Q3: How do they perceive it?
  Determine to what extent focus is shared:
    Are common criteria being used?
    Are common authorities appealed to?

For a given situation, each stakeholder will have his or her own perception of it. We should not be surprised if for each stakeholder a given situation is perceived differently. If persons dealing with a problem do not understand it as the same thing, then solution is unlikely.

For concrete problems, we can easily identify the perceptions of at least one stakeholder, the complainant. Most people cast the situation they are complaining about in terms of their own perceptions, so the original statement of problem contains that perception. (See Chart 3.6.) Why did we bother to analyze the original if all we do is get back to it? Because we recognize now that the situation embedded in the perceptions of the complainants may involve other stakeholders. These other stakeholders, for example, the principal, other people in John Doe's department, and Sam's students, may have different perceptions of the situation.

Parents, teachers, and general public often complain about schools having "discipline" problems.[6] But when we look more closely at what each group understands by "discipline" we often come up with quite a range of conceptions. In the *American School Boards Journal* of June 1988 we find the following warning:

It is ... important to define vague terms in discussing discipline. The difficulty with defining a general set of rules for a school system is that every

---

[6]Cf. "19th Annual Gallup Poll of the Public's Attitudes Toward the Public Schools." in *Phi Delta Kappan* (Sept. 1987) p. 28.

person has a different idea of what constitutes appropriate behavior. Individual values and levels of tolerance come into play ... differences of
opinion extend to what constitutes serious misbehavior ... the vagueness
of ... terms makes them subject to abuse or to culturally biased interpretations.[7]

"Discipline" tends to be used in a sloganistic manner. Everyone agrees that it
is a problem. Few agree about how to solve it since it means different things
to different people.

Slogans "defocus" perceptions. They obscure differences in the criteria in
terms of which people understand crucial terms like "discipline." In addition,
slogans obscure the even more profound dissensus that exists when people
do not recognize the same authorities to settle their disputes over the criteria.
Think how teenagers and their parents might disagree on what "good music"
is. Realize how profound this disagreement is if it turns out, as it usually does,
that they do not even agree who should be the judge of what good music is.

School disputes may be no more easily settled. A principal or parent may
understand one thing by "discipline"; we, another. Why should we agree to
accept one or the other's understanding as the common one? To come to
a practical agreement we have to focus our perceptions of a problematic
situation.

Looking for Common Criteria

Perceptions are commonly shared among people under two conditions:

a.   the different parties use the same criteria, i.e., they agree why something is what it is;
b.   the different parties invoke the same authorities to settle the differences
they may find in the criteria.

Thus, for different individuals, their perceptions may turn out to be focused
according to individually different criteria and authorities.

Let us imagine a community, call it Anytown, where a broad consensus
exists that "discipline" is a problem in Anytown High School. But when we
inventory the various stakeholders we find the following. Different groups
think "good behavior" has been achieved, that is, the "discipline problem" has
been solved, under the following conditions:

■   the parents want classrooms to be happy places and their children to
get good grades;

---

[7]William Thomas, "To Solve 'the Discipline Problem,' Mix Clear Rules with Consistent Consequences," *The American School Boards Journal*, June 1988, p. 30.

- the teachers want to be able to get their students through the specified curriculum;
- the principal wants the students not to do anything that would shock Mr. Jones, a prominent schoolboard member;
- Mr. Jones wants the students to behave in ways he likes to believe he and his friends behaved when they were in school, e.g., they were "regular guys";
- the mayor (who dislikes Mr. Jones) wants the students to avoid acting the way he remembers Mr. Jones and his hooligan friends did when they went to school together.

In a sense, although they are using the same word, "discipline," they are "speaking different languages." The nature of the communication among people depends on the nature of the consensus on criteria that they share. Certainly, the criteria for identifying a solution to the "discipline problem" vary among the stakeholders. An even greater problem may develop if they were to come together to try to forge a common set of criteria to deal with it. The "authority" each group of stakeholders might invoke runs the gamut from parental "rights" to professional and career commitments on the part of the teachers and the principal, to Mr. Jones' and the mayor's disparate personal senses of right and wrong. Yet the possibility of dealing with "the discipline problem" depends upon the possibility of reconciling them.

Who Says So?

If people cannot agree on criteria and whether they are being met, they will have to agree on an **authority** to settle the following questions, that is:

a. What should the criteria be? and,
b. Have those criteria been met?

These are crucial questions faced every day by people in schools. Without agreement about them, disputes cannot be settled by negotiation.

Generally, except for what we call "cults," an authority is not a person as an individual. Rather it is a person *in a role*, who has followed a specific procedure. John Smith, M.D., does not pronounce on your physical condition by virtue of his being John Smith. It is his pronouncement as a medical doctor having performed a diagnosis that leads many people to acknowledge his authority on the matter.

Most people concede the authority to individuals to decide what they see, hear, and feel. After all, those are their perceptions. But teachers, priests, and psychiatrists may deny them that authority with respect to what they claim to know, even about their own motivations. On issues of life, death, and morals—and education—there is controversy.

To illustrate, we should consider that the very existence of something like Special Education presupposes the ability to reclassify as impediments needing treatment what were at one time thought to be moral failings. Dyslexic students were once dismissed as "lazy." Learning disabilities were just "stupidity." It is not surprising, then, to discover that in both theory and practice Special Education is controversial.[8]

Different Sources of Authority

Many different kinds of authority are recognized in our pluralistic society. And it is rare to find a broad consensus on any of them. Some kinds of authority often given to justify particular criteria are found in Chart 3.7. The *Examples of Possible Authority* were chosen so that it would be unlikely that the reader would acknowledge them all to be sources of authority. Of course, many people do not agree which items in the chart are authoritative. Even where there is agreement, there may be different rankings, so that for some, religious beliefs rank above scientific theories, or vice versa. The intense controversy about teaching evolution versus teaching Creationism centers on a dispute over authority.

Consensus on authority determines the nature of the community that exists among people. Pluralisms tend to recognize a few authorities broadly but shallowly. The conflict of law versus morality is characteristic of this kind of consensus. Moral communities recognize their authorities both broadly and deeply. But in a pluralistic society they are generally in the same position as technical communities: consensus is deep but not broad. Figure 3.1 shows these possibilities.

There is a circumstance in which pluralism can look very much like moral community and is critical to understanding how a pluralistic society is pos-

---

[8]See Frank R. Vellutino, "Dyslexia," *Scientific American*, Vol. 256, No. 3 (March 1987), pp. 34–41. See also Carol A. Christensen, Michael M. Gerber, and Robert B. Everhart, "Toward a Sociological Perspective on Learning Disabilities," *Educational Theory*, Vol. 36, No. 4 (Fall 1986), pp. 317–331; Mary Saily, "Learning Remains Elusive for Handicapped Children," *Educational R&D Report*, Vol. 4, No. 4 (Winter 1981–1982), pp. 2–5; Nathan Glazer, "IQ on Trial," *Commentary*, June 1981, pp. 51–59; Diane McGuinness, "Facing the 'Learning Disabilities' Crisis," *Education Week*, February 5, 1986, p. 28.

Chart 3.7 **Examples of Possible Authority**

- personal judgment/experience
- other's judgment/experience
- religion
- science
- law
- scholarship
- astrology
- news media
- government publications
- Tarot cards

Figure 3.1

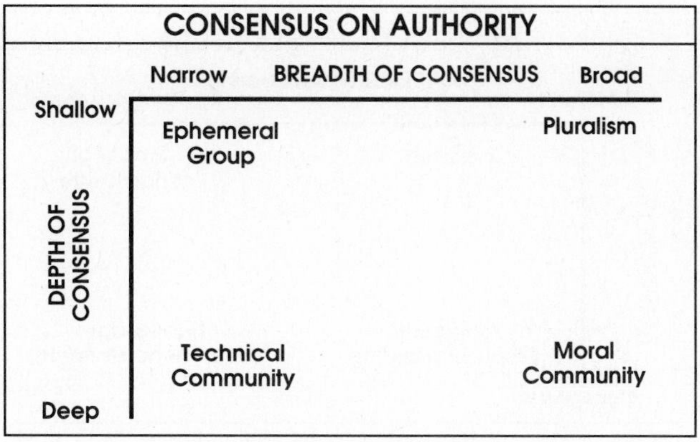

CONSENSUS ON AUTHORITY		

To understand the figure: A two-dimensional chart titled "CONSENSUS ON AUTHORITY." The horizontal axis is "BREADTH OF CONSENSUS" running from "Narrow" (left) to "Broad" (right). The vertical axis is "DEPTH OF CONSENSUS" running from "Shallow" (top) to "Deep" (bottom). Four quadrants are labeled: Ephemeral Group (shallow, narrow), Pluralism (shallow, broad), Technical Community (deep, narrow), and Moral Community (deep, broad).

sible. If different authorities agree on criteria or explanations, this has the effect of increasing the depth of consensus. For example, there is a great deal of agreement among different authorities as to what is good and bad social behavior. One group might cite the Bible, another the law, yet another a sense of common humanity. But all may agree that unprovoked aggression is wrong. Various moral communities, who disagree profoundly about ends, can maintain themselves in a pluralism precisely because, for most of the pedestrian activities of life, they happen to agree on the value of simple judgments.

To understand why a problem resists solution or a controversy persists, we look to determine the **focus** of the stakeholders: Are they employing common **criteria**? Do they recognize the same **authorities**? Whether a stakeholder *ought to* recognize someone or something as authoritative is another question. It involves us in the dispute, rather than helping us to analyze it.

If we compare consensus and dissensus on criteria and authority, we can illustrate the possibilities of productive interaction for a group of people. Practical knowledge requires only consensus on criteria: we need only agree on what is what, and how we control them. We need not agree on why it works that way.

Criteria are often neutral with respect to authority. That is, they may be recognized by competing authorities. The theories underlying practical knowledge may well be different—the reason why people of very different religions can all be engineers. However, if the very conception of knowledge rests on the recognition of certain authorities, it is not possible to accept those authorities neutrally. One cannot be a Roman Catholic atheist, or a behaviorist mystic. Figure 3.2 locates some important items.

Criteria are the what's and how's of human action: *this* is what an IQ score is and *this* is how we compute it, we might be taught. And *this* is why, says your principal, it is important to know a student's IQ. Authorities provide the why's. Consensus on both criteria and authority provides what communities call deep understanding, or (well-founded) knowledge. Knowledge is a term

Figure 3.2

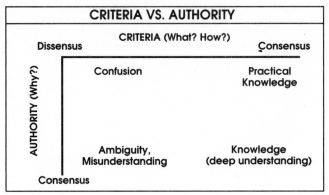

of respect that communities reserve for those beliefs that rest upon shared criteria and authority. When the what's and how's, the criteria, are not in dispute, but the why's are, the community will still recognize such items as practical knowledge. A teacher may know how to get students to learn algebra and may agree with psychologists on the criteria for knowing algebra. But the psychologists may disagree with each other and with the teacher as to why the teacher's method is effective. The practical knowledge is not denied; the deep understanding is.

Some examples illustrate the important relationships between criteria and authority:

■ Two psychologists wish to determine Johnny Jones' intelligence. One uses an IQ test based on the theory that IQ is a comprehensive, unitary characteristic of the individual. The other uses tests based on a theory of multiple intelligence, i.e., there are different and independent kinds of intelligence. The results turn out to be very different. Here both the criteria and the authority upon which they are based are different. We have confusion.[9]

■ Two teachers get into a discussion of Johnny Jones' writing ability. They disagree about its quality and consistency. Each trusts the other's professional judgment. This is the commonly recognized authority. Why the disagreement? It turns out one used Johnny's daily journal— a free-form composition—to make his evaluation. The other teacher made her evaluation on the basis of formal composition assignments. The criteria are different. This causes misunderstanding and ambiguity.[10]

---

[9]Cf. Stephen Jay Gould, *The Mismeasure of Man* (New York: Norton, 1981), for a discussion of the variety of competing authorities and criteria used in the assessment of human characteristics.
[10]Cf. Jane A. Stallings, "Are We Evaluating What We Value?" *Action in Teacher Education*, Vol. IX, No. 3 (Fall 1987), pp. 1–3; see also Linda Shalaway, "For High Scores, Test What You Teach," *Educational R&D Report*, Vol. 5, No. 3 (Washington, D.C.: Council for Educational Development and Research, Fall 1982), pp. 2–6.

■ Everybody in town knows Johnny Jones. They've all heard about his difficulties in school. They know too that Johnny's father paved over an old cemetery and was cursed along with his family by Old Lady Smith for the desecration. For many people in Johnny's community, this explanation constitutes knowledge. They agree on the criteria and their common authority is a system of traditions and beliefs.

■ Johnny's adviser, Miss Parker, sees Johnny's difficulties, too. She believes, however, that it is not the curse in and of itself that is Johnny's problem. Rather it is the expectation by Johnny and members of his community that he will suffer which brings him to do so. Miss Parker cites different authority although she agrees with the community on the criteria identifying the problem. She and Johnny's parents can cooperate to some extent on remediating Johnny's problems. They share practical knowledge, even though they disagree on the explanations for its effectiveness.[11]

If we compare the last few charts we can begin to see the relationship among the existence of a moral community, consensus on authority, and the idea of knowledge. Elsewhere we will discuss the complex issue of the relationship between consensus, objectivity, and truth.

There are a number of situations where disagreements over criteria and authority cause schooling controversy. The following sets of questions indicate some of them:

■ What is child abuse? How is it different from discipline? Who is to determine the distinction? On what authority? What moral right has the school or the state to intervene in what may be a matter of parental authority? Why should teachers be forbidden the use of corporal punishment if it might be effective in dealing with problematic behavior?

■ Should the school provide information about birth control and/or abortion despite the contrary wishes of parents? When should community expectations override respect for the student's individuality?

■ Which authority ought to take precedence in the school: science or religion? Should students be required to learn about evolution if they believe it is falsehood? What if students and their parents believe that certain ethnic groups are inferior and deserving of bad treatment? Do educators have the right to insist that whatever authority they base this belief on is wrong?

Questions about authority lead us to the next section. Who is to decide what is problematic about a situation? What are the concerns of the stakeholders that bring them to see a problem?

---

[11]However, for a criticism of expectations effects see Christopher J. Hurn, *The Limits and Possibilities of Schooling* (Boston: Allyn & Bacon, 1978), pp. 147–155.

Concerns and interests

> Behind opposed positions lie shared and compatible interests, as well as conflicting ones. We tend to assume that because the other side's positions are opposed to ours, their interests must also be opposed. If we have an interest in defending ourselves, then they must want to attack us. . . . In many negotiations, however, a close examination of the underlying interests will reveal the existence of many more interests that are shared or compatible than ones that are opposed.[12]
>
> ———— *Fisher and Ury*

Fisher and Ury focus on the concerns that underlie a problem and suggest that reconciliation might be possible because many times people share many more concerns than they suspect. On the other hand, some concerns may not be reconcilable. Let us look at this dichotomy more closely.

Sorting Out Interests

The fourth Analysis Question is:

Q4: **Why does it concern them?**
Uncover the underlying interests.
Are they instrumental values?
Are they intrinsic values?

The most direct, and tactless, way to uncover interests is to ask any of the following questions when someone expresses a concern:

a. So what?
b. Why does that concern you?
c. Can you explain what that has to do with you?

A general rule of thumb is this: When people believe their concerns to involve intrinsic interests—that is, ends—they will forgo further justification by some statement beginning with, "Because . . ." They also often get angry or upset if they believe you should recognize such interests as intrinsic. On the other hand, if people understand their concerns as involving instrumental interests—that is, means—they will be able to justify them with an explanation involving a further goal.

Imagine the following conversation:

"I have a problem. My grades are not in."
"So what?"

---

[12]Fisher and Ury, op. cit., p. 43.

"My principal will demand to know why."

"So what?"

"I'll get in trouble and get a bad rating!"

"So what?"

"I could lose my job!"

"So what?"

"What's wrong with you? How am I supposed to live?

Clearly, because earning a living is as intrinsic an interest as most people will have, the first speaker loses his patience with the second. But, given special circumstances, he might as well have answered,

"You're right. Why sweat it? I can dip into my savings and take a cruise for a year."

Moral justifications tend to be intrinsic. People often try to duck a question by using a moral justification when their reasons are really extrinsic. For example, a person might express worry about illiteracy by explaining that his concern rests on the principle that all people have a right to equal educational opportunity. We might suspect there are other reasons, particularly if he is the author of a series of reading textbooks.

We have a procedure now, for getting at interests:

> **To identify underlying interests:**
> Persist in asking, "So what?" of stated interests.
> ▬ The final answer is an intrinsic interest.
> ▬ All the preceding ones are instrumental.

This procedure explains why so much public justification of behavior sounds saintly. For public relations purposes, everybody tries to appeal to widely accepted intrinsic interests. For example, when a tax hike is passed to fund a teachers' contract, the teachers' union president celebrates the city council's having recognized the city's schoolchildren "as a priority."[13]

In a similar manner, E. D. Hirsch, a fellow at the National Endowment for the Humanities, worries that a lack of "cultural literacy" will undermine our ability to communicate with one another. He proposes wide exposure to broad areas of humanities topics. Of course, he does not explain what consequences we stand to suffer from such "cultural illiteracy," and why, for example, the Japanese—who by Hirsch's standards are culturally illiterate—don't suffer them.[14] Perhaps Hirsch's occupational relationships throw light on more instrumental motives.

---

[13]Marvin E. Schuman, "A Letter of Thanks to the PFT Rank and File" *The PFT Reporter* (Philadelphia: Philadelphia Federation of Teachers), June 1988, p. 2.
[14]See "Cultural Literacy and the Schools: 2 Views," *Careers in Teaching*, May 13, 1987, p. 20.

Some Incompatible Interests

Different stakeholders may have different, even incompatible interests (see Chart 3.8). Let's recall "the discipline problem" that concerned the citizens of Anytown and look at some possibilities in Chart 3.8. We'll assume that all the stakeholders like seeing happy children who get good grades. However, they might be willing to sacrifice a child's happiness and grades to the listed interests.

Because it is generally easier to reconcile clashes between extrinsic or instrumental values than clashes between intrinsic (final) values, for effective problem solving it is important to sort out concerns as intrinsic as opposed to instrumental.[15] It might be possible, for example, for the mayor of Anytown to get the principal to adopt the mayor's criteria if he were to assure the principal that his contract would be renewed even if Mr. Jones objected. If the teachers were assured their ratings would not go down if they did not finish the course of studies, they might be more focused on a happy learning environment.

Denying Concerns and Interests

Every way of a man is right in his own eyes...

———————— *Proverbs, 21, 2*

Have you ever been called lazy just because you didn't feel like doing something? Or because you had something you believed was more important to do? The person who called you lazy was doing something it is important you take note of. He or she was denying that your concerns and interests were legitimate.

A common way of dealing with concerns or interests we don't like is that we dismiss or ignore them. If a woman worries about her son's first overnight

---

[15]William Glaberson, "Coping in the Age of 'Nimby'" *New York Times*, June 19, 1988, p. A1. Also see Susskind and Cruikshank, pp. 165–175.

Chart 3.8	Stakeholder	Interests
	The parents	specific parents would like their children to win recognition.
	The teachers	they want to get a good rating from their principal
	The principal	Mr. Jones votes on his contract
	Mr. Jones, boardmember	he hates "sissies"
	The mayor	he wants to bring the school system up-to-date

camping trip we can dismiss her anxiety as a concern of ours by calling her "overprotective." On the other hand, we might show our approval of her concern by characterizing her as an "involved parent."

We call a person "irrational" to resist conceding legitimacy to the reasons he or she offers for acting. If a student will not work for the incentives we are prepared to provide, he or she is "lazy." If he or she does not bear our remarks patiently and answers back, we call such challenge "insolence."

Our language provides us with many terms for disapproving or approving the interests that underlie a person's perception of a problem. It is important to avoid them if our purpose is analysis. Chart 3.9 compares terms of rejection with terms of recognition of interest. It is important to realize that terms such as those in the left column of the chart are very judgmental. And you can't expect to understand people's motivations if you indulge yourself in descriptions of them which deny legitimacy to their interests and concerns. It makes a big difference whether a teacher sees himself or herself faced with a class that is "lazy" or a class that is "insufficiently motivated." Such delegitimating characterizations are often part of the traditions of a school or institution, for example, "nerds," "jocks," "heads," and "Speds." In fact, the Temple image of the school tends to reinforce itself with such characterizations.

Proposals for Change: "Solutions" and Positions

Normally, when people declare a situation to be a problem, they have a ready proposal to change it. It is easy to claim that a solution is at hand. But it is rare to have one. Let's develop a critical technique for examining proposals.

The next Analysis Question is:

Q5: **What changes, if any, do they propose?**
Examine their positions.
Is the proposal sloganeering?
Is the proposal technically usable?

Chart 3.9

Rejection of Interest	Recognition of Interest
lazy	insufficiently motivated
irrational	having reasons different from mine
insolent	self-assertive
obsequious	very concerned about tact
infantile	focused on the here-and-now
pig-headed	insistent, committed
gutless	cautious
fanatic	single-minded

Just as "problems" can be slogans, so also can "solutions." The "technical feasibility" rule given next helps distinguish sloganistic, "formal" solutions from potentially workable, "technical" solutions:

technical feasibility
THE RULE:

Ask of the solution-proposal, **Can it fail?**
- **No** identifies slogans.
- **Yes** identifies real possibilities.

Formal solutions are not identified independent of the problem situation. Technical solutions are. Consider the pairs of problems and solutions in Chart 3.10. The odd-numbered ones will be formal solutions. The even-numbered ones will be technical solutions. Can you see why?

We can see that the odd-number solution proposals are safe. They cannot fail. Logically they are denials of the problem. You can't possibly have the problem if the formal solution is achieved. We don't even need to test them. But the even-numbered solution proposals could well fail. They must pass the test of experience to determine their effectiveness.

Real, practical attempts at solving a problem are risky. They can fail. "Formal" solutions are dead certain. If you fail you haven't done it right. But they don't really tell you what to do, because they are merely reformulations of the problem situation in the form of a solution. Formal solutions do not specify tasks that would change the situation. They say little more than "Do something that will solve this problem!" Technical solutions specify tasks. "Do this," they indicate, "and it will **cause** the change you desire!"

An important function of formal solutions in a political environment is to keep technically knowledgeable people under the control of their appointed leaders. By issuing vague directives, "Motivate at-risk youth!", "Get kids to say No to drugs!" school people are burdened with a mission of unquestionable concern. But the very vagueness of the directive both evades commitment to provide resources and denies school people an objective standard for judging their efforts. The anxiety this conflict produces makes for stressed-out but docile school people.

Chart 3.10	Problem	Solution
	1. Kids are noisy.	1. Quiet them down.
	2. Kids are noisy.	2. Get them to work.
	3. No homework is done.	3. Motivate students sufficiently.
	4. No homework is done.	4. Threaten lunch detentions.
	5. Kids don't learn.	5. Hire really competent teachers.
	6. Kids don't learn.	6. Feed them Wheaties.
	7. Funds are wasted.	7. Increase efficiency.
	8. Funds are wasted.	8. Decentralize purchasing.
	9. Kids use drugs.	9. Really educate them not to.
	10. Kids use drugs.	10. Give them support and counsel.

The first reaction many people have when this distinction between formal and technical solutions is pointed out to them is to claim disbelief that anyone would use "formal" solutions as change proposals. But they are by far the most common. Just listen to anyone on a public platform talk about solutions. He or she cannot be technical, or the audience either won't understand or might think the proposal too risky. The following is a true story:

> A psychologist was sent to a state senate hearing as an expert witness for a local school district. He was to assure the funding agency heads that Special Education funds were being appropriately used. He began by describing the intake process, the tests used and the assignment procedure. Right in the middle of a sentence, a commissioner interrupted him and said, "Look, Professor, cut out this technical jargon and tell us what is being done!" The psychologist thought a minute then said, "Appropriate tests are being used in an efficient placement process to remedy the problem!" The hearing board was satisfied.

Powerholders

Why do reform movements come and go and schools stay substantially the same? A key reason is that the stakeholders are often not the powerholders. The stakeholders, alone, are often unable to overcome the conflict. Identifying the powerholders is an important step in addressing schooling problems.

The next analysis question is.

Q6: **Can and will anything be done?**
Locate the Powerholders. Are they stakeholders?
Are the power holders willing to change or is conflict preferred?
Are they able to change?

It might seem strange to ask if conflict is preferred, especially when all involve profess the most sincere desires to find an amicable solution. But, as we will see in Chapter 4, conflict has many benefits, especially for the leadership of conflicting groups.

From time to time it becomes the educational fashion to talk of school reform as a matter of identifying "change agents." But change agents are stakeholders—if only for the sake of a consultant's fee—who are also powerholders, that is, someone *able* to make the change and *willing* to do it. If no such people exist, a problem cannot be dealt with.

The Outcomes

Every change proposal implicitly redefines who the potential stakeholders are: who pays the costs and who receives the benefits. This is why change is threatening; not simply because it is change. Our final question addresses this issue:

Q7:   **Who gains and who loses from the change?**
   Specify
      costs and benefits, and who suffers or enjoys them.

To understand the difficulties in bringing about change, we have to realize that every situation provides costs and benefits in varying degrees to various people. To propose a change is to propose a reallocation in costs and benefits. Of course, that something is a cost or a benefit depends upon the perceptions of specific persons. Implementing change successfully requires getting stakeholders to agree that the reallocation of costs and benefits does not generate more conflicts for them than the status quo.

SCHOOL PROBLEMS AND CONSENSUS

We should recognize that solving school problems depends on many different consensus:

- The problem itself is *a consensus of concern*, resting on *a consensus of perceptions*.
- These perceptions themselves require *a consensus on criteria* and to some extent *a consensus on authority*.
- Selecting a change proposal depends upon *a consensus of expectations*. If the proposal is a technical, rather than a formal one, *consensus on a specified task* is at issue.
- But a consensus of stakeholders is not sufficient. What is needed is *a consensus of powerholders* on resources, on willingness and ability to make the change.
- But because change means a reallocating of costs and benefits, consensus on change must ultimately be founded on *a consensus to bear new costs in order to enjoy new benefits*.

In the next chapter we will look at the nature of controversy in education and apply the techniques developed in this chapter to better understand them. Second, we will use slogans productively to generate a normal model of school functioning that relates consensus to expectations, tasks, and resources.

SUMMARY

1.   Underlying school problems are conflict situations. Problems in schooling are generally stated as abstract problems. Although this practice generates a consensus of concern, it also makes it difficult to determine whose concerns are involved. It may be possible to formulate abstract "solutions" for abstract problems, but they may not address the concrete realities that underlie the problems.

2. Problems are treated as situations that concern people. Proceeding from this perspective we can identify as pertinent items that remain hidden when only abstract problems are discussed. These items are: the situation, the stakeholders, their perceptions, their concerns, their proposals for change, the powerholders, and the outcomes of the proposed change.

3. The fundamental consensus is consensus on authority. Failing this, practical knowledge is possible if common criteria are accepted. Pluralistic societies tend to share a broad but shallow consensus on authority.

4. Proposals for change are often empty formalisms: verbal solutions that cannot fail because they do not really indicate a course of action. Feasible proposals are always risky. A common but important strategem to recognize is the use of words like "lazy" or "irrational" which delegitimate concerns and interests.

QUESTIONS

1. "Teenage suicide is a problem." Is this statement a slogan? Explain your answer.
2. Are the expectations indicated by what people call school problems divisible or indivisible? How do you justify your answer?
3. What kind of evidence would it take to decide the merits of the "degeneracy hypothesis"?
4. Write down a problem you have. Identify the situation which affects you. Is the situation the problem or the fact that it affects you?
5. Most people would agree that there is a drug problem in our schools. Far fewer would agree that there is a smoking problem of equal or greater severity. Why is this?
6. Who are the stakeholders for the drug problem and the smoking problem? How many of them are in school?
7. The number of smoking-related deaths each year is approximately 300,000. Drug-related deaths number under 5,000. Should educators be more concerned with the drug problem than the smoking problem?
8. Write down a problem of yours. Use the so-what technique to get at intrinsic values.
9. Find terms which express a recognition of an interest for each of the following terms used to reject interest:
    a. immature
    b. cold-blooded
    c. aggressive
    d. sneaky
    e. incoherent.
10. List five school problems. For each one write a sloganistic solution proposal and a technical solution proposal.

CONTROVERSY, CONFLICT, and the SCHOOL

Chapter 4

PREVIEW

In this chapter we look at controversies about schooling. We will see that controversy indicates conflict. But conflict is not a social illness. On the contrary, conflict is a normal occurrence where many people have to coordinate their activities. Also, conflict serves important functions in preserving and enhancing groups. Handling conflict productively in schools requires political skill and the wisdom to understand that not all conflicts are adversarial in nature.

Using the Analysis Questions developed in the last chapter, we will analyze a controversy over contraceptive clinics in schools. Other controversies we will examine are those dealing with control of the schools and teacher certification. We will consider the general conditions necessary for the resolution of controversy.

In the last section of this chapter we develop a model of effective education, putting slogans to practical use to develop a framework for assessing schooling practice.

INTRODUCTION

Rural visitors to a large city like Chicago or New York are at first startled by the noise, the bustle, and the closeness of massed humanity. In a short while, though, they will stop hearing the blare of traffic or feeling the press of the crowds. It becomes a normal and thus invisible experience.

Most of us have spent years and years in schools. Situations that would strike us as remarkable in any other context are overlooked as normal. To understand schooling we have to be like city-dwellers opening themselves up again to the noise of traffic or to intrusive encounter with strangers. We have to consider what is "normal" in schools and try to place it in other contexts. We have to look at other organizations, such as churches and corporations, and ask what parallels and dissimilarities exist in schools. This is very much like paying close attention to your own breathing: somewhat unnerving, perhaps worrisome. But so far as schools are concerned, it can be enlightening.

We have already taken the first steps toward resensitizing ourselves by contemplating the school in the images of temple, factory, and town meeting. Also, we have the Analysis Questions at our disposal. Precisely because they appear overly inquisitive or even impertinent, they function to penetrate the assumptions that make schooling look so pedestrian.

Because schooling touches so many kinds of people so deeply, controversy and conflict are at the core of the experience. There are available numerous books that present educational controversies.[1] Yet many people, locked into the image of School-as-Temple, think they should be models of serenity. Kids know differently. So do teachers and administrators who remain sensitive to

---

[1]E.g., James W. Noll, ed. *TAKING SIDES: Clashing Views on Controversial Educational Issues* (Guilford, Conn.: Dushkin, 1987), or Dwight W. Allen and Jeffrey C. Hecht, eds., *Controversies in Education* (Philadelphia: W. B. Saunders, 1974).

the difficulties we all experience in reconciling our individual needs to the demands of the social order.

Education has been controversial since ancient times. Recall the comment made in the first chapter by Aristotle:

> . . . mankind are by no means agreed about the things to be taught, whether we look to virtue or the best life. Neither is it clear whether education is more concerned with intellectual or moral virtue.[2]

More than two thousand years later, things have not changed. To understand why, it helps to recapture a certain sense of naivete, as if we were newcomers to the scene. Our concern in this chapter is educational controversies: controversies often obscured by the routine of daily school practice. With our "outsider's" sense of novelty we will try to understand how controversy develops naturally out of the routine.

LIBERTY AND CONTROVERSY

> I maintain that those who blame the quarrels of the Senate and [of] the people of Rome condemn that which was the very origin of liberty, and that they were probably more impressed by the cries and noise which these disturbances occasioned in the public places, than by the good effect which they produced.[3]
>
> —————— *Niccolò Machiavelli*

Conflict occurs whenever one course of action impedes another. Controversy is substantially rarer. **Controversy** occurs only when people have the freedom to give voice to their conflicts. So it was that among the free citizens of the Roman Republic conflict could gain expression as controversy. The citizens of many modern dictatorships do not enjoy similar liberties. One does not find such controversies raging among them.[4] Where liberty is lacking, controversy is sedition.

---

[2]Politics, Book VIII.

[3]Niccolo Machiavelli, *Discourses on the First Ten Books of Titus Livius*, Book 1, Chapter IV, Christian E. Detmold, trans. (New York: Carlton House, undated), p. 119. Machiavelli is commonly misunderstood as an adviser to tyrants. However, he suffered for his republican ideals. See Thomas Babington Macaulay, "Machiavelli," in Charles W. Eliot, ed. *The Harvard Classics*, Vol. 27 (New York: Collier, 1910), pp. 381–421.

[4]Popular protest in the Soviet Union against nuclear power plants was officially unrecognized for some time. Because it could not be contained, it became the basis for controversy. See Bill Keller, "Soviet Scraps a New Atomic Plant In Face of Protest Over Chernobyl," *New York Times*, January 28, 1988, p. 1.

Figure 4.1

CONTROVERSY

		YES	NO
C O N F L I C T	**Y E S**	FREEDOM OF EXPRESSION	SUPPRESSION
	N O	NOT POSSIBLE	NOT UNDER CONSIDERATION

Figure 4.1 displays the possibilities. Three important points can be drawn from the chart:

1. Controversy is the indicator of conflict.
2. Conflict can occur without controversy.
3. Without conflict there can be no controversy.

Controversy is primarily debate, dispute, or quarrel. Once conflict has escalated past a certain point, we no longer talk about controversy. World War II was **not** a controversy between the Allies and the Axis. But participation in it was still a matter of controversy in many religious groups whose members enjoyed the liberty of dissent without risking their fellowship. By way of contrast, there was dispute among members of the German High Command, even to the point of confrontations with Adolf Hitler himself, over tactical matters.[5] In general, however, Nazi Germany was free of controversy. We should not think, however, that totalitarian societies avoid conflict by suppressing controversy. This is an illusion. Freedom from controversy may indicate freedom from conflict. More likely, however, it indicates the loss of important human liberties.

ARE SCHOOLS THE PLACE FOR CONTROVERSY?

Despite the fact that controversy is a by-product of liberty, many people believe that it has no place in the school. In their concept of a moral community, conflict is subversion. Controversy is considered to be harmful and moves are made to squelch it or cover it up,[6] even though conflict serves many beneficial purposes. Robert G. Owens writes,

[5]John Keegan, *The Mask of Command* (New York: Viking, 1987), p. 291.
[6]"Stop the Student Presses. The Supreme Court Says Educators Can Censor School Newspapers," *Time*, January 25, 1988, p. 54.

A controversial principal. But is he a powerholder?

> Whereas conflict was once thought to signal a failure of the or-
> ganization, it is being increasingly recognized as a normal and le-
> gitimate aspect of human social systems. Thus conflict is not only
> inevitable but, contrary to earlier views, it can serve a useful func-
> tion by stimulating creative solutions to problems.[7]

Any teacher who has had to face a classroom of recalcitrant students will
find Owens' comment overly optimistic. Getting a job done often means putting an end to dispute. But educators also know all too well how their own
professional judgment is often overridden for the sake of avoiding controversy.

School people have to function under a variety of conflicting demands.
Teachers are supposed to treat each child as an individual yet move the class
along through externally determined curricula. Principals are asked to maintain a just authority, yet respond to individual differences. Keeping costs down
is an almost universal criterion of administrative competence. Yet education
costs money. Along with the real joys of teaching and running a good school

---

[7]Robert G. Owens, *Organizational Behavior in Education* (Englewood Cliffs, N.J.: Prentice-Hall,
1970), p. 262.

often goes a considerable amount of stress due to the conflicting demands placed upon school people.

What is the proper balance between a commitment to educational goals and the airing of conflicts? Who should have the right to decide this balance? The many chapters of this book aim to inform this debate.

THE FUNCTIONS OF CONFLICT

Reflective people are often dismayed that the leaders of opposing factions profess the desire for peace, even as they wage war. Union and schoolboard leaders express severe misgivings about closing down the schools as they wrangle themselves, inevitably, it seems, into a strike. To the uninformed eye, this looks like blatant hypocrisy. It is not.

Public expressions of desire are not merely a method of disseminating information. "I sincerely wish to put an end to this conflict" is not meant to inform the public about some leader's state of mind. Rather, it is a move in a negotiation process that may well result in peace. But there is a hidden proviso.

"I sincerely wish to put an end to this conflict" has to be understood as meaning "I sincerely wish to put an end to this conflict provided that the costs of ending it do not outweigh its benefits." Wars **could** be avoided if one side would agree to accept the aggression of the other. School strikes **could** be avoided if teachers would uncomplainingly accept lowered salaries, staff cutbacks, increased class sizes, and arbitrary administrative decisions. But wise negotiators understand that every unresisted encroachment on the prerogatives of a group invites additional ones. Conflict cannot be avoided by capitulation renamed "cooperation." Sociologist Charles H. Cooley comments,

---

POINT/COUNTERPOINT: IS CONFLICT AVOIDABLE?

There are in Western culture three deeply opposed schools of thought on the nature of conflict. The first, based on religious traditions, teaches that humankind's basically perverse nature causes perpetual conflict in this world. The individual's susceptibility to evil causes conflict. In another world, more perfect than this, conflict will not exist.

The second school of thought purports that conflict is avoidable, for each individual within himself or herself, at least. Rational, principled persons, says this theory, cannot experience internal conflicts. Principles, rationally prioritized through critical reflection, cannot cause conflict. The conflicts that do occur will be only with irrational, unreflective, or unprincipled persons. Adherents of this theory may perceive themselves as rational, reflective, and principled and those who disagree with them as either irrational, unreflective, or unprincipled.

The third school of thought, generally followed in this text, is that principles are too general and not clearly prioritizable, whereas reality is too full and complex, to avoid conflict. What we have to do is learn how to handle conflict reasonably and humanely.

The more one thinks of it, the more he will see that conflict and cooperation are not separable things, but phases of one process which always involves something of both.[8]

If a person sees the school in the image of a moral community, a Temple, conflict seems to be an indication of something wrong. Similarly, the image of the school as Factory tolerates little conflict. These views occur primarily because under both images the school is seen as **monocratic**, ruled by a single person or group of people. Consequently, it is the perceptions of the powerholders that become the norm for the entire organization. The principal as moral leader speaks for the school. How subversive, how immoral, to suggest his interests might be narrower than those of the entire community! As director of production in the school factory, the principal looks at conflict as "inefficient," impeding production. Again, to suggest that the principal might favor personal goals is to attack his or her competence or sincerity! So it is that our fixation with either image of the school blinds us to the way conflict serves to maintain and enhance groups.

Conflict serves five basic functions both among different groups and within a single group. They are connection, definition, revitalization, reconnaissance, and replication.[9]

Connection.   Conflict makes connection. It is a basic form of exchange and interaction. It is a negotiation. Nine-year-old boys and girls, teachers complain, seldom interact except when they quarrel or fight. The people who everyone describes as "not getting along" are doing just that, but in a way that is often considered socially undesirable. No one has to fight. He or she can just walk away. But what will the person lose if they do? Conflict provides a basic way of asserting one's relationship with another person. **Among groups** conflict maintains a form of negotiation. **Within groups** it does so by releasing tensions among members that might harm the group. One of the hallmarks of professional conduct is that persons who do not like one another personally can nonetheless work together.

Definition.   Conflict **among groups** sharpens their exterior boundaries. It heightens the sense of "us" versus "them." **Within groups** conflict focuses the differences between ranks and social levels. The teacher demonstrates his or her rank and authority in the process of ordering students what to do.

Revitalization.   Conflict **among groups** revitalizes traditions and norms. School spirit has a lot to do with interscholastic games. Indeed, the major purpose of sports is the group solidarity the conflict promotes. **Within groups**, the individual is confronted with an opportunity to recommit himself

---

[8]Charles H. Cooley, *Social Process* (New York: Scribner's Sons, 1918), p. 39. Quoted in Lewis Coser, *The Functions of Social Conflict* (New York: Free Press, 1956), p. 18.
[9]This is adapted from Coser, *The Functions of Social Conflict.*

or herself to the values that underlie membership in the group. This is the reason that harassment and hazing form part of the initiation ritual in so many groups. Hazing may drive many away, but those who remain are the more tightly bonded for it.

Reconnaissance. Information gathering, reconnaissance, is a function of conflict. Small-scale conflicts often determine whether large-scale conflicts are worth the trouble. New teachers face "testing" by their students to see how serious the teachers are about school rules and procedures. Students will deliberately break small rules to see how safe it would be to break bigger ones. **Among groups** conflict serves this information-gathering purpose. **Within groups** reconnaissance often serves to determine whether some members will accommodate or reject a deviant member. Students who are seen as "different" often become "troublemakers" in the eyes of adults. This reputation gives them leverage in their personal negotiations with those considered "normal."

Replication. Groups that are potential adversaries often reflect (replicate) each other's complexity. **Among groups**, conflict causes replication. One does not find, for example, teachers in a large school district represented by several small unions. Rather, one large, complexly organized union serves the function. Because conflict among groups serves to revitalize mores and traditions, we can expect to observe a greater conformity in the behavior **within the group**. Each person replicates, in some way, the next. In many schools, the big Thanksgiving day game is preceded by a "school spirit week" during which students and staff are expected to wear school colors. Also, many schools promote contests among classes over attendance and grades with the intention that group pressure will persuade individual students within a class to perform up to the level of the group.

Figure 4.2 shows how the functions of conflict parallel each other among groups and within groups. We can see that conflict can benefit a group. But it is important to ask, whom does conflict benefit when it benefits a group?

Symbolic and Substantial Benefits

One thing becomes clear early on: not everyone in a group may benefit equally from group membership. Nor does everyone pay the same costs. In addition, some costs and benefits are much more substantial than others. The parents whose sons fall in battle bear much more substantial costs than the political leader who regrets their loss. Similarly more substantial are the benefits of physical safety over the honors bestown on the fallen and the wounded.

The issue of substantial benefits and costs can be set out apart from questions of individual value commitments. **Substantial benefits and costs** are those recognized as benefits and costs by people who are not members of a specific group or not committed to the values of that group. Other benefits and costs we will call **symbolic.** Many people value symbolic benefits even

Figure 4.2

THE FUNCTIONS OF CONFLICT (adapted from Coser, 1956)		
function	among groups	within groups
1. Connection	Asserts relationship to other group	Maintains relations by releasing tension
2. Definition	Sharpens exterior boundaries	Sharpens internal boundaries
3. Revitalization	Revitalizes mores and traditions	Strengthens underlying values of membership
4. Reconnaisance	Gets information for peace-making or war	Gets information for cooptation or persecution of deviants
5. Replication	Given a balance of power, generates similarity of structure	Generates a similarity of behavior

to the point of sacrifice of life and limb. In such a case symbolic honors outweigh their substantial costs. Every cultural group makes such tradeoffs.

The distinction between substantial and symbolic benefits is not a clear-cut division, but rather a continuum, as Figure 4.3 shows. To simplify things, we will refer to all such items as benefits, understanding that they may as well be perceived as costs, depending upon who exactly it is that perceives them. Gold and jewels are recognized across many groups as something of value; less so cash, which fluctuates in value, as do stock certificates. Real estate may not have widespread recognition. Esteem, as such, is valued in many groups but its value usually depends on whose esteem it is. Goodwill is often recognized as a cash-value asset for businesses. Baseball cards have value among certain small groups. A high school class pin is recognized by even fewer people outside specific groups as something of value. A lover's letter or memento may be valued highly by an individual, but not have much value to others.

One measure of the substantiality of a benefit is whether it can be used in an exchange among groups. This indicates that substantial benefits are most likely to be seen within groups as instrumental means, rather than ends. Sym-

Figure 4.3   **SUBSTANTIAL AND SYMBOLIC BENEFITS**

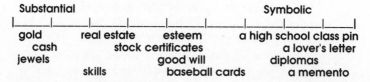

A symbolic or substantial benefit?

bolic benefits are valued within groups as intrinsic, valuable in and of themselves.

Substantiality depends upon consensus, particularly upon consenses about values (see Figure 4.4). In coming to understand the allocation of substantial and symbolic benefits and costs among individuals in a group, and among groups, we uncover the dynamics of organizational change. In distinguishing between symbolic and substantial benefits we can see why, historically, moral communities of all kinds warn against concern with material goods. It is reasonable to expect that the leaders of moral communities would stress that symbolic benefits are of higher value than material goods.

Substantial benefits undermine the moral community by giving their possessors options. They can move out, join another community, and have those substantial goods recognized as such by the new community. Symbolic goods,

Figure 4.4

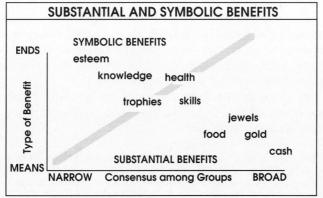

SUBSTANTIAL AND SYMBOLIC BENEFITS

ENDS

SYMBOLIC BENEFITS
esteem
knowledge   health
Type of Benefit
trophies   skills
jewels
food   gold
cash
SUBSTANTIAL BENEFITS
MEANS
NARROW   Consensus among Groups   BROAD

recognized only within a community, bind one to the community and ensure preservation of its traditions.

ADVERSARY AND CONSENSUAL POLITICS

Conflict handling is a political skill. It often happens in the context of the school that politics are equated with the promotion of narrow interests. In this way, a negative view of politics becomes the caricature by which an essential interpersonal skill is disparaged.

Politics is the art of reconciling competing ends to common means. Those with political skills can often get people who pursue different ends to avoid conflict. Politics is the productive management of controversy. Skill in negotiation is at the heart of it. Yet it is not uncommon to hear educators exclaim, "If only politics could be removed from education." This is not merely an empty hope. The attitude that politics "pollutes" education supports authoritarian control processes within organizations. Politics legitimates dissent. For this reason, in a monocratic organization politics is reduced to a minimum.

What people often mean when they decry politics in education is that schools are influenced by considerations other than those that serve the public goals of schools. So it is that school buildings are built with coal furnaces to provide business to coal-producing counties of a state. In exchange, the legislature supports funding bills that benefit those schools. The practical result of this exchange may be badly heated school buildings and consequent impairment of learning. Effective financing may undermine such traditional schooling objectives.

We see in the example above a tradeoff of *institutional goals* for *educational goals*. That is, obtaining general financial support for a school system may impair the publicly professed goals of that system, for example, learning. Understanding schooling is understanding what such tradeoffs are, how they come to be, and what can be done about them. The real world of the schools[10] is filled with conflicts of that most stubborn kind, between one good and another good. The art of politics provides one means of reconciling them, particularly in a democracy. The vacuum left by removing politics is often filled by coercion.

It is important to distinguish conventional **adversarial negotiations** from **consensual negotiations**. Not every conflict makes us enemies. People who want to do away with dissent confuse this issue. Adversarial negotiations tend to suppress controversy without addressing the underlying conflict. Consensual negotiations try to get at that conflict.

Susskind and Cruikshank identify five difficulties with conventional adversarial negotiations that make long-term settlement of the underlying conflicts very difficult. These are[11]:

---

[10]See Harry S. Broudy, *The Real World of the Public Schools* (New York: Harcourt Brace Jovanovich, 1972), for many examples.
[11]Lawrence Susskind and Jeffrey Cruikshank, *Breaking the Impasse: Consensual Approaches to Resolving Public Disputes* (New York: Basic Books, 1987), pp. 35–79.

Surgeon General C. Everett Koop, an educator who did not shrink from conflict.

- **the tyranny of the majority**. As we will see elsewhere, majorities often ignore or suppress the real needs and rights of minorities. When this inequity happens, redress may be sought through the courts.
- **short-term political commitment.** Majority decision is often unstable. Old coalitions re-form themselves and different majorities come into being. A small swing-group can often command power far in excess of its numbers. Educators are understandably reluctant to expend energy on such politics, as it affronts the image of both the Temple and the Factory. Mansbridge points out that what is needed here is more respect among persons, rather than efforts to maintain equal protection of interests.[12]
- **the inadequacies of voting.** Voting is often untimely; ballots are cast long after the need has passed. Also, you can't take your vote back if your candidate doesn't deliver. Consensual negotiations can be made contingent on performance. This practice keeps them both satisfactory and timely. Large-group voting legitimates conflict but often does not settle it. Consensual approaches allow reopening of the matter of concern if any stakeholder feels the need for reconsideration. There is something of a dilemma here for educators. We consider voting to be such an intimate part of our culture that to suggest some other way to settle disputes seems undemocratic. Underlying the apparent student and faculty apathy in the recognized formal voting process of the

---

[12]Jane J. Mansbridge, *Beyond Adversary Democracy* (New York: Basic Books, 1980), p. 5.

school—for example, student council and faculty senate—is the assumption of common interest. This assumption may be false, of course, but Mansbridge claims it removes the necessity to participate.[13] What we take to be apathy might actually be consensus.

■ **winner-take-all.** It is not necessarily the case that every conflict need have a winner and a loser, particularly if the situation is complex. Tradeoffs can be made so that each party gains something.

As conflicts occur in the school, it is important to ask whether they need be treated adversarially in an I-win-you-lose-fashion. What would be the costs and benefits of such an approach? Is it possible that a consensual, I-win-and-you-win-too-approach might serve everyone's interests better? Conflict may be inevitable, but not every concession is a capitulation.

The increasing professionalization of educators requires they be able to recognize the nature of school conflict and that they develop the political skills to deal with it. By treating politics as a contamination, educators turn away from participation in the central reality of our society and from the enhancement of their own status. Politics is the market mechanism of liberty. Those who are above politics are soon under someone's thumb.

ANALYZING CURRENT CONTROVERSIES

Complaints about American schools are nothing new. In May 1911 the editors of the *Ladies Home Journal* complained, "on every hand the signs are evident of a widely growing distrust of the effectiveness of the present educational system in this country."[14] In the various chapters of this book we will try to understand many of the controversies and complaints that have been made about the schools. For the moment, however, let's look at some prominent ones that are featured regularly in the news.

Controversy 1: Sex Education and AIDS

The distinction between education and schooling is never more telling than when it touches on human sexuality.[15] It is not for lack of advertising skill that school people do not promote sex education as "sexual schooling." Rather they recognize a widespread fear that the innocence of childhood might be contaminated by the mere knowledge of sexuality. The idea that children are asexual—and that they therefore ought to remain so—is one that is historically

---

[13]Mansbridge, xii.

[14]Cited in Raymond E. Callahan, *Education and the Cult of Efficiency* (Chicago: University of Chicago Press, 1962), p. 48.

[15]Debra Viadero, "AIDS Threat Providing Impetus for Sex-Education Mandates," *Education Week*, June 3, 1987, p. 1.

recent[16] and restricted to particular social classes in Western European cultures. So, the reality in most American schools is that learning about sex is not seen on a par with learning about quadratic equations.[17]

The AIDS problem makes the normal controversy[18] about sex education even fiercer.[19] On the face of it, the solution seems simple: tell kids how to prevent AIDS. But this requires bringing up subjects that many adults fear would be "cheapened" in the process. Even as Surgeon-General Koop warned against an "explosion" of AIDS,[20] recommending that children be given straight information about its causes and means of prevention, President Reagan advocated abstinence as its only preventative.[21] Meanwhile, researchers find that sexual activity among teenagers is on the increase.[22] We know that 25 percent of sexually active teenagers never use contraceptives and only one-third of them use them consistently.[23] Thus the majority of sexually active teenagers are vulnerable to AIDS.

Yet, upon the disclosure that nine school health clinics in New York City had been dispensing contraceptives without a formal authorization from the board of education, the vicar of education for the Roman Catholic archdiocese of New York called the practice "outrageous" and "a betrayal of fundamental parental rights." Some board members joined in the criticism and voiced "suspicions" that the clinics were primarily in areas with large minority populations because they might be part of a plot to limit their numbers. So, board members have pressured principals of schools with those clinics to discontinue dispensing birth control aids on school grounds. In California, Governor Deukmejian vetoed a bill that would have financed three such facilities.[24]

We must recognize here that the controversy is by no means merely over the issue of the causal efficiency of contraceptives to prevent pregnancy or AIDS, although this is probably the foremost consideration in the minds of their proponents. Not even the physical well-being of the students is crucial to some parties to the dispute. What have been raised in New York are underlying interests of moral authority[25] and racism.[26]

---

[16]See, for example, "From Immodesty to Innocence," *Centuries of Childhood*, Philippe Aries, ed. (London: Jonathan Cape, 1962), Chap. 5, pp. 100–127.

[17]Cf. John Passmore, "Sex Education," *The New Republic*, October 4, 1980, pp. 27–32.

[18]Debra Viadero, "Wide Distribution of Contraceptives Advocated," *Education Week*, December 12, 1987.

[19]Blake Rodman, "Sex Education Said Key to Stemming Spread of AIDS," *Education Week*, October 29, 1986, p. 1.

[20]"Koop Warns of an 'Explosion' of AIDS Among Teenagers," *Education Week*, June 24, 1987, p. 10.

[21]"Reagan Again Urges Abstinence to Fight AIDS," *Education Week*, April 5, 1987, p. 4.

[22]"Research and Reports: More Girls Becoming Sexually Active by 16," *Education Week*, June 17, 1987, p. 3.

[23]*Covering the Education Beat* (Washington, D.C.: Education Writers' Association, 1987), p. 57.

[24]"Debate Intensifies Over School-Based Health Clinics," *Education Week*, October 15, 1986, p. 9.

[25]See also Kirsten Goldberg, "Catholic Bishops Sharply Attack School Clinics," *Education Week*, November 25, 1987, p. 1.

[26]Debra Viadero, "Clinics' Birth-Control Efforts Aim To Control Growth in Black Population, Some Charge," *Education Week*, November 11, 1986, p. 1.

Analyzing the AIDS Controversy

Let's use the analysis questions to see what we can make of the AIDS controversy. Given the information we have we can hardly expect to do more than scratch the surface. There is controversy here because the solution to one group's problems is seen as a problem by another group.

ANALYSIS QUESTIONS

Q1. What is the situation?
Q2. Whom does it concern?
Q3. How do they perceive it?
Q4. Why does it concern them?
Q5. What changes do they propose?
Q6. Can and will anything be done?
Q7. Who gains and who loses from the change?

Q1. What is the situation? Sexually active teens run the risk of AIDS. Perhaps it would be better to answer: teens who engaged in x acts of intercourse with y different partners run a risk of probability p that they will contract AIDS. Why is this better? It requires specifics of the sort that would tend to tone down the controversy. Pressing for facts often calms rhetoric. It would, however, be very difficult to get the specifics. But the numbers are crucial. They will affect considerably our strategies for dealing with the situation.

Q2. Whom does it concern? A variety of people. But it is not clear that either the Archdiocese of New York nor the minority leadership protesting the clinics sees that in this controversy the situation given above is the problem. Let's restrict ourselves to two groups and work out the situation—artificially, of course—for them alone.

Group 1:   the Catholic Archdiocese of New York.
Group 2:   the principals in the schools with clinics.

We have picked these two because the proposals to open clinics were apparently supported by group 2 and opposed by group 1. Why is this?

Q3. How do they perceive it? We can suppose that both groups see sexual activity as a danger, direct or indirect, threatening the teenagers.

Q4. Why does it concern them? Both groups consist of people whose normal charge it is to identify and express such concerns. But the risk run by each group on the issue of the clinics is quite different. It is not clear, for example, that the vicar of education risks anything by opposing the clinics. But the principals who allowed them to open in their schools without the express directive of the board of education may risk their jobs. On the other hand, principals are sometimes paid more for accepting additional programs in their schools. It may also be the case that the leaders in the school com-

Chart 4.1

	Group 1: NY Archdiocese	**Group 2: Clinic School Principals**
Q4. Why does it concern them?	Teens are sexually active.	Teens will get and spread the disease.
So what?	This opposes Church teachings on chastity.	Attendance wil fall; panic will spread.
So what?	This is immoral.	This is undesirable.

munity strongly approve of the principals' initiatives. This approval strengthens the principals politically in their dealings with central administration. (Principals often have to fight for what they get for their schools by bringing community pressure to bear.) These are only some indications of what the underlying interests might be. The controversy is actually far more complex because it is not restricted to the two groups we have chosen.

We have to work in two columns in Chart 4.1 because the list of interests generated by reiterating **So what?** varies with the two groups. It would be unfair to suggest that either group is less concerned than the other that the students who get AIDS will die. The question is how this concern fits in with other ones. Does morality take precedence over survival? Does a school atmosphere free of panic or high absenteeism take precedence? Suppose AIDS were perceived not to be contagious and it took twenty symptom-free years to kill you. Would the principals still have opened the clinics?

For lack of information we have gotten rather quickly to intrinsic interests, for example, morality and undesirability. What this restricted exercise does show is that the underlying interests can be quite different from one another. The principals' response bears some more inquiry. It likely hides some instrumental concerns.

Q5. What changes, if any, do they propose? We will guess at the Archdiocesan proposal[27] and put it in Chart 4.2 together with the next question:

Q6. Can and will anything be done?

---

[27]Cf. Michael D. Schaffer, "Promoting Teen Chastity Is Troupe's Act of Virtue," *The Philadelphia Inquirer*, February 7, 1989, p. B-1. Acting troupe, Inasense, from Bishop McDevitt High School, tours with morality play.

Chart 4.2

	Group 1: NY Archdiocese	**Group 2: Clinic School Principals**
Q5 What changes do they propose?	Emphasis on chastity.	Clinics in schools.
Q6. Can and will anything be done?	Increased instructional effort.	Opening of the clinics.

Chart 4.3

	Group 1: NY Archdiocese	Group 2: Clinic School Principals
Q7: Who gains and who loses?	Parents' authority is undermined.	School morale is not affected.
Q7: Who gains and who loses?	Church's authority is undermined.	Principals are seen to show concern.

Q7. Who gains and who loses from the change? It is about this question that the controversy devolves. The clinics opened. The two groups saw the reallocation of costs and benefits differently as they affected different groups. (We give four in Chart 4.3.)

It's clear that what is involved is lack of consensus on very basic issues. This is an obvious clash of the Temple with the Factory. Another way to understand the conflict is that it is a conflict between symbolic and substantial benefits. The substantial benefit of reduced disease will be recognized across many communities and thus the clinic program promises broad political support. But the symbolic costs to the Archdiocese of New York were shared with other religious denominations.[28] These were able to be translated into greater political power, since the dispensing of contraceptives by the clinics was halted. Power is still an important factor even if symbolic costs and benefits are recognized only within a specific moral community. Let's turn now to another dispute.

Controversy 2: Control of the School

In 1986 the Carnegie Task Force on Teaching as a Profession issued a report titled *A Nation Prepared: Teachers for the 21st Century*.[29] Meaningful educational reform, it insists, requires nothing less than the full professionalization of teaching. The report endorses revamping the school bureaucracy to permit a professional level of autonomy and responsibility for teachers. It advocates restructuring the teaching force, and introduces a new category of "lead teachers." And it states flatly that teachers' salaries and career opportunities must be competitive with those of other professions. The School District of Rochester, New York, has undertaken many of the proposals of the Carnegie commission in its present contract with its teachers.[30] The teachers have applauded the greater autonomy and increased salaries.[31]

---

[28]See Robert Rothman, "Church Groups Attack Sex-Education Plan," *Education Week*, December 17, 1987, p. 1.
[29]*A Nation Prepared: Teachers for the 21st Century* (San Diego: The Task Force on Teaching as a Profession, The Carnegie Forum on Education and the Economy, 1986).
[30]"Friendship and Trust: Unusual Key to Radical Pact," *Education Week*, September 30, 1987, p. 1.
[31]See "A Blueprint for Better Schools," *U.S. News & World Report*, January 18, 1988, pp. 60–65.

On the other hand, the 10,000 member American Federation of School Administrators (AFSA) is seeking to halt efforts by the American Federation of Teachers (AFT) to acquire responsibilities traditionally held by principals. The AFSA has complained that the AFT, a sister union, is violating the constitution of the AFL-CIO to which both belong. A similar complaint was made in a suit filed in state court in December 1986 by administrators in Rochester, New York, that sought to dismantle the "mentor teacher" program on the grounds that it encroached on their authority.[32]

Let's quickly lay out the problem using the Analysis Questions.

Q1. What is the situation? The situation here is that teachers in Rochester make decisions that were previously reserved to administrators.

Q2. Whom does it concern? The teachers and the administrators.

Q3. How do they perceive it? The teachers see it as gaining control over the factors that most directly influence their teaching. The administrators see it as a loss of decision-making prerogatives.

Q4. Why does it concern them? The teachers now directly control factors that influence their teaching. The administrators have less say over matters than they did formerly.

So what? The teachers see it as a proper recognition of their professional status. The administrators see it as undermining their professional status. That we have escalated quickly here to intrinsic values is significant, as we will discuss below.

Q5. What changes, if any, do they propose? The teachers have no proposal. The administrators want to change back to their former status.

Q6. Can and will anything be done? The American Federation of School Administrators has initiated a complaint to the AFL-CIO against the American Federation of Teachers. Whether this will have any effect remains to be seen.

Q7. Who gains and who loses from the change? If the situation can be reversed, the administrators believe they will gain from the exchange.

Through our analysis we can see that the major impediment to the productive resolution of this conflict is the manner is which it is being perceived by both the AFSA and the AFT. We can understand the call to professionalism as an attempt to transform the conflict into one over symbolic benefits. Symbolic benefits are a lot harder to negotiate with than are substantial benefits because they do not lend themselves to compromise. They tend to make conflicts adversarial rather than consensual.

Perhaps this quick escalation into a conflict over symbolic values indicates a deeper antagonism between the two groups: why couldn't they compromise on who decides what? Or, perhaps the administrators feel vulnerable because

---

[32]"Grievance Targets A.F.T. Efforts on Professional Role," *Education Week*, May 13, 1987, p. 1.

the schoolboard, which demands the evaluation of administrative performance and threatens their jobs on the results, has contracted away the resources and authority the administrators believe are necessary to perform well. With the information we have, we cannot answer these questions with finality, but the Analysis Questions have helped us identify some interesting areas for investigation.

Controversy 3: Certification and the Nature of Teaching

A critical shortage of teachers has been predicted beginning in the 1980s and lasting into the 1990s.[33] An important question to be considered is whether what is desired is warm bodies to fill up classrooms or whether stronger criteria will be used in addressing the teacher shortage.

A close examination of the Carnegie Task Force's professionalization recommendations reveals there is no direct attempt to define the nature of teaching even though there is little consensus regarding this issue. Some argue, for example, that teaching is an art best compared to the craft of a painter or perhaps a pianist. Some even maintain that teacher education should follow the same patterns as the training of an actor.[34] Here teaching is seen as essentially, perhaps inevitably, unscientific. In this view, teaching is something akin to a calling.

Some educational "reforms" that reflect this model of teaching have already been implemented. The New Jersey "Alternative Route" to teaching, paralleled in other states, is one example. It permits school districts to hire individuals to teach who have little or no training in pedagogy.

If teaching is really a calling that cannot be learned and that depends upon a combination of **subject matter knowledge** and **charisma**, there is little reason to suspect that the Carnegie Task Force's "professionalization" can amount to anything more than "improving teacher status." And such improvement would not necessarily bear at all on the improvement of instruction.

But, while the Carnegie Task Force does not reject these alternative routes to certification, it implies that teaching is an occupation that can and should be informed by causal knowledge. The Task Force also implies that teaching can only be professionalized by ensuring that teachers know how to cause learning. But what the Task Force does **not** do is state this operative principle clearly while explicitly rejecting the noncausal view described earlier. The absence of consensus on the matter is simply ignored.

The charismatic model of teaching is particularly well suited to the Temple image of the school. The causal model is obviously a Factory concept. The cleverness of the charismatic appeal is that it appears to invoke the symbolic benefits of the Temple image, while obscuring the substantial benefits to be

---

[33]*Staffing the Nation's Schools: A National Emergency* (Washington, D.C.: Council of Chief State School Officers, January 1984). A report of the Council of Chief State School Officers Ad Hoc Committee on Teacher Certification, Preparation and Accreditation.
[34]H. Dawe, "Teaching: a performing art," *Phi Delta Kappan*, Vol. 66, No. 3 (1984), pp. 548–552.

gained by schoolboards if teachers can be hired who needn't have undergone a rigorous professional training.

Here, too, professionalism is invoked to enhance the appeal of the causal model. This symbolism obscures the substantial benefits to be gained by teacher-preparation institutions and strictly certified teachers from the restricted market they would enjoy.

Let's lay out the problem using the Analysis Questions.

Q1. What is the situation? There are different and conflicting conceptions as to the nature of teaching.

Q2. Whom does it concern? Many people, including prospective teachers, teacher educators, and school district administrators.

Q3. How do they perceive it? All the groups mentioned are unclear about what being a teacher will mean.

Q4. Why does it concern them? Prospective teachers want to know what their professional preparation will look like and what kind of job awaits them. Teacher educators want to assure themselves a role in the preparation of future teachers. School district administrators want to avoid encroachments on their own prerogatives.

So what? Each group can see a variety of costs and benefits tied into each concept of teaching. Space does not permit a detailed analysis here.

Q5. What changes, if any, do they propose? The teacher educators and the administrators tend to advance or support proposals that support their own interests. (See Q7, below.)

Q6. Can and will anything be done? This remains to be seen.

Q7. Who gains and who loses from the change? The Carnegie Commission's proposals tend to benefit teacher educators and incumbent teachers, **given the present structure of our schools**. Alternate Route proposals tend to benefit prospective teachers in the short run by helping them reach entry level faster. Also, school district administrators are benefited by quickly increasing the supply of available teachers.

THE RANGE OF CONTROVERSY

As the previous section illustrated, the range of controversy in education is wide and we will explore many educational disputes in this book. It will not be our intent to jump into the fray, but to examine the issues as dispassionately as possible in order to understand their origins, their contexts, and their point. This is one reason we have come to develop the set of Analysis Questions. It is the authors' belief that any controversy that persists does not do so out of stupidity or blindness but, rather, because values are threatened which parties to the dispute hold dear. In this book we seek an understanding of these conflicts.

Some controversies we will consider in later chapters are:

- Should states take over ill-functioning school districts?
- Should values (which ones?) be taught in schools?
- Should the schools serve the economy?
- Who should receive what instruction?
- Should schooling be centralized?
- Who should play what role in controlling the school?

Framed as general questions these may not seem controversial. But their specifics invariably are. Educators constantly deal with the conflicts that underlie these questions. But the realities of schools are such that little would get done were they to surface frequently as controversies in the classroom.

But, invariably, these conflicts do surface, disguised as "problems": Johnny's bad behavior may be a question of values, health, or bad teaching. In dealing with such problems as they arise, by not seeing them as related to a wider controversy, educators are socialized into passivity and taught to disdain conflict. And this is, basically, to give up on effectiveness.

Can Educational Problems and Controversies Be Resolved?

It is beyond the scope of this text to provide the reader with more than reasons for studying how to negotiate. Prospective teachers who think this is a secondary matter should realize that administrators are, as a matter of course, prepared in their professional training to expect conflict in the school and to deal with it through negotiation. And teachers are treated as potential adversaries. Those who do not understand how organizations work are put off by the possibility of such conflict and complain, "Can't we just learn to all work together? Why must we have conflict?" This is the wrong question. Learning to work together *is* learning to deal with conflict and learning to negotiate differences among people.

What can we say in general about settling controversies? Negotiation theorist Chester L. Karass gives us an insight.

> ... It is better to start talks with easy-to-settle issues than highly controversial ones. ... Agreement on controversial issues is improved if they are tied to issues on which agreement can easily be reached.[35]

There are three ways to settle an educational problem or controversy:

- dissolve it;
- solve it;
- abandon it.

---

[35]Chester L. Karass, *Give & Take: The Complete Guide to Negotiating Strategies and Tactics* (New York: Crowell, 1974), p. 146.

We can dissolve a problem by showing that the lack of any one of the conditions is needed to provide an answer to some of our basic questions. For example if John says he feels alienated we cannot describe the situation in a manner that is independent of John's reporting on the difference. The independence of situation and person cannot be achieved. Chart 4.4 illustrates other ways problems can be dissolved if conditions necessary to framing the problem are not met.

If we are skillful, we might actually solve the problem by following through the questions and finding people *willing and able* to implement a *technically feasible* change proposal. In the final section of this chapter we will provide a basic model for achieving educational goals based on these conditions.

There is one other circumstance where the pursuit of resolution is abandoned. Negotiation theorists have noticed that deep divisions can often be avoided if small areas of agreement between the conflicting parties are reached first. In effect, increasing the depth of consensus on many small issues has the psychological effect of broadening the consensus as well. But these same theorists caution that dispute based on dissensus on basic authority cannot be negotiated.[36]

Of the kinds of conflicts that can occur between different parties we can identify three basic types:

- conflicts between symbolic benefits, for example, innocence versus knowledge; the sex-education controversy is an example of this conflict.
- conflicts between substantial benefits, for example, time versus money; the dropout problem is an example of this conflict.

---

[36]Cf. Susskind and Cruikshank, op. cit., p. 17, on distributional and constitutional disputes.

Chart 4.4	Question	Condition of Failure
	Q1. What is the situation?	Can't be independently described.
	Q2. Whom does it concern?	Cannot be determined who is concerned.
	Q3. How do they perceive it?	No consensus on focus, i.e., criteria and authority.
	Q4. Why does it concern them?	They are mistaken that their interests are involved.
	Q5. What changes, if any, do they propose?	No technically feasible proposal has been made.
	Q6. Can and will anything be done?	Powerholders are not stakeholders.
	Q7. Who gains and who loses from the change?	Reallocation of costs and benefits opposed by powerholders.

■   conflicts between symbolic and substantial benefits, for example, justice versus schooling costs; the controversy over equal educational opportunity is an example of this conflict.

Although negotiation theorists say that only conflicts over substantial benefits can be resolved, we should remember that conflicts can be dissolved, too. If a conflict is a matter of perception, and perception is a matter of criteria, it is not too hard to imagine a conflict's being defined out of existence in a moral community. This exercise is called—in some communities—apologetics or reconceptualization. It may be resorted to where power is lacking to coerce a settlement in a conflict over symbolic value.

For example, reconceptualization is the process by which sex-blind IQ tests have been developed. The fact is that any test will show differences among different groups of people. Only scores wholly determined by chance will show no bias.[37] To make a sex-blind IQ test we must use an IQ test and select those items that correlate along sexual lines. The remaining items—with some technical adjustments—constitute a sexually unbiased IQ test. IQ thus becomes independent of sex and we have eliminated "bias" by reconceptualizing IQ.

A deep understanding of how to productively handle conflicts requires further study. Real conflict situations have a variety of complications. Howard Raiffa[38] suggests the following questions to examine the complexity of the negotiations:

1. Are there more than two parties? Who is to negotiate?
2. Are the parties groups? Are internal conflicts possible?
3. Is future bargaining at stake?
4. Will precedents be set? Are there connections to other disputes?
5. Is there more than one issue? Can tradeoffs be made?
6. Is an agreement required? Can somebody just quit?
7. Is ratification required? Can constituencies void an agreement?
8. Are threats possible?
9. Are there time constraints?
10. Are the agreements binding?
11. Are the negotiations done in public?
12. What are the group norms? Is cooperation possible?
13. Is third-party intervention possible?

Clearly, these complexities of negotiation merit much more study than we can provide here. All we can do is to present in Chart 4.5 a set of basic principles that provide a good start in handling conflicts in schools.

---

[37]L. J. Cronbach, G. C. Gileser, H. Nanda, and N. Rajaratnam, *The Dependability of Behavioral Measurements: Theory of Generalizability for Scores and Profiles* (New York: Wiley, 1972), p. 385.

[38]Howard Raiffa, *The Art and Science of Negotiation* (Cambridge, Mass.: Belknap Press, 1982), pp. 11–19.

Chart 4.5 **Principles for Dealing with Conflict**

1. **Accept Conflict.** It is not an affront, an immorality, or a sign of incompetence. It is a normal occurrence for complex activities.

2. **Determine whether the involved parties are really adversaries.** Separate the person from the situation. Use the Analysis Questions developed in this book.

3. **Don't confuse public posturing with actual attitudes.** Don't demand trust as a prerequisite, earn it. Look behind the public positions to the underlying interests.

4. **Avoid debate over final, intrinsic values.** See if the conflict can be recast in terms of instrumental values.

5. **Know your Best Alternative to a Negotiated Agreement.** It may allow you to dictate terms. But don't be short-sighted. You could win the battle now and lose the war later.

6. **Look for trade-offs and exchanges.** Avoid making it a win-lose situation. See if all parties can come away with something.

7. **Don't try to settle it once-and-for-all.** Allow for the possibility of reconsideration if the situation changes. Forcing closure often produces bizarre results.

Conflicts can be handled productively. However, we close this section with a somber reminder. Problems and controversies may not find permanent resolution, not only because people change, but also because they may lack consensus on fundamental authorities. This is not a tragedy, but a reality of American Pluralism.

THE BASIC MODEL: ACHIEVING EDUCATIONAL GOALS

Up to now in this chapter we have been trying to understand controversy. We have used the Analysis Questions to push aside the slogans and dig up the specifics of the conflicts underlying them. Controversy indicates a lack of consensus and it is important that we understand just exactly why that consensus is lacking.

In this last section, however, we will reverse the procedure. We will use slogans to develop a model of schooling that will, we hope, enjoy broad consensus. This model will provide the framework for a good deal of the discussion that follows in later chapters.

Using Slogans

We saw in the last chapter how slogans work to support consensus and impede implementation. General statements are easy to agree with. Specifics are needed, however, to get the job done. The problem is that there is often more than one job to be done and not every job is understood as a specification of the slogan.

Slogans can be useful for more than patching together a consensus. We can use them to indicate where to look for problems when things are not working.

Suppose we ask, "How can we achieve school goals?" If we were responsible for implementation, it would do well for us to ask, "*Which* school goals?" Because we are *not* looking to find statements for consensus on implementation, analysis is not to the point right now.

To the question, "How can we achieve school goals?" let's answer, "Through effective implementation." Clearly, this is sloganistic. It cannot fail. Something is not effective if it fails.

Putting the question and answer together we come up with the slogan:

A. School goals are achievable through effective implementation.

"Implementation" is commonly used technical jargon for "tasks feasible for some purpose." Statement A is hardly disputable and nearly vacuous. But it is not just empty verbiage. It can easily be transformed into:

A′: If school goals are not being achieved, implementation is not effective.

We then look to see in what ways effectiveness has been frustrated. Some common reasons for ineffectiveness are

- The task outcomes do not satisfy the goal conditions.
- Other tasks conflict with ours.
- Other goals conflict with the one we pursue.

Notice that these reasons are a mixed bag. To explain failure by saying the task outcomes do not satisfy goal conditions is a longer way of saying that the task is ineffective. But the important point here is that we now have something else to tie down: goal conditions. If someone complains that the schools are failing to turn out literate graduates, we have to determine what "literate" means. Experts disagree.[39]

That other tasks or goals conflict with ours does not necessarily mean our implementation is ineffective. So this is not sloganistic. We have a useful indicator here: If your efforts are ineffective, look for task or goal conflicts. (See Chapter 1, Figure 1.7, which indicates common conflicts in proposed school reforms.)

The Basic Model: the general slogan.

What do we need to carry out a task? What makes a task feasible? Adequate resources. This answer gives us our second slogan:

B. Adequate resources are necessary for feasible tasks.

And this gives us:

B′. Infeasible tasks result from inadequate resources.

What could we count as inadequate resources? Any of the following:

- A certain level of funding.
- A certain level of student motivation or readiness for school.
- A certain level of teacher or administrator competence.
- A certain physical location.
- Certain support activities, for example, duplication, equipment maintenance.

We can put A and B together to get a basic model of a successful schooling process, a statement capturing broad consensus (a slogan) that focuses our efforts to account for failures.[39]

- The Basic Model: School goals are achievable when adequate resources are provided for effective, feasible tasks of implementation . . .

Figure 4.5 illustrates the stages leading to this model.

The Venn diagrams in Figure 4.5 illustrate that

- only tasks that pursue goals are effective tasks;
- only tasks that are provided (sufficient) resources are feasible tasks;
- goals are achievable only when they are pursued by feasible tasks.

We can generate a number of useful slogans from these points, for example, "Goals are achieved by effective, feasible tasks," or the much more intriguing, "Without goals, there is no efficiency."

The model given in Figure 4.5 is simple because we have ignored one thing: consensus. Each item—resources, tasks, or goals—is practically tied into some sort of consensual procedure. What creates difficulty is that the consensus may not be connected, so that those who allocate resources may not agree with those who choose the tasks that define implementation. Nor does either consensus have to depend on the consensus that defines goals. When all is taken into account, the model becomes somewhat more complex.

Some Complexities of Consensus

The greater the variation in expectations, tasks, and resources, the deeper the consensus needed to support action. We can understand the temptation of school people to overlook or deny legitimate variation in goals, methods, and resources such as student abilities and cultural background: these all create consensus problems. But past denials have not made these problems go away.

---

[39]Cf. Education Writers' Association, "Myth #1: There is an Epidemic of Illiteracy in American Society," *The Literacy Beat*, Vol. 1, No. 3 (September 1987).

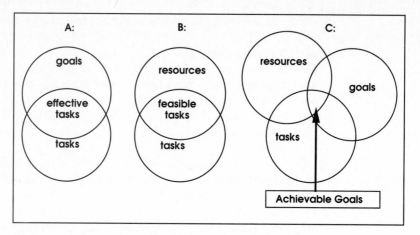

Figure 4.5 Stages Leading to the Basic Model.

The public goals of schools derive from consensus about expectations. Public goals, to be implemented, have to be transformed into specific **tasks**. These educational goals are achievable only if tasks can be derived from them.

Tasks, too, may require a consensual process. The depth of consensus about a goal may affect what tasks are viable operationalizations of it. For example, instruction in art education may enjoy considerable support. But using live nude models may reduce such consensus to nonviability.

Consensus may not be uniform about all items but may involve trade-offs where one group specifies an expectation to be broadly supported and then supports another group's expectation. Such coalitions provide depth of consensus for items that would otherwise not be seen as connected, but such consensus is as stable as the coalitions that support it.

Feasible tasks require resources. But resources may be subject to consensual processes that make specific tasks difficult to sustain. Certain resources require a consensual process for their availability. Examples of these consensual resources are taxes, tuitions, and contributions. Nonconsensual resources include things like endowments, reserve funds, or earnings. The stability of the consensus affects the continued availability of consensual resources. Politically unacceptable tasks can affect the resources needed for their completion.

We have seen that the more specific the task, the less likely the breadth of consensus about the resources it needs. This status encourages appeals to nonconsensual authorities, for example, the courts or commissions to maintain resource levels where consensus is lacking. Similarly, where consensus falters, previously conceded expertise may be challenged through litigation.[40]

A major complication is that the consensual process that selects the expectations may not be the same one that identifies the relevant tasks, nor the

---

[40]Cf. Stephen Goode, "Nation's Schools Courting Trouble," *Insight*, July 11, 1988, pp. 56–57.

one that supports the allocation of resources. Thus, in order to convert political rhetoric into reality, several conditions must be met simultaneously. (See Item B in the Technical Appendix to Chapter 4.) There must be

- **consensus on expectations**, that is, **goals**, translated into
- **effective tasks** selected, possibly, by some other **consensus**, supported by
- **adequate resources**, also selected, possibly, by yet some other **consensus**.

Many other circumstances can prevent the achievement of school goals. For example, the life-spans of each of the factors, consensus, expectations, task, and resources. Will any of the consenses disappear before the others? Will expectations change? Will the task outlive the resources? Suppose, for example, that implementing meaningful educational reform took a minimum of twelve years. Which stakeholders could maintain power for that length of time? What consensus would hold together long enough to get the job done? Let us continue to search for reasonable answers to such questions in the chapters that follow.

SUMMARY

1. Liberty permits the expression of conflict as controversy. The image of the school as Temple or Factory is hostile to the recognition of controversy as a positive force.

2. Conflicts may persist because they provide group definition, revitalize values, and strengthen structure. But benefits within groups may vary. Symbolic benefits are recognized within groups; substantial benefits, across groups.

3. Politics seeks to bring a disparity of ends to a consensus on means. Negotiation may be either adversarial or consensual. The Temple image of the school disparages politics as undermining community. The Factory image finds politics inefficient. The real issue is whether and how conflict is recognized and handled.

4. Controversies in education derive from a variety of circumstances. Most basic are perceptions of conflict among symbolic and substantial benefits. The resolution of controversy can be done by dissolving, resolving, or abandoning the underlying conflict.

5. Slogans can be used to construct a general model for achieving school goals. These do not specify tasks to be done, so much as indicate sources of difficulty when goals are not achieved. At the bottom of all attempts to achieve school goals is the problem of consensus: to what extent and for what aspects of the schooling process is consensus needed?

QUESTIONS

1. Here are some practices common to schools but rarely found elsewhere:
   - asking permission to go to the bathroom
   - raising the hand to be recognized
   - saying the Pledge of Allegiance
   - regularly practicing fire drills
   - being subject to surprise tests

   Can you think of others?

2. Consider the three images of the school. To what extent is controversy tolerated under each image? What relation do you think this has to the age of the children involved. (See Chapter 1, Question 10.)

3. Who has a stake in avoiding or suppressing controversy in the school? What might their concerns be?

4. Consider the functions of conflict. Can you see what benefits there are to school sports? Who benefits from them? Who pays their costs? Why do you think that school sports are emphasized in well-established private schools?

5. Are the following schooling outcomes symbolic or substantial? The ability to
   - compute square roots with pencil and paper
   - read
   - play outstanding basketball
   - recite the poetry of Wordsworth
   - speak Spanish, or
   - read ancient Greek.

6. Consider the situation that sexually active teenagers run the risk of AIDS. Let's recast it as: teens who engage in x acts of intercourse with y different partners run a risk of probability p that they will contract AIDS.

   Consider what might be critical values for x, y, and p as far as identifying different stakeholders are concerned. (Where could you find out the actual statistics for the variables x, y, and p?)

7. Who are the stakeholders in the controversy about the way teachers should be certified? What is at stake?

8. Suppose there were a learning pill. Who would gain and who would lose from such an educational innovation?

9. Who might be the stakeholders and what might be their concerns for the following controversies:
   - Should schools have dress codes?
   - Should kids with AIDS be allowed in school?
   - Should kids be paid for grades?
   - Should values be taught in schools?

10. Give examples of school conflicts of the following types:
    - symbolic values versus symbolic values
    - symbolic values versus substantial values
    - substantial values versus substantial values.

Section II

The Social Foundations of Education

Education in the United States responds to tradition and novelty in the wider social universe, but it has never been a passive hostage to history. It has exerted a strong influence on events both as a major resource in the industrialization process and as an instrument for preserving the continuity of political and social institutions. As such its influence has been simultaneously revolutionary and conservative.

— *Marvin Bressler*

This section of the text is devoted to the study of the relation of school to society. It emphasizes the fact that the school is a **social** institution that exists in complex relationship to the broader society that controls and supports it. This perspective provides a basis for understanding the true limits and possibilities of schooling.

One of the most fundamental things you will discover here is how important nonschool factors, like family dynamics, are to school achievement. Other approaches to education often fail to emphasize their importance. Perhaps these reflect a desire to accentuate the positive, or to highlight only those elements within the teacher's control.

Unfortunately, however, such a celebrationist approach also encourages a superficial understanding of the relationship of school and social realities while simultaneously discouraging critical inquiry. Worse, it promotes unrealistic expectations that ultimately interfere with effective teaching.

SOCIETY, CULTURE, and SCHOOLING

Chapter 5

PREVIEW

In this chapter we explore the nature of **society** as it relates to education and schooling. Using three models of society, the consensus model, the individualistic model, and the conflict model, we show how our assumptions about society help shape our view of schooling. We then outline the essentials for societal survival, showing how education and schooling fit in, and exploring schooling's various social functions. We also compare and contrast different types of societies by evolutionary type, defining them and commenting on how each type has distinctive educational needs and practices.

Turning our attention from society to **culture**, we point out that educators must be aware that much of it is "transparent," escaping our notice while profoundly influencing our actions and perceptions. Dividing culture into its formal, technical, and informal levels, we develop the educational dimensions of each, paying particular attention to how these relate to school-related conflict.

We close with observations concerning professionalism and the changing nature of teaching.

THREE MODELS OF SOCIETY

Human beings are profoundly social. Indeed, the very qualities we associate with being human are learned through social living. Everywhere, the necessity of survival has brought human beings together, compelling them to conform to a common social order that we call society. Broadly speaking, a **society** is a group of humans occupying a common territory and accepting common political authority, sharing language, customs, values, ideas, and material goods that reflect a way of life.

If this were all there was to society, it would be relatively easy for us to determine how education and schooling fit in. However, once we are past the broad and deep consensus that supports this initial definition, things become more complicated. Some fundamental disagreements have yet to be worked out.

Because this is not a primer in sociology, the reader might wonder why these disagreements would be of any interest in a text on the foundations of education. But our assumptions about the nature of society are fundamental to our understanding of education and schooling. We will demonstrate why this is the case by describing three models of society and showing how each leads to very different conclusions concerning education and schooling.

The Consensus Model

From the point of view of the "**consensus**" model, social facts are *not* reducible to individual facts. Rather, each society has a collective reality that somehow transcends its individual members. Prominent early sociologists such as Emile Durkheim (1858–1917)[1] and Talcott Parsons (1902–1979)[2] first advanced this point of view.

Those who embrace the consensus model emphasize the forces and mechanisms that keep societies stable, pointing out the central importance of *common* perceptions, values, and morality. Stressing the importance of orderliness and complementarity, they develop the idea that societies resemble living organisms. Each part complements the whole, and the whole is greater than the sum of its parts.

Those who accept the consensus model stress that education functions as a transmitter of traditional values. Downplaying the importance of individual differences, they stress the **holistic** view that schooling properly encourages stability and maintains the existing social order. They emphasize that schooling harmonizes values, and encourages consensus, and integrates individuals into the social structure. Similarly, those who consciously or unconsciously accept this model make broad-based claims on schools because "America" has certain wants, or "the nation" requires some sort of action. Their critics argue that such claims fail to adequately consider the role of individual interests.

The Individualistic Model

According to extreme individualists, such as the famed English philosopher Thomas Hobbes (1588–1679), a "society" has *no* substantial reality of its own. *All* of its attributes, they claim, are ultimately reducible to the relations and actions of particular individuals.

Recall that in Chapter 1 we highlighted the difference between indivisible and divisible benefits. The consensus model stresses the indivisible. Those who accept the **individualistic** model, stress the divisible. In fact, individualists claim that it is hard to identify any benefits that are, in the final analysis, truly indivisible. Referring to things like "America's needs," they argue, simply serves to obscure *which* American's needs, or wants, we are really talking about.

Individualists understand education in terms of what it does to, or for, particular people. And so far as schooling is concerned, individualists point out that schools do different things for, or to, different people. If, for example, you are the scion of a wealthy family attending a prestigious prep school, this schooling provides the opportunity to network with other future members of the power elite. If you are the child of an impoverished single mother attending an inner-city high school, this opportunity does not present itself. So when the claim is made that schooling offers benefits, individualists immediately want to know "for whom?"

---

[1]See, for example, Emile Durkheim, *Education and Sociology*, Sherwood Fox, Trans. (Glencoe, Ill.: The Free Press, 1956).
[2]See, for example, Talcott Parsons, "The School Class as a Social System," *Harvard Educational Review*, Vol. 29, Fall 1959.

The Conflict Model

For those who endorse the conflict model, societies are political arenas in which various groups seek antagonistic goals. Whenever a special interest group gains power, they claim, it can be expected to try to preserve it by imposing its values and understandings on the less privileged. This tendency explains, claim the conflict theorists, why societies are arranged so unequally.

Conflict theorists like Samual Bowles[3] or Margaret Weir emphasize the inherent disequilibriums of society.[4] They consider antagonisms and conflicts between social institutions and groups to be fundamental. They point out what they regard as built-in inequalities, and the role of coercion in the maintenance of order. They propose that social institutions and status groups often work at cross-purposes, and that conflict, change, and instability are the natural order of things.

From a conflict perspective, education is the product of an unequal socio-economic structure that greatly profits only a few, and schooling reflects and further reinforces fundamental inequalities of opportunity for personal development and economic reward. Proponents of this model also claim that schooling reinforces repression and domination by fostering complementary forms of consciousness, interpersonal behavior, and personality.

[3]Samual Bowles and Herbert Gintis, *Schooling in Capitalist America* (New York: Basic Books, 1976).
[4]Ira Katznelson and Margaret Weir, *Schooling for All* (New York: Basic Books, 1985).

Are conflict, change, and instability the natural order of things?

A Nation At Risk?

The immediate practical importance of the models just outlined becomes evident when we turn to one of the most influential school reform reports in the history of the nation.

In their landmark 1985 report, *A Nation at Risk: The Imperative for Educational Reform*, the National Commission on Excellence in Education declared:

> Our Nation is at risk. Our once unchallenged preeminence in commerce, industry, science, and technological innovation is being overtaken by competitors throughout the world. This report is concerned with only one of the many causes and dimensions of the problem, but it is one that undergirds American prosperity, security and civility. We report to the American people that while we can take justifiable pride in what our schools and colleges have historically accomplished and contributed to the United States and the well-being of its people, the educational foundations of our society are presently being eroded by a rising tide of mediocrity that threatens our very future as a Nation and a people.
>
> If an unfriendly foreign power had attempted to impose on America the mediocre educational performance that exists today, we might well have viewed it as an act of war. As it stands, we have allowed this to happen to ourselves.... We have, in effect, been committing an act of unthinking, unilateral educational disarmament.
>
> Our society and its educational institutions seem to have lost sight of the basic purposes of schooling, and of the high expectations and disciplined efforts needed to attain them. This report ... seeks to generate reform of our educational system in fundamental ways and to renew the Nation's commitment to schools and colleges of high quality throughout the length and breadth of our land.[5]

As intended, these pronouncements served as the goad for a flood of school reform efforts. Significantly, however, there was little discussion of the *central assumption* that gave *A Nation at Risk* its focus. This assumption concerned the Commission on Excellence's understanding of the nature of society.

The Assumption

The authors of *A Nation at Risk* assume the correctness of the consensus model. Clearly they accept the idea that American society has a reality that

---

[5]The National Commission on Excellence in Education, *A Nation At Risk: The Imperative for Educational Reform* (Washington, D.C.: Superintendent of Documents, U. S. Government Printing Office, 1985), pp. 5–6.

transcends its individual members. Note that they claim,"*Our society* and its educational institutions seem to have lost sight of the basic purposes of schooling." They also speak of renewing "... *the Nation's* commitment to schools and colleges of high quality" (italics are the present authors').

Such statements are slogans, and beg crucial questions. Individualists would ask, "Which individuals have lost sight of things?" and "Whose basic purposes are we talking about?" Of course, conflict theorists would go further. They would probably claim that it is not "the Nation" that is at risk, but the vested interests of a relative handful of very wealthy and powerful people. And they would understand the general concerns expressed in *A Nation At Risk* to actually reflect the specific concerns of special interests.

Consider how different *A Nation at Risk* might have been if the Commission had at least considered these alternative models. Had it been written only from an individualistic or from a conflict model perspective it would have been wholly different. Imagine, for example, if it had reflected a conflict perspective. Perhaps it would read something like this:

> The wealth and profits of some very influential Americans are at risk. The once unchallenged preeminence in commerce, industry, science, and technological innovation of the corporations they control is being overtaken by competitors throughout the world. This report is concerned with only one of the many causes and dimensions of the problem, but it is one that undergirds some very influential people's prosperity and security. We report too that while some of us can take comfort in how our schools and colleges have further reinforced fundamental inequalities of opportunity for personal development and economic reward in the United States, the educational foundations of this system are presently being eroded by a rising tide of resentment, resistance, and alienation that threatens the very repression and domination that fosters and perpetuates unequal economic rewards.

This illustrates how so much of what we think about education and schooling is tied to our basic assumptions about the nature of society. We see, then, that when the authors of *A Nation at Risk* claim that "American society" can lose sight of things, or "the Nation's commitment to schooling," they are begging some very important questions.

EDUCATION AND SOCIETAL SURVIVAL

We have established that how we understand the processes of education and schooling to fit in to the social order is very much determined by which model of society we think is valid. In this section we go beyond competing models of society to explore what basic prerequisites must be met for any society to survive. Then we consider how education and schooling fit in.

Functional Prerequisites

One way of understanding how education and schooling fit in to the social order is to consider how societies survive from generation to generation. Once formed, societies can last for thousands of years. But some have proved far more durable than others. It all comes down to whether or not a particular society can satisfy nature's performance criteria. Sociologists call them the **"functional prerequisites."** They are:

- **Subsistence.** Food and shelter must be secured.
- **Distribution.** Subsistence must be distributed among group members. Equal access is not necessary, but the young need someone to provide them with food and shelter.
- **Reproduction.** At least some members of the group must biologically reproduce.
- **Protection.** There must be some sort of defense from external threats, both physical and social. Some means of keeping members from destroying one another must also be found.
- **Communication.** Members must be able to communicate with one another.
- **Socialization.** The existing culture must be transmitted to the young through osmosis (it just soaks in through daily contact), education and, possibly, schooling.[6]

Failure to accomplish any of these functional prerequisites results in the destruction of the social system. And education and its more formal version, schooling, have a clear role in making sure at least two of them work.

First, education and schooling are very directly involved with the communication prerequisite. At the simplest level children learn language by just being around it. But they are also deliberately taught. In a modern society this happens first at home, then at school. Consider the 3 Rs. They are but three methods of communication, and nearly everyone regards them as the heart of the formal school curriculum.

Second, socialization is one of the most vital functions of education. It is also a central function of any school. Indeed, schools are particularly useful in this regard because they make it possible to put much of the increasingly complicated socialization process in a public place where it can be monitored. To illustrate, American schoolchildren are tested and retested using standardized measures of achievement. One way of understanding recurrent testing is that it is a way of checking up on socialization. We worry that the disarray so common to modern societies—crime, alienation, drug addiction, and the like—is symptomatic of a deeper hidden failure that could be bringing us all to ruin; so we test the young to get some measure of how they are developing.

---

[6]Ibid.

Teachers socialize.

SOCIALIZATION, EDUCATION, AND SCHOOLING

Our consideration of the functional prerequisites points out the fundamental importance of socialization and its subordinate processes, education and schooling. In this section we examine socialization in greater detail, then compare and contrast it with education and schooling.

Socialization

We have already seen that for any society to survive, it is necessary to transmit to all new members (newborns or previous members of other cultures) the system of shared meanings, language, customs, values, ideas and material goods that we call **culture**. This process of cultural transmission is termed **socialization**.

In one sense, there are as many different types of socialization as there are roles in a society. One is socialized to be a truck driver, Ukrainian-American, mother, rock musician, student, Roman Catholic, or even Hell's Angel. But interrole cooperation, a necessity for cultural survival, can only be assured if each of these roles also incorporates a common cultural core. One function of the public schools is to instill this core.

Socialization is not accomplished willy-nilly in accordance with personal tastes. Every society has developed specific ways and means of accomplishing it. For one thing, many members of the society have social roles that incorporate this function. (**Roles** are culturally prescribed behaviors relating to social position.) The most obvious example is the role of parent. Typically, parenting includes a major responsibility for socialization.[7] Other social roles

---

[7]Harry Johnson, *Sociology: A Systematic Introduction* (New York: Harcourt, Brace and World, 1960), p. 110.

also include this function. Religious authorities have responsibility for certain aspects of socialization. So do many others.

In complex societies part of the process of socialization is given over to a social institution that specializes in the process. (An **institution** consists of formalized statuses, roles, and norms centered on an important social need.) This institution is staffed by members of the society who have been given specific responsibility and authority required for them to specialize in socialization. We refer, of course, to schools and teachers.

Education

Socialization often occurs through a kind of cultural osmosis. It is not a question of deliberate teaching, or of a conscious effort to learn.... Culture just soaks in, becoming how one lives. This type of socialization has been going on since the very beginnings of culture. In modern societies, however, the scope has broadened enormously. The media, particularly television, now expose us to an amazing variety of cultural messages. How much rubs off is difficult to say but there is no question that the exposure is changing us and the culture by changing how we are socialized.

Despite the importance of accidental socialization, the transmission of certain aspects of culture, usually formal or technical in nature, often requires *deliberate and systematic teaching over a sustained period of time*. It is this variety of socialization that we call "**education**."[8]

Thus we should not think of education too narrowly as simply synonymous with schooling. Throughout the greater part of human history most education has been accomplished in families, apprenticeships, churches, and the like, rather than schools. Indeed, when parents try to get their baby to say "Daddy," or "Mommy" for the first time, they are educators, teaching that most vital of cultural skills, language. Similarly, when a plumber shows his or her apprentice how to thread pipe, and a priest instructs engaged couples in the duties and responsibilities of marriage, they too are educators. They are going beyond chance learning to ensure that specific aspects of the existing culture—the group's shared customs, values, ideas, and artifacts—are deliberately transmitted to the uninitiated.

Schooling

Schooling is formalized education. It is accomplished by specialists, and commonly takes place in buildings specifically set aside for instruction. This developed very slowly. For the vast expanse of human existence there were no schools. Even when they did come into being, they served a very small percentage of the population. Only in the last 100 to 150 years have they become common.

---

[8]Lawrence A. Cremin, *American Education: The Colonial Experience 1607–1783* (New York: Harper & Row, 1970), p. xi.

The Manifest Functions of Schools

The manifest functions of schools are those that are intended, and stated openly. Therefore, it is not difficult to identify them.

Richard L. Derr surveyed the written objectives of 10 percent of the nation's public school districts in developing a taxonomy of the manifest functions of public schools.[9] (A **taxonomy** is a system of classification.) In this taxonomy, Derr divides the manifest functions into two major categories. He labels them "social" and "individual." These terms parallel what in Chapter 1 we called "indivisible" and "divisible." (You will recall that, in simplest terms, indivisible benefits are those that satisfy broad social needs, and cannot benefit one without benefiting many. Divisible benefits can benefit some without benefiting all.) Derr's taxonomy is shown in Figure 5.1.

Conflicting Manifest Functions.   Derr's taxonomy, derived from the actual policy statements of school authorities, reveals some of the conflicts which make schooling problematic. The most basic of these is the tension between the divisible and indivisible benefits highlighted in Figure 5.1. (Recall from Chapter 1 that we defined these two types of benefits.)

Consider the following example. In a world where nations wage war, there is a social need to have individuals who will do combat with members of other cultures, killing and risking their own maiming or death in the process.

---

[9]Richard L. Derr, *A Taxonomy of Social Purposes of Public Schools* (New York: McKay, 1973).

Figure 5.1

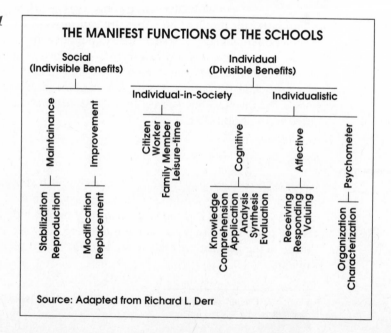

THE MANIFEST FUNCTIONS OF THE SCHOOLS

Social (Indivisible Benefits) — Maintainance, Improvement; Stabilization, Reproduction, Modification, Replacement

Individual (Divisible Benefits) — Individual-in-Society: Citizen, Worker, Family Member, Leisure-time; Individualistic: Cognitive (Knowledge, Comprehension, Application, Analysis, Synthesis, Evaluation), Affective (Receiving, Responding, Valuing, Organization, Characterization), Psychometer

Source: Adapted from Richard L. Derr

In other words, when a nation gives a war, it is essential that those who are invited, come.

Thus, one function of the social maintenance aspect of schooling is to encourage nationalistic patriotism, and the related notions that some wars are just, that personal sacrifice on the battlefield is heroic, and so forth. On the other hand, as Figure 5.1 shows, one of the individual manifest functions of the school is to teach kids facts; and also how to tear these facts apart, put them together in new ways, and evaluate their meaning.

It is not difficult to imagine individuals whom schools have made more knowledgeable, and also have taught to analyze, synthesize, and evaluate what they have learned, concluding that a particular war is not for them. They might even decide that all wars are such a bad idea that they accept imprisonment or flee to a neutral country rather than participate.

How are we to reconcile these potentialities? Is there some way to do both without total confusion or utter hypocrisy? If not, who decides which function schools should emphasize? These are questions that no thoughtful educator can avoid.

Other conflicts invite our attention. Note, for example, that schools have the social function of both *maintaining* a society's culture while also *improving* it. If we think carefully about the matter, it becomes obvious that this generates some real difficulties. Clearly, it is difficult to stabilize the existing order while simultaneously replacing it. Yet school boards and other educational authorities list *both* of these as things as functions of our schools. So we see that the social functions of the school are, in themselves, problematic.

Obviously, no thinking person should expect schools to simultaneously accomplish mutually contradictory ends. Yet, prompted by the circumstances of the moment, such individuals often do expect both functions somehow to be accomplished. Also, we should not forget that there are a lot of people out there who do **not** think—at least not about things like this. And they too are perfectly capable of demanding that schools stabilize and replace, reproduce and modify, all at the same time.

The Latent Functions of Schools

Latent functions are harder to identify than manifest ones simply because they are, by definition, the sorts of functions that school officials either do not intend or do not recognize. Attempts to isolate and highlight them tend to be controversial. Predictably, they are often pointed out by conflict theorists.

Caretaking.   **Caretaking** is one of the easiest latent school functions to identify. Although schools do not intend to be in this business, they are because children who are in school need not be cared for at home. In the past, when women were not commonly employed outside the home, this consideration was not as important as it is today. Like it or not, millions of American families now depend on schools for most of the caretaking that makes two-parent employment possible.

Few realize what a bargain schools are in this regard. Putting instruction aside, if an elementary teacher has 25 children in class, he or she is providing a total of approximately 28,000 hours of caretaking per schoolyear. Assuming a bargain in-home cost of $3.00 an hour for babysitting, the teacher provides the equivalent of $84,000 worth of caretaking services per year. But in 1987 the average teacher salary—that is, the median income among all teachers, not just beginners—topped $26,000 for the first time.[10] Thus, given an average class size of 25, teachers are babysitting the nation's youth for an average of 93 cents an hour per child and throwing in instruction in the bargain.

Status.   As we will learn in detail later, early civilizations, such as those found in Sumer or Egypt, developed an elaborate and well-defined social status hierarchy distinct from previous simpler cultures. And there was a clear connection between this class structure and the first schools. Only the upper classes, such as the clergy, the landed aristocracy and the nobility, were able to attend them.[11] Schooling thus provided them with another form of authority and legitimacy.

This arrangement has been maintained, in one form or another, since the first schools were built in Sumer 6,000 years ago. Throughout history, schooling has helped legitimate the power and privilege of the upper classes. In many cases it still works that way. Of course, in developed societies nearly everyone goes to some kind of school. But nearly everyone does *NOT* go to elite residential preparatory schools like America's Lawrenceville School, or the most famous of the English "public"[12] schools, Eton College. Such prestige schools are intimately connected to the upper ranks of the social status system of their respective societies. "Prepping" at the "right" school, and then graduating from the "right" college or university has a **status function**. In other words, one of the latent functions of schooling is to act as a mechanism of socioeconomic selection and control.[13]

We must remember that latent functions operate in the background, at an unknowing and unthinking level. Often they take subtle forms which are not readily evident. Take, for example, what schools count as valid knowledge. Inner-city youngsters learn volumes on the street, but they derive little benefit from this knowledge so far as their grades are concerned. Schools do not test for "street smarts." Kids from affluent circumstances fare much better in this regard. What they learn outside of school frequently pays off on their report card.

The Parallel Operation of Manifest and Latent Functions.   Manifest and latent functions often operate simultaneously in parallel fashion. In his best

---

[10]"Teachers for Tomorrow," a report of the Standing Committee on Instruction and Professional Development of the National Education Association, Washington, D.C., July 1987, p. 16.
[11]See Chapter 7 for details.
[12]In England the term "public school" refers to a privately owned and operated residential preparatory school.
[13]Philip Wexler, *The Sociology of Education: Beyond Equality* (Indianapolis: Bobbs-Merrill, 1976), p. 56.

Lawrenceville School is one of the nation's premier prep schools.

seller *Cultural Literacy* E. D. Hirsch argues that teaching his "List" of dates, names, and other status-oriented information should be a manifest function of American schooling.[14] Perhaps he is right, perhaps not. But, before deciding we should consider the possibility that his proposal unknowingly or unthinkingly promotes unintended consequences. Might it, for instance, make school easier for students coming from affluent backgrounds while simultaneously penalizing the less affluent? If so, a latent function of Hirsch's type of schooling would be to further legitimate wealth and privilege while simultaneously reinforcing the second class citizenship of other Americans. Hirsch claims it will not have this effect. His critics believe that he is wrong.

TYPES OF SOCIETIES/PATTERNS OF EDUCATION

There is a pattern of historical development that reveals a general trend of sociocultural evolution. Various societies have not followed this pattern, remaining relatively fixed in their culture for thousands of years. But we can say generally that there is growing complexity accompanied by a significant increase in specialization as the division of labor grows more and more refined. There is also an accumulation of surplus wealth as culture becomes capable of producing more than is necessary for sheer survival. And all of this is accompanied by a gradual transition from reliance on informal education to formal schooling.[15]

The thousands of different cultures that have existed on this earth can be classified into five evolutionary types. They are diagrammatically represented in Figure 5.2.

---

[14]Hirsch, op. cit., p. 2.
[15]Ian Robertson, *Sociology*, 3rd Ed. (New York: Worth, 1987), p. 101.

Figure 5.2   **TYPES OF SOCIETIES/ PATTERNS OF EDUCATION**

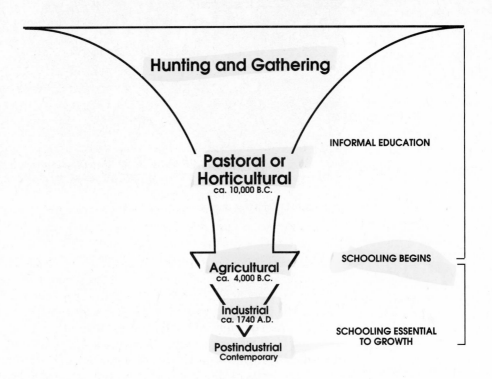

Hunting and Gathering Societies

The most ancient of human groups, hunting and gathering societies are small, nomadic, and based on kinship. As the name suggests, hunting and gathering provide subsistence. There is little social status except that based on sex, age, or kinship, and the means of subsistence is distributed relatively evenly. Specialization is uncommon and wealth does not accumulate. Reproduction is troubled by a very high infant mortality rate. Protection is a critical issue, but technological resources are very limited. Communication is rudimentary.

Socialization is entirely informal. All education is conducted by individuals with other primary roles. There are no paid teachers and no schools.

Pastoral Societies

Nomadic societies evolved about 10,000 to 12,000 years ago. With subsistence based on herding, they are larger and more complex than hunting and gathering groups, often numbering in the thousands. The means of subsistence is unevenly distributed. Wealth, in the form of herd animals, accumulates. Social status is well defined, family related, and often passed on to the next generation. Such ascribed status (ascribed status depends on birth) takes precedence over individual achievement. Protection and communication remain critical but basic.

Socialization remains totally informal. Parents and other adults teach by example and demonstration. Schools are unknown.

Horticultural Societies

Evolving about the same time as pastoral societies, horticultural societies—settled groups of several thousand people—are based upon a simple hand agriculture. The means of subsistence, material culture, such as houses, is often well developed. The accumulation of surplus permits a few wealthy, powerful families to gain control over the distribution system. It also encourages specialized statuses and new roles such as trader or craft worker. These tend to be passed from father to son. Protection is still critically needed, but unsophisticated. Communications grow in complexity.

Because there is much to learn, socialization is more problematic. Nevertheless education remains informal and schools are nonexistent. As in simpler societies, children are still taught by adults, principally parents, who have other primary functions. However, apprenticeships are used more and more often to train young craft workers.

Agricultural Societies

The invention of the plow about 6,000 years ago made agricultural civilizations possible. Residents of some such communities number in the millions. Large surpluses of food make subsistence less problematic and cities common. Population is divided into very distinct social classes. Political and social inequality is ascribed at birth. Power and the means of subsistence are concentrated in the hands of a hereditary elite, often associated with organized religion. This elite controls the governmental bureaucracy which collects taxes, develops roads and other public works and keeps detailed records. Protection now requires the maintenance of a permanent military. The invention of written language advances communications in a dramatic fashion and compels a new type of formal education—**schooling**. Despite all of this, the family generally remains the basic social and economic unit.

For the vast majority, education remains informal. Most children learn from their parents. Some are apprenticed to learn a trade. But the elite few who must master the newly invented written language, and similar abstract skills, for the first time in human history, rely on schools and full-time teachers. This new social institution not only teaches technical skills, it also further distinguishes the social elite from the broad mass of humanity. Nearly all such schools have religious sponsorship, and the teachers are often priests. This complements the religious emphasis common throughout the society.

Industrial Societies

First born in England about 250 years ago, the industrial type of society is based upon mechanized production derived from scientific technology. Highly urbanized communities with members numbering in the tens or even hundreds of millions are common. In such a society a small minority can feed and house everyone. Corporations and governmental bureaucracies grow ever larger as the economy becomes vast and complex. At first, social inequalities are enormous. But in later stages of development, they are reduced as ascribed status (conferred at birth) gives way to achieved status (earned through accomplishments). Large armed forces are maintained equipped with technological weapons of tremendous power. Massive domestic police forces also develop. The family is no longer the primary economic unit. Its emotional support function remains, but all of its other functions are partially replaced by other institutions such as the hospital, the poorhouse, insane asylums, retirement homes, and schools. Scientific and technological development promote rapid advances in communications.

Formal schooling is universal and primarily sponsored by national governments rather than by religious groups. They customarily promote a sense of nationalistic patriotism that matches the growth in power of the modern nation state. Instructing the young, particularly in technical matters, is given over more and more to teachers trained and paid to perform this function. One obvious purpose served by this is that it frees the majority of the society to do other things, such as produce wealth.

Was this a new form of motherhood?

Postindustrial Societies

Postindustrial societies are still forming, and the United States is thought to have been the first. Based on a global economy and international cooperation, basic subsistence is pretty much taken for granted. A minority of its members still engage in highly automated food production, or the manufacture of sophisticated products unsuited for mass production in less technologically advanced societies—producing enormous surplus in the process. But the majority provide services. There are high-end service jobs such as those in basic research, computer design, teaching, medical care, and investment banking. There are also low-end service jobs in fast food restaurants, custodial work, and the like. These jobs reflect differences in social status that are still great, but more of this status is achieved than acquired. "Protection" now requires weapons so destructive as to threaten all life on earth. There is no satisfactory defense against them. Police continue to be vital to domestic order although in some societies they are a law unto themselves.

Knowledge, particularly technical knowledge, is one of the primary means of creating wealth in a postindustrial society. From it come new jobs, new products, and still more sophisticated services. Thus a postindustrial society depends upon the effectiveness of its schools—particularly elite schools specializing in advanced technical studies as well as pure and applied research. Wealth has come to depend on the quality of this schooling even more than on natural resources.

Reflecting the need for information, communications in a postindustrial society are enormously sophisticated. Linking the earth in an instant, modern information technology makes it possible to carry on electronic "conversations" around the world.

Because of rapid change and the technical nature of things, lifelong education is also a necessity. Without it, one's skills soon become obsolete.

Table 5.1 shows how educational developments **correspond** with broader social developments. The origin of schools corresponded, for example, to the development of the first agricultural civilizations. Similarly, the recent development of postindustrial societies has seen a corresponding growth in support for schools.

UNDERSTANDING CULTURE

We know from the preceding section that all groups of people are *NOT* societies. In a **society** a group shares common meanings, language, customs, values, ideas, and material goods that are the products of a way of life. We call this interacting, interdependent, and evolving system a **culture**.

Culture is enormously powerful in shaping human behavior. In a sense it is its own gigantic personality that accounts for the differences between ourselves and all the other cultures of the earth.

Sometimes we are able to deliberately shape or change certain aspects of

Table 5.1

			TYPES OF SOCIETIES	
TYPE (AGE)	SIZE	SUBSISTENCE	EQUALITY/ INEQUALITY	SOCIALIZATION
Hunting & Gathering (4 Million Years)	Small, kinship bands	Hunting and Gathering	Very Equal	Entirely Informal
Pastoral (12,000 Years)	Thousands	Herding of Domestic Animals	Inequality Based Primarily on Ascription	Entirely Informal
Horticultural (12,000 Years)	Thousands	Simple Subsistence Agriculture	Inequality Based Primarily on Ascription	Entirely Informal
Agricultural (6,000 Years)	Millions	Commercial Agriculture	Inequality Based Primarily on Ascription	Primarily Informal, but Apprenticeship & Schooling
Industrial (250 Years)	Hundreds of Millions	Industrial Production	Balance Changing to Achievement	Informal & Universal Schooling
Postindustrial (Contemporary)	Hundreds of Millions	Service & Knowledge Production	Balance Changing More to Achievement	More and More Emphasis on Schooling

our culture. But try as we might, some of it seems beyond our direction. In his *Notes Toward a Definition of Culture,* the poet T. S. Eliot observed:

> Culture is the one thing we cannot deliberately aim at. It is the product of a variety of more or less harmonious activities, each pursued for its own sake.

Cultural Transparency

One reason much of our culture is beyond our conscious direction is that we are unaware that it is acting on us. We are so caught up in it and shaped by it, that it is often transparent to us. This lack of awareness is particularly true about basic social roles that are closely tied to our personal identity.

The distinction between gender and sexuality provides a vivid example of cultural transparency. Gender is biologically defined. One is born male or female by virtue of one's chromosomes. But sexuality is the cultural expression of gender. It consists of social roles, man or woman, boy or girl, that are *learned*, not inherited.

Sexuality differs markedly from culture to culture. In fact, what is encouraged as masculine in one, may be considered feminine in another. For example, Hall reports that in Iran men are prompted to read poetry, show emotion, be sensitive and develop their intuition. Women, on the other hand, are encouraged to be coldly rational. In short, these particular traits are pretty much the reverse of those which, until recently, were thought to be masculine or feminine in the United States.[16]

Remembering that sexuality is learned behavior, ask yourself **how** it is learned. Are there any lectures or demonstrations on the topic?

Culture shapes an individual's consciousness in thousands of ways. It becomes an omnipresent yet largely invisible lens through which we view ourselves and the world. Its contents seep into the very marrow of our being.

Scholarly studies of cross-cultural differences reveal an amazing variety of attitudes, behaviors, ideas, and values. We might wonder if it is "human nature" to be almost infinitely malleable with respect to culture.

A few of the many things shaped by cultural differences are:

- technology
- manners
- morals
- family life
- attitudes toward school
- social relations
- attitudes toward work
- relations and procedures in the workplace
- conversation
- nonverbal communications
- public behavior
- gestures
- eye and body contact
- proximics (the way people handle space in communicating with each other)

Levels of Culture

There is a way of organizing and understanding this bewilderingly diverse list and understanding some of its implications for education and schooling. Edward T. Hall proposes that culture operates at three levels: the formal, the technical, and the informal.[17]

Formal Culture

The **formal level of culture** spans a wide range of human behaviors. It includes relatively trivial things such as manners, "proper" and "improper" language, appropriate tone of voice, and so forth. It also includes fundamental values. For example, the Ten Commandments are at the formal level of culture. So are all other religious admonitions.

Formal culture is explicit. Members of a society are well aware of its rules and understandings. Nevertheless, "proper" behaviors are seldom questioned.

---

[16]Edward T. Hall, *The Silent Language* (Greenwich, Conn.: Fawcett, 1959), pp. 49–50.
[17]Ibid.

They are taken at face value, and simply understood to be true, proper or right.

Thus formal culture is taught by precept and admonition. If, for example, a child were to ask, "Why must I take my hat off in school?" the answer would probably be, "Because it is good manners." And if a child should ask, "Why is it wrong to steal?" the response would likely be, "Just because it is!" or "It is against the law!" At the formal level there would be no attempt to advance an explanation based on the practical reasons why we should not take someone else's property.

The formal level of culture is tied up with feelings and is very resistant to change. Individuals found violating the formal culture are almost certain to incur social disapproval and/or criminal penalty.

Although many aspects of formal culture are taught informally, education and schooling also have important roles. For example, the Ten Commandments and other fundamental religious values are routinely inculcated by religious institutions and schools affiliated with them. The Reagan administration made repeated demands that the public schools pay more attention to the teaching of values. Similarly "Proper English" is encouraged in all schools, as is teaching children "good manners." Teachers also can and do grade for behavior and the like. And classmates can be ruthless with any of their number who violate those aspects of the formal culture that schoolchildren value. All of these illustrate the ways schools are involved with teaching the formal culture.

Schooling is involved in another aspect of the formal culture. Over the years schools themselves have become very formalized institutions. Many things are done by ritual rather than with rational planning. In such a setting, technical considerations become less important than customs, traditions, and even habit. Elsewhere in the text we will see that this process, called **institutionalization** is very important to our understanding of what goes on in schools.

Technical Culture

The **technical level of culture** has expanded greatly with the evolution of societies. In modern societies it includes things like designing satellites, building automobiles, landing an airplane, solving an equation or programming a computer. Like the formal culture, the technical culture is explicit. But at the technical level things are not "proper" or "improper" so much as they are "effective" or "ineffective." Procedures are carefully and logically developed by experts, and justified in terms of getting the job done.

Technical culture carries little emotional charge. Rather, it is characterized by the suppression of feelings. Television provides an example of a character who is memorable because of his uncommon ability to operate at the technical level of culture. Star Trek's Mr. Spock goes about his business with the calculated precision and near absence of emotion characteristic of this level of culture.

"Live long and prosper."

Technical culture is taught systematically, rationally, and deliberately by experts—usually in schools. Corporate training programs and the military are also in the technical culture business in a big way. Because the technical culture is essentially pragmatic, at the technical level of culture—unlike at the formal level—learners are encouraged to question and analyze. This level of culture changes if new techniques are better suited for the ends pursued. Conflicts are at a minimum.

Informal Culture

The **informal level of culture** involves subtle things like how men and women cross their legs, hold their hands, or touch their bodies in public. It also involves eye contact, body language, and proximics—the way people handle space when communicating. And there are hundreds of similar practices.

The informal is picked up unconsciously by simply living in a society and is the least visible level of culture; not because it is deliberately hidden, but because it operates primarily out of our awareness. Only when deviations occur do we notice something "strange."

Strong emotions typically accompany violations of informal culture. If, for example, a person touches another in circumstances where this is not commonly done, the recipient is usually uncomfortable and more than a little offended. But conformity to the unstated norms is taken totally for granted. Take, for example, the practice of football players patting each other on the behind for a job well done. This is not a violation of informal culture and the receiving player is certainly not supposed to be offended. On the other hand, imagine the principal of the local elementary school giving a pep talk to his or her faculty and then standing at the door and giving each of them an encouraging swat on the fanny as they go out to face the day. That, we think you will agree, is another matter entirely.

Table 5.2

		THREE LEVELS OF CULTURE	
LEVELS	*FORMAL*	*TECHNICAL*	*INFORMAL*
examples	manners, dirty words	driving, typing, writing	posture, tone of voice, sexuality
awareness	explicit	explicit	out of awareness
how learned?	as right and wrong	as efficient or not	violations are "wrong"
affect	strong	weak	strong for violations
changeability	low	high	?

adapted from Edward T. Hall

Table 5.2 summarizes the levels of culture. Pay particular attention to the category "How Learned" and then think back over your own school life. No doubt you can remember learning all sorts of technical level things. But can you remember instances where you were taught or otherwise learned formal cultural content? How about informal?

Social Conflict and the Levels of Culture

Understanding culture in terms of its three levels is very helpful in analyzing issues relating to consensus and the impact of social conflict on our schools. At its simplest, two different groups within a society can have profoundly different understandings of the same phenomenon even though both understand the matter to be at the same level of culture. For example, at the informal level of culture what one group sees as "sensitive" another might see as "effeminate." Things get more complicated when we consider that different groups might understand the same situation to fall under two different levels of culture. A typical school-based conflict situation occurs, for example, when one group thinks a particular matter should be dealt with as a formal cultural issue while a contending group sees it as a technical level matter. We will offer some examples shortly.

Table 5.3 highlights some of these possibilities by showing how two cultural groups might interpret the same situation.

Formal/Formal Conflicts

In a pluralistic society, such as the United States, several different formal cultures relate to the major subcultural divisions of the society. These formal cultures are often in conflict. Heated debates at several universities have highlighted conflicts of this type.

Table 5.3

	CONFLICTS BETWEEN CULTURAL SUBGROUPS		
GROUP B \ GROUP A	FORMAL	TECHNICAL	INFORMAL
Formal	property/greed law/repression	theft/business fair price/ extortion	sensitive/ effeminate cultured/ snobbish
Technical	free market/ exploitation gang/union	effective/ ineffective promotes/ impedes	tactful/ cowardly leader/ tyrant
Informal	"natural"/sexist, racist	normal/ obstructive	"natural"/ "weird"

Group A's perceptions/Group B's perception

The most well-known concerns Stanford University. Stanford requires all freshmen to take a course in Western Culture. A polarizing controversy erupted when a number of faculty recommended that the required reading list of 15 classics be altered to include non-Western, women, and minority authors. Proponents of the change felt that it was necessary in order to reflect the sexual and ethnic diversity of Stanford and contemporary America. (Stanford's undergraduates include 14 percent Asian-Americans, 9 percent Hispanics, 8 percent blacks, and 1 percent American Indians.) Opponents contended that it compromised our deepest cultural values.[18]

Former Secretary of Education William Bennett propelled the controversy into the headlines when he took sides in the dispute. Charging that attempts to change the core readings were an attempt to "trash Plato and Shakespeare," Bennett denounced the move.

Ultimately, the matter was resolved by compromise. The list was pared to six required readings and one non-European work to be chosen by the professor with "substantial attention to issues of race, gender and class."[19]

One way of minimizing these formal/formal conflicts is to focus on technical concerns. With respect to schooling, for example, we avoid formal clashes over what **should** be taught by "technicalizing" the matter as a "curriculum decision." This technicalizing moves the disagreement to a less emotional level and enhances the authority of school officials. It also promotes breadth of consensus at the cost of depth.

[18]*Insight*, March 7, 1988, pp. 58–60.
[19]*Time*, May 16, 1988, pp. 75–76.

Technical/Technical Conflicts

The technical level of culture tends to be the least troubled by conflict. The technical nature of the culture, the relative absence of strong emotion, and the tentative nature of truth all combine to keep disagreements civil. This is one reason why school officials tend to concentrate on this type of instruction. Nevertheless, conflicts still exist. For example, within the technical field of psychology there are conflicts between strict behaviorists and cognitivists relative to the nature of learning. A number of similar technical/technical conflicts are highlighted in various chapters of this book in the boxes labeled Point/Counterpoint.

Informal/Informal Conflicts

The informal level of culture has proved very prone to conflict, and is particularly problematic for schools and teachers. Its transparency promotes this. For example, Americans who are descendants of Northern Europe stock tend to have internalized an informal cultural trait termed **monochronism**, that is, in social situations they deal with people one at a time. In a school setting a teacher from such a background, seeing children informally at his or her desk, for example, would take care of one student at a time.

People who are descendants of Southern European stock, particularly Hispanics, tend to exhibit **polychronism**. They deal socially with as many as five persons at a time. To return to our school-based example, imagine the teacher described above talking to one child when a second "interrupts" and tries to join in the conversation. From the teacher's cultural point of view, the child is being rude. If that child is Hispanic, however, he or she comes from a culture where interruptions to conversations are completely permissible. In fact, from an Hispanic polychronistic perspective, it is the teacher who is being discourteous in expecting the child to wait.[20]

We often fail to even recognize the nature of these misunderstandings because it is hard to distance ourselves from the socially derived knowledge, values, and behaviors that we have **internalized**. They operate in the background, below the level of conscious awareness. Of course, others are operating just as blindly, but often in a very different frame of reference. This leads to profound misunderstandings and conflicts that have proved particularly troublesome in a school setting.

Cross-Level Conflicts

Perhaps the most explosive of all cultural conflicts are those that cross levels. One social group presumes a particular matter to be at one level of culture, while a second group places it at another.

---

[20]Judith Nine-Curt, "Non-Verbal Communication and English as a Second Language," *B.E.S.L. Reporter*, Vol. 1, No. 1 (January 1975) pp. 1–2.

Clarence Darrow (center) defending John T. Scopes.

One of the most durable and persistent cross-level school-based conflicts concerns the teaching of evolution versus Biblical accounts of creation. The most famous example concerns John T. Scopes, a teacher of biology who violated a 1925 Tennessee state law forbidding the teaching in the public schools of that state "any theory which denies the story of the Divine creation of man as taught in the Bible," and from teaching "instead that man is descended from a lower form of animal." Scope's trial quickly became the focus of national attention. The prosecution of the case was handled by none other than Tennessee's own attorney general, assisted by the famous William Jennings Bryan. Scopes was defended by the nation's most controversial criminal lawyer, Clarence Darrow. Scopes was eventually found guilty and fined $100, but not before his prosecution had provoked a storm of ridicule.

Among other things, what this trial was about was the level of culture that should be used in school to explain the origins of human life. Would it be the formal culture from the Bible, or the technical culture from the science of biology? As we learn elsewhere in this book, this controversy still persists.

Technical Culture and Teacher Professionalism

It is important to appreciate that this entire text emphasizes the development of a technical level understandings of education and schooling, rather than the traditions and so-called "common sense" resident in the formal culture. The intention is to encourage the development of an expert knowledge base that will permit educators to make reasoned judgments superior to those made by intelligent laypersons. In this chapter, for example, the discussion of the levels of culture helps us appreciate the basic dynamics of school-related conflicts—a critically important skill. Similarly, the other chapters of this text offer procedures and knowledge that enhance and enrich our ability to dissect educational issues with precision.

Appreciating the full importance of this material is not always easy. It requires not only making the effort to master new knowledge, but also laying aside a wide assortment of cultural conceits and prejudices. Admittedly, these are uncommon abilities, but they are the measure of a true professional.

SUMMARY

1. Different models of society emphasize different aspects of social organization. The consensus model emphasizes regularities, the individualistic model emphasizes differences, and the conflict model emphasizes social inequalities. Each of these has major implications for education and schooling. Also all societies must meet functional prerequisites to survive. In that connection, schooling—a formalized subspecies of education—is particularly involved with the prerequisites of communication and socialization.

2. Schools have both manifest and latent functions and these may be in conflict, particularly if improving social conditions is an aim together with maintaining them. Another consideration is that societies can be grouped by evolutionary type. When they are, their educational practices correspond to their type.

3. Culture can be understood to have three levels—the formal, the technical, and the informal. Cultural conflicts crucial to schooling occur at or across any of these levels. To be true professionals, it is necessary for educators to develop technical level understandings of schooling, teaching, and learning. However, much of what is distinctive about culture is transparent and invisible to those in it, and that makes this understanding difficult to achieve.

QUESTIONS

1. Our understanding of the phrase, "the Nation," depends on whether we use a consensus model of society, an individualistic model, or a conflict model. What would be some differences in understanding? How do you think these differences would affect the tone of the reform proposals in *Nation at Risk*?

2. Can you draw any parallels among the three models of society and the three images of the school given in Chapter 2?

3. Socialization into one role may conflict with socialization into another. For example, learning to be a soldier permits displays of aggression not tolerated in other contexts. Can you think of role conflicts teachers may face in the school (for example, disciplinarian versus "counselor")?

4. List five manifest and five latent functions of school.
5. Are the items you listed in 4 above compatible or do they conflict?
6. Ascribed characteristics are those you are "born with." Achieved characteristics you "earn." Can you list some of each that we recognize in our society? How do schools support or undermine them?
7. List what you consider masculine and feminine traits. What kind of consensus can you find among your friends or classmates?
8. Do you see any parallels between levels of culture and the three images of the school?
9. Classify the following items in terms of formal, informal and technical culture:
   a. a table place setting, that is, fork, knife, spoon, napkin.
   b. fixing a flat.
   c. being manly.
   d. stringing a guitar.
   e. sending thank-you notes.
   f. washing yourself in a shower.
   g. conducting fire drills in school.
10. We learn in an upcoming chapter that many male children are raised without another male present in the home. From whom could these children pick up the informal aspects of the culture pertaining to "maleness"? Do you think there is a greater need for such youngsters to have male teachers in the primary grades? Is there any available research on this subject?

THE SOCIOEDUCATIONAL SYSTEM

Chapter 6

PREVIEW

Among other things, the last chapter emphasized that education is much broader than schooling. This chapter further develops the importance of this distinction by demonstrating how education is really an interrelated and interdependent process involving the individual, his or her family, peers, schooling, and a variety of other cultural and subcultural elements. The existence of this socioeducational system helps to explain why attempts to use schooling to solve the nation's most persistent social ills often fail. Nonschool factors keep getting in the way. Nevertheless, research indicates that educators can make schools more effective.

We begin by offering historical background that shows how research has led us to assign greater importance to nonschool factors in influencing schooling outcomes. We describe how the family has the greatest influence. We then consider the socioeducational importance of peer groups, selected subcultures based on status, ethnicity, and race, and geographic factors.

Noting that the socioeducational system has changed dramatically over time, we explore some of these changes by focusing on the impact of radio, television, and the recording industries. We then reevaluate the limits and possibilities of schooling. We close the chapter by exploring what kind of a difference educators can realistically expect to make.

EXPECTATIONS AND REALITIES

This section provides historical background. It highlights changing expectations and troublesome realities that have emerged during the evolution of American schooling.

Historical Background

At the founding of the nation, most Americans were unenthusiastic about schooling. But by the mid-twentieth century, it had become an article of popular faith that schools could deliver a wide variety of benefits. The most ambitious of these was acting as a "great leveler." It was thought that public schools could offer all Americans more of an equal chance.

It was understood that some children went to better schools than others. But it was hoped that differences in quality could be eliminated. Then schools could offer Americans the opportunity to play the game of life on a level field.[1]

This hope was powerfully reinforced by the Supreme Court's historic desegregation decision in *Brown* v. *The School Board of Topeka*, 1954. In ruling

---

[1]Godfrey Hodgson, "Do Schools Make A Difference?" in *The Sociology of Education: A Sourcebook*, Holger Stubb, ed. (Homewood, Ill.: Dorsey Press, 1975), p. 34.

that segregation was inherently unequal, and requiring that the South integrate its schools "with all deliberate speed," the Court did more than establish that segregated education violated the Thirteenth, Fourteenth, and Fifteenth Amendments of the Constitution. It also suggested that equal schooling could create social equality.[2]

Disappointing Discoveries

In the 1960s the Johnson administration launched a series of ambitious social reforms. The 50 million poor living in "the other America" were to be brought into the mainstream.[3] Discrimination against minorities was also targeted for elimination.

At first, schooling was only a part of this massive federal initiative. But as social action programs proved to be political liabilities, the schools took up more and more of the burden of reform.[4] Many claimed, however, that there were vast differences in school quality. They said that some schools, particularly in affluent suburbs, were well financed and well maintained. Others, usually in pockets of rural poverty or inner cities, seemed poorly supported and ramshackle. If this could be changed, it was hoped that schooling could enable the poor and minorities to claim better lives.

If schools were to carry the major burden of reform, the first order of business was to find out just how bad school inequalities were. To that end, in the Civil Rights Act of 1964, Congress ordered the Commissioner of Education to conduct a survey concerning the lack of equal educational opportunities for individuals by reason of race, color, religion, or national origin.

Harvard Professor of Education James Coleman was selected to head the study team. Despite neglected studies suggesting otherwise, Coleman confidently predicted that the study would show that it was the difference in the quality of schools that retarded the academic achievement of the poor and minorities.[5]

Coleman's prediction turned out to be dead wrong. The data collected by studying 600,000 children in all fifty states pointed to a *lack* of difference in the quality of schools that black and other minority children attended.

Coleman's study also showed that minority children had serious educational deficiencies when they started school. Sadly, these deficiencies got worse with each year spent in school.

Coleman reluctantly concluded that his massive survey pointed to the critical importance of nonschool factors, particularly family background, in variations in school achievement. His report, entitled *Equality of Educational Opportunity*, stated:

---

[2]Ibid.

[3]For an influential contemporary account of this problem see Michael Harrington, *The Other America* (Baltimore: Penguin, 1962).

[4]Hodgson, op. cit., p. 35.

[5]J. S. Coleman et al., *Equality of Educational Opportunity* (Washington, D.C.: U. S. Government Printing Office, 1966), p. 325.

One implication stands out above all: That schools bring little influence to bear on a child's achievement that is independent of his background and general social context; and that this very lack of an independent effect means that the inequalities imposed on children by their home, neighborhood, and peer environment are carried along to become the inequalities with which they confront adult life at the end of school.[6]

Sobering Realizations and Angry Accusations

Without intending to do so, Coleman demonstrated that schools are only one element of an interrelated socioeducational system which includes family, peers, and socioeconomic factors, as well as ethnic, sexual, and racial factors.

Subsequent Research

Subsequent research has confirmed the importance of this socioeducational system. Perhaps the most extensive study bearing on Coleman's research was published in 1972 by Christopher Jencks. His book, *Inequality,* was the product of a massive three-year study of American social differences as they related to schooling. Like Coleman, Jencks found school results to be influenced almost solely by the characteristics of the entering children. He concluded:

> ... children seem to be far more influenced by what happens at home than what happens in school. They may also be more influenced by what happens on the streets and by what they see on television. Everything else—the school budget, its policies, the characteristics of the teachers—is either secondary or completely irrelevant.[7]

Jencks came away from his study thoroughly convinced that schools were an ineffective force for reshaping society. Pointing to the fact that the top 5 percent of the population had 25 times the income of the bottom 5 percent, Jencks concluded that many of the nation's problems would have to await a more equal distribution of wealth. And his research suggested that this redistribution would require far more radical measures than reforming schools.[8]

About the same time that Jencks was publishing his results, Lester Thurow released research revealing that although school attainment was increasing within the population, there was *NO* corresponding increase in income. In fact, Thurow found that while the bottom fifth of the white male population

---

[6]Ibid.
[7]Christopher Jencks, *Inequality: A Re-assessment of the Effect of Family and Schooling in America* (New York: Harper & Row, 1972), pp. 255–256.
[8]Ibid., p. 264.

increased its share of schooling 25 percent between 1950 and 1970, their share of national income *decreased* by 20 percent. In contrast, while the top fifth of white males *decreased* their share in education during that period 6 percent, their share of income *increased* 3 percent.

Thurow's research also revealed that the top fifth of the population ended up with 1,800 percent of the income of the lowest fifth.[9] In other words, in terms of income, America was a *very* unequal place. And schooling did not promise to change that.

It was becoming apparent that schools were not the solution to poverty, racism, and social injustice that many had hoped they would be. Findings such as those of Jencks and Thurow suggested the need to directly address disparities in status, power and income rather than tinkering with schools. Schooling was too limited by the nonschool aspects of the socioeducational system to even begin to resolve these issues.

Angry Accusations

Eventually some scholars began to speculate that schooling, particularly public schooling, was not only not the solution, but part of the problem. Economists Samual Bowles and Herbert Gintis, for example, charged that America's schools had never provided equality of opportunity, either for personal development or for economic reward. Indeed, Bowles and Gintis maintained that providing youngsters with ready access to schooling not only failed to reduce the inequalities among individuals from different social backgrounds; it actually reinforced them.[10]

Bowles and Gintis's pessimism is not widely shared. Despite evidence that schools sometimes reinforce inequalities we thought they were altering, the enthusiasm that made schooling one of the nation's biggest enterprises remains.[11] But *informed* enthusiasm must now be tempered by the knowledge that schools are only one part of a complex process.

THE SYSTEMIC POINT OF VIEW

The realization that schools are only one part of a complex, interdependent *system*, in which *everything influences everything else*, has striking parallels in other fields. Again and again, contemporary researchers in a wide variety of disciplines have come to appreciate that nothing can be fully understood in isolation. As the pioneer system theorist Ludwig von Bertalanffy observed,

---

[9]Lester Thurow, "Education and Economic Equality," *The Public Interest*, No. 28, Summer 1972.
[10]For a well-known example of this type of criticism see Samual Bowles and Herbert Gintis, *Schooling in Capitalist America* (New York: Basic Books, 1976).
[11]Richard Pratte, "Public Education and Its Public: The Changing Relationship," *Philosophy of Education* 1976, pp. 34–44. Proceedings of the thirty-second annual meeting of the Philosophy of Education Society. (Champaign, Ill.)

"In one way or another, we are forced to deal with the complexities, with "wholes" or "systems" in all fields of knowledge. This implies a basic reorientation of scientific thinking."[12]

Von Bertalanffy was referring to a growing awareness of how important it is to study how various phenomena interact and play off one against the other. This new conceptual scheme, this change in basic categories of thought, has been revolutionizing all fields of knowledge, not just education.

Nonschool Factors and School Achievement

We see that the schools are not the only, not even the primary, institution of education. Each individual comes to maturity in an all-enveloping, many-layered, socioeducational system that is interdependent, and involves multiple causations. This socioeducational system can be conceptualized in the manner illustrated in Figure 6.1.

The Family and the Socioeducational System

Schools begin educating a child relatively late in his or her life. The transformation from a purely biological being to a social one is already well developed. The child has already learned to speak, to expect certain behaviors, and to play out social roles.[13] Thus, whatever schools attempt, they attempt with individuals who have already been educated, and continue to be educated, in the family. *but not always the case.*

Parents, or parent surrogates, are the primary teachers of young children. Often not fully aware of their pedagogical responsibilities, they teach by mod-

---

[12]Ludwig von Bertalanffy, *General System Theory* (New York: George Braziller, 1968), p. 5.
[13]William Goode, *The Family* (Englewood Cliffs, New Jersey: Prentice-Hall, 1964).

Figure 6.1

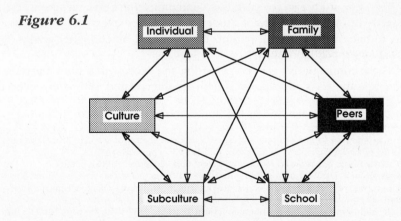

THE SOCIOEDUCATIONAL SYSTEM

eling, showing and telling. Affection and approval, or the withholding of same, is another key element.[14]

Schooling and Parenting.   Many kinds of family dynamics are of importance to school outcomes. For instance, research reveals that parental rejection, incest, and other forms of child abuse can have a devastating effect on school performance. Similarly, children raised by parents who model low frustration tolerance, in homes featuring verbal and physical violence and socialization based on threats and abuse, are also likely to relate poorly to teachers and experience problems in school.[15] Sadly, a recent study by the U. S. Department of Health and Human Services estimates that at least 1 million children each year are victims of abuse or neglect. About half of the cases involve physical, sexual, or emotional abuse. The other half involve neglect of the child's needs for clothing and shelter, or neglect of educational and emotional needs.[16]

Veteran teachers are well aware that the family is crucial to school success. A recent national poll revealed that a majority of teachers think that the chief reason their students have learning difficulties is that they are "latchkey children." The teachers surveyed singled out children being left unsupervised after school as the major cause of trouble in school. They selected this factor over poverty, broken homes, and the like.[17]

Research on educational achievement suggests a basis for the teacher's opinion. A 1985 study of 58,000 high school students by the National Center for Educational Statistics, found that students whose parents closely supervise their activities tend to get the highest grades in school (see Figure 6.2).

We can see from Figure 6.2 that the overwhelming majority of "A" students (88 percent) reported that their parents or guardians closely monitored their activities. They knew where they were and what they were doing. At the opposite end of the scale, only 61 percent of the "D" students reported that their parents knew.

The same study also revealed that communication between parent and child is related to success in school. Students who talked every day or almost every day to one or both of their parents tended to get much higher grades. Figure 6.3 shows this relationship.[18]

These connections between parenting and success in school illustrate how factors in the socioeducational system are interrelated. Ultimately, everything in it depends on everything else.

---

[14]For a somewhat dated but useful overview of modeling behavior see Urie Bronfenbrenner, *Two Worlds of Childhood* (New York: Pocket Books, 1973), pp. 128–147.

[15]Thomas Good, *Educational Psychology* (New York: Longman, 1986), p. 626.

[16]Spencer Rich, *The Washington Post*, July 3, 1988. (The actual statistics were compiled by Westat Inc., a private research organization for the Department of Health's Office of Human Development Services.)

[17]"The Metropolitan Life Survey of the American Teacher, 1987," The Metropolitan Life Insurance Company, New York, N.Y.

[18]Christopher Connell, "Study Finds Link Between Parents and High Grades," *Philadelphia Inquirer*, April 7, 1985.

Figure 6.2

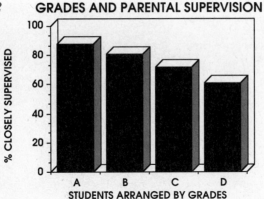

GRADES AND PARENTAL SUPERVISION

What Works? There are specific things that parents could do to increase the probability of their child's success in school. These have been highlighted in a governmental publication titled, "What Works."

- Children who are told stories by their parents are motivated to read.
- Children who are read to by their parents do better in school.
- Children who are encouraged by their parents to do leisure reading have larger vocabularies and greater reading fluency.
- Children whose parents encourage the counting of everyday objects are more likely to succeed at higher level mathematical tasks.
- Children who are encouraged by their parents to draw and "write" develop crucial language skills.
- Children who are engaged in thoughtful discussions on anything they have an interest in are likely to have higher academic achievement.

Figure 6.3 **GRADES AND COMMUNICATIONS WITH PARENTS**

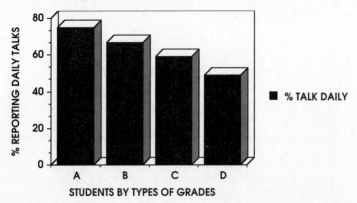

The overwhelming majority of "A" students (88%) reported that their parents or guardians closely monitored their activities.

▬ Children who are encouraged by their parents to value hard work, personal responsibility, and respect for learning are likely to experience greater success in school.[19]

If parents follow these practices the evidence suggests that they could improve their child's success in school. But from a systemic point of view the question becomes, "Under what conditions are parents likely to follow these practices?" We can think of several:

▬ The parents know what the research indicates.
▬ The parents feel that doing better in school will ultimately mean something positive for their children.
▬ The parents have the time and energy.
▬ The parents believe that it is appropriate to their role. (For example, in certain cultures, fathers might not feel that reading to little children is manly.)
▬ The parents believe that these suggestions do not violate the proper lines of authority between parent and child. (For example, some subcultures do not encourage the discussion of ideas with children.)
▬ The parents are able to afford materials that could be "wasted" by children in practicing drawing and writing.

These considerations illustrate the *many* factors that are at work. It is not sufficient to treat the outcomes of research as a recipe for success in school. The socioeducational system is far more complex than that.

---

[19]This research summary is derived from *What Works: Research About Teaching and Learning*, United States Department of Education, 1986.

Schooling and Peer Groups

In a system, *all factors are interrelated*. And in the socioeducational system we can see that principle in action when we note that the power of the peer group is inversely related to the strength of the family. If the child has a strong emotional bond to parents, he or she is more likely to consider their wishes and concerns. On the other hand, lack of family support or disruptions caused by divorce or separation are likely to increase the influence of the peer group. Systemic elements are also revealed by research that finds that the child's gender has a significant influence on susceptibility to antischool influences from peers. Boys are particularly vulnerable.[20]

Ironically, the widespread development of schooling itself has had the unintended consequence of strengthening the power of the peer group. Coleman and others have pointed out that compulsory schooling has promoted the segregation, by age, of the nation's young. As a consequence, the socially isolated age-graded peer groups of the school exercise considerably greater influence than peers ever exercised before.[21]

With the possible exception of hermits, all of us belong to peer groups. Peers are equals—individuals who share the same rank or standing. It is this similarity that is the basis of the mutual attraction. When a youngster first ventures out beyond the limits of the family, it is commonly his or her peers who supplement the socialization and education done by parents. Long before schools have their turn, the peer group has been at work. Sometimes the peer group's "lessons" complement those learned at home. Sometimes they do not. Sometimes peers help a child succeed in school. Sometimes they are a major reason for failure.

As the child develops and matures, the peer group becomes ever more important. The normal maturational process of separating from parents invests peers with growing significance. They can be a source of approval, encouragement, and understanding as the young person moves toward adulthood. The unwritten peer rules for behavior are a potent socializing force. In fact, peers often teach certain facts of life more effectively than either school or parents. Ordinarily, this peer teaching is helpful. For example, in forming close or satisfying relationships, children learn social skills which are important throughout life. The ability to initiate and maintain social relationships and to resolve conflicts are invaluable skills that peers can encourage.[22]

Peers can also enhance the process of schooling. Some adolescent peer groups, particularly those in more affluent areas, prize academic excellence. Peer groups of this sort add meaning to grades and awards. They also enhance the task of the teacher, acting as informal tutors and spurring each other to greater efforts through friendly competition.

---

[20]Frank Schneider and Larry Coutts, "Person Orientation of Male and Female High School Students: To the Personal Educational Disadvantage of Males?" *Sex Roles*, Vol. 13, No. 2 (July 1985).
[21]James Coleman, *The Adolescent Society* (New York: Free Press, 1961).
[22]S.R. Asher, R.S. Hymel, and P.D. Renshaw. "Loneliness in Children," *Child Development*, Vol. 55 (August 1984), pp. 1456–1464.

"Sometimes peer group lessons complement those learned at home; sometimes they do not."

However, there is a down side to the importance of peers. Children without close relationships often suffer the pain of isolation and alienation.[23] Frequently, youngsters who are socially rejected are different in some way. Ethnicity, race, physical unattractiveness, handicaps, or being a newcomer are common reasons for rejection.[24]

Whatever the reason, peer rejection can make school a very unpleasant experience. Ultimately, the rejected child may become truant or drop out altogether.[25] They might also seek out a group of delinquent or drug-abusing peers who will accept them if they conform to antisocial values.[26] The interests and values of such adolescent peer groups can diverge sharply from those of adults. They often model and reinforce behaviors that parents or school officials oppose. They may, through praise and attention, reward young people for doing that which is forbidden. Such social forces exert a powerful influence on schooling.[27]

Significantly, research suggests a relationship between peer rejection and low grades. In one particularly interesting study, children who were equal in IQ and achievement test scores, were grouped by their level of peer acceptance. It was found that children who were rejected had significantly lower grade point averages.[28] As is often the case in a complex system, it is difficult

---

[23]S.R. Asher, P.D. Renshaw, and S. Hymel, "Peer Relations and the Development of Social Skills," in *The Young Child: Reviews of Research*, Vol. 3, S. G. Moore and C. R. Cooper, eds. (Washington, D.C.: National Association for the Education of Young Children, 1982).

[24]Ibid.

[25]J.B. Kupersmidt, "Predicting Delinquency and Academic Problems from Childhood Peer Status," paper presented at the biennial meeting of the Society for Research in Child Development, Detroit, Mich., April 21–24, 1983.

[26]S. Isaacs, "Popularity," *Parents Magazine*, August 1985, pp. 58–62.

[27]See Christine Burton, "Children's Peer Relationships," *ERIC Digest*, ERIC Clearinghouse on Elementary and Early Childhood Education (Urbana, Ill.: University of Illinois), for an excellent summary of peer relationship factors.

[28]Donna Clasen, paper presented at the Biennial Meeting of the Society for Research in Child Development, Baltimore, Md., April 23–26, 1987.

to determine which is cause and which effect. The central question is, are such children rejected because of their low grades, or is it the rejection that depresses their grades? If it is the latter, there is hope that informed teaching could ease the situation, for research suggests that classroom characteristics and pedagogical practices influence the formation of friendship cliques.[29]

Certain peer groups regard the good student as a "wimp," and often support delinquent behavior. In such groups, which can occur at any social level, academic achievement is not valued, achievers are ostracized, and status is determined by the trouble you cause. Students who are pessimistic about their future and who are headed toward low status jobs tend to seek out such peer groups.[30]

Inner-city educators are particularly aware of the negative persuasive power of some adolescent peer groups. For example, Marie Valentine is employed at a North Philadelphia junior high school where three-fourths of the families are poor enough to qualify for welfare, and most of the students come from single-parent homes. She directs a school program designed to offset the negative power of peers. "You can't emphasize the effect of peer pressure too much," says Valentine. "A lot of the students are interested in school when they first come here," she explains, but "the peer pressure just takes them over."[31]

Formal research backs up Valentine's sense of things. For example, a research study focusing on Hispanic students experiencing academic problems, surveyed twenty-five counselors in southern California high schools. In interviews, these counselors were asked to rank the causes of the problems Hispanic students were facing in their schools. Seventy-five percent listed peer pressure number one on their list of causes. Language differences and poor study skills were listed as secondary reasons.[32]

Gangs.   Deviant adolescent peer groups which reject school and all it stands for can become extraordinarily powerful. For example, 387 people died in gang-related violence in Los Angeles County in 1987. The violence continued into 1988, provoking the police to make massive sweeps through gang-infested neighborhoods, arresting more than 2,000 people. At one point the situation got so desperate that a county supervisor demanded National Guard reinforcements.

The presence of the gangs has made normal life impossible for residents of the involved communities. Youth workers describe entire neighborhoods as "battlefields." Mothers teach their toddlers to take cover at the sound of shots. Young people choose clothing carefully, since wearing colors associated with

---

[29]Maureen Hallinan and Stevens Smith, "Classroom Characteristics and Student Friendship Cliques," paper presented at the Annual Meeting of the American Educational Research Association, Washington, D.C. April 20–24, 1987.

[30]Arthur Stinchcombe, *Rebellion in a High School* (Chicago: Quandrangle Books, 1964).

[31]Dale Mezzacappa, "Donning an Achieving Attitude," *The Philadelphia Inquirer*, February 5, 1987, p. B-1.

[32]Margaret Cooney, "Education and Job Training Needs of Hispanic Students," California State University, San Bernardino, School of Education, 1986.

POINT/COUNTERPOINT

Although scholars agree that schooling has promoted the power of the peer group, they do not agree on how we should view this situation. Some child development experts, Urie Bronfenbrenner, for example, argue that isolation and concentration of the young promotes alienation, indifference, antagonism, and even violence. Bronfenbrenner maintains that the transmission of higher order moral values requires the participation of older members of the culture. Concentrated in schools, and then left to their own devices unless their conduct disrupts instruction, he explains, young people are left with a moral and emotional vacuum filled by television and a search for thrills.[33]

Other scholars have a much more benign interpretation of the growth of peer group influence in the lives of children. R. Bauman, for example, warns that researchers tend to be "adultcentric," judging children's behavior against adult standards. But, says Bauman, children must be studied on their own terms. Children in a peer group do have their own distinctive subculture that interacts with the adult world in a cross-cultural way. But, although the way this peer group acts on and makes sense of the world is admittedly different from adults, it is neither incompetent nor malignant. It is just different.[34]

---

warring gangs invites death. Neighborhood "turfs" are spelled out in graffiti that children learn to decipher before they learn to read.

Police estimate that there may be as many as 80,000 members in 700 gangs in Southern California. Most of them are concentrated in predominantly black and Latino low income neighborhoods of Los Angeles.[35] Big-city gang culture is also spreading to neighborhoods and cities that have never before experienced the problem. In the words of U. S. Representative George Miller, "Gangs are beginning to slop over into middle America."[36]

We can imagine how difficult it is for educators to overcome the impact of gangs. But sometimes, say the experts, school officials are slow even to recognize the problem. And when they do recognize it, they may take the position that gangs are not an issue unless they disrupt instruction—perhaps because school administrators are ill-equipped to meet the costs of a more active interpretation of their role.[37]

Selected Subcultures and the Socioeducational System

The United States is one of the world's most pluralistic societies. There are vast differences among Americans as to what they believe and how they be-

---

[33]Bronfenbrenner, op. cit., pp. 120–121.
[34]R. Bauman, "Ethnography of Children's Folklore," in P. Gilmore and A. A. Glathorn, eds., *Children in and Out of School: Ethnography and Education* (Washington, D.C.: Center for Applied Linguistics, 1982), pp. 172–186.
[35]This account of gang-related violence in Southern California is based on Paul Nussbaum, "Youth Gangs Bring Death to L.A. Streets" *The Philadelphia Inquirer*, April 15, 1988, p. A-1.
[36]Debra Viadero, "Big-City Gang Culture Spreading to New Turf," *Education Week*, April 20, 1988, p. 1.
[37]Ibid.

have. Often these differences indicate the existence of subcultures. Although not differentiated enough to constitute separate cultures, **subcultures** possess their own common traditions, mutual sense of identity, and distinctive customs.[38] They often reflect age groups, occupational specializations, religious affiliations, social stratification, ethnicity and race.

Subcultures Based on Status and Class.   A number of subcultures are based largely on social status. 'Yuppies,' or young urban professionals are an example. **Social status** refers to rank or social position.[39] This rank or position reflects a complex of interrelated attributes including:

- occupation
- income
- housing
- education
- religion
- ethnicity
- race

All of these subcultural variables tend to correlate into clusters. When they do, they contribute to the formation of a **social class**, a category of people with roughly equal social status.

Many researchers hold that there is a strong relation between academic achievement and social status. Indeed, this "truth" is so widely accepted that educators routinely encounter quotes such as this:

> To categorize youth according to the social class position of their parents is to order them on the extent of their participation and degree of success in the American educational system. This has been so consistently confirmed by research that it can now be regarded as an empirical law. . . . [Status] predicts grades, achievement and intelligence test scores, retentions at grade level, course failures, truancy, suspensions from school, high school dropouts, plans for college attendance, and total amount of formal schooling.[40]

Concerned that things may not be as they seem, researcher Karl White analyzed almost 200 studies that considered the relation between social status and academic achievement. He concluded that although social status is a factor, the relation between it and *individual* academic achievement is so weak as to be of limited use to educators. He found that it is how parents rear their children, not their social status, that really makes most of the academic difference when it comes down to individual children.[41] He did not deny, how-

---

[38]Caroline Persell, *Understanding Society: An Introduction to Sociology*, 2nd Ed. (New York, Harper & Row, 1987), p. 91.
[39]Persell, op. cit., p. 56.
[40]W. W. Charters, Jr., "The Social Background of Teaching," in N. L. Gage, ed., *Handbook of Research on Teaching* (Chicago: Rand McNally, 1963), pp. 739–740.
[41]Karl White, "Socioeconomic Status and Academic Achievement," Exceptional Child Center, UMC 68, Utah State University, Logan, Utah 84322 (undated).

ever, that certain educationally unhelpful styles of parenting *tend* to be associated with poverty.

Underclasses.   Often specific subcultures will occupy socially inferior positions within a culture. Usually assigned on the basis of ethnicity, race, or religion, these minorities are isolated from the social mainstream and confined by custom and prejudice to very limited opportunities. Such caste-like minorities exist around the world. The Harijans, or "untouchables," of India, the native Maoris of New Zealand, and the Burakumi of Japan all exemplify groups occupying inferior social positions.

Significantly, the IQ scores of such groups average 10 to 15 points below children of the dominant group. But when members of these groups are taken out of their socially inferior positions, scores change dramatically. For example, when Burakumi children are raised in the United States, where their alleged inferiority is unknown, they do as well on IQ tests and in school as any other Japanese-Americans.[42] Unfortunately, the identities of all underclasses are not so easily forgotten as that of the Americanized Burakumi.

In America, as elsewhere, underclasses are often associated with ethnic or racial minorities. Of course, it would be a mistake to think of all ethnic and racial minorities in this way. White Anglo-Saxon Protestants, or WASPS, are a minority subculture, for example, but are hardly members of an underclass.

In what follows we will examine the role of ethnicity and race in the shaping of distinctive socioeducational systems and in school achievement.

Ethnic Subcultures.   Ethnic groups are distinguished by common cultural traditions and a mutual sense of identity, language, religion, and distinctive customs. They are among the most easily identified subcultures in the nation. In order to qualify as "ethnic" a subculture must incorporate a past-oriented group identification emphasizing origins, and include some conception of cultural and social distinctiveness.[43] It is this heritage that helps shape the development of children, and encourages some traits and preferences over others.

Comparing group differences on an international basis reveals the remarkable power of the ethnic subculture. Thomas Sowell, author of *Ethnic America* and *The Economics and Politics of Race*, has shown how the Italians of Australia and Argentina, for example, show social, economic and school related patterns which are remarkably similar to those of Italians in Italy or the United States. Similarly, Chinese students in Malaysia specialize in much the same academic areas as they do in American universities—differing markedly from the specializations of other groups.[44] This points up the fact that *socioeducational systems can be more or less self-contained and relatively*

---

[42]Daniel Goleman, "An Emerging Theory," *New York Times Education Life*, April 10, 1988, p. 22.
[43]Wendell Bell, "Comparative Research on Ethnicity: A Conference Report," *Social Science Research Council Items*, Vol. 28 (December 1974), p. 61.
[44]Thomas Sowell, *The Economics and Politics of Race: An International Perspective* (New York: William Morrow, 1983.)

resistant to outside influences. No matter the nation of residence, nonschool ethnic factors continue to influence school outcomes in the same way.

The connections between ethnicity and American schooling have always been remarkable. Consider that in the early twentieth century more than half of the children of southern Italian origin were behind their normal grade. Only one-fifth of the children of Dutch origin were in a similar situation. Less than one in ten of the southern Italian origin children were ahead of their grade level. Among the Dutch origin children the rate was one in four. In this same time period, high school graduation was one hundred times higher among Germans and Jews than among Irish and Italians.[45]

We should notice that these statistics refer only to the quantity of schooling, not to the quality. But qualitative differences only add to the disparity. Groups with above average amounts of education—Jews, Chinese, Japanese—also tend to attend demanding colleges and specialize in highly competitive fields such as law, medicine, and biochemistry. In other words, emphasizing quantitative differences understates the actual ethnic differences.[46]

Today, ethnically related educational differences are smaller than in the past. Nevertheless, they remain very real. For example, Hispanics tend to drop out of school far earlier and at a greater rate than any other ethnic subculture. By age 19 only about one-half of Hispanics complete high school, compared with two out of three blacks and three out of four whites.[47] Hispanics are also significantly lower than whites or blacks in the years of college completed by individuals 25 to 34 years old. More than 25 percent of whites had four or more years of higher education. About 14 percent of blacks were in that category. Hispanics were not quite at the 10 percent level.[48] Figure 6.4 summarizes these differences. (Remember, we are describing statistical averages,

---

[45]Ibid., p. 193.
[46]Ibid., pp. 196–197.
[47]Center for Educational Statistics, *The Condition of Education: A Statistical Report, 1987 Edition* (Washington, D.C.: Office of Educational Research and Improvement, U.S. Department of Education), p. 26.
[48]Ibid., p. 195.

Figure 6.4   **% HIGH SCHOOL AND COLLEGE GRADUATES**

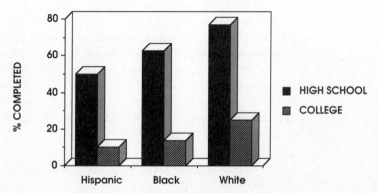

not individual children of Hispanic background. It is also important to keep in mind that the term "Hispanic" is imprecise. Cubans, Puerto Ricans, Argentinians, and so forth each have their own distinctive characteristics.)

These statistics have complex origins reflecting the systemic nature of the socioeducational complex. For example, a greater percentage of black and Hispanic youngsters are poor, and research reveals a clear relationship between socioeconomic status and educational achievement. Also, many of the Hispanic students have substandard English skills, and their parents may not speak English at all. We can readily imagine the relevance of these and similar considerations.

Another example of the scholastic significance in ethnicity can be found in the achievements of some Asian-American groups. Youngsters of Chinese, Korean, and Vietnamese backgrounds, for example, are finishing high above the national average on the mathematics section of the Scholastic Aptitude Tests. A higher percentage of them also complete high school and college than do white Americans. Like the Jews before them, Asians from countries where Confucianism is the dominant value tend to see schools as gateways to a better life. Their Confucian ethic, stressing the value of work, the importance of schooling, and the need to repay debts owed to parents, lends itself to school success. Children from Buddhist cultures, such as Cambodia, for example, tend to be less remarkable in their academic achievement.[49]

Racial Minority Subcultures.   Race is also a factor in school achievement. But we have to be careful not to overgeneralize because it is hard to imagine a subject more prone to mythology and misinformation than race. Explorations of race have always featured a mixture of fact and fiction with a tendency to turn ugly. It is associated with pseudosciences such as craniology, and the homicidal racism practiced with such deadly effect by the Nazis.

Unlike the concept of ethnicity, which can be used with some precision, the concept of race is slippery and prone to misuse. In biology, race is used to classify local variations of a single species into subdivisions based on genetically inherited physical features. In human beings, skin color, eye color, hair type, the shape of facial features, the roundness of the skull, blood type, and the measurement of various body parts have all been considerations.

Despite all of these delimiters, however, great difficulties have been encountered in classifying humankind into races. Many individuals and groups do not fit easily into any racial classification. Contrary to popular belief, *there are no pure races*. Human beings are all one species (*Homo sapiens*) and can be described adequately only in terms of the frequency that certain genetically inherited traits occur. As the pioneer geneticist Gregor Mendel demonstrated with finality in 1865, even if a population of individuals became isolated from other populations so that no cross-breeding can occur, the status of a "pure race" could never be reached.

---

[49]David Brand, "The New Whiz Kids: Why Asian Americans Are Doing So Well, and What It Costs Them," *Time*, August 31, 1987.

POINT/COUNTERPOINT

Race is not the only term that is hard to pin down. Deciding whom to count as a "minority" is also more problematic than one might think. Many definitions do not rely solely on numbers. Louis Wirth, of the University of Chicago, emphasizes inferior status when he defines a minority as "groups distinguished from the rest of society by racial or cultural characteristics which have become the objects of differential and inferior treatment, and have developed a consciousness of their inferior status."[50]

As a result of emphasis on inferior status rather than percentages some numeric minorities are denied the benefits that can accompany such a distinction. Jews, for example, though they comprise about 5 percent of the population, are not legally classified as a minority. Thus, they are not eligible for "affirmative action"-type programs. *Affirmative action* refers to legal requirements for taking positive steps to overcome the effects of past discrimination. Typically, affirmative action plans encourage policies that give preference to individuals from historically disadvantaged groups. For example, the courts have encouraged colleges and universities to give preferential admissions treatment to minorities that the institution wants more adequately represented among its students.

Recently, because of certain advantages related to being legally classified as a minority, groups have sued to establish their claim to this distinction. For example, Louisiana's Cajuns (Americans of French Acadian background) won a state court case that established that they are a minority. They were opposed in this by several black groups. This curious situation reflects an historic realignment of costs and benefits which is altering the nature of American society.

Thus we see that the differences in the "races" are more social than they are biological.[51] And it is these social differences, shaped by culture into distinctive subcultures, that are particularly significant in the operation of the socioeducational system. For example, the most complete measure available is the National Assessment of Educational Progress. It measures national samples of students in key subject areas. NAEP testing does reveal racial differences. On average the writing performance of Asian and white students, for example, is higher than that of black. Reading proficiency scores show similar differences.[52]

No one doubts that these academic achievement differences exist. But the central question is, why? Is race really the key, or are other things at work here? For instance, having examined the importance of the family and the peer group, we already know that both are factors in school achievement. And in the case of black Americans evidence suggests that these families have been particularly hard hit in the years since World War II. Prior to that war 80

---

[50]Louis Wirth, observations delivered at the World Congress of Sociology, Zurich, Switzerland, September 1950.
[51]Theodosius Dobzhansky, "On Species and Races of Living and Fossil Man," *American Journal of Physical Anthropology*, Vol. 2 (1944), pp. 251–265.
[52]These differences are highlighted in *The Condition of Education: A Statistical Report, 1987 Edition*, pp. 19 and 31.

percent of black children lived in two-parent families.[53] Today, only 45.5 percent have two parents in the home.[54] Therefore, the support system that once existed for black children, more specifically, poor black children, has changed dramatically. This has an impact on school achievement directly and also, as observed earlier, increases the probability that peers will exercise a negative influence.

We should also remember that if "race" is defined as significant, it is significant in its consequences. For example, if race is used to legitimate and perpetuate enslavement, or exploitation as in the case of Afro-Americans, this usage imposes very different cultural experiences on those who are victimized. And it is very likely these negative cultural experiences, rather than any alleged genetic inferiority, which accounts for differences in academic achievement.[55]

Countercultural Subcultures

Some subcultural variations are not merely different from those of the larger culture, but define themselves in terms of their opposition to it. These *affiliations based upon a set of norms and values that contradict the norms and values of the broader culture are called* **countercultures.**

Many countercultures are overtly hostile to their host society and particularly troublesome to schools. The juvenile gangs discussed earlier would be one example. Another more recent expression of a hostile counterculture is the small but growing "skinhead" movement. Sporting close-cropped hair, combat boots, and Nazi insignias, skinheads menace blacks, Jews, homosexuals, and even the police while also promising to become a growing problem for the nation's educators.

Law enforcement officials note that most skinheads come from middle income families. They also tend to come from homes where parents are either not present, or not interested.[56] Once again, this finding illustrates the interaction of elements within the socioeducational system.

Countercultures need not be overtly antisocial. In fact, the "flower children" of the Vietnam War era were noted for their "love-ins" and nonviolence. While they rejected the materialism of the cultural mainstream, and were highly critical of its competitiveness, "*the* counterculture," as they were called, championed passive resistance. This rejection of hostility was central to their identity.

"Flower children" and their allies had a profound, if chiefly temporary, impact on America's schools. They excoriated them for being mindless and

---

[53]"Illiteracy: Chicken or Egg?" *The Literacy Beat: A Special Newsletter of the Education Writers Association*, Vol. 1, No. 2 (August 1987), p. 1.
[54]*Statistical Abstract of the United States, 10th Edition, 1987* (Washington, D.C.: U. S. Department of Commerce, Bureau of the Census), p. 49.
[55]Significantly, the fact that an estimated 70 percent of those affected had some white ancestry was considered irrelevant.
[56]Paul Nussbaum, " 'Skinheads': Youth United to Vent Hatred." *The Philadelphia Inquirer*, May 14, 1988, p. A-10.

mean spirited.[57] They also accused educators of being obsessed with power and discipline.[58] They even indicted them for graduating noncomprehending automatons who would murder children if their commanding officer so ordered.[59] These and similar criticisms gave birth to a whole host of "reforms," recounted in Chapter 13, which present reformers regard as foolish and excessive.

Other Factors

We have only partially examined the many elements of the socioeducational system. Churches and synagogues, voluntary organizations such as Scouting or the 4H, libraries, museums, newspapers, radio, the recording industry, television, and so forth also share in the education of America. And in each case, educators need to ask whether what is taught complements or contradicts the work of the school.

Geographic Considerations.   The socioeducational system also has a geographic dimension that vitally influences its "curriculum." The importance of the geographic dimension comes into focus if we compare and contrast socioeducational systems operating in the heart of a big city and in an isolated and relatively inaccessible corner of the nation. Consider, for example, the differences between the socioeducational system at work on students in a public school serving a public housing project in the South Bronx with the system educating the students who attend the one-room Currie School (enrollment 7) in the Nevada desert. (There are still 772 one-room schools out of total of 84,173 public schools in the nation.)

Peer pressure in Currie must be practically nonexistent. As a consequence, parents and other adults would have a far great influence on the socioeducational curriculum and on the school. In contrast to the South Bronx, there is no opportunity for Currie children to learn the intricacies of the drug trade by hanging on street corners; and their sexual knowledge is more likely acquired by observing ranch animals than prostitutes. The down side is that Currie children have less chance to make their own mistakes—often a very educational experience. Also, there is no YMCA, Scout troop, or summer day camp to supplement the education provided by school and family.

The Interplay of Factors in a System

Social systems are complex, and elements within them interrelated. Things are seldom as simple as they seem. Consider, for example, that a typical three-person family headed by a single mother operates on a little more than a third of the income of an average four-person family headed by a mother and

---

[57]Bel Kaufman, *Up The Down Staircase* (New York: Avon, 1964).
[58]Herbert Kohl, *The Open Classroom* (New York: Vintage, 1969).
[59]Jonathan Kozol, *The Night is Dark and I am Far From Home* (New York: Bantam, 1973).

father.[60] As a result, unless researchers control their studies very carefully, they may measure differences that have more to do with family income or socioeconomic status than single-parenting.

Although well-designed research studies routinely do have such controls, it is always problematic to isolate and study one aspect of a complex system. We know, for example, that 33 percent of black families are headed by a mother who never married. Little research has been done to determine if this sort of arrangement produces an effect on schooling different from that of divorce. Perhaps the presence of extended families and community networks may make the single-parent experience different for black children.[61]

Similarly, we must keep in mind that families are, in part, products of the economy. How well off people are has a lot to do with whether or not the father is present, who works outside the home, the life-styles of family members, how decision making is divided, and the opportunities available for children.[62]

Thus, different factors play off against one another as we seek to understand the workings of the socioeducational system. This is the nature of a system—everything influences everything else.

Changes in the Socioeducational System

One of the most overlooked aspects of the U. S. socioeducational system is how it has changed over time. Many of these transformations were outlined in Chapter 5 and are covered in detail in the upcoming section on the history of education, but a few examples will help clarify the point. For instance, many of the opportunities and difficulties facing contemporary educators derive from the changes imposed on the socioeducational system by the urbanization of America. In 1930 half of the 262,000 schools in the United States were single-teacher schools. As late as 1960 there were still nearly 60,000 of them. Today there are only 772, less than 1 percent of all the schools in the nation. Urbanization and improvements in transportation have eliminated the rest, and with them went an adult/parental influence on the socioeducational system that will never be recaptured.[63] In the days when transportation was slow and there was only modest movement of people and ideas in and out of communities, teachers were almost totally integrated into the local social structure. They lived side by side with the parents of their students, shopping at the same stores and attending the same church. Under such circumstances, teachers generally shared community views of what was right or wrong, good

---

[60]J. Orth and S. B. Zacariya, "The School and the Single-Parent Student: What Can Schools Do to Help" *Principal*, Vol. 62, No. 1, 1982.

[61]Heatherington, op. cit., p. 780.

[62]Maxine Zinn and D. Stanley Eitzen, *Diversity in American Families* (New York: Harper & Row, 1987), p. xiii.

[63]Paul Nussbaum, "Readin', Writin' and the Rebirth of a One Room School," *Philadelphia Inquirer*, October 10, 1988, p. 1.

or bad. They were a part of a moral community that accepted a common authority.[64]

Teaching in such a setting could be a suffocating experience for those who valued autonomy and individuality; but the schooling process was often reinforced by other elements of the socioeducational system. If a child caused trouble in school, parents might learn about it from the pastor at church, or from other parents in the local grocery store. And if they did not take action, they risked becoming outcasts in their own community—an outcome that was likely to have economic as well as social costs. On the other hand, cooperative children generated benefits for their parents.

In such a setting educators were less likely than they are today to be troubled by a lack of support in dealing with behavior problems, by "careless" attitudes, or by children more interested in selling or taking drugs than in learning how to solve an equation.

Radio, Television, and the Recording Industries

Radio, television, and the recording industries provide another vivid illustration of the way the socioeducational system has changed over time.

The first scheduled radio program in the United States went on the air on Election Day, November 2, 1920. By 1928 over 7 million radio receivers were in nearly 20 percent of American homes where they could be tuned to a total of 677 commercial stations. By 1949 diversified programs of national interest and importance broadcast coast-to-coast had been a daily occurrence for twenty years, and 94 percent of all American homes were able to tune in.[65] Millions of Americans listened to "Fibber McGee and Molly," "Jack Benny," "The Shadow," the New York Philharmonic, and the NBC Symphony, news, political conventions, inaugural ceremonies, disasters, sports, public affairs, religion, variety, and drama. All with access to a radio, and that was nearly everybody, could put their ear to the world. This effected vast educational changes.

Commercial television was inaugurated in New York on April 30, 1939. However, the real growth of the industry began in 1946. By 1949 there were more than 2,500,000 TV sets in American homes and new ones were being purchased at the rate of a quarter million each month. About 25 years later, in the mid-1970s, television sets were nearly universal and children under five years of age were averaging 24 hours of television watching per week or one-fifth of all their waking hours. By the time these children graduated from high school they had spent 15,000 to 20,000 hours watching television compared to only 11,000 to 12,000 hours in school.[66]

There is a lot we do not know about the impact of television on the so-

[64]For an interesting treatment of this and related issues, see James Comer, "Is 'Parenting' Essential to Good Teaching?" *NEA Today Special Edition*, January 1988, pp. 34–40.

[65]Niles Trammel, "Radio and Television Broadcasting," *The Encyclopedia Americana* (New York: Americana Corporation, 1962), Vol. 23, pp. 120–124.

[66]Evelyn Kaye, *The Family Guide to Children's Television* (New York: Pantheon, 1974), p. 7.

Johnny Rotten sang with the Sex Pistols and is now a member of the rock group PIL. What does he teach the young?

cioeducational system, but we do know some things. For example, there is no doubt that young people obtain much of their political and social information from television—though how they interpret it seems to depend on parental influence.[67] We also know that children view an incredible amount of violence, and some research suggests that seeing violence on television increases the probability that a child will be aggressive.[68] Some maintain that the single most important impact of television is that it encourages too much passivity among American youngsters.[69] Perhaps so. In any case, television is a major player in the socioeducational system of modern America. Does it complement the work of the schools? In some cases, yes. Programs like "Sesame Street," "Mr. Rogers," or "Nova" clearly enhance and enrich the school curriculum. But one wonders about wrestling, "Soul Train," or "Dallas," for example.

In the years since 1900, when the first recordings were molded commercially, the recording industry has also come to play an important role in the socioeducational system. Presently, many recordings and music videos are aimed at the youth market. Here they have considerable opportunity to educate the young—particularly in the realm of values.

For the most part this influence is relatively benign. But the so-called "heavy metal" and "punk" aspects of the industry are a different story. The late Sid Vicious and the Sex Pistols provides an example. Sid's song "Anarchy in the U.K." from their "Flogging a Horse" album begins, "I am an antichrist! I am an anarchist!" and goes down hill from there. Whatever else it might be, this is not the sort of stuff that helps schoolteachers do their jobs.

---

[67]George Comstock et al., *Television and Human Behavior* (New York: Columbia University Press, 1978).
[68]Ibid.
[69]Marie Winn, *The Plug-in Drug: Television, Children and the Family* (New York: Viking, 1977).

Reevaluating The Limits and Possibilities of Schooling

Understanding that schools are only one part of a complex and dynamic socioeducational system is essential to making intelligent judgments regarding their limits and possibilities. It also leads us directly to other key considerations. We will list several.

An Open System

The socioeducational system is an **open system**, that is, it is influenced by changes in its basic environment, or in other systems. We know, for example, that changes in the economy affect the schools. Some of these effects are direct. Hard times reduce school revenues, for example. Other effects are more subtle but just as real. We can imagine the following sequence:

- Hard times result in parental unemployment.
- Unemployment reduces parental self-esteem.
- The decline in self-esteem promotes child abuse.
- The child abuse produces the school-related results described earlier.

Equifinality

The principle of **equifinality** states that within a system there are many ways of producing the same results. In other words, systems involve multiple causation.

The concept has telling implications as far as the socioeducational system is concerned. It means, for example, educational reforms could be achieved by reforming things other than schools. We have already seen that the family is a critical, but troubled, component of the socioeducational system. We can readily imagine that steps to strengthen the family could also strengthen schooling. Similarly, anything that might make the peer group support or encourage schooling makes the teacher's job easier.

Equilibrium

Unfortunately, the fact that strengthening the family or improving the peer groups support for school achievement has to be tempered by the recognition that systems tend to remain in **equilibrium**; that is, systemic powers and influences are in a balanced state. Sometimes, changing one variable can make all the difference. But in a system in equilibrium, changing one factor might only cause the others to take on more importance while the overall situation remains unchanged.

The extent to which the socioeducational system is in equilibrium has yet to be established. This emerges, however, as a critical question.

The Point of Saturation

Sometimes the socioeducational system is in a particularly delicate equilibrium. If it is, small perturbations can set off major changes the consequences of which are hard to forecast. If a class is already close to the critical point of saturation with troubled children, for example, it could be extra sensitive to a last small difference. A single child who is troubled by parental abuse being added to the balance might be all that is needed to throw the classroom into educational turmoil.

Under these new circumstances, educational methods that previously worked could become nonproductive or even counterproductive. New strategies would be essential. Moreover, "memories" of the incident and its consequences will linger in the system for years to come. We are not referring here to the memory of teachers or students, but to the "memory" of the system in which incidents create consequences that bound and rebound off one another.

Making A Positive Difference

We do not imply that teachers are incapable of making a positive difference in the lives of children. Indeed, some studies suggest very practical steps to improve instruction, and simultaneously to improve the academic achievement of children from disadvantaged backgrounds.

Michael Rutter's *Fifteen Thousand Hours*, a classic study of the the academic achievement of students from the inner-city of London, England, suggested that school can make a difference in the education of such children. Specifically, Rutter's investigation revealed that teachers with well-prepared lessons, who gave frequent homework assignments, had a clear-cut system of rewards and punishments, and expressed high academic expectations to their students were able to get better attendance, better student behavior, and better examination scores. These positive results were further facilitated if the schools were clean and well maintained, if the entire staff planned the curriculum and discipline, if there were shared activities between students and staff, and if students were given positions of responsibility.[70]

Rutter's study reinforced the findings of American researchers working on the same problem. Scholars like Ron Edmunds—particularly in working with children from disadvantaged backgrounds—had also found that some schools were more effective than others. This research, which commonly used standardized test scores as their measure of efficacy, found that the more effective schools had the following characteristics:

- ■ A shared sense of high expectations on the part of faculty, administrators, and students.

---

[70]Michael Rutter et al., *Fifteen Thousand Hours* (Cambridge, Mass.: Harvard University Press, 1979).

- Strong school ties with parents.
- A student-centered environment.
- Specific educational goals.
- Constant feedback to students on their rate of progress.
- Strong leadership by the principal, but shared ownership of policies and programs by the teachers.
- A safe school.
- Lots of instructional materials.[71]

We see, then, that nonschool limits on school achievement can be at least partially addressed, and that real school reform can be accomplished. We are beginning to form a clearer understanding of what aspects of schooling make a difference, and how great a difference.

Schooling is a tough job that cannot be accomplished by political posturing, sloganeering, or even authoritative commands. It requires, at a minimum, thorough lesson preparation, well-defined rules, clear-cut rewards and punishments, parental outreach, a student-centered outlook that gives them responsibility commensurate with their maturity, administrative leadership, teacher involvement in policy making, a positive attitude, and loads of perseverance. It also requires a clean, well-maintained and safe school with plenty of instructional materials. Is this a tall order? Maybe so, but who ever said that effective schooling was either easy or cheap?

In Chapter 8 which deals with the school as an organization, we will identify those models of organizations that promise most in the way of educational reform. We will also explore some of the reasons why previous reforms have fallen short, and discover that we can understand the findings just discussed in terms of organizational considerations.

FINAL CONSIDERATIONS

In this chapter we emphasized that schooling is one component of a complex and interdependent socioeducational system. The major point of making these observations is not to provide a litany of excuses for poor teaching or ineffective schools, but to point out that social variables must always be considered if we are to develop comprehensive understanding of educational issues. The social and cultural circumstances in which education occurs are absolutely critical. They determine the who, what, when, where and how of learning.

Teaching is not like the labor of Sisyphus—a mythical King of Corinth condemned in Hades to roll a heavy stone up a steep hill only to have it roll down again when he nears the top. A caring, professionally competent teacher can make an enormous difference in the lives of many children. However,

---

[71]Summarized in *Covering the Education Beat: A Current Guide for Editors and Writers* (Washington, D.C.: Education Writers Association, 1987), p. 45.

getting most students to achieve at an acceptable level is tough, complicated work that requires time, effort, and the cooperation of a lot of people — many of them outside the school. Sometimes if instruction is to benefit children it must even run contrary to the interests of entrenched social and economic interests. Simple fixes and instant results are very unlikely, and the consequences of any particular attempt at improvement are unpredictable. What is more, love of teaching and knowledge of subject matter, while necessary, are rarely sufficient.

Those who would be teachers want to make a difference—and if they don't, they should. But we have to be careful that zeal does not create unrealistic expectations that, in turn, lead to disillusionment and despair. No one survives and prospers in teaching who does not come to recognize that there are many problems that are beyond their control, and many individuals whom they can neither reach nor help. When educators who have come to this practical knowledge the hard way confront the glib recommendations of those in remote positions of "authority," they often get cold chills. A letter from an angered teacher to the editor of *Education Week*, illustrates this point. She is referring to a policy proposed by the Council of Chief State School Officers that schools "guarantee" a certain minimum level of learning, much as automobile manufacturers back their cars for, say, 5 years or 50,000 miles.

To the Editor:

I read with disbelief your article on the "guarantees" policy proposed by the Council of Chief State School Officers.

As a classroom teacher, I will be the one who must "guarantee" that my students will learn. Every brainstorm of groups like this puts the burden of implementation on the teacher.

I will be happy to guarantee that leaning takes place if the following conditions are met:

- The parents certify that neither has ever used drugs.
- A doctor certifies that the mother had proper prenatal care and the child was properly nurtured by both parents the first five years of his life.
- The child scores above 100 on an I.Q. test.
- An inspection is made of the home to see that a quiet place to study is available.
- An attitudinal survey is given to the parents to determine the degree of importance they place on education.
- The parents present a sworn statement that they will not divorce or consume alcohol to excess while their child is being educated.
- The child and the parents promise that the child will follow the school district's code of behavior.

- A secretary is provided to handle routine paperwork so that I have time to plan and teach.

Of course, given the conditions of society, these requirements are as ridiculous as the "guarantees" that are being pushed by the state chiefs. I don't hold any child responsible for his home life. Neither do I take the responsibility for all of the problems that are inflicted upon him.

I get cold chills every time I read another national report or another proposal for "improvement." These are all prepared by people far removed from the classroom who don't have the foggiest notion about the realities of our schools.

Rachel Hampton
5th Grade Teacher
La Porte, Texas

Educational strategies designed for quick reform or certain success are attractive—particularly to politicos facing elections every few years. And there is a certain temptation to appeal to the idealism of future educators by ignoring or obscuring the realities of the socioeducational system. But in the real world of the schools, quick fixes seldom work, certain success is never guaranteed, and Pollyannas just get in the way.

A report released in 1989 by the Rand Corporation's Center for the Study of the Teaching Profession illustrates this point. The Rand researchers concentrated on the big city schools of Atlanta, Cincinnati, Miami, Memphis, Pittsburgh, and San Diego where efforts at reform were under way. They found that improvements were possible, but that they required the following conditions:

- The same sort of business and civic coalitions are required that are brought together to revitalize downtown areas.
- Meaningful change requires two strands of support, one inside the school, one outside.
- There must be popular support for long-term solutions rather than gimmicks or panaceas.
- School authorities must be open concerning existing deficiencies.
- Superintendents must be active and able to win strong support, yet not dominate the process.
- Coalitions of school administrators, teachers' union officials, business leaders, and local politicians are necessary.
- Business leaders must play a key role in placing schooling high on the public agenda and providing strategic thinking.
- Real change requires the active cooperation of a strong, well-led teachers' union.

■ Parental choice plans that emphasize private schools are not necessary.[72]

The Rand study suggests that meaningful school reform requires a systemic approach. And this conclusion is hardly surprising when we take into consideration the chief points of this chapter.

SUMMARY

1. The school is part of and systemically interrelated with other elements of complex socioeducational system. For this reason nonschool elements such as the family and the peer group can greatly affect student performance in the schools. The research conducted by Coleman as well as Jencks confirms this. Rutter found, however, that schooling could still be effective despite hostile external conditions.

2. The family, not the school, is the key element of the socioeducational system. The peer group, accidentally strengthened by mass schooling, is another key element in the socioeducational system. Ethnic or racial subcultures are another aspect of this system which have an effect on school performance. "Race" has two senses, one biological, the other cultural. It is the latter conception that ties in with social expectations that can influence school performance. The socioeducational system has also changed dramatically over time.

3. The limits and possibilities of schooling can be effectively reevaluated using systemic considerations. Knowing your subject matter or having detailed professional knowledge will not lead to success with all students in all settings. But what can be realistically pursued is being a very positive difference in the lives of some children every year.

QUESTIONS

1. How does the research of Coleman, Bowles and Gintis, and Thurow relate to the kinds of expectations of the schools we discussed in Chapter 1, that is, professed and unprofessed expectations, competing and noncompeting expectations, and expectations as expressions of disappointment?
2. Name some factors in the home that affect school performance.

---

[72]Paul Hill, Arthur Wise and Leslie Shapiro, "Educational Progress: Cities Mobilizing To Improve Their Schools" (Santa Monica, Calif.: Rand Corporation Center for the Study of the Teaching Profession, 1989).

3. Is it reasonable to expect that a child's grades will rise if his or her parents increase only supervision and communication? Take into consideration that 10 percent of the students getting As and 20 percent of those getting Bs are not closely supervised.

4. What conditions might prevent "What Works" from being tried out in the home?

5. How do Rutter's findings compare with those of Bowles and Gintis? Is it possible to reconcile them?

6. Is there a relationship between peer groups that prize academic achievement and actual student achievement? If so, describe it.

7. a. What is the relationship between peer groups that prize achievement and student achievement?

    b. Why might the formation of a student honor society not automatically pick up the school grade point average?

8. What is a "minority?"

9. What are the costs and benefits of belonging to a group officially recognized as a minority?

10. Are blacks and whites "races" in the biological sense? How is this seemingly theoretical question relevant to schooling?

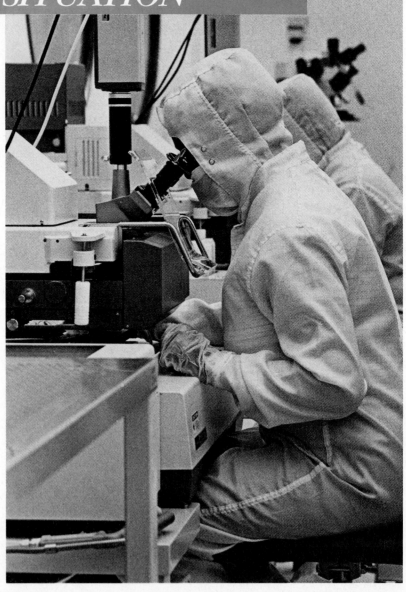

SCHOOLS and the CHANGING SOCIAL SITUATION

Chapter 7

PREVIEW

Sentimentalists would have schools be islands of innocence and hope, untroubled by the changing and sometimes frightening world that surrounds them. Nonetheless, as we saw in the last chapter, the world finds its way in, and all of its possibilities and problems find their way in with it.

In this chapter we seek to further develop your understanding of these forces by exploring key aspects of the changing social situation in the United States. It is a view that, through its emphasis on recent developments, complements and enhances that already developed in the last chapter on the socioeducational system. We examine some of the same topics, such as the central importance of the family, but our emphasis on change strengthens your appreciation of the subtleties and complexities of the educational process. It also encourages informed opinions concerning the future.

Space limitations prevent this discussion from being more than a reconnaissance. But it is at least suggestive of the many ways our schools are intertwined with different aspects of America's changing social situation. Key topics include: schooling and the changing family; schooling and the new demographics; and schooling and the changing economy.

SCHOOLING AND THE CHANGING FAMILY

As you saw in the last chapter, the family has long been the most basic of educational institutions. For that reason we highlighted its central role in the socioeducational system. Here, in this section, we further develop this theme by emphasizing the American family's changing nature, and the school-related consequences of these changes.

The Mythical American Family

Nostalgia would have it that there was a time when "the American family" was unchanging, cohesive, communicative, free of conflict, and only politely sexual.[1] Love, duty, responsibility, work, and self-denial welded individual interests into an inseparable whole.

This ideal is one of the most powerful images in our culture. It is something many of us yearn for, and its appeal to our emotions is used to sell us everything from laundry detergent to Presidential candidates. The problem with it is that the "typical" American family has little counterpart in reality. As Louise Howe puts it:

---

[1]Maxine Zinn and D. Stanley Eitzen, *Diversity in American Families* (New York: Harper & Row, 1987).

The ideal family is one of the most powerful images in our culture.

> ... the first thing to remember about the American family is that it doesn't exist. Families exist. All kinds of families in all kinds of economic and marital situations, as all of us can see ... The American family? Just which American family did you have in mind? Black or white, large or small, wealthy or poor, or somewhere in between? Did you mean a father-headed, mother-headed, or childless family? First or second time around? Happy or miserable? Your family or mine?[2]

There has always been a gap between family imagery and family reality. The intense privacy of family life conceals the difference between public norms and private behavior. For some, the family has always been less a haven than a horror. Indeed, even murder is most commonly a family affair.[3]

Family experiences are differentiated by many factors. For one thing, the family is profoundly influenced by the capabilities of its members. Whether a father is capable or incapable of love, for example, has a profound influence on the family. Also, the family has always been embedded in a larger social context. When the social situation changes, the family changes with it. Throughout history major economic forces and demographic trends have created a wide variety of family structures.

In what follows we highlight some crucial changes. The central point for educators is that they must have a reasonably objective understanding of family life if they are to properly serve *all* of the children in our schools. If their professional judgments involving family considerations are infused with mythical ideals or excessively influenced by their own experiences, they are

[2]Louise Howe, *The Future of the Family* (New York: Simon and Schuster, 1972), p. 11. Quoted in Zinn and Eitzen.
[3]Suzanne Steinmetz and Murray Strauss, *Violence in the Family* (New York: Harper & Row, 1974).

likely to be wrong. Indeed, such distortions are the cause of many of the thoughtless cruelties that make school such an unpleasant place for some children.

Divorce and Separation

There is great concern over the current high rates of marital dissolution in the United States. Although it differs from group to group, divorce rates have generally been rising since at least 1860. In fact, the United States leads the nations of the world by a wide margin in divorces per thousand.[4] (Whether the recent brief downturn shown in Figure 7.1 is indicative of a long-term trend remains to be seen. But the general trend since 1900 has been upward.)

Family breakup is one of the most painful experiences a child can endure, and over 1 million children go through it every year. A high remarriage rate often adds to these difficulties.

Consider these facts concerning the changing American family:

- Approximately 40 percent of all children born to post-1966 marriages (about one in three white children and two of every three black children under age 16) will experience the long-term separation or divorce of their parents.
- One child in three will experience another disruption in the step-family.
- One child in ten will experience three or more family dissolutions.
- Less than half of children from broken families saw their absent father during the last year.
- If both parents remarry, only about one child in ten has at least weekly contact with the absent parent.
- More than nine out of ten children of divorce live with their mother.

---

[4]Zinn and Eitzen, op. cit., p. 338.

Figure 7.1   **U.S. DIVORCE RATE (1900 TO 1986)**

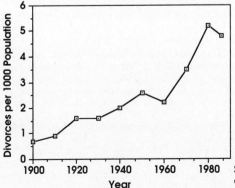

Source: Department of Health and Human Services

- One half of all the children of divorce have not seen their father in the last year.
- Most research reveals that divorce and separation have strongly negative effects in the life of a child.[5]

The Impact on Schooling

A cost of divorce familiar to teachers is that it often disrupts and distorts the educational process. The recent research of William Shreve, for example, reveals the adverse affect of single parenthood on school achievement. Shreve surveyed a very homogeneous population of seventh- through twelfth-grade students by administering the California Achievement Tests and comparing their grade point averages. In every instance but one, single-parent students scored lower than their two-parent counterparts. Such dramatic results caused Shreve to speculate that for many students single parenthood may be the deciding factor in school success.[6]

Researchers generally agree that children of one-parent families:

- are absent, truant, and tardy more often.
- have less efficient work or study habits.
- are more disruptive in the classroom.
- are more likely to drop out of school.[7]

Ideally, parents should help children come to terms with family dissolution. However, many parents have more than enough to handle just coming to terms with it themselves. This leaves their youngsters to deal with the emotional by-products on their own.

Anger is one of the most typical responses on the part of the child, and youngsters tend to work out such hostility in school by lying, stealing, and fighting.[8] Problems of this sort are particularly intense in the two years immediately following the dissolution of the family.[9] Educators must try to reconcile their appreciation of the origin of the child's problem behavior with their obligation to protect the rights of other children. An educational career is full of tough choices like this.

The dissolution of a marriage can also reduce a child's emotional bonding to family members. Such a reduction lessens sensitivity to parent's wishes and

---

[5]All of the statistics listed below, and the research studies listed under "Schooling and Family Disruption," were taken from David R. Miller, "Sensitizing New Teachers about Father-absent Boys," *Action in Teacher Education*, Vol. VIII, No. 3 (Fall 1986), pp. 73–77.

[6]William Shreve et al., "Single Parents and Student Achievement — A National Tragedy," Research Report conducted in 1984 by Eastern Washington State University Department of Education. 1988 EDRF 262028.

[7]"A Closer Look at Children in Single-Parent Families," ERIC/Clearinghouse on Urban Education Digest, No. 23, June 1984.

[8]J. S. Wallerstein and J. B. Kelly, "The Effects of Parental Divorce: Experiences of the Child in Later Latency," *American Journal of Orthopsychiatry*, Vol. 46, No. 2, pp. 256–269.

[9]M. A. Fine et al., "Long-term Effects of Divorce on Parent-Child Relationships," *Developmental Psychology*, Vol. 19, No. 5, pp. 703–713.

concerns. It also increases the possibly negative influence of peers. When the family breaks up, parents sometimes also lose their ability to supervise and control the behavior of their children. This loss further increases the potential negative influence of peers, as well as the likelihood that the child will experience school problems.

Dependent behavior is another by-product of family dissolution. Like the children of alcoholics, the children of divorce often need more than usual approval from teachers and other authority figures. Psychologist Abraham Maslow argues that such dependent behavior is probably a by-product of the child's unmet need for security, belonging, and esteem. Looking for the gratification of these basic needs, children are often distracted from any real appreciation of what Maslow understands as their need for knowledge, understanding, and beauty.[10]

Recent research suggests that the negative effects of broken marriages are particularly evident with boys.[11] In elementary and middle school more than half the boys experiencing a family dissolution evince a pattern of lower grades, and low intelligence and achievement test scores. Anger and "anxiety interference" appear to be the chief culprits.[12]

Experienced teachers also report that family changes produce noticeable changes in a child's mood. They find that a child is often excited and distracted prior to a visit with a noncustodial parent, or exhibits abrupt mood changes in the week following such a visit.[13]

Family changes appear to have a differential effect, depending on the developmental age of the child at the time of the dissolution. Apparently, parental breaks occurring late in the child's adolescence have fewer negative effects on the child. The fact that much of the child's socialization will have already occurred is the critical element.[14]

Some school-related problems associated with divorce and separation reflect the severely reduced income of the single parent. Often there is a decline of as much as 70 percent.[15] Such changes can be profoundly disruptive.

We should not lose sight of the fact that some of the consequences of family dissolution may be the lesser of evils. Often it is better for parents to divorce if the alternative is a home filled with rancor, hate, or abuse. In fact, several studies have shown that children of divorced parents function better in school than children in families characterized by conflict.[16]

---

[10]Abraham Maslow, *Motivation and Personality* (New York: Harper, 1954).

[11]O. C. Moles, "Trends in Divorce and Effects on Children," presented at the meeting of the American Academy for the Advancement of Science, Washington, D.C., January 1982.

[12]E. Heatherington et al., "Cognitive Performance, School Behavior and Achievement of Children from One-Parent Households," prepared for the Families as Educators Team of the National Institute of Education, Washington, D.C., 1981.

[13]Karen Appel, *America's Changing Families: A Guide for Educators* (Washington, D.C.: Phi Delta Kappa, 1985), p. 28.

[14]J. H. Rankin and L. E. Wells, "The Preventive Effects of the Family on Delinquency," in Elmer Johnson, ed., *Handbook on Crime and Delinquency Prevention* (New York: Greenwood, 1987), p. 262.

[15]Appel, op. cit., p. 9.

[16]Ibid.

Figure 7.2

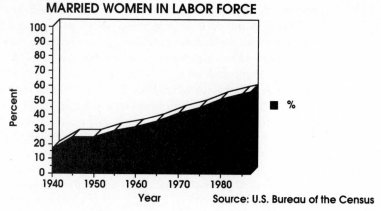

MARRIED WOMEN IN LABOR FORCE

Source: U.S. Bureau of the Census

Mothers in the Work Force

The growth of parental separation is only one of many family changes influencing schooling. The increase of women working outside the home is another obvious example. Thirty years ago two out of three U.S. families had a bread-winning father and a mother who was a full-time homemaker. In 1988 only one in five families fits that description.[17] By the year 2000 less than one family in twelve will fit the pattern of wage-earning father and homemaker mother with two children.[18]

Figure 7.2 shows the dramatic increase in married women in the labor force.

Long-term data were not available on married women with children. However, in recent years married women with children are in the labor force in percentages greater than their childless counterparts. For example, Figure 7.3

---

[17]Lance Morrow, "Through the Eyes of Children," *Time*, Vol. 132, No. 6 (August 8, 1988), p. 33.
[18]Thomas Payzant, "Making a Difference in the Lives of Children: Educational Leadership in the Year 2000," *Basic Education: Issues, Answers and Facts*, Vol. 2, No. 3 (Spring 1987), p. 1.

Figure 7.3 **EMPLOYMENT OF MOTHERS WITH CHILDREN UNDER 18**

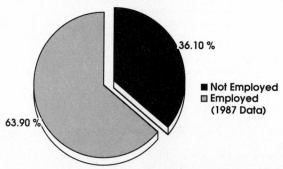

36.10 %

63.90 %

■ Not Employed
□ Employed
(1987 Data)

Source: U.S. Bureau of Labor Statistics

shows that 64.7 percent of married women with husbands present were employed outside the home. The rate for their childless counterparts was only 48.4 percent.

Today's family is frequently economically locked into the employment of both parents. In 1987, for example, the typical family's income was about the same as in previous periods of economic expansion even though more members of the family were working. The family that does not send another family member out to work actually falls behind in real income.[19] More often than not, mothers or older children need a job outside the home if the family is to maintain its standard of living.

The Importance of Actions Rather Than Labels

We must realize, of course, that what parents **do** is the key element in all of this. It is far more important than parental education, income, ethnicity, or race. To illustrate, we know that children with extremely permissive parents tend to do poorly in school. Children with extremely authoritarian parents do even worse. But inconsistent parenting produces the very worst results of all.[20] Research shows that the tendency to be permissive, authoritarian, or inconsistent is often related to parental education, income, ethnicity, or race. But it also shows that one can be rich or poor, black or white, Irish-American or Amish and still be a consistent and moderate parent. In short, it is the actual behavior that counts.

Competent educators recognize that changes in family life influence schooling. But being aware of the situation is only the first step in dealing with it. There is also a requirement for action. Some school districts, for example, have tried special school-based counseling and support services for children from broken homes. These seem to be helpful. Unfortunately, however, given the resources educators have at their disposal, it appears that they will not be able to deal effectively with family-related school issues without diverting very substantial resources from other priorities. And even if they do, it is unlikely that they will be able to remediate all the damage.

SCHOOLING AND CHANGING DEMOGRAPHICS

One of the most basic elements in America's social situation is the changing characteristics of its population. Demographic trends all have major implications for the process of schooling.

---

[19]Census Bureau Data interpreted by the Economic Policy Institute and reported in the *Philadelphia Inquirer*, September 5, 1988, p. 6.

[20]Sandy Dornbusch, "Helping Your Kid Make the Grade" (Reston, Va.: National Association of Secondary School Principals, 1987).

Figure 7.4

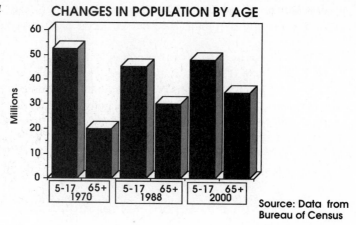

CHANGES IN POPULATION BY AGE

Source: Data from
Bureau of Census

The Graying of America

Because of an ever-increasing life span, America is well on the way to becoming the world's first four-generation society. And separated by age, income, educational levels, and value differences, these generations are often at odds as far as our public schools are concerned. For example, America's ever-growing number of elderly citizens whose children have grown are often caught in a squeeze between rising prices, escalating property (school) taxes, and a relatively fixed income. In this situation, seemingly remote from the benefits, and very concerned about the costs, they constitute the single most effective community voice against increased school spending.

Figure 7.4 illustrates why this trend promises to become even more important in the future. Notice the dramatic increase in the portion of the population that is over 65.

How do we balance the needs of the aged with the needs of the young? How do we reconcile these apparently conflicting interests? What will happen to public schools when there are fewer children and more elderly, both desiring costly benefits? These are the key questions arising from the graying of America.[21]

The Changing Balance

The profound changes in America's population are not limited to aging. It is also significant that the white population is diminishing relative to other groups. For one thing, Hispanics and African-Americans are having more

---

[21]Cf. January 1, 1987, news release of the Macomb Intermediate School District, Mount Clemens, Mich.

Figure 7.5 **AVERAGE AGE OF AMERICANS BY RACE OR ETHNICITY**

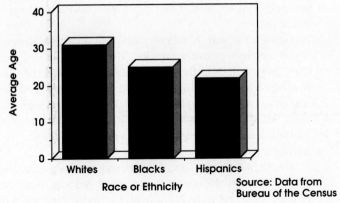

Source: Data from
Bureau of the Census

babies than are whites—in part, because of their lower average age. In addition, since the Immigration Act of 1965, which ended the quota system restricting the number of migrants who could come from certain countries, large numbers of Hispanics and non-European immigrants having been coming to America. This change has resulted in the gradual transformation of America from a largely European culture to a truly international one.

By the year 2000, one in three Americans will be nonwhite. Among the school age population the proportion of nonwhites will be even greater.[22] Thus, the traditional educational and occupational gaps between blacks, Hispanics, and whites, should they persist, take on a new significance. In the past it has been possible for the white majority to shrug off differences in achievement as "their problem." But as blacks and Hispanics become a greater and greater percentage of the U.S. work force, it is becoming "our problem."

---

[22]Payzant, op. cit., p. 1.

The emerging world culture?

Of course, we look to the public schools for a solution. Whether or not we are prepared to muster the necessary resources to secure this benefit is another matter.

Figures 7.6 and 7.7 show that the racial and ethnic diversity of American society is also growing rapidly. This change poses a significant challenge to the past practices of the public schools. Traditionally concentrating on **assimilating** or merging minority peoples into the cultural mainstream, many Americans now want our schools to promote **pluralism**. This pattern of ethnic or race relations involves the pursuit of economic and political unity while simultaneously encouraging the preservation of the minority's own cultural heritage.

Whether such tolerance can survive the cultural mainstream's contacts with truly different cultures, such as the fast-growing body of immigrants from Asia, remains to be seen. In the meantime, those who want the schools to promote assimilation, or even domination, of the foreign-born must wait restlessly on the sidelines.

It is not clear just how many linguistically and culturally different youngsters are enrolled in our schools. Apparently, it all depends on who is counting. The U. S. Department of Education estimated a 1987 total of 840,000 and claimed that 94 percent of these were receiving special bilingual services. Others use the Department's own standards, and Bureau of the Census data, to maintain that as many as 5.3 million children are different enough to need special help with English.[23]

Regardless of the exact numbers, until the mid-1970s many school districts inflicted most of the costs of dealing with cultural differences on the children

---

[23]*Covering the Education Beat: A Current Guide for Editors and Writers* (Washington, D.C.: Education Writers Association, 1987), p. 27.

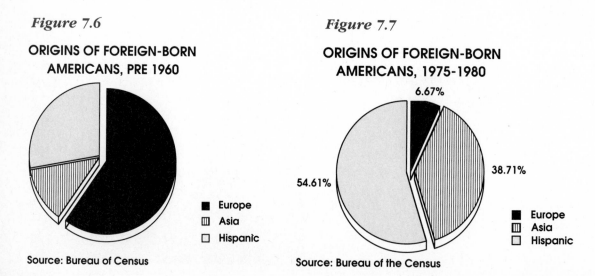

Figure 7.6

ORIGINS OF FOREIGN-BORN AMERICANS, PRE 1960

Europe
Asia
Hispanic

Source: Bureau of Census

Figure 7.7

ORIGINS OF FOREIGN-BORN AMERICANS, 1975-1980

6.67%

54.61%

38.71%

Europe
Asia
Hispanic

Source: Bureau of the Census

and their classroom teachers. Provided with very little in the way of resources, they were simply expected to cope. In *Lau* v. *Nichols*, 1974, however, the Supreme Court ruled that the failure of the San Francisco School District to provide special instruction to non-English-speaking Chinese students violated the Civil Rights Act of 1964. Thus the costs of dealing with the situation were placed squarely on the shoulders of school officials and the taxpayer.

Presently, there is a heated debate over how this special instruction should be accomplished. There are several options. **Transitional programs** provide students with the opportunity to study basic subjects in their native language while they learn English through special instruction. These programs are not intended to preserve the child's original culture or language, though they are not hostile to such an outcome. **Maintenance programs** are far more pluralistic in orientation. They are intended to maintain the child's original language and culture while simultaneously introducing English. Both of these approaches make use of English for Speakers of Other Languages instruction. **ESOL** emphasizes the practical aspects of English usage. **Immersion programs** are the third alternative. They feature massive doses of English on a nearly continuous basis. Critics maintain that, in fact, this approach is the practical equivalent of no program at all.

Some Americans, feeling that apparent concessions to the foreign-born have been melting the cultural glue that holds the country together, argue that the best way of dealing with the situation is to make English our official language. Presently, seven states have passed, or are considering, English-only initiatives. Such measures have proved particularly popular in states like California where Hispanics are a well-established force in the community. Clearly, these initiatives are hostile to the maintenance model of bilingual education.

SCHOOLING AND THE CHANGING ECONOMY

The relationship of schooling and the economy is becoming more and more publicized. For example, the two most influential of the reform reports of the 1980s, *A Nation at Risk* and *A Nation Prepared* (both detailed in a previous chapter) highlighted the economic challenge from abroad and called for the revamping of schools as a catalyst for fueling a new era of prosperity and productivity.

The Question of Subsistence

Recall that in Chapter 4 we laid out the "functional prerequisites" that any society must satisfy in order to survive. The first of these was subsistence. Food and shelter must be secured. About half of the world's people suffer from malnutrition and live in very marginal housing.[24] For them, subsistence

---

[24]R. Byrnes and G. Stone, *Economics* (Glenview, Ill.: Scott, Foresman, 1987), p. 676.

Figure 7.8

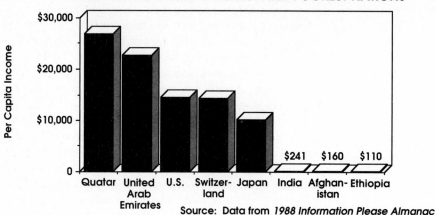

SOME OF THE WORLD'S RICHEST AND POOREST NATIONS

Source: Data from *1988 Information Please Almanac*

is a daily problem. By comparison most of the citizens of the United States lead a relatively abundant life. The United States is one of the richest nations of the world, and subsistence is simply not a problem for most of its citizens.

The Question of Distribution

The most accurate way of comparing differences in the distribution of the means of subsistence is not by income, but by **wealth**—the total value of what is owned. And the fact is, the top 20 percent of the population of the United States owns or controls three-quarters of all the wealth in the nation. The remaining 80 percent share the other fourth. The bottom 20 percent have less than 0.2 percent to divide among themselves.[25]

Figure 7.9 shows the approximate distribution of wealth in the United States. Note the extreme difference between the top and bottom 20 percent. The consequences of this distribution are very evident in schools. One of the most obvious consequences is that the top 20 percent tend NOT to send their children to public schools. This choice deprives these schools of the full support of those who control most of the nation's resources.

In a previous chapter we observed that there was no logical need for an equal distribution of the means of subsistence as far as societal survival is concerned. We can see that this is certainly the case in the United States. And the U.S. distribution of wealth is not unusual. Indeed, it is typical of nations that have an advanced degree of economic development. The reader may be surprised to learn that underdeveloped nations have an even less equitable distribution. Advanced nations have greater equality of wealth than less well-developed nations even if they are socialist societies like those of Cuba or

---

[25]Lester Thurow, *Generating Inequality* (New York: Basic Books, 1975).

Figure 7.9   **DISTRIBUTION OF WEALTH IN THE UNITED STATES**

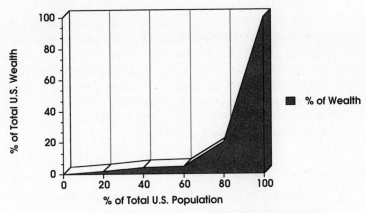

Source: Statistical Abstract
of the United States 1988

Nicaragua.[26] Unusual or not, however, it has a profound effect on the process of schooling.

Attempting to Reconcile Equality and Excellence

It is particularly relevant to bring up the uneven distribution of wealth in a text on schooling because as we have previously pointed out, promoting social equality has traditionally been one of the major acknowledged purposes of our public schools. As far back as 150 years ago when Alexis De Tocqueville was making his famous journey through America he found a uniquely American faith in the power of schooling to even the odds. "All of the people I have seen up to now," remarked De Tocqueville, "to whatever rank of society they belong, have seemed incapable of conceiving that the advantages of education might be doubted. They never fail to smile when told this opinion is not universal in Europe."[27]

Concerned about the growing gap between rich and poor, some Americans, like Christopher Jencks, author of *Inequality*, insist that the United States must become a far more equal society. Wealth, they say, must be redistributed in fairer shares if we are ever to address the root cause of crime and other social ills. Other Americans shy away from the promotion of general equality on the grounds that it would destroy initiative and promote mediocrity. (It would also be very costly to those with the greatest power and influence and, therefore, unlikely.) They would be content if they thought that every American enjoyed **equality of opportunity** or fair play. With equality of opportunity everyone is *not* guaranteed equal pay or equal status, but he or she does at

[26]Ralph Byrns and Gerald Stone, *Economics* (Glenview, Ill.: Scott-Foresman, 1987), p. 681.
[27]Quoted in Richard Reeves, *American Journey* (New York: Simon and Schuster, 1982), pp. 67–68.

least have an equal chance to compete for the best jobs and the high status and pay that go with them. (See Chapter 20.)

Of course, the public schools are one social institution these Americans pin their hopes on in regard to educational equality. If educators could just ensure that no child is left behind, they reason, things would really be evened up. But in our exploration of the socioeducational system we have learned that nonschool factors are critical to school success. This reality raises the paradoxical issue of how we can ensure that children enjoy equality of *educational* opportunity when the very social problems we are concerned about have a major negative impact on schools.

The Changing Situation of the Poor

Twenty-five years ago Michael Harrington wrote *The Other America*—the book that reportedly sparked Lyndon Johnson's massive "War on Poverty." One of Harrington's key points was that the poor in the United States tend to be invisible, off the beaten track, hidden in ghettos, migrant labor camps, Appalachian "hollers," or shelters for the homeless, far from the emotional experiences of millions of middle class Americans.[28] Harrington predicted that this "other America," this politically invisible land of the nation's poor, would grow less and less obvious. These new poor, he observed, were numerous enough to constitute "a subculture of misery," yet were sufficiently "invisible" and powerless to be ignored.

Perhaps Harrington was correct. But one place in American society where this "other America" is neither invisible nor easily ignored is in our public schools. Here their presence is indelibly recorded in low test scores and higher dropout rates.

If there were a small number of children involved it could be argued that this situation is chiefly *their* concern. But there are approximately 12 million poor children; and that figure has been steadily increasing. Figure 7.10 clearly shows this disturbing trend. These impoverished children represent nearly one in five of the nation's future workforce—nearly one in five at a time when the number of young available to replace our rapidly aging working population is proportionately smaller than ever. In this context continued national prosperity for those now living in relative comfort may well require most of these children to be well schooled and productive.[29] If so, the situation should be of concern to most Americans.

The poverty that affects a disproportionate number of U.S. children is far from uniform. For example, it directly reflects both race and ethnic origin, as Figures 7.11 to 7.13 show.

We should note that even though poverty has a disproportionate impact on young blacks and Hispanics, most impoverished youngsters are white. As

---

[28]Michael Harrington, *The Other America: Poverty in the United States* (Baltimore: Penguin Books, 1963), p. 10.
[29]Marian Wright Edelman, "Children's Time," The 1988 Martin Buskin Memorial Lecture, delivered at the National Seminar of the Education Writers Association, April 16, 1988, in New Orleans.

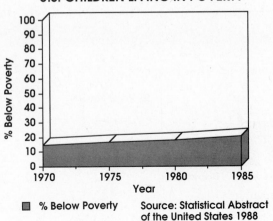

U.S. CHILDREN LIVING IN POVERTY

■ % Below Poverty   Source: Statistical Abstract
of the United States 1988

Figure 7.10

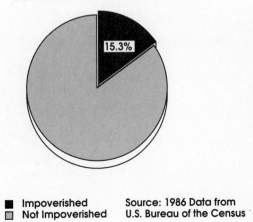

STATUS OF U.S. WHITE CHILDREN

■ Impoverished   Source: 1986 Data from
☐ Not Impoverished   U.S. Bureau of the Census

Figure 7.11

shown by Figure 7.14, the condition of America's poor cannot be explained by prejudice alone. Nevertheless, there is a black and Hispanic ghetto underclass whose social condition has worsened in recent years. And it is this underclass, plagued with joblessness, violent crime, out-of-wedlock births, female-headed families, and welfare dependency, that educators find the most difficult to teach.[30] This particular group of poor Americans is concentrated

---

[30]In his controversial book, *The Declining Significance of Race* (Chicago: University of Chicago Press, 1978), William Wilson called attention to the widening gap between the black underclass and the black middle class in order to stress that racism alone was an insufficient explanation of black poverty.

Figure 7.12

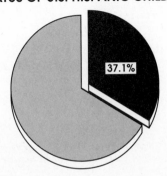

STATUS OF U.S. HISPANIC CHILDREN

■ Impoverished   Source: 1986 Data from
☐ Not Impoverished   U.S. Department of the Census

Figure 7.13

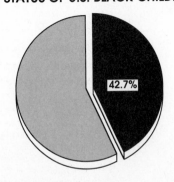

STATUS OF U.S. BLACK CHILDREN

■ Impoverished   Source: 1986 Data from
☐ Not Impoverished   U.S. Bureau of the Census

Figure 7.14

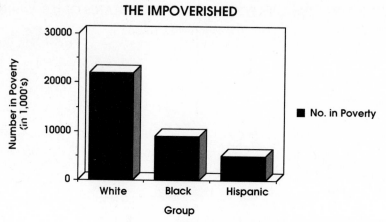

THE IMPOVERISHED

Source: Statistical Abstract of the United States 1988

in urban areas, and has been particularly hard hit by their transformation from industrial centers to centers of administration and information exchange. This change has caused many low-skilled laborers to lose their jobs and to have little hope of finding new ones in white-collar clerical industries. All that is left is welfare or the low-skill, low-pay, nonadministrative jobs available, for example, at fast food restaurants or car washes.[31]

As a result of these changes, certain urban areas have become inhabited almost exclusively by the very poor.[32] Cities like Jersey City, Irvington, and East Orange, New Jersey, are examples. Existing in the shadow of the "Big Apple," these communities have the highest taxes in New Jersey,[33] yet their resources are so limited and their children so troubled by poverty that they have become the educational equivalent of underdeveloped countries. As a matter of fact, Essex County School Superintendent Franklin Williams calls Irvington the "New Delhi" of New Jersey.[34]

Immunity to Progress

In *The Other America*, Harrington noted that the U.S. poor of the 1960s were "the rejects of society and the economy." They were, he claimed, a people "immune to progress." He explained:

---

[31]The number of jobs in the fast-food industry now outnumber the production jobs available in the steel, auto and textile industries combined.
[32]William Julius Wilson, *The Truly Disadvantaged* (Chicago: University of Chicago Press, 1988.)
[33]Craig McCoy, "New Jersey Judge to Rule in School Tax Case," *Philadelphia Inquirer*, August 25, 1988, p. 5B.
[34]Laura Quinn, "Educators See a Victory for N.J. Schools," *Philadelphia Inquirer*, August 25, 1988, p. 1.

Certain urban areas are inhabited
almost exclusively by the poor.

As the society became more technological, more skilled, those who
learn to work the machines, who get the expanding education,
move up. Those who miss out at the very start find themselves at
a new disadvantage. A generation ago in American life. the majority
of the working people did not have high-school educations. But at
that time industry was organized on a lower level of skill and competence.... Today the situation is much different. The good jobs
require much more academic preparation, much more skill from
the outset. Those who lack a high-school education tend to be
condemned to the economic underworld — to low paying service
industries, to backward factories, to sweeping and janitorial duties.... The very rise of productivity that created more money and
better working conditions for the rest of society can be a menace
to the poor.[35]

Harrington's observation is even more true today than it was in the 1960s.
Today, there are even more Americans who are "immune to progress." Sadly,
educators are having great difficulties in their efforts to change this on their
own. Given the magnitude and complexity of the situation, it can best be
addressed by a comprehensive program combining employment policies with
social welfare policies that are systemwide rather than group specific. If these
were tied to a national child care strategy and some sort of family support
program, urban school reform would be far more likely.[36]

[35]Harrington, op. cit., pp. 18–19.
[36]Wilson, op. cit., p. 163.

The Web of Poverty and "At Risk" Students

One of the most insidious aspects of poverty is that its effects are systemic. The difficulties of schooling impoverished youngsters are multiplied many times because when a child is poor there are a multitude of interrelated educationally negative consequences—for example, the approximately 22 percent of America's children living in poverty tend to be unhealthy. This, in turn, often influences what can or will happen in school.

It also happens that many children born into poverty are conceived by school-age youngsters who are ill-equipped to handle their own lives, much less the financial or emotional responsibilities of parenting. Indeed, children having children account for 700,000 of the 3.3 million births annually. Every day 40 teenage girls give birth to their third child.[37]

In recent years educators and policymakers have come to lump together children from poverty-level families, unmarried teenage parents, the children of poorly educated immigrants, and so forth as *at risk*. This means that without some sort of special attention, these children are likely to become dropouts or school failures. There are many "at risk" children in America, and their numbers are growing.

The Enduring Situation of the Rich

There are communities that stand in stark contrast to the nation's Jersey Cities, Elizabeths, and East Oranges. Swank suburbs like Greenwich, Connecticut, Mill Neck, New York, or Alpine, New Jersey, have average home prices of approximately $1.2 million.[38] Here, secure in their estates, guarded by social secretaries, recreating at exclusive clubs or resorts, associating with others who have made the *Social Register*, the wealthy need have little contact with "ordinary" Americans.

Their children are in a similar situation. Utterly removed from the influence of the public schools, such children come of age with those of similar circumstance in elite private schools. This arrangement is anything but an accident. It is a deliberate act of social segregation that resembles what went on in the very first schools in ancient Sumer nearly 6,000 years ago. As one upper class mother commented to educational researcher Susan Ostrander, "You don't go to private school just for your education. You go there to be separated from ordinary people."[39]

Given enough money, such an intention is easy to satisfy. Most Americans of humble circumstance are unable even to identify the following as schools, much less know that, according to Baltzell and Kavaler, they are America's elite private boarding schools where the nation's most privileged children prepare for power:

---

[37]Payzant, op. cit., p. 1.
[38]Source: Relo Broker Network, September 13, 1987.
[39]Susan Ostrander, *Women of the Upper Class* (Philadelphia: Temple University Press, 1984), quoted in Cookson.

Swank neighborhoods like Greenwich, Connecticut, Mill Neck, New York, or Alpine, New Jersey, have average home prices of approximately $1.2 million.

- **Ashville** (Ashville, N.C.)
- **Buckley** (New York, N.Y.)
- **Choate** (Wallingford, Conn.)
- **Cranbrook** (Bloomfield Hills, Mich.)
- **Deerfield** (Deerfield, Mass.)
- **Episcopal** (Alexandria, Va.)
- **Exeter** (Exeter, N.H.)
- **Groton** (Groton, Mass.)
- **Hill** (Pottstown, Pa.)
- **Hotchkiss** (Lakeville, Conn.)
- **Kent** (Kent, Conn.)
- **Lake Forest** (Lake Forest, Mich.)
- **Lawrenceville** (Lawrenceville, N.J.)
- **Loomis** (Windsor, Conn.)
- **Middlesex** (Concord, Mass.)
- **Milton** (Milton, Mass.)
- **Phillips** [Andover] (Andover, Mass.)
- **Pomfret** (Pomfret, Conn.)
- **Portsmouth Priory** (Portsmouth, R.I.)
- **St. Andrews** (Middletown, Delaware)
- **St. George's** (Newport, R.I.)
- **St. Mark's** (Southborough, Mass.)
- **St. Paul's** (Concord, N.H.)
- **Shattuck** (Faribault, Minn.)
- **Webb** (Bellbuckle, Tenn.)
- **Woodberry Forest** (Woodberry Forest, Va.)[40]

These private schools, and the elite universities they feed into, are a centrally important social institution of America's upper class. Indeed, Baltzell comments that in the nineteenth century the proper boarding school replaced the family as the chief socializing agent of that class.[41]

Educational sociologists such as Randall Collins have repeatedly observed that schools prepare students for assuming social and cultural positions in society.[42] And these elite schools, which teach fewer than 1 percent of the nation's high school students, assist in the maintenance and transmission of

---

[40]This list was compiled from the work of Baltzell and Kavaler by G. William Domhof in *Who Rules America?* (Englewood Cliffs, N. J.: Prentice-Hall, 1967), pp. 34–35.
[41]Cited in Ibid., p. 16.
[42]Randal Collins, *The Credential Society* (New York: Academic Press, 1979).

privilege. They turn out a disproportionate number of our business, professional, and governmental leaders.[43] They also cream off some of the best and brightest children from the lower social classes, helping to reinvigorate the "establishment."[44] Most importantly, they develop a style and state of mind that legitimates unequal relationships, conveying a new sort of authority to those with power.[45] In our changing social situation, this is one thing that has not changed.

Educational sociologist Earl Hopper has pointed out the crucial difference between the amount of schooling one receives and where that schooling takes place. Nowhere is this distinction more important than in the case of elite schooling.[46] Attending one of these "status seminaries" conveys certain advantages that attendance at Altoona High School cannot hope to match, even if the child attending the latter learned more.

Most textbooks of this type completely ignore elite schooling. And educators are often reluctant to stress this aspect of schooling in America. As Cookson and Persell perceptively note:

> Power and privilege are not usually central issues in discussions of education. After all, part of the tradition of democracy is that individuals should be allowed to succeed according to their abilities; barriers to mobility are an affront to the frontier spirit of American life. Of course, we recognize that barriers do exist; demonstrating that education does little to reduce social inequalities has become something of a growth industry in academic circles. To the general public, however, the purpose of education goes largely unquestioned. Schools are places where students learn to read and write, and do their sums, and because students are evaluated according to their abilities, the great status race starts off fairly if not exactly evenly. If some students excel while others fall behind it is a personal, not a social problem. Like the Statue of Liberty, education should be blind to race, religion, sex, or national origin.[47]

The mere assertion that elite schools exist, goes against the American grain—democracy is supposed to begin at the schoolhouse door. But it is utterly clear that certain private schools represent an elite alternative to the public educational system in much the same way that private cars are alternatives to public transportation. Private transport is easier, cleaner, often safer, and a good deal quicker. Yet it may also be more expensive and wasteful of resources.

---

[43]Peter Cookson, Jr., and Caroline Persell, *Preparing for Power: America's Elite Boarding Schools* (New York: Basic Books, 1985).
[44]E. Digby Baltzell, *The Protestant Establishment* (New York: Random House, 1964), p. 344.
[45]Cookson, op. cit., p. 26.
[46]Earl Hopper, "Stratification, Education and Mobility In Industrial Societies," in *Readings in the Theory of Educational Systems*, Earl Hopper, ed. (London: Hutchison, 1971).
[47]Cookson, op. cit, p. 14.

Schooling, Knowledge and the Creation of Wealth

Much of America's affluence is a product of abundant natural resources. They are, however, no longer sufficient. In order to maintain the level of subsistence to which we have become accustomed we are increasingly dependent on research and a highly educated labor force that must be capable of competing on an equal basis in an intensely competitive international economy.

In Chapter 4 we noted: "Knowledge, particularly technical knowledge, is one of the primary means of creating wealth in a postindustrial society. From it comes new jobs, new products and still more sophisticated services. A postindustrial society depends upon the effectiveness of its schools—particularly those schools that specialize in advanced technical studies as well as pure and applied research."

Fine colleges and universities now serve a dominant role in this type of economic development. As *U.S. News & World Report* comments: "It was no accident that California's famed Silicon Valley sprang up around Stanford and the University of California or that the Route 128 corridor surrounds Harvard and the Massachusetts Institute of Technology."[48] Similarly, North Carolina's prosperous Research Triangle is near three major universities and the fast growing hundred-mile-long slice of Texas software firms, computer companies, and research centers known as Silicon Prairie shares its backyard with the 46,000 students of the University of Texas at Austin.

Modern academics are often not only researchers but also enterprising entrepreneurs who help transform university towns into major high-tech hubs of commerce. For example, Frank McBee, an engineering professor at the University of Texas at Austin, and three of his colleagues began with a part-time consulting firm and eventually created a cluster of high-tech companies that generated 6,377 new jobs. In the last decade, professors and students at the same university have formed at least twenty-five other companies and the presence of the university has proven pivotal in attracting many other major high-tech firms to the area.[49]

This pattern of development is not confined to the United States. In France a complex of high-tech firms at university- and government-sponsored research centers has brought prosperity to places like Villeurbane outside Lyon.[50] In Japan, the government is sponsoring the creation of new research and manufacturing cities known as "technopolises."[51]

Sometimes research results spawn whole new industries. Bioengineering provides an example.

---

[48]Kenneth Sheets, "Welcome to Silicone Gulch," *U.S. News & World Report*, September 12, 1988, p. 51.
[49]Ibid.
[50]One of the authors lived there during the summer of 1987. The most common sight was building cranes.
[51]Sheets, op. cit., p. 51.

Figure 7.15   **PREDICTED SALES OF BIO-ENGINEERED AGRICULTURAL PRODUCTS**

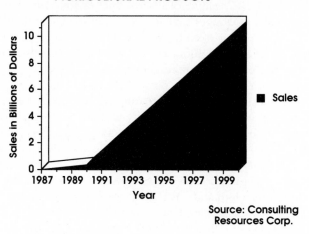

Source: Consulting
Resources Corp.

Bioengineering

In the world of agriculture, biotechnological research is blossoming as never before. Advances in plant tissue culture, genetic alteration, recombinant DNA techniques—splicing genes from foreign organisms into a plant's genetic material—and similar techniques resulting from knowledge gained at the University of Pennsylvania, Rutgers University, Cornell University, the University of Iowa, the University of Wisconsin, and dozens of other schools across the country promise an agricultural revolution the full consequences of which cannot yet be imagined.

Researchers at the federal Office of Technology Assessment think that the potential uses of agricultural biotechnology will be even more far-reaching than those in the fields of medicine and pharmaceutical products.[52] It promises to produce more nutritious plants with higher yields and improved resistance to disease and pests; crops that create their own fertilizer; varieties that can withstand drought and global climate change; and plants that can manufacture perfumes, plastics, oil and pharmaceuticals. Other very real possibilities are cows that yield skim milk, low fat pigs, farm animals whose growth can be turned on and off, commercially grown fish that gain weight three times faster, and laboratory animals with selected human genes that will be almost identical to humans with respect to their susceptibility to disease.[53]

Such research promises to be enormously lucrative. According to a study by the Consulting Resources Corporation in Lexington, Massachusetts, world-wide sales of bioengineered plant and animal products will increase more than

---

[52]Jim Detjen, "Planting New Ideas in the Lab," *Philadelphia Inquirer*, September 3, 1988, p. 1.
[53]Gene Bylinsky, "Here Come the Bionic Piglets," *Fortune*, Vol. 116, October 1987, p. 74.

four hundredfold from 1987 to the year 2000 when it is predicted to become a $10.6 billion per year industry.[54]

Reiterating the Point

Our example shows that schooling at least *some* of the population to a very high level of technical proficiency is no luxury. At the least, our general affluence as a nation depends on it. At the most, the very survival of humanity itself could be at stake.[55]

Scholastic Excellence and the Economic Competition Among Nations

Present demands for scholastic excellence commonly reflect the realization that schooling now serves as an engine for the generation of wealth. Chapters 1 and 4 quoted the highly influential *A Nation At Risk*, which launched the first wave of school reform in 1983. Remember that in this "open letter to the American people" this "Blue Ribbon" commission selected by the president of the United States warned that the United States risked losing the economic competition among nations due to a "... rising tide of [educational] mediocrity that threatens our very future as a Nation and a people."

It went on to observe schooling's role in the generation of wealth:

> Knowledge, learning, information, and skilled intelligence are the new raw materials of international commerce and are today spreading throughout the world as vigorously as miracle drugs, synthetic fertilizers, and blue jeans did earlier. If only to keep and improve on the slim competitive edge we still retain in world markets, we must dedicate ourselves to the reform of our educational system for the benefit of all—old and young alike, affluent and poor, majority and minority. Learning is the indispensable investment required for success in the "information age" we are now entering."[56]

In 1986 the Carnegie Forum on Education and the Economy launched the second round of school reform with the release of *A Nation Prepared: Teachers for the 21st Century*. Saying that better teachers were the key to reform, it too emphasized the role of schools in maintaining the nation's standard of living in an intensely competitive world economy. The report noted that:

> America's ability to compete in world markets is eroding. The productivity growth of our competitors outdistances our own. The

---

[54]Detjen, op. cit., p. 8.
[55]Fritz Machlup, *The Production and Distribution of Knowledge in the United States* (Princeton, N.J.: Princeton University Press, 1972), p. 27.
[56]*A Nation at Risk: The Imperative for Educational Reform*, The National Commission on Excellence in Education, U.S. Department of Education, Washington, D.C., 1983, p. 7.

capacity of the economy to provide a high standard of living for all our people is increasingly in doubt. As jobs requiring little skill are automated or go offshore, and demand increases for the highly skilled, the pool of educated and talented grows smaller and the backwater of the unemployable rises."[57]

The Task Force went on to point out that the changing nature of the world economy makes it necessary not simply to reverse the decline in performance of the schools, but to meet higher standards than ever before.

The stakes seem to be high. If our schools fail to produce at least an elite cadre of competent scientists and scholars, American society will lose its present high standard of living. That is a key aspect of the present social situation.

Other Key Factors in Economic Competition

We have seen that schools are a very important factor in America's international competitiveness. However, there exist other important aspects as well. In an earlier chapter we encouraged readers to be analytic, pointing to the necessity of exploring the answers to key questions before drawing any conclusions. The first question concerned the nature of the situation. The following discussion about changes in America's ability to compete with foreign nations illustrates why this consideration is so critical.

America's negative balance of trade situation reflects far more than inadequate schooling. In fact, a brief consideration reveals that schooling is far from the only factor in America's declining international competitiveness.

Investment Rates

International differences in labor productivity, or output per person per hour, not only reflect the knowledge and work habits of the work force, but also the quantity and quality of the equipment workers use. Obsolete and inefficient machinery is replaced by investment. And the U.S. rate of investment is less than half that of Japan. In fact, for the last four decades, Japan has been investing at a rate of about 20 percent of its GNP, while net investments in the United States have averaged less than half that.[58]

Profits Invested Overseas

Often, instead of investing in improvements in productivity, U.S. corporate profits go overseas or are invested in other ways that don't increase compet-

---

[57]*A Nation Prepared: Teachers for the 21st Century* (Washington, D.C.: The Carnegie Forum on Education and the Economy, 1986), p. 4.
[58]Data for 1951–1980: OECD *National Accounts*, Vol. 1, 1951–80, ed. 1982, pp. 30, 32, 48, 68, 74. Data for 1981–1984: *United Nations, National Accounts Statistics: Main Aggregates and Detailed Tables, 1984,* pp. 563, 835, 1602, 1649.

itiveness or create jobs. Since the late 1970s U.S. investment in foreign countries has slowed. Nevertheless, in 1985 about 30 percent of all after-tax profits of U.S. corporations was earned abroad. Significantly, these are taxed at lower rates than profits made at home.[59]

Value of the Dollar

The value of the dollar is still another consideration. A strong dollar does not necessarily lead to a strong economy. It makes imports cheaper, affecting our balance of trade unfavorably, while it drives up the price of American exports, depressing sales. The value of the dollar rose steadily through the first half of the 1980s, causing an imbalance in trade that led more dollars to go out of the United States than came in. The high value of the dollar also means that U.S. workers are paid more than their foreign counterparts, making our products more expensive.

Labor-Management Relations

Poor labor-management relations is another factor in declining U.S. competitiveness. Greater worker involvement in decision making, in the manner of the Japanese, could help. In fact, Japanese-style management was able to turn around GM's Freemont, California, assembly plant. Troubled by an allegedly uncooperative work force, it was slated for extinction. But Toyota, heading a joint venture to build the new Chevy Nova, reorganized labor-management relations along Japanese lines. Now the Nova, since renamed the Geo, is widely recognized as the most trouble-free car in the GM line and the Freemont plant is a model of efficiency.

These considerations reveal that the present changing situation is far more complex than school critics acknowledge. Clearly, schooling is more important to our economy than ever before, and there is little doubt that schools could do better in adjusting to this new reality. But we must wonder if corporate executives and government officials sometimes scapegoat schools and teachers.

We also must keep in mind that the payoffs from economic development are distributed very unevenly, varying from individual to individual, social class to social class, and ethnic group to ethnic group. This suggests that such development does not necessarily lead to social progress. Indeed, there are a host of well-reasoned arguments that dispute this notion.[60]

A Troubling Question

There are those who question whether our schools should be in the economic development business at all. For example, E. F. Schumacher argues that there

---

[59]Data from *Survey of Current Business*, U. S. Department of Labor, July 1986, p. 77.
[60]These are nicely summarized in Alan DeYoung, *Economics and American Education* (White Plains, N. Y.: Longman, 1989).

are very definite limits to economic growth because the earth's irreplaceable natural resources are already being used up at a rate the planet cannot sustain.[61] Since the earth's population will likely double within the next 40 years, further economic development will put an even greater strain on the earth's resources and ecosystem. Also, humankind now has the ability to annihilate itself with thermonuclear weapons. These considerations make it apparent that educators must at least consider pursuing longer-term ends.

Given the present emphasis on economic development, it will be difficult for educators to focus on issues that transcend economic growth. But it might be that the focus needs to be shifted nonetheless. Rather than just setting out to make children into more efficient human resources for economic development, as many present reform reports seem to suggest, the human condition also requires that educators also address ecological issues, questions of justice and democracy, and the matter of appropriate social behavior. Above all, moral and ethical issues are of paramount importance.

SUMMARY

1. Schooling is intimately connected to other aspects of the social system. For example, recent changes in the American family are intertwined with recent pressures on schools. Demographic changes are also "graying" America, and undermining support for public school expenditures. The children of the wealthy have never attended public schools; thus those with power and influence have never had an immediate personal stake in their quality.

2. The acquisition and distribution of wealth is intimately related to schooling practices. Moreover, there is an ever-increasing connection among schooling, knowledge, and the creation of wealth that makes it foolhardy for the leaders of any modern nation to neglect the schools. Nevertheless, there may well be limits to growth, suggesting that educators must pay more attention to ecological issues, questions of justice and democracy, and the matter of appropriate social behavior. Also, moral and ethical issues are of paramount importance.

QUESTIONS

1. Television sitcoms present us with various images of the family. What different types are there? Which programs present which family image? Do they deal with the benefits and costs of different family structures?

2. In many schools, Parent Organization meetings are held in the early afternoon. How would this schedule affect the nature of participation? What might this indicate about parental input into the schooling process?

---

[61]E. F. Schumacher, *Small Is Beautiful: Economics As If People Mattered* (New York: Harper & Row, 1973).

3. How might the school adjust to the characteristics of children of divorced parents? What would the costs and benefits be of changing the school program so that students could be
    - absent or late more often
    - less efficient in their work habits
    - less decorous in the classroom, and
    - more likely to drop out of school?

4. What are the costs and benefits of a child's disrupting a class? For whom are these costs and benefits? Consider such things as
    a. per pupil loss of instructional time
    b. entertainment value to students of the disruption
    c. opportunity for the teacher to demonstrate authority
    d. release of tension
    e. attention received by the disruptive pupil
    f. value of curricular topic interrupted versus value of moral lesson to be learned by teacher's handling of problem
    g. frustration to teacher and students caused by disruption.

5. What school policies and routines make it difficult to address the special problems of children suffering from the effects of divorce and parental alcoholism?

6. What has been the effect on the schools of new job opportunities for women?

7. Suppose parents of school-aged children were required to pay additional school taxes for each school-age child in their family. Recipients of Social Security, on the other hand, would be exempt from school taxes. What would be the costs and benefits of such a plan? For whom?

8. Considered together, what do the following situations portend?
    a. Ten percent of the American people own 86 percent of the stocks, bonds, and real estate.
    b. Twenty percent of the American people own or control 75 percent of all the wealth of the nation.
    c. The gap between rich and poor grew between 1979 and 1987.
    d. The wealthiest members of our society do not send their children to public schools.
    e. Public schools are funded through taxation.

9. What type of new knowledge tends to generate the most wealth? In that connection, can you see how emphasizing this type of knowledge might generate important costs as well as benefits?

10. Book companies require literate people to keep them in business. By promoting literacy, schools create the possibility of future customers for book publishers. Can you relate other habits or skills acquired in school to the consumption of goods and services that support some part of our economy?

Section III

Organization Theory and the Schools

...Organizations are not, *by nature*, cooperative systems ... Like the broom in the story of the sorcerer's apprentice, they occasionally get out of hand.

— *Charles Perrow*[1]

While doing the preparatory research for this text, we were struck by an anomaly: very few books written as introductory texts in the foundations of education dealt with any aspect of organization theory. In fact, none

[1]Charles Perrow, "A Short and Glorious History of Organizational Theory" in Jay M. Shafritz and Philip H. Whitbeck, eds., *Classics of Organization Theory* (Oak Park, Ill.: Moore Publishing Co., 1978), p. 320.

of the five most widely used texts in teacher preparation does. On the contrary, every book we reviewed intended for use in supervisory or administrative programs—some twenty, in all—gave extensive coverage to organization theory. Why is it that this important discipline, full of insights for any educator, is so differentially taught?

We need not imagine there is any conspiracy here. Rather, this is just another consequence of the Temple and Factory images of the school: viewed as low functionaries of the Temple or the Factory, teachers are not seen as "needing" such information. We disagree. Everyone who wants to understand how schooling in America works, especially prospective teachers, has to acquaint himself or herself with the insights offered by organization theory.

Just how badly school people need the insights of organization theory was indicated by reviews of the rough drafts of this text. Reviewers who were not involved in the day-to-day activities of primary or secondary education tended to accept with little comment the information that organizational structures undermined individual efforts and that schools tended to supplant learning goals with other less educational ones. Teachers new to practice, no matter what their age, conceded this only begrudgingly. "That's just an excuse!" they would sometimes say. Or, "A dedicated individual can overcome such obstacles!" Frontline school staff tend to be socialized into disregarding organizational factors. The point of studying organization theory is to anchor our zeal in the knowledge that will make our efforts to improve schooling effective. Hopes and dreams are necessary but insufficient.

THE SCHOOL
as an
ORGANIZATION

Chapter 8

PRINCIPAL

There is a strong tendency in human society for the unorganized group to develop organization and for organizations to develop even where there has been no consciousness of a group previously, in which case the organization itself creates the group it expresses and embodies. Consequently, group conflict tends easily to pass over into organizational conflict, and the growth of organizations themselves may create conflict where no previous consciousness of conflict existed.

Kenneth E. Boulding, Conflict and Defense: A General Theory[1]

PREVIEW

In this chapter we look at the school as an organization. Many people, when they think of an organization, tend to think of it as a group of people working toward a common goal. Much literature about education depicts schools in this way. This conception of organization, however, is strongly biased by Temple and Factory images of the school. In fact, by focusing on presumed common goals, we easily lose sight of the conflicts that generate schooling controversies.

We will approach organizations from a different perspective. We will consider an organization to be a social structure that allocates costs and benefits, both symbolic and substantial. This way of looking at the schools is made possible by the development of **organization theory**. There are many different aspects to this broad subject and we can go into only a few of them here. Organization theory ranges, for example, from studies of the effects of management, of bureaucratic structures, or of technology, to the systems of motivation and learning established in an organization. Of particular interest is the ability of organization theory to account for the failure of past school reform efforts. It also gives us indication as to what kinds of school reform are likely to take hold.

To begin the chapter, we examine some standard kinds of conflict that arise in organizations and how they show up in schools. We will learn that different conceptions of human nature underlie different conceptions of organizations. We will see that relations of power among people determine to some extent these perceptions of human nature. Finally, we will look at different models of organizational structure and relate them to our images of the school: Temple, Factory, and Town Meeting.

The images of the school we presented in Chapter 2 were based primarily on expectations. Temple, Factory, and Town Meeting are

---

[1]Kenneth E. Boulding, *Conflict and Defense: A General Theory* (New York: Harper Torchbooks, 1963), p. 145.

expectation models of the school. A model is a schematic, an image that depicts the relationship of parts to the whole. So far, we have dealt with rather informally conceived models based on the expectations of people traditionally involved with schools, for example, parents, students, teachers, and administrators. Now we will consider a set of rather formal organizational models deriving from a concern with implementation. Contrasting and comparing implementation models with our expectation models, we will see that the notion of authority, control, and policy varies with them.

INTRODUCTION: MAKING SENSE OF IT ALL

To the untutored eye, many things make no sense. To someone who knows nothing about the depth of cultural difference the situations of cultural conflict described in Chapter 5 would make no sense. Similarly, not knowing about the functions of conflict, many people fail to understand why conflict persists when all involved desire to end it. Organization theory gives us another dimension of understanding. It helps us realize that many situations we might otherwise consider a matter of personality conflicts, or maybe incompetence, are in fact a matter of organizational structure.

In a large eastern city, half-day classes are held for about one week in the middle of the year for "reorganization." The children are sent home while teachers are given twelve hours to do paperwork. Because this paperwork needs no special skill to do, everybody's first reaction is that the situation "makes no sense." Why should teachers be given secretarial work, while the children lose out on instruction? Narrow focus on the professed mission of the school, instruction, provides no answer. Organizationally, however, we can discern a rationale. Indeed, if we examine the costs and benefits of the practice, its reasonableness becomes clear.

- The paperwork done is absolutely essential for the continuance of certain funds by the state and federal government.
- Requests for budget money allotted for the additional secretarial help needed to complete the "reorganization" paperwork would be subject to review by a cost-conscious school board.
- The costs of using teachers are easily hidden. They get no additional salary for doing paperwork. It is merely a reallotment of time that needs no budget review and remains at the discretion of school administration.

This practice is clearly an intelligent trade-off in a tight situation. Its benefits are clear and its costs are hidden. But it takes an overview of the school *as an organization* to understand it as "making sense," even if we still believe it is an undesirable practice.

Schooling: Education vs. Organization

We know that schooling and education are not the same. Education pursues values that may not be realized in actual schools. And neither are socialization and education the same. As children learn to adapt themselves to the social situations they must cope with, they may not reach the goals their community aspires to. In studying the organization of the schools we learn how different organizational structures influence the socialization of children in ways that may undermine as well as support educational goals.

The way schools work often has greater effect on what students learn than what their teachers try to do. Here is an example. For administrative convenience, some schools require final grades to be entered weeks before summer vacation begins. This is supposed to be a top secret. Invariably students find out about it. When they question their teachers about it, the teachers—following administrative directive—reply that no grades are final and that any slacking off will be reflected in a lower grade. The students not only disbelieve this, they understand the teachers to be lying. Worse, they take them for fools to persist in lying in the face of common knowledge. Imagine the moral lessons these students come to learn, just for the sake of organizational convenience!

Here is another real example where crossed purposes produce questionable results. A principal of a large high school, feeling that school spirit is low, has senior and junior students brought to the auditorium for a pep rally the day before a major football game. At first the students are unenthusiastic, but as trumpets blare and drums boom interest is aroused. Finally, the whole auditorium is on its feet, shouting, "Go! Go! Go Team! Go!" Then the bell rings for change of class. "Go! Go! Go Team! Go!" the students continue to chant, in their frenzy oblivious of the bell. The vice-principal in charge of assemblies runs onto stage and turning up the volume of the PA system yells at the students to shut up and sit down. His thundering commands, electronically amplified to the point of auditory pain, eventually overpower the crowd. Red-faced, he tells the students that he is disgusted by their blatant disregard for school procedures. "That bell is the signal for you to quiet down and pass on to the next class!" he scolds. The students shuffle out, no doubt having learned a sad lesson about the meaning of school spirit and the need to respect school procedures.

Teachers work hard at trying to develop industriousness in their students. They also try to get them to develop an interest in their studies that will motivate them through much of the drudgery of learning. But what happens all too often when they have their classes humming along through a lesson? An announcement on the loudspeaker interrupts the class. Or the bell signals the end of the class period. Or a suprise fire drill or visit from the principal stops the lesson. No doubt these all serve organizational purposes. But what lessons do the students learn about the relative importance of their studies to the importance of announcements, scheduling convenience, fire drills, and principal observations? Is it any wonder that the most common complaint of high school teachers is that students show little, if any, interest in their studies? Perhaps they have been socialized out of it.

To reiterate, it is important for school people to recognize that many school problems are generated by organizational structure rather than to mistake them for shortcomings in themselves or their students. They should also be careful of those who firmly deny this possibility. Anyone who insists that there are no organizational problems may have a hidden agenda to reinforce his or her authority through guilt and feelings of inadequacy.[2]

BASIC INTERNAL CONFLICTS

The school is a complex organization. Complex organizations, by mere virtue of their complexity, run up against four basic internal conflicts.[3] These are

- following policy vs. sensitivity to individual differences.
- delegating authority vs. pursuing authorized goals.
- process vs. product.
- power vs. morale.

Dealing with these school conflicts is not merely a matter of more dedication or self-discipline on the part of individuals. Nor is it a matter of patience or forbearance or charisma. What must be addressed is the structure of relationships that constitute the organization. We will examine each of the four conflicts in this way.

Following Policy vs. Sensitivity to Individual Differences

A basic organizational conflict is that of following policy vs. being sensitive to individual differences. Robert K. Merton[4] investigated how following policy reduces sensitivity to individual differences. This conflict, for example, is the basis of the persistent tension in trying to follow a school policy providing equal educational opportunity that also tries to address the individual needs of the child. This issue first came up in Chapter 2 as a conflict in disciplinary goals between the Temple and the Factory. Is consistency more desirable than the effectiveness of individualized treatment? We can find this tension between policy and sensitivity in a variety of school problems and practices.[5] For example,

- the conflict of teaching a class according to a standardized curriculum vs. making adjustments according to the readiness of individual students.

---

[2]See Richard Sennett, *Authority* (New York: Vintage, 1981), pp. 97–99, for an example of the use of indifference to create guilt and assert authority. The organizational issue of how compensation gets negotiated is obscured in this exchange.

[3]James G. March and Herbert A. Simon, *Organizations* (New York: Wiley, 1958).

[4]Robert K. Merton in Ibid., p. 41. See also Robert K. Merton, *Social Theory and Social Structure* (New York: Harcourt Brace Jovanovich, 1976), or Robert K. Merton, *Sociological Ambivalence and Other Essays* (New York: Free Press, 1976.)

[5]See Joseph Berger, "New York's Principals Tell Why They 'Break the Rules,'" *New York Times*, February 21, 1989, p. B-1.

- restrictions, for fear of legal liability, on outside-of-school activities to enhance the curriculum.
- establishment of mathematical formulas for generating grades rather than reliance on teacher judgment.
- use of standardized tests for college admissions to supplement, sometimes replace, secondary school records and recommendations.

Delegating Authority vs. Pursuing Authorized Goals

Philip Selznick[6] finds that as authority is delegated to them, organization members pursue their personal goals more strongly. Teachers have moral and professional goals and these not infrequently come in conflict with school procedures and policies. For example, a teacher may be put in charge of discipline and ignore a policy that requires students who fight to be automatically suspended. He or she may take into consideration that students who are bullied ought not be punished along with the bullies.

On the other hand, principals have neither time nor energy to check on every detail of the school's functioning. A well-running school necessarily involves teachers in much of what the public would consider administrative work, for example, rostering, discipline, trip planning, admissions. This puts teachers in the position of exercising discretion on matters of policy. They often then make decisions on the basis of what they consider the merits of the case rather than on the basis of policies and procedures.

The basic conflict between delegation of authority and the pursuit of authorized goals is a matter of the extent to which resources allotted for the public goals of the schools, for example, instruction, are diverted to other uses. This is not a matter of dishonesty but a difference in perception of what is needed to carry out a task. School boards and citizens' committees tend to underestimate the resources needed—from an educator's point of view—to accomplish the goals they profess to esteem. The organizational reality is that people on-site have to have a good deal of discretion in determining how resources are used, or the job has no chance of getting done.

Some common practices that negotiate the conflict between delegation of authority and the pursuit of authorized goals are the following:

- Teachers use instructional time to have students decorate the classroom or the halls.
- Principals call special assemblies to free staff for committee work.
- Teachers change the curriculum at will to reflect their personal tastes and priorities.

Of course, every one of these practices is given an educational justification so that it appears to be serving the pursuit of the goals it is deviating from. In

---

[6]Philip Selznick in James G. March and Herbert A. Simon, op. cit., p. 43. See also Philip Selznick, "Foundations of the Theory of Organization," in Jay M. Shafritz and Philip Whitbeck, eds., *Classics of Organization Theory* (Oak Park, Ill.: Moore, 1978), pp. 84–95.

fact, these practices often serve worthy goals but they are not ones for which there is wide consensus on funding.

Process vs. Product

Luther Gulick[7] finds a conflict between a focus on product and a focus on process. The essential questions are how should we divide our attention between these two concerns? And, when they conflict, which should take precedence?

Are people given projects which they follow to completion? If so, this is **product** orientation. If they are given repetitive, piecemeal things to do, this is **process** orientation. Teaching is a bit of both. Lessons can be planned with product orientation. Teachers usually get to see some development and completion over a span of time. On the other hand, they don't get to see really long-range effects, say, from first through twelfth grade. Process orientation can be accomplished more cheaply if common activities are pooled, but no one is responsible for seeing that completion occurs. Someone in the previous stage of the process can always be blamed for failure. In this sense, schools are process-oriented. Children are pooled for common treatment because it is less expensive to do so, and no overall attention is given to students' careers. Economies of scale reduce the effectiveness with which goals are achieved.

Situations that point to an underlying conflict between process orientation and product orientation are these:

- School district consolidation vs. "small school" virtues such as school spirit, a feeling of sharing, a personal knowledge of all members of the school community.[8]
- Subject-matter focus and departmentalization in high schools vs. learner-centered focus and concern with development.[9]
- Standardized testing and curriculum vs. the concern for the "specialness" of students.
- Class size and teacher feelings of frustration in reaching children.[10]

[7] Luther Gulick's work is summarized in James G. March and Herbert A. Simon, op. cit., p. 41. Also see Luther Gulick, "Notes on the Theory of Organization" in Jay M. Shafritz and Albert C. Hyde, eds., *Classics of Public Administration* (Oak Park, Ill.: Moore, 1978), pp. 38–47.

[8] Cf. Roger G. Barker and Paul V. Gump, *Big School, Small School: High School Size and Student Behavior* (Stanford, Calif.: Stanford U. Press, 1964).

[9] See procedures developed by the Coalition for Essential Schools aimed at recapturing the "small community" environment and the focus on learner development. Contact Coalition of Essential Schools, Brown University, Education Department, Box 1938, Providence RI 02912, for their newsletter, *Horace*.

[10] See Seymour B. Sarason, *The Culture of the School and the Problem of Change* (Boston: Allyn & Bacon, 1971), pp. 152–154.

Power vs. Morale

Coercion is as essential a component of command as prescription or kinship. Ideally it should remain implicit, and when made explicit should manifest itself as rarely as possible as physical force, except in extreme emergency never falling arbitrarily or threatening the majority. Once a commander becomes as much an enemy to his followers as the enemy himself—and what else is a commander who breathes fire and sword against his own men?—the mystification of his role is destroyed and his power, essentially an artificial construct, dissipated beyond hope of recall.

—————————— *John Keegan,* The Mask of Command[11]

So strong are the images of Temple and Factory that people are reluctant to admit to the use of power both in individual motivation and in school relationships. People tend to find issues of power discomforting. Focusing on policies, rules, procedures, and so forth, offers an escape from dealing with the role of power in organizations. Abraham Zaleznick comments:

> ... executives are reluctant to acknowledge the place of power both in individual motivation and in organizational relationships. Somehow, power and politics are dirty words. And in linking these words to the play of personalities in organizations, some managers withdraw into the safety of organizational logics.[12]

Alvin Ward Gouldner,[13] studying **highly monocratic** organizations, found that the desire to hide power relations conflicts with getting more than minimal cooperation from organization members. If you don't yell, they don't work! However, some theorists take this to be an indication of organizational pathology. Why should we expect people to perform only when intimidated? What is it about an organization that necessitates that its goals can be achieved only through compulsion?

The issue of power in schools goes right to the heart of the professionalization controversy presented in Chapter 4. Schools are in flux with respect to the power issue. Thus the power vs. morale conflict varies depending upon the prerogatives accorded school people throughout the organization. Some situations that illustrate the power vs. morale conflict follow:

■■■ Teachers are demoralized to discover that their textbooks have been selected for them by their local school board committee.

---

[11]John Keegan, *The Mask of Command* (New York: Viking, 1987), p. 324.
[12]Abraham Zaleznik, "Power and Politics in Organizational Life," in *Harvard Business Review: On Human Relations* (New York: Harper & Row, 1979), pp. 375–396.
[13]Alvin Ward Gouldner, in March and Simon, op. cit., p. 45. See especially Alvin Ward Gouldner, *Patterns of Industrial Bureaucracy* (Glencoe, Ill.: Free Press of Glencoe, 1954).

Chart 8.1   **BASIC ORGANIZATIONAL CONFLICTS**

CONFLICT	EXAMPLE
following policy vs. sensitivity	standardization vs. individualization of curriculum
delegating authority vs. authorized goals	instructional vs. noninstructional use of time and material
process vs. product	Big-School vs. Small-School outcomes
power vs. morale	coercion vs. commitment

■ Classroom morale may be negatively affected by a teacher's unnecessary expressions of authority.[14]

■ School spirit sinks as bullying becomes widespread: With his baseball bat New Jersey principal Joe Clark raises the morale of those students he protects from the illegitimate power of bullying as he lowers the morale of staff members, who see him as a kind of bully himself.

Chart 8.1 summarizes the basic conflicts with examples.

THEORY X, THEORY Y, AND THEORY Z

We saw in the previous section that there is a basic conflict between power and morale. How much use of power is necessary in an organization? Is low morale a disadvantage? Answers to these questions depend upon what one believes about human nature.

Why do people join an organization, stay in it, and work for its goals? Chester I. Barnard's classic response to this question is that the benefits outweigh the costs.[15] But how one perceives human beings and their relationship to organizations has a lot to do with costs and benefits. An interesting and pertinent set of contrasts has been developed by Douglas McGregor.[16] McGregor calls these contrasts **Theory X** and **Theory Y**. William Ouchi,[17] examining successful Japanese corporations, expanded McGregor's distinctions with his own **Theory Z**. These theories are, of course, idealizations. They purport less to describe how organizations in fact function than to prescribe how organizations should be structured in order to function best.[18]

---

[14]See "war games" in Alfred S. Alschuler, *School Discipline. A Socially Literate Solution* (New York: McGraw-Hill, 1980), pp. 27–38.

[15]Chester I. Barnard, *The Functions of the Executive* (Cambridge: Harvard U. Press, 1938), p. 44.

[16]Douglas M. McGregor, *The Human Side of the Enterprise* (New York: McGraw-Hill, 1960).

[17]William Ouchi, *Theory Z: How American Business Can Meet the Japanese Challenge* (Reading, Mass. Addison-Wesley, 1981). But see also B. Bruce Biggs, "The Dangerous Folly Called Theory Z," *Fortune*, May 17, 1982, pp. 41–46.

[18]McGregor is ambivalent as to whether Theory X management elicits Theory Y behavior or vice versa. See Michael A. Oliker, "Douglas McGregor's Theory Y and the Structure of Educational Institutions," *Dissertation Abstracts International*, Vol. 37, No. 10, pp. 6158A-59A.

Human Nature and Commitment

Theory X basically describes people as lazy and needing compulsion to work. Theory Y says that if people are committed to the organization, they show all sorts of leadership qualities. Theory Z recommends that the organization, rather than demand commitment **from** its people, be committed **to** its people. Chart 8.2 presents these contrasts with additional information about the theories.

If we reconsider our basic organizational conflicts in light of Theories X, Y, and Z, it would seem that organizations that conformed to the different theories could avoid certain conflicts, particularly those having to do with internal relations. Theory X, expecting the worst of people, would find all four of the basic conflicts possible. Theory Y, on the other hand, by pursuing relationships that trust and empower organization members to act, would probably avoid the conflict of power with morale. Theory Z, by looking to organizational members for the goals to pursue, might undercut the possibility of the conflict between delegating authority and authorized goals. Chart 8.3 illustrates these points.

Whether people espouse Theories X or Y or Z is going to determine whether the conflict between morale and power will arise. But this is a two-

Chart 8.2

THEORIES X, Y AND Z

	Theory X	Theory Y	Theory Z

It is Human Nature to	Avoid work
	Need compulsion
	Shirk responsibility
	Seek to be
	   commanded
	Value security
	Lack ambition
		Find work natural
		If committed, show
		  initiative, self-
		  control, self-
		  direction
		Seek responsibility
		Value creativity
			(Same as Y)

Commitment	Irrelevant	People need to commit to the organization	The organization needs to commit to people

Chart 8.3

BASIC CONFLICTS AND THEORIES

	Theory X	Theory Y	Theory Z
following policy vs. sensitivity	possible conflict	possible conflict	possible conflict
delegating authority vs. authorized goals	possible conflict	possible conflict	**NO CONFLICT**
process vs. product	possible conflict	possible conflict	possible conflict
power vs. morale	possible conflict	**NO CONFLICT**	**NO CONFLICT**

way relationship. There is evidence that whether they adopt X or Y or Z in their relationships with others depends upon the nature of those relationships.

This analysis jibes with our common experience in schools. Teachers who complain that administrators are "autocratic," often tend to be as autocratic when they become administrators. This consideration leads us to suspect that **role** has a lot to do with behavior and perceptions. In the next section we will examine how members of different groups tend to see others in an X or Y framework depending upon the roles they play in an organization and the power relations among them.

Monocratic Power

Power tends to corrupt. Absolute power corrupts absolutely.

———— *Lord Acton*

Lord Acton's saying is famous. But is it true? How exactly does power corrupt? It does so by changing our perceptions of the people over whom we have power or who have power over us. This status tempts us to deal with them in ways that may undermine both our personal and our common interests.

An interesting set of studies by Kenwyn K. Smith[19] indicates that when organizations are monocratic, that is, power is concentrated rather than distributed, certain ways of perceiving subordinate or superior groups develop. These fixed ways of perceiving others, which Smith calls "encasements," generate very difficult problems for each of the groups in an organization.

If we consider a monocratic organization as comprised of three groups, powerholders, implementers, and lowers,[20] we can map out the relationships among them. **Powerholders** control resources, money, influence, police power. **Implementers** attempt to adjust the directives of the powerholders to the realities of the situation to which their directives are addressed. **Lowers** are those left in the organization, subject to the will of the powerholders, and the administrations of the implementers, lacking power of their own. Smith found that these three groups had different ways of perceiving themselves and others. They also handled conflicts in characteristically different ways.

If we look at schools, we find that the monocratic relationships of powerholder–implementer–lower are relative. They depend upon whom we are focusing on. In the school building, a principal may be a powerholder, whereas at a school board meeting he or she may be a "lower." In a small New England

---

[19]Kenwyn K. Smith, *Groups in Conflict: Prisons in Disguise* (Dubuque, Iowa: Kendall/Hunt, 1982).
[20]Smith uses the terms "uppers," "middles," and "lowers," respectively for what we are calling here "powerholders," "implementers," and "lowers." An analysis of his terminology shows the identicalness of the two sets of terms.

town Smith found that the relative position of different parties in a monocratic relationship depended upon the parties in question. The parties he considered were:

- The Public
- Local Politicians
- The Board of Education
- The Superintendent
- Principals
- Teachers
- Students

Smith focused on the Board of Education, the Superintendent, and the Principals and found that each filled the role of powerholder, implementer, and lower with respect to someone else. Chart 8.4 shows the relationships. If we focus on the principals we can see that they are powerholders in relation to the teachers, who are implementers, and the students, who are lowers. The principals are implementers in relation to the superintendent, who is a powerholder, and the teachers, who are lowers. The principal is a lower in relationship to the Board of Education, who are powerholders, and the superintendent, who is an implementer.

Chart 8.4   **THE RELATIVITY OF POWER**

focus \ role	Powerholders	Implementers	Lowers
Board of Education	Board of Education	Superintendent	Principals
	Politicians	Board of Education	Superintendent
	Public	Politicians	Board of Education
Superintendent	Superintendent	Principals	Teachers
	Board of Education	Superintendent	Principals
	Politicians	Board of Education	Superintendent
Principals	Principals	Teachers	Students
	Superintendent	Principals	Teachers
	Board of Education	Superintendent	Principals

Adapted from Kenwyn K. Smith, Groups in Conflict, *1982.*

The Pathology of Domination

*I don't want her to work, and I don't want her to go to school. What for?
She doesn't have to. She's got plenty to keep her busy right here.*

———————— *Husband speaking of his wife in* Worlds of Pain[21]

The warning in Smith's research is that when monocratic relationships stabilize, they "encase," that is, imprison, the perceptions of particular groups in a pathological manner. Powerholders tend to have little insight into the consequences of their own behavior on other people. They are pessimistic about the competency of other groups and tend to delegate responsibility but not sufficient resources. They also tend to withhold information to create dependencies in other groups upon them, the powerholders. They react to conflict with other groups by being punitive and assertive and by withholding resources. Within their own group, however, they tend to ignore conflict and tolerate dissidence. Those most charismatic among them dominate.

In contrast, implementers find themselves caught up in the need to relate to both powerholders and lowers. They tend to be optimistic and systemic thinkers who base their decisions in moral and ethical frameworks. They are information sharers and brokers. But faced with conflict from other groups they become disoriented, indecisive, and impotent. Within their own ranks they handle conflict by seeking common understandings, employing what they believe are effective techniques of conflict resolution. (The irony in Smith's research came with his realization that as a researcher he was not someone external to these encasements. He was, willy-nilly, by virtue of his interests and pursuits, an implementer.[22])

Lacking power, lowers suffer from yet another encasement. They are caught up in behavior that maintains group protection and unity. They may give the appearance to others that they "just don't care." They are suspicious of implementers and powerholders and adopt a reactive attitude toward them. Like powerholders they withhold information, but being unable to create dependency they do it to preserve group unity. They handle conflict from without by increasing cohesion and commiting to group unity and from within by suppression of dissent.

Chart 8.5 summarizes and compares the particulars of monocratic power relationships.

Depending upon the extent to which schools fit different models of organization, the possibilities of domination can be reduced.[23] By relating the theory of encasements to Theories X, Y, and Z, we can begin to understand how the power relationships among people work their way into the structure

---

[21]Cf. Lillian Breslow Rubin, *Worlds of Pain: Life in the Working Class Family* (New York: Basic Books, 1976), p. 180.
[22]Kenwyn K. Smith, op. cit., pp. 248–249.
[23]See Richard Sennett on making authority visible and legible, op. cit., pp. 168–190.

Chart 8.5   MONOCRATIC RELATIONSHIPS AMONG ROLE GROUPS

	Powerholders	Implementers	Lowers
Encasements (Constraints on Perceptions)	No insight into consequences of own behavior	Caught up in need to relate to both other groups	Caught up in unity and protection devices; "don't care"
Perceptions and Attitudes	See other groups as less competent; are pessimistic	Are systemic thinkers; optimistic	See others as manipulative and self-serving
	Delegate responsibility but not resources	Use moral and ethical frameworks	Are suspicious; assume reactive posture
Use of Information	Withhold info to create dependency	Are information sharers and brokers	Withhold info to preserve unity
Handles External Conflict by	Being punitive, assertive; withholding resources	Becoming disoriented, indecisive, impotent	Increasing cohesion; commiting to group unity
Handles Internal Conflict by	Ignoring it. Charismatics rule, Dissidents tolerated	Seeking common understandings. Believing in techniques	Suppressing minority viewpoints

Adapted from Kenwyn K. Smith, Groups in Conflict, *1982.*

of schools. Both Temple and Factory tend to be monocratic. Power flows from the top downward and sets the stage for encasement problems. A benefit of the Town Meeting image of the school is that it does not have the unidirectional flow of power that can produce the encasement pathologies. Power flows in many directions. People within the Town Meeting are exposed to various power roles. This variation undermines perceptual encasements. We might well worry that any attempt to strengthen the Temple or Factory aspects of schooling risks producing encasement pathologies.

MODELS OF ORGANIZATIONS

An organization is social structure that allocates costs and benefits, both symbolic and substantial. Because Organization Theory is an independent discipline with its own history, it treats organizations in a way different from that we have used with our images of the school as Temple, Factory, and Town Meeting. (The reader is encouraged to further study of this important discipline.[24]) But there are other ways of looking at the school. Important research

---

[24]An introduction to the field might begin with the highly readable Charles Perrow, *Complex Organizations* (Glenville, Ill.: Scott Foresman, 1979). Further study would be well pursued with Jeffrey Pfeffer, *Organizations and Organization Theory* (Boston: Pitman, 1982). See also other citations throughout this book.

on how programs have succeeded or failed explains their results in terms of **implementation models**. We will examine a set of organizational models that derives from such a concern with the implementation of reform legislation, and contrast these models with our original images, **expectation models** of the school.

Expectation vs. Implementation: A New Set of Organizational Models

In Chapter 2 we proposed three models of the school. Each model had associated with it an image. The basis for the distinction among the models was a sorting out of different kinds of **expectations**, respectively, for propriety, community, and nurturance, for effectiveness, and for negotiability.[25] Chart 8.6 shows these relationships.

There are many kinds of moral community and many kinds of productive organization. Because it simplifies the discussion, we have let the images from Chapter 2 associated with each model represent the model. This will suffice for this chapter, although we will also have reason in later chapters to distinguish among different images of different models. For example, there are different kinds of productive organization and the Factory is only one image of it. We will suggest that a different kind of productive organization might be able to handle the difficulties in present school organization. But in this chapter, Temple, Factory, and Town Meeting serve as our **expectation models** of the school as an organization.

Who exactly carries out the tasks in an organization can substantially affect its success. In a school, implementation power affects student achievement. Richard F. Elmore, focusing on problems of the **implementation** of social programs, presents four models of the organization.[26] Chart 8.7 compares our expectation models of the school with Elmore's implementation models.

The boundaries in the two kinds of models are somewhat different from one another. Whereas we place Temple and Factory in the expectation models, Elmore has broken them up into the Organizational Development model, the Systems Management model, and the Bureaucratic model. These new implementation models share characteristics of the expectation models

---

[25]See Frank W. Lutz and Aaron Gresson III, "Local School Boards as Political Councils," in *Educational Studies*, Vol. 11 (1980), pp. 125–144.
[26]Richard F. Elmore, "Organizational Models of Social Program Implementation," *Public Policy*, Vol. 26, No. 2 (Spring 1978), pp. 185–228.

Chart 8.6	**Model**	**Image**	**Related Expectations**
	Moral Community	Temple	Propriety, community, nurture
	Productive Organization	Factory	Effectiveness
	Political "Marketplace"	Town Meeting	Negotiability

Chart 8.7

EXPECTATION VS. IMPLEMENTATION MODELS

Contrasts Basis	Organizational Model or Image		
Expectation	Temple	Factory	Political Arena
Implementation	Organizational Development	Systems Management	Bureaucratic	Conflict and Bargaining

they overlap. Elmore's Conflict and Bargaining Model corresponds to our Town Meeting. The importance of distinguishing among these models is that program implementation can fail in different ways, depending upon the model used to examine the organization.

If we wish to ask of a proposed reform "What can go wrong?" we have to consider which model of the school we are using for our analysis. The Systems Management model conceives the school to be something like a large computer that the proper programming controls. Its failures are primarily failures in planning. The **Bureaucratic model** recognizes that in complex organizations implementation power is spread throughout the organization. Most actions that are taken are routine and derived from policy. Success in this model is a matter of adapting routines to reflect policy and making sure that power centers deliver the goods. The **Organizational Development model** sees effective organizations as reflecting the consensus and commitment of its members. If such consensus is lacking, failure follows. Finally, the **Conflict and Bargaining model** sees success as a matter of one group's having sufficient power to impose its conceptions of policy on others. Chart 8.8 illustrates these differences.

Why must we complicate things with an additional set of models? Because important research has been done with them. And because they give us another perspective by which to examine that very complex reality that is the school. In fact, there are other models we might use, but they don't serve our

Chart 8.8

ANALYZING THE FAILURE OF REFORM EFFORTS

Model	How Does Implementation Fail?
Systems Management	A lapse in planning, specification or control.
Bureaucratic	No change in routines to reflect policy. Policymakers overlook delivery problems.
Organizational Development	Lack of consensus and commitment among implementers.
Conflict and Bargaining	No unit of the organization is powerful enough to impose its conception of policy.

purposes as well. We need only distinguish between our original expectation models of the school, Temple, Factory, and Town Meeting, and these four new implementation models. Clearly, however, we must understand more about these new models and how they illuminate that organization we call the school.

Task Analysis: How Can Things Go Wrong?

It's a simple task to row your friend across a stream in a canoe. But it's not a simple thing, even if it's possible, for the U.S. navy to transport 2,000 sailors across that same stream in an aircraft carrier. Simple tasks may not be simple for a complex organization.

It's not unusual for a parent to drop into school and ask that his or her child's forgotten gym shorts be taken to the child by a certain period. The bigger the school, the less likely this simple task will be accomplished. Why is this? For the same reason it is difficult to get an error corrected on a utility bill. Or to find someone who can do something about a fixing a defect in your brand new car. Individuals can perform simple and amazingly varied tasks. Organizations function best with socially complex and routine tasks.

Organizations are composed of individual persons. Organizational tasks and products are developed from the tasks and products of individual persons, too. We learned in previous chapters that our expectations about schools affect what we believe the structure of the school to be and how people in the school should relate to one another. In this chapter we will see how an individual performs a simple task and then how this simple task changes in different organizational structures. In order to better understand the figures illustrating different organizational models, let's begin with a figure that represents the performance of simple tasks performed by an individual, for example, building a bird house or baking a cake.

At the end of Chapter 4, we developed a general slogan, a basic model for achieving educational goals: *School goals are achievable when adequate resources are provided for effective, feasible tasks of implementation.* To keep things simple, we will try to restrict ourselves to items introduced by this slogan, goals, tasks, and resources. Figure 8.1 captures the Basic Model of Chapter 4.

How should we understand Figure 8.1? Let's go through it bit by bit to make sure we understand what the flowchart means. We will use this basic chart, making it more and more complex, to illustrate what is involved in getting something done in different models of the school. Also, by seeing how different organizational models affect the complexity of a task, we gain insight into how simple tasks might go awry.

Firstly, Goals control Tasks. That is, the goals we choose determine what the appropriate tasks will be. For example, if we decide to build a bird house, selecting wood and nails, and cutting, would be tasks appropriate to that goal. If we choose to bake a cake, we select edible ingredients, rather than wood and nails.

Figure 8.1

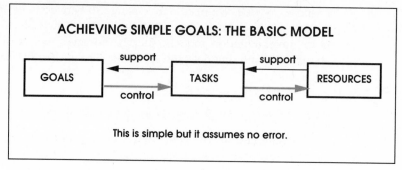

Secondly, Tasks control Resources. Once we decide how to pursue our goal, that is, what our tasks are, this decision determines what resources we will look for.

Next, Resources support Tasks. Without resources, tasks cannot be accomplished.

Finally, Tasks support Goals. Goals without tasks through which they are implemented remain only plans.

There is a certain artificiality about this task analysis because as individuals we do not often perceive tasks to be composed of separate parts: goals, tasks, and resources. We tend to blend these distinctions together into a harmonious whole. But we do this only as long as we succeed. When we fail, an analysis such as this becomes indispensable to intelligent troubleshooting.

The point of developing this flowchart of a simple task is to help us understand how different organizational structures affect how tasks are done. Tasks are done differently in small schools from the way they are in big schools. Different people may share different parts of the task. This structure requires our reconceptualizing what we might have thought of as a unified action into coordinated subtasks.

The advantage of the basic model in Figure 8.1 is that it is simple. Its drawbacks are that it doesn't account for error. People seldom just do something and have it satisfy what they set out to do. There is a lot of trial and error involved, especially as the tasks become complex and require coordination. Let's complicate our first model with the addition of a new item: **Benefits and Costs**, which are **organizational outcomes** to be evaluated to see if goals have been met (see Figure 8.2)

Figure 8.2 is not very different from Figure 8.1, our flowchart of a simple task. What we see here is a slight change in the relationship of the items. Tasks are not assumed automatically to support goals. Rather, they generate (support) outcomes that are Benefits and Costs. These outcomes must be evaluated to determine to what extent they support goals. And they are often evaluated by people other than those who produced them. How far the outcomes are from the goals will determine how tasks need to be adjusted. If many people are involved in this process, a complex communication system will have to be established. And it is a widely recognized "maxim" of systems

Figure 8.2

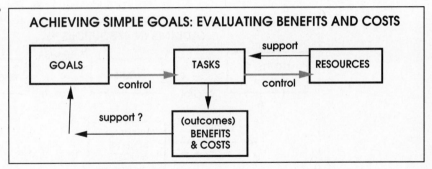

theory that as complexity increases, potential for failure does, too. This is hedged against in military and business systems by building in redundancy, that is, systems that duplicate one another's functions. School budgets are generally too tight for this kind of safeguard.

The "Benefits and Costs" in Figure 8.2 include **all** outcomes of the Tasks—not only what is created or transformed, but also what is used up. People tend to think of outcomes as only those new valued things produced by an activity. Costs tend to be overlooked or put into a special category. But someone's costs are another person's benefits. The trash produced by a school which it pays to dispose of is what provides benefits to the trash haulers and new resources to factories that recycle paper and cans. Whatever they may be, Benefits and Costs must be evaluated to see if they support Goals.

The task-analysis model shown in Figure 8.2 is the model underlying the vast majority of reform proposals directed at the schools. It is the simplest form of what we will call below the Systems Management model. Comparing Figures 8.1 and 8.2 we see the first difference between tasks undertaken by individual persons and those undertaken by organizations: the outcomes of tasks do not easily relate back to goals. As we have seen in Chapter 2, organizational goals are often sloganistic and relating outcomes to them may involve a complicated process of evaluation.

The Coleman Report, discussed in Chapter 7, asserted that merely putting more money into the schools had no effect upon student achievement, whereas student achievement was found to correlate with parent SES. (We can consider parent SES to be a kind of resource.) Adding in Resources of any kind and expecting a corresponding increase in Benefits (and Costs), we get a **production model** (see Figure 8.3), which assumes the use of the simple Systems Management model.

The production model tends to make people look for a direct relationship between increasing resources ($$$ + $) and increasing outputs (☆☆☆ + ☆) to meet goals. Researchers[27] have argued that the school is not organized in a way that makes the production model appropriate. We will encounter below

---

[27]See Rebecca Barr and Robert Dreeben, *How Schools Work* (Chicago: U. of Chicago Press, 1983).

Figure 8.3

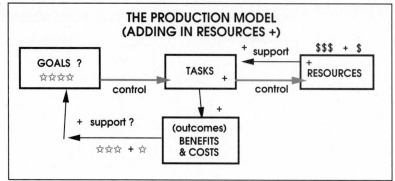

some ways of conceptualizing the school organization which explain why simply increasing Resources will not increase the output of Benefits and Costs supporting Goals.

We should understand that our basic model is simplistic. More resources do not necessarily lead to more benefits. In a complex organization, tasks have to be coordinated. **Coordination** is a kind of task and uses time, energy, and money. The resources used for coordination purposes are part of what is called **overhead** costs. Figure 8.4 shows the relationship, ignoring Benefits and Costs, and Goals, for simplicity's sake.

It is possible to use up new resources as overhead—for example, when new programs are started because a large part of start-up costs are for administration, staff training, and liaison, that is, coordination tasks. Or a teacher may get several sets of new textbooks with the expectation that they will improve his or her teaching. But it may take the teacher so much time and energy just to develop lessons that use the text material that the instruction itself suffers. As another example, simply admitting more new students at a university brings new resources in the form of tuitions. However, against these must be weighed the costs of additional staff and facility use. When budgets expand and production doesn't, administrators should check to see if overhead has gone up.

As practically important as these complexities are, let's leave them and build upon our simple model. We will examine the differences between models of Systems Management, Bureaucracy, Organizational Development and Conflict and Bargaining.

Figure 8.4

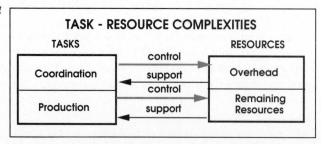

The Implementation Models

Most people think of reform as a top-down process. Without necessarily intending to, they adapt the viewpoint of the powerholders in a monocratic relationship. Thus, when reforms fail, they blame the implementers (school personnel) or the lowers (students).

Knowledge of organization theory, however, opens up a new perspective. We will see how and why effective school reforms have come about despite severe limits on resources, because teachers and principals were given the discretion to determine organizational changes at the local level. Let's begin our review of Elmore's implementation models.

The Systems Management Model

Let's first look at the **systems management** model. Here the school is conceived as a sort of computer aimed at maximizing goals. Historically, this concept precedes the others in organization theory. It is the ultimately rational factory. To reiterate an earlier point, it is the model of the school most reform proposals assume. It is monocratic, is programmed at the top, and executes directives unquestioningly. The lower levels, being parts of the computer, have no special needs of their own, and certainly no independent goals that could conflict with the basic computer program. In a school system, the basic program is policy, translated instructionally into curriculum. (The quote from John Franklin Bobbitt in Chapter 2 alludes to this model.) If the computer has undesirable outputs, the program is at fault—or maybe there is a hardware malfunction. Policy must be changed or parts replaced.

We can see our simple Systems Management model in Figure 8.2. We make one change in it, however. As a concession to the complexities of the school organization, **Goals** becomes **Goals & Related Policy** (see Figure 8.5), since the day-to-day functioning of an organization is normally accomplished in terms of policies rather than by reference to the Goals themselves. What we see in Figure 8.5 is our simple task flowchart complicated in a second way.

Is this how a school works?

Figure 8.5

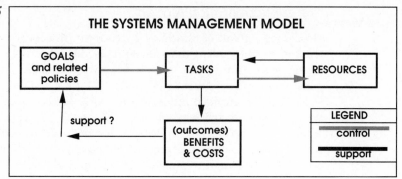

At first, we broke the easy connection between tasks and goals, placing outcomes between them. Now, goals become complicated with policies. And policies invariably need interpreters. As individuals, we have no need of policies for the sake of performing simple tasks. But, for reasons we look at in Chapter 9, organizations develop policies to coordinate the actions of the different individuals in them.

As the flowcharts get more complicated, try to trace the elements of the basic task flowchart and to relate them back to Figure 8.1.

The Bureaucratic Model

The second model developed by Elmore is the **Bureaucratic model**. Like a bureau for clothes, a bureaucratic model sees the organization as compartmentalized; more complex than a simple input-output systems model. It has departments to which different tasks are assigned. These departments may work independently, in that the master program, the policy, need not govern the day-to-day work.

School systems are bureaucracies. So are departmentalized schools or any organization where different tasks are given, by rule or by tradition, to different people. Thus, most large religious organizations are bureaucracies, too, with this important difference: their ultimate focus is not on effectiveness or efficiency, but on propriety or morality.

In all but the smallest schools, the new teacher's first task on the job is to learn how to function in a bureaucracy. Bureaucracy is not meant here as a term of condemnation. It represents instead what some consider to be the most humane, equitable, and rational form for a large, complex organization.[28] Bureaucracy tends to limit favoritism, despotism and inconsistency in organizations. It also imposes controls that less complex organizations cannot[29] and

---

[28]Charles Perrow, op. cit., pp. 5–16.
[29]Cf. Randall Collins, "Some Comparative Principles of Educational Stratification," *Harvard Educational Review*, Vol. 47, No. 1 (February 1977), pp. 1–27.

Philadelphia Board of Education
Administration Building: School
systems are organized
bureaucratically.

is subject to its own kind of organizational politics: department vs. department. The reforms of political Progressivism of the late nineteenth and early twentieth centuries brought about the bureaucratization of the schools. The costs of this are reflected in the four standard conflict situations of complex organizations.

The Bureaucratic model is still monocratic as far as basic goals are concerned. But, whereas in the Systems Management model discretion resides only at the top, in a bureaucracy there is discretion at the departmental level. Established routines are supposed to support the goals and their related policies. But **discretion** as to whether and how a routine is followed rests with the department. The major problems of control in a bureaucracy from the point of view of the policymakers are how to control departmental discretion and how to assure that routines support rather than undermine goals.

Personal goals are not recognized although conflict among departments is.[30] Range of departmental control becomes a concern. Responsibilities rest with the top administration to "optimize" coordination. **Optimize** is an important word here. It means to do as best as considerations of cost and benefit allow. This contrasts with that for the systems management model in which **maximization** of goal values is pursued. Costs are usually not considered important unless they are suffered by the powerholders.

Because a major difference between the Systems Management model and the Bureaucratic model is the way in which discretion is distributed, let's digress for a moment to look at discretion more closely.

The Locus and Span of Discretion

People tend to underestimate the amount of discretion they have even when they are given a direct order. Any teacher, however, who has had to quiet

---

[30]Cf. Richard Weatherley and Michael Lipsky, "Street-Level Bureaucrats and Institutional Innovation: Implementing Special Education Reform," *Harvard Educational Review*, Vol. 47, No. 2 (May 1977).

down a large group has learned how differently students can respond to the directive, "Be quiet!" Even in the military, a paradigm of systems management in the minds of many, discretion is hard to control.[31] Between a superior's evaluation of a person's response to a directive as adequate or as inadequate often lies a very considerable **span of discretion**. Telling someone to do something still leaves to that person the choice of how.

We saw in Chapter 2 that goals statements with broad consensus generally lacked specificity. The vaguer the directive, the more discretion we have in deciding what is an adequate response to it. This risks the possibility that some people will judge that our response was less than adequate. There is a tension here which traps educators to their disadvantage. The broader, the more sloganistic, the goal they pursue, the greater the span of discretion they enjoy. But the greater the likelihood their response will be seen to be inadequate. In the discussion in Chapter 9 on Institutionalization, we will look at this dilemma more closely to see what the schools have done to extricate themselves from it.

Let us introduce one more new item into our analysis: **the discretionary unit**. A discretionary unit, **DU**, is a *person or group of people that controls goals, tasks, or resources in the organization*. We can use the discretionary unit to compare and contrast the notions of stakeholder and powerholder in an organization. For example, a stakeholder is a person or group supported by the products of an organization. A powerholder is a **discretionary unit** that controls resources in an organization, even if indirectly. (We should recall from Chapter 3 that stakeholders may not be a powerholder, that is, DU.) Figure 8.6 illustrates these relationships.

Why is it important to spell out a conception of discretionary unit? Not only because it helps strengthen the distinction between stakeholders and powerholders, but also because it helps us understand how it is that school people can exercise great discretion in a school and still remain relatively

---

[31]See James F. Dunnigan, "Leadership," in *How to Make War* (New York: Quill, 1983), Chapter 14, pp. 216–222.

Figure 8.6

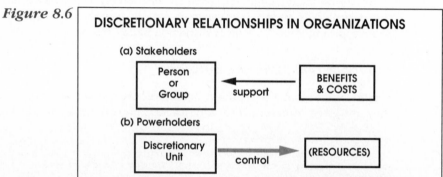

DISCRETIONARY RELATIONSHIPS IN ORGANIZATIONS

(a) Stakeholders

Person or Group ← support — BENEFITS & COSTS

(b) Powerholders

Discretionary Unit — control → (RESOURCES)

Figure 8.7

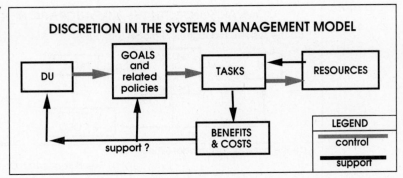

DISCRETION IN THE SYSTEMS MANAGEMENT MODEL

powerless. School reformers often concede that principals and teachers must be given more responsibility, that is, discretion. But if having discretion means little more than letting school people decide how to make the best of a bad situation, giving them more will not bring about school improvement. Judging results is only fair if those responsible for decisions control the resources to support them.

In monocratic organizations, the discretionary unit is found at the top. In bureaucracies, discretionary units are distributed throughout. For example, many large schools not only have principals, but also have deans and department heads, all of whom can exercise discretion. If we include the discretionary unit in our simple diagram of the systems management model, we get Figure 8.7. This flowchart brings up an interesting point: Discretionary Units require resources. There may be Benefits and Costs that support the goals and policies of the organization but do not support the discretionary unit, and vice versa. As we will see in a later section, policies can constrain the powerholders to the benefit of others in an organization. But powerholders can use the organization to pursue their own goals rather than the stated public goals of the organization.

Comparing the Two Models

For the sake of a simple diagram, let's compare the systems management model and the bureaucratic model, ignoring the resources, which we will remove from the figure. In comparing the Bureaucratic model with the Systems Management Model in Figure 8.8, we should note not only the division of tasks into routines in a bureaucracy, but also the introduction of new centers of discretion.

How can we relate the Bureaucratic model back to the original flowchart for simple tasks (Figure 8.1)? To begin, we deleted resources to simplify the figure. (We can imagine them attached on the right.) What is new about the bureaucratic model is that the task is broken up into routines and each routine is controlled by its own DU. For example, a principal may be charged with promoting the education, generally speaking, of the students in his or her

Figure 8.8

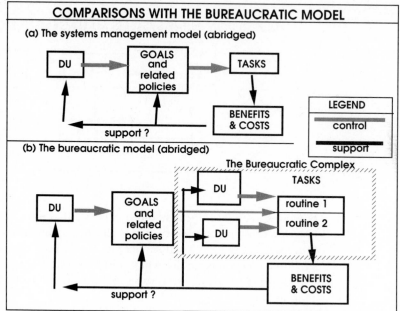

COMPARISONS WITH THE BUREAUCRATIC MODEL

(a) The systems management model (abridged)

(b) The bureaucratic model (abridged)

school. But the foreign language department head is certainly going to have more to say specifically than the principal about what is to be done in the foreign language department. And in most cases, particularly if the school is large, the department head will have far more influence on what is actually learned in foreign language classrooms than will the principal.

The top level DU of a bureaucracy tries to maintain control with Goals and Related Policies, not only because of coordination problems, but also because of the tendency of each DU to pursue goals other than those authorized by the top level DU on the far left. As discretionary units develop to control ever more complex subroutines, the control and coordination problem increases.

We can see in Figure 8.8 that bureaucracies have various centers of discretion and that they use up resources. The outputs, that is, the costs and benefits, may support any of the DUs or the goals and related policies, each in different ways. For example, it is not unusual for a school to attract students for its strengths in a particular department, say, mathematics. But the high enrollment helps support even the weakest department of the school. (For the sake of future simplification, the next flowchart will treat as a simple block the group of elements enclosed within the border marked "The Bureaucratic Complex.")

We should note that in a bureaucracy simple tasks can only be accomplished as part of a departmental routine. If some specific department is not given the responsibility for a task, it will be done, at best, haphazardly. Or the task may be redefined as a complex, organizational task requiring interde-

Figure 8.9

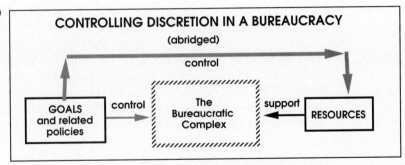

partmental coordination. Bigger may not be better for getting certain things done.

How is discretion in a bureaucracy controlled? By several means. The first is that people are socialized to subordinate their personal goals to those of the organization. A second means of controlling discretion is that policy governs routine in the bureaucracy. But the most important control is that goals and related policy are established to control resources (see Figure 8.9).

Whether such means work, of course, is another matter. The School Laws of the State of New Jersey, for example, mandate a "thorough and efficient education." But more impressive is the ability of the state to take over a school district found to be inefficiently run. This has actually happened in Jersey City. Resource control is by far the greatest source of power.

The control of discretion by controlling resources has particular interests for school people trying to professionalize teaching. Both lawyers and doctors, in comparison to schoolteachers and administrators, exercise great discretion in the performance of their jobs. But lawyers and doctors also control their most important resources: access to their profession and monopoly on the performances characteristic of their field (and therefore funding). Teachers control neither of these; state officials do.

But school people are far from being mere pawns in the hands of school boards and state officials They can often exercise discretion in the face of apparently strong directives. (Recall comments made earlier about span of discretion.) For example, attempts at control of school bureaucracies by state legislatures sometimes result in lack of sufficient resources to carry out a mandate. Weatherley and Lipsky tell how school people authorized to implement Chapter 766, a special education law in Massachusetts coped with the tensions of a comprehensive mandate and limited resources:

- they rationed the number of assessments performed;
- they placed limits on children held for the program;
- they took behavior problems first;
- they favored group over individual treatment;
- they used trainees, rather than experienced teachers;

■ they short-circuited time-consuming procedures aimed at securing the rights of parents.[32]

This application demonstrates how the authority conferred by law can be substantially transformed by those who have the power of implementation. Each DU not only consumes resources but may also transform the goals and policies of an organization (that is, of the powerholders in an organization) to something quite different from what was originally intended.

Organizational Development

An attempt to restore moral community to the systems management and bureaucratic models comes in the form of another model: the **Organizational Development** model. This model starts off with its fundamental goals set at the top but ends up inviting participation in the very process of policy-making. Elmore comments that the effect of this model is to "turn the policy-making process on its head." The major concern here is that members "buy into" the goals of the organization. This kind of model underlies many of the current proposals to professionalize teaching; for example, sharing of policy-making authority with teachers, or the determination of budget by building staff rather than central administration.

The general appeal of this model is that the organization will be most effective in reaching its goals when the personal needs of the individuals in it are recognized and provided for. We have here a sort of democratic moral community in which commitment is shared. This corresponds somewhat with our image of the school as Temple, but a Temple that is democratically controlled. What we have in the Organizational Development model is the organization conceived of as a single discretionary unit (see Figure 8.10). As far as getting work done, however, this model seems to offer no improvement over a monocratically controlled bureaucracy.

We have stripped down the flowchart in Figure 8.9 to the bare essentials

---

[32]Richard Weatherley and Michael Lipsky, op. cit., p. 194.

Figure 8.10

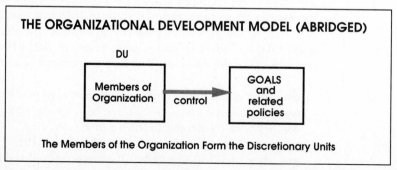

THE ORGANIZATIONAL DEVELOPMENT MODEL (ABRIDGED)

DU

Members of Organization → control → GOALS and related policies

The Members of the Organization Form the Discretionary Units of the Organizational Development model. We have left out not only resources but also tasks and outcomes. This model may strike us either as utopian or as running against the grain of our intuitive images of the school as Temple or Factory. However, the model does reconceive the school to be a democratic moral community, giving much more weight to school personnel in the determination of goals and related policies than our actual school systems are structured to do. Is the Organizational Development model just wishful thinking? Or is there evidence that it is workable?

A Rand Corporation study[33] of four federally funded educational programs aimed at innovation in the public schools turned up the following results:

■ Project success depended primarily upon the existence and mobilization of local resources, over which federal administrators had no control.

■ Among the important factors in determining that success were the use of voluntary, highly motivated participants and the development and use of local resources.

We see attempts along these lines in the Dade County, Florida, experiments and the Buffalo, New York, reorganization mentioned elsewhere in this book.

The Conflict and Bargaining Model

The final model, the **Conflict and Bargaining model**, corresponds to our Town Meeting image. A major difference between this model and the previous three is that it **assumes no consensus about goals**. For the Systems Management model and the Bureaucratic model, goals are provided by a discretionary unit (DU) at the top of the organizational hierarchy. The Organizational Development model develops consensus on goals among all the members of the organization. But the Conflict and Bargaining model requires only that participants in the organization agree that maintaining the bargaining relationship, that is, staying in the organization, is worth more than leaving the organization.[34]

We can picture a Conflict and Bargaining model of the organization to be a group of resource-controlling DUs that come together to form and maintain an organization. They may pool their resources but are unlikely to relinquish control over them entirely. All DUs are stakeholders and powerholders, but the public goals and policies of the organization will tend to express most clearly the expectations of the most dominant DUs (see Figure 8.11).

[33]See Paul Berman and Milbrey Wallin McLaughlin, *Federal Programs Supporting Educational Change*, Vol. VIII, *Implementing and Sustaining Innovations*, R-1589/8-HEW (Santa Monica, Calif.: Rand Corp., May 1978).

[34]Cf. Chester I. Barnard, op. cit., p. 44, "The total motivation of a cooperative system ... is determined by the marginal contributor." Barnard would reject the conflict and bargaining model since he preferred to believe that organizations could have goals apart from the goals of its members.

Figure 8.11

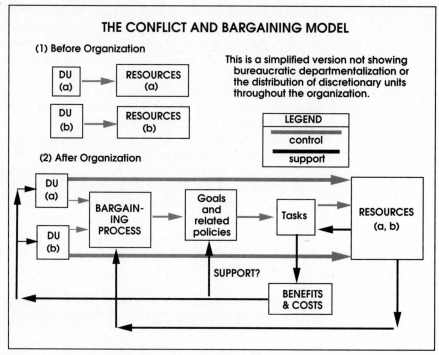

What we find in Figure 8.11 is a kind of "chemical reaction." Before organization, only individual DUs that control their own resources exist. But the bargaining process brings them together to form an organization whose structure we can recognize in the way it relates Goals and Related Policies to Tasks, Resources, and Costs and Benefits (outcomes). The Conflict and Bargaining model is the first model to concede that something occurs among DUs to bring about goals and related policies, that is, bargaining. Goals and related policies in this model do not just come into being mysteriously as they seem to in the other models.

We can understand why this model is unattractive compared to the Systems Management model, or even the more involved Bureaucratic one: it is complicated. We must consider a whole range of variables to predict the possible outcome of some new policy or reform. The Conflict and Bargaining model is a complex model even in its simplified form. But reality, too, is often not simple.

Can we discern the components of our original simple task and the flow of control and support within this new model? Whether simple tasks can be defined will depend mostly upon the number of people involved with them. If we imagine that only two people are involved, this model gives a good analysis of what goes on when one person enlists the aid of another to complete a task: one person negotiates for the resources of the other, for example,

Chart 8.9   **IMPLEMENTATION MODELS OF ORGANIZATIONS**

Dimension / Type	Central Principle	Theory of Power	Theory of Decision	Implementation Process
Systems Management	Should Maximize Goals	Hierarchical Top down	Optimal Allocation of Responsibilities	Objectives Monitoring Goal Directed maximizing
Bureaucratic Process	Balance discretion with routine	Power dispersed Front line discretion	Controlling discretion Changing routine	Devise alternative routines
Organizational Development	Satisfy individual needs for autonomy and control	Maximize participation Reduce hierarchy	Create effective groups Build consensus	Accommodation between policy makers and implementers
Conflict and Bargaining	Organizations are arenas for competing for resources	The distribution of power is never stable	Decisions are the resultants of bargaining	Success is relative

Adapted from R. F. Elmore, 1978

time, money, or effort, in such a manner that both can look forward to outcomes that support their mutually recognized goals.

We should note:

■ The bargaining process requires support from resources. In the bureaucratic complex this is called "overhead."
■ Evaluation tends to be focused on those Benefits and Costs that are intended to support goals.
■ The potential exists for resources to be diverted away from supporting goals and policies to other uses. We will deal with this in detail in the next chapter on Institutionalization.

Chart 8.9 compares and contrasts information given by Elmore about the four models. These implementation models enhance and inform our own intuitive expectation models of the school, temple, factory, and town meeting but do not necessarily supersede them.[35]

Elmore distinguishes his four models in terms of:

---

[35]Graham Allison, in *Essence of Decision: Explaining the Cuban Missile Crisis* (Boston: Little, Brown, 1971), presents three models of organization that correspond more tightly to the images of the school. His focus, however, is on strategic decision making.

- a central principle, operating as an organizational rationale
- a theory of power, that is, how power is distributed throughout the organization
- a theory of decision, that is, how decisions are best thought to be made in the organization
- the implementation process, that is, how decisions are thought to be best put into practice

Which of these models best describes schools in a large system in a pluralistic society? To some extent, they all provide some insight into the process of schooling. Clearly, however, in our pluralistic society the Conflict and Bargaining model deserves much more attention by educators than it tends to get. We will see in the next chapter that the Conflict and Bargaining model lends itself more readily than the others to an explanation of the process of **institutionalization**.

Decision in Organizations

Models of organizations can help us understand connections that would be otherwise hard for us to discern in the daily hustle and bustle of schooling. Models can clarify. But they can also create expectations of tidiness that do not match reality. Our most complex model so far has been the Conflict and Bargaining model. But even within that model, the DUs, though they may be in conflict, stand out as little islands of rationality. There, it seems, things are thought out. Means pursue ends, even if ends vary from unit to unit.

The model introduced in Chapter 4 was, in effect, a paradigm of rational decision making: goals were pursued by effective, feasible tasks. The analysis questions of Chapter 3 also contained a model of decision making embedded in them. The questions suggested that problems were to be approached with a procedure similar to the following:

1. Analyze the problem situation to determine present allocations of costs and benefits;
2. Examine goal proposals for feasibility;
3. Determine the likelihood of implementation;
4. Determine postimplementation allocations of costs and benefits.

The question we must ask is whether, even in the most monocratic or technically developed organizations, such a procedure is actually followed.

How Problems Are Dealt With

March and Simon,[36] in their classic work **Organizations**, suggest that problem-solving behavior takes a different form:

---

[36]James G. March and Herbert A. Simon, op. cit.

In a search for programs of activity to achieve goals, the focus of attention will tend to move from one class of variables to another in the following general sequence. (1) Those variables that are largely within the control of the problem-solving individual or organizational unit will be considered first. There will be a serious attempt to elaborate a program of activity based on control of these variables. (2) If a satisfactory program is not discovered by these means, attention will be directed to changing other variables that are not under the direct control of the problem solvers ... (3) If a satisfactory program is still not evolved, attention will be turned to the criteria that the program must satisfy, and an effort will be made to relax these criteria so that a satisfactory program can be found.[37]

What people do with problems in organizations is what some people tend to do when their cars don't run well. At first they kick the bumper and flip the switches on the dashboard. If these tactics don't work, they may let the car warm up longer when it's cold or start using high-test gas regularly or put additives in the oil. Finally, they may give up trying to drive at high speeds or for long distances.

Schools do similar things. If a cross-racial fight occurs in school, an assembly on Brotherhood may be held. Then, if the conflict continues, the parents of children from the different racial groups may be contacted. If this approach brings no improvement, all fighting may be treated as a suspension offense. And in each step along the way the goal, the breadth of expectations, is diminished. We go from enhancing Brotherhood to enlisting parental control to squelching fighting of any kind. The underlying animosities that the fighting was a symptom of may remain untouched.

The Costs of Analysis

Why is problem solving in organizations so haphazard? Are people basically irrational? Don't they really care?

The answer is that careful analysis costs time, effort, and—ultimately—money. A detailed cost-benefit analysis can have political costs, also. Unless people perceive a situation to involve their own interests, they don't look for the "best" answer. They don't even look for the most cost-efficient answer. They generally accept what will do to answer the concern, if only for the moment. A tight budget or a tradition of making do aggravates this.[38] According to March and Simon, as problem solvers people are neither goal-maximizers nor goal-optimizers, but **goal-satisfiers**. They do what works for them, and that is good enough.

---

[37]Ibid., p. 179.
[38]Cf. Bob Cole, "Teaching in a Time Machine: the 'Make-Do' Mentality in Small-Town Schools," *Phi Delta Kappan*, October 1988, pp. 139–144.

Unless participants individually believe the stakes are high, they don't personally want to bear the costs of careful analysis, particularly because prediction involved in feasibility studies is so uncertain. Instead they prefer to make whatever it is that is "the problem" not their problem.

Garbage Can Decision Processes

In another important work, March and Olsen[39] characterize the organization as a bunch of solutions looking for a problem. The routines and the skills of individuals in an organization are the tools available to attack problems, that is, someone's concern about a situation. If a concern arises, these routines and skills are applied to it, willy-nilly, for those are the tools at hand. If we only have a hammer, everything begins to look like a nail.

This process of problem solving March and Olsen call the **garbage can decision process**. In a garbage can decision process a decision within an organization is an outcome of the following randomly related factors:

- problems, that is, someone's concerns
- solutions, someone's product, often waiting to be applied to something
- participants, often whoever happens to be available
- choice opportunities, occasions when a decision is expected

Figure 8.12 depicts this mix.

An organizational choice is, according to March, "a somewhat fortuitous confluence."[40] Within a garbage can process, decisions are made either by oversight, by flight (running away), or by resolution, the only method rec-

---

[39]James G. March and Johan P. Olsen, *Ambiguity and Choice* (Bergen: Universitetsforlaget, 1976).
[40]James G. March and Johan P. Olsen, Ibid., p. 27.

Figure 8.12

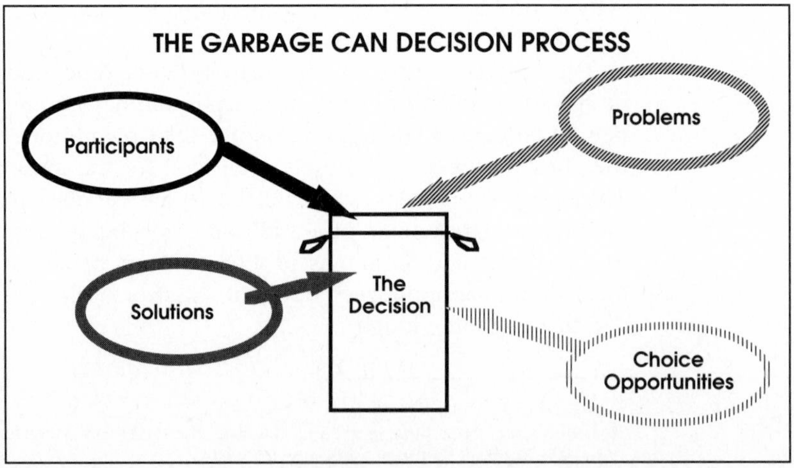

THE GARBAGE CAN DECISION PROCESS

Participants

Problems

Solutions

The Decision

Choice Opportunities

ognized within the classical perspective. And resolution is the kind of careful analysis we have provided an example of in earlier chapters.

The garbage can decision theory says that resources brought to bear on a problem will primarily be what happens to be available. A problem is solved when it ceases to be a concern. But when do people decide really to look at a problem or to treat it lightly? March and Olsen suggest that both big problems and small problems are given the same short shrift. In general, only modestly important problems will be resolved through any structured procedure. This approach gives us an important clue. If we consider what a "big problem" might be, we may see why thorough analyses are avoided.

As we learned in Chapter 3, a problem is a perception by someone that a situation concerns them or other people. March and Olsen say much the same thing. A "big problem," let us postulate, is one or both of the following:

a. a situation uniformly perceived by powerholders to be a concern because solutions would involve substantial reallocations of costs and benefits, or

b. a situation perceived generally to be a concern but for which there is no broad consensus for solution

In a situation like **a** we should not expect any more care to be taken with a decision than seems necessary to protect the interests of the powerholders, unless, of course, such decision is made within a moral community where broad concern for all stakeholders is acted upon. Decisions will not be made public and will be dealt will summarily.

In situation **b**, where consensus is not likely to be forthcoming, we should expect the powerholders to make the decision according to their own lights for the following reasons: (1) any decision will be criticized; and (2) widespread perception of lack of consensus and of the leadership's inability to deal with it undercuts the legitimacy of that leadership. (We will look at this more closely in the next chapter.) For such reasons we can expect that powerholders in a school system will not invite careful analysis of either school budget allocations or the implementation of controversial programs such as sex education. So we can expect a participative, analytic decision process to be used only where the powerholders are not in agreement that their concerns are at stake, or a great consensus exists among all stakeholders as to what costs should be borne to address the problem.

Figure 8.13 maps out areas of decision processes. The dimensions defining the problem space are: reallocation prospects, the amount of reallocation of costs and benefits threatened by the decision, and breadth of consensus.

March and Olsen's analysis seems to indicate that the very possibility of developing reasoned approaches to solving problems requires the kind of "buying into" the process envisioned by theorists of the Organizational Development model. Without this shared commitment, the very costs of analysis will cause the process to collapse into a perfunctory garbage can decision process.

Figure 8.13

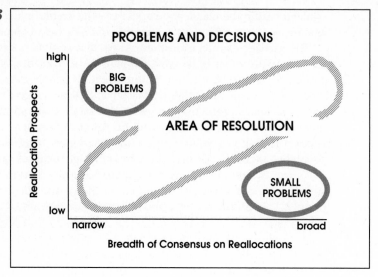

Reform Proposals from an Organizational Perspective
Reform Proposals from an Organizational Perspective

Naive reformers, including educators, work at the level of expectations. There is public outcry for, among many other things, increased literacy, higher mathematical skills, reduction in teenage sexual activity, and greater concern for the elderly. Naive reformers seem to think it is sufficient to inaugurate a policy, a rule, or a procedure to eliminate their problem. "Encased" in the images of Temple and Factory, often ignoring the complexities of Bureaucracy or the Town Meeting, they fail to address concerns about implementation. But as Elmore and many others point out, structures of implementation in organizations are absolutely crucial to the fulfillment of expectations.

Many who see the complexities tend to believe that monocratic power is needed to address the problem. The Factory model in its traditional forms tends to stress the centralization of power. Recall Bobbitt's quote from Chapter 2 to the effect that managers alone should decide "the order and sequence of all of the various processes through which the raw material or the partially developed product shall pass" and "must see that the raw material or partially finished product is actually passed on from process to process." To Winston Churchill the comment is attributed that democracy is a very troublesome form of government, but all other forms are worse. The risk of monocratic leadership, even in schools, is that it ignores costs to others that it does not itself suffer.

Our awareness of organizational issues allows us a more sophisticated view of who the stakeholders and powerholders are and what the costs and benefits to them might be. For a given reform proposal, stakeholders and powerholders are found both within and without the school. They are found at the policy-making level, at the implementation level, and elsewhere. A careful mapping of the benefits and costs of change implementation becomes essential.[41]

"There oughtta be a law ... " is the naive response to a problem. Organization theory helps us develop a more sophisticated view of command, control, and policy. This should bring about a reconsideration of what can be commanded, controlled, and affected through policy. In the next chapter we will look at how authority, control, and policy differ according to the image of the school under consideration. Sometimes a new policy serves merely as a ritual expression of concern rather than a commitment to focusing the resources of the school on a problem. Such policy requires the wisdom not to worry too much about its implementation. If what we expect to see at any given level of an organization is change of behavior, we will have to look beyond policy and formal control to effect it.

Finally, organization theory reinforces our increasing sensitivity to the language of reform proposals, to the important distinctions set out in the first section of this book between formal and technical change proposals. It helps us determine with greater accuracy where slogans may or may not be useful in the schooling process.

SUMMARY

1. Organization theory is useful in helping us understand how the structure of schools can undermine professed goals and individual efforts to achieve them. Our expectation models of the school, Temple, Factory, and Town Meeting, have been supplemented with implementation models, Systems Analysis, Bureaucratic, Organizational Development, and Conflict and Bargaining.

2. Complex organizations tend to have four basic conflicts, following policy vs. sensitivity, delegating authority vs. authorized goals, process vs. product, and power vs. morale. Theories X, Y, and Z rest on different conceptions of human nature and the relationship of commitment in organizations. Organizations structured according to the different theories may avoid certain of the basic conflicts.

3. Monocratic power relationships can produce "encasements," perceptual fixes that can lock persons into pathologies of domination. In our pluralistic society, however, relationships are flexible and the roles of Powerholder, Implementer, and Lower are played by different people in different circumstances. It is important, however, that we understand to what extent behavior may be determined by such roles.

---

[41]See John P. Kotter and Leonard A. Schlesinger, "Choosing Strategies for Change," *Harvard Business Review*, March-April 1979, for a simple cost-benefit analysis of change methods.

4.   A major concern is the span and locus of discretion in the organization. Studies indicate that enhancing teacher and principal discretion is a major factor in making significant school reforms. A consideration of the garbage can decision process also indicates that without commitment to support the possible costs of analysis, we can expect perfunctory participation to degenerate into a hit-or-miss problem-solving approach.

QUESTIONS

1.   How might organization theory affect our ideas of responsibility and blame in assessing how an organization functions? If a school does not live up to expectations, how can you respond to someone who feels that either the administration, the teachers, or the students must be at fault?

2.   Can you give other examples from your own experience of situations involving the basic internal conflicts of an organization? What was your reaction at the time (assuming you did not know anything about organization theory)?

3.   Different kinds of organizations tend to operate under Theory X and Theory Y. Make two lists of organizations that in your experience seemed to be run on the basis of one theory rather than the other.

4.   What are the possible costs and benefits of running an organization on Theory X rather than Theories Y or Z? Chart these costs and benefits in terms of the risks run in case the situation does not fit with the theory used. When is Theory Y risky? Theory X? Theory Z?

5.   Give separate examples of domination behavior as part of the formal, the technical, and the informal culture of some group. What is the response of those dominated at each level of culture? You might recall a topic from Chapter 3, "Denying Concerns and Interests," and examine how domination is reflected in the language people use to deal with one another. Who calls whom by his or her first name? Who is referred to, even when absent, by a formal title?

6.   Analyze the task of preparing for a party in terms of a Simple Systems management model. Do it also in terms of the Bureaucratic model (divide the tasks up among your friends.) How does discretion vary in each case? On what items does it vary?

7.   What additional insights do we get from the conflict and bargaining model? What does it explain about organizations you are familiar with, for example, your family and your school?

8.   When the costs of planning become burdensome, the garbage can decision process takes over. At what point did you stop planning your party in detail (see question 6) and just "play it by ear"? (For example, did you consider whether you would have several kinds of refreshment and where the best prices were available? Or did you just delegate it to someone with the directions, "Get the Brewski"?)

9. What kinds of organizational models do different reform proposals presume? Is there a relationship between who sponsors a reform proposal, what organizational model they presume is operating, and a perceptual encasement due to a relationship of domination?

10. What is the relationship between different organizational models and the nature of the consensus needed to run an organization? Do you think there may be a relationship between the model people prefer and their willingness to take other peoples' concerns into consideration?

CONTROLLING
the SCHOOL:
INSTITUTIONALIZATION

Chapter 9

...The idea of unlimited ... growth, more and more until everyone is saturated with wealth, needs to be seriously questioned on at least two counts: the availability of basic resources ... and the capacity of the environment to cope with the degree of interference implied.

—E. F. Schumacher[1]

PREVIEW

In the last chapter we learned that different implementation models of the school located power at different sites in the organizational structure. In this chapter, we look more closely at authority, control, and policy. Depending upon our expectations for the school, they relate to power in very different ways. Next we consider whether a technical notion of production jibes with the realities of teaching practice. How much like a well-run factory is the school?

We noted earlier that schooling is not education. This precept is crucially important in understanding a major development in American schooling: **institutionalization**. Institutionalization occurs when concern in an organization shifts from efficiency to formality. Seen from one point of view, institutionalization is an attempt to reconstruct the Temple, a moral community, from the Factory. From another point of view, institutionalization is the sacrifice of productive activities to political pressures.

INTRODUCTION

A large school district in the Eastern United States spends $20 million dollars a year auditing $3 million in discretionary funds given to principals.[2] The public scandal of misuse of funds by a principal some years back makes top school officials feel particularly vulnerable on the issue. Although we can understand the desire for school officials to be above reproach, does it make sense to spend $17 million a year to guard against the rather remote possibility that a principal will embezzle petty cash?

In this case the reality is that the city council, which controls school district funding, resists budget requests with the argument that school finances are not administered well. With budget requests for the district approaching a billion dollars, their criticisms excite a wide audience. Here are power and control unrecognized by the Temple image of the school! So the audit money is spent, although a standard audit is not a cost-effective means of control. Its virtue is its impartiality and its public relations value. In deference to the

---

[1]E. F. Schumacher, *Small is Beautiful: Economics as if People Mattered* (New York: Harper & Row, 1975), p. 30.
[2]From private conversations with an auditor who wishes to remain anonymous—E.G.R.

Town Meeting, the resources of the Factory are sacrificed to maintain the purity of the Temple.

AUTHORITY

In the previous chapter our models of the school varied depending upon whether we considered *expectations* or *implementation*. Within those dimensions we considered how power is distributed in the school organization. We will return to the expectation models in this chapter to show that authority, control, and policy vary depending upon the image of the school. We will see that for the Temple, authority derives primarily from *tradition*. For the Factory, authority derives from *knowledge of causes*. For the Town Meeting, authority is based on *power*. Controlling the school is a substantially different process, depending upon the image of the school that is considered.

Discipline and Authority

In the 19th Annual Gallup Poll of the Public's Attitudes Toward the Public Schools, the greatest problem believed to be facing community schools, after drug abuse, was lack of discipline.[3] Perhaps this is so. But we should take care to distinguish two important and different concepts of discipline: the discipline of cause[4] and the discipline of form. They differ according to the reasons that are given for a command:

- **the discipline of cause**: Do it this way! Why? Because it **works**.
- **the discipline of form**: Do it this way! Why? Because it's **right.**

Children have little trouble understanding the discipline of cause. They will happily go along with it if there is something they want to learn how to do. When adults complain about discipline, it's generally the discipline of form that is at issue.

The discipline of form and ideas of deference and esteem are bound together. There is an intimate connection between authority and what many people perceive as an important part of discipline: showing deference to particular people. When adults worry about discipline in the schools, they worry whether their children will come to esteem those things they, as adults, esteem.

It is important for us to realize that the role of the teacher is different in each of these two cases. For the discipline of cause, the teacher is a guide or a coach. For the discipline of form, he or she is a socializer, a molder of character. The discipline of form clearly is a concern of the Temple; the

---

[3]The 19th Annual Gallup Poll of the Public's Attitudes Toward the Public Schools, p. 28.
[4]Cf. John Dewey, *Democracy and Education* (New York: Macmillan, 1916), Chap. 10, "Interest and Discipline," pp. 124–138.

Is this an exercise of authority?

discipline of cause, a primary concern of the Factory. Conceptions of authority and control will vary with these images.

Let's look at the relation of power and authority and examine what the sources of authority are for the different image of the school. These have an important bearing on the "problem" of discipline.

Authority and Power

> The ability to exercise power may, of course, be a necessary condition for the exercise of authority. It may also be a ground of entitlement as in the old saying, "no legitimacy without power." But a necessary condition for the exercise of authority or a ground of entitlement to it should not be confused with what "authority" means.
>
> —————— *Benn and Peters*[5]

Power rests on *resources* and the influence they confer; authority rests on *consensus*;[6] ultimately, upon assent. To have power is to be able to act despite lack of consensus. To have authority is to be conceded a decision-making role.

---

[5]S.I. Benn and R.S. Peters, *The Principles of Political Thought: Social Foundations of the Democratic State* (New York: Free Press, 1965), p. 22.

[6]Cf. Paul Hersey and Kenneth H. Blanchard, *Management of Organizational Behavior* (Englewood Cliffs, N.J.: Prentice Hall, 1988), pp. 214–218. Hersey and Blanchard call authority "legitimate power" and dispense with the contrast between power and authority. But to call power "legitimate" is to beg some very important questions.

It is common to muddle these distinctions, but the maxim, "Might does not make right" expresses ancient yet accurate wisdom. In our terms this translates to "Power does not confer authority."

Tyrants presume that might makes right. But power, by itself, does not confer authority, although it may inspire fear. A gun in your hand gives you power. It may frighten others into conceding you a decision-making role: they obey when you say, "Hands up!" But your "authority" such as it is has no moral status. Its sole support is physical force and will disappear with your gun. However, if you hold the gun long enough, people may adapt traditions that legitimize your authority so that it is recognized even when the gun is no longer visible.

The other side of the story is that recognized authority may have little power. Educators are often given authority with no power: they are assigned a decision-making role but are not provided with the resources to accomplish the job. Authority alone does not suffice to get the job done.

Tradition and Uncertainty

Authority may be conceded to elders, teachers, or policemen, for example, as a result of our having been socialized at both the formal and informal levels of culture to showing deference. Authority is acknowledged through displays of deference. These traditions of displaying deference are a primary basis for authority.

Who are our authorities? Those people we habitually show deference to whether that habit of deference has its beginnings in custom or fear. One source of the "discipline problem" mentioned earlier may be that students are not acculturated into the forms of deference behavior that certain people in the school expect of them.

Granted that we can be socialized at both the formal and informal levels of culture in deference behavior toward certain people. But ought we to show them that deference? This question pushes for a rational basis to support the authority of the Temple. It dismisses the consensus that forms a moral community. This question also estranges us from that community, making it an object of investigation rather than a forum of participation. It leads us from the Temple to philosophy.

Some theorists suggest that where traditions of deference are weak, authority ultimately derives from **mystery**. Mystery supports command. Military historian John Keegan comments:

> Orders derive much of their force from the aura of mystery, more
> or less strong, with which the successful commander, more or less
> deliberately, surrounds himself; the purpose of such mystification
> is to heighten the uncertainty which ought to attach to the con-
> sequences of disobeying him. The taskmaster who eschews mys-
> tification, who makes himself, his behavior and his responses fa-
> miliar to his subordinates, must then evoke compliance either by

love or by fear. But love and fear . . . are ultimately self-limiting in effect.[7]

In the language of organization theory, mystery is called "uncertainty." Slogans that incorporate unanalyzed concepts such as "the pursuit of Truth," "improving American competitiveness," and "strengthening democracy" call up ideas that are mysteries to the great majority of those who concede them authority. So it is that the most materialistic philosophies invoke uncertainty in much the same manner as the most otherworldly religions. What distinguishes them are their approaches to consensus. We will look more carefully at this elsewhere. It is enough now to note that those things that allay our most basic uncertainties we concede to be (or are acculturated to accept as) our basic authorities. If someone can manipulate these uncertainties, their power over us is substantial.

Now, uncertainty (or "mystery") is not merely a psychological reaction by people who feel uncertain about something. We are all uncertain about the existence of plant life in other galaxies, but we do not feel any compulsion to concede authority to someone on that basis. What seems to be necessary for us to concede deference, is the possibility that we will suffer some sanction. This possibility tends to create an exaggerated perception of its likelihood.[8] What we fear, we believe more likely to happen. So we are disposed to treat with deference anyone we think has the power to control such sanctions. We hedge against a potential evil by controlling our own behavior instead of trying to control the threat.

Some cross-cultural research indicates that avoidance of uncertainty correlates directly with "power distance," the readiness to concede authority to persons with power.[9] People who need to know in detail "who can boss who" are most likely to accept something "because the boss said so." This finding supports the connection we are making here between uncertainty and authority.

An "authority," therefore, may be someone toward whom we show esteem on the chance that some possible threat will be averted. If students are neither socialized to show deference behavior, for example, "good manners," nor fearful of sanctions, or if they believe the teacher not to have the power of sanction, how can we expect them to show the discipline of form? "Discipline problems" may be no more—and no less—than an indication of cultural pluralism. And if schools pursue or support cultural pluralism, they may well have to look for bases of authority other than tradition or the mysteries of rank.[10]

---

[7]Keegan, op. cit., pp. 315–316.

[8]Cf. Daniel Kahneman and Amos Tversky, "Judgment Under Uncertainty: Heuristics and Biases," in Daniel Kahneman, Paul Slovic, and Amos Tversky (eds.), *Judgment Under Uncertainty: Heuristics and Biases* (Cambridge: Cambridge University Press, 1982), pp. 3–20.

[9]Geert Hofstede, "Motivation, Leadership and Organization: Do American Theories Apply Abroad," *Organizational Dynamics,* Summer 1980, pp. 42–63, cited in Nancy J. Adler, *International Dimensions of Organizational Behavior* (Boston: Kent, 1986).

[10]Cf. Edward G. Rozycki, "Values, Rationality and Pluralism: A Plea for Intolerance," *Philosophy of Education 1979,* Proceedings of the Thirty-fifth Annual Meeting of the Philosophy of Education Society (Champaign, Ill.: McKee, 1980), pp. 195–204.

Knowledge and Charisma

There are other bases of authority. They are knowledge and charisma. Once the basic goals are set, authority in the Factory is the authority of knowledge. To recognize someone as possessing knowledge is to concede authority to those who can produce. This tends to disperse authority (and often, power) throughout the organization. The distinction between authority and power is again underscored.

Why is it that in our pluralistic society, authority is conceded to the most charismatic among us? Celebrities of all kinds regale us with answers to deep questions. Charisma relies upon individual ability to psychologically manipulate other people, not actually upon tradition or implied threat of sanction—although it may invoke both tradition and threat to create a mood.

We should realize that the authority of knowledge may conflict with the authority of tradition or charisma. No small part of the sex education controversy is that a technical approach to sex is considered by many parents to be a threat to the esteem they wish their children to demonstrate for certain systems of belief and attitude. Knowledge threatens to "demystify" certain traditional authorities, undercutting the esteem thought to be their due. Remember, what Adam ate was the fruit of the tree of the **knowledge** of good and evil.

Discussion of knowledge and charisma brings us to a consideration of the main source of political authority. It is **power**—that is, control of resources, including such resources as charisma, skill at intimidation, or persuasion, together with the uncertainty about its focus. Power is not authority, but it can generate authority by compelling a practical consensus about patterns of deference. However, such coerced political authority may be criticized as immoral or illegal.

We should again consider an important point: power derives from resources, but authority depends upon consensus on the concession of esteem and the decision-making roles that go with it. Powerholders of all kinds want us to ignore the distinction between power and authority. But there are two important consequences if we muddle the difference:

- If we treat power as conferring authority in and of itself, we undermine our ability to criticize power as illegitimate; teachers could not, for example, legitimately resist racist school boards.
- If we treat authority as a kind of power, we undermine our ability to criticize delegations of authority as empty gestures, failing to provide resources. Being appointed a teacher would be sufficient to raise student test scores.

Both religion and philosophy can provide a basis for the concession of authority. These invoke traditions of esteem or acculturations of deference behavior that can generate authority in the Town Meeting. (The Declaration of Independence, for example, invokes "unalienable Rights"—a mysterious concept—as a basis for political authority.)

Control

> While most people will agree that there is much overlap between skill and luck, a full understanding of how inextricably bound the two are has yet to be attained. In principle the distinction seems clear. In skill situations there is a causal link between behavior and outcome. Thus, success in skill is controllable. Luck, on the other hand, is a fortuitous happening. Success in luck or chance activities is apparently uncontrollable. (Is) this distinction generally recognized (?). (I)t is not. While people may pay lip service to the concept of chance, they behave as though chance events are subject to control.
>
> —————— *Ellen J. Langer, "The Illusion of Control"*[11]

In many books, including this one, you will find charts such as the one in Figure 9.1. They indicate the formal structure of an organization.[12] What do they mean? Figure 9.1 depicts a chart of formal control. It starts at the top and flows down. Such charts are generally used to indicate lines of authority. They are generally constructed as an administrative aid. As a result, they tend to muddle the distinction between power and authority in order to persuade compliance from lower levels. We can avoid this confusion of power and authority if we interpret such charts to be defining **lines of authority**. In this one, for example, the governor's authority is derived from the state consti-

[11]Ellen J. Langer, "The Illusion of Control," in Daniel Kahneman, Paul Slovic, and Amos Tversky (eds.), *Judgment Under Uncertainty: Heuristics and Biases* (Cambridge: Cambridge U. Press, 1982), p. 231.
[12]Cf. Jacob W. Getzels, James M. Lipham, and Roald F. Campbell, *Educational Administration as a Social Process: Theory, Research, Practice* (New York: Harper & Row, 1968); Wayne K. Hoy and Cecil G. Miskel, *Educational Administration* (New York: Random House, 1982).

Figure 9.1

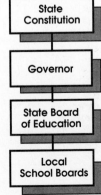

tution. The authority of the state board of education derives from the governor, and so forth.

Informal Control

Many organizational theorists distinguish formal from informal control.[13] Formal control is official authority. **Informal control is power to influence, in an unofficial way, what gets done.** If we were to indicate on the chart of formal control how influence really flows, our chart might look like that of Figure 9.2. Note that influence flows in two directions, as the arrows show. Even the state constitution can be influenced through the legislature (not shown on this chart) from lower sources. Newberg and DeLone comment on control in a large school system:

> Neither the board nor the top administrators of a large school district have ability to control what happens in other layers of the system. They may shift marginally some allocations of resources; they may block some thing from happening; they may set instructional standards, revise curriculum, or launch teacher training programs. But with the possible exception of improving the quality of professional staff appointed to key positions . . . , their support and official actions, while often necessary to instructional change, are not sufficient. The normal processes of policy making, planning and management do not constitute a strategy for instructional changes in a loosely coupled bureaucratic system owned by the employees. The system adapts to such processes—but it is not changed by them.[14]

---

[13]For classic examples of this distinction see Chester I. Barnard, *The Functions of the Executive* (Cambridge: Harvard U. Press, 1938), and Charles E. Lindblom, "The Science of 'Muddling Through,'" *Public Administration Review*, Vol. 19 (Spring 1959), pp. 79–88.

[14]Norman Newberg and Richard H. DeLone, "Bureaucracy as the Milieu for Educational Change," *Education and Urban Society*, Vol. 13, No. 4 (August 1981), p. 44.

Figure 9.2

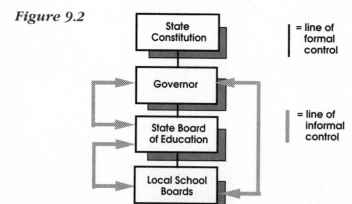

Different Modes of Control

The nature of control depends upon the school image under consideration. For the Temple, control is **command**. For the Factory, control is **cause**. For the Town Meeting, it is **rationale**.

These distinctions have a very practical import. Principals and teachers are often judged as good or bad depending upon whether they have things "under control." Is the school under control? If so, we have a good principal. Is the class under control? If so, a good teacher! The reality, however, may have less to do with being a good principal or a good teacher than with having good luck. If you have no causal control over events so that all you can do is issue commands and hope, or rationalize after the fact, then you are indeed a hostage to fortune.

Control as Command

In the beginning was the Word ... (St. John 1,1)

Only in the most egalitarian groups does the leadership help implement commands. Every organization tends to be a Temple with respect to the way its leadership controls: leaders command and the mystery of command gives the spoken word the appearance of cause. The distinction between command and implementation mirrors the distinction between authority and power. That a divide between the two is possible is caught by the saying, "If you want something done right, do it yourself."

When we look at formal control charts it is important that we understand what they do **not** indicate. Nothing put into a state constitution guarantees that a governor will behave in a certain way. No directive from the governor guarantees specific behavior from a member of a state board of education. And so on down the line. Neither the written nor the spoken word is a cause in and of itself. It must be supported by an intricate social organization.

Many of us tend to overestimate the power of command. All events in an organization, we convince ourselves, are commandable, thus controllable. So it is that the expectation develops that if there is a social problem, say, drug abuse, school authorities need only command an appropriate curriculum and the problem is addressed, if not already on its way to solution.

Control as Cause

In the factory, control is cause. If you can't produce results, you don't have control. March and Olsen point out that there is no causal justification for supervision (which they call "attention structures") if front-line decisions are necessary to keep things working.

Control: command, cause.

As a result, we would expect symbolic, educational and traditional factors to rise in relative importance ... The definition of attention structures under conditions of ambiguity will be somewhat more attentive to discovering and communicating meaning, and somewhat less to decision efficiency.[15]

In other words, ambiguous school goals and the technical expertise of teachers make supervision less causal and more ceremonial. This circumstance ties into the "discipline problem" in the following way: if school goals are ambiguous then what is demanded of students is the discipline of form, rather than the discipline of cause. Are students learning? becomes less important than Are students behaving? Consequently, supervision shifts its focus from teaching technique to class control.

Administrative control and technical control are distinct and not infrequently in conflict. In highly politicized societies such as China during the Cultural Revolution or Kampuchea under Pol Pot's Khmer Rouge technical control was sacrificed for uniformity in political command. The technological, economic, and educational consequences were devastating. But these are only extreme examples of the commonplace trade-off between what is thought to be socially or morally desirable and what is technically possible. To recall an example from Chapter 2, think of how highly we could motivate students if

---

[15]March and Olsen, op. cit., p. 43.

each school had a torture chamber and a brothel! But only if the ends justified any means.

Below we will examine the extent to which the school is a Factory to see whether control in the school is a matter of knowledge of causes.

Control as Rationale

We often try to understand people's behavior as determined by "socialization," or "culture" or "community norms." In a similar vein, organization theorists talk of "premise setting," by which they mean socialization within an organization to a way of thinking that prevents serious challenge to that organization. Charles Perrow comments:

> (Organization theorists do not) . . . measure the more powerful and subtle form of control found in premise setting. . . . We are content to speak of socialization, or culture, or community norms, thus making it both sanitary and somehow independent of the organization. But we could just as well label premise setting as indoctrination, brainwashing, manipulation or false consciousness.[16]

Control in the political arena is accomplished through **premise setting** that provides **rationales.** Rationales are narrative patterns that structure what people accept as reasons for acting. The informal culture of the organization works to restrict the very possibilities of reasoning by inculcating rules about what may and may not be brought up for discussion. For example, in many schools, particularly those without standard pay scales, discussion of salaries is taboo. Not only is such discussion frowned upon, but any attempts to determine how people are remunerated may be criticized as "unprofessional." This practice, of course, benefits some at the expense of others.

Wasting others' time is one of the ritual displays of superior rank in our culture. But it is rationalized as a display of good will. For example, premise setting prevents criticism of superiors who use meeting time to ramble on about personal interests. For example, if a peer were to preface a report by talking about his vacation or his hobbies, most people would complain that he was wasting their time. Doesn't he realize they have better things to do? But if the boss does the same thing, he or she is merely "being one of the guys." By mere display, powerholders within an organization come to define for their inferiors what acceptable powerholder behavior is. It takes a courageous person to invoke other authorities to bring them to task. In many organizations, "whistleblowers" lose their jobs.

If competition within an organization is not to escalate into a costly conflict, the use of power has to be rationalized so that all parties can appear to have been fairly treated. Premise setting helps remove many of the bases of criticism so that there are socially acceptable explanations available to support any change. So, we may be told, people who have "higher level" jobs deserve

---

[16]Perrow, op. cit., p. 152.

more pay because, even though they may appear to work less, they "bear more responsibility." Symbolic benefits are stressed where substantial ones are not well distributed.

Premises of action are part of the informal culture of groups. Premise setting is generally done indirectly. No one stands up and declares, "These are the premises from which we will reason in this organization!" First of all, to do so would be to invite inspection, even criticism of the premises. What happens is that premises are developed through a tradition of rationales.

Rationales are stories, explanations that are accepted because they give insight, save face, are backed up by power, and so forth, and become part of a network of precedents upon which organizational decision is justified. Rationales may be causal explanations that have predictive power. Or they may be after-the-fact rationalizations that give an appearance of intelligence to what was in fact a haphazard, garbage can decision process. Corporate researchers Deal and Kennedy comment,

> People tell stories to gain power and influence—and because they enjoy doing it. Storytellers are in a powerful position because they can change reality. Storytellers simply interpret what goes on in the company—but to suit their own perceptions. And what is power anyway but the ability to influence people's perceptions—without their realizing it, of course.... The tales that storytellers tell, like myths in a tribal setting, explain and give meaning to the workaday world.[17]

In Chapter 19 we will examine in detail the mechanism of premise setting using rationales. We will find that the structure of rationales is remarkably universal. Indeed, the fact that the procedures developed in this book can be used among people who recognize even the conflicting authorities mentioned in Chapter 3, from science to religion to tarot cards, is an indication of the broad consensus that exists on what rational action is.

We should understand that constructing rationales is not manipulating causes. Very few participants in the Town Meeting may have causal power for any length of time. But everyone needs to understand their behavior as reasonable within that context: they do what they have to in order to make the best of the situation. This is their rationale and the extent of their control.

People provide rationales in even the most exploitative situations. Teams of professional swindlers usually have a member whose function it is to "cool the mark out," that is, convince the victims that it is in their best interests to not make a fuss.[18] In schools, too, a similar kind of rationalization occurs. Teachers want students to obey. So they ask them to "cooperate." But co-

---

[17]See Terrence E. Deal and Allen A. Kennedy, *Corporate Cultures: The Rites and Rituals of Corporate Life* (Reading, Mass.: Addison-Wesley, 1982), p. 87.

[18]Cf. Erving Goffman, "On Cooling the Mark Out: Some Aspects of Adaptation to Failure," *Psychiatry: Journal for the Study of Interpersonal Processes*, Vol. 15, No. 4 (November 1952), pp. 451–463.

operation, unlike obedience, presumes common goals that the students may in fact not have with their teachers.[19]

Policy

> Policy manuals: Don't bother. If they're general, they're useless. If they're specific, they're how-to manuals—expensive to prepare and revise. . . . The only people who read policy manuals are goldbricks and martinets. The goldbricks memorize them so they can say (1) "That's not in this department," or (2) "It's against company policy." The martinets use policy manuals to confine, frustrate, punish and eventually drive out of the organization every imaginative, creative, adventuresome woman and man.
>
> —— *Robert Townsend,* Up the Organization[20]

Here is a true story. In a large urban school district, the principal of a high school called together his best, most creative teachers to develop new ideas and programs for the next year's reorganization of the high school. Formerly admitting only tenth through twelfth graders, the school would now accept ninth graders. The present high dropout rate was a problem and there was great concern among the staff that the new students find the school an interesting place to come and to stay in until graduation. After many months of extra effort a series of proposals were presented. Every single item was rejected. They were "against school district policy."

Policy is often thought to be a set of general rules of operation for an organization. It is distinguished from procedures in that it addresses more directly the goals publicly espoused by members of the organization. Recall from Chapter 2 the characterization by Elmore and McLaughlin of policy as abstract, often not useful for solving concrete problems, and in conflict with practice. Policies are usually slogans. A formal control chart indicating lines of downward authority from goals through policies to procedures is illustrated in Figure 9.3.

The Functions of Policy

What are policies for? Why not jump from goals to procedures? If we recall some of the basic internal conflicts of a complex organization, we can begin to understand how policy functions. Remember that organizations tend to have conflicts of the following sort:

---

[19]Sharing a common goal is a criterion offered by a variety of authorities, e.g., *The Compact Edition of The Oxford English Dictionary* (New York: Oxford U. Press, 1971), p. 963. Also, Caroline Hodges Persell, *Understanding Society* (New York: Harper & Row, 1987), p. 67. This criterion of common goal is omitted in the school dictionary, *Thorndike Barnhart Junior Dictionary*, 7th ed. (New York: Scott-Foresman, 1968), p. 139.

[20]Robert Townsend, *Up the Organization* (New York: Fawcett, 1971), p. 129.

Figure 9.3

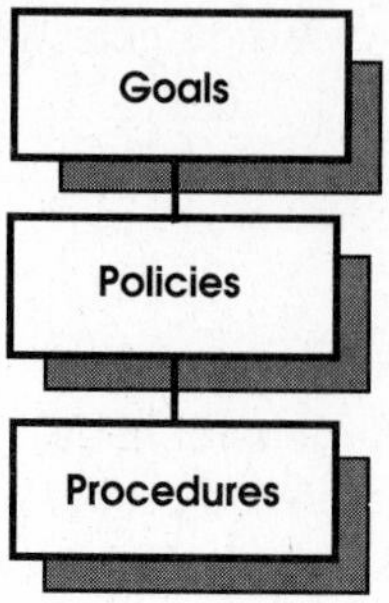

1. following policy vs. sensitivity to client need,
2. delegating authority vs. pursuing authorized goals,
3. process focus vs. product focus of activities, and
4. power vs. morale.

Policy addresses itself to these conflicts in the following way:

- It restricts the discretion of members of the organization.
- It sets priorities among conflicting goals and procedures.
- It emphasizes and defines the flow of authority.
- It depersonalizes organizational discipline.

We can expect policy to decrease organizational sensitivity, suppress the pursuit of unauthorized goals, be process-oriented, and emphasize power over morale. These may seem like heavy costs, but policy has its benefits also. Let's look at some of these.

The Costs and Benefits of Policy

Depending upon a person's situation in an organization, policy has different costs and benefits. If we distinguish between the powerholders of the organization, the implementers, and others, we realize that benefits for one group do not necessarily mean benefits for the others.

The benefit for powerholders is that policy restricts negotiation. They can dismiss pleas for special consideration by saying, "that's against policy" without having to be responsible for a personal decision. Policy also tends to reinforce their position as powerholders while obscuring the realities of that power. Policy is, after all, made by powerholders, even if it is afterward treated as though it were divinely inspired and written in stone.

But policy can be used by implementers and lowers against powerholders. Policy reduces uncertainty by stating publicly commitments to which powerholders may be held accountable. It also reduces the scope within which powerholders can exercise favoritism. Policies may be supported by lowers as a sign of fairness.

For implementers the benefits of policy are that commitments are made clear, priorities are set, and the scope of personal decision is restricted. They, too, can refuse a request on the grounds that it is against policy, rather than having it be seen as a personal denial. But policy has its costs, too. It reduces their independence and the scope of their professional decision.

For lowers, the benefits of policy have already been mentioned: reduction of uncertainty and the promotion of fairness. Its costs are that it obscures the relations of power that determine who is a powerholder, an implementer or a lower. In particular, it obscures the why of these arrangements.

The benefits of policy to one group may be costs to others. The costs of policy to one group may be benefits to others. Figure 9.4 indicates this dichotomy. Note again how what are benefits for one group may be costs for another.

Figure 9.4

	THE COSTS AND BENEFITS OF POLICY		
Groups / Effects	**Powerholders**	**Implementers**	**Lowers and Others**
Benefits — **Restricts Discretion**	restricts negotiation	states commitments / restricts negotiation	reduces favoritism / states commitments
Restricts Discretion — Costs	states commitments	reduces independence / reduces scope of technical decision	reduces independence
Benefits — **Sets Priorities**	further restricts negotiation	settles some conflicts	clarifies choices
Sets Priorities — Costs	makes more commitments	reduces discretion further	reduces sensitivity
Benefits — **Defines Authority**	enhances position / reduces goal displacement	reduces uncertainty	reduces uncertainty
Defines Authority — Costs	reduces uncertainty	reduces discretion further	restricts access
Benefits — **Depersonalizes Discipline**	obscures interests / hides power relationships	obscures interests / promotes fairness	promotes fairness
Depersonalizes Discipline — Costs	impedes intervention	reduces special appeals	reduces special appeals

Ritual, Program, and Treaty

The power of policy over spoken command rests on an ancient magic. The written word seems more substantial, more constant, more real. Linguistic scholar Karl-Heinz Osterloh comments:

> In developing societies ... what is written is ... associated with absolute truth. Since both context and the form of texts are in principle solemn, holy, and incontestable, it follows that language learning becomes very difficult when it comes to analyzing a text and testing its validity. In order to do so a student will have to go through a series of new social experiences. He has to learn that in Western civilization something written is something man-made, and that everything written is to be seen as an individual presentation or personal opinion which can be contested.[21]

An examination of the costs and benefits of policy indicates that policy is a device for dealing with conflict. To the extent that we can distinguish policy from the morality of the Temple or the efficiency of the Factory, policy, after power, becomes the primary basis of judgment in the Town Meeting. Thus, in a pluralistic society, morality and efficiency will generally be subordinated to political policy. This is precisely what happens as organizations become institutionalized! But more on this below.

We should expect that the nature of policy, like the sources of authority and the nature of control, depends upon the image of the school under consideration. In the Temple, where authority is not under challenge, a policy serves primarily a symbolic, **ritual** function. It celebrates traditions of command and deference.[22] Within the Temple, policy is treated as Scripture and may elicit commentary and exegesis, but not a critical review of its basic assumptions.

In the Factory, policy is a **program**—much like a computer program—that sets the basic goals and allays conflicts among them. Recalling Elmore's systems management and bureaucratic models we can see how this notion of policy is supposed to work. These models also gives us insight into why public interest focuses on policy debate rather than concerns with implementation. People tend to believe that policy change suffices to get things done. To use Kenwyn Smith's terms, this belief shows that they are "encased" in the image of school as Temple or Factory.

Finally, in the Town Meeting, policy functions like a **treaty**. It sets up structures of authority and provides a focus for the negotiation of conflict among groups. Policy provides the rationale in terms of which different DUs

---

[21]Karl-Heinz Osterloh, "Intercultural Differences and Communicative Approaches to Foreign Language Teaching in the Third World," *Studies in Second Language Acquisition*, Vol. 3, No. 1 (Indiana University, Fall 1980), p. 65.

[22]Jeffrey Pfeffer, "Management as Symbolic Action: The Creation and Maintainance of Organizational Paradigms," *Research in Organizational Behavior*, Vol. 35 (JAI Press, 1981), pp. 1–52.

Figure 9.5   **AUTHORITY, CONTROL, AND POLICY**

	Temple	Factory	Arena
Source of Authority	Tradition, uncertainty	Knowledge	Power, uncertainty
Control	Command	Cause	Rationale
Policy	Ritual	Program	Treaty

in the school settle their conflicts. This process not only interprets "what is there" but actually recreates policy, transforming it from the vague and problematic to something more specific and useful. The ebb and flow of this political process of policy making is described by Lindblom:

> Policy is not made once and for all; it is made and remade endlessly. Policy-making is a process of successive approximation to some desired objectives in which what is desired itself continues to change under reconsideration.... A wise policy-maker consequently expects that his policies will achieve only part of what he hopes and at the same time will produce unanticipated consequences he would have preferred to avoid.[23]

Figure 9.5 summarizes the relationships between the images of the school and sources of authority, control, and policy.

In the next section we will examine the extent to which the teacher functions in a school as a technician in a Factory. The previous figure gives us the basic elements of authority, control and policy in the Factory model. We will see to what extent they are to be found in actual school practice.

THE TEACHER AS TECHNICIAN

As organizations become institutionalized, political considerations come to dominate decision making rather than those of morality or efficiency. Science, however, can resist politics because although Nature may be ignored, it cannot be negotiated with. To the extent that schools perform needed technical functions, to that extent they can resist political pressure. But are schools very much like factories? Or is that more metaphor than substance? Let's consider the extent to which teachers perform as technicians. Perhaps that will give us an indication of the school's political vulnerability.

To get certification, teachers have to take professional education courses. Goodlad writes that many teachers feel, however, that their training in pedagogy left much to be desired. They complain that it didn't prepare them to

---

[23]Charles E. Lindblom, op. cit., pp. 79–88.

function in their actual schools.[24] How do you cause learning in students, given the realities of the schooling situation?

It is hard to deny that teachers in some circumstances **cause** students to learn. On the other hand, that causation is difficult to control and when it doesn't occur, explanations abound to rationalize the failure. (We will see in Chapter 18 that the relationship between teaching and learning and the place of causation in it are problematic.) What we have to examine is a technical conception of teaching. This will give us a standard of comparison to judge the extent to which schools have been institutionalized.

Formality and Efficiency

> "... the only measure of the efficiency of a cooperative system is its capacity to survive."
>
> ———————— Chester I. Barnard, The Functions of the Executive[25]

Under the Factory image of the school, teachers are expected to be technicians. Their goal as technicians is to maximize student achievement as efficiently as possible. School instructional policies embodied in a curriculum provide a program to direct daily teaching.

Every experienced teacher knows activities that bring students to learn and knows that some are more efficient than others. What is involved in this notion of efficiency?

Levin suggests the following criteria of efficiency that might be suited to a technical conception of teaching:[26]

- Knowledge of the technical production process
- Substantial manager control over the input mix
- A basically competitive environment
- Managerial knowledge of input and output prices
- The goal of maximizing output (not necessarily just profits)
- Clear signals of success or failure (profits, losses, market shares, etc.)

Let's look at each of these conditions to see to what extent they can be met in a normal school environment.

Knowledge of the Technical Production Process.   This criterion is what methods courses try to encompass. Many teachers are superb technicians and get results with all kinds of children. Unfortunately, it is difficult to say ex-

---

[24]See Goodlad, op. cit., pp. 183–186.
[25]Barnard, op. cit., p. 44.
[26]Henry D. Levin, "Concepts of Economic Efficiency and Educational Production," in J. Froomkin, D. Jamison, and R. Radner (eds.), *Education as an Industry* (Cambridge, Mass.: Ballinger, 1976).

plicitly just what it is they do—the very reason why many educators believe teaching is more an art than a science.[27] Unfortunately, pedagogical knowledge is still greatly a part of the informal culture of teaching. Many of the causal factors in pedagogy await discovery. It is difficult to generalize from one successful classroom the circumstances that led to its particular success. Also, the application of research results is often constrained by political and moral concerns. This limitation tends to make people believe that good pedagogy is a mysterious matter, and to exaggerate charisma.[28] In the popular media, good teachers are evangelists, magicians, or entertainers.

Substantial Manager Control over the Input Mix.   If we take this criterion to mean that the teacher or principal controls **who** will be taught, the reality in schools is that such control is minimal. Public schools must take whoever applies. What the teacher can do, if resources permit it, is to control student groupings within the classroom. This seems to be an important factor in school success,[29] but it is far from the ability to reject students who promise little success.

A Basically Competitive Environment.   This criterion requires that incentives exist for experimentation to find efficient means of production. Outcomes should not be indifferent to technique. This is the point of proposals to provide educational vouchers so parents can select schools they believe are more effective. There are two problems with this. First, schools, even private schools, for reasons we will see below, avoid such competition. Second, and even more basic, it is not clear what would count as more efficient technique. Is a technique more efficient if it brings a few students to higher achievement, or if it brings more students up to a lower common standard? Which outcomes should take precedence in a school, divisible or indivisible ones, or absolute or positional ones? (Recall Chapter 1.) At whose cost should someone else's achievement be gained?

Managerial Knowledge of Input and Output Prices.   To attain this criterion necessitates some standard method of gauging costs and benefits so that a teacher could decide among different techniques on the basis of those costs and benefits. Not only does such a standard method not exist, but both law and tradition militate against this practice in the school. For example, "teaching to the middle" is a practice teachers engage in because it shows greatest gain for a given amount of effort. But special education laws and moral considerations often direct teachers to expend effort on students whose achievement will cost many times that of a normal student—measured in teacher hours. This speaks to the next criterion of efficiency.

---

[27]Cf. H. Dawe, "Teaching: A Performing Art," *Phi Delta Kappan*, Vol. 66, No. 3, pp. 548–552.
[28]Cf. Edward G. Rozycki, "Review of *Teaching with Charisma* by Lloyd Duck," *Educational Studies*, Vol. 13, No. 1 (Spring 1982), pp. 70–73.
[29]Cf. Barr and Dreeben, Chap. 4, "Social Organization of Classroom Instruction," pp. 69–104.

The Goal of Maximizing Output.   This condition is not a priority in schools. Both moral and legal restraints prevent its realization—not to mention a lack of consensus on what would count as a measure of input and output. Teaching efficiency, for example, is constrained by considerations of morality and status. Let's look more closely at this.

Consider our previously mentioned examples of motivational devices of ancient though ill repute: the torture chamber and the brothel. No one doubts that certain kinds of behavior could be motivated by the use of torture or the promise of sex. No doubt standard learning outcomes could be enhanced through these means. Why are they not used? Many people would find them morally objectionable, particularly if children were involved.

Teachers are careful not to single out or group students by race, sex, SES, or other characteristics possibly pertinent to school achievement. (See Chapter 5.) Although such grouping might increase the efficiency of instruction, other outcomes are feared, such as stereotyping. In fact, there are legal barriers to grouping students on the basis of these characteristics.

Not only means, but also ends come under moral restriction. Who would teach any of the following in an American public school: cheating at cards, safecracking, mugging, or begging? Why are the following highly useful things—economically speaking—not taught in the public schools? For example, slaughtering pigs, fixing toilets, or handicapping horse races? Why not the following pastimes: mumblety-peg, tree-climbing, half-ball, or solitaire? Some of these are thought to be inappropriate to the school, out of place because of their status as crude, low class, or trivial. We will see elsewhere that to include something in the school curriculum is to make a public declaration as to its morality and status.

Clear Signals of Success or Failure.   For the reasons mentioned above, there are no such signals that enjoy wide acceptance. Good grades or bad grades, for example, are only a sign of success or failure if you trust the process that generates them. The fact is that the majority of parents trust this process, to judge from Gallup Poll results.[30] We can begin to understand why parents, for one group, prefer the Temple image of the school. The Factory image does not seem to jibe with the considerations that actually underlie schooling practice. The common complaint that students are insufficiently interested in their studies identifies an important factor, motivation, to be beyond the control of the classroom teacher. The quote from Langer at the beginning of the chapter indicates that people tend to treat chance events as controllable. But it might instead be that events controllable only in ways forbidden by tradition or ethics may be treated as chance events.

Lecture is the most common teaching technique. When students fail to learn, we seldom look to see if the lecture technique can be replaced by something else. Rather, we look to SES, culture, race, and parenting to account for the failure. These are beyond our control! We can use the concept of the

---

[30] 19th Annual Gallup Poll of the Public's Attitudes Toward the Public Schools, p. 17.

socioeducational system as an excuse, as well as a tool. The Temple permits command; when this fails, otherwise controllable factors are relegated to chance.

It would seem that despite all the talk of schooling processes as technical parts of the image of the Factory, the realities are quite different. The conditions for the technical control of the pedagogical process are routinely impeded in the school. In the next section we will see to what extent a technical approach to some common school problems is permissible.

Technical Problems: Ritual Solutions

What is the answer to the problem of increasing schooling efficiency? Would it suffice to train teachers to a higher level of technical adeptness? There are, after all, numerous complaints that American students aren't learning what they should. For example, American students don't know as much math as do Japanese students.[31] They don't know where the Seine is.[32] They don't know who Herbert Hoover is.[33] They read with difficulty[34] and can't write a coherent paragraph.[35] They can't function in a second language. They have little if any conception of science.[36]

Such complaints overlook an important fact. Even though specific knowledge in specific subjects may be highly esteemed, it is just a small part of the outcomes of the schooling process.[37] Just training teachers to be educational technicians will not be enough. When we look at the wide range of outcomes expected of the schools including who benefits from them and who pays the costs, we begin to understand why learning technology takes a back seat. Let's consider a few examples that will indicate the degree to which schools have been institutionalized.

Evaluating with Grades

Evaluation is indispensable to the factory. But are school grades anything like a technical evaluation system? Does the fact that grades are used to motivate

---

[31]Cf. Robert Rothman "Mathematics Scores Show U.S. Is a 'Nation of Underachievers,' " *Education Week*, January 21, 1987, p. 1. Also, see David Brand et al., "The New Whiz Kids," *Time*, August 11, 1987, pp. 42–50.

[32]Cf. Alvin P. Sanoff et al., "What Americans Should Know," *U.S. News and World Report*, September 28, 1987, pp. 86–94. But see, Robert Rothman, "Teachers Dispute Studies' Counsel on Humanities. 'Fact Based' Courses Unwise, They Contend," *Education Week*, September 16, 1987, p. 1.

[33]Robert Rothman, "Students' Knowledge of History, Literature 'Shameful,' National Assessment Indicates, *Education Week*, September 9, 1987, p. 1.

[34]Cf. Kathleen Starr and Bertram C. Bruce, "Reading Comprehension: More Emphasis Needed," *ASCD Curriculum Update* (Washington, D.C.: Association for Supervision and Curriculum Development, March 1983), p. 1.

[35]But see Robert Rothman, "U.S. Pupils Fare Well in Study of Writing Skills. Positive Results are Called 'a Big Shock,' " *Education Week*, September 23, 1987, p. 1.

[36]Cf. Robert Rothman, "Groups Foster 'Hands On' Approach to Science in Early Grades," *Education Week*, September 17, 1986, p. 10.

[37]Cf. Lynn Olson, "Saying Reforms Fail Most Pupils, Shanker Argues for a 'New Type' of Teaching Unit," *Education Week*, April 6, 1988, p. 1.

students as well as evaluate them undercut their use as a technical measure of achievement?

You can grade apples, beefsteaks, and turkeys. You can also, for example, grade the turkey farm by the quality of the turkey it produces. Then why is there a problem with grading students? Meyer and Rowan comment:

> Schools use elaborate tests to evaluate pupils and to shape the course of their present and future lives. But the same data are almost never used to evaluate the performance of teachers, schools or school systems.[38]

Why does the situation described by Meyer and Rowan exist? Teachers will say, with some justification, that it is not fair to evaluate them on the basis of student achievement because they have no control over whom they get as students or over what happens to students outside of school. This is true, yet children are evaluated, sorted, and their lives are affected by the grades teachers give them.

In fact, teachers do give students a break by taking into consideration their prior level of knowledge and whether they have made an effort. Many teachers make allowances. But Goodlad suggest that such "individualization" creates an inequality of educational opportunity![39] Note that this criticism is precisely parallel to charging a principal with inconsistency if he or she takes individual differences into account. (See Chapter 2.) It is another conflict between the Temple and the Factory.

---

[38]John Meyer and Brian Rowan, "The Structure of Educational Organizations" in Victor Baldridge and Terrence Deal (eds.), *The Dynamics of Organizational Change in Education* (Berkeley, Calif.: McCutchan, 1983), pp. 60–87.
[39]Cf. Goodlad, op. cit., pp. 132–138.

Whom do these grades grade?

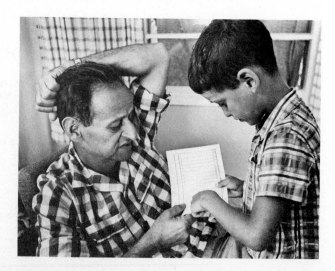

Why not give exams a year after a course is taken?[40] Why not judge the mathematics achievement of a nation by testing 35-year-olds rather than high school kids? This would certainly place the emphasis on retained and presumably useful knowledge. Why not put an expiration date on diplomas and require their renewal by test? Again, these suggestions overlook the fact that knowledge is only one of many outcomes of the schooling process. Even though knowledge is accorded high esteem, there are other outcomes for which a broader consensus establishes greater importance. There is more to schooling than technical process.

Special Programs: Who Is Not Normal?

Another way of evaluating a technical process is to see how inputs are measured and compared with outputs. Lacking clear standards at either end of the process undercuts whatever technical expertise is brought to bear on it.

What do we generally find in the schools? To begin, there is no broad consensus on what a typical student is supposed to know. What math skills should a typical ninth grader have? What knowledge of history, science, and languages? There are proposals, often in the form of curriculum documents, that teachers follow in their classrooms. But there is, of course, almost always a discrepancy between the various conceptions of what kids should know and what in fact they do know. And these are the "normal" kids.

What then are we to make of special populations? By various criteria they are judged to need special treatment to help them overcome an impediment to achievement. But achievement with respect to what? What normal students are supposed to learn? Or what normal students do in fact learn? And which population of normal students? Teachers of special students are often pressured to prepare them for the mainstream.[41] But what exactly is the "mainstream"?

Public School Textbooks

Another hallmark of a technical process is instrumentation. Devices of production have to function in reliably consistent ways. One "device" normally found in schools is the textbook. Are textbooks produced and treated like the productive machinery of a factory? Let's see.

Textbook costs represent about one percent of the public school budget,[42] about $1000 per teacher per year. Yet complaints about the quality of texts

---

[40]Cf. Grant Wiggins, "11 Suggestions for Reform That are Radical—But Shouldn't Be" (Providence, R.I.: Coalition of Essential Schools, Brown University, 1988).

[41]Cf. Jack W. Birch, *Mainstreaming: Educable Mentally Retarded Children in Regular Classes*, University of Minnesota Leadership Training Institute/Special Education. Undated monograph. Available from The Council for Exceptional Children, 1920 Association Drive, Reston, Va. 22091.

[42]"Textbooks," *Covering the Education Beat* (Washington, D.C.: Education Writers Association, 1987), pp. 97–99.

used in public schools abound.[43] This would seem to be a relatively easy matter to resolve. Why should it be a matter of controversy? If we assume that textbooks are tools to aid learning, we can set up a simple test: have some students use them, others not, and see if there is any difference in what is learned.

But the issue does not even get to the test. Parents complain when their children don't have books. They would complain particularly loudly if they found out it was for the sake of an experiment. Students expect to get books no matter how poor somebody thinks they are, and teachers rely on some kind of text to support their efforts in the classroom.

Publishers complain that their best efforts are thwarted by technically untrained, often politically motivated textbook review committees who accept and reject books on widely disparate criteria. The same book may be criticized by one group as "soft on Communism" and by another as "soft on apartheid," depending on the political commitments of the reviewers. In such circumstances, book selection becomes less a technical and more a political decision.

It may be that these anomalies are a matter of expecting a Factory model of the school always to be pertinent. This expectation may well be wrong. The dominant images of the school seem by far to be the Temple and the Town Meeting. In the next section we analyze this interpretation more closely. Because their constituencies are so broad, schools have traded off certain productive functions for an institutional stability that ensures their continued funding in a highly pluralistic society.

It is disputable whether teaching does or should uniformly and universally aim at production. There is a great deal of ritual in schooling.[44] There are many rituals of participation for which it is extremely difficult to identify divisible benefits, skills, knowledge, and so forth, as outcomes. Pledging allegiance to the flag, singing the school song, and attending the Thanksgiving Day football game are examples of these. In a sense, such rituals may produce for the group that practices them indivisible benefits, for example, a feeling of community.

This is important. A practice may be ritual with respect to divisible benefits but causal with respect to indivisible benefits (or vice versa). That is, school assemblies may cause no particular individual benefits, but produce benefits for the school as a whole. Or a specific student may learn in a disorderly, stressful school environment just as easily as in a calm, well-managed one. School assemblies might have the effect of reducing disorder in classrooms. Individual grades might not be affected but the indivisible benefit of participating in an orderly classroom might. On the other hand, individual students may be affected negatively by rituals of participation that have only a mythical benefit for the institution, for example, forced competitions, or mass detentions.

---

[43]Cf. Harriet Tyson-Bernstein, *Improving the Quality of Textbooks* (Secaucus, N.J.: Matsushita Foundation, 1987). Also, see Michael W. Apple "The Political Economy of Text Publishing," *Educational Theory*, Vol. 34, No. 4 (Fall 1984), pp. 307–319.

[44]James G. March, *How We Talk and How We Act: Administrative Theory and Administrative Life*, Seventh David D. Henry Lecture (Urbana-Champaign: University of Illinois, 1980).

INSTITUTIONALIZATION

> To speak of practices or procedures that are continued and transmitted without question, to speak of meanings that become typified and transmitted to newcomers in the organization and shared without thought or evaluation, is to speak of the process of institutionalization.
>
> ——————*Jeffrey Pfeffer*[45]

Institutionalization theory helps us understand why bigger is not necessarily better. Often, the reverse is true. Institutionalization occurs when concern in an organization shifts from production to formality. It explains why the technical criteria of production we looked at above are not applicable. Size and political control are two factors that organizational theorists suggest affect productivity.

Many American school systems are big. And they are dependent upon local resources. They cannot allow themselves to look too bad to local taxpayers. Thus they tend to emphasize (quietly) the production of substantial benefits, such as child care. But it is the symbolic benefits of learning that they celebrate. These are seldom thoroughly and consistently evaluated.[46]

The separation of certain learning from the processes of evaluation and control produces a situation called **loose coupling**.[47] Parts in a loosely coupled system work independently of each other. When teachers close the classroom door, for example, it's generally as if they have stepped onto a desert island.[48] What will matter for public purposes is what grades they give, not what they do in the classroom, so long as it doesn't attract critical attention.

As organizations become institutionalized, they tend to become more loosely coupled for activities whose outcomes cannot be highly controlled. They cannot afford to be judged on haphazard outcomes.

Schools engage in some activities because they look right, or are traditional, or are required by law. These activities may actually interfere with the learning processes of the classroom. Surprise fire drills are a good example. At the very least, these activities use up resources that might otherwise support the teaching mission. How much knowledge of mathematics or French does a football team cost? Meyer and Rowan put it succinctly:

[45]Jeffrey Pfeffer, *Organizations and Organization Theory* (Boston: Pitman, 1982), p. 239.

[46]John W. Meyer and Brian Rowan, "Institutionalized Organizations: Formal Structure as Myth and Ceremony," *American Journal of Sociology*, Vol. 83, No. 2, p. 341.

[47]Karl Weick, "Educational Organizations as Loosely Coupled Systems," *Administrative Science Quarterly*, Vol. 23 (December 1978), pp. 541–552. Also see Arthur Wise, "Why Educational Policies Often Fail: The Hyperrationalization Hypothesis," *Journal of Curriculum Studies*, Vol. 9, No. 1 (1977), pp. 43–57, and Edward F. Pajak, "Schools as Loosely Coupled Organizations," *Educational Forum*, Vol. 44 (November 1979), pp. 83–95. But, see Frank W. Lutz, "Tightening up Loose Coupling in Organizations of Higher Education," *Administrative Science Quarterly*, Vol. 27 (1982), pp. 653–669.

[48]Goodlad, op. cit., pp. 186–188.

> ... the formal structures of many organizations ... dramatically reflect the myths of their institutional environments instead of the demands of their work activities.[49]

That is, schools are structured according to expectations of a broad community rather than according to teacher and administrator concerns for the implementation of learning-oriented policies.

Principals and teachers who get their school's name in the newspapers for musical or artistic productions, for sports or community service, or for having the mayor speak in the assembly, are better thought of than those who merely take average children and make them slightly better than average readers and writers. The symbolic learning goals of the school are not hot news. School people and parents appreciate them. Others tend not too. For example, the Gallup Poll indicates that parents tend to think more highly of public schools than does the general public.[50] This may be less a matter of lack of information than of interest.

Zero-based budgeting and "sunset-laws," which require justification of every budget item, represent attempts to counteract institutionalization in organizations. Without them, most school items are budgeted this year because they were budgeted last year. Assessed from one point of view, institutionalization represents the triumph of form over function, of ritual over reality, of symbol over substance. It is, in this view, a tragedy.

But from another perspective, institutionalization represents the ascendency of wider social goals over narrow instrumentalist interests, the transformation of administration into statesmanship, a developing sensitivity to moral concerns that tempers a compulsive need for efficiency. Institutionalization happens to the degree that the Factory transforms itself into the Temple. This is a desirable, almost heroic transformation. In the celebratory words of a famous organizational theorist:

> ... the executive becomes a statesman as he makes the transition
> from administrative management to institutional leadership.[51]

The most alarming part of institutionalization theory is that it claims that certification interests, the gaining of grades and diplomas, takes precedence over educational interests of all kinds.[52] It is not the content of what children learn that matters, but that they get a grade for a class. If this interpretation is true, then institutionalization goes a long way to explaining the lack of student interest in subject matter.

---

[49]Meyer and Rowan, "Institutionalized Organizations: Formal Structure as Myth and Ceremony," p. 341.

[50]Alec M. Gallup and David I. Clark, The 19th Annual Gallup Poll of the Public's Attitudes Toward the Public Schools, *Phi Delta Kappan*, September 1987, pp. 17–30.

[51]Philip Selznick, *Leadership in Administration: A Sociological Interpretation* (Evanston, Ill.: Row, Peterson, 1957), p. 4, sees institutionalization as primarily a positive development in which narrow organizational goals and competitiveness yield to wider social goals and cooperation among organizations.

[52]Cf. Randall Collins, *The Credential Society* (N.Y.: Academic Press, 1979.)

Products of Schooling: Substantial and Symbolic

> An institutional leader ... is primarily an expert in the promotion and protection of values.
>
> _____ *Philip Selznick*[53]

We can approach institutionalization theory from another angle. Let's recall the distinction introduced in Chapter 4 between symbolic and substantial benefits. That distinction rested on the notion of consensus. If something is recognized **across many communities** as a benefit (or a cost), it is a **substantial** benefit (or a substantial cost). Gold is a paradigm (perfect example) of substantiality. If, on the other hand, something is recognized as a benefit (or a cost) only **within a community** (or narrow range of communities), it is a **symbolic** benefit or cost. A certificate of award is a paradigm of a symbolic benefit. Recall also that substantial benefits tend to be regarded as means within a community, whereas symbolic benefits are regarded as ends.

If we now consider the various outcomes of the schooling process, we can rank them as primarily symbolic or primarily substantial. When we speak of outcomes of the schooling process, most people tend immediately to think of such things as diplomas, knowledge, skills, tastes, varsity letters, attitudes, and so forth. These are the **celebrated** outcomes: they're announced, written up in the newspapers, discussed in public, and worried about in reform reports.

Schooling aids in socialization and people who study a little about schools readily recognize it as an outcome, as they also do with child care. But unless you're an economist, you probably overlook employment and consumption as outcomes of the schooling process also. Schooling provides employment and consumes materials. These uncelebrated outcomes are very important to school employees and to the many, many businesses that provide supplies and services to schools.[54] Socialization, child care, employment, and consumption are not normally celebrated. Too pedestrian, they are seen only as means to greater ends. But, it turns out, they are of vital importance to understanding the organizational dynamics of schooling.

In Figure 9.6 we see schooling process outcomes charted in terms of their being symbolic or substantial. Whether, for example, specific tastes, attitudes, and knowledge are benefits depends very much upon which community we focus on. Such outcomes tend to be valued intrinsically as ends—as what it means to be educated. At the other extreme, the fact that schools provide child care and employment and consume goods produced by a wider society is recognized as benefits across many kinds of communities. Yet few people see them as anything more than means to other more important ends.

---

[53]Selznick, op. cit., p. 28.
[54]Cf. William Montague, "Contractors See Lucrative Market for School Services," *Education Week*, October 21, 1987, p. 1.

Figure 9.6

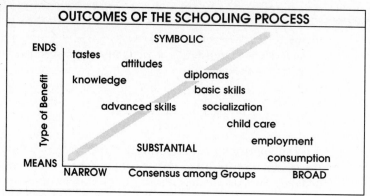

The celebrated benefits of schooling are the most symbolic. It's important to realize though that public declarations about the importance of tastes, attitudes and knowledge are almost invariably made in slogans; specifics are avoided. When was the last time that anyone praised a school because its students had an extensive knowledge of any of the following?

- the poems of Robert Frost;
- the theory of functions;
- distinctions among annelidae;
- the writings of Charles Dickens

There exist communities where such knowledge in its specificity is highly prized. But they are small.

Grades and diplomas represent knowledge, we would think. But everyone knows that grades are highly variable in what they represent. Consequently, so are diplomas. These function more as passports to other more substantial benefits than as guarantees of educational achievement. Grades and diplomas are more the symbols of a rite of passage than they are the outcomes of a measurement procedure. The existence of such things as the College Board exams attests to the extent to which schools have been institutionalized.

Symbolic or substantial benefits?

Teachers' employment or school funding is a more substantial benefit than are student grades. To use grades to evaluate a teacher or school system threatens benefits in a way that would probably not withstand legal challenge. In addition, the teachers' organizations involved here tend to be politically powerful. Trying to avoid local political influence by developing national assessment procedures might help in evaluating teachers and school systems, but it might also be deemed as taking decision-making authority away from local government.

Organizational Environments

The specific symbolic academic values celebrated in the school do not enjoy a sufficiently widespread consensus to keep the river of money that nourishes the schools flowing from year to year. So schools come to closely control and subtly emphasize those things that appeal to the broadest general public. Have you seen the following slogans?

- If you think education is expensive, try ignorance.
- Education for Democracy
- Open your mind.
- Open your life.
- We prepare today's professionals to meet tomorrow's challenges.
- Can management education solve ethical problems?
- Education for Leadership
- Celebrate your originality!

They also try to decouple from any procedure that might reveal the academic mission to be a failure. Thus, grades stand in for, rather than stand for, achievement. Diplomas, rather than learning, become the benefit pursued. Schools become credentialing agencies. Education comes to be understood by what Meyer and Rowan call the schooling rule:

- **The schooling rule**: Education is a certified teacher teaching a standardized curricular topic to a registered student in an accredited school.[55]

Notice that learning outcomes are not mentioned at all. The schooling rule is compatible with both the Temple and Town Meeting images of the school. Like any model of schooling it has its costs and benefits. We will be examining them throughout this book and determining whether other models of schooling might preserve the benefits of the schooling rule while providing something more explicit in the way of production.

There is another concern. Because of its size schooling creates what is

---

[55]Meyer and Rowan, op. cit., p. 73.

called a "turbulent environment."[56] What happens in the schools affects the situations that other institutions have to deal with and plan for.[57] Consider, for example, how a heavy snowfall affects a city. Administrators who have to deal with snow days find themselves in a dilemma. If they make the kids come to school, they will contribute to the traffic jams and bring about a certain level of sickness from exposure to the elements. But if they close the schools, they create an immense child-care problem. Many parents won't make it into work, children will be left alone in the house, and so forth.

It is important to emphasize that the schools are **not** unproductive in some absolute sense. The situation is that they do not consistently produce the benefits, mostly symbolic, that they celebrate, for example, academic knowledge. (For a flowchart representation of an institutionalized organization and an example of an institutionalized school, see the Technical Appendix to Chapter 9.) They do produce other benefits. The child care, alone, provided by the school is a real bargain (see Chapter 1). But this is not the kind of benefit that attracts the resources for schooling activities that pursue the visions of our greatest educators: the School as the instrument of Enlightenment and Liberation, the firmest foundation of our democratic society.

Faith vs. Evaluation

Loosely coupled organizations replace evaluation with faith. Rowan and Meyer comment:

> Organizations whose structures (reflect) the myths of the institutional environment—in contrast with those primarily structured by the demands of technical production and exchange—decrease internal coordination and control in order to maintain legitimacy. In place of coordination, inspection and evaluation, a logic of confidence and good faith is employed.[58]

In productive organizations tightly coupled to a market, policy making relies heavily on knowledge gathering. In loosely coupled organizations, efficiency is not a measure of administrative effectiveness; compliance with policy is the primary concern.

Members of tightly coupled organizations can use organizational resources for their own purpose only to the extent that efficiency is not affected, for example, you can make "free" duplicate copies only if duplication doesn't "get out of hand." Members of highly institutionalized organizations like schools, however, can make a variety of claims for resources; a predominant one in

---

[56]F.E. Emery and E.L. Trist, "The Causal Texture of Organizational Environments," *Human Relations*, Vol. 18, No. 1 (February 1965), pp. 21–32.
[57]Dennis A. Connors and Donald B. Reed, "The Turbulent Field of Public School Administration," *The Executive Review*, Vol. 3, No. 4 (Institute for School Executives, The University of Iowa, January 1983).
[58]Meyer and Rowan, "Institutionalized Organizations: Formal Structure as Myth and Ceremony," p. 340.

schools is equity. Educational programs are funded not because they are proven to produce mathematical or other skills in certain groups of students, but because they are fair, or their funding is required by law.

Compliance with policy rather than evaluation of results is the institutional form of accountability. Little evaluation information gets used internally. For example, educational innovations are adopted not because they are found to work, but because they have been adopted by "good schools."[59] If, by reading Plato in your seventh-grade classes, you get your school name into the newspapers, you might expect that the "Plato curriculum" will become an item of conversation—for a while at least—in the popular media. E.D. Hirsch's "Cultural Literacy" proposal is an example of this phenomenon.

Let's recall the four situations we considered above, actual school practices of grading, special programs, exit tests, and textbooks. We will compare them with correlative technical processes of a productive organization, a factory. Also, we will compare them with the procedures that would be followed in an institutionalized organization. (See Table 9.1.) When we compare actual

---

[59]See Zucker; also summarized in Pfeffer, pp. 246–250. See also Karl Weick, "Educational Organizations as Loosely Coupled Systems," *Administrative Science Quarterly*, Vol. 23 (December 1978), pp. 541–552. Also, Arthur Wise, "Why Educational Policies Often Fail: The Hyperrationalization Hypothesis," *Journal of Curriculum Studies*, Vol. 9, No. 1 (1977), pp. 43–57. Both are reprinted in J. Victor Baldridge and Terrence Deal (eds.), *The Dynamics of Organizational Change* (Berkeley, Calif.: McCutchan, 1983).

Table 9.1

ACTUAL SCHOOL PRACTICE	FACTORY	INSTITUTION
grades, diplomas Rite of passage. No clear requirement. Renewal not necessary.	Guarantees of competence. Can become outdated. Need refreshing.	An honor. An award. A tradition. A first step. A ceremony. A sign of ambition.
program goals No clear goals. Need to justify special placement. Fear of legal action.	Learning outcomes are identified. Tasks are found which cause them. Adequate resources found.	We're expected to have this program. We've always had it. To drop it would disappoint.
textbooks Textbooks are criticized as bad. They are used anyway.	Test to see if kids learn better with or without texts. Make decision to retain texts on that basis.	Good schools use textbooks. They allow us to control what the kids are doing. The publishers give rebates.

school practices with the technical processes of the Factory and the moral-political processes of the Institution, it is quite clear that the school is highly institutionalized. The most technically adept teachers and administrators will not prevail against a system whose very foundations undercut the technological enterprise. If we are really serious about increasing learning across the board for all students careful attention must be paid to restructuring the schools.

SUMMARY

1.   Power rests on resources; authority, on consensus. The sources of authority and the nature of control and policy vary with the organizational model of the school under consideration. Consequently, there will be ambiguity in such concepts as discipline, effectiveness, and reform.

2.   Concerns for production do not dominate in school situations. A variety of circumstances discourage the teacher from developing a technical orientation. Neither grading, program criteria, nor textbooks are treated in technically efficient ways.

3.   The predicament that the school as Temple participates importantly in the Town Meeting, a turbulent environment, provides the conditions for the development of institutionalization. Institutionalization is seen by many as a reduction in concerns about production and an increase in politics. Others, however, understand institutionalization as the reconstruction of a moral community.

4.   Schooling benefits and costs can be divided into those that are substantial and those that are symbolic. Symbolic benefits of schooling seem to be the celebrated ones. Their production tends to be uncertain because of the technical interference of institutionalization. Institutionalization emphasizes the production of noncelebrated, substantial outcomes. The evaluation of symbolic outcomes is replaced with faith in the adequacy of the schooling rule: Education is a certified teacher teaching a standardized curricular topic to a registered student in an accredited school.

QUESTIONS

1.   As learning becomes formalized, more emphasis is placed on the discipline of form and less on the discipline of cause. For example, consider the difference between "picking up" a skill on a musical instrument as opposed to being instructed in it in school. Can you list some activities that have formal and informal counterparts? Do they, too, emphasize form over cause as they become formalized?

2. Make a two-by-two chart. The columns should be headed "Much Power" and "Little Power." The rows should be named "Much Authority" and "Little Authority." Into the four identified categories enter different school-related jobs, according to whether persons in that role have the authority and power to do what is generally expected of them.

3. Mystery begins where inquiry is commanded to stop. What kinds of questions are you dissuaded from asking in different social situations? For example, what would be considered unseemly or prying for you to ask
   a. the president of the United States
   b. your parents
   c. your religious leader
   d. your roommate
   e. your professor?
   How does this "boundary of impropriety" define the social relationships involved?

4. What kinds of uncertainty do fashion designers control? For whom? What kinds do teachers control?

5. People with specific knowledge or direct control of resources tend to exercise informal control in organizations. Can you cite some examples, for example, head secretaries, janitors?

6. What kind of control, command, cause, or rationale does a teacher have
   a. over the behavior of students in the classroom?
   b. over reports and plans he or she must submit?
   c. over the implementation of the curriculum?

7. A teacher puts a list of classroom rules on the board. What premises are set by this action? A student may violate the rules without violating the premises. Explain how.

8. Name a school policy you are acquainted with. What are its costs and benefits? For whom? Does this policy tend to reinforce a structure of powerholders, implementers, and lowers?

9. Review the different conceptions of education presented in Chapter 1 for their symbolic and substantial content.

10. Use institutionalization theory to:
    a. explain why teachers' and administrators' salaries tend to be based on seniority and degrees attained, rather than subject taught and skill at teaching or administering.
    b. predict the probable outcomes of some presently topical curriculum proposal, for example, substance abuse education, sex education, critical thinking criteria.

The Historical Foundations of Education

> If education is considered apart from the historic causes upon which its shape depends it becomes incomprehensible.
>
> — *Emile Durkheim*

All of our plans and actions are based on our memories and assessments of the past. Every one of us, even young children, make our choices with this consideration in mind. Most have a perspective of months or years. But the wise among us take a much longer perspective. They realize that they represent just one of more than 50,000 generations of thinking and feeling human beings who have peopled this planet.

Many of the trivialities that pass for thought about schools are fatally flawed because they lack this historic dimension. The recent spate of reform literature provides far too many examples. Devoid of any real sense of what preceded them, many of these reports are distinguished by an extraordinary historical ignorance that betrays their essential superficiality.

The primary purpose of this section is to encourage the student to increase the length of the past that they see as relevant. This is particularly useful in developing a fuller appreciation of that fundamental distinction between education and schooling which we make throughout the text. It also encourages a far more sophisticated appreciation of what is possible and/or desirable with respect to both education and schooling.

A HISTORY of EDUCATION: THE EARLY YEARS

Chapter 10

PREVIEW

In this chapter on the history of education we emphasize the long perspective, inviting readers to extend their vision back to the dawn of humankind. By exploring the education of early humans and ancient civilizations we develop a truer sense of where we have been, what we can plan for, and even what we might hope for. In short, we gain the historical imagination necessary for meaningful insights regarding education and schooling.

Education and Schooling

We begin our account of the educational past in prehistory. Attempts to examine the education of humankind which fail to take this prehistoric period into account ignore about 99.85 percent of the human experience. And in so doing they create the false impression that schooling has always been a part of the educational experience. It has not.

EARLY HUMANS

The search for our ancestors takes us back at least 4 million years, to the age of *Australopithecus afarensis* (Southern ape of Africa), the oldest hominid fossils yet recovered. ("Hominid" refers to the family of man.) These distant "faint whispers of humanity" walked upright, but they had a primitive brain structure and only one-third of our cranial capacity. Because of the structure of their brain and voicebox they were incapable of articulate speech. They must have operated at a near instinctual level.

Their biological characteristics placed severe limitations on Australopithecus' ability to develop culture or to pass on learning to their offspring. For this reason both socialization and education were comparatively unimportant to their survival. Instinct was a central feature of their behavior.[1]

Homo habilis (Man the handy), the earliest known member of our own genus, appeared on the scene approximately two million years ago. Their cranial capacity was double that of Australopithecus, though still half of ours.[2] Their more sophisticated brain structure enabled them to control fire, fashion stone tools, and, most important of all, to accumulate discoveries over multiple generations.[3] This ability placed a great premium on socialization and education. All of their ever-increasing store of skills and primitive technology had to be passed on to their youngsters if they were not to be lost.

---

[1]Kenneth F. Weaver, "The Search for Our Ancestors," *National Geographic*, Vol. 168, No. 5 (November 1985), p. 588.
[2]Anastasia Toufexis, "Lucy Gets a Younger Sister," *Time,* June 1, 1987, p. 63.
[3]John J. Putnam, "The Search for Modern Humans," *National Geographic*, Vol. 174, No. 4 (October 1988), p. 452.

Figure 10.1   **HUMAN EVOLUTION**

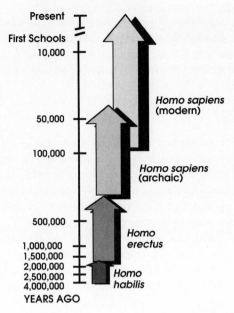

This process was facilitated by the brain structure of *Homo habilis*, which contained the so-called Broca's area—the brain region essential to speech.[4] Its presence made possible *Homo habilis'* most crucial cultural invention, the development of spoken language for simple communication.[5] They were not able to utter the full range of sounds that modern humans can. They did not have full command of articulate speech.[6] Nevertheless, this new process vastly increased their capacity to adapt to new and changing conditions through learning. Of course, it also greatly increased the importance of education.[7]

Homo erectus, or "upright man," dates back at least 1.6 million years. This species of hominid had an average brain size about 75 percent of that of modern humans. With this larger brain, *Homo erectus* was capable of controlling fire, cooking food, and making sophisticated stone tools and weapons. He or she was also capable of intellectual curiosity, and may have developed more advanced speech.

Having much greater capability for learning to exploit the environment than *Homo habilis*, *Homo erectus* moved far beyond the original biological niche in the earth's ecosystem that early humans had occupied. Indeed, they

---

[4]Weaver, op. cit., p. 600.
[5]Richard Leakey, op. cit., p. 127.
[6]Weaver, op. cit., p. 600.
[7]Nancy Tanner, *On Becoming Human* (New York: Cambridge U. Press, 1981), p. 265.

were the first humans to leave the African cradle of humanity to roam the earth in search of new resources and experiences.[8]

Homo erectus was very dependent on culture, the system of shared meanings, language, customs, values, ideas, and material goods that are common to a way of life. Thus, any failure to teach their culture's contents to their offspring threatened their very survival. It was in this way that education became of central concern.

Homo Sapiens

The archaic version of the first modern humans, *Homo sapiens*, first appeared approximately 300,000 years ago. Their name (*Homo sapiens* or Man the thinker) denotes their most distinctive characteristic—the ability to wonder and reason. Their brain size and structure were essentially what ours are today. Specialized biology also enabled *Homo sapiens* to produce the great variety of distinct sounds necessary for speech as we know it.[9]

Not only were the archaic *Homo sapiens* anatomically like us, they also shared our curiosity, creativity, and talent for learning.[10] Their culture was complex when compared to *Homo erectus*. Social bonds were also strong, and altruism and social conscience seem to have been common.[11]

More and More to Learn

The story of humankind is essentially the story of culture gradually becoming more elaborate. As *Homo sapiens* advanced, for example, hunting and gathering gave way to pastoral or horticultural societies. This development reflected the growth in sophistication of their technical culture. Their formal culture also gained sophistication, as these early humans sought to give greater meaning to their suffering, striving, and yearning through religion. Their informal culture also grew more complex, and posture, tone of voice, and proximics gained more and more subtle meanings. (See Chapter 5 for a description of formal, informal, and technical culture.)

This growing cultural sophistication made education even more essential while simultaneously making it more complex. Unlike *Homo habilus*, who had been very dependent on instinct, *Homo sapiens* had become totally dependent on culture. Thus, each new generation had to be taught a complex way of life that had been painstakingly constructed by the doings and sufferings of preceding generations.

The Total Absence of Schools

Despite the ever-growing importance of education, however, there were, as yet, no schools. Example, emulation and informal instruction were still suffi-

---

[8]Weaver, op. cit., pp. 608–610.
[9]Bernard Campbell, "The Roots of Language," *Biological and Social Factors in Psycholinguistics*, John Morton, ed. (Urbana, Ill.: U. of Illinois Press, 1970), p. 6.
[10]Putnam, op. cit., p. 440.
[11]Weaver, op. cit., p. 615.

cient. Neither formal nor technical culture was complex enough to require schooling.

We know then that for nearly 4 million years schools played **no** role in human affairs. This consideration is inevitably humbling for any educator. Yet we must accept it if we are to develop a sense of where schools fit in the human scheme of things. Put in its simplest terms, schools are **not** inevitable. They are an outgrowth of broader social developments, which we depict below.

Socialization, Education, and the Family

We learned in Chapter 5 that early societies were organized in small, nomadic units based on the family and dependent on hunting and gathering for their survival. There was little social status except that based on sex, age, or kinship, and the means of subsistence were distributed relatively evenly. Specialization was uncommon and wealth did not accumulate. Technological resources were very limited and communications elemental.

In such hunting and gathering cultures children learned much of what they needed to know by accident—simply by being around. This socialization was supplemented by a deliberate but informal educational process that was the principal responsibility of the family. By "family" is meant a social organization in which members communicate with one another in terms of their roles as mother, father, husband, wife, grandfather, grandmother, daughter, son, brother, or sister.

The slow maturation of human infants provided plenty of time for the child to learn the technologies and skills of that day—fire making, tool making, animal skinning, hunting, and the like—through simple imitation and im-promptu demonstrations. Children learned the prevailing norms, values, beliefs, and behaviors of the clan or tribe in like manner. Of course, other adult members of the clan or tribe played a role in this process of socialization and education. Indeed, from what we know of present-day hunting and gathering societies, it is highly likely that unrelated adults took a greater interest in other people's children than they do today.

This family-based pattern of socialization and education would utterly dominate the socialization and education of ordinary people until well into the nineteenth century. Indeed, despite compulsory school attendance laws, research evidence (summarized in Chapter 6) suggests that the family is still the principal socializer and educator of the young.

EDUCATION IN EARLY CIVILIZATIONS

Throughout the vast bulk of human development the family was the fundamental, indeed, very nearly the only, social unit. It functioned as a system of governance, a defense organization, a court system, a factory, a church, and a school. Nothing had been surrendered to the state, the Church, or industry.[12] Not even one of these existed.

Some six thousand years ago, in the fourth millennium B.C. (4000–3000 B.C.), changes in the technical level of society resulted in the development of agriculture. This, in turn, led to the formation of very complex societies with central governments, formalized religion, and, eventually, schools, all of which augmented the functions of the family.

The most significant of these agricultural civilizations was that of the Sumerians in Mesopotamia,[13] the Egyptians in the valley of the Nile, and the Chinese in the valley of the Hwang Ho. Here we find the formation of the first cities, and a rush of technical developments. Cloth was woven, the wheel and the sail were invented, pottery making was perfected, and metal was first extracted from ore.

Writing, one of the most crucial technical level cultural developments, evolved in both Sumer and Egypt around 3500 B.C. The development of this treasury of symbols which could be multiplied to infinity, assured the retention of acquired ideas, and facilitated their communication. It also established new educational needs that set the stage for the creation of schools.

Meanwhile, at the formal level of culture, myth and ritual became more complex and more formalized as human beings sought to give new meaning to life and death. The shamans and prophets of simpler cultures, whose deities were personal and whose authority came out of psychological experience, gave way to priests, whose gods were historic and whose authority was conveyed by formal training and social ordination.[14] This process was also crucial to the development of the first schools.

Status groups reflecting occupational specializations evolved simultaneously with the culture of agricultural civilizations. A new occupationally based power elite, most of them priests, replaced leadership based on age and kinship. Concentrations of wealth and power also increased as critical resources began to be monopolized by this class. Only their children were served by the first schools.

In all of these ancient civilizations some of the traditional roles of the family were augmented by the state and related formal institutions like government, organized religion and schools. These formal institutions were altogether different from their informal predecessors. Formalized government offered public works, defense against aggression, and systematically adjudicated interpersonal disputes. Formalized religion offered elaborate temples, complex rituals, and authoritative dogma. Formalized education, schooling, taught complex technical skills like reading and writing, established greater social control over key members of the society, and confirmed the superior status of the elite. (**Social control** refers to the patterned and systematic ways in which mem-

---

[12]Francis and Joseph Gies, *Marriage and the Family in the Middle Ages* (New York: Harper & Row, 1987).
[13]Mesopotamia is in present-day Iraq, in the lowlands between the Tigris and Euphrates rivers. "Mesopotamia" literally means "between the rivers."
[14]Campbell, op. cit., pp. 100–101.

bers of a society are guided and restrained so that they act in predictable and desired ways.)[15]

Sumer

Ancient Sumer developed in the fertile area between the Tigris and Euphrates Rivers. An elaborate system of irrigation, developed in the period 5000 to 4000 B.C., resulted in an agricultural revolution that led to the gradual merger of a network of villages into the world's first great civilization.

Because, in an agricultural society, wealth accumulated as it never had before, tremendous social advantage could be passed from one generation to the next.[16] This process encouraged the development of dynasties. Empires also evolved as military conquest became more and more rewarding. Planting and harvesting were regulated by lunar calendars constructed by the priestly class, and mastery of this technical invention facilitated their control over agricultural production. This, in turn, led to vast increases in their wealth and power. Eventually, they claimed universal authority over the culture, completely dominating the other classes. Beneath them were artisans and merchants, and far beneath them were thousands upon thousands of peasants and slaves.[17] Social and political life centered more and more on the palace and the temples.

Eventually, all aspects of life came to be controlled by a single Priest/King. He alone interpreted the will of the Gods and enjoyed supreme authority. Below him ranked thirty categories of lesser priests who enforced the Priest/King's edicts and supervised the affairs of government. And with the advent of empire, government had become a major undertaking, requiring the services of thousands of skilled people.[18]

Writing

Writing, a critically important development of Sumerian technical culture, made the governance of the empire possible. It facilitated the keeping of detailed records of ownership, the development of written communications carried over vast distances, the codification of laws, and similar conventions that we now take for granted.

Although writing's origin is not completely clear, the Sumerians were among the first to fully develop the art of recording ideas by means of characters or figures. By approximately 3500 B.C. they had developed 2000 pictographic signs that they recorded on clay tablets. Five centuries later this complicated and unwieldy system had been replaced by the use of wedge-shaped cuneiform writing that substituted phonetic for ideographic values.

[15]Caroline Percell, *Understanding Society: An Introduction to Sociology* (New York: Harper & Row, 1987), p. 169.
[16]Ibid., pp. 50–51.
[17]J. Kelly Sowards, *Western Civilization to 1660* (New York: St. Martin's, 1964), pp. 22–23.
[18]Marvin Harris, *Cannibals and Kings: The Origins of Culture* (New York: Vintage, 1977).

The First Schools

How were individuals to be trained to master the complex business of reading and writing? Who could be relied upon to have the right attitude and also command the necessary skills?

Apprenticeship proved a cumbersome, inefficient, and unreliable answer. It could not train a large number of people to perform sophisticated functions using a minimum of scarce talent for the teaching. What was needed was a way of mass-producing literate individuals. This need led to the development of schools—a brand new social institution.[19]

These very first schools, circa 3500 B.C., concentrated numbers of children in one place for the purpose of teaching them efficiently. Predictably, they educated only the Sumerian power elite.[20] Often located in temples, they were chiefly a priestly prerogative.[21]

Temples were particularly appropriate sites for schools because literacy itself was viewed with reverential awe. Writing was not even regarded as a human invention. It was believed to have been created by a god. For this reason, learning to read and write was considered a sacramental act. We see, then, that the Temple image of the school discussed earlier has an historic basis.

The Three Functions of Sumerian Schools

Like other early civilizations, Sumer's early schools served three functions. First, they taught the technical skills necessary for a priestly/governmental vocation. Second, they reinforced the superior status of the upper classes. Third, they established more effective social control over key members of the society.

In terms of its vocational function , we have already seen that Sumerian schooling satisfied the staffing needs of the Sumerian government and related religious bureaucracy. They initiated a select few into the mysteries of reading and writing the enormously complex text that was the world's first written language because these technical skills were essential to critical vocations, such as that of scribe or priest.

The status function operated more subtly. The elaborate and well-defined social hierarchy of Sumerian society was primarily based on birth; but schooling gave the upper classes, such as the clergy, the landed aristocracy, and the nobility, another form of authority and legitimacy. Literacy was a badge of membership in the upper classes. In theory, admission to Sumerian schools was open to all males. However, in practice, it was restricted to male children from high status families. Students were the sons of government officials, mil-

---

[19]V. Gordon Childe, *Social Evolution* (New York: Henry Schuman, 1951), p. 161.

[20]The earliest school ever excavated, located in the ancient Sumerian village of Mari, dates back to 2000 B.C. Circumstantial evidence, such as the discovery of hundreds of clay tablets containing what appear to be educational exercises, suggests that earlier schools existed, but none has yet been unearthed.

[21]James Bowen, *A History of Western Education,* Vol. 1 (New York: St. Martin's, 1972), pp. 14–15.

Figure 10.2

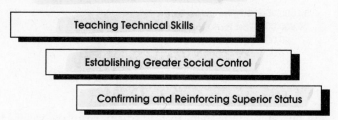

THREE FUNCTIONS OF SCHOOLING

Teaching Technical Skills

Establishing Greater Social Control

Confirming and Reinforcing Superior Status

itary officers, ship captains, priests, scribes, and other individuals of rank. Females appear to have been excluded altogether.[22] One way that the poor were excluded was that tuition fees, rather than public moneys, funded these schools.

With respect to the social control function, Sumerian government officials required a small army of loyal functionaries. Through strict discipline and stress on the myths and values central to Sumerian life, schooling encouraged attitudes and behaviors that were at least as indispensable as literacy.[23] It was, in effect, the cement necessary for the maintenance of an elite moral community.

We see then that there was a close correspondence between Sumerian social structure, social values and norms, and school practices. Such "correspondence" is a universal feature of schools. The history of education is literally filled with examples. Indeed, it is so common that there is recognized a **principle of correspondence**, which states that schooling conforms to the social structure, social values, and norms of the host society.

We should note here that the fact that Sumerian schools served these three functions (see Figure 10.2) does not prove that the powerholders who directed them had them in mind. Conscious purpose should not be confused with social function. There is not always a one-to-one-correspondence.

At this point we might review where schools fit in the overall development of humankind. Since it is difficult to think in terms of millions, much less billions of years, we can better understand by restating the relative age of humans and schools in terms of imaginary days, weeks, months, and years. If we reduce the 4.6 billion years of our planet's existence to one imaginary planetary year, *Australopithecus* did not evolve until the 365th day at 4:18 P.M. The first schools evolved only 30 seconds before midnight on this last planetary day. It has been only in the last second of this last day, 11:59:59 P.M., that schools have attained a central place in the lives of most humans.

The More Things Change, the More They Stay the Same

Regardless of their correspondence to the needs of Sumerian society, the archaeological record shows that Sumerian children often hated school. It was

---

[22]S. M. Kramer, *History Begins at Sumer* (London: Thames and Hudson, 1976), pp. 229–248.
[23]Ibid.

Figure 10.3   **How Many Years Ago?**

4,500,000,000 Origins of the Earth
4,000,000 First Proto Humans
40,000 First Homo Sapiens
6,000 First Schools

not uncommon for them to play truant, roam the streets, and loiter in public places in much the same way as some young people do today.

The concerns of the parents of school children were also remarkably similar to those of our time. For example, a surviving 3700-year-old clay tablet contains the angry inscriptions of a father berating his son for poor work habits, ingratitude, and laziness. His tablet demands that his son begin doing his assignments, making sure his homework is correct, and coming straight home after school. He points out that he has never asked his son to get a job or even to do chores as other fathers do. Yet, despite his consideration, he laments, he is bedeviled day and night by a son who is a whining wastrel more concerned with enjoyment than a meaningful existence.[24]

Egypt

Shortly after the founding of Sumer, another great agricultural civilization began taking shape along the Nile. Egyptian developments paralleled those of Sumer, and the culture exhibited similar characteristics. Schools developed later than in Sumer, but by 2000 B.C. schooling had begun to supplement family-centered education for members of the upper class.[25]

The Preeminence of Organized Religion

Egyptian schooling was also controlled by religious authorities. This practice corresponded with the fact that the priesthood was the controlling element in the society. Predictably, most schools were in temples and were taught by priests. Here young boys learned reading and writing. Older students studied a relatively wide variety of subjects including astronomy, music, law, medicine, arithmetic, and architecture. Tuition was usually charged.[26]

Government Schools

The Egyptian government did run some schools of its own. Operated by the Treasury, they specialized in preparing boys for careers in governmental bureaucracies. Admission was open to any male youngster regardless of class,

---

[24]Kramer, op. cit., pp. 243–246.
[25]S. E. Frost, *Historical and Philosophical Foundations of Western Civilization* (Columbus, Ohio: Merrill, 1966), pp. 16–20.
[26]Ibid.

and it was at least theoretically possible for a poor child to attend.[27] However, Egyptian society was based on a plantation economy that afforded the many a bare subsistence while providing the few, primarily aristocratic landowners and priests, with unparalleled luxury.[28]

Given such a system, few youngsters from the vast peasantry found their way into governmental schools for scribes. However, these schools did provide a means of upward mobility to the children of lower level aristocrats and church officials.

Vocational, Control, and Status Functions

Egyptian schools emphasized copying, memorization and recitation in order to develop literacy. In 2000 or 1000 B.C. this was a technically advanced skill with great vocational utility.

The routine was often grinding and cheerless, and they made liberal use of corporal punishment for control and motivation. Characteristically, an educational slogan of the time remarked, "A boy's ears are on his back; he hears when he is beaten."[29] As in Sumer, this emphasis on "discipline" reflected the importance Egyptian authorities attached to establishing social control over children who would be future functionaries of the government.

By the time Egypt had become a great empire, its social classes were caste-like. Mobility from class to class was nearly impossible. Schooling reinforced the privileged existence of their upper classes. It was heavily involved in furthering the political control of this social elite through a structure of grades, ranks, degrees, and other credentials very reminiscent of those in use today.[30]

So it was that Egyptian and Sumerian schooling did not encourage the search for truth, the development of theories, or the exploration of knowledge.[31] One went to school to gain useful technical skills, to be exposed to formative discipline, and to preserve high social status. When that was taught, all was taught.

The Unschooled Majority

Although the Sumerians and Egyptians virtually invented literacy and schooling, the vast majority of their citizens remained illiterate and totally unschooled. Though some middle class merchants and artisans were highly skilled, their expertise was established informally through example and apprenticeship. As for the masses, the peasant farmers and slaves whose toil built and fed these civilizations, they learned only from bitter experience.

---

[27]Edward Burns and Philip Ralph, *World Civilizations from Ancient to Contemporary*, Vol. I (New York: Norton, 1958.).
[28]Charles Smith and Grady Moorhead, *A Short History of the Ancient World* (New York: Appleton-Century-Crofts, 1939), p. 21.
[29]Graves, op. cit. p. 39
[30]Bowen, op. cit., p. 33, and Collins, op. cit., p. 5
[31]James Breasted, *A History of Egypt from the Earliest Times to the Persian Conflict* (New York: Scribner, 1937), p. 98.

Figure 10.4   TYPICAL EDUCATIONAL STRUCTURE
OF AN ANCIENT CIVILIZATION

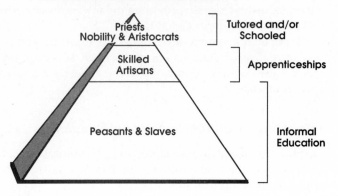

Decline

Both the Sumerian and Egyptian civilizations eventually withered. Why, is a matter of debate. We do know that their educational systems passed through a process of early development, significant accomplishment, rigid formalism, and then decline that mirrored processes at work in the broader society. Institutionalization seems to have been a factor. Their governmental bureaucracies, once established, turned away from the tasks they were created to perform, and instead worked mainly at administering themselves. Their schools also became involved in a similar process that constantly confused means for ends. Practices originally intended to promote more effective skill acquisition became, instead, hollow rituals required only because they had been required before.

China

Because of the distinctive importance of schooling in their culture, some mention should be made of Chinese civilization. Chinese schools date back to at least 1000 B.C. and continued their traditional practices well into the twentieth century.

As in Sumer and Egypt, the development of schooling in China was promoted by a revolution in agriculture which promoted the growth of cities, the emergence of a socially stratified society, the birth of an empire, and, most important, the invention of writing. Chinese writing consisted of thousands of different characters, and was even more complex than that in Sumer or Egypt. Understanding this system of writing virtually required formal instruction, and schools provided it.

Chinese civilization developed later than that of Sumer or Egypt. It began to reach an extraordinary sophistication in the period 800 B.C. to 200 B.C. In this period feudal warlords were pushed aside by the Emperor's forces and

Confucius was a teacher and philosopher who became China's most influential moral leader.

an imperial government was consolidated. By 500 B.C. the original feudal elite had been totally replaced by a new governing bureaucracy under the authority of the Emperor. It was staffed by a formally educated upper class that had been schooled in the Chinese literary tradition.

Schools and Social Mobility

At first these were primarily patronage positions, but competition between Chinese states pushed rulers to select the most capable people to serve government. A system of rigorous examinations eventually replaced patronage as the basis for appointments. Schooling in the Chinese classics, particularly the writings of Confucius, ca. 551–471 B.C., became a must if one was to have any hope of passing these tests.

More practical subjects, such as mathematics and calligraphy, were also examined; but these were considered merely technical skills leading only to low positions. There was no alternative. Anyone wishing the status of a high government post had to master a literary education. Because it was essentially Confucian, such an education incorporated a strong emphasis on ethical principles, decorum, social solidarity, and loyalty to authority.[32] In other words, it was deeply involved in reinforcing the formal level of culture.

This emphasis was useful in promoting social solidarity and control. But the examination system also resulted in an unprecedented degree of social mobility. Often the children of the old power elite had to give way to a cadre of bright young men of humbler circumstances (women were excluded) who had been selected on the basis of competitive examinations. In this way the schools helped reinvigorate Chinese government and revitalize the ruling

---

[32]Fairbank, Reischauer, and Craig, *East Asia: Tradition and Transformation* (Boston: Houghton Mifflin, 1973), pp. 102–103.

Figure 10.5   **THE FOURTH FUNCTION OF SCHOOLING**

Social Renewal

class. Such *social renewal* is a fourth function of schooling. It should be added to the social control, vocational, and status functions cited earlier.

All Chinese did not have an equal opportunity to get the schooling essential for upward social mobility. Government-sponsored schools in the capital were restricted to sons of great families. Even the extensive network of government subsidized local schools, theoretically open to all, were dominated by the younger sons of aristocrats and lesser ranked scholar officials. This arrangement did not remain unchallenged. As the examination system became more and more refined, the ambitious children of merchants and minor officials made inroads into the upper class. By the eleventh century a new ruling class had arisen, based partially on birth, but also on schooling.[33]

In the centuries which followed, the examination system was corrupted by various forms of favoritism and the introduction of patronage. Chinese schooling also lost its vitality. Emphasizing empty ritual and formalism, it ultimately failed to adapt to changing conditions. Classic writings, such as those of Confucius, were literally engraved in stone. Classroom practices took on a similar rigidity. In other words, as in Sumer and Egypt, Chinese schools became institutionalized.

Ultimately, in the early 1900s, nearly a thousand years after the initial reforms, traditional Chinese government and the schools that served it crumbled into ruin.

THE GREEKS

The educational heritage of the Sumerians and Egyptians was passed to the Hebrews, Arabs, and Greeks. The Greeks refined and modified it, then passed it to the rest of the Western world through the Romans. For this reason, it is essential to know something about Greek educational history.

Ancient Greece was a society of city-states at the agricultural level of development. The most influential were Sparta and Athens. Their cultures present a striking contrast, and their vastly different educational practices are a perfect illustration of correspondence.

Sparta

In the eighth century B.C. the already powerful Greek city-state of Sparta greatly expanded its influence and resources by conquering the neighboring

---

[33]John Lewis, "Chinese History," *Encyclopaedia Britannica Macropaedia*, Vol. 14 (Chicago: Britannica, 1975), pp. 305–312.

Messenian people. A small number of Spartans now not only controlled thousands of dependent subjects in surrounding towns and villages, but also had thousands upon thousands of Messenians to control and exploit.[34]

More or less constantly at war, and preoccupied with controlling their subjects and slaves, Spartan society was organized as a military garrison. The Spartan educational system, totally integrated with the military, was an arm of this garrison state. It taught the skills of war and fostered valor, fitness, and fidelity to the end that absolute control could be maintained over Sparta's subject peoples.

Spartans served the state unconditionally. Consensus was absolute, dissensus punished by death. Even the family was distrusted because it menaced group interests and the national consensus.[35]

Totally integrating the formal, informal, and technical levels of culture to the end of conquest, the Spartans also demanded the total subordination of self to the collective. Males were educated to wage war and dominate others, females were systematically toughened for childbirth.

Educating Boys for War

Boys in Sparta began to be drilled in training schools, really little more than military encampments, at the age of seven. Though state control was total, the boy's father was expected to pay. These "schools" gave little or no attention to the development of literacy much less cultivation, eloquence, or refinement. Instead the boys were brutalized, and required to communicate with as few words as possible.[36]

Living in a barracks, sleeping on a bed made of rushes, deprived of shoes and all but a single garment for all seasons, a young Spartan roamed the countryside in a "herd" of 64 headed by older boys.[37] They were encouraged to steal what they required from the serfs, called helots, who were owned by the government and allotted to local landowners. If caught, the boys were beaten, not for stealing, but for getting caught. Sometimes they ambushed and murdered helots for the sake of the experience. This practice was not regarded as a crime. In fact, it was legitimized and regulated by declaring a sort of war, called the "Cryptia," on helots once a year.[38] Presumably, it was intended to "educate" the helots as much as the Spartans.

Spartan boys gave out only a bit worse than they got. Brutal beatings were routinely administered by "whip bearers." They were administered primarily for the sake of encouraging stoicism in the face of pain. Boys also volunteered for brutal floggings at the alter of Artemis Orthia. Here they vied with one

---

[34]J. Kelley Sowards, *Western Civilization to 1660* (New York: St. Martin's, 1964), p. 91.
[35]Bowen, op. cit., p. 52.
[36]The term "laconic" (meaning given to speaking with very few words) is derived from Laconia, the name of the region containing Sparta.
[37]H. G. Good, *A History of Western Education* (New York: Macmillan, 1960), p. 20.
[38]Paul Monroe, *Source Book of the History of Education for the Greek and Roman Period* (New York: Macmillan, 1939), p. 22.

A Spartan boy endures the pain of a fox tearing at him to conceal his possession of the forbidden animal.

another for the honor of enduring the most pain without flinching. A prize was awarded to the winner.[39]

Higher Education

At seventeen boys were released from their "herds." They then joined private military units sponsored and controlled by prominent citizens. These private armies competed with one another in sports and martial contests. On special days they even fought battles to the death.

Universal Military Service

After three years in these private militia, the boys entered the ranks of the army. From their twentieth to their sixtieth year all male Spartans were obliged to serve the state, living in barracks, eating the simplest food, and enduring hardship without complaint. Family life was limited and highly regulated. In fact, family loyalties were so suspect that Spartan men often visited their wives in stealth.[40]

Educating Women

Spartan girls lived at home rather than in barracks as the boys did. Nevertheless, they were encouraged by their mothers to be obedient, uncomplaining, courageous, and modest. Their bodies were strengthened, primarily for child-

---

[39]J. F. Dobson, *Ancient Education and Its Meaning To Us* (New York: Cooper Square, 1963), pp. 15 and 18.
[40]A. Gordon Melvin, *Education: A History* (New York: John Day, 1946), p. 42.

birth, through participation in sport. These competitions were also designed to reinforce Spartan values.[41] Above all, they were made to understand that the state came first.

Even mother love was expected to give way to the needs of the collective. Mothers with children judged defective by the Council of Elders were required to abandon their babies to the elements.[42] When sons went off to war, Spartan mothers were expected to hand them their heavy shields, which they would have to drop in order to run away, and tell them to return bearing their shields or lying dead upon them.

An Example of Cultural Lag

Within its limitations the Spartan educational system was a great success. It virtually guaranteed complete social control and the domination and exploitation of others. It also preserved Spartan independence long after most other Greek city-states lost theirs. But Sparta remained remarkably brutal long after her military might was overcome. Despite the fact that after Rome's conquest of them they served no greater purpose than satisfying the morbid curiosity for Roman tourists, Spartans continued to sponsor festivals in which young men volunteered for bloody, sometimes fatal, floggings.

Cultures often cling to customs or educational practices that no longer serve the functions that gave them birth. Sociologists refer to this as **cultural lag**.

Athens

Around 500 B.C. another city-state challenged Spartan dominance. Overthrowing tyranny and establishing democratic government, Athenians quickly established their city-state as a leading power. In the period 499–477 B.C. they established its preeminence among the Greek city-states by leading the repulse of Persian invaders. This made them masters of the Aegean and its islands while encouraging the rivalry of Sparta.

Class, Literacy, and Democracy

Athenian society was clearly divided along social and sexual lines. Wealthy landowners held the highest social position. Anyone who worked with his hands, even a skilled artisan, was looked down upon. Unskilled laborers were near the bottom of the male social hierarchy. Foreigners and slaves constituted the lowest two classes. Women led separate secluded lives, invariably subordinate to the men of their class.

Athenian males enjoyed a degree of personal freedom unknown in any other ancient civilization. This was facilitated by a remarkably efficient alphabet, the simplicity of which eliminated many of the difficulties associated with mas-

[41]Bowen, op. cit., pp. 55–56.
[42]Good, op. cit., p. 20.

tering the more formidable pictorial scripts of Sumer, Egypt, or China. This technical invention undermined the scribal monopoly on literacy. Evidently, even females and those males unable to afford formal instruction could often read and write with modest proficiency.[43] This expansion of knowledge through literacy opened the way for an unprecedented assault on the bonds of ignorance, and provided fertile ground for the cultivation of a limited democracy.[44]

This historic example raises the question of whether literacy is a necessary condition for freedom. Clearly it is not a sufficient condition, for there are many examples of highly literate societies that were also tyrannies. But one is hard-pressed to come up with one society in which illiteracy and freedom are both the norm.

Elementary Education

A Greek boy of noble birth customarily had a pedagogue permanently assigned to him. Commonly a slave, though sometimes a freedman, this individual was entrusted with the child's physical safety and moral development. His title literally meant "leader of a child."[45]

The pedagogue was the child's first teacher. Later, if the family was wealthy enough, this task was taken over by a better educated private tutor. If the family could not afford a tutor, they resorted to schools. In this case, the pedagogue accompanied the child, carrying his school gear, and keeping him out of trouble en route. He also helped with homework.[46]

Schools were an accepted part of male upper and middle class life even in the infancy of Athens. As early as 600 B.C. laws had been passed regulating their governance. Solon's Code, a series of ancient laws, required parents to

---

[43]Ibid., p. 76.
[44]Bowen, op. cit., pp. 60–61.
[45]The term has since become synonymous with "teacher."
[46]F. A. G. Beck, *Greek Education 450–350 B.C.* (London: Methuen, 1964), pp. 106–107.

Athenian education was very different from that of the Spartans.

ensure that their sons learned to read, write, and swim—though these skills could be learned at home. It also established full scholarships for boys whose fathers had died while serving Athens. Other laws regulated the daily activities of these schools. Significantly, Solon's Code did not provide for the education of females of any class.[47]

Despite state encouragement and regulation, however, Athenian schools were private. Teachers (*didaskalos*) were entrepreneurs who charged fees for their services. Parents shopped around. School was usually conducted in the home of the teacher or even in some corner of the marketplace. There were few schoolhouses. As in all other schools for many thousands of years, instruction was entirely individual. The other students were expected to busy themselves with seat work. (Simultaneous instruction of groups of youngsters was pioneered by St. Jean Baptiste de la Salle much later in the history of schooling.[48])

By 500 B.C. Athenian schooling had become routinized and teaching specialized. "Elementary" education was divided among three specialist teachers. The grammarian taught reading and writing, the citharist music, and the paedotribe, gymnastics. This division into specialties mirrored the increasing complexity and specialization of Athenian culture. At first, these three areas were accorded equal importance. In time, however, music declined in importance.[49]

Ultimately, elementary schooling was divided between instruction in reading, writing, and counting on the one hand (arithmetic was little taught because of its association with the "vulgar" world of commerce) and physical education on the other.[50] The Athenian view was that both were of equal importance in the educational process.

Teachers

Though they were supervised in a general way by state authorities, teachers received no special preparation for their work. Some Athenian teachers operated schools as a business, fixing their own fees and employing other teachers. They earned a moderate income and enjoyed a status equal to other skilled individuals such as doctors and sculptors. They usually made more than skilled workmen. Others worked as private tutors. Those working for wealthy families generally enjoyed high status and an enviable standard of living.

The fact that some ancient Greek writers referred to teachers with contempt, encouraged many historians wrongly to conclude that Athenian teachers were despised. They were not. We should understand, however, that aristocratic Greeks thought it unfortunate, even vulgarizing, to have to do any work for a living. They had complete disdain for labor with the hands or at a

---

[47]Frost, op. cit., p. 50.
[48]Power, op. cit., pp. 128–130.
[49]Ibid., p. 134.
[50]Good, op. cit., p. 26.

desk maintaining that such work "feminized" the body and marred the soul.[51] Teaching was no exception. Moreover, aristocrats had contempt for those who were taught in a classroom rather than privately tutored.[52]

Control and Status Concerns

Methods of classroom teaching were similar to those used in Sumer, Egypt, and China. Pupils memorized and then recited their lessons. Often these consisted of long passages of poetry containing moral admonitions and mythology. Superior students could recite formidable epics, such as the *Iliad* and *Odyssey*, entirely from memory. Students also painstakingly copied writing samples provided by the teacher. Discipline was severe and corporal punishment common. Fear was often the sole motivation.

The rigidity, coercion, and relentless demands for conformity suggest that social control was a major function of Athenian schooling. The emphasis on literature and grammar, as opposed to technical skills that had no place in Athenian schooling, indicates that it also reinforced status distinctions.

The "Good Old Days"

Given its drudgery, canings, and mindless memorization, Athenian children often hated school. As in ancient Sumer, it was not uncommon for the older students to play hooky, and to pass the day carousing with their friends. This caused some Athenians, such as the writer Aristophanes, to lament the disappearance of the good old days when children had been quiet, orderly, and studious. He claimed to remember when youngsters would fight their way to school in "snow thick as meal." But today's children were another matter. These "chattering wastrels," lamented the great writer, were "narrow chested, broad of tongue, ill-disciplined and soft—clearly not made of the same stern stuff which had won the day against the Persians."[53]

The Absence of Technical Level Pedagogical Knowledge

The Athenians were no more sophisticated than the Sumerians, Egyptians, or Chinese so far as pedagogy is concerned. Their teaching methodology was based nearly entirely on tradition, enjoying almost no understanding at the technical level of culture.

The Guerard-Juguet document, discovered in Athens shortly after World War II, illustrates this lack of pedagogical sophistication. This ancient student workbook, covering the entire Athenian reading curriculum from the first days of school up to the reading of Homer, reveals that it took four years for Greek children to learn a simple sentence. Pupils started by memorizing the alphabet.

---

[51]G. Lowes Dickinson, *The Greek View of Life* (New York: Collier, 1961), pp. 91–93.
[52]Beck, op. cit., pp. 111–116.
[53]Aristophanes, *Clouds*, p. 961.

They recited it forward, backward, and in every other conceivable way. They then learned to recognize and pronounce all possible two-letter syllables before moving on to three- and four-letter syllables. Altogether they were required to spend three years memorizing 750 syllables before finally proceeding to words and sentences.[54]

Higher Education

As the society developed, private teachers began to go from city to city selling a form of higher education. Known as Sophists, these teachers attracted wealthy and ambitious young men to lectures emphasizing rhetoric and argumentation, but also covering mathematics, astronomy, and the study of the Greek language. This curriculum reflected upper class vocational concerns. The skills developed were those necessary for success in patrician republican Athens.

The Sophists taught small classes of five to six students. This exclusivity required high fees that few could afford, restricting higher education to the wealthy. It had the latent function of reinforcing Athenian status distinctions. It also emphasized the power of personal contacts.[55]

The Sophists were not the only teachers of higher education in ancient Athens. In fact, this civilization produced educators of such surpassing skill and wisdom that their names are still synonymous with higher learning. These pathbreaking educators who made lasting contributions to schooling in the West included the following three:

Socrates, 469–399 B.C., a teacher loved and admired by the brightest and wealthiest youth of Athens, played a crucial role in the development of speculative thought. Although he left no writings, his lessons were popularized by

---

[54]Robert M. W. Travers, "Unresolved Issues in Defining Educational Goals," *Educational Theory*, Vol. 37, No. 1 (Winter 1987), p. 30.
[55]F. A. G. Beck, op. cit., pp. 270–271.

POINT/COUNTERPOINT

Learned individuals, like Socrates, have often questioned traditional values. In effect, they reduce formal culture to the technical level. As a result, many have been imprisoned, banished, or executed and their scholarly works burned. Frequently reviled in their lifetimes, some are now remembered as geniuses, saints, even prophets—perhaps because there is a fine line between the stability needed to maintain social control and the flexibility needed to adjust cultural values to adapt to changing conditions. Without a certain level of conformity to formal culture, societies disintegrate. But if conditions change and attitudes and values do not, societies also fall apart. Such tensions have a particularly strong impact on schools. In the United States, for example, some citizens place a premium on stability and urge that our schools enforce and encourage conformity to the formal culture. Others urge that the educators encourage its technical dissection.

Plato, his most famous pupil. While strolling in the gardens of a public park known as the Academy, Socrates skillfully questioned his students' most basic values. Teaching through questioning thus became known as the "Socratic method." His technical dissections of Athenian formal culture led to his denunciation and trial. He was convicted and condemned to death for corrupting the morals of Athenian youth and heresy.

Plato, 427?–347 B.C., was a wellborn Athenian influenced by the teaching of Socrates. His writings included the dialogues that brilliantly portray Socrates' method of inquiry and popularize his views. Plato subjected virtually every problem that has occupied subsequent generations of thinkers to painstaking analysis, reframing many at the technical, rather than the formal, level of culture. In approximately 387 B.C. he established a school in the quiet groves of the Academy. It eventually became the most influential school of the ancient world. His teaching career must be ranked among the most influential in the history of Western civilization.

Aristotle, 384?–322 B.C., along with his teacher Plato, is the most revered teacher and philosopher of Greek antiquity. His work had a particularly great influence on Christian philosophers of the Middle Ages. He made contributions to all areas of philosophy and his writings occupied hundreds of volumes. His most enduring contribution was the almost single-handed creation of the science of logic. This greatly strengthened the power and influence of the technical level of culture, permitting the most incisive criticisms of formal level "truths." Aristotle tutored Alexander the Great and subsequently founded the so-called Peripatetic school in the Athenian Lyceum. Funded by Alexander's contributions of money and provided with scientific specimens from the four corners of his empire, this famous school stressed natural science. Even after Aristotle was forced to flee Athens following charges of impiety, the Lyceum continued to prosper for nearly 900 years.

Also established were additional schools of higher learning that reflected

Plato and Socrates at the School of Athens.

different philosophical positions. Many flourished and became a long-term presence in Greek life. Even today we reflect this history by referring to "schools" of philosophy when we speak of philosophical differences.

The Greek Legacy

All of Greece was eventually conquered by the Romans. But Athens had established a culture of unprecedented richness which refused to die. Under Roman rule, Athens eventually prospered once again, becoming the great center for the schooling of aristocratic Roman youth. Subsequently, Roman conquest spread Athenian culture and educational practices throughout its enormous empire. Here it survived long after Rome's greatness had passed.

THE ROMANS

Rome, a sophisticated agricultural society, had already conquered the Italian peninsula by the time Athens entered her Golden Age. For more than six centuries Roman power increased while that of Greece declined. Eventually the Roman Empire became a colossus, controlling most of Europe and the Middle East, parts of Asia Minor, and much of North Africa.[56]

Early in their history the Romans educated their children by means of the family. Indeed, the Latin root of the English word "education," did not refer to schooling, but to a child's upbringing. If Roman children were well-schooled they were termed "**eruditus.**"

The Athenian Model

Although they were very sophisticated in technical skills, the Romans never equaled the Athenians in intellectual or artistic refinements. When they came into contact with Athenian culture through conquest, however, they recognized its value. As the Roman poet Horace observed, the conqueror was itself conquered by the civilization of the Greeks.

Though deeply conservative, the Romans eventually adopted Athenian upper class religion, philosophy, and ideas. They also adopted the Athenian system of schooling.

Throughout Roman history the artisans and the citizen farmers that were the backbone of early Roman society learned their skills by apprenticeship and example. The Roman lower classes had no notion of Athenian civilization.[57]

---

[56]Edward Burns, *Western Civilizations: Their History and Culture* (New York: W.W. Norton, 1968), p. 207.
[57]James Breasted, *The Conquest of Civilization* (New York: Harper Brothers, 1926), p. 559.

Pedagogues and Tutors

The Roman *familia* consisted not only of parent and child, but also of other relatives, servants, and slaves. It was the fundamental economic, social, legal, religious, and educational unit of society.[58] As Roman civilization developed, the biological family delegated more and more of its responsibilities to surrogates. In addition, the state claimed an ever greater share of familial authority.

One of the first functions to be delegated was child care and education. Shortly after birth upper class Roman children were turned over to a wet nurse. (Breast feeding by an aristocratic natural mother was not the fashion.) The wet nurse's duties went far beyond offering the child her breast. She was, in effect, a substitute mother with whom the children lived and took their meals—dining with their biological family only in the evening or on holidays. Until the age of puberty it was her responsibility to educate the children in conjunction with a pedagogue.[59]

Literacy was required of an upper class child, and teaching this was delegated to the pedagogue. As in Greece, this educated slave or freedman (former slave) functioned as a surrogate father. He was charged not only with teaching basic academic skills, but also with the child's moral and physical well-being.

The nurse and pedagogue functioned as surrogate parents. Under the supervision of the paternal grandmother, whose role was to be a strict enforcer of social convention, they often lived in the countryside with their charge, far removed from the temptations of Rome. In such a setting the love between nurse, pedagogue, and child became strong indeed, usually lasting a lifetime.

Roman history affords many examples of emotional attachments between the child and his or her nurse and pedagogue. One of the most notorious concerns the Emperor Nero, who murdered his biological mother with the help of his pedagogue. Later, as he faced certain death at the hands of his enraged subjects, only his nurse stood by him.[60]

The services of the pedagogue and nurse were often supplemented with those of a better-schooled tutor who usually charged a hefty fee. Having been tutored became a distinguishing feature of a Roman upper class child.

This system of education had a clear-cut status function. Indeed, the prestige of a family could easily be measured by the fame of the tutor it employed. Members of the royal family were tutored by academics of the greatest reputation. Seneca the philosopher and Quintilian the rhetorician are two examples. There was considerable competition for the services of such teachers, and they were well paid.[61]

---

[58]Gies, op. cit., p. 18.
[59]Paul Veyne, *A History of Private Life from Pagan Rome to Byzantium* (Cambridge, Mass.: The Belknap Press of Harvard U. Press, 1987), p. 14.
[60]Ibid.
[61]Stanley J. Bonner, *Education in Ancient Rome* (Berkeley: U. of California Press, 1977), pp. 10–33.

Roman Schools

Although Romans greatly preferred private tutors, most could not afford them. For them the *ludus*, or primary school, was the only alternative. Here, for a fee, a fairly substantial proportion of Roman children, boys and girls together, were taught reading, writing, and counting. Many *ludi* were conducted on street corners or in public arcades. Others were established in the teacher's home or in rented shop space. Parents paid only after services were rendered, and many looked for an excuse not to pay at all. The child's pedagogue also expected a cut; otherwise he would use his influence to undermine the teacher. In general, it was a mean business involving little pay, less status, and even less technical sophistication so far as teaching skill was concerned.[62]

By the age of twelve girls were considered nubile, and were often married. Sexual maturity marked the end of their schooling.[63]

Less well-to-do boys also had to drop out at that age because they could not afford to continue. Those who could, attended a higher tier of schools emphasizing Latin grammar and literature. The equivalent of our secondary schools, these Latin Grammar Schools were operated by well-educated freedmen or Romans of high birth who had come upon hard times. Attracting boys in the general age range of twelve to sixteen, these schools were unregulated and ranged from street corner makeshifts to prestigious enterprises run by famous grammarians who had become affluent by teaching the sons of Rome's "best families."[64]

Following completion of Latin Grammar school, at approximately sixteen years of age, the more privileged boys enrolled in Schools of Rhetoric. These were the equivalent of modern higher education. At first Romans were reluctant to adopt this Athenian institution. By the time of Christ, however, there were many tutors and even more schools specializing in rhetoric.

Schools of Rhetoric were at the top of the prestige hierarchy. True, their importance was partially vocational, reflecting the usefulness of many of the techniques of the rhetorician in governance and legal matters. But these schools served status better than vocation. Their requirement of hefty doses of vocationally useless Greek bear witness to that fact.

At one point the Roman Senate even attempted to require the study of Greek in all Schools of Rhetoric. This was intended to effectively limit rhetorical training to the children of the aristocracy. (Apparently Latin-based Schools of Rhetoric were becoming popular with the middle class.) Requiring Greek was intended to make such training too expensive for those of limited means.[65]

The Roman government neither created nor sustained schools. A formal education was not compulsory, literacy was haphazard and there were not

---

[62]Bonner, op. cit., p. 46.
[63]Veyne, op. cit., p. 19.
[64]Dobson, op. cit., p. 26.
[65]Good, op. cit., p. 49.

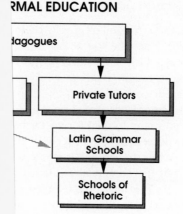

RMAL EDUCATION

dagogues

Private Tutors

Latin Grammar Schools

Schools of Rhetoric

even any buildings designed as schools. Teachers were untrained in pedagogy, were for the most part unregulated, and received no government funds. They were left entirely to the mercy of a free market economy. For this reason inequality of educational opportunity was the order of the day.[66]

The social functions of Roman schooling were vocational, status maintenance, and social control just as they were in Sumer, Egypt, China, and Athens. As in Athens, the "vocational" function must be thought of in the broadest sense. But it did prepare upper class males for government and the law. Social renewal was also involved, though neither the Roman Senate nor Emperors were interested in an elite selected from the ranks of the schooled by rigorous examination.

The main difference between Roman schooling and its Greek parent was that Greek schooling was a very public business with half of the day devoted to sport. Roman schooling was a far more private affair, and physical education was relatively unimportant.[67]

The Education of Roman Women

Although more honored and unimpeded than their Greek counterparts, Roman women were still educated only for homemaking. However, the great importance of family life, coupled with the fact that the mother expected to personally rear and educate the younger children, did much to legitimize the formal schooling of upper class Roman women. By the second century B.C. it was possible for aristocratic woman like Cornelia, mother of the great liberal

---

[66]Bonner, op. cit., pp. 328–329.
[67]Veyne, op. cit., p. 20.

tribunes Tiberius and Gaius Grachus, to have acquired a classical Greek education. She put it to use teaching her children—achieving such remarkable results that she became famous for her contribution to Roman history.[68]

Basically, however, Roman attitudes toward women and their education were similar to those of the Greeks. The father governed the all-important family with absolute authority. If women received formal education, this was done grudgingly as a concession to class distinctions and the requirements of aristocratic motherhood. It was also done with deep misgivings, for it was widely held that educated women were troublesome. The Roman dramatist, essayist, and tutor of Nero, Lucius Seneca (c. 4 B.C.–65 A.D.) spoke for many Roman men when he commented in Hippolytus, "When a woman thinks . . . she thinks evil."

Schooling and Bureaucracy

Throughout most of its history the Roman world did not rely upon a vast bureaucracy to govern and administer. During the early years, when Rome was a Republic, governing was accomplished through citizen participation with rapid turnover in office. It did not depend upon career bureaucrats selected through formal education and examinations. Even in the early Empire the administration of local affairs was still in the hands of wealthy citizens rather than career bureaucrats. Only in the later stages of Roman history (in the fourth through the sixth centuries A.D.) did the government begin to use large numbers of professional officials. Characteristically, this period also featured the imposition of regulations governing teachers and schools.[69]

The form of classical schooling corresponded to this style of governance. For the most part, a "liberal education" amounted to teaching upper class students of independent means how to read carefully and to write and speak in accordance with the ostentatious eloquence then popular in governmental circles. Whatever they knew of subjects, such as geography, natural philosophy (science), mathematics, and history, they picked up indirectly by reading the classical writings.[70]

Roman Educational Ideas

The Roman lack of emphasis on teaching technical subjects corresponded with their attitude, shared with classical Athens, that the virtuous life lived by a man of quality had to be one of "idleness." Thus, wealthy Romans had to be educated for the type of life which, while not actually idle, was the exclusive

---

[68]Gary Clabaugh, "A History of Male Attitudes Toward the Education of Women," *Educational Horizons*, Vol. 64, No. 3, p. 131.
[69]Randall Collins, "Some Comparative Principles of Educational Stratification," *Harvard Educational Review*, Vol. 47, No. 1 (1977), pp. 15–16.
[70]Norman F. Cantor, *Medieval History* (New York: Macmillan, 1963), p. 70.

province of men who could afford to do as they pleased according to their ideals, rather than the dictates of necessity.[71]

The Romans developed their own distinctive ideas about teaching and learning which reflected this point of view. For example, Marcus Tullius Cicero (106–43 B.C.), Rome's leading orator, statesman, and man of letters during the later part of the Republic, articulated an elitist educational value system that still remains influential.

In *De Oratore* (*The Orator*) Cicero maintained that a well-rounded background in the liberal arts is what makes an individual truly educated. To this end he outlined the type of study necessary for a class of wealthy, cultivated notables who exalted idleness because it permitted the cultivation of virtue. The elitist curriculum he articulated was later codified into law, and eventually became a basic model for higher education even to the present day.

The Remnants of Empire

Latin outlived the Roman Empire to become the language of educated people throughout the Western world. What is more, the writings of Romans, such as Cicero and Quintilian, eventually helped inspire the Renaissance. But Rome's greatest educational contribution was the preservation and extension of Athenian culture. Part of the very essence of the vast Roman empire itself, these principles and practices eventually held sway from the Sahara in the south to Scotland in the north, from Portugal in the west to the Euphrates River in the East. By the time Rome's Western Empire crumbled, centuries of Roman rule had made Athenian educational practices and ideals an integral part of Western culture.

The Nature of Roman Teaching

Throughout most of this Roman period there were few schools, and little formal instruction. When these did finally develop, teachers received no formal training in pedagogy. Teaching methods were based solely on tradition. There was a "right" and "wrong" way of conducting instruction, and knowledge of subject matter was regarded as both necessary and sufficient preparation. There was no sense that more efficient instruction could be derived from a systematic study of children or learning. Motivation was primarily based on the threat of physical punishment. All these characteristics indicate that teaching was conceived and executed at the formal level of culture.

It is true that Socrates pioneered the teaching method of asking a series of questions that led the student to an ever deeper understanding. Although this Socratic method was based on the philosopher's erroneous theory that we are born knowing all there is to know, and simply need to be reminded, at least one of its consequences was a systematic inquiry into the nature of knowledge.

---

[71]Veyne, op. cit., pp. 119–120.

Of all the educators and teachers of this
Fabius Quintilianus (A.D. 35–97) seemed
schooling and teaching could be understo
than the formal level of culture. Indeed, Q
Oratoria, an elaborate treatment of Roma
foundations of teaching must be derived
rather than from tradition. In this same
knowledge of child growth and develo
educator.

The ancient notion that teaching shou
in terms of tradition and knowledge of subject matter
us. For example, William Bennett, the Secretary of Education during
the Reagan administration, seemed convinced that there was little technical
level knowledge concerning pedagogy or students that teachers need to know.
As the history of schooling developed, however, more and more key thinkers
came to the conclusion that the way to improve teaching and schooling is to
ground them both in the technical level of culture by making use of scientifically derived knowledge, research on teaching and learning, and in an understanding of the basic principles of human growth and development—a view
that Quintilian would have found congenial.

SUMMARY

1. For nearly 4 million years schools played *no* role in human affairs. People
were educated only informally. Schooling did not emerge until the development of writing approximately 6000 years ago. These first schools, in ancient
Sumer and Egypt, were involved in vocational preparation, social control, and
status reinforcement with children of the upper class. Later, China added
another function, that of social renewal.

2. The Spartans and Athenians practiced very different types of education
which corresponded to essential elements in the broader culture. The Spartans
demanded total devotion to a garrison state and subordinated the family to
this end. The Athenian upper class stressed preparation for a cultivated life of
leisure. The most privileged were tutored at home. The less privileged attended schools. The Athenian model provided the basis of many Western
traditions of higher education. These were passed on to the West by way of
the Romans.

3. The distinction between the formal, technical, and informal levels of culture provides a useful way of understanding the early evolution of teaching
and schooling. None of the civilizations discussed in this chapter developed
a technical level understanding of teaching and learning. All relied upon tradition, and a formal level kind of understanding.

QUESTIONS

1. How long ago did schooling first originate in our "planetary year"? Translate that into actual years.

2. The very existence of a culture depends upon the effective education, though not necessarily the formal schooling, of the young. Imagine that a whole generation of Sumerian children somehow failed to learn anything about their culture whatsoever. What would have happened to their civilization?

3. We argued that the capacity for language and symbolism are uniquely and vitally human. Looking back on your own experience in school, was the development of language and symbolic competence a central feature of the curriculum of the schools you have attended? How?

4. Identify the four functions of schooling described in the chapter.

5. The correspondence principle holds that the functions of schooling are consistent and compatible with broader societal practices. Thus, for example, Sumer developed schools that taught a governing elite socially necessary technical skills that also legitimized and reinforced their high social status. Recently, critics of the correspondence principle have argued that it fails to explain how schools and societies change. Accordingly, the critics have added a contradiction principle. It states that change arises out of incompatibility and tension between school practices and the broader social situation. It further claims that when education no longer fulfills broader social needs, change of some kind is inevitable. Do you see any evidence that the contradiction principle may have been at work in the period of history described in this chapter? If so, where and when? (For a summary and examples of these principles see Betty A. Sichel, "Correspondence and Contradiction in Ancient Greek Society and Education: Homer's Epic Poetry and Plato's Early Dialogues," *Educational Theory*, Vol. 33, No. 2 (Spring 1983), pp. 49–59.)

6. In a previous chapter we distinguished between powerholders and stakeholders. In this chapter we noted that women were systematically discriminated against with regard to access to formal schooling in the early years. How does the distinction help us understand the discrimination?

7. What intellectual tool is Aristotle credited with developing which made it possible to subject formal culture to more effective technical analysis?

8. Until the late 1960s most experts held that fostering socially necessary technical skills and socializing the young were the chief motives for the development of schooling. Recently, however, several new reasons for this development have been suggested. Focusing on the development of public education, for example, various Neo-Marxist historians, such as Michael B. Katz, have argued that public schools have historically imposed middle class interests on an often reluctant working class. They have been, say these theorists, an instrument of domination and exploitation. Can you cite any evidence in this chapter which supports or undermines the Neo-Marxist point of view?

9. What is the significance of the complexity or simplicity of methods of writing with regard to the image of the school as Temple?
10. How do Quintilian, formal and technical levels of culture, and teaching methodology relate?

Chapter 11

A HISTORY of EDUCATION: THE AGE of FAITH THROUGH the RENAISSANCE

PREVIEW

In this chapter we trace the history of education from the Age of Faith to the Renaissance. We emphasize broad social trends that had a great impact on education and schooling. The first concerns the shift of emphasis from the family to broader social institutions, such as the government, the Church, and schools. The second concerns the conflict between the technical culture, which is changeable and understandable in terms of efficiency, and the formal culture, which is more enduring and understandable in terms of right or wrong, good or evil. The last concerns the degree of social consensus and the related presence or absence of conflict and bargaining.

We highlight the precipitous decline of schooling that accompanied the fall of Rome, then describe its slow redevelopment within the Christian Church. We recount the slow breakdown of the Church's control of schooling which was initiated by the rise of towns and hastened by the Renaissance, the Reformation, and the scientific revolution. We also describe the impact of the invention of printing, stressing its educational implications and relating it to the Renaissance and humanism. Finally, we summarize the educational impact of the Reformation and the Counter-Reformation, preparing the ground for a more sophisticated understanding of colonial American educational practices. Throughout we offer different illustrations of the principle of **correspondence,** which emphasizes that developments in education and schooling are reflections of far broader events in the society as a whole.

SCHOOLING AND THE AGE OF FAITH

In the late fifth century A.D. the last remnants of Rome's military empire fused with Germanic or barbarian society.[1] The result was a decline of trade, a reversal of urbanization, and general disorder. Commercial agriculture gave way to essentially agricultural villages little more sophisticated than those of the horticultural age. Education reverted to the family and the Church. These changes accompanied the disintegration of Rome's advanced technical culture.[2]

The formal level of Roman culture faired better than the technical. In its last years Rome had been strongly influenced by the spread of a Christianity modified by Greek thought and Roman concepts of law and administration. Originally hated and feared as subversive, Christianity became the state reli-

---

[1]Frances and Joseph Gies, *Marriage and the Family in the Middle Ages* (New York: Harper & Row, 1987), p. 16.

[2]Paul Moorhead, *A Short History of the Ancient World* (New York: Appleton-Century-Crofts), 1939, p. 609.

gion. Intent on eliminating dissensus and establishing Christianity as the sole source of spiritual authority in the Roman Empire, Emperor Theodosius II decreed that followers of other religions were "mad and demented," "guilty of infamy," and "subject to the wrath of both God and the state."[3]

When Rome fell, Romanized Christianity remained widely practiced. Although it was at the mercy of local lords, badly fragmented, and ill-disciplined, the Christian Church represented a broad, though shallow, consensus in a sea of dissensus. It was almost universally regarded as the only guide that could show both nobleman and commoner their way to Heaven.

A New Social Order

A new, more primitive, technical culture slowly took root, replacing the commercial agricultural and civil engineering emphasis of the Romans. It depended for its foundation on a technique of open fields agriculture, passed on from grandfather to father to son, which required everyone to do the same thing in the same way at the same time. When, for example, the Church bells rang on Lammas Day (August 15th), they signified the end of harvest and the opening of the crop fields to the village livestock. It was simply too bad for anyone foolish enough to experiment with a new crop that was still maturing.[4]

Such a system discouraged technical level innovation while simultaneously fostering a broad yet deep consensus regarding the formal level of culture that was reflected in the religious values of the age.

The stability and seeming unchangeability of both the technical and formal levels of medieval culture produced regular, repetitive lives in an apparently unchanging world. Those of us who are troubled by the transience of modern life might envy such stability and permanence; but it sustained a system that was often cruel, harsh, and exploitative. The peasantry, for example, lived in the shadow of their local warlord who compelled them to pay heavy market tolls and handicraft taxes, forbade them to carry weapons, regulated their marriages, required their wageless labor, and inherited their goods, even if they had surviving relatives.[5]

Household Education

Even more than in Roman times, the family was the heart and soul of this new social system. Traditionally patriarchal, it provided food, clothing, shelter, religious affiliation, social status, economic opportunities, and education to all classes of society.

---

[3]The Theodosian Code, 438 A.D.
[4]Herrell DeGraff, "History of Agriculture," *The Encyclopedia Americana*, Vol. 1 (New York: Americana Corporation, 1962), p. 256.
[5]E. Belfort Bax, *The Peasant War in Germany* (New York: Russell and Russell, 1899, reissued 1968), pp. 42–43.

The educational aspects of family life involved imitation and explanation either in one's own or in someone else's home. Because crafts and trades were performed within the household, such an arrangement was eminently practical. Indeed, it worked so well that this informal system of education proved perfectly adequate to meet most of European society's educational needs for the next thousand years.

The putting out of male children into another's home was necessitated by the fact that they did not universally follow their father's occupation. If a boy's father wanted him to learn blacksmithing, for example, he would try to locate a blacksmith to train the lad in return for his doing most of the menial chores around the forge.

The Educational Functions of the Church

The great authority and educational importance accorded the family in the medieval world were complemented and reinforced by the Church.[6] Indeed, in some ways church attendance was very much the medieval equivalent of public school attendance. From its inception Christianity had an essentially educational character, and this made it perfectly natural for the Church to supplement the family and draw together the community in much the same way that public schools do today.

Man, woman, boy, and girl attended church services on a regular basis both on Sundays and in response to the seasonal round of holy days. Here they heard sermons intended to exhort, educate, and instruct them concerning matters both spiritual and practical. The ceremonial was also seen as "a book to the lewd [uneducated] people, that they may read in imagery and painture what clerks [clerics] read in the book."[7] To this end the churches were filled with statuary, relics, and paintings intended to educate and inform. Even the church windows were filled with educational messages in the form of beautiful displays of stained glass. Stories, biblical and secular, individually and in series, were depicted with the intention of informing the faithful, who were also required to memorize the Paternoster, the Apostles' Creed, and the Decalogue.[8]

In addition to regular services, the Church also promoted morality plays based on Christian teaching. Intended to instruct the laity, these plays were often entrusted to a single craft guild to carry out. Good natured rivalry encouraged these organizations of persons with common occupational interests to compete with one another in the elaborateness of their sets and costumes. In time these productions moved from the Church into the village square where there was more room for ambitious productions.[9]

---

[6]James Burke, *The Day the Universe Changed* (Boston: Little, Brown and Company, 1985), p. 91.
[7]Quoted by Lawrence Cremin in *American Education: The Colonial Experience* (New York: Harper & Row, 1970), p. 139.
[8]Ibid., p. 140.
[9]Janet Roebuck, *The Shaping of Urban Society* (New York: Scribners, 1974), p. 58.

The Near Disappearance of Schools

In Roman times the middle class had taken school attendance pretty much for granted. In the early middle ages this class itself had nearly disappeared and the corresponding educational institutions and practices had nearly disappeared with them. Moreover, because books and teachers were very scarce, schools themselves were practically nonexistent.

The Roman upper classes had been even better schooled than the middle class. Now an educated sword arm was more practical. The medieval upper classes needed skill at arms, not rhetoric or Greek. Predictably, a corresponding educational system that taught upper class youngsters the skills of knighthood largely replaced classical studies.

Upper class churchmen still required some measure of literacy in order to read the scriptures. But classical learning, as Aristotle understood it and both the Greek and Roman upper classes experienced it, was no longer widely valued and very nearly disappeared. Also, there were many within the Church who were suspicious of schooling. Like many of the Latin fathers of the Church who had preceded them, they frowned on all books except the Bible, and shunned scholarship as a source of damning pride.[10]

Even the more sympathetic Church fathers discouraged the study of "heathen" authors and "pagan" classics. However, the intellectual leaders of the Church were still men who had received a classical education, and they almost unconsciously transposed the fundamental attitudes of Roman thought into Latin Christianity. This process had been bitterly resisted even in Roman times by radical fundamentalists like Tertullian, the North African church father of the early third century, who denounced Greco-Roman philosophers as "hucksters of wisdom and eloquence," and "animals of self-glorification." He even proclaimed that the "pitiable Aristotle," the very embodiment of intellectual authority in the classical world, was a "fountain of heresy."[11]

Classical Culture and the Reemergence of Schools

Despite this sort of opposition, Christian thought eventually adopted classical culture. This step was due, in large measure, to the fact that as products of classical schooling themselves, most of the church fathers could not imagine another system and curriculum than the one that had been universal in the Mediterranean world for nearly a thousand years.[12]

The influence of St. Jerome (ca. A.D. 340–420) and St. Augustine (A.D. 354–430) were decisive in this regard. Jerome was a classically educated scholar whose work, most particularly a brilliant translation of the Bible from Hebrew into Latin, demonstrated that classical humanism could render enormous service to the faith. Augustine, while less sympathetic to the values of classical culture, was a highly persuasive advocate of Christian adoption of the

---

[10]Justo Gonzalez, *The Story of Christianity*, Vol. 1 (San Francisco: Harper & Row, 1984), p. 143.
[11]Quoted in Norman F. Cantor, *Medieval History* (New York: Macmillan, 1963), p. 69.
[12]Ibid.

Roman system of education. He also drew heavily on Platonic philosophy in developing his highly influential theological writings such as *The City of God.*[13] Despite Jerome's and Augustine's contributions, however, a fundamental tension remained between the authority of the Bible on the one hand, and classical humanism on the other.

Monastery Schools

Ultimately, the Christian Church kept the remnants of Romanized Greek learning alive.[14] As a matter of fact, it found a particularly sympathetic refuge in monasteries operating in the Benedictine tradition. Growing out of an Eastern tradition that held the material world in disdain, monasteries developed in Western Europe during the sixth century under the direction of St. Benedict. He adopted Eastern monasticism's life in religious communities with strict rules of poverty, obedience, labor, and devotion. But, whereas Eastern orders shunned formal study, Benedict required it as an act of devotion and discipline.

Benedict did not intend monastic scholarship to be motivated by a search for truth. That, he believed, was already at hand. His purpose was to encourage piety, discipline, and, above all, the dignity of work, because, "To work is to pray."

As a consequence of Benedict's belief that scholarly work was an act of devotion, the monks of monasteries, such as the Abbey of Monte Cassino (founded A.D. 529) and Cluny Abbey (founded A.D. 910), copied priceless manuscripts, wrote most of the books, and maintained the only libraries in the Europe of the Early Age of Faith.[15] They toiled to capture the purity of God's truth and offered their lives in the prayer of work, but in so doing they also preserved the pagan classical values that had been abandoned in the world outside.

In the early years candidates for the order were taken from all social levels. Since few monastic novices were literate when they arrived for training, monasteries had to provide some sort of schooling. Monastic formal education was further encouraged by the work of the Roman aristocrat and scholar Cassiodorus, who, in St. Benedict's day, set out to establish a large monastery that would serve as a center for Christian education and scholarship. It featured a school, a library, and a scriptorium that prepared copies of the works to be studied in the school. In the two centuries after the founding of Cassiodorus' scholarly monastery, Benedictine communities all over Europe established similar schools, libraries, and scriptoria. By 800 the more important Benedictine monasteries had flourishing schools and large libraries. In addition, the monks were producing the manuscripts that kept Christian scholarship alive.[16]

The early Benedictine monasteries did not accept children as novices; their only students were adults. Eventually, however, parents were permitted to

---

[13]Ibid., pp. 76–77.
[14]William Ker, *The Dark Ages* (New York: Mentor, 1958; original publication, 1904), p. 25.
[15]James Bowen, *A History of Western Education*, Vol. I (New York: St. Martin's, 1972), p. 345.
[16]Cantor, op. cit., p. 188.

Cluny Abbey, one of the most influential of the Benedictine monastaries.

offer their youngsters for training and initiation into Holy Orders. Later, when schooling had regained some of the substantial value it enjoyed in Roman times, other parents, uninterested in monastic life for their children, began enrolling them in monastery schools for a fee. These children were drawn almost exclusively from the class of the nobility. Despite initial reluctance on the part of many Abbots, such children eventually became a very important part of the student body.

Because of the almost universal illiteracy of the age, monastic schools had a disproportionate impact on early medieval society. Cantor estimates that fully 90 percent of all the literate men between A.D. 600 and 1100 were trained in monastery schools.[17]

Monastery schools were very much in the Temple image described in Chapter 2. All of the benefits of this type of school were present. Authority was clearly established, there was a great sense of community, the ends controlled the means, role models were readily available, and consensus was very deep. On the other hand, the costs of this model also made themselves felt. Suppression of variety and dissent and the fact that ends were not open to discussion led to intellectual aridity and the persecution of the very people who could have provided the system with the renewal it required.

Governance and the Substantial Value of Schooling

During the tumultuous centuries following Rome's collapse the Church assumed more and more of the governmental functions that the state could no

---

[17]Ibid.

longer sustain. Church officials developed administrative offices, courts of law—even an army.

The growth of this infrastructure required increasing numbers of literate administrators and clerks. (Significantly, "clerk" is a derivation of "cleric," the medieval term for clergyman.) This requirement, in turn, corresponded with an increased need for schools.[18]

The growth of the Church's governmental role also increased individual incentives for attending school. Being schooled now gave an individual great advantage within the Church's growing administrative bureaucracy. Also, because clerics were virtually the only ones able to read and write, only they could record treaties, read letters, draft contracts, register births and deaths, probate wills, and draw up deeds, and all of these services were a source of considerable income. Most important, only the literate could read and interpret the word of God. Since the medieval period is chiefly characterized by the fact that thirty generations of human beings defined their conduct in terms of God's word, this was an enormous advantage.[19]

Church officials also had organizational incentives for making certain that priests were schooled. It helped them solidify administrative control through uniform training of Church bureaucrats. A common school experience also promoted group solidarity and a similar perspective on the world. Finally, because literacy of any kind was utterly distinctive, schooling further legitimated the high social status of the clergy.[20]

Despite these individual and organizational incentives, an almost universal scarcity of resources and educated persons meant that many of the lower ranking early churchmen were nearly illiterate. Also, a goodly number of the high clergy were political appointees, long on connections but short on learning.[21] Thus the ideal of a fully literate clergy was not realized. However, churchmen were so distinctive in their literacy that throughout the early Age of Faith it was assumed that an educated man had to be some sort of clergyman. If, for example, it were discovered that an individual accused of a crime could read and write, it was considered proof of his status as a religious and he would be turned over to the Church for trial.[22]

Schooling Women

Initially, monasticism was not confined to men. Women had their own monasteries and monastic leadership. In fact, many early monasteries enrolled both men and women. Thus, with the cautious encouragement of Gregory I (540–604), the early medieval church benefited from the accomplishments

---

[18]Thomas Mendenhall et al., *Ideas and Institutions in European History* (New York: Holt, 1948), p. 23.
[19]G. B. Adams, *Civilization During the Middle Ages* (New York: Scribner, 1932), p. 190.
[20]Robert Arnove and Harvey Graff, "National Literacy Campaigns: Historical and Comparative Lessons," *Phi Delta Kappan*, Vol. 69, No. 3 (November, 1987), p. 205.
[21]J. O'Sullivan and J. Burns, *Medieval Europe* (New York: Crofts, 1946), p. 302.
[22]Loren MacKinney, *The Medieval World* (New York: Farrar & Rinehart, 1938), p. 655.

of well-educated women such as Hild of Whitby, Hildegard of Bingen, and Roswitha of Gandersheim.

As the revolutionary fervor of Christianity faded, a more reactionary attitude toward women began to assert itself. As a result, the public activity of women declined, their place in the church receded, and their schooling became more and more unlikely. Ultimately, the Gregorian "reform" movement of the eleventh century severely discouraged female monastic orders. This effectively stifled the schooling of women.[23]

Court Schools

Monasteries did not operate the only schools in the early period of the Age of Faith. A few Court schools were also available to a very limited number of upper class children. A remnant of the Roman tutorial system, these schools addressed the status and, to some extent, the vocational concerns of aristocratic families. The most influential was sponsored by Charlemagne (crowned Emperor by the Pope in A.D. 800).

To ensure the preeminence of his Court school, Charlemagne recruited Alcuin, a famed English schoolman, to be its principal teacher. Gathering scarce intellectual talent from throughout Europe, Alcuin established a school that enrolled the Emperor, his family, and courtiers.

Charlemagne's Educational Initiatives

Charlemagne also issued edicts upgrading the schooling of the clergy and directing "ministers of God's altar" to school all children, rich and poor. He also supported scribal activity that improved libraries throughout Europe.

---

[23]Gary Clabaugh, "A History of Male Attitudes Toward the Education of Women," *Educational Horizons*, Vol. 64, No. 3 (Spring 1986), pp. 131–132.

POINT/COUNTERPOINT

In the past historians have often emphasized a "Great Man" theory of history. They assumed, without much validation, that history was, in the words of nineteenth-century historian Thomas Carlyle, "the biography of great men" like Charlemagne or Alcuin. Serious challenges to this assumption developed in the mid-twentieth century—possibly as a consequence of the democratization of Western culture. Some historians began suggesting that history was really written by the actions of thousands of obscure and quite ordinary individuals. Others argued that powerful impersonal forces, such as economics, class interests, or even hidden psychological mechanisms, shaped human affairs. Though these disagreements remain unresolved, contemporary historians have come to recognize the limitations of the "Great Man" theory.

The "Great Men" and women in this history were included for three reasons: first, in the hope that by identifying past educational trends with historic individuals we will help the student understand and remember the trends; second, because it is possible to identify individuals whose accomplishments have forever changed some particular aspect of education; and third, because tests required for teacher certification often include questions on famous individuals.

Ambitious as they were, these efforts produced little of lasting consequence. Not even the commands of an Emperor could alter the basic tenor of the times. Schooling simply had little substantial value outside the Church.

Necessity, Scarcity, and Schooling

Scarcities of all kinds also stood in Charlemagne's way. There were very few literate individuals who could act as teachers, and there was also an extreme scarcity of books. It took a monk approximately a year to handcopy an average volume and books were so valuable they were sometimes traded for vineyards or houses. Libraries were small, enormously difficult to establish, and meaningful to only a handful of people. Textbooks were an impossibility, paper was unavailable, and parchment was very expensive.[24]

THE RISE OF TOWNS

By the twelfth century the changes initiated by the collapse of the Roman empire had been accommodated. A subsequent improvement in public order encouraged a revival of trade. European culture was beginning a slow transformation from a rural, agrarian to an urban, commercial base.[25]

The old knightly nobility had always looked with suspicion upon the merchants and craftsmen who had gathered for protection behind town walls. There was not even an official place in the medieval social structure for those who made their living in them. But despite harassment, blackmail, and oppressive taxes by the nobility, towns—and the economic activity and rule of law which they sheltered and promoted—were now becoming the dynamic element of medieval life.[26]

The type of community one lives in has a decisive influence on the character and destiny of its inhabitants, and for this reason the revival of towns was a very important development in the history of education and schooling. Not only did town growth encourage the development of new and dynamic forms of schooling, which we will review shortly, but they also were educative simply because they represented a broader world than that of the medieval village.

Guilds and Education

During the 1100s and 1200s many new occupations developed within the protection of city walls. Most were associated with guilds of merchants and craftsmen who regulated commerce and industry. Created for the defense of free citizens against the nobility, and the furtherance of trade monopoly, guilds came to dominate medieval city life. And as cities grew, the influence of the guilds grew with them.

---

[24]O'Sullivan and Burns, op. cit., pp. 302–303.
[25]Mendenhall et al., op. cit., pp. 3 and 88.
[26]Cantor, op. cit., pp. 278–279.

In time guilds became extraordinarily powerful. They often were able to successfully oppose the nobility and prevail upon kings to grant their members certain privileges and immunities. In some parts of Europe, North Germany, for example, they also managed to totally regulate the practice of trades, set tough standards for the training of apprentices, and demand real competence from aspiring masters.

The guild's carefully structured educational systems were modeled loosely on the family. Apprenticeship training was widely employed for those who wished to learn a trade and gain membership in the guild. During these apprenticeships young unpaid novices lived as surrogate members of the master's household. Here they learned trade or merchant skills from a master craftsman or merchant who provided supervision, training, and room and board. In turn the apprentice provided cheap labor and, ideally at least, familial faithfulness.

The workplace was commonly in or near the master's home, and the apprentice was obliged to live within his family. Because he was not a true family member, he had more independence than at home. In fact, when he was not working, he often lived in a condition of semi-independence that many young men found very congenial. It was not all that pleasant for the townsfolk, however, for after the working day was over they had to put up with roaming bands of adolescent apprentices getting into all sorts of trouble.[27]

---

[27]Michael B. Katz, "Connections Between the Origins of Public Education and the Major Themes in American Social History," unpublished paper distributed at the University of Pennsylvania.

Guilds set up carefully structured apprenticeship systems modeled loosely on the family.

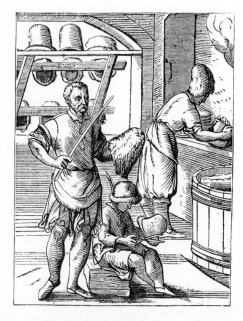

Figure 11.1 **TYPICAL STEPS IN THE EDUCATION OF A MASTER CRAFTSMAN**

The apprenticeship system was part of the hierarchical structure of guilds. The apprentice was at the bottom of the hierarchy. After a number of years of training, typically seven, the apprentice was promoted to journeyman. In this capacity the master was required to pay him. After several years of journeyman status he might qualify to become a master himself, if, in examining his "masterpiece," the guild was satisfied with the excellence of his skills (Figure 11.1).

Guilds provided social welfare services to their members. Sometimes guild officials went beyond providing relief to destitute and disabled members and set up funds to pay for the formal schooling of members' children. This practice supplemented the apprenticeship system. In time, as the wealth and power of the guilds grew, it also became increasingly common for them to start their own schools. They offered elementary instruction to their members' children. As with municipal schools, the Church was not in direct control.[28]

Cathedral Schools

A few careers required more formal education. Bankers, lawyers, physicians, notaries, clerics, teachers, and others had to be able to read and write. As a result, schooling became more desirable as it opened more and more occupational doors. Schooling was regaining more and more of the substantial value it had enjoyed in Roman times.

At first, monasteries offered virtually the only schooling available. With the increase in demand, however, bishops began to establish schools. At first the next bishop might be a semiliterate who would disband the faculty and sell off the library.[29] However, as the Age of Faith progressed, the growth of cities increased the wealth and power of the bishops, while undermining that of the

---

[28]S. E. Frost, *Historical and Philosophical Foundations of Western Education* (Columbus, Ohio: Merrill, 1960), pp. 151–153.
[29]Cantor, op. cit., p. 189.

abbots in their rural monasteries. These developments were accompanied by a new and sustained commitment to schooling on the part of the bishops. Using their abundant resources, they not only erected magnificent cathedrals, but also began offering schooling on a continuous basis.

Cathedral schools were customarily located in or near the bishop's palace. The teachers were paid by the diocese. Their urban locations meant they could easily attract both students and teachers. They also benefited from every increase in urban life and wealth. Soon they replaced monasteries as the chief educational institution of the age. By the 1200s Cathedral schools were playing a major role in providing higher education throughout Europe.

Originally stressing religious instruction, many of these schools added a general education component based loosely on the so-called seven liberal arts. This curriculum, remnants of which we described in the last chapter, was derived from the Greeks and further defined by the Romans.[30] The program of study was divided into the Trivium, composed of grammar, rhetoric, and logic, and the Quadrivium, consisting of arithmetic, music, geometry, and astronomy.[31]

These "liberal arts" were taught unevenly in Cathedral schools. The Quadrivium was widely neglected. The Trivium faired better, but its rhetoric component faded as Latin grammar and Aristotelian logic emerged all powerful.[32]

Although they appealed to status interests, Cathedral schools also had a distinctly vocational function. A Master's degree, the typical terminal degree from a Cathedral school, helped one qualify for the growing ecclesiastical bureaucracy, Cathedral school teaching positions or similar high status careers. Later in their development Cathedral schools added training in vocational specialties like theology, philosophy, and canon and civil law, as well as medicine to their curriculums.[33]

Because of this vocational connection, energetic and ambitious young men of low birth, such as Thomas à Becket, were able to use such schooling as an avenue of upward social mobility.[34] It was not easy, however, requiring about six years of study and a final examination that some scholars likened to the "Last Judgment."

Instruction in Cathedral schools, as in Monastery schools, was entirely in Latin. Students were penalized for lapsing into their native tongue or dialect, and informants, nicknamed "wolves," specialized in reporting violations. Latin was essential to both Church and scholar because Europeans spoke many languages and these broke down into even more dialects. Indeed, the dialect spoken in one village was often nearly incomprehensible in a village fifty miles away.[35]

---

[30]The liberal arts were most likely passed to the Middle Ages in a book written in the fifth century by Martianus Capella.
[31]Frost, op. cit., p. 84.
[32]Haskins, *The Rise of the Universities* (New York: Holt, 1923), pp. 39–41.
[33]O'Sullivan and Burns, op. cit., p. 306.)
[34]Roebuck, op. cit., p. 58.
[35]Burke, op. cit., p. 92.

Latin was the language of power and privilege. Mastering Ovid and Cicero was a badge of membership in the upper classes. Such learning would have startled an illiterate nobleman of the eighth century.[36]

Correspondence Between School Practices and the Broader Society

The lack of room in Cathedral or Monastery schools for individuality, personal initiative or innovation corresponded to the medieval world outside the school. In this world the collective, be it the family, the village or the Church, took precedence over the desires of the individual. Neither individual privacy nor autonomy were recognized as desirable. Similarly, medieval schooling's rigidity, authoritarianism, and preoccupation with the next world reflected the rigid group-mindedness of the Age of Faith.[37]

As far as the students were concerned, they did not welcome whippings, nor look forward to the mindless memorization and recitation so characteristic of the schools of that period. But their underlying resentments were tempered by the fact that personal accommodation to social circumstances, necessity, and authority were required in all aspects of their life.[38]

The Medieval View of Children

Another elemental reason for the rigidity and inflexibility of medieval school-ing was that school practices corresponded with medieval attitudes toward and practices in regard to children. Children were not seen as particularly special, nor were they understood to be fundamentally different from adults. Indeed, childhood was not generally understood as a period of life worth cherishing or extending.

This medieval view of children had a great influence on school practice. Ground-breaking historians, such as Philippe Ariès, point out that the lack of emphasis on cumulative or incremental learning (for example, starting with the easy, ending with the hard) reflected the absence of our present-day appreciation of human growth and development.[39]

Similarly, medieval teachers made nearly universal use of physical punish-ment, particularly whipping, to control and motivate students. This too was a reflection of the broader societal view that physical coercion was desirable, not only because it changed behavior but also because it properly subdued the child's self-assertiveness. Until this was accomplished, it was believed, little true education or spiritual growth could take place.[40]

---

[36]Gies, op. cit., p. 254.
[37]Lawrence Stone, *The Family, Sex, and Marriage In England 1500–1800* (New York: Harper & Row, 1977), pp. 4–5.
[38]Ibid.
[39]Philippe Ariès, *Centuries of Childhood* (London: Jonathan Cape, 1962).
[40]Carl N. Degler, *At Odds* (New York: Oxford U. Press, 1980), pp. 86–87.

Parish Schools

Cathedrals and monasteries were not the only source of church-sponsored schooling. By approximately A.D. 1000 parish priests were being officially urged by high Church officials to promote teaching and support the growth of literacy. In large parishes this often resulted in schools that were bigger and better staffed than those of the monasteries. In such parishes it was now possible for boys whose parents could afford the tuition, to learn to read and write, to study scripture, and to begin the mastery of Latin.[41]

Municipal or Town Schools

The growth of towns and cities, which began with the revival of trade in the tenth century signaled the emergence of a new urbanized social order based on commerce. They were a power base that had the potential for rivaling both the Church and the landed aristocrats.

As towns and cities developed, their residents began throwing off the limitations of feudalism. Alternative institutions formed which corresponded to the needs of a new social order. Town schools were one of these institutions. Sponsored by municipal authorities rather than the Church, such schools were originally concerned with providing the children of the town's upper classes with a status-related Latin Grammar kind of literary education similar to that offered in Cathedral and Monastery schools.

It was not long, however, before some municipalities were also sponsoring elementary level schools taught in the vernacular language rather than Latin. Such schools were intended to instruct middle class males in technical skills relating to the growing complexity of business and commercial life.

These elements allowed some very limited aspects of a Town Meeting image of the school to assert themselves. Close connection to business and commercial life encouraged greater changeability and responsiveness. However, Town schools still tended to correspond to the Temple image. The age was too authoritarian to permit otherwise. Nevertheless, major changes were just over the horizon, and their imminent dawning was announced by two conflicts that were becoming more and more apparent.

The first conflict involved a struggle between the sacred and the secular for place and power in the world. This struggle was clearly embodied in this Church-town competition over control of schooling.[42]

The second conflict involved two levels of culture, the technical and the formal. (These are described in detail in Chapter 5.) This struggle found expression when, much to the horror of some Church officials, elements of the technical culture, mainly Aristotle's logic, were put to work to analyze the faith. We will learn the results shortly.

---

[41]Edward Power, *Main Currents in the History of Education* (New York: McGraw-Hill, 1970), p. 290.
[42]Mendenhall, op. cit., p. 45.

The End of the Church's School Monopoly

Town schools were a fundamental threat to the Church's control of schooling. But that was already being threatened by the freelance instruction available from itinerant teachers. Satisfying a growing popular demand for schooling, these entrepreneurs had multiplied as towns grew.

Church officials felt that Town schools would deal these itinerant teachers a heavy blow. For this reason they were inclined to tolerate them. They were the lesser evil.

For their part, most municipal officials felt they had to compromise with Church officials regarding schooling. Religion was still very much a part of the Town school curriculum, and Church officials had no intention of losing control over this aspect of instruction. They demanded an oversight role, and they got it.

Church officials had another major concern. Local clerics suffered a loss of income once those educated in Town vernacular schools no longer had to pay them for writing wills, keeping records, reading letters, and the like. To allay this concern, municipalities often paid the Church an amount equal to the estimated loss. Given these concessions, Church officials lapsed into uneasy silence regarding their increasingly formidable secular competitors.

As the centuries advanced many Town schools became exceptionally well supported. Some even had the resources to offer very substantial wages and special privileges in order to recruit first-rate teaching talent. These Town schools came to rival all but the finest Cathedral schools, joining them as a source of the first medieval universities.[43]

The Rise of the Universities

The 1100s saw the origin of the great universities of Western Europe. First referred to as *Studium Generale*, these institutions evolved from Cathedral or Town schools. Technically, to become a university a Cathedral or Town school required only the incorporation of its masters into a universitas or guild.[44] *Universitas* means "corporation" in Latin. Members of the *universitas* had no common library or buildings of their own. They were simply a society of masters and scholars with their own corporate organization. In Paris, for example, students merely registered for instruction with a particular master. It was up to him to furnish accommodations. These were usually rented on the left bank of the Seine in the vicinity of the Cathedral of Nôtre Dame. Congregating here in great numbers, this community of scholars gave the area its nickname, the Latin Quarter.

Most universities grew quickly. In Paris, for example, the transformed Cathedral school rapidly became so extensive that it attracted teachers and students from all of Christendom. This growth was due, in large measure, to the

[43]Haskins, op. cit., pp. 119–126.
[44]Cantor, op. cit., p. 395.

In time, particularly in England, colleges such as Kings College at Cambridge University became centers of university life and teaching.

fact that under the patronage and protection of the Bishop of Paris, the original Cathedral school had attracted to its faculty some of the great leaders of European thought.

Who was permitted to teach in these fast-growing institutions? At first Church officials had sole authority regarding this matter. But when the teachers gained control, they developed a licensing process that became the basis for our present system of academic degrees. The faculty also gained control of the disciplining of students. This too was originally under the authority of Church officials.[45] The gradual erosion of Church authority corresponded with the progressive secularization of medieval society.

The teachers' guilds eventually became very powerful and came to command special rights and privileges. They could try their own members, were exempt from local taxes, could not be conscripted into the military, and had the right to suspend classes in protest of unjust treatment.[46] (Notice that teachers' strikes are about 800 years old and very much part of the university tradition.)

Colleges

As students and teachers crowded into university towns, residents realized that renting accommodations could yield handsome profits. Rents soared, and many students, already impoverished by fees for tuition and the rental of books, found it impossible to continue their studies.

Wealthy individuals sometimes endowed a hospice, hall, or residence for these poor scholars. These were called **colleges**. In time, particularly in

---

[45]Loren C. MacKinney, *The Medieval World* (New York: Farrar & Rinehart, 1938), p. 663.
[46]Frost, op. cit., p. 142.

England, these colleges became centers of university life and teaching. After all, they had buildings and endowments while the corporation controlling the university had none.[47]

Scholasticism

The system of study and writing that developed in the universities was called **Scholasticism.** The term applied to a wide variety of philosophical studies guided by Aristotelian logic, but dominated by theology. At its best the scholastic method cut to the heart of complex questions, revealing contradictions and truth with startling clarity. At its worst, it became "decoupled" from the actual requirements of scholarship, becoming, instead, the chief instrument of those who loved empty formalism more than truth.

Scholastics did **not** subject **all** things to logical scrutiny. The teachings of the Church set limits beyond which logic dared not stray. But even when Scholasticism worked within these boundaries, laboring to prove Christian truths, the results were sometimes more embarrassing than helpful. An unresolved tension between the formal and the technical culture was building just beneath the surface of things.

Scholars and Students

When a scholar published a work that was perceived to threaten the existing order it was commonly burnt. Unauthorized translations of the Bible were a favorite target. To make a point, the offending book was often consigned to the flames by the public hangman. It was also common practice to place the author, usually a professor, in the pillory. In fact, after his head was placed through the hole, he was often nailed to the board by his ears. After a suitable period of public abuse he would be released by the simple expedient of cutting off his ears. These were left on the pillory as a warning.[48] (We learn from this that academic freedom is a relatively recent convention.)

Most professors did not risk their ears. Few offered more than bookish formalism.[49] Some, however, were brilliant teachers and daring scholars. They were the stars of the university system, attracting hundreds of students and persecution.

Pierre Abelard (1079–1142), philosopher and theologian, was such a teacher. His lectures attracted hundreds of students to the infant University of Paris. However, his brilliant logical explorations of Church doctrine, while helping to renew the Church, also attracted official disapproval. Dissecting theology with Aristotle's logical scalpel proved a dangerous procedure. Abelard was first compelled to burn one of his treatises with his own hand. Ulti-

---

[47]A.B. Cobban, *The Medieval Universities: Their Development and Organization* (London: Methuen, 1975), p. 47.
[48]William Andrews, *Old Time Punishments* (London: Tabbard Press, 1890), pp. 90–103.
[49]Hayes, Baldwin, and Cole, op. cit., p. 247.

mately he was condemned to prison for heresy. However, this did not prevent his methods from eventually winning out. They were to influence theology for over 300 years.

Most medieval professors were not like Abelard—risking all in the pursuit of truth. Indeed, many professors taught safe, practical subjects like letter and document writing.

Each professor was an independent entrepreneur, existing on his students' fees. Naturally, they competed for students. Favorite tactics were to water down requirements and to cater to popular tastes. One enterprising professor at the University of Bologna, for example, urged prospective students to forget Cicero, whom the professor could not recall having read himself, and learn to write letters, wills, and other documents instead. Remote both from logic and scholarship, such professors frequently attracted record numbers of students.[50]

As a matter of fact, despite the rhapsodic fantasies of some present-day conservative reformers, the focus of the medieval university was very vocational. Virtually all of the instruction was designed with practical ends in mind.

We should also note that medieval scholars were not necessarily musty intellectuals whose biggest thrills were the products of logic. Abelard's personal life refutes this myth. He was the principal figure, along with the beautiful Heloise, in one of the world's most famous love stories. While teaching in Paris the passionate cleric fell in love with, impregnated, then secretly married his 17-year-old student. When Heloise's condition and marriage were revealed, her uncle, a high Church official, vowed revenge. He hired a band of thugs who, on his orders, brutally castrated Abelard. This mutilation made Abelard ineligible for clerical advancement. It also convinced him to join a monastery. In response, Heloise took the veil. Their love continued from afar for a lifetime. Eventually they were reunited, but only after death when they were buried side by side. Their story, popularized in literature, is celebrated to this day.

Like Abelard, medieval students were also interested in extracurricular activities. More than one contemporary professorial account of university life laments the "students" who spend their time drinking and wenching, going to class only once or twice a week. One professor noted dryly that when they finally have to return home, these so-called scholars fill their book bags with imposing volumes to impress their parents, traveling "with a full sack and empty mind."[51]

Violence was also a common feature of university life. Drunken brawls, sword fights, stone-throwing incidents (even in chapel), and occasional full-scale combats between "town and gown" were not at all unusual. Such behavior corresponded to the generally violent nature of medieval life. It also reflected the fact that many national and regional antagonisms came to a boil when students from all over Europe got together.

---

[50]Haskins, op. cit., p. 45.
[51]Ibid., p. 87.

Eventually, university officials were compelled to hire marshalls, complete with uniforms and head-cracking maces, just to keep order. Today, their traditional costume and mace are used only to add color to academic processions where they are visual reminders of the way the past always influences the present.

Secular Knowledge

For centuries religion, like other aspects of the formal level of culture, had been taught by precept and admonition. But the great medieval schoolmen tried to harmonize the technical level methods of the Greeks, particularly Aristotle's logic, with the doctrines of the Church. Often, as with Abelard, the task of reconciling the secular and the sacred was risky and the results were limited by the power of Church officials. Nevertheless, Aristotle's logic was put to work on questions of faith. Technical experts were now analyzing religion systematically, rationally, and deliberately. But the question was, could this be done without killing Christianity?

Reconciling Faith and Reason

In the thirteenth century, the famous Dominican Thomas Aquinas came up with an answer that proved definitive for Christendom. Aquinas was a scholar of uncommon devotion. As a student he had pursued his studies in such dogged silence that his companions nicknamed him the "Dumb Ox." As an adult, he addressed the reconciliation of faith and reason with the same purposeful intensity. In so doing he produced a systematic exposition on Christian theology based upon Aristotelian logic. In his work *Summa Theologica*, still a standard authority in the Roman Church, Aquinas painstakingly developed the idea that faith and reason have two distinct spheres that, he claimed, *cannot* logically be in conflict. Thus, said Aquinas, they can live happily side by side.

Many now regard the *Summa Theologica* as the greatest achievement of medieval philosophy. It was certainly the ultimate triumph of Scholasticism. This accomplishment eventually won Aquinas the more flattering nickname "the Angelic Doctor." Today he is one of the most celebrated saints of the Catholic Church.

Like Abelard before him, Aquinas' contribution can best be understood as an example of the social renewal function of schooling. He temporarily reinvigorated a heavily **institutionalized** Church by applying Aristotelian logic to theology. (See Chapter 8.)

The Death of Feudalism

In the 1300s Europe entered into a crisis lasting more than one hundred years. Economic stagnation set in, population declined, and land remained untilled as civil wars between competing cliques of feudal lords laid waste to the countryside. Mass insurrections of desperate peasants and the urban poor spread throughout Europe. Compounding all of this, in the later half of the century came the greatest disaster of all—the Black Death, or bubonic plague. Before it was over one-third of the population of Europe was dead. Things were coming apart. Old ways were disintegrating before new ways could be born.

Nearly a thousand years after its beginnings, feudalism—the political, economic, and social basis of medieval civilization—was dying. Emerging national monarchies filled the vacuum.[52] So did a new upper class of wealthy merchants, bankers, and traders.

As far as the socioeducational system was concerned, medieval schooling's rigidity and inflexibility eventually became counterproductive, even in an age when such characteristics were the norm. Schooling had become almost totally institutionalized. (See Chapter 8.) Meanings and routines had become typified, and were coercively transmitted to newcomers without sufficient thought or evaluation.[53] Assignments that once had deeper meaning were now copied by teachers and students alike in a simple, imitative way. Thought puzzles were still resolved according to the dictates of Aristotelian logic, but the process had often become wooden and mechanical. Even students' letters to parents reflected, at least by modern standards, a curiously generic and artificial quality.[54]

Ultimately, broad social changes compelled major educational reforms. With a conservatism characteristic of education, many of its forms, such as apprenticeship and the university, survived. But their substance was altered so substantially over time as to make schools virtually new institutions.

SCHOOLING, THE RENAISSANCE, AND HUMANISM

The disorder of the 1300s reflected exciting developments. The use of gunpowder, an invention of the technical culture, was leveling the distinction between knight and commoner. Travel and discovery were bringing people in touch with new ideas and inventions. Spurred on by ever widening patterns of trade, local loyalties were taking on regional and even national character as the rustic Latin spoken in different parts of southern Europe became languages of their own and, in the process, supported the growth of national consciousness.[55] All of this supported the emergence of a new confidence that both man and nature was worthy of study; a view that was to have a profound impact on schooling.

[52]Jerome Blum, Rondo Cameron, and Thomas Barnes, *A History of the European World* (Boston: Little, Brown, 1966), pp. 4, 5.
[53]Meyer and Rowan, "Institutional Organizations," p. 346.
[54]Haskins, op. cit., p. 41.
[55]S. E. Frost, Jr., *Essentials of the History of Education* (New York: Barrons, 1947), p. 86.

The Revolutionary Impact of Printing

These developments were followed by a technical revolution that had an enormous impact on education and schooling. In fact, printing with movable type was one of the most important technological advances in human history. It was made possible by the happy confluence of the invention of the printing press and the newfound availability of inexpensive paper.

Printing appears to have originated in Europe around 1440. About this same time, as a result of the Crusades, paper imported from Egypt began replacing the expensive parchment that had helped make books scarce. This inexpensive print medium, which, unlike parchment, was porous enough to take the ink from the typeface, made it possible to mass produce books on a previously unimagined scale.[56]

By 1500, sixty years after its invention, there were approximately forty printing presses in Europe that had already printed about 8 million volumes. Significantly, few of these presses were in university cities. Most were in centers of business, banking, or royal government.[57]

Initially, there was a limited market for the printed word because few could read. But print technology made it both possible and desirable for a wide variety of people to become readers. And as they did so, often through self-instruction, education entered a new era.

Printing spread knowledge far beyond its customary boundaries of monastery, church, and university. Men of science and letters were able to share ideas and discoveries with great facility. Theologians and philosophers carried on dialogues with hundreds, even thousands, of colleagues.

But printing was not confined to scholarly uses. Most printed material concerned the how-to of trade and industry. Europe's skilled artisans had been decimated by the Black Death. This, and the restrictive practices and lengthy apprenticeships of the guilds, had created a desperate need for craftsmen. With the printing press, technical knowledge became the property of anyone who could read.[58]

This new opportunity greatly increased demands for schooling. As the great scientist Francis Bacon put it, "Printing made mighty for the advancement of learning."[59]

Not since the dawn of the written word had there been such a revolution in information technology. Nearly everyone desirous of influencing others or bettering themselves sought to use it. Centralized monarchies enhanced their control and revenue collection. The Church disseminated devotional literature and decrees. It even printed thousands of indulgences, the sale of which was intended to pay for the construction of St. Peter's in Rome. Most importantly, thousands upon thousands of ordinary people set about to teach themselves to read, or to learn the skill informally from someone who already knew how.

---

[56] Will Durant, *The Story of Philosophy* (New York: Pocket Books, 1960), p. 105.
[57] Burke, op. cit., p. 113.
[58] Ibid., p. 116.
[59] Edgar Knight, *Twenty Centuries of Education* (Boston: Ginn, 1940).

Printing had an enormous
impact on education and
schooling.

All in all, most of the developments encouraged by the explosive growth of printing bode well for schooling, but ill for established authority. As we have seen elsewhere, withholding or influencing the flow of information is a key element in social control. With the invention of print technology, those in power found such control far more difficult. What is more, the proliferation of books encouraged private reading as opposed to public reading or the oral tradition. With private reading, communication could occur without the social interaction of members of society. Such communication in seclusion encouraged a new sort of individualism that is probably one of the most important differences between traditional and modern societies.[60]

The Renaissance and the Growth of Humanism

The Renaissance was a particularly powerful expression of individualism. It began in the period 1350–1450, in rich and independent city-states in northern Italy such as Milan, Florence, and Venice. These cities were ruled by a new upper class of rich merchants and displaced landed aristocrats who had accumulated wealth from the growth of banking and trade. Unaligned with traditional power, their influence soon created a social climate different from that in any other part of Europe. Their material wealth focused attention on things of this world, and the various city-states vied with one another for economic and cultural preeminence. Wealthy men put their surplus capital into art, beautiful buildings, and patronage for scholars and writers.[61] This was the beginning of the modern, as opposed to the medieval, outlook.

The term Renaissance refers to the revival of classical learning, and it was this that captured the imagination of the leaders of the northern Italian city-states. They fell in love with the nearly forgotten legacy of the Greek and Roman classics.

---

[60]Jack Goody and I.P. Watts, "The Consequences of Literacy," in Jack Goody, ed., *Literacy in Traditional Societies* (Cambridge: Harvard U. Press, 1968), pp. 27–68.
[61]Blum, op. cit., p. 66.

Studying the classics was known as **humanism** from *studia humanitatis*, the Latin term for studies that empower a human being to express personal individuality in conduct, speech, and writing.[62] Many of these works had been studied by the scholastics during medieval times, but scholars of that period had attempted to reconcile them with Christianity. Humanist scholars did no such thing. They accepted the classics on their own terms because they reflected their own secular and individualistic notions of how humans should live and act.[63]

The reverence for authority once reserved for the Church was now directed toward the ancients. This was a step toward emancipation from Church dogma, since the ancients disagreed with each other and individual reason was required to choose among them.[64]

Now that knowledge could be picked up from a book, the age of unquestioned authority was over.[65] Propelled by the optimism inherent in this realization, the humanists reaffirmed the importance, dignity, and possibilities of humankind. The spirit of this new age was captured in the boast of the Renaissance architect, painter, and writer Leon Alberti, "A man can do all things if he will."

Fortified by the ready availability of the printed word, newly optimistic about the human prospect, and independent of the universities by virtue of their wealthy patrons, scholars turned their attention to things human rather than divine. During the Age of Faith, St. Anselm (1033–1109) had once declared, "I do not seek to know that I may believe, but I believe in order that I may understand." These new scholars stood this dictum on its head. They sought to know in order to understand. Belief, for them, was largely irrelevant.

The Renaissance spread slowly throughout Europe. The study of Greek became a new enthusiasm, supplementing the study of Latin. Inexpensive printed editions of Greek and Roman classics greatly stimulated interest in "Pagan" sources. Philosophers, too, asserted their independence from theologians and even defied the censorship of the Church.

Finally, the Church itself made peace with humanism. Nicholas V (1447–1455), the first humanist Pope, went so far as to give papal offices to men of learning regardless of their orthodoxy.[66] And the Jesuits turned humanism into immensely valuable educational coinage when they incorporated it into their school curricula.

The Latin Grammar School

Many humanists were intent on revolutionizing schooling. Rejecting the medieval model, they reinvestigated the value of the classics, the relationship of

---

[62]Blum, Cameron, and Barnes, op. cit., p. 67.
[63]Ibid., p. 66.
[64]Bertrand Russell, *A History of Western Philosophy* (New York: Simon & Schuster, 1945), p. 495.
[65]Burke, op. cit., p. 122.
[66]Russell, op. cit., p. 498.

content to teaching style, the education of women, the value of physical education, and the schooling of the common man. Since many humanists were employed as secretaries, officials, or teachers by men of wealth and power, they were able to effectively promote their conclusions.[67]

The Renaissance and its attendant humanism reflected fundamental alterations in European status relationships. The medieval universities had served the old feudal order well. But when a new elite of merchants and bankers rose to positions of power and wealth, university officials failed to accommodate their interests. Perhaps they were tied too tightly to the old institutional order and the related scholastic way of thinking. In any case, the new class found it necessary to support the establishment of a new type of school, called the **Latin Grammar school**. It was devoted to humanistic studies, as well as to the status concerns of this mercantile elite.

Latin Grammar schools accepted children of late elementary school age and retained them through part of what today would be college. Their name derived from their emphasis on the study of Latin grammar AND literature. They also emphasized social control concerns like good manners and athletics.

Latin Grammar schools became very popular and survived for three hundred years as the schooling of choice for upper and middle class boys.[68] In fact, many school practices still reflect the Latin Grammar school curriculum. The present emphasis on giving students a liberal education intended to broaden and deepen their intellect is a direct reflection of this tradition.

Schools that still retain some elements of the Latin Grammar School, such as Boston Latin Grammar in Massachusetts and "prep" schools like Phillips Academy, tend to be strongly status oriented. The contemporary vocational utility of Latin is not what it was in the 1500s.

Transforming the University

Eventually humanistic influences led to changes in the Cathedral school and the university. But before that happened many universities were wracked by conflict between the "ancients" representing scholasticism, and the "moderns" representing humanism.

Scholasticism, once totally dominant in Cathedral school and university, was now subject to increasingly effective ridicule by humanistic scholars. Conservative scholastics, such as the famous John Duns Scotus (1274–1308), were accused by humanists of being unwilling or unable to learn. The charge stuck. The term Dunsmen or Dunse came to signify someone of invincible stupidity.[69]

The chief impact of humanism was on the university curriculum rather than on methods of teaching. Rhetoric and public speaking were supplanted by prose composition, letter writing, and even business administration.[70]

---

[67]Blum, op. cit. p. 68, and Power, op. cit., p. 379.
[68]William T. Kane, S. J., *History of Education* (Chicago: Loyola U. Press, 1954), p. 254.
[69]*The Encyclopedia Americana*, Vol. 9 (New York: Americana, 1962), pp. 401–402.
[70]Burke, op. cit., p. 68.

Desidarius Erasmus (ca. 1466–1536), one of the most famous scholars of the Renaissance, typified the humanist educator. His widely read publications did much to popularize humanism in northern Europe. Though he remained a Catholic throughout his life, his merciless attacks on empty formalism and vice within the Roman church complemented the Lutheran revolt.

Thanks to the printing press, Erasmus was a widely sold author. His many publications included several popular books on schooling, *The Right Method of Instruction* and *The Liberal Education of Boys*. In them he advocated what were then radical goals for schooling, such as refining taste, correcting ecclesiastical abuse, and promoting world peace. Such goals stood in interesting contrast to the piety and obedience commonly promoted during the Age of Faith.

Schooling Women During the Renaissance

Women remained largely outside the scope of the Renaissance. Schooling still played an unimportant role in their education; and even the most enlightened humanistic scholars still clung to views substantially similar to those of Aristotle, who declared that women were "mutilated males." Erasmus offers an example. In his *Colloquia* the otherwise enlightened humanist noted, "I do not know the reason, but just as a saddle is not suitable for an ox, so learning is unsuitable for a woman." It remained for the Protestant Reformation to make major changes in the schooling of women.

SCHOOLING AND THE PROTESTANT REFORMATION

Early in the 1500s officials of the Christian church found their authority challenged by the Protestant Reformation. The ascendancy of urban life, the rise of industry and commerce, the creation of a new class of capitalists, and the emergence of nation-states had all provided a helpful environment for the Renaissance. It provided Protestantism with similar support.

Martin Luther

Martin Luther (1483–1546), a German priest, theologian, and teacher, was moved to protest by a Church decision to finance the building of St. Peter's in Rome by selling large blocks of printed indulgences. They guaranteed the remission of certain sins. Foiled in his attempt at reform from within, a surprised Luther soon found himself at the head of a massive protest, swelled to remarkable proportions by the power of the printing press, with the support of the emerging economic, political, and intellectual forces of the day.

Luther went beyond mere condemnation of clerical abuses. He declared that there was a "Priesthood of All Believers," and even suggested that in the eyes of God there was no difference between priest and layman. Relying on the Bible's new availability, Luther declared that all Christians had the re-

Martin Luther

sponsibility to interpret the scriptures for themselves according to the inner light of faith.

The flaw in this prescription was that while printing presses were turning out millions of Bibles, many people still could not read. Fully half the men and more than half the women of this era were illiterate.[71] As a remedy, Luther championed universal schooling. Everyone—adults as well as children, females as well as males, poor as well as rich—was to be schooled.

Luther was *not* a social revolutionary. Indeed, he was as socially conservative as he was religiously radical. And he quickly became associated with conservative German national affiliations. A staunch supporter of the political and economic status quo, he had no intention of changing the powerholder/ stakeholder alignment. For him, the social order was a gift of God, and schools were simply its servants.[72] He wanted to school everyone for religious reasons—nothing more.

Luther was convinced that government had a responsibility to support his proposal. Consequently, in his "Letter to Mayors and Aldermen" (1524) and his "Sermon to Parents" (1530), he urged the organization of government-sponsored German language primary schools for boys AND girls. Attendance would be compulsory "for an hour or two a day."

This was the beginning of the Protestant practice of support for government-sponsored compulsory schooling that continues to this day. Later, during the formative early years of colonial American history, this tradition would provide the basis for our first schools.

[71]R. R. Bolger, "Education and Learning," in *The New Cambridge Modern History*, Vol. III, R. B. Wernham, ed. (Cambridge: Cambridge U. Press, 1968), p. 427.
[72]R. Pascal, *The Social Basis of the German Reformation* (London: Watts, 1933), pp. 221–226.

John Calvin

This matter of religious authority represented a fundamental difference between Protestants and Catholics. Lacking the authority of Pope and universally
accepted dogma, Protestants found it impossible to establish a broad consensus based on biblical interpretation. Schism and denominationalism followed.
These had the effect of accidentally widening the scope of tolerance.[73] They
also increased the availability of colleges and seminaries as each new denomination sought to marshall its own school resources.

Schooling was the one area of agreement. Despite their quarrels regarding
the meaning of the Bible, Protestant reformers unanimously echoed Luther's
call for common schooling. Among the most influential was John Calvin, a
Frenchman.

Calvin (1509–1564), a theologian and religious reformer noted for his
scholarship and stern morality, insisted that the Bible was the supreme authority for *every* aspect of life. From this it followed that universal literacy
was a nonnegotiable objective.

Like Luther, Calvin set out to promote basic literacy for the broad masses.
Because he enjoyed secular as well as religious power in his refuge in Geneva,
he was able to move quickly. He founded the college at Geneva, and also
promoted secondary education in Latin, Greek, theology, logic, and rhetoric
for all church leaders.

Untrammeled by the national affiliations of Lutheranism and informed by
Calvin's comprehensive scholarship, Calvinism eventually became the international form of Protestantism. Its influences spread far and wide, even to New
England. Here the Calvinistic Puritans established schools that were of central
importance in the history of American education.

A New System of Schools

In Protestant areas the Reformation led to a massive redistribution of wealth
and land from the Church to civil government. This was often the price secular
authorities put on their cooperation with Luther and similar reformers. This
development crippled many Monastery, Church, and Cathedral schools while
also weakening the universities. Only the Town schools escaped unharmed.

Urged on by Luther and other Protestant reformers, newly powerful secular
governments used confiscated resources to build and staff new schools. Directed by famous Protestant schoolmen such as Philip Melanchthon
(1497–1560) and Johann Sturm (1507–1589), municipal authorities built vernacular language Town schools for the broad masses and Latin Grammar
schools for students of exceptional ability. A few charged a fee, but most were
free. Girls were included, though they were often taught at a lower level and
always in the vernacular.[74]

---

[73]W.H. McNeill, *The Rise of the West: A History of the Human Community* (New York: Mentor,
1963), p. 644.
[74]Frost, op. cit., pp. 184–195.

Chart 11.1

PROTESTANTISM'S CONTRIBUTIONS TO SCHOOLING

Laid Basis for State and National Control of Schools
Emphasized That All Children Should Be Schooled
Stressed Educational Obligations of Parents
Encouraged Idea of "Progress"
Provided Basis for First American Schools

Protestant enthusiasm for the creation of schools derived, in part, from the divided nature of the movement. Early disagreements about the meaning of the scriptures had led Protestantism into denominationalism. Since each denomination needed to train its own cadre of ministers, much of the effort that went into the establishment of Protestant Latin Grammar schools, seminaries, and universities had this as a goal. Protestantism's stress on individual biblical understanding and knowing one's spiritual destiny also contributed to the growth of schools (Chart 11.1).

Protestantism and the Schooling of Women

Despite the Protestant belief in the necessity of schooling females, we should not imagine them as champions of women's rights. Martin Luther provides an example. He still relegated women to the kitchen and the nursery. Citing anatomy, he even argued that women had broad hips " . . . to the end that they should remain at home, sit still, keep house and bear and bring up children."[75] Nevertheless, his call for female literacy, to be accomplished by government compulsion if necessary, was direct and unapologetic. It would eventually have an effect far beyond what the Protestant reformers of the time could ever have anticipated.

SCHOOLING AND THE COUNTER-REFORMATION

At the Council of Trent (1545–1563), Catholic Church officials hammered out policies intended to deal with a wide assortment of threats, the chief of which was Protestantism. Establishing tighter control over schooling in order to reestablish social control was one of their principal objectives. This led to standardization of the training of the clergy and redoubled support of reorganized Parish schools.

In this same period the newly formed Society of Jesus (1540) was assigned the mission of reforming and reinvigorating Catholic secondary and higher education. Motivated by mystical visions, some of which brought charges of heresy, a young Basque aristocrat who had been invalided out of military service and rejected by the Franciscans, won papal approval to found a new religious order. Ignatius of Loyola (1491–1556) demanded that its members

---

[75]Martin Luther, *Table Talk*.

Ignatius of Loyola

give complete obedience to the Roman Catholic Church, declaring: "To attain the truth in all things, we ought always to hold that we believe what seems to be white to be black, if the Hierarchal Church so defines it."

By the time of Ignatius' death it was clear that he had launched a movement of great educational significance. His order, the Society of Jesus, organized "to employ itself in defense of the Holy Catholic Faith," was developing Latin Grammar schools for boys and what they called "Colleges" for young men all over Catholic Europe. These schools combined the development of Catholic faith with selected aspects of the humanistic culture of the Renaissance. Latin was their only language, and religion dominated their curricula. Social control and status concerns were a key element. They also had a vocational aspect.

Using the actual experience of thousands of teachers, the Jesuits devised a complete master program for their schools. Revised and refined over the years this *Ratio Studiorum* was issued in final form in 1599. It spelled out a standardized curriculum as well as classroom methods and management. There was study of the classics, math, cosmology, geography, rhetoric, good manners, and Holy Scripture.[76] Instruction was self-paced, floggings were reduced to a minimum, and rewards were substituted for punishment as a means of motivation.[77] Never had schooling received such a careful formulation. The Jesuits were advancing pedagogy one more step from the formal into the technical level of culture.

DISSENSUS AND THE DAWN OF THE MODERN AGE

As the Jesuits worked to reestablish Catholic hegemony over Europe, the leaders of the various Protestant fragments of Christianity labored to establish

---

[76]Burke, op. cit., p. 128.
[77]Kane, op. cit., p. 268.

their own preeminence. Each wanted to reestablish the Christian consensus on their terms; and they used persuasion, schooling, printed propaganda, and threats to do it. But their efforts proved fruitless.

In the face of persistent failure, Luther became increasingly dogmatic and intolerant, Calvin persecuted those who disagreed with him, and the Pope set up the Holy Inquisition to hunt down and destroy those seen as heretics. But the extremity of the efforts mirrored the desperation of the practitioners. Try as they might, none of them could put the consensus back together.

Eventually, the ambition to impose one or another total truth plunged Europe into a series of devastating wars. But the religious conflicts of the 1500s, vicious struggles with no quarter given, simply strengthened the intellectual ferment.

Broad social changes were abroad in the land, and no amount of repression or reaction could undo them. A torrent of books was being printed; the practical arts were flourishing; nations were forming; monarchs were gaining unprecedented power; a New World was being discovered; and a new middle class was displacing the feudal aristocracy while also claiming many of the old prerogatives of a now divided church.[78] All of these developments were working their profound effects, destroying the last remnants of the medieval consensus.

The modern age was at hand, and neither education nor schooling would ever be the same again. Chief among the changes was a gradual acceleration of the shift of education away from the family to broader social institutions such as the school. Compared to what happened in the nineteenth century, the seventeenth century developments were merely a trickle rather than a flood—though it must have looked like a torrent compared to what came before.

While this was happening, the medieval consensus of faith was also being replaced in schools by the dissensus, conflict, and bargaining so characteristic of the modern era. The socioeducational system now serviced a transformed economy in a reformulated society and the adjustments necessary to accommodate these differences would continue for many years.

SUMMARY

1. A precipitous decline of schooling followed the fall of Rome. Then it slowly redeveloped within the Christian Church.

2. The family gained renewed importance with the Roman collapse, but then once again gave ground to broader social institutions, such as the government, the Church, and schools.

---

[78]Ibid., p. 242.

3. There developed an ever-growing competition between the technical culture and the formal culture which often found expression in school controversy and conflict.

4. Monastery schools, Cathedral schools, Parish schools and Municipal schools were new forms of schooling developing during the Age of Faith.

5. Municipal schools represented a significant inroad on the Church's educational monopoly that was already threatened by independent itinerant teachers.

6. The origins, structure, and governance of the medieval university and the humanistic Latin Grammar school reveal the continuing importance of status, vocational, and social control concerns to schooling. Social renewal was, to some extent, also encouraged by the schools.

7. The principle of correspondence is illustrated in the changes in schooling that were set in motion by the decline of Rome, the Age of Faith, the Reformation, the Counter-Reformation, and the Renaissance.

8. There was a shift in authority from dogma to reason and from piety to passion associated with the loss of the medieval consensus, and the rise of a revolutionary new culture that is still working its changes on education and schooling.

QUESTIONS

1. Some intellectual historians, such as Christopher Lucas, have suggested that a substantial part of history could be profitably analyzed in terms of recurrent cycles of optimism and despair regarding the human condition and the nature of society. Lucas argues that the tension between opposing views has been perennial, and that each historic period can be measured by its degree of optimism or despair. (Christopher J. Lucas, "Twilight of the Evening Lands and the Striptease of Humanism," *Educational Studies,* 1977, pp. 343–356.) Assuming Lucas is right, is there a prevailing view of humanity and society that typifies the age in which we live? If so, how is it reflected in attitudes toward children, education, and schools?

2. Can you see a relationship between
   a. adopting a religion as a "state religion" and
   b. suppression of other religions? What are the costs and benefits of both **a** and **b** and for whom?

3. A formal culture can be maintained unintentionally through technical means. How did early Medieval Christianity preserve formal pagan culture?

4. Do you see a parallel in the growth of the medieval Church to fill social functions and the growth in the twentieth century of the public school to fill social functions? What similarities and dissimilarities can you detail? Consider the expansion of learning opportunities.

5. Can you see any parallels between the educational use of books in Charlemagne's time and the educational use of computers today? Consider scarcity of materials, cost, and widespread lack of appropriate skills.

6. From the powers granted to the teachers' guilds, can you surmise what kinds of problems they were faced with?

7. Printing eventually disseminated knowledge far beyond its customary boundaries of monastery, Church, and university. Consider the personal computer. What long-term effect do you think it will have on the dissemination of knowledge? Are the cost/benefit elements similar?

8. Women were not included in the full educational benefits of either the Reformation or the Renaissance. What do you think would account for this? Consider the relationship of powerholders and stakeholders, of costs and benefits.

9. What interests of Lutherans required schooling of women as well as men? Did Calvin support this interest?

10. How would you summarize the major educational developments of the Reformation?

A HISTORY of EDUCATION: THE EARLY DEVELOPMENT of AMERICAN SCHOOLING

Chapter 12

The public schools do not teach reading, say some; they are weak in mathematics and science, say others; the able are given short shrift; youth are not required to do homework. Most of these criticisms are, at least in part, unjustified. . . . [And] the fact that they are made often, with such venomous outrage, shows a vast ignorance of why schools were established in this country. No set of Americans in any generation in the past has ever argued for schools for such a puny purpose as the teaching of any set of specific subjects. The purposes were always more profoundly conceived and more broadly stated.

Gladys Wiggin[1]

PREVIEW

We begin this chapter with a review of educationally relevant European developments immediately preceding and accompanying the colonization of America. This is followed by a brief review of English educational and schooling practices that were particularly influential in colonial America.

We then highlight the educational practices of three Colonial regions: New England, the Middle Colonies, and the South, showing how each had distinctive educational practices that corresponded with their patterns of settlement. Focusing on the workings of their respective socioeducational systems, we illustrate how the many different institutions within those systems interrelated. (See Chapter 6.) We describe colonial higher education, primarily in order to illustrate the educational importance of colonial American class distinctions and status concerns.

We also focus on fundamental shifts in authority, pointing out the impact on the educational process. By describing constitutional responsibility for school governance and finance, we prepare the ground for the development of both of these matters later in the text. We also establish a context for describing America's socioeducational system in the years immediately following the American Revolution. Finally, we describe the beginning of the great common school crusade that culminated in the present U.S. public school system.

EUROPEAN ORIGINS OF AMERICAN EDUCATION

Colonial America was settled by Europeans concerned about transmitting their values to their children and anxious to reproduce familiar social, political, economic, and religious systems.[2] They soon found that life on the frontier

---

[1]Gladys Wiggin, *Education and Nationalism* (New York: McGraw-Hill, 1962), p. vii.
[2]Carl N. Degler, *Out of Our Past: The Forces That Shaped Modern America* (New York: Harper & Row, 1984), p. 171.

imposed its own realities. What is more, the very European civilization they were attempting to transplant was undergoing wrenching changes. In the place of the consensus, certainty and permanence of the Age of Faith, the first settlers took with them the accelerating dissensus, uncertainty, and imper-manence of a Europe in ferment. And this had a profound impact on colonial education.

With respect to politics, in-group loyalty was shifting from the parochial interests of growing towns and shrinking feudal estates to much broader na-tional loyalties.[3] In terms of economics, the growth of commerce, hastened by technical level improvements in transportation, was developing far beyond the feudal estate and the self-governing town. Interregional, even transoceanic commerce was expanding explosively. All of this had a profound impact on education and schooling, while causing the old tension between the formal and the technical, the secular and the sacred, and the Hellenic and the Chris-tian to resurface.[4] Aquinas had not settled the matter after all.

The Age of Reason

Change, and the growth of political and religious diversity which it encour-aged, weakened traditional religious authority with its locus in the formal culture. It was replaced, in part, by a growing belief in the value of religious toleration and a new respect for secular authority.

As tradition and dogma became less compelling, a new breed of philoso-pher, men like Copernicus, Harvey, Galileo, Bacon, and Brahe, turned from the formal to the technical culture, especially science and mathematics, for answers. Encouraged by skeptical habits of thought stressing proof not dogma, and fortified by progress in the practical arts as well as the rapid evolution of instruments like the telescope, they soon produced them in astonishing and disconcerting abundance.[5]

The French philosopher and mathematician René Descartes (1596–1650) exemplifies the radical skepticism toward traditional authority which reliance on reason encouraged. In his famed *Discourse on Method*, Descartes advised that we doubt *everything*. Take as false that which is probable, he advised, and only that which is "certain" should even be considered likely.[6] Only one thing can safely be regarded as truly certain—our own existence. And the only key to this certainty is that one cannot doubt that one doubts. In other words, in the fact that our doubt exists, we find our only proof that we exist. "Cogito ergo sum" (I think, therefore I am) was the way Descartes put it.

It was now possible to challenge nearly everything. Even the authority of kings, of bishops, and of received opinion was suspect. In addition, some of the doubters were discovering an astoundingly powerful new order and unity

---

[3]W. H. McNeill, *The Rise of the West: A History of the Human Community* (New York: Mentor, 1965), pp. 632–633.
[4]Ibid., p. 642.
[5]Ibid., p. 649.
[6]Ibid., pp. 154–155.

in nature through experimentation, observation, and the cultivation of the habit of truth, not as dogma but as process.[7]

All of this proved a formidable challenge for school authorities. Schooling traditionally reinforced and legitimated established authority. What is more, change ran contrary to the interests and instincts of educators who made their living and reputation in schools that had institutionalized the medieval.[8] What were school authorities to do? For a time many hunkered down, changed nothing, and became increasingly irrelevant.

The English Educational Model

North America was colonized by a wide variety of Europeans. But when the initial settlement period was over, the English were preeminent. As they set about building colonial communities, they modeled them on those they left behind. Of course, their educational practices were also based upon English patterns.[9] For this reason it is illuminating to briefly summarize English educational practices at the time of colonization.

The Continued Centrality of the Family

The family still shouldered the vast majority of the educational burden in English life. Indeed, at the time of the first American settlements Tudor social policy was both emphasizing and enlarging the role of the family as a systematic educator. The clergy were encouraged by royal injunction to oversee and encourage household religious instruction. All fathers, mothers, masters, and governors were also required to teach their children and servants some form

---

[7]Jacob Bronowski, "The Creative Aspects of Science," in *Exploring the Universe*, Louise Young, ed. (New York: McGraw-Hill, 1963), p. 4.

[8]James Burke, *The Day the Universe Changed* (Boston: Little, Brown, 1985), p. 169.

[9]Lawrence Cremin, *Traditions of American Education* (New York: Basic Books, 1977), pp. 4–5.

Figure 12.1   **CHANGING SOCIAL BOUNDARIES**

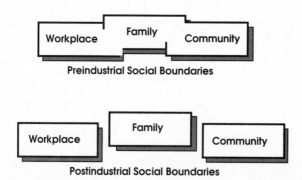

Preindustrial Social Boundaries

Postindustrial Social Boundaries

of honest occupation and to link their efforts, whenever possible, to the traditional institution of apprenticeship.[10] Because the boundaries between home and workplace were not yet as sharply drawn as they would be during industrialization, this linkage represented simply a variation on the theme of learning in the family.[11]

The Role of the Church

Churches were second only to households in their importance to English education. In the previous chapter we already indicated something of the educational functions of the church, and this certainly applied to both the English established church and the dissenting sects.

Schooling

Officials of the Church of England, the established church, did not embrace the cause of schooling the broad masses with the same zeal as that of the Puritans or other dissenting denominations. They did, however, inherit from the Reformation the belief that schooling should nurture children in the faith.[12]

This belief, coupled with the educational efforts of dissident denominations, and the growing sophistication of an urbanizing culture, made schools relatively common in the England of this period. They were, however, haphazardly arranged in a curious amalgam of privately funded grammar schools, parochial charity schools, and dissenting academies (schools serving religious dissenters who were excluded from Cambridge and Oxford in 1662) that most children still did not attend. Many of those who did got only a year or two of indifferent instruction.[13]

The tenuous nature of Protestantism in England—there had been a restoration of Catholicism under Queen Mary (1553–1558)—encouraged a narrow, defensive, and very self-conscious religiosity in the schools. Control concerns were central and school authorities were expected to defer to the authority of the official Church of England.[14]

Classical Studies and Status Concerns

Ordinarily it was only children of the upper and merchant classes who received reasonably competent formal instruction by tutors and in privately funded Latin Grammar schools, and/or universities. Such elite schooling in-

---

[10]Lawrence Cremin, *American Education: The Colonial Experience 1607–1783* (New York: Harper & Row, 1970), p. 118.
[11]Bernard Bailyn, *Education in the Forming of American Society* (New York: Norton, 1972), p. 17.
[12]Gerald Gutek, *Education and Schooling in America* (Englewood Cliffs, N.J.: Prentice Hall, 1988), p. 8.
[13]Ibid., p. 13.
[14]Ellwood P. Cubberly, *A Brief History of Education* (New York: Houghton Mifflin, 1922), p. 172.

corporated the Renaissance definition of a well-educated person as competent in Latin and Greek composition, versification, and literature. This criterion pertained even though there had been a decline in the practical value of Latin. (It had been retained as an official language only by the Catholic branch of the Christian Church, and had given way to French as the language of diplomacy.[15])

The popularity of Latin and Greek was due, in part, to the "Doctrine of Formal Discipline"—an elaborate technique for "training the mind."[16] However, it also reflected status concerns. Such studies were, in a sense, a form of conspicuous consumption. Pursuing Latin or Greek, rather than more practical arts, was akin to cultivating lawns rather than crops. Both lawns and Latin demonstrated the superior status of practitioners by making it abundantly clear that they could afford to transcend the merely practical.

It is hard to overemphasize the importance of status concerns in English education and schooling. The dominating influence in England during the American colonial period was class. The lower classes were widely regarded as inferior and born to obey rather than govern. The privileged were commonly considered innately superior and uniquely qualified to rule.[17]

Class differences were not all that divided England. There also were regional and religious differences. The resultant lack of consensus led to a ruinous civil war (1642–1648).

EDUCATION AND SCHOOLING IN COLONIAL AMERICA

English heterogeneity was reflected in American colonial settlements. North American climate, soil types, and topography also imposed other distinctions, as did religious beliefs, and economic institutions. For these reasons, English colonial settlements quickly took on regional characteristics.[18]

Each region developed its own educational and schooling practices, illustrating the systemic interdependence of education, schooling, and culture detailed in Chapter 6. We will sketch the broad outline of all three.

New England

New England was settled by Congregationalist "Puritans." These stern, hardworking, frugal, and law-abiding Calvinists gathered together in close-knit villages. This strengthened the influence of their church, and helped them

[15]Stephen Duggan, *A Student's Textbook in the History of Education* (New York: Appleton-Century, 1927), p. 182.
[16]Ibid., pp. 186–187.
[17]Edgar W. Knight, *Education in the United States* (Boston: Ginn, 1941), pp. 64–65.
[18]S. E. Frost, *Historical and Philosophical Foundations of Western Education* (Columbus, Ohio: Merrill, 1960), pp. 215–216.

New England was settled by Congregationalist "Puritans" who established a theocracy.

maintain the broad and deep consensus necessary for the maintenance of a religious state.[19]

Even though their colony was divided along class lines, all male Congregationalist Church members did have the privilege of voting in frequent town meetings. This gave their dogmatic moral community an apparently democratic quality. Nevertheless, it was traditional Calvinist belief that only the enlightened elect, the "saints," are capable of true righteousness. For that reason it was God's will that a small band of the elect still held positions of greater power over the unregenerate many.[20]

The Impact of the Wilderness

Despite their tightly woven theocratic communities, life in the wilderness gradually weakened the Puritan social fabric. In the years from the landing at Plymouth to the Revolution, cheap land and a scarcity of labor undermined both the apprenticeship system and parental authority. In addition, children frequently adapted to the demands of life in the New World more quickly than their elders. This upset traditional teaching and learning roles, eroded adult credibility, further weakened the family, and undermined consensus.[21]

Of course, these unforeseen consequences of life on the frontier were not confined to Puritan New England. All along the eastern seaboard, colonials found themselves confronted with similar situations.

The Centrality of Reason

The Puritans' great respect for schooling was an outgrowth of Calvinistic religious beliefs and a related devotion to logic and reason. Unlike many other

---

[19]Bailyn, op. cit., p. 11.
[20]Christopher Hill, *Society and Puritanism in Pre-Revolutionary England* (New York: Schocken, 1967), p. 243.
[21]Cremin, op. cit., pp. 16–17.

religionists who found fulfillment in unrestrained emotion, the Puritans were convinced that the mere emotion of religion had to be mediated by reason. The English Puritan Richard Baxter expressed it succinctly when he insisted,

> The most religious, are the most truly, and nobly rational.

This respect for reason reflected the old scholastic impulse to reconcile faith with logic; but not in the medieval way. The Puritans' leadership had added the humanism of the Renaissance.[22] For this reason, the Congregationalists maintained a remarkably well-schooled cadre of ministers who prided themselves not only in their erudition and in the unemotional, ordered logic of their sermons,[23] but also in their knowledge of classical studies and Latin, Greek, and Hebrew—the "holy" languages of ancient scripture.

Puritan Schooling

Concern that these ministerial standards be maintained in New England led to the establishment of Harvard College in 1636. In the words of the Puritan founders, the college had been initiated so that they would not,

> ... leave an illiterate ministry to the churches, when the present ministers shall lie in the dust.

The need to prepare youngsters for Harvard led to the creation of Latin Grammar schools—the very rough equivalent of modern secondary schools. The Calvinist commitment to reason and to literacy as a tool in the search for salvation, coupled with the fact that each Puritan had the terrifying personal responsibility of learning the full meaning of God's word, also encouraged the founding of elementary schools.[24]

The Old Deluder, Satan

In 1642 the Puritan fathers, through their General Court, passed a law requiring parents to see to it that their children could read and understand Congregationalist doctrine, and the laws of the Commonwealth.[25]

In 1647, concerned with the further deterioration of traditional values the Congregationalist General Court declared:

> It being one Chiefe project of ye ould deluder, Satan, to keepe men from the knowledge of ye Scriptures, as in former times by keeping ym in an unkowne tongue, so in their latter times by perswading

---

[22]Cohen, op. cit., p. iii.
[23]Quoted in Degler, op. cit., p. 17.
[24]Ibid.
[25]Gutek, op. cit., p. 10.

from ye use of tongues, yt so at least ye true sence & meaning of ye originall might be clouded by false glosses of saint seeming deceivers, . . . It is therefore ordered that every towneship in this jurisdiction, after ye Lord hath increased ym number of 50 house-holdrs, shall then forthwth appoint one within their towne to teach all such childeren as shall resort to him to write & read, whose wages shall be paid either by ye parents or masters of such children, or by ye inhabitants in genrall, . . . it is further ordered, yt where any towne shall increase to ye number of 100 families or hous-holdrs, they shall set up a grammar schoole.

The law did not require school attendance. It only compelled communities to establish schools for those who wished to attend.[26] Similarly, officials of the General Court did *not* provide financial resources to accomplish their requirements. Like other public authorities past and present, they tried to assure the benefits of schooling, while passing the costs to others.[27] The village elders did likewise, and most village schools charged parents tuition. Over the years, however, local Puritan communities did gradually make their schools tax-supported. In fact, by 1750 schooling in New England had generally become "free" to any child. It would be years before any other part of the United States made schooling available to all children regardless of their ability to pay.[28]

This "Old Deluder, Satan" law is often referred to as the foundation of America's public schools. This, however, is misleading. Puritan schools were a very different sort of endeavor from the public schools that evolved a hundred years later. The Puritans' efforts were backed by a community that had such depth of consensus that it did not find it necessary to distinguish even between individual and collective interests. They were simply assumed to be identical. This was not the case with the first truly public schools. They were the distinctive product of a heterogeneous society, which lacked such consensus.

The Puritan View of Children

Puritans understood children to have been conceived in sin and born in corruption.[29] For this reason, if the rod was spared, they were in grave risk of becoming "undutiful, unsubmissive and disorderly"—"a curse on persons in this world."[30] This perception grew out of the traditional Calvinist belief that,

---

[26]Frost, op. cit., p. 256.
[27]Ibid.
[28]Ibid., p. 257.
[29]Standord Fleming, *Children and Puritanism: The Place of Children in the Life and Thought of the New England Churches, 1620–1847* (New Haven, Conn.: Yale U. Press, 1933).
[30]H. Norman Gardiner, ed., *Selected Sermons of Jonathan Edwards* (New York: Macmillan, 1904), p. 148.

Man is sinful; he is by his nature an enemy of God, a rebel and a traitor; he cannot understand and consequently cannot will the things acceptable to God.[31]

Michael Wigglesworth's widely popular *Day of Doom*, first published in New England in 1662, clearly portrays Puritan attitudes toward the young. One part of it depicts unbaptized infants pleading for mercy at the Last Judgment only to be told:

> You sinners are, and such a share
>   As sinners may expect,
> Such you shall have; for I do save
>   None but my own elect.
> Yet to compare your sin, with theirs
>   Who lived a longer time,
> I do confess yours so much less
>   Tho' every sin's a crime.
> A crime it is, therefore in bliss
>   You may not hope to dwell;
> But unto you, I shall allow
>   The easiest room in Hell.

Social Control

Ever mindful of the power of Satan, the Puritans were determined to make the costs of sin and disobedience clearly outweigh the benefits. Whipping posts were common in the schoolroom, or close by, and beatings were regarded as religiously therapeutic. Disobedient children literally had the Hell beaten out of them. Young people over sixteen found guilty of striking their parents, or of being incorrigible, could even be put to death. Of course, these punishments corresponded to a harsh public penal code that featured branding, public whipping, the pillory, the stocks, and capital punishment for a wide variety of crimes.[32]

Town Meetings and School Boards

We noted previously that the Puritans used town meetings to determine many matters of government. And every aspect of the governance of the local village schools was a concern of these meetings. Thus began the American tradition of involving local elected boards in the governance of public schools. Such

---

[31]This is a paraphrase of the orthodox sixteenth-century Calvinist John Penry in Hill, op. cit., p. 243.
[32]Ibid.

boards have since become an integral part of the governance of America's public schools.[33]

The Middle Colonies

The Middle Colonies lacked New England's cultural and religious uniformity. As a consequence they developed a greater variety of educational practices.

The Example of Pennsylvania

The Quaker Commonwealth of Pennsylvania provides a particularly good example of the Middle Colony pattern. The Society of Friends, who were very influential in early Pennsylvania, had much less impulse toward popular schooling than the Puritans. This attitude was due to their emphasis on the importance of the "Inner Light," rather than reason, and their belief in universal salvation.[34]

Although they had control over schooling, the Quaker principle of tolerance, which stood in stark contrast to the intolerance of the Puritans, made it difficult for them to force their religious principles on anyone. For this reason Quaker dominance soon gave way to educational initiatives sponsored by a bewildering array of religious denominations attracted to the colony by its religious freedom.

Protestant denominations were inclined to educate their own in a "guarded" atmosphere intended to promote group solidarity. Quaker tolerance gave this inclination free rein. The Lutherans, for example, quickly created German language schools modeled on those of Germany. They were intended to keep Lutheran traditions alive by separating the denomination's children from the "corrupting" influences of the outside world. The Mennonites and Amish took this biblical principle of "total separation" one step further. They organized a socioeducational system deliberately isolated from the

---

[33]Frost, op. cit., p. 257.
[34]Degler, op. cit., p. 20.

A typical colonial school scene.

"worldliness" of the broader community.[35] This proved so effective that these "Pennsylvania Dutch" are still able to maintain a style of life remarkably free of outside influences.

The Absence of Consensus

In general, then, the Middle Colonies lacked the consensus necessary to launch a colony-wide school initiative similar to the one in Massachusetts. There was no "moral community" (see Chapter 2) from which it could spring. However, most of the denominations shared the characteristic Protestant commitment to schooling. Because limited resources were divided among a multitude of groups quality suffered. Often teachers were barely literate, facilities primitive, and standards lowered to fit necessity.[36] And as long as each denomination insisted on schooling its own teachers, professors, ministers, and church officials, school credentials had little substantial value outside the congregational sphere.

Still, a common system of schooling seemed out of the question. There were too many competing interests. Incompatible status systems and disagreements concerning the Bible made them impractical.

The South

Some historians have remarked that it was the South that should have been named "New England," because here the English country way of life was replicated with the greatest authenticity. Southern colonial settlements were organized by middle and upper class members of the Church of England seeking economic advantage. And once in America they set out to replicate the life of the English country gentleman.[37]

The Plantation Economy

In some ways, the colonial South did come to bear a curious resemblance to parts of England. The primarily agricultural economy was organized into a two-tiered social system in much the same manner as Devon, Dorset, or East Anglia. Large landholdings of up to 200,000 acres were owned by upper class gentry, while agricultural labor was provided by the lower classes.[38] To facilitate this, a large number of "indentured white servants" and African slaves were imported into the region.[39]

The key to this southern way of life was the cultivation of tobacco. European demand for this product skyrocketed shortly after its introduction, and

---

[35]Frost, op. cit., pp. 266–267.
[36]Ibid., p. 267.
[37]Ibid., p. 268.
[38]Ibid.
[39]Cubberly, op. cit., p. 200.

the South had exceptionally suitable soil and climate for its production. Thus, there were fortunes to be made in southern tobacco plantations.

The Plantation Economy's Significance to Schooling

Officials of the Church of England, predominant among the upper class in the South, did not share the same enthusiasm for mass schooling as most other Protestant denominations. Indeed, upper class Southerners frequently adopted the view of traditional English conservatives who had always lacked enthusiasm for mass education because they knew it had a social renewal potential and believed it dangerous to their interests. After all, once schooled, the lower classes might revolt.[40] The South also lacked the denominational competition characteristic of the Middle Colonies.

These factors, combined with a more unrestrained pursuit of personal advantage, a widely dispersed rural way of life, and the mercenary interests of English officials concerned with tobacco revenues, produced conditions that were largely hostile to schooling. When, for example, the Virginia Assembly sent James Blair to England to secure a charter and financial aid for a college now known as William and Mary, he reminded the custodian of the crown's purse that a college was needed to train ministers. Otherwise, Blair explained, souls might be lost. "Souls!" roared the official. "Damn your souls! Raise tobacco!"[41]

As a consequence of these circumstances, most southern colonial youngsters not only failed to go to school, but could not even sign their own names to legal documents. About half of all boys were capable of a signature. Girls were generally incapable of forming any letters at all.[42]

Even in those rare instances when southern colonial officials tried to carry out educational initiatives, they often failed. Concerned about social disruptions, for example, they tried, through legislation, to force the children of the poor to become apprentices. This type of compulsory education was routine in England, but the southern colonial socioeducational system simply did not fit together in the same way and the initiative was of no consequence. The semi-slavery of indentured servitude was not a stable base upon which to construct an apprenticeship system. Neither was slavery.

Familial Education

The relative isolation of southern agricultural life put a particularly great educational burden on the family. Wealthy planters were able to employ private tutors to supplement their own efforts just as country gentlemen did in

---

[40]Michael B. Katz, "Connections Between the Origins of Public Education and the Major Themes in American Social History," unpublished paper distributed at the University of Pennsylvania. (Undated.)

[41]Quoted in Knight, op. cit., p. 86.

[42]Rhys Isaac, *The Transformation of Virginia* (Chapel Hill, N.C.: The U. of North Carolina Press, 1982), p. 123.

England. The planter's children were also often sent to England for the university phase of their education. Poorer white families had a tougher time schooling their children. Spread out across a rural landscape largely devoid of towns, the yeoman farmers and indentured servants who constituted about 80 percent of Southern white settlers had none of the resources that were available in the nucleated settlements of New England or the Middle Colonies.

Slavery and the Education of Afro-Americans

There was one underclass of Southerners who received a rather extensive nonfamilial "education." Thousands upon thousands of enslaved blacks had their family life and traditional patterns of education deliberately destroyed as a part of the "educational" practices of their owners. Then, cut off from their native cultures, unable to love with any hope of permanence, and unsure that they could ever raise their children to maturity, they were "re-educated" in a manner calculated to keep them in chains. The disabilities imposed by this "education" were then used as "proof" that black Americans were essentially inferior and incapable of freedom.

One of slavery's most eloquent apologists, J.D.B. De Bow, summed up this circular reasoning when he wrote,

> The physical differences between the two races are so great as to make what is wholesome and beneficial for the whiteman, as liberty, republican and free institutions, etc., not only unsuitable to the Negro race, but actually poisonous to its happiness.[43]

With respect to slavery and schooling, there were scattered efforts to teach black children to read; but these initiatives were limited. Despite the good

---

[43]Quoted in Degler, op. cit., p. 189.

Slaves were "educated" by their owners.

intentions of English missionary societies, like the Society for the Propagation of the Gospel, and the heroic efforts of a few black men and women, such as the scientist Benjamin Banneker, the vast majority of slaves remained illiterate.[44]

The Legacy

The southern United States still suffers from school problems that originated in this period. Weak public school systems, made all the weaker by years of official racial segregation, plague efforts to improve the economic vitality in a number of southern states. Also, the "great migration" of large numbers of poor whites and Afro-Americans to America's industrial cities, which began during World War I, spread the costs of generating benefits for a handful of planters far beyond southern boundaries.

Colonial Secondary Schooling

What we would call secondary schooling was offered in Latin Grammar schools and Academies in colonial America. We will briefly highlight each.

Latin Grammar Schools

The Latin Grammar school, discussed in the previous chapter, specialized in preparing the sons of upper class colonials for college. In addition, it was one of the traditional steps in preparation for the "higher professions," such as the ministry, law, medicine, and college teaching.

These European style schools catered almost exclusively to the upper and middle classes. In other words, relatively few of the total population attended.[45]

The Academy Movement

In his influential "Proposals Relating to the Education of Youth in Pennsylvania," published in 1749, Benjamin Franklin proposed a practically oriented, secular "Academy" for the colonies. It would train students in the skills required to build and maintain a civilization on the edge of the wilderness.[46] Franklin's publication helped promote the evolution of this distinctively American school. They were secondary schools, not usually preparatory for college. Chiefly serving the middle class, many even were open for girls, a striking innovation for the time.[47]

---

[44]Cremin, *American Education*, pp. 354–355.
[45]R. Freeman Butts, "Search For Freedom—the Story of American Education," *NEA Journal*, March 1960.
[46]Joel Spring, *The American School: 1642–1985* (White Plains, N.Y.: Longman, 1986), pp. 20–21.
[47]H. Warren Button and Eugene F. Provenzo, Jr., *History of Education and Culture in America* (Englewood Cliffs, N.J.: Prentice Hall, 1989), pp. 46–47.

From their inception academies took on a form different from Franklin's proposal. Most retained Latin in their curriculum, but also emphasized studies more closely connected to vocational rather than status interests. Among them were "useful" subjects such as English, geography, drawing, writing, arithmetic, algebra, and science. Most also retained religion, but were often free of denominationalism.[48]

Academies quickly eclipsed Latin Grammar schools, which were something of a struggle to maintain in the colonies. Eventually they were established in the thousands, becoming the precursors of our present-day comprehensive high schools. Some, usually the ones that stuck more closely to the old status-oriented Latin Grammar school curriculum, also metamorphosed into elite secondary "prep" schools such as those described in Chapter 7.[49]

Colonial Higher Education

Colonial higher education was modeled on that of England. In 1636 when Puritan officials voted to establish Harvard College, for example, they emulated Emmanuel College, Cambridge. The one significant departure from the English tradition was that Harvard was not governed by its faculty, which was poorly organized and often composed of part-timers. It was controlled by its president and an outside board of trustees—a pattern that became general for American colleges and remains with us to the present.[50]

Vocational Concerns

Harvard's original purpose was to train a new generation of ministers. Soon, however, it was also busy further legitimizing the superior status of Puritan "gentlemen." Predictably, the curriculum combined the seven liberal arts and Latin and Greek classics with formidable doses of Calvinistic theology.[51]

Most lower level schooling in New England developed *after* Harvard's founding. Significantly, it was originally intended to prepare the most capable youngsters for study there. This pattern of setting up basic schooling in anticipation of the demands of higher schooling was typical throughout the colonies and is still very much with us. It has always been one of the indirect controls on primary and secondary schooling.

Control Concerns

Social control was often near the top of a colonial college administrator's list of "things to do." One reason for this was that it was not uncommon to have youngsters attending college who were ten or eleven years of age.

Sometimes the enforcement of social control became a bit too vigorous

---

[48]Cubberly, op. cit., p. 248.
[49]Ibid.
[50]Ibid.
[51]Cremin, op. cit., pp. 210–212.

even for Puritan tastes. The first preside
missed for cruelly whipping students, "g
a time," and for beating his assistant in
dismissal did not mark the end of corp
for instance, a student convicted of utt
before a solemn assembly of all the sc
the library, was preceded and followed

Status Concerns

It is difficult for students to fully appr
social distinctions dominant in colonia
education provides a particularly clear-cut case. From its inception, —
ample, the names of the students in the Harvard catalogue were not listed
alphabetically but in an order indicating the social rank of their families. This
practice continued for 136 years. When Yale was established in 1701 it also
used family pedigree to determine a student's place on the list. In addition,
freshmen at both institutions took their places in classes, dining rooms, and
chapel according to carefully graded precedence.[53]

SCHOOLING AND THE AGE OF REASON

As the eighteenth century advanced, it became more and more apparent that
novel social and economic forces were encouraging and reinforcing a skeptical
view of traditional authority and received opinion. The spirit of revolution
was abroad in the land.

This spirit found a particularly congenial home in England's American colonies. Far removed from London, yet conscious of their rights as Britishers,
prominent American colonials chafed under the British government's regulations and taxes.

Schooling and the Idea of "Progress"

Changing views of authority were accompanied by a gradual, yet fundamental,
change of opinion concerning the human condition. Unlike the great thinkers
of the Age of Faith, who awaited a better life in the next world, the radical
thinkers of the Age of Reason were convinced that all humankind could continually improve their condition in this world. The key to this social renewal,
perhaps reform is a better word, was attaining and disseminating knowledge
of the natural laws that governed the physical world. Armed with this knowledge humankind could subject the physical world to the requirements of
human welfare and even reshape the social order itself.

This view reflected the growth of an idea that the historians Charles and

---

[52]Knight, op. cit., pp. 128–129.
[53]Ibid., p. 78.

ary Beard have labeled "the most dynamic social theory ever shaped in the history of thought."[54] Today, we call it "progress."

A seventeenth-century Czech teacher, Protestant pastor, and educational theorist by the name of Johann Amos Comenius (1592–1670) penned one of the earliest and most influential elaborations of this idea. Significantly, Comenius maintained that schooling was the key. Properly conceived, he argued, it could transform the human condition.

In dozens of popular publications on education, the most famous being *The Great Didactic,* Comenius urged that instruction be fitted to the individual child. He also pointed out that children learn by doing, and that learning is more efficient if it is correlated with other learning. Comenius developed these insights while attempting to understand schooling in the same way that physical scientists were coming to understand the natural world. His efforts represented another major step toward placing pedagogy in the technical, rather than the formal, culture.[55]

The school curriculum Comenius proposed was breathtaking in ambition. In *Pansophiae Prodromus* he discussed amassing all knowledge, organizing it to be in reach of ordinary persons, and then teaching it to everyone, regardless of their economic or cultural status. If this were possible, and Comenius thought it was, people would be not only their own priest, as Luther had advocated, but also, to a large extent, their own authority on secular matters as well.

New Sources of Authority

Such faith in the power of reason and optimism regarding the human condition represented a new force in human affairs. Many of the influential thinkers of this new "Age of Reason" believed that rationalism could provide truly comprehensive knowledge that would provide a new source of authority free of the inertia of received opinion.[56] Such an idea had vast implications for education and schooling.

The English teacher, physician, philosopher, and social theorist John Locke (1632–1704) helped pioneer this revolutionary spirit. Locke stressed the necessity of absolute clarity of expression, of tracing our beliefs to their psychological origins and basing conclusions on observations of the natural world rather than received opinion or emotion. Again and again he insisted that it was these procedures, and these procedures alone, that could lead to true knowledge.

With respect to learning, Locke proposed that the human mind is a "tabula rasa" or "blank slate" at birth, and then is furnished by experience. This not

---

[54]Charles and Mary Beard, *Rise of American Civilization*, Vol. I (New York: Macmillan, 1927), pp. 434–435.
[55]Will Monroe, *Comenius and the Beginning of Educational Reform* (New York: Scribner, 1900).
[56]*The Age of Enlightenment: The 18th Century Philosophers*, selected and with Introduction and interpretive commentary by Isaiah Berlin (New York: Mentor, 1956), p. 113.

only held forth the hope that humankind could be bettered, but also suggested the more dangerous conclusion that given equality of opportunity there should be no difference between the mind of a king and that of a commoner.[57]

With respect to politics, Locke argued that the just powers of government derive from the consent of the governed. In other words, legitimate power-holders base their authority on the consent of the stakeholders and use their power to defend the right of the individual to life, liberty, and property.

Partly because of his devotion to the rights of property, Locke assumed the exclusion of women and the poor from these full rights of citizenship.[58] However, he still helped provide a justification for the American Revolution, as well as for the basis of American government which Jefferson so elegantly summarized in the Declaration of Independence.[59]

Damnable Heresy and High Treason

In the years following Locke's death the prestige of rationalism grew rapidly as more and more thinkers became convinced that the universe operated according to patterns or laws; and that, through science, they could be discovered. Once they were, the affairs of humankind could be reorganized and social and personal perfection would become more likely. Of course, enlightened education and/or schooling would be required to free humanity from the dead weight of superstition and received opinion.[60] Then the possibilities were nearly infinite.

Such ideas were not simply an update of the classical humanism of the Renaissance. Nor were they similar to those that gave rise to the demands for spiritual probity and biblical authenticity during the Protestant Reformation. Rationalism was representative of a revolutionary spirit, a general intellectual

---

[57]J.J. Chambliss, "Reason, Conduct and Revelation in the Educational Theory of Locke, Watts and Burgh," *Educational Theory*, Fall 1976, pp. 372–387.

[58]Bertrand Russell, *A History of Western Philosophy* (New York: Simon & Schuster, 1945), p. 631.

[59]Degler, op. cit., p. 89.

[60]Gutek, op. cit., pp. 27–28.

Figure 12.2   **SHIFTING AUTHORITY DURING THE AGE OF REASON**

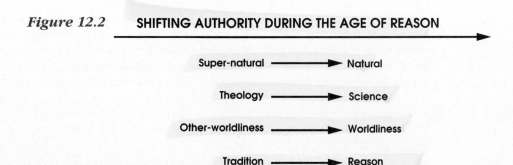

revolution, viewed by Protestant and Catholic traditionalist as a damnable heresy, and by the officials of established governments as high treason.

As rationalism increased, protests against established authority and settled opinion gained momentum in both Europe and the colonies. Indeed, radical points of view developed under particularly favorable conditions in the colonies, where established authority had already been undermined by the realities of living in the New World.[61] "The Revolution," as John Adams said years later, "was effected before the war commenced." It occurred "in the hearts and minds of the people."[62] And it should not escape the attention of educators that this was the consequence of the spread of an idea.

Schooling and the New Rationalism

The Age of Reason did not always find its way to the schoolroom. Locke himself failed to appreciate that his writings provided a basis for developing a true science of instruction based in the technical rather than the formal level of culture. He even failed to recognize that schooling had utopian possibilities if people were really a product of their environment, as he claimed. Instead, he rejected schooling in favor of the private tutor, and confined himself to writing about educating gentlemen of "good character."[63] Other thinkers, deeply influenced by Locke's ideas and the tenor of the times, drew far more radical conclusions.

The Romantic Reaction

The formal, precise, and detailed rationalism of Locke, or of other empiricists such as Bacon, Hobbes, Spencer or Mill, enjoyed a great influence but also provoked opposition. In particular, a romantic reaction soon became an integral part of the general culture of the late eighteenth century. Like the rationalists, the romanticists stressed the central importance of humanity and nature, and despised the old "proofs" of scholasticism. They also put considerable emphasis on reason and investigation. But in place of the authority of the scientific method, they substituted generalities about "human nature," and some sort of social consensus model of the "general will," based largely on emotion and their own personal "sense" of right and wrong.[64]

The writings of Jean Jacques Rousseau (1712–1778) were among the most famous and influential of this genre. A French Swiss writer, social critic, and educational theorist strongly influenced by Locke, Rousseau's writings reflected the growing impatience among some European thinkers for sole reliance upon observed facts and reason and their profound contempt for tradi-

---

[61]Frederick Jackson Turner, *The Frontier in American History* (New York: H. Holt, 1920).
[62]Quoted in Faulkner, op. cit., p. 76.
[63]Duggan, op. cit., pp. 192–193.
[64]Russell, op. cit., p. 691. (See Chapter 5 for a description of the consensus model of society.)

tional authority. More important, claimed Rousseau and those like him, were the emotions of the heart.

In a number of popular books Rousseau attempted to make hamburger out of a wide variety of societal sacred cows. He reversed the Christian conception of original sin, for example, to argue that in a purely natural state "man is good, and only by institutions is he made bad." Despite his debt to Locke, Rousseau also attacked science, contending that it had developed from ignoble origins, astronomy from the superstition of astrology, for example. For this reason, Rousseau argued, science was an enemy of virtue. And because technology, sciences' stepchild, created wants, it too was bad—a source of enslavement. Even schooling and printing promoted corruption.

In short, Rousseau boldly maintained that everything that distinguishes civilized humans from the "noble savage" is evil.[65] Thus he prayed that humanity would be delivered from "the fatal arts and sciences of our forefathers" so that we might return to "ignorance, innocence, and poverty which alone can make us happy."[66]

In contrast to Locke, Rousseau claimed that children were not born a "tabula rasa," but were "naturally good." They became evil, he claimed, only to the extent that they were corrupted by tyranny, faulty institutions, and, most important of all, improper education. For this reason he recommended that children should be schooled in nature, as far as possible outside society.

In *Emile* (1762), one of the most influential books on education of the eighteenth century, Rousseau described a program of instruction following this naturalistic principle. The teacher sets aside conventions and preconceptions, studies the natural child, then constructs a learning environment based upon the child's development. The educational setting is designed to make it possible for learning to take place when the child experiences the necessity. In this manner, claimed Rousseau, education empowers the learner, rather than serving as an instrument of oppression or exploitation.[67] How all of this is to be reconciled with conformity to the "general will" is not clear.

Paradoxically, earlier in his life, before addressing the matter of education, Rousseau had placed all five of his own common law children in an orphanage as soon as they were born.[68] Much of his educational commentary was written after he had begun to long and grieve for them.

The Changing View of the Child

Locke and Rousseau took completely different positions with regard to their source of authority. But the uncompromising empiricist and unapologetic romanticist were united at one critical juncture. They both were convinced that children were fundamentally different from adults. In this they helped

---

[65]Ibid, p. 687.
[66]Quoted in S. E. Frost, *Essentials of History of Education* (New York: Barrons, 1947), p. 138.
[67]Joel Spring, *The American School: 1642–1985* (White Plains, N.Y.: Longman, 1986), p. 25.
[68]Carlton Hayes, Marshall Baldwin, and Charles Cole, *History of Western Civilization*, Vol. II (New York: Macmillan, 1967), p. 490.

mark a revolutionary change in the attitude of adults toward children which began to gain great currency around the turn of the eighteenth and nineteenth centuries. It has since become nearly universal.

Rousseau's educational publications, characteristic of a romantic genre of educational writing that persists to this day, were influential in shaping public opinion. His observations that schooling should be adapted to the unfolding capacities of the child, and that memorization should be replaced by the development of reason, gained wide acceptance.

The philosopher Bertrand Russell points out that the essential difficulty with Rousseau's speculations and prescriptions, is that there is no reason to suppose that they are based on anything substantial. He asks how one refutes an argument that does not attempt to prove its points? Rousseau's "heart" may have told him that "savages" are noble and children both free and good, for example, but Russell wants to know why anyone should accept his feelings as authoritative.[69] We should note, however, that Locke's source of authority was not his emotions, but reasonably careful application of the methods of scientific investigation to a study of the mind.

Figure 12.3 summarizes key differences in the three most influential views of children, comparing it with sources of authority. These differences are still very much with us.

EDUCATION AND SCHOOLING IN A NEW NATION

Both rationalism and romanticism helped inspire the American Revolution, but the English tradition of constitutional government and liberty under law were used as a basis for freeing the colonies from the mother country. By

---

[69]Russell, op. cit., p. 694.

Figure 12.3

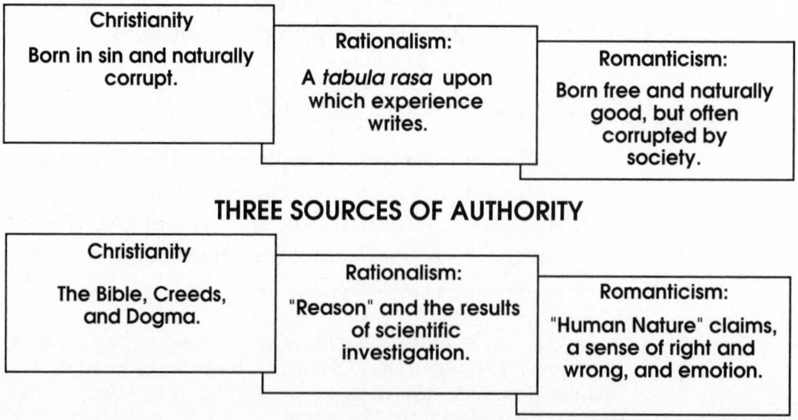

THREE VIEWS OF THE CHILD

Christianity
Born in sin and naturally corrupt.

Rationalism:
A *tabula rasa* upon which experience writes.

Romanticism:
Born free and naturally good, but often corrupted by society.

THREE SOURCES OF AUTHORITY

Christianity
The Bible, Creeds, and Dogma.

Rationalism:
"Reason" and the results of scientific investigation.

Romanticism:
"Human Nature" claims, a sense of right and wrong, and emotion.

1789, George Washington was framing his first administration under an American constitution.

Recall that in the years between Jamestown and the first Continental Congress in Philadelphia, America had already been caught up in a hidden educational revolution. The institutions that had served so well in England and on the Continent formed a new and problematic socioeducational system in the New World. As a consequence, schooling had acquired a new importance.[70]

For a time this development went largely unrealized. The prevailing agricultural life of that time did little to encourage schooling. Even if one wanted to be a blacksmith, woodwright, or wheelwright rather than a farmer, it was not necessary to go to school. Apprenticeship was the route to take.

The Absence of Federal Responsibility

The strength of apprenticeship was one reason why the Constitutional Convention—which was essentially a process of compromise in order to establish consensus—did not include schooling among the functions of the Federal Government. Perhaps some of the framers simply could not foresee the future importance of schooling. Most, however, just did not consider it to be among the basic rights of American citizens. After all, they crafted the Constitution and its Bill of Rights in terms of civil and political rights, not affirmative rights, and the Constitution is just as silent regarding the right to a job, shelter, or food as it is about schooling. Under the Tenth Amendment, this omission left it to the respective states or, if state officials did not see it as their responsibility, to individual citizens.

Schooling and the Preservation of the Republic

Despite the omission of schooling from the Constitution's list of rights, many prominent leaders of post-Revolutionary America were convinced that the preservation of the Republic required a system of distinctly American tuition-free public schools. Men like Thomas Jefferson, George Washington, James Madison, Noah Webster, and Benjamin Rush maintained that free public schooling was essential for a strong democracy, for only educated citizens could fulfill the obligations of self-government. Madison, who provided the basic plan of the Constitution, put it this way:

> A popular Government, without popular information, or the means of acquiring it, is but a Prologue to a Farce or Tragedy; or, perhaps both. Knowledge will forever govern ignorance; and a people who mean to be their own Governors must arm themselves with the power that knowledge gives.[71]

[70]Bailyn, op. cit., p. 21.
[71]Quoted in Butts, op. cit., p. 8.

Madison and the others did not want to develop the same style of nationalism that common schooling supported in Prussia. Like Prussian leaders, they wanted to enhance group loyalties. And some of Jefferson's plans for education in America excluded large numbers of children, white as well as black, by emphasizing the schooling of a gifted few.[72] But the Founders also wanted to encourage civil rights and the liberty of the individual by restricting the power of government.[73] This required an informed rather than obedient citizenry; and it was this which men like Jefferson, Madison, and Webster were determined to promote through a system of publicly financed common schools.

Schooling and Self-Governance

Federal legislators considered various plans for encouraging the growth of schooling. There were some, George Washington chief among them, who championed establishing a federally controlled and financed school system, grade school through university, in spite of the fact that the Constitution gave the federal government no such power.[74] Respect for the Tenth Amendment, a scarcity of resources, and the jealous guarding of state prerogatives by state officials, eventually prevented federal officials from taking such an action. They turned, instead, to indirect methods of encouragement.

Indirect Federal Support

When, in 1787, the Congress of the Confederation of States began selling the wilderness of the Northwest Territory to land companies, they decided to adopt Jefferson's concept of allocating land for the support of public education. The land was divided into townships of 36 square miles. Each square mile constituted a "section" of a township. Congress required that as land was sold, purchasers were required to set aside the cash equivalent value of every sixteenth section for the support of schools. Two townships were also sold to fund higher education. These established the original endowment of Ohio University.

The "Northwest Ordinance of 1787" was the first of many federal efforts to promote schooling in the somewhat indirect ways permitted under the Constitution. Similar initiatives followed.

The Demands of an Infant Democracy

Setting up and operating the institutions that should replace colonial rule was a very difficult undertaking. In the first place, the Americans who won the war were really more English, Scottish, German, Dutch, Swedish, and so forth, than

---

[72]Colin Greer, *The Great School Legend* (New York: Basic Books, 1972), p. 50.
[73]Carlton Hayes, *The Historical Evolution of Modern Nationalism* (New York: Macmillan, 1950), pp. 1–4, cited in Wiggin, op. cit., pp. 5–7.
[74]Frost, op. cit., pp. 318–319.

they were American. Often, too, those that had been successfully Americanized thought of themselves more as Virginians, Pennsylvanians, or New Yorkers, than as citizens of the United States. Some means of creating a closer knit national community was required.[75] It was also widely believed that self-government demanded a different sort of citizen: one who could participate wisely in his own governance. (Women were disenfranchised and could not vote; hence the masculine pronoun.)

There was little to build on. Throughout the new nation elementary schooling was largely undeveloped. Although many states made direct constitutional provisions for schooling, only in New England was it free and open to all. Outside this region the only children able to get publicly supported schooling were those too poor to pay. As a result, free public schooling in most of the United States was tainted with the stigma of poverty.[76] Wealthy Americans continued to employ private tutors, send to Europe for teachers, or even send their children to Europe for schooling.

Worried about the long-term effects of this arrangement, which were seen to be "... directly opposite to our political interests," prominent patriots like Noah Webster called for a distinctly American system of public schooling.[77] Thus it was that a deliberate cultural nationalism became one of the most important characteristics of the Common School crusade that emerged on the American scene in the 1820s and 1830s.[78]

Tax-Supported Public Schools

The old tax-supported "public" schools of colonial New England were essentially religious institutions. This affiliation is not what Webster, Jefferson, Madison, and others like them, were thinking of. They wanted to use public schools to promote an American "state of mind."[79]

Religious Liberty and Secular Schooling

Denominationalism was a major barrier to all such efforts to establish public schools. There was no state church in America and very little consensus among the prevailing Protestant denominations as to religious truth. In such circumstances it was difficult to imagine how common schooling could ever proceed. Should the state governments fund the educational efforts of every denomination desirous of running schools? And if they did, how could they be assured that this would contribute to the creation of a nation?

When the framers of the Constitution confronted the question of religion, they had taken a practical course and forbade Congress ever to establish a

---

[75]Butts, op. cit., p. 8.
[76]Frost, *Essentials*, op. cit., p. 173.
[77]Noah Webster, *A Collection of Essays and Fugitive Writings on Moral, Historical and Political Subjects* (Boston: Thomas and Andrews, 1790), pp. 30–33.
[78]Button, op. cit., p. 65.
[79]Wiggin, op. cit., p. 8.

state religion or impose a religious requirement for office holding. Ultimately, it was these Constitutional provisions that were the basis for a solution to the religion question in public schooling.[80] In the end, there would be a strict separation of religion and publicly financed schools. But this solution would be more than 150 years in the making; and in the meantime, the religious question remained problematic.

Opposition to Public Schooling

The idea of a public school system did not inspire universal enthusiasm. It was vigorously opposed by many taxpayers, private school leadership, and those with interests in charity schools. Farmers often viewed schooling as unnecessary, and even artisans and tradesmen were often either indifferent or downright hostile. Even the urban lower classes, whom upper class and upper-middle class reformers depicted as the chief beneficiaries of public schooling, were often very reluctant to enroll their children.[81]

This opposition makes more sense if it is remembered that with the exception of a few professions, schooling had little value in the marketplace.[82] Job skills were usually learned informally. Diplomas and the like were not well integrated into the cultural exchange system.

POINT/COUNTERPOINT

Some historians, particularly those embracing the conflict theory highlighted in Chapter 5, argue that the reason public schooling continued to expand despite opposition was that traditionally powerful groups were pushing it in order to revitalize and preserve a traditional middle class morality of hard work and perseverance which was being challenged by the urban, industrial lower class and immigrants.[83]

Other historians, who usually embrace a consensus or individualistic view of society, are less skeptical. They point out that there were a multitude of pro-school groups, each with their own motives, and the schooling that their efforts created was broad enough to give a range of choice to individuals who had no such choices before.

Both factions agree, however, that schooling did not bring liberty to slaves or survival to the culture of Native Americans.[84] As a matter of fact, for many years schooling remained largely unavailable to both. Immigrants also found their school opportunities more limited, as did women of all backgrounds. In addition, all agree that these groups also experienced physical and psychological barriers once they gained admission.[85]

---

[80]Cubberly, op. cit., p. 270.
[81]Randall Collins, *The Credential Society* (New York: Academic Press, 1979), pp. 106–107.
[82]Ibid.
[83]Ibid., p. 107.
[84]Cremin, *Traditions*, op. cit., p. 85.
[85]Lawrence Cremin, *American Education: The National Experience, 1783–1876* (New York: Harper & Row, 1980), p. 300.

In spite of opposition to its expense, and in spite of its lack of full integration into the cultural exchange system, however, the popularization of American public schooling developed, albeit in fits and starts.

European Developments

While the popularization of schooling was finding expression in the United States, there were corresponding developments in Europe.

The Decline of English Privatism

During the seventeenth and eighteenth centuries there was a substantial increase in English school attendance. For the most part it came from the growing English middle class who began enrolling their children in Latin grammar schools. This motivated upper class parents to withdraw their children, and to rely more and more on tutors and elite boarding schools such as Winchester, Eton, Harrow, and Rugby.

Increasingly ambitious attempts were also made to school the English lower classes. The need was great. The massive conversion of farmlands to pasture for sheep raised for the wool industry had displaced many farmers and disrupted the family-centered socioeducational system that the agricultural way of life had always supported. Also the replacement of hand power by machines had caused the decline of home industry, and dealt a heavy blow to the apprenticeship system. The subsequent growth of the factory system only intensified the destruction of this tradition.

Spurred on by this decline of informal education, by 1800 several thousand privately funded "charity schools," including Sunday schools, were providing free, although very limited and uninspiring, elementary education to poor children no longer well served by traditional methods of education.

Monitorial Schools

"Monitorial Schools" were the most distinctive of these charitable activities. Initiated by the Englishman Andrew Bell (1753–1832), and further developed by the flamboyant English emigre to America, Joseph Lancaster (1778–1838), these factory model schools were directly inspired by the Industrial Revolution. Bell even boasted that Monitorial schools were a "mechanical system of education"; and Lancaster referred to them as "the steam engine of the moral world."

The most distinctive feature of Monitorial schools was the use of a hierarchy of pupil "monitors" to teach hundreds of less advanced students in immense classrooms. This was accomplished through a systematic mass process based on the division of labor characteristic of factories. Significantly, those controlling the process were called "operatives," not "teachers," and the older

Monitorial schools were inspired by the industrial revolution.

children who read out the lesson according to detailed plans were termed "dictators."[86] Learning relied heavily on the memorization of facts.

In *Hard Times,* Dickens describes an industrial pedagogue of this type:

> Thomas Gradgrind sir. A man of realities. A man of facts and calculations. A man who proceeds on the principle that two and two are four, and nothing over, and who is not going to be talked into allowing anything over. Thomas Gradgrind sir, peremptorily Thomas—Thomas Gradgrind. With a rule and a pair of scales, and the multiplication table in his pocket, sir, ready to weigh and measure any parcel of human nature and tell you exactly what it comes to. It is a mere question of figures, a case of simple arithmetic.[87]

Dickens charged that such teachers were "Murdering the Innocent."

How did "operatives" ever control such large numbers of children? Lancaster theoretically rejected the corporal punishment common to schools of his era. But that did not mean he was uninterested in social control. Instead of the birch, he substituted tags hung around the neck announcing misdeeds.[88] He also devised yokes, shackles, a technique of sewing boys into blankets where they were left overnight, and, perhaps the most inventive, the procedure of placing malefactors in baskets and then hoisting them to the ceiling.[89]

---

[86]Ibid.

[87]Ibid., p. 12.

[88]Gerald Gutek, *Education in the United States: An Historical Perspective* (Englewood Cliffs, N.J.: Prentice-Hall, 1986), pp. 62–63.

[89]Button, op. cit., p. 76.

Significantly, a letter published in 1977 suggests that Lancaster devised these "innovations" for personal reasons. Apparently, he was a practicing sadist.[90]

Arousing Expectations, Setting Patterns

Monitorial schools helped prepare the way for the development of public schools.[91] But the rigid mechanical methods of the Lancastrian system remained as a less positive legacy. Monitorial techniques promoted the idea that the chief end of schooling was the rote mastery of facts and skills by a submissive child. It also encouraged the view that good teaching involved little more than proficient repression and following a printed course of study "by the numbers."[92]

Lancaster's ideas were widely popular in America. DeWitt Clinton, Governor of New York, even called them "a blessing sent down from heaven to redeem the poor and distressed of this world from the power and dominion of ignorance."[93]

In England his reception was more mixed. Despite the obvious need, schooling the poor concerned many among the privileged classes, who feared that they were becoming overeducated and, hence, would become rebellious.[94] Nevertheless, in 1833 the first government aid was given to schools. In 1847 schooling was nationalized, though tied in with the official Church of England.

Changes in France

England was not the only European nation where schooling was expanding. With the encouragement of the Council of Trent, there was a new emphasis on broadening the availability of schooling in Roman Catholic countries. There was to be a Catholic answer to Protestant efforts to school the children of the poor. In France, for example, it was not long before various newly formed religious orders took up the task.

The French cleric Jean Baptiste de la Salle (1651–1719) started one such order. Scion of an aristocratic family and heir to a fortune, La Salle gave away his wealth and devoted his life to establishing free elementary schools for poor boys. To this end he established a religious teaching institute, the Brothers of the Christian Schools, which has since become the largest teaching order in the Roman Catholic Church. He also devised a method of simultaneous instruction that permitted more efficient teaching of large groups. Heretofore

[90]H. deS. Honey, *Tom Brown's Universe: The Development of the English Public School in the Nineteenth Century* (New York: Quadrangle, 1977), pp. 202–203, cited in Button, op. cit., p. 76.
[91]Richard Stephens, op. cit., p. 64.
[92]Ravitch, op. cit., p. 82.
[93]Quoted in ibid., p. 12.
[94]David Snodin, *A Mighty Ferment: Britain in the Age of Revolution* (New York: Seabury, 1978), p. 43.

teachers dealt with each child individually while the others waited their turn.[95]

Following the success of the French Revolution, the Law of 1791 established a national school system intended to serve nationalism. In 1802 Napoleonic Law founded the French secondary educational system that featured status-oriented classical *lycées* emphasizing the traditional Latin. A national university was established in 1808, and state grants for elementary schools followed in 1834.

Prussian Developments

Recalling Luther's urgings that the state promote schooling, it is not surprising that during the late seventeenth and early eighteenth centuries most of the German states organized state-church school systems. They involved elementary and secondary schools, as well as the beginnings of compulsory education.[96]

Prussia was the first German state to organize and centralize a universal and compulsory system of schooling. Frederick Wilhelm I (r. 1713–1740) and his son, Frederick the Great (r. 1740–1786), recognized the social renewal and social control potential of schooling and made a state system of schools part of their general plans to promote the unity, power, and prosperity of this once backward kingdom.[97] Frederick I, for example, established nearly 2000 elementary schools with money saved by economizing in the royal household. He also founded one of the world's first successful teachers' training academies at Stettin (1735). His son, Frederick the Great, more in sympathy with the Enlightenment than his father, encouraged academic freedom in universities, strengthened and codified secondary classical schools, and, in 1763, decreed that all Prussian children from age five to thirteen must attend schools taught by licensed and examined teachers.[98]

This decree was opposed by teachers who feared they could not pass the required examinations, by farmers who thought schooling useless, and by nobles who feared an educated peasantry; and Frederick died before he could bring it to fruition. Nevertheless, these initiatives set in motion a chain of events that culminated in the General Code of 1794. Issued by Frederick Wilhelm II (r. 1786–1797), it declared:

> All schools and universities are state institutions, charged with the instruction of youth in useful information and scientific knowledge. Such institutions may be founded only with the knowledge and consent of the state.[99]

---

[95]W.J. Battersby, *De La Salle, A Pioneer in Modern Education* (New York: Longmans, 1949), p. 41.
[96]Elwood P. Cubberly, *The History of Education* (Boston: Houghton Mifflin, 1920), pp. 552–553.
[97]Edward Burns and Philip Ralph, *World Civilizations from Ancient to Contemporary*, Vol. II (New York: Norton, 1958), pp. 20–21.
[98]Cubberly, op. cit., p. 283.
[99]*Allgemeine Landrecht*, as quoted in Ibid.

Pestalozzi with children.

The principles of the famed Swiss teacher Johann Heinrich Pestalozzi (1746–1827) were particularly influential in the schools of Prussia. His principles also carried considerable weight in the rest of Europe and America. Teaching, said Pestalozzi, should be motivated by love of children, not efficiency. Of equal importance was that it be informed by a detailed understanding of how instruction could be integrated, step by interlocking step, with the organic development of the child. Above all, he was insistent that mechanical learning and harsh discipline were harmful.

When Pestalozzi put his method to work in his own boarding school for boys at Yverdon, it enjoyed remarkable success. As a result of this, and the fame won by his books on education, Pestalozzi's boarding school became a mecca for famous visitors and scholars. The king of Prussia was so taken by the ideas in operation at Yverdon that he ordered the famous Prussian *Volksschule* (elementary school) reorganized along the same lines.[100] Pestalozzi eventually became something of an international celebrity. Among many other honors, he was made a "Citizen of the French Republic," and even knighted by Tsar Alexander of Russia.[101]

Pestalozzi's influence on schooling was so great that the German philosopher Johann Fichte compared it with that of Martin Luther.[102] His followers and enthusiasts included Phillip von Fellenberg, developer of model schools for the rural poor; Johann Herbart, pioneer in the scientific approach to schooling; Friedrich Froebel, "Father of the Kindergarten"; and Horace Mann, "Father of the American Common School."

---

[100]Edgar Knight, *Twenty Centuries of Education* (Boston: Ginn and Company, 1940), pp. 359–360.
[101]S.E. Frost, *Historical and Philosophical Foundations of Western Education* (Columbus, Ohio: Merrill, 1966), pp. 344–360.
[102]Edgar Knight, *Twenty Centuries of Education* (Boston: Ginn and Company, 1940), p. 358.

Figure 12.4   **A KEY TRANSITION IN THE CONTROL OF SCHOOLING**

Religious Authority   Civil Authority

The Age of Faith   Modern Times

The Sacred to Secular Transition

These developments in England, France, and Prussia were all expressions of a process that began during the Age of Faith—the shift in the control of schooling from the Church to civil government. (See Chapter 11.) In Prussia, there was even a decree that *all* schooling exists at the sufferance of the secular state. A century later some governments would make schooling a total state monopoly.

There was also an American movement from a religious to a secular-based society in the formative days of the republic.[103] And even though American public schools remained nominally Protestant they were under the control of civil rather than religious authority. One only need think back to the Puritans to see how dramatic this transformation really was.

SUMMARY

1. American enthusiasm for public schooling was the consequence of a gradual but constantly intensifying commitment that began with largely religious motives within an essentially English context. Colonial America had three regions each with different social, political, and economic realities. However, in all three regions the educative functions of the extended family, church, and apprenticeship system was eroded by the restless and fluid social situation.

2. As the informal elements of the socioeducational system faltered, schooling acquired more importance. Teachers were expected to teach what had previously been soaked up through social contact.[104] With the Revolution, American statesmen like Washington and Jefferson insisted upon the necessity of schooling for the preservation of a free nation. Nevertheless, the Constitution gave the responsibility for school governance and finance to the respective states.

---

[103]Greer, op. cit., p. 55.
[104]Bailyn, op. cit., pp. 22–23.

3.   European educational developments illustrate the growing importance of schools. Also the marked transition from religious to secular control of schools that developed in the United States was mirrored by developments in key European countries.

QUESTIONS

1.   What new problems did the Age of Reason tend to generate for school authorities which they did not have to deal with in the Age of Faith?

2.   How would New England's educational history have been changed if that region had been settled by Anglicans rather than Puritan Congregationalists? Use the Southern Colonial experience as a reference.

3.   In 1672 Governor William Berkely of Virginia told authorities in England that he thanked God that there were no free schools and no printing presses in the province of Virginia. Why do you think he was grateful for this?

4.   In the chapter it was argued that Colonial era studies of Latin and Greek were, in a sense, a form of conspicuous consumption. "Pursuing Latin or Greek, rather than more practical arts, was akin to cultivating lawns rather than pastures." What present-day college majors do you think are examples of this same phenomenon?

5.   In an earlier chapter we discussed the economic emphasis of **A Nation At Risk.** Would the emphasis of that reform report been different had it been written by individuals who shared Washington, Jefferson and Webster's educational concerns?

6.   "The whole education of women out to be relative to men. To please them, to be useful to them, to make themselves loved and honored by them, to educate them when young, to care for them when grown, to consel them, console them, to make life agreeable and sweet to them— these are the duties of women at all times and should be taught them from their infancy."

—Rousseau

Comment on the costs and benefits of such an arrangement.

7.   Suppose the Founders had included the following in the Constitution: "Congress shall make no laws respecting the establishment of schools, nor prohibiting the free development thereof." What sort of major changes would we see today?

8.   Early in our history deliberate cultural nationalism became one of the most important characteristics of the Common Schools. Is that still true today?

9.   The early public schools stirred vigorous opposition from a wide variety of special interest groups. Identify at least one contemporary group that is hostile to the public schools.

10.   Identify a nation or nations where schooling is presently monopolized by the state and where private schools are totally disallowed.

A HISTORY of EDUCATION: THE LATER DEVELOPMENT of AMERICAN SCHOOLING

Chapter 13

PREVIEW

In this chapter two periods of the later development of American schooling are reviewed. The first, 1800–1865, describes the chief events that defined the essential characteristics of the American public schools. The second, 1865-Present, outlines how these characteristics achieved their present configuration.

The development of American schooling is placed in the broader context of social institutions, processes, and ideas. Nationalism, immigration, industrialization, and urbanization are seen in the context of the perpetual struggle for consensus regarding the ends and means of American schooling.

DEFINING AMERICAN SCHOOLING (1800–1865)

Despite the fact that influential men like Jefferson, Madison, and Webster were convinced that an educated citizenry was essential to the survival of the United States, schooling remained private rather than public, and unregulated and voluntary rather than state regulated and compulsory, in the early years of the Republic.[1] Such schools were widely available and steadily increasing in numbers throughout the Northeast as early as 1800. They were, however, largely restricted to people of means. Religious schools and private academies did waive tuition for a few, but such benevolence fell far short of equal and universal schooling. The majority of Americans were still educated outside of schools.

The public generally shared the anxieties of the Founding Fathers with respect to maintaining the Republic. But, at least initially, they were apparently convinced that the informal education provided was already sufficient.[2] During the period 1830–1840 this situation began to change. There was both a steady increase in school enrollment, particularly in smaller towns rather than cities, and a gradual but decisive shift from private to public schools throughout the northern United States.[3]

This process occurred in three stages. At first, state legislators *permitted* local communities to establish public schools, subject to the approval of voters. Later, they *encouraged* the establishment of local schools by providing state funding. Finally, they *required* the establishment of local school districts, and *specified* minimum school tax rates and a minimum curriculum.

The Common Schools

Many citizens felt that public schools were needed to deal with the effects of immigration, industrialism, and urbanization. They also hoped that such

[1]Bernard Bailyn, *Education in the Forming of American Society* (New York: W.W. Norton, 1972), p. 11.
[2]Carl Kaestle and Maris Vinovskis, *Education and Social Change in Nineteenth-Century Massachusetts* (Cambridge, England: Cambridge U. Press, 1980), p. 9.
[3]Ibid., p. 20.

schools could create the common bonds necessary to support new and vital conceptions of democracy that were then emerging in America. State constitutions were being revised or replaced to permit wider political equality and responsibility. Property qualifications for voting were being eliminated, the basis of representation in state legislatures was changing from wealth to population, and the number of public offices filled by popular vote increased.[4]

It was *not* intended that these would be schools just for the common people, such as the *Volksschule* of Prussia were, but schools common to all the people. Such a community of children living and studying together would, it was hoped, build bonds of friendship and respect that would provide the basis for a truly American consensus.[5]

We have seen that influential federal officials were enthusiastic about this endeavor. But one consequence of the Constitution's not giving the federal government authority over schooling was that it was left to the various state governments to set such schools in motion.

New England Sets the Pace

At first, many state officials did not support free public education; providing every child a tax-supported free education was a radical idea. In New England, however, conditions were particularly favorable. Compact settlements made it relatively easy for the children to get to school, and traditional religious attitudes encouraged the belief that common schools were a good idea. Also, a history of community-sponsored religious schooling provided a fairly extensive preexisting infrastructure. In addition, influential citizens were concerned about controlling the children of impoverished factory workers and immigrants who were crowding into fast-growing industrial cities. And an increasingly heterogeneous society made it necessary and prudent to distinguish between individual and collective interests.

Horace Mann and the Common School Crusade

Despite these favorable factors the prodding of a number of extraordinarily dedicated "public school men" was needed to really get things moving in New England. It was their activities that encouraged sufficient consensus to support the founding of the first public schools during the early nineteenth century.[6]

Horace Mann (1796–1859), often referred to as the "Father of the Common School," was the most famed of these activists. Mann accepted the apparently powerless job of Secretary of the new Massachusetts State Board of Education because, like many other reformers of his day, he was convinced that free common schools were the key to social renewal and the improvement of

---

[4]Knight, op. cit., p. 258.
[5]Lawrence Cremin, *The Transformation of the School* (New York: Vintage, 1961), p. 10.
[6]R. Freeman Butts, "Search for Freedom—the Story of American Education," *NEA Journal*, March 1960.

Horace Mann

humankind. He was also very concerned about controlling "the giant vices which now invade and torment" society.[7]

Charged only with collecting and disseminating information, the State Board Mann headed had no authority. But through talks, publications, and a particularly influential series of reports, Mann persuaded Massachusetts authorities to build hundreds of new schools, lengthen the school term, increase teacher's salaries, establish a state "normal school" to train teachers, and encourage the use of the best in European teaching methodology.

Mann was determined to supplant private schooling. He believed that it was divisive, drew off the support of wealthy and powerful parents, and diverted some of the best students from the public schools.[8] Of course, his efforts were not without opposition. Private school interests naturally worked against him. He was also bitterly attacked by orthodox churchmen because it was Mann's view that common schooling should empower children to decide for themselves what their religious obligations were.[9]

Mann also offended many schoolmasters because of his advocacy of the teaching methods of the Swiss educator Johann Heinrich Pestalozzi.[10] Mann was concerned that group teaching undermined the democratic importance of the individual, and he believed that Pestalozzi's emphasis on adjusting instruction to the individual differences of children could counteract this tendency. Predictably, however, many teachers thought such a method un-

---

[7]Quoted by Nassaw, op. cit., p. 81.
[8]Kaestle and Vinovskis, op. cit., pp. 32–34.
[9]Joel Spring, *The American School: 1642–1845* (White Plains, N.Y.: Longman, 1986), p. 85.
[10]Frost, op. cit., pp. 393–396.

Figure 13.1

**AN UNDERLYING TENSION
IN A DEMOCRACY**

As we have seen elsewhere in the text, it is always problematic to convert
dermined their authority and was an impertinent assault on "tried and true"
methods.[11]

Consensus and the Common Schools

Encouraged by leaders like Mann, friends of the common schools organized
associations, published journals, and released a flood of sloganeering advocat-
ing free public schools.[12] One reformer proclaimed, for example, that common
schools would be "the best police for our cities, the lowest insurance for our
houses, the finest security for our banks, the most effective means of pre-
venting pauperism."[13]

Such rhetoric was eventually effective in building a broad but shallow consensus in support of public schooling. Unfortunately, however, this consensus
proved hard to maintain under the pressures of implementation. David Nassaw
describes it thus:

> While there appeared to be widespread agreement among Ameri-
> cans on the importance of schooling for their children, there was
> no consensus on the shape that schooling should take. There were
> differences of opinion over how the schools should be funded; over
> what form religious instruction should take; over the qualifications
> for schoolmasters, the facilities for schoolhouses, the content and
> objectives of school books, and the proper language of classroom
> instruction.[14]

As we have seen elsewhere in the text, it is always problematic to convert
slogans into actual tasks backed by adequate resources. And this was particularly true in founding American common schools. As soon as implementation
began, the crusade met with bitter opposition. It took a quarter of a century
of sloganeering, struggle, and compromise to establish sufficient consensus to
bring about change. Battles were waged in every state. Lawmakers who voted

---

[11]Ibid.
[12]Ibid., p. 399.
[13]Knight, op. cit., p. 172.
[14]David Nasaw, *Schooled to Order: A Social History of Public Schooling in the United States*
(Oxford, England: Oxford U. Press, 1979), p. 81. He is quoting Horace Mann.

for public schooling were often turned out of office in the next election. Legislation passed one year was sometimes repealed the next. Even among liberal Jackson Democrats, support was only partial.[15] Objection to taxation was the main obstacle.[16]

Significantly, much of the support for public schooling came from businessmen. In fact, their interests sometimes gained dominance over educators and school programs—particularly after 1900.[17] As a result, concern for human problems often became a secondary consideration, even with schoolmen.[18] Social control and the maintenance of the status quo became even more important considerations.

Over time consensus supporting the common schools broadened. It became more and more widely accepted that they were the institution through which the United States could hold itself together and prepare citizens for life in a democracy. Some assumed this stance meant establishing control over the lower classes and foreign born. Others assumed it involved the encouragement of egalitarian change. But the slogans supporting the movement temporarily glossed over these contradictions as the public schools became the carriers of American dreams.

Massachusetts adopted free public schooling in 1827. Gradually other states fell in line. By the Civil War (1860–1865), thousands of tuition free public elementary schools had been founded all over the North.[19] Only the South continued to rely on private schooling.

Schooling and Americanization of Immigrants

The importance of the common schools was heightened as more and more immigrants began arriving in the United States. Between 1820 and 1860 over five million (more than the entire population of the United States in 1790) tumbled ashore and spread out across America.[20] Had they been similar to the preexisting population, this influx would still have been difficult to absorb. But because there were a disproportionate number of Irish, most of whom were Roman Catholics, assimilation was even more problematic. Figure 13.2 illustrates the extent of Irish immigration in the period 1820–1840.

Predictably, most Americans looked to common schooling as a means of dealing with this influx of foreigners. Most thought the public schools should aid in the assimilation of the newcomers by deliberately weakening their ties to an alien faith and foreign land. Others, far fewer in number, thought their beliefs and culture should be accommodated—at least to some extent. But all

[15]Ibid., p. 161.
[16]Knight, op. cit., pp. 270–271.
[17]Raymond Callahan, *Education and the Cult of Efficiency* (Chicago: U. of Chicago Press, 1962).
[18]Maxine Greene, *The Public School and the Private Vision: A Search for America in Education and Literature* (New York: Random House, 1965).
[19]Carl N. Degler, *Out of Our Past: The Forces That Shaped Modern America* (New York: Harper & Row, 1984), p. 172.
[20]Vincent Parrillo, *Strangers To These Shores* (New York: Macmillan, 1985), p. 114.

Figure 13.2   SOURCES OF IMMIGRATION, 1820–1840

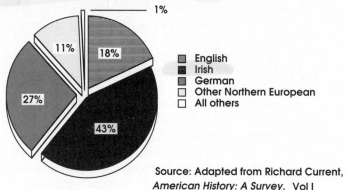

Source: Adapted from Richard Current,
American History: A Survey, Vol I

agreed that the public schools should play a central role in their Americanization. Many of the Irish, however, were uncooperative.

The Catholic Issue

The central problem for all Roman Catholic immigrants was that the "nonsectarianism" of the early public schools was really a sectless form of Protestantism.[21] For this reason the school curriculum was broadly Protestant, and many textbooks contained anti-Catholic sentiments. Here is a sample biographical entry from a textbook used in New York:

> Huss, John, a zealous reformer from Popery, who lived in Bohemia, towards the close of the fourteenth, and the beginning of the fifteenth centuries. He was bold and persevering; but at length, trusting himself to deceitful Catholics, he was by them brought to trial, condemned as a heretic, and burnt at the stake.[22]

Moderate Catholics preferred public schooling. But they wanted it to embrace children of all religions equally. They thought this could be accomplished by confining religious training to the home and church.[23] But many Protestants were furious at the mere suggestion of eliminating religion from the public schools. After all, why should the arrival of foreigners with alien religious ideas disrupt a shallow and somewhat unstable Protestant consensus that had just been painstakingly put together?

Militant Protestants denounced compromise as a sell-out to "Popery." Their vitriolic tirades against the Pope, alleged Jesuit plots, and the like silenced

[21]Ibid., p. 35
[22]Joel Spring, op. cit., p. 104.
[23]Diane Ravitch, *The Great School Wars: New York City, 1805–1973* (New York: Basic Books, 1974), p. 41.

moderate elements of the Catholic faithful. Conservative elements within the Church gained the upper hand in pushing the idea that Catholic parents were obliged to provide their children with an education based on religious principles and subordinate to religious authority.[24]

When it became apparent that Catholic immigrants could not be ignored, a few public officials made belated efforts to accommodate them. Governor Seward of New York proposed using state money for Catholic schools, and public school officials in Philadelphia permitted Catholic youngsters to read their own version of the Bible, and even excused them from other religious instruction. But these measures were too little and too late. The initial conflicts had sharpened the boundaries of both the Catholic and Protestant communities and revitalized old antagonisms.

In the early 1840s, this controversy got out of control and violent anti-Catholic riots erupted in a number of American cities. Mobs roamed the streets, Catholic churches were burned to the ground, and dozens died.

In the end, neither side prevailed. Enough native-born Americans had been convinced that Americanism meant Protestantism to prevent accommodation of a minority committed to a different authority. As far as public schools were concerned, it was assimilation or nothing. But the Catholics had also refused to renounce their faith. Eventually, at great cost, they developed their own parallel system of schooling.[25]

Paradoxically, however, as these schools were being established they too became involved in a bitterly divisive situation within the Catholic community. All American Roman Catholics came under the nominal authority of the Church, but there still were many differences principally involving the various ethnic groups which made up that community. After much conflict, often over the use of the English language in church and parish elementary schools, Church authorities coped with the dissensus by permitting separate churches and schools for single nationalities *within* the boundaries of the parishes established by the diocese. This arrangement kept things from falling apart.[26]

---

[24]Spring, op. cit., pp. 106–107.
[25]Ibid.
[26]Theodore Maynard, *The Story of American Catholicism* (New York: Macmillan 1941) pp. 219–228.

In the early 1840s controversy turned into conflict when anti-Catholic riots erupted.

Other Minorities

Catholics were not the only group refused accommodation in schools that were theoretically for all. Many African-Americans were also excluded or segregated. Significantly, they did not have the organizational equivalent of the Roman Catholic Church to fall back on. For this reason it was nearly impossible for them to escape the educational consequences of prejudice, discrimination, and exploitation.

There was one other minority that did not participate in the common schools—those with power and wealth. Such individuals had employed tutors or sent their children to elitist private schools since before the Revolution, and most continued to do so even when public schooling became available. Thus, those with the most power and influence had no personal stake in their operation, and only an indirect interest in their quality.

This lack of commitment to, and involvement with, the public schools on the part of the nation's most influential citizens has proven highly significant. No one can say for certain how different our public schools would be if this situation had been otherwise.

We realize, then, that broadening and deepening the national consensus through public schooling was far more problematic than was expected.[27] Many were left out; others opted out. The reality did not match the dream.

The Matter of Compulsion

Another difficulty with the common school crusade was that some parents were indifferent or downright unenthusiastic about sending their youngsters to school. Many depended upon the wages their children earned for family survival. Others were simply unconvinced that schooling was necessary.

When persuasion failed, compulsion seemed the only solution. There was some precedent for such action. Since colonial days, public officials had been empowered to remove children from their natural parents *if* it was determined that they were not being properly cared for. "Neglected" children were routinely "placed out," or apprenticed to individuals who agreed to accept responsibility for their rearing in return for their labor.[28]

Social control and having the child learn a vocation were the considerations behind "placing out." And much the same motivation was behind compulsory school attendance. For instance, Diane Ravitch reports that thousands of poor children, some no more than six years old, were living in the streets of New York and other major cities. During the day they shined shoes or sold newspapers and other items. Many were beggars or thieves. At night they slept wherever they could, just as street people do today.[29]

Massachusetts authorities were the first to compel school attendance. Hor-

---

[27]David Tyack (ed.), *Turning Points in American Educational History* (Waltham, Mass.: Blaisdell, 1967).
[28]Nassaw, op. cit., p. 10.
[29]Ravitch, op. cit., p. 89.

POINT/COUNTERPOINT

The particular model of society an historian subscribes to has a great deal to do with how he or she interprets the public school movement. Radical historians who subscribe to a conflict model of society argue that the common schools were designed from the very beginning as agencies through which the prosperous and propertied could control and contain the poor. They also emphasize that the poor have always failed in school, and that those who did "make it" often did so by dropping out and falling back on native customs and skills.

Historians with a consensus perspective agree that common schooling encourages stability and maintains the existing social order, but go on to argue that schooling promotes value integration, encourages consensus, and works individuals into the social structure. Scholars with a more individualistic notion of society maintain that there were as many motivations for initiating common schools as there were initiators. (See Chapter 5.)

---

ace Mann had seen compulsory schooling in action while visiting Prussia. On his return he urged a similar measure for Massachusetts. In 1852 state authorities passed legislation compelling all children from 8 to 14 years of age to go to school twelve weeks out of the year. Other states followed this example. By 1918, when the Mississippi legislature passed its compulsory attendance law, every state in the United States compelled children to go to school.[30]

These laws represented a fundamental shift in authority over the lives of children. The educational efforts of every family was to be supplemented by schools through compulsion.

At first, compulsory attendance laws were poorly enforced—in part, because of a widespread lack of enthusiasm for the requirement. The poor, both native and immigrant, for example, were completely unenthusiastic. Also, public school officials were already coping with a lack of resources and severe overcrowding. In New York City, for example, classrooms intended to hold 50 to 70 students had between 100 and 150 under one teacher.[31] School officials did not need all the additional problems that enforced compulsory attendance would bring.

There was also the curriculum question to deal with. Does one try to teach academic subjects to children who in previous years were beggars, thieves, or sweatshop workers? If not, what should they be taught?

Despite these practical problems, state after state gradually strengthened its compulsory attendance provisions and enforcement. The age of entrance was lowered, stiff penalties for noncompliance were provided, and the length of the school year was increased. Compulsory schooling slowly became a fact of American life.

Significantly, private schooling satisfied compulsory attendance laws. This option, for those upper class parents who could afford it, alleviated status

---

[30]Frost, op. cit., p. 400.
[31]Ravitch, op. cit., p. 89.

anxieties generated by the prospect that their children might have to attend the same schools as the children of the poor.

Given the anti-Catholicism of many Americans, the private school option was not always a welcome feature of compulsory attendance laws. It could be used by Catholics to escape the Protestant values of nominally public schools. In 1922, the private school option was put to the test when Oregon voters, motivated by a groundswell of anti-Catholic agitation, passed a petition virtually requiring public school attendance of everyone. In 1925 this law was declared unconstitutional by the U. S. Supreme Court. (See Chapter 15 for details.)

Over the years the original dream of a school experience common to all American youngsters was not fulfilled. Catholics started their own system of schools; the wealthy opted for private schools; blacks were usually either segregated or systematically excluded; and public officials wanted only some of the remaining children to attend. For instance, the "mentally weak" or otherwise handicapped were granted "exemptions."[32]

Common Schools In A Rural America

In their first years most public schools developed in a largely rural setting simply because that is where the vast majority of Americans lived. For this reason common schooling was often heavily influenced by the nature of rural life. In the mid-nineteenth century, for example, the school year, city or country, was divided into summer and winter terms that fit between the spring plowing and the fall harvest. It was only after 1900—slightly more than 30 percent of Americans lived in cities at that time—that the school year was standardized into the nine-month term still common today.

Figure 13.3 illustrates the extremely rural nature of American life in the period when public schooling was rapidly expanding.

---

[32]Ibid., p. 434.

Figure 13.3

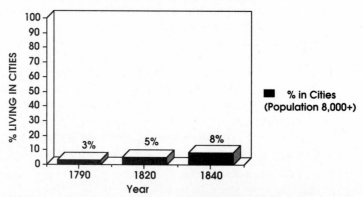

U.S. URBAN POPULATION 1790–1840

Source: Data from U.S. Bureau of Census

Country Schools

Unlike Europe, most American rural communities were not sharply defined, but strung out along the roads.[33] Thus, country schools, too, were scattered all over the landscape. Usually crude one-room affairs, they used poorly educated teachers under the control of rural schoolboards with very limited interests. As the historian Carl Kaestle notes:

> . . . rural schools of the early nineteenth century reflected the close local control, the broad parental discipline, the parsimony and the limited educational needs of rural communities in the early American Republic.[34]

Rural schools commonly accepted everyone from children as young as four to adult farmhands and immigrants. Country teachers were usually required to teach them all together in just one room. This configuration necessitated ability grouping, the preparation of lessons to accommodate a broad range of learning, and the older children's helping to teach the younger. Children could also advance at their own pace.

The stinginess of country school officials was legendary. They would not buy books; cord wood for the pot belly stove was often bought in inexpensive sled lengths that had to be cut and split by the older children; and experienced teachers were often fired to keep salaries at a minimum.[35] More often than not, the schools were unventilated cubicles, averaging about 8 by 16 feet with 30 or so youngsters packed inside. In 1848 the Commissioners of the Common Schools of Connecticut even reported that of the 1,663 school houses in that state, 745 had no sanitary facilities whatever.[36]

Primitive as they were, country schools quickly became the centers of rural social life. They were the only place that people of different Protestant de-

---

[33]Jack Larkin, *The Reshaping of Everyday Life* (New York: Harper & Row, 1988), p. 7.
[34]Carl F. Kaestle, *Pillars of the Republic: Common Schools and American Society, 1780–1860* (New York: Hill and Wang, 1983), quoted in Andrew Guilford, *American Country Schools* (Washington, D.C.: Preservation Press, 1984), p. 39.
[35]Ibid.
[36]Daniel Boorstin, *The Americans: The National Experience* (New York: Random House, 1967), p. 44.

A well-appointed country school.

A brush arbor school in Live Oak County, Texas—1887.

nominations could meet on common ground. John Steinbeck offers this description of the role of the country school in *East of Eden*.

> In the country the repository of art and science was the school, and the school teacher shielded and carried the torch of learning and of beauty. The schoolhouse was the meeting place for music, for debate. The polls were set in the schoolhouse for elections. Social life, whether it was the crowning of the May queen, the eulogy for a dead president, or an all-night dance, could be held nowhere else.[37]

Country Teachers

Most country teachers were young. It was common for them to be in their late teens. Also, they were little better educated than the children that they taught. Literacy plus "good moral character" was usually the only requirement. Regarding professional knowledge, teacher training was virtually nonexistent, and certification was not even available until the 1880s.[38]

Country school teachers were expected to model faithfully the *professed* values of the communities in which they taught, and their practical circumstances made this more than a theoretical challenge. Although the country teacher's pay usually included room and board, he or she was merely shuttled from one child's home to another.

Living conditions in parental homes were often uncomfortable and devoid of privacy. Country schoolteacher Phoebe Nater describes her accommodations:

---

[37]John Steinbeck, *East of Eden* (New York: Viking Press, 1952), quoted in ibid.
[38]Guilford, op. cit., p. 63.

> The door was warped out of shape. It lacked four inches at the top of being closed. The door hung with icicles and heavy frost.... Lying in her bed this country teacher was nearly insane with anger. Shivering under blankets and dressed in a flannel robe and pajamas, a coat and socks, her breath made a thin sheet of ice around the pillow and covers as she kept her head under the covers and tried to sleep.... The supreme test came at dawn one morning. Two coyote trappers, relatives of the family, pushed the frosty door open, and smoking corn cob pipes, walked across the bedroom floor with traps slung over their shoulders and dead coyotes resting outside the door.[39]

When country teaching was in a frontier school, it took an especially tough and resourceful individual to succeed. Here discipline was usually a matter of the rod or, in the case of a male teacher, even fists, because school officials assumed that a schoolmaster would overcome all challenges to his authority on his own. If a teacher lost the struggle he would simply be driven out.[40] Frank Grady, a country schoolteacher in Nebraska in the early 1900s recalls;

> The first teacher in Raymond school was run out by the boys, who used stones as weapons of assault. The second met the same gang, but when he had soundly thrashed one boy and the youth's father coming to take up the battle shared the same fate, the reign of terror ended abruptly, and a new respect for the school was established.
>
> [Another teacher] was already in the school on New Year's Day, and [the students] threw brimstone—sulphur, I reckon its called—down the chimney and smoked him out, getting possession of the premises.... Quite a percentage of the big fellows considered the teacher Public Enemy Number One.[41]

Such incidents corresponded with life in a society where casual violence was a part of the daily fabric of existence. Tavern brawling was common, dueling and no holds barred wrestling were customary means of settling disputes, and men traveled armed throughout much of the country.[42]

The Feminization of Teaching

In the early days of the common schools, male teachers were much preferred, especially in the winter term when the older boys attended, because it often took the two-fisted approach described above to get such boys to cooperate.

---

[39]Quoted in Guilford, op. cit., p. 68.
[40]Larkin, op. cit., pp. 288–289.
[41]Quoted in ibid., p. 64.
[42]Ibid., p. 288.

Women teachers were a lot cheaper to hire than men teachers. (E. L. Henry, *Country School*, 1890)

In time, however, single women teachers became predominant. (Those who married were automatically fired.)

There were several reasons for the popularity of women teachers. First, there was the matter of nurturance. Horace Mann emphasized this when he noted in 1840:

> ... females are incomparably better teachers for young children then males.... Their manners are more mild and gentle, and hence in consonance with the tenderness of childhood.[43]

Mann neglected to mention that there was also a matter of cost. Most Americans wanted the benefits of common schooling, but balked at paying for it. Consequently, teacher's salaries and working conditions were notoriously awful, and there was a scarcity of male applicants. Because women's job opportunities were severely restricted, they could be hired much more cheaply than men—their pay was perhaps one third that for men. This made their "natural" talents with children look especially promising. Catherine Beecher unconsciously reveals this dimension of the popularity of female teachers in an 1845 recruitment pamphlet:

> It is WOMAN who is to come in at this emergency and meet the demand. Woman, whom experience and testing have shown to be the best, *as well as the cheapest*, guardian and teacher of childhood.[44]

It was in this way that women, particularly young unmarried women, came to pay a disproportionate share of the costs of establishing common schooling. And they gained very meager benefits for their efforts.

Despite the poor pay and unpleasant working conditions, however, teaching provided women with significant autonomy at a time when that was a very scarce commodity. In fact, frontier teaching was particularly attractive to an

---

[43]Quoted in ibid., p. 65.
[44]Quoted in ibid.

independent breed of older woman who, in the words of historian Polly Welts Kaufman, "... demonstrated a greater will to direct their own lives than was usual for the majority of women of their time."[45]

TRANSFORMING AMERICAN SCHOOLING (1865–PRESENT)

The end of the Civil War marks the beginning of the modern era in American public schooling. In the years that followed, the idea that every child ought to go to school gained nearly universal currency. As a consequence, schooling was gradually transformed into one of the nation's most ambitious, and expensive, enterprises. Schools were joined rung by rung into a single articulated system, and a market for cultural credentials developed that linked diplomas, degrees, and licenses with social stratification. State governments also assumed more and more educational authority, severely limiting the original control and freedom of action of local communities while consolidating school districts into ever larger entities.

Schooling in the Post-Civil War South

In the pre-Civil War South common schools were virtually undeveloped. African-Americans and poor whites were educated at home and in the community. The wealthier whites depended on private schools and tutors to supplement their families. Following the Civil War, however, federal officials took initiatives that dramatically increased the schooling available to poor Southerners of both races.

With respect to newly freed slaves, the federally sponsored Freedmen's Bureau used federal funds to provide "Negro education" in over 2,600 bureau schools. Private northern philanthropic organizations also sponsored schools for freedmen, as did blacks themselves. Although these schools encouraged very modest vocational ambitions, most southern whites viewed them with a mixture of alarm and resentment.[46]

During the 1870s Reconstructionist southern legislatures initiated common school systems serving both whites and blacks. At first, there was some thought that these schools might be racially integrated. But when federal military occupation ended in 1877, a powerful, conservative white oligarchy regained political power. Southern public schools were then segregated in the same systematic legal fashion as all other institutions, facilities, and services.[47] Passage of compulsory education legislation in the South also lagged way behind that of the rest of America. Figure 13.4 clearly shows this.

Despite their late start for compulsory schooling, by 1880 more than half

---

[45]Polly Welts Kaufman, "A Wider Field of Usefulness: Pioneer Women Teachers in the West, 1848–1854," quoted in ibid.

[46]Gutek, op. cit., p. 138.

[47]Ibid., p. 156.

Figure 13.4

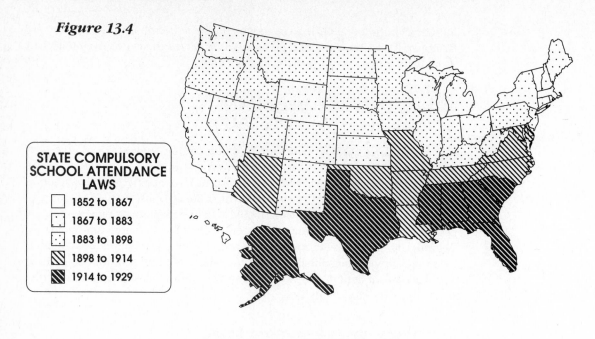

STATE COMPULSORY SCHOOL ATTENDANCE LAWS

☐ 1852 to 1867
⬚ 1867 to 1883
⬚ 1883 to 1898
⬚ 1898 to 1914
⬛ 1914 to 1929

of all white children and about 40 percent of all black children were attending southern public schools.[48] However, the opportunity to integrate African-Americans into the mainstream of American life had been set aside in favor of defining them as a legally segregated underclass.

Toward Universal Schooling

The ideal of universal free education slowly became a reality in the decades after the Civil War. By 1900 public schooling had become widely available, and compulsory attendance laws had been adopted by thirty-one states and territories.[49]

Common Schools in an Urbanizing and Industrializing America

In this same period cities became more and more important as immigration and rural to urban migration, due largely to industrialization, promoted their explosive growth. In 1790, there was not one U.S. city of over 50,000 people. In 1830, just 40 years later, almost half a million Americans lived in cities that

---

[48]Richard N. Current et al., *A Survey of American History Vol I: Since 1865* (New York: Alfred Knopf, 1983), p. 465.
[49]Ibid., p. 555.

Figure 13.5

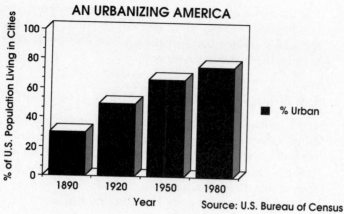

AN URBANIZING AMERICA

% of U.S. Population Living in Cities

■ % Urban

Year   Source: U.S. Bureau of Census

size.[50] By 1920 more than half of all Americans lived in urban areas. In 1980 the number had grown to about three out of four. Figure 13.5 summarizes this trend.

City schools were markedly different from their country counterparts. Because urban children were concentrated, it was possible to build large schools organized in ways that corresponded with the factories and business organizations that made cities possible.

Such factory-type schools grouped children homogeneously by age. They were then required to take a uniform course of study formulated by the superintendent, supervised by the building principal, and taught by teachers who specialized in teaching one particular age group and/or subject. These developments were elements in the evolution of a formalized, routinized, hierarchical, and bureaucratic model of organization for American public schooling which has since become universal.[51] (See Chapters 8 and 9.)

The Changing Role of the Family

City schools were a more pressing necessity than were country schools. Factory employment weakened the bonds of the urban family and limited what parents could teach their young about making a living. Previously, the similarity in occupations from one generation to the next meant that the family was a invaluable educational unit within which older family members; often grandparents too aged to work a full day, could pass on vocational knowledge to the young. With industrialization, income derived from cooperative effort on the farm or home workshop was replaced by the pooled industrial wages of individual family members who worked at whatever jobs they could find.

---

[50]Nassaw, op. cit., p. 12.
[51]Diane Ravitch, op. cit., p. xiv.

The urban middle classes encountered a similar phenomenon when the family firm began giving way to the modern corporation. In both cases, adults outside the family trained the young while the vocational skills of family members became more and more superfluous.[52]

The Struggle for Recognition and Accommodation

From their inception city public schools were battlefields where social, religious, and ethnic groups struggled for recognition and accommodation. Over time a very shallow consensus would be worked out. But no sooner was that accomplished than there would be a wave of new immigration that would start up the struggle again.[53]

Historian Diane Ravitch describes it thus:

> Though the issues in each instance were different, the public school was the battleground where the aspirations of the newcomers and the fears of the native population met and clashed. . . . In each case, the role and purpose of the public school were bitterly disputed by intense and hostile factions. The political system of the city and state, which usually aims to compromise differences and pacify discontent, on each occasion engineered a political solution which satisfied both wants and fears, terminating the contest.[54]

Differences over the matter of authority were central to these disputes. A Catholic spokesman summarized his co-religionist's views on that matter:

> The Catholic Church tells her children that they must be taught by authority. The sects say, read the Bible, judge for yourselves. The Bible is read in the public schools. The children are allowed to judge for themselves. The Protestant principle is therefore acted upon, silently inculcated, and the schools are sectarian.[55]

The Second Wave

In the late nineteenth century a decided shift occurred in the origins of American immigrants which made their accommodation even more problematic. Northern and western Europeans were supplanted by eastern and southern Europeans. Instead of English, Scandinavians, Germans, and Irish, it was Italians, Sicilians, Poles, Ukrainians, Russians, Czechs, Slovenes, Jews, and dozens of others, each one seemingly more foreign than the last. In astounding num-

---

[52]Janet Roebuck, *The Shaping of Urban Society* (New York: Scribners, 1947), pp. 142–143.
[53]Ibid., p. xiii.
[54]Ibid.
[55]Quoted in W. Richard Stephens and William Van Til, *Education in American Life* (Boston: Houghton Mifflin, 1972), p. 81.

bers, they came to America as a part of the greatest migration in the history of the world.

By 1890, fully 43 percent of New York City's population of 1.5 million were foreign born, and that figure skyrockets to 80 percent if we include those of foreign parentage. The physical and cultural differences of these newcomers, as well as the fact that most were often illiterate, unskilled, rural peasants, made them easier to identify and harder to assimilate. Plunged into a bewilderingly new environment with virtually no resources, they were forced to live in squalor in tightly packed poverty stricken communities.[56] And as these wretched slums expanded, so did poverty, illiteracy, ignorance, disease, filth, crime, and vice. Thousands of children ended up living on the street. Even slums were beyond their means.

Growth and More Growth

Predictably, many hoped that public schooling could bring this situation under control. But it soon turned out that this goal required greater resources than most Americans were willing to provide. Thus, as the children of these newcomers flooded into public schools, educators were often left with tasks that they did not have the resources to carry out.

School buildings, which were often unsanitary, poorly ventilated, and inadequately heated to begin with, became vastly overcrowded. Newly arriving farm children rubbed shoulders with young immigrants in classes averaging sixty or more per teacher.[57]

Pestalozzi and Mann had both stressed the importance of considering the needs of individual children, but in this situation it was simply impossible. At best, the classroom could be little more than an assembly line as educators found themselves overwhelmed.

Many of the children were similarly overwhelmed. More often than not the

---

[56]Parrillo, op. cit., pp. 150–151.
[57]Cremin, op. cit., p. 21.

Thousands of children lived on the streets in America's growing cities.

public schools did not match up well with the nonschool aspects of the socioeducational system that informed and shaped their lives. Lessons learned from immigrant parents or on the streets of impoverished city neighborhoods were often completely at odds with those taught in schools. As a consequence the rate of school failure among children from poor and/or immigrant families was consistently and remarkably high. In the end such children dropped out in great numbers—sometimes falling back on the customs and skills their families brought with them to America, sometimes relying on the savvy they had picked up on the street.[58]

Undeterred by their lack of success with many children, a failure that we have seen continue to the present day, school officials launched ambitious expansion plans. These made public schooling an ever bigger business.

Science, Darwinism, and the Matter of Authority

Massive waves of immigration were not the only reason that educators found consensus and authority to be problematic. New ways of looking at humankind and the world were creating additional difficulties. For example, when in 1859 Charles Darwin published *On the Origins of the Species*, he presented convincing evidence that life on Earth had evolved from simple to complex forms through a long process of "... universal struggle for existence [in which] the right of the strongest eventually prevails." This new vision of the past represented a profound challenge to traditional religious authority. In Darwin's creation there was no Adam and no Eve, and humans were no longer God's special creation. They were subject to the same evolutionary forces as all other life forms.[59]

Some liberal religionists came to terms with Darwin. But because of biblical pronouncements on the origin of life, most religious authorities, and most of the faithful, considered evolutionary theory totally unacceptable. This belief encouraged a feeling of "us versus them" that revitalized Christian traditions and norms while making the evolutionists even more determined to prevail. (See the functions of conflict in Chapter 4.)

Concerns stirred by Darwin's work quickly focused on the public schools. Responding to popular pressure, a number of states passed laws forbidding the teaching of evolution. As we learned in Chapter 5, matters finally came to a head in 1923 when John Scopes, a Tennessee biology teacher, was arrested for violating a state statute forbidding the teaching of any theory that denied "the story of divine creation of man as taught in the Bible." In the subsequent "Monkey Trial," Scopes was found guilty. His appeal to the state Supreme Court was denied, and the Tennessee law remained on the books until 1967.[60]

Authority conflicts concerning evolutionary science and creationism still persist. In recent years several states have passed laws requiring that any

---

[58]Colin Greer, *The Great School Legend* (New York: Basic Books, 1972), p. 4.
[59]Ibid., p. 260.
[60]Frost, op. cit., pp. 505–506.

teaching of evolutionary science be matched by equal time given over to biblical creationism. Although the courts have generally concluded that such laws are unconstitutional (note the authority that governs here), efforts to circumvent these rulings persist.

The longevity and intensity of this struggle illustrates how central the matter of authority is to schooling. Time and again it has turned out to be *the* critical factor.

Science and Democracy

As the twentieth century progressed, scientific authority became more and more powerful despite the opposition of those who claimed a unique authority for the Bible. The scientific method was well suited to America's changing technological civilization, and also seemed to some to be appropriate to a highly pluralistic democratic society.

A number of influential thinkers, known as "pragmatists," were particularly interested in integrating science and American democracy. They maintained that in a pluralistic democratic society decisions should not be based on received opinion, but on their practical consequences. For pragmatists the ultimate test of any institution, value, or idea was, "Does it work?" In essence, they argued that all social institutions, values, and ideas should be measured in terms of their usefulness. And, just as nature ruthlessly sorted the fit from the unfit, so Americans should retain institutions or values only if they accomplished desired ends.[61]

John Dewey (1859–1952), philosopher and educator, was one of the most famous and effective spokesmen for this point of view. Supremely interested in applying his ideas to the moral, social, and political problems of his time, he saw schooling as one way of accomplishing this.

The Progressive Era

Pragmatism first found expression in the late nineteenth and early twentieth century during the Progressive Era. In short order its practical problem-solving approach was making itself felt.[62]

As their name implies, Progressives were devoted to progress. But while this diverse coalition of social reformers was convinced that American society could be improved, its various members disagreed on how that could be accomplished. The "Social Gospel" movement equipped "Christian soldiers" to wage war on misery and poverty. The Settlement House movement established outposts of civilization on the urban frontier. Municipal reformers launched major efforts to reform urban politics. Suffragettes set out to win voting rights for women because this promised a better tomorrow. Those advocates of the Temperance Movement worked for the prohibition of drink

---

[61]Current, op. cit., p. 555.
[62]Ibid., p. 597.

which, they believed, would also eradicate the many problems generated by its abuse.[63]

Progressive Education

However much Progressives disagreed as to fundamental tactics, most agreed that public schooling could be a significant means of reform.[64] Unfortunately, however, many public school systems had been overwhelmed by municipal corruption, and were overcrowded, understaffed, riddled by patronage, and housed in substandard buildings. As if these problems were not enough, teaching frequently consisted of a machine-like inculcation of facts, reinforced with stiff doses of repressive discipline from poorly educated teachers.

Largely motivated by pragmatist thinking, a Progressive school reform movement began to take shape. It would have an important influence on American public schooling.

John Dewey soon became Progressive Education's most influential spokesperson. Dewey and other pragmatists placed great value on scientific knowledge and technological expertise. It was science, enlightened experts, and well-designed bureaucracies that they thought held the key not only to school reform, but to positive human evolution as well.[65]

Dewey was motivated primarily by humanistic concern for the **dignity of the individual**. He championed educating the "whole child," arguing that the school should be a sort of "embryonic community" in which children could learn by doing rather than by rote.[66] He and his followers also maintained that American schools should be places suffused with cooperative and mutually helpful living, not blind obedience, docility, and submission. Otherwise children would grow up rendering lip service to democratic ideals, while still requiring the tyranny they had lived in school.[67]

Working from within the school hierarchy, and capitalizing on the changing public climate, progressive educators like Dewey managed to have many of their methods and programs adopted. Working to capitalize on the instinctive, impulsive attitudes and activities of children, they tried to integrate originality and learning. They also tried to maintain discipline through student involvement, popular agreement, and appeals to reason.

The problem with all of these methods and programs was that they were being applied in schools that were under pressure from soaring enrollments of students from increasingly diverse backgrounds. Progressivism called for

---

[63]In 1921 the National Origins Quota Act limited new immigrants to only 3 percent of the number of people of that nationality already in the United States. In 1924 that was reduced to 2 percent of those already in the United States in 1890. These restrictions remained in effect until the Immigration and Nationality Act of 1965 once again opened the United States to immigrants who are significantly different from natural-born Americans.

[64]Ravitch, op. cit., p. 234.

[65]Ibid., p. 603.

[66]John Dewey, *The School and Society* (1899) in *John Dewey: The Middle Works, 1899–1924*, edited by Jo Ann Boydston (15 vols.; Carbondale: Southern Illinois U. Press, 1976–1983).

[67]John Dewey, *Democracy and Education* (1916), in ibid.

Figure 13.6   **TWO COMPETING ASPECTS OF PROGRESSIVISM**

Dignity of the Individual vs. Social Efficiency

dealing with the "the whole child," but school authorities had barely enough resources to deal with traditional academics on a production line basis. To make matters worse, external factors, such as child labor laws, were encouraging more and more children to stay in school who did not appear to have the slightest desire to master traditional school subjects.

Given these sorts of pressures, some Progressives began endorsing a formalized, routinized, hierarchical, and bureaucratic model of school organization that emphasized **social efficiency** more than individual human dignity. In the end this became the "flip side" of Progressivism. School officials adopted standardized achievement tests that were intended to measure progress through the system. They worked to relate learning to the children's experiences, and to use "scientific" management techniques in school administration.[68] They began using psychological testing to group children according to ability.

The tensions between the humanists and the bureaucratizers often produced unfortunate results. Harried teachers with hordes of youngsters and insufficient resources were often chided "to involve all the children," "to appeal to each of their interests," and "to encourage creative self-expression." But they were also engulfed in the forms, reports, and other clerical details characteristic of institutionalized "scientific management." Despite these aberrations, however, Progressivism left the schools better than it found them. Physical and instructional conditions that had been unbelievably bad, an affront to even modest humanitarian instincts, generally became better for teachers and children alike.

Teaching and the Professions

The rise of Progressivism coincided with a tremendous expansion in the number of Americans engaged in managerial, technical, administrative, and professional jobs. And throughout the Progressive era such occupational groups worked to stabilize and protect their positions by building organizations and establishing standards.

Physicians were the first to form a national association that insisted on strict standards for admission to the practice of medicine. Lawyers followed with the establishment of professional bar associations and central examining boards composed of lawyers.[69]

Some teachers were similarly inclined, and Progressivism gave their professional aspirations a boost. Emphasis on scientific authority encouraged research, and, despite organizational structures that cast teaching as a semi-

---

[68]Dewey, ibid., pp. 234–235.
[69]Current, op. cit., pp. 604–605.

skilled occupation, a body of knowledge began to accumulate that could support a teaching profession.

Small improvements had already been made in teacher preparation. Despite the opposition of taxpayers and private schools, both of which were threatened financially, a growing network of two-year normal schools had begun offering training to novices in basic pedagogical techniques. Now, under the influence of progressivism, normal schools turned into four-year teachers colleges and many universities established colleges of education. Teacher preparation was becoming more and more a part of the technical culture

Before professionalism could be fully realized, teachers needed to gain control of licensure; but this proved extremely problematic. Even though they founded the influential National Education Association (NEA) in 1906, teachers were unable to emulate the American Medical Association by wresting control of their occupation from state government. After all, state officials had a vested interested in forestalling the establishment of rigorous standards. They would depress supply, raise costs, and make teachers harder to control.

Eventually, minimal requirements for teacher licensure were established. To this day, however, they remain weak when compared with medicine, law, podiatry, certified public accountancy, and the like. This failing has degraded occupational prestige, depressed salaries, and encouraged factory model schools in which the impact of teacher incompetence is minimized.

The continued triumph of the factory model encouraged the NEA to metamorphose into a labor union. In so doing they were simply emulating the more militant, and more successful, tactics of their avowedly union rival, the American Federation of Teachers, or AFT (founded in 1916).

Teacher unionization was not the end of the story. Officials of both these organizations were and still are very interested in the full professionalization of teaching, and are encouraging a number of initiatives to gain that end.

The Swinging Pendulum of Reform

Progressivism was neither the first nor the last school reform movement to influence American schooling. As a matter of fact, during the twentieth century American public schooling has been the subject of repeated and competing demands for reform which swing back and forth from collectively oriented to individually oriented extremes like the pendulum of some great historic clock. These oscillations of national consensus are described in a special report by the National Association of Secondary School Principals in 1986:

> Our schools are on the receiving end of every conceivable and inconceivable prescription for reform. In one era the prescription is for the schools to do something they are not doing. In a succeeding era, it is to undo the something they are now doing as a result of having adopted the earlier prescription. Special-interest groups that seek to impose their solutions on the schools might

well be saying, "If you think you have problems now, just wait until you see our solutions."[70]

In what follows we will briefly examine the swinging pendulum of school reform.

Back to the Basics

Progressivism slowly lost its reformist vitality. Finally, in the late 1940s and early 1950s its surviving remnants came up against a new breed of school reformer. Claiming that academic standards had eroded under the baleful influence of Progressivism, they argued for the reimposition of stricter discipline, and a new emphasis on excellence, particularly in science and mathematics.

Denouncing the humanistic "life-adjustment" schooling that had developed out of the Progressive school reforms of the early twentieth century, these critics urgently demanded that the schools produce more and better scientists and engineers in order to serve collective interests. Such demands were given enormous vitality when the Soviet Union was able to launch the world's first man-made satellite. As Sputnik beeped its way through space and American launch vehicles blew up on their pads, school critics like Harvard's Jerome Bruner denounced our national "neglect" of the nation's brightest youth and called for a return to basics.[71]

A billion-dollar program was hastily launched by the National Science Foundation to give top priority to science and mathematics in the school curriculum. For example, some of America's best scientists carefully crafted a new way to teach kids physics. Stressing the "why" of things, it was intended to produce scientists to better the Soviet Union. Students were also provided the opportunity to scratch their heads over the "New Math." It had been carefully crafted by a number of mathematical experts in order to improve quantitative skills.

The New Romantics

Many of these reforms did not work out as planned. Ten or so years after their introduction the number of students taking high school physics had plunged to half the pre-reform rate. Apparently the "why" of things interested the students less than "American Bandstand" and a host of other new elements in the socioeducational system. Discouraged with its results, even some prominent scientists were now denouncing the revised science curricula as "... a crime against a generation." As if this were not bad enough, national testing revealed a marked decline in student ability to make mathematical applications

---

[70]Danniel Tanner, "Are Reforms Like Swinging Pendulums?" in *Rethinking Reform: A Principal's Dilemma*, Herbert Walberg and James Keefe, Eds. (Reston Va.: National Association of Secondary School Principals, 1986), p. 5.

[71]Jerome Bruner, *The Process of Education* (Cambridge, Mass.: Harvard U. Press, 1960), p. 10.

despite the "New Math."[72] The "back to the basics" consensus was breaking up.

But new and very different reforms were now in the works. Thanks to an investment of hundreds of billions of dollars, America was now way ahead in the space race. Urban riots, student activism, various human rights movements, "flower power" the counter culture, and a frustrating war in Vietnam were now the new front page news. As a consequence, schools were no longer being criticized for graduating technical nincompoops. Instead, they were being widely criticized for their inhumanity, "lock-step" scheduling, cell-like classrooms, and stress on mindless memorization.

Vocal radical and romantic critics convinced many that schools were too centralized, overly bureaucratized, and intellectually and spiritually stifling. Science and math requirements slowly gave way in the face of romantic raptures about choice. The work ethic was denounced in favor of self-generated enthusiasms that educators hoped derived from the "natural curiosity" of the child.

Schools were also enlisted in a "War On Poverty" rather than in the Cold War. Instead of being criticized for neglecting space-engineering skills, schools were now denounced for failing the nation's poor. Critics soft-pedaled excellence, instead emphasizing how schools were neglecting the kids at the bottom. Jerome Bruner, for example, supplemented his earlier complaint that the schools neglected the top quarter of the nation's youth, by now stressing that they were overlooking the bottom tenth.[73]

The Pendulum Swings Again

For a decade or so schools were regarded as the key to a more fully human existence and a more individualistic nation. Reforms were hastily implemented to bring about these ends in schools all over the country. Soon there were schools without walls, schools with open classrooms, alternative schools, and so forth.

Ironically but predictably, no sooner were these humanistic reforms in place than they too went out of style. To make matters worse, their lingering consequences were destined to be cited as evidence of "unilateral educational disarmament" by the previously discussed and highly influential reform report *A Nation At Risk*, released in 1983. Written by a "Blue Ribbon" commission selected by the president of the United States, this "open letter to the American people" made headlines when it warned that the United States risked losing the economic competition among nations because of a ". . . rising tide of [educational] mediocrity that threatens our very future as a Nation and a people."

Since *A Nation At Risk* there have been more than 50 additional national reform reports from "blue ribbon" or "high level" commissions and between

---

[72]Tanner, op. cit., pp. 6, 7.
[73]E. Hall, "Bad Education—A Conversation with Jerome Bruner," *Psychology Today*, No. 4, 1970, p. 51.

275 and 300 state rep
courage excellence persu
of some particular constituen
ated still another broad, but s
reformed.

Lasting Changes

The metaphor of a swinging pendulum of refor
lasting changes in our schools. But this is not the
have been organized that have encouraged lasting
deliver educational services in the United States. For ins
mentary schools were well established by the mid-nineteer
secondary education was generally available only in private o
schools for which a tuition fee was charged.

Gradually public demand grew to include a new type of higher sch
would be supported by taxation. Years of sloganeering and politicking v
required, but eventually the **High School** emerged as a part of the commo
school system. Its curriculum emphasized "useful and practical studies" such
as English composition, the study of 'the best' English authors, mathematics,
natural philosophy (science), geography, and history.[75] This more vocationally
oriented approach, and the public funding of these schools, distinguished them
from the more status-oriented private academies with their classically oriented
curriculum.

By 1900 the American high schools had expanded from 100 in 1860 to a
total of 6,000.[76] Reflecting the recommendations of the National Education
Association's status-oriented Committee of Ten (1892), they tended to be
heavily oriented toward preparation for college.[77] However, dissatisfaction
with this arrangement, encouraged by broadening enrollment and fast-moving
changes in the economy, led to the N.E.A.'s Commission on the Reorganization
of Secondary Education (1918). This commission's recommendations,
adopted on a massive scale, were that the high school be made over into a
truly comprehensive institution that met business, commercial, industrial and
domestic as well as college preparatory needs.[78]

This arrangement worked reasonably well for more than half a century. But
in recent years radical changes in the job market and a steady increase in the
percentage of youngsters graduating from high school have dramatically reduced the market value of the high school diploma. Non-college-bound high
school graduates now find themselves facing shrinking opportunities for "a

[74]Martin Haberman, "Recruiting and Selecting Teachers for Urban Schools" (New York: ERIC
Clearinghouse for Urban Education, Teachers College, Columbia University, 1987), p. 7.
[75]*Proceedings of the School Committee of the Town of Boston, Respecting an English Classical
School*, June 17, 1820, pp. 2–7.
[76]Current, op. cit., p. 555.
[77]Stephens and Van Til, op. cit., p. 67.
[78]Commission on the Reorganization of Secondary Education, *Cardinal Principles of Secondary
Education*, Bulletin No. 35 (Washington, D.C: Government Printing Office, 1918), p. 1.

high unemployment, and a
eneration of people with this

hool type emerged to take its
These **Junior High Schools**,
of criticism of the academic
asses in traditional elementary
rollment loads of overcrowded
effects of the post-World War
schools were virtually indistin-
noving from class to class and
hat this organizational structure
ort needed to make the transition

n to give way to **Middle Schools**,
980s the number of these schools
ional Middle School Association,
ools in 1988 alone.[79]
to create a better developmental
ls are also tailored to the needs of
ers with either elementary or sec-
eing broken down into managerial
ch. The units are led by a team of
ne. In some schools they also teach

teachers who share a comm_____ _____ together.

Public school **Kindergartens** also began to be established in the late nine-teenth and early twentieth centuries. They enrolled a minimal number of students until women began to enter the labor market in increasing numbers during the 1920s. The kindergarten's popularity has increased steadily since then. In 1980 they enrolled nearly 37 percent of the nation's four-year-olds, and more than 93 percent of five-year-olds.[81]

In the 1950s, in addition to a vast growth in the number of Americans attending colleges and universities, there was also a great proliferation of **Junior Colleges**, two-year **Branch Campuses** sponsored by major univer-sities and two-year **Community Colleges**. For example, in 1948 there were about 250,000 students attending 450 such schools. By 1985 there more than 4.5 million students in 1,311 two-year schools.[82]

This incomplete sample of the evolution of school types in the United States illustrates substantial linear development rather than simple swings of a pen-dulum between collectivist and individualistic extremes.

---

[79]William Warren, "Middle Schools Grow in Academic Importance," *New York Times*, April 12, 1989, p. B7.
[80]Ravitch, op. cit., pp. 547–549.
[81]Ibid., p. 547.
[82]U.S. Bureau of the Census, *Statistical Abstract of the United States: 1988* (Washington, D.C.:, U.S. Government Printing Office, 1987), p. 141.

Figure 13.7   STUDENTS IN U.S. TWO-YEAR COLLEGES

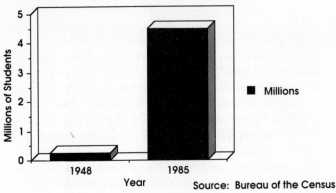

Source: Bureau of the Census

Broadening the School Community

There were other enduring changes as well. Despite the fact that public schooling effectively paved the way to a more abundant life for some Americans, the original vision of who should be served by public schooling was very narrow. Those with wealth went their own way; immigrants often dropped out in bewilderment or disgust; women were granted very limited opportunities; and minorities and the handicapped were either excluded altogether or segregated.

Over time, however, we have seen these limitations eased as we broaden our vision of who should be included among the beneficiaries of public schooling. The results of this revolution, still in its formative stages and incomplete, can be found on all sides. Some examples follow.

African-Americans

The U. S. Constitution itself proclaimed that slaves were not full persons in the eyes of the law. We also saw in the last chapter that the discrimination and racial prejudice common to America were reflected in school practices that included exclusion and segregation. In 1954 all that began to change when, in *Brown v. Board of Education, Topeka,* the Supreme Court ruled the racially segregated public schools common throughout the South to be unconstitutional. The extraordinary bravery of individuals in the civil rights movement like Rosa Parks, who in 1955 refused to sit in the back of a Montgomery, Alabama, bus, and Dr. Martin Luther King Jr., who successfully challenged racial discrimination despite enormous personal risk, encouraged broad support for a reexamination of the nation's racial policies. In 1957, 1960, 1964, and 1968 Congress passed civil rights acts intended to protect voting rights and guarantee equal protection under the law, mandating equal access to public accommodations and requiring full civil rights in employment and education. (See Chapter 15.) These were backed up by numerous court decisions.

In 1971, in *Swann v. Charlotte-Mecklenburg Board of Education*, the Supreme Court also ruled that busing was an acceptable means of school integration and that future school construction must not be used to perpetuate segregation. Subsequent lesser court decisions extended desegregation orders to include the de facto (in fact, not in law) segregation of northern schools.[83]

These decisions were intended to integrate African-Americans into the social mainstream through a nonsegregated common public school experience. "White flight" to the suburbs and private schooling have effectively forestalled total integration. And much remains to be done to improve inner city schools. Nevertheless, black Americans have greater access to schooling than at any other time in American history.

Schooling Handicapped Children

Traditionally, handicapped youngsters were either excluded from public schooling, or segregated in special programs. Like blacks, they often were not part of the common school experience.

During the 1970s and early 1980s there was substantial progress in breaking down these barriers. Judicial decisions established that the right to access to educational services was protected by the Fifth and Fourteenth Amendments. In addition, a series of Public Laws, culminating in Public Law 94–148, set forth as national policy that no handicapped child may be denied a "free and appropriate public education." It also gave parents or guardians the right to protest decisions made by school officials and provided that educational services must be provided in the "least restrictive environment" possible. These laws have encouraged the "mainstreaming" of handicapped youngsters in regular classrooms. (See Chapter 15.)

Establishing more effective education for handicapped students is still an ongoing process. Nevertheless, public schooling has been established as a fundamental right for all handicapped children.

Schooling Females

Earlier chapters on the history of schooling demonstrated an almost unbroken pattern of discrimination against females. Although much remains to be done, substantial progress has been made in getting away from this legacy of prejudice. Progressive reforms were instrumental in expanding women's school opportunities. Encouraged by the the pluck of woman reformers like Elizabeth Cady Stanton, more and more Americans came to share the opinion that women deserved equality of educational opportunity. By the 1920s even some

---

[83]Gerald Gutek, *Education and Schooling in America* (Englewood Cliffs, N. J.: Prentice Hall, 1988), pp. 31–32.

conservatives, like the writer H. L. Mencken, had joined the ranks of those calling for complete equality of educational opportunity for women. The idea that they should be schooled in ways more suited to their alleged "delicacy and sensitivity" was fast coming to a close. As Mencken put it in *In Defense of Women*,

> That it should be necessary, at this late stage in the senility of the human race to argue that women have a fine and fluent intelligence is surely eloquent proof of the defective observation, incurable prejudice, and general imbecility of their lords and masters.

In the 1960s and 1970s Federal legislation advanced female rights including those relating to schooling. For instance, Title VII of the Civil Rights Act of 1964 prohibited discrimination in employment on the basis of sex, and Title IX of the Education Amendments of 1972 forbade discrimination against women in federally assisted education programs. Other gains include efforts to reduce sex stereotyping in curriculum materials; the removal of admission restraints in traditionally male vocational programs; greater encouragement of female athleticism; special programs to encourage female participation in science and mathematics; and special programs to encourage female participation in school administration.

A Word of Caution

None of these remarks is intended to suggest that we have reached the educational promised land. Much remains to be done. Poor people of all colors and national origins are not well served by our schools. Large-scale and long-term poverty still survives despite massive school-based efforts to wage war on it. Social discrimination also persists despite elaborately planned curricula and much conscientious effort.

Some of our frustration is due to our putting too much faith in what schooling alone can accomplish. After all, we have seen that nonschool factors are terribly important to school outcomes. And we need to be careful not to let our faith in schooling become a convenient way to put off dealing with fundamental social and economic issues like the distribution of wealth in America.

Lack of consensus and related conflict are also at the heart of why it is so hard to get public schools working the way we would like. But this situation has been with us since before the Revolution, and has always been as much a part of the nation's genius as its folly.

Despite our frustration and the swings of the pendulum from individual to collective interests and back again, more Americans have greater school opportunities than ever in our history. In a little over 200 years we have built a school system that is at least theoretically dedicated to providing everyone with equality of educational opportunity. And that is no small accomplishment.

Yes, we continually fall short of the mark in numerous areas. And the nonschool aspects of the socioeducational system have repeatedly confounded our best efforts at providing equally valuable educational benefits for every child. But it is a wonderfully difficult challenge that we have accepted.

SUMMARY

1. The basic characteristics of America's public schools were defined in the period 1800–1865. From 1865 to the present these essential characteristics were transformed into contemporary educational processes and institutions. During this later period nationalism, immigration, industrialization, and urbanization all left their mark on schools and school practices.

2. Throughout American history there has been a protracted struggle to establish a meaningful consensus regarding both the ends and means of American schooling. Because of this, school reforms swing pendulum-like between extremes. The issue of authority is of central importance in these controversies and conflicts.

3. In recent years there has been an expansion of educational opportunity for minorities, the handicapped and women. Much remains to be accomplished, but America now offers more educational opportunities to a broader range of citizens than almost any other nation on earth.

QUESTIONS:

1. Contrast and compare the motives supporting common schooling in the United States and Prussia.
2. What concerns supported the public schooling movement in the United States?
3. What problems would the monitorial school have encountered, had they tried to implement a Pestalozzian approach?
4. The conditions in New England which favored the growth of public schooling can also be seen to impede its further development. Explain.
5. Recalling the conditions in New England which favored the founding of public schools, use their absence to account for the slow development of public schooling in the South.
6. How does the conflict between Catholics and Protestants over religion in the public schools illustrate the five functions of conflict?
7. Consider the relative rank of these different authorities as they bear on educating children:

    federal government
    state government
    local school board
    church
    family

School Governance, Law, and Finance

The business of running the schools ultimately comes down to issues of governance, law, and finance. This section of the text deals with those issues.

Professional educators need to know who governs schools and, more importantly, what difference that makes. Similarly, they must have a working knowledge of what is legal or illegal and constitutional or unconstitutional, and what they can be sued for doing or failing to do. Of course they also need an understanding of how this is paid for. After all, it is they who must deal with the presence or absence of the resources school finance provides on a daily basis. All of these concerns are covered in this section.

It is impossible to cover all the significant topics of school governance, law, and finance in three chapters. Therefore, we will address crucial issues with an emphasis on their impact for the practitioner.

SCHOOL GOVERNANCE and ADMINISTRATION

Chapter 14

PREVIEW

In this chapter we describe the governance and administration of America's public schools. Examining the levels and branches of government, we highlight their respective jurisdictions and explore the consequences of overlapping authority. The shifting balance of school governance is another key concern.

We also examine the legal basis of school governance and administration. Using key statutes and court decisions, we develop an understanding of the legal foundations of American schooling at all levels of governance.

We make no attempt to say who **should** control our schools. However, we do provide information and techniques relevant to a systematic consideration of this issue.

AN OVERVIEW OF SCHOOL GOVERNANCE

Just how are the nation's public schools governed? They are a **federal concern**, a **state responsibility**, and conducted with **local control**.[1]

Three **levels** of American government—**federal, state, and local**—are involved in schooling. And three **branches** of government—**executive, legislative, and judicial**—also share legal authority for school-related matters. This arrangement reflects the larger constitutional design of American government.

Overlapping Authority and Jurisdictional Conflict

How these various levels and branches of government are to share legal responsibility and authority with respect to schools is not always clearly delineated. Responsibilities and authority sometimes overlap.

A key consequence of these blurred responsibilities is that the actions of one level or branch of government can overlap those of another. This necessitates cooperation while provoking jurisdictional conflicts as well as certain measure of imprecision in administration.

Figures 14.1 and 14.2 illustrate the overlaps that occur with respect to levels and branches of government.

Jurisdictional Conflict in Action: Desegregating Schools

The potential for jurisdictional conflict set up by these overlapping responsibilities is illustrated by the events surrounding the Supreme Court decision, *Brown v. Board of Education, Topeka* (1954). In this famous case the High Court ruled that racially segregated schools were unconstitutional.

---

[1]"Education Governance: Overview," *Covering the Education Beat* (Washington, D.C.: Education Writer's Association, 1987), p. 5.

Figure 14.1

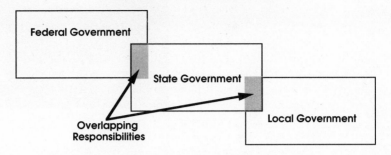

THREE LEVELS OF GOVERNMENT SHARE
AUTHORITY OVER SCHOOLS

Figure 14.2

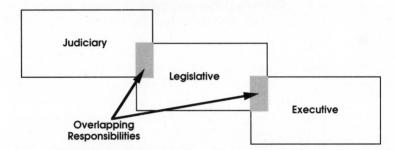

THREE BRANCHES OF GOVERNMENT SHARE
AUTHORITY OVER SCHOOLS

The ruling immediately provoked a bitter jurisdictional dispute. Claiming that the federal level of government was trespassing on the proper jurisdiction of the state level, several southern governors announced that they had no intention of obeying the High Court's "illegal" edict. Governor Faubus of Arkansas even ordered out the state's National Guard to prevent blacks from attending all-white schools.

The High Court did not command the means to enforce its own decision. It was up to the executive branch of the federal government to assert the preeminence of the federal judiciary.

Although President Eisenhower privately disapproved of the Court's action, he believed that it was his duty to execute the law. He first nationalized the Arkansas National Guard, bringing it under federal control, and then used the fixed bayonets of the 101st Airborne Division to protect the nine black students attempting to integrate Little Rock's Central High School. Reluctantly, he also ordered federal marshalls into the South to secure the newly declared rights of black Americans to attend integrated schools.[2]

---

[2]Richard Morris, William Greenleaf, and Robert Farrell, *America: A History of the People* (New York: Rand McNally, 1971), pp. 682–83.

Federal troops integrating
Little Rock schools.

Meanwhile, in Congress, segregationist Senators and Representatives denounced the High Court, claiming that the *Brown* decision represented a judicial usurpation of legislative power. They also said that the federal level of government was violating the state level's rights.

We see, then, that the *Brown* decision involved a number of jurisdictional disputes. First there was a dispute between the federal level of government and the governments of 17 southern and border states. It also involved a dispute between the judicial branch of government and conservative segregationist elements within the legislative branch. Finally, it could have involved a dispute between the federal judiciary branch and the federal executive branch if President Eisenhower had proved reluctant to use his authority to deal with southern defiance.

Usually the normally blurred lines of authority with respect to schools do not provoke jurisdictional disputes of such dramatic intensity. But it is important to understand that this sort of thing comes up again and again.

Other Consequences of Blurred Lines of Authority and Competing Interests

Jurisdictional disputes are not the only important consequence of these blurred lines of authority. Here are a few of the most prominent. Notice that some are positive.

- It ensures that a wider variety of interests will be represented in the determination of school policy.
- It encourages state government to mandate school programs without passing revenue measures to pay for them. Local education authorities are thus forced to pay the costs from their own tax revenues while state officials get credit for having secured the benefits.
- It permits the federal government to bypass state authorities and directly influence local school districts.
- It allows priorities established at one level of government to be imposed on programs and policies operated by other levels of government.

▬ It makes it possible for individuals or groups with grievances to seek redress from a wide variety of authorities. If one is dissatisfied with a local school situation, for example, one can seek a variety of remedies from the state or federal courts, the state department of education, the state school board, the chief state school officer, the state legislature, or the U.S. Congress.

▬ It promotes diversity while discouraging unified action.

▬ It permits legal directives that schoolboard members can perceive as conflicting. For example, in Title VIII of Public Law 98–377 Congress stipulated that schools receiving federal funds and allowing noncurricular student clubs to meet must provide facilities to all groups regardless of their religious, political, or philosophical nature. However, four different federal court decisions and a California state court decision bar devotional meetings from public schools.[3]

The Shifting Balance of School Governance

The history of American schooling shows a continual shift in the balance of school governance. In terms of levels of governance, as late as the 1930s schools were principally a local responsibility. They were in the hands of 127,000 local school boards who raised most of the revenues and enjoyed considerable autonomy in the operation of their respective school districts. Today as a consequence of state-imposed consolidation, theoretically to promote greater efficiency and economies of scale, there are only 15,427 local school boards, just 12 percent of the 1930s total.

In that same time period the funding of schools has shifted from the local property tax to state funding. Local autonomy has also given way to a surge of state regulation.

---

[3]Lawrence Rossow, "Conflicting Directives from Congress and the Courts Put You in the Hot Seat," *American School Board Journal*, Vol. 174, No. 2 (February 1987), pp. 38–39.

Figure 14.3   **ONE EFFECT OF SCHOOL DISTRICT CONSOLIDATION**

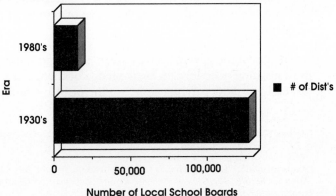

Number of Local School Boards

At the local level, with the exception of some dramatic recent experiments reported at the end of this chapter, building principals and teachers have been losing discretion to central offices. This trend has been fueled by a loss of confidence in the local capacity to maintain high academic standards.[4]

As far as the federal government is concerned, its involvement in schooling increased dramatically throughout the 1960s and 1970s. The Reagan administration intended to reverse this trend and entered office having pledged to do away with the recently established cabinet-level Department of Education. Administration officials also tried to cut federal funding of schools. They quietly backed away from this stance when schooling emerged as an issue of national concern. By 1987, however, federal spending on schooling was down by about 29 percent in real dollars from its 1980 level. It would have been reduced further had it not been for an uncooperative Congress.[5] George Bush, who campaigned as the "Education President," seems to be modestly more enthusiastic about federal spending for schooling.

The relative importance of the various branches of government to school policy making has also shifted over time. Since the late 1950s, for instance, there has been a dramatic increase in judicial involvement in the governance of schools. More conscious of their rights and less intimidated by authority, parents and teachers who might once have compromised have been taking a host of novel cases to court.

Perry Zirkel, a professor of education and law at Lehigh University, estimates that federal courts rendered four times as many school-related decisions in the period 1977–1986 as they did from 1957 to 1966. Cases before state courts more than doubled over the same period.[6] Recently, however, the courts have become less involved in school related matters.

Most recently, the trend has been a shift to the executive branch of government at the state level. The nation's governors have become very involved with schools. The essence of this involvement was summarized in 1986 when the National Governor's Association released a headline-grabbing report on education called, "Time for Results." Here the governors declared,

> We are ready to provide the leadership needed to get results on the hard issues that confront the better schools movement. We are ready to lead the second wave of reform in American public education."[7]

Since then the governors have been active, promoting in their home states the legislation necessary for their agenda of change. It includes career ladders for teachers, more parental choice in the **public** schools their children attend,

---

[4]Michael Kirst, "Who Should Control Our Schools?" *NEA Today: Special Edition*, January 1988, p. 76.
[5]Ibid.
[6]Stephen Goode, "Nation's School's Courting Trouble, *Insight*, July 11, 1988, pp. 56–57.
[7]*Time for Results: The Governor's 1991 Report on Education* (Washington, D.C.: National Governor's Association, 1986), p. 2.

more detailed evaluation of school results, better use of technologies for instruction, and the power to declare local school districts educationally bankrupt preparatory to a state takeover.[8]

Their proposals have met with a variety of fates. State legislators have their own agendas.

A Fourth Branch of Government?

Recently, school governance has become increasingly involved with the work of specialized state commissions. Sometimes described as a fourth branch of government, these semi-independent agencies enjoy considerable authority over specific areas of public policy. They are created, assigned a specific responsibility and funded by an act of the legislature. Daily control is accomplished by a board usually appointed by the governor.

The Pennsylvania Human Relations Commission is typical. Created and funded by an act of the state legislature, it is directed by a board appointed by the governor. The Commission is charged with enforcement of state anti-discrimination statutes.

The Commission accepts complaints, conducts investigations, renders findings, and directs remedies. If, for example, a college student feels that he or she has been denied admission to a college or university because of race, religion, national origin, sex, ancestry, or handicap, the student may seek remedy with the Pennsylvania Human Relations Commission. If Commission staffers determine that the complaint may involve an actual violation of Pennsylvania's Fair Educational Opportunities Act, they serve the school with a complaint. A fact-finding conference follows. If this fails to resolve the matter, a formal investigation produces a finding. If there is no cause to believe that a state statute has been violated, the case is closed. But if probable cause is found, the Commission orders school officials to remedy the situation.

Should they fail to comply, a public hearing is conducted. If compliance still does not follow, school officials are taken before a state court. Because Commission staffers are considered expert in the interpretation of state anti-discrimination statutes, the court usually agrees with their finding and enforces their remedy.[9]

We realize from this example above that **commissions can have considerable discretionary authority**. They have the latitude to make judgments with regard to specifics that are not spelled out in detail by the laws they are charged to enforce. The existence of this discretionary authority means that the manner in which commissioners are selected and rewarded can have a dramatic effect on the work of the commission. Their economic backgrounds and political attitudes are also crucial. The existence of discretionary authority also enhances the influence of outside forces. Political superiors, interest

---

[8]Ibid., p. 3.
[9]Interview with Stuart Gross, Supervisor, Pennsylvania Human Relations Commission, August 3, 1988.

groups, legislators, and the media all play a part in shaping school policy through the work of the commission.[10]

A Highly Politicized, Loosely Coupled System

The process of governing schools is highly politicized. Not only do the various levels and branches of government play off one another, but the special interests of many groups continually clash as school-related issues are advanced and resolved.

Contrary to the charts that show authority flowing from the top down (we include one in this chapter), the reality is that every level of governance has some options relative to their degree of compliance. In fact, they have a good deal of power to render directives impotent.

Experts argue that this highly politicized system works only because the policy process and its implementation are not tightly coupled—that is to say, that levels of government often adopt school policies and then fail to follow up. This omission often gives school authorities room to maneuver.[11] We offered a more detailed description of this phenomenon in Chapter 9.

SOURCES OF SCHOOL LAW

School governance is based on law, and these laws have a number of different origins. This reflects the multiple levels and branches of government involved in school governance.

Federal Level

The federal government has authority in some school-related matters. This authority is based on the U. S. Constitution and is actualized in statutes passed by Congress and in case law established by federal court decisions.

U.S. Constitution

In an earlier chapter we learned that the U.S. Constitution makes no mention of schooling. The absence of any specific mention of schooling has been interpreted by the Supreme Court to mean that it is not a fundamental right, like the right to the free exercise of religion, specifically guaranteed to all Americans.[12] It has also come to mean that the respective states have assumed

---

[10]James Wilson, *American Government: Institutions and Policies* (Lexington, Mass.: D.C. Heath and Company, 1986).

[11]Thomas Sergiovanni et al., *Educational Governance and Administration* (Englewood Cliffs, N. J.: Prentice-Hall, 1987), pp. 33–34.

[12]This was most recently reiterated in *Kadrmas v. Dickenson Public Schools*, U.S. Supreme Court, June 24, 1988. The decision reads in part: "Nor is education a 'fundamental right' that triggers strict scrutiny when government interferes with an individual's access to it."

primary authority over schooling. The Constitution permits them this in the Tenth Amendment, which states:

> The powers not delegated to the United States by the Constitution, nor prohibited by it to the states, are reserved to the states respectively, or to the people.

Article I of the Constitution does charge Congress with providing for the "General Welfare of the United States." While it does not provide Congress with a totally free hand, this is the legal basis for most federal school legislation. The Fourteenth Amendment has also proved a crucial source of Federal authority on school related matters. This amendment, enacted after the Civil War, was originally intended to protect the rights of newly freed slaves. But in time it also came to provide general protection to the Constitutional rights of Americans from actions by state government. It reads in part:

> No State shall make or enforce any law which shall abridge the privileges or immunities of citizens of the United States. Nor shall any State deprive any person of life, liberty or property, without due process of law, nor deny to any person within its jurisdiction the equal protection of the laws.

The most far-reaching application of the Fourteenth Amendment came in 1954 when the U.S. Supreme Court ruled that state-imposed racial segregation of schools, practiced in seventeen southern and border states, violated the Fourteenth Amendment.

Federal Statutes

The U.S. Congress has passed a number of highly significant federal statutes pertaining to schooling. They target the following priorities:

- **Support for postsecondary education.** This is the most ambitious of all federally funded efforts. It cost $14 billion in fiscal 1987. The largest of the seven programs is the Guaranteed Student Loan Program. It cost $8 billion in fiscal 1987.
- **Remedial services for disadvantaged children**. The Federal government spent $3.9 billion on these services in 1987.
- **The education and rehabilitation of handicapped children**. The U.S. Department of Education distributed about $3 billion for such services in fiscal 1987.
- **Vocational education.** About 10 percent of the money spent nationwide on vocational education comes from the federal treasury. This amounted to $882 million in fiscal 1987.

The U.S. Congress has passed a number of highly significant federal statutes pertaining to schooling.

- **Impact aid** to local school districts who have federally owned property in their districts and or employees who live or work on federal property. This cost $666 million in fiscal 1987.
- **Basic literacy skills for adult illiterates**. About $106 million was provided in fiscal 1987.
- **Enforcement of statutes that prohibit discrimination** in programs and activities receiving federal funds. This cost $43 million in fiscal 1987.[13]

Some of the most significant school-related statutes enacted in the second half of this century by Congress are listed below.

- **National Defense Education Act of 1958** (P.L. 85–864). Spurred by popular reaction to the Soviet Sputniks, this legislation involved federal support for the improvement of school curricula, the training

---

[13]"U.S. Department of Education," *Covering the Education Beat* (Washington, D.C.: Education Writers Association, 1987), pp. 167–168.

Figure 14.4   **CHIEF CONCERNS OF FEDERAL SCHOOL LEGISLATION**

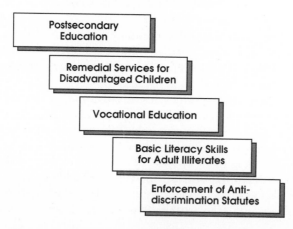

of teachers, and aid to students. All areas of science were also given major direct support in universities.

- **Civil Rights Act of 1964** (P.L. 88–352). Passed only after the longest filibuster in the history of the Senate, this act authorizes the attorney general to initiate law suits to compel compliance with school desegregation guidelines. It also authorizes withholding federal funds from school districts which practice discrimination.
- **Elementary and Secondary Education Act of 1965** (P.L. 89–10). Originally part of Lyndon Johnson's "Great Society" program, this act continues to provides billions of federal dollars for compensatory programs for disadvantaged students, mostly in the primary grades.
- **Bilingual Education Act of 1968** (Section 701 of P.L. 89–10 as amended by P.L. 90–247 and 93–380). This law is intended to aid students with limited proficiency in English. Federal funds are provided to initiate or augment transitional bilingual programs.
- **Title IX of the Education Amendments of 1972** (P.L. 92–318). This law forbids sex discrimination in any education program or activity receiving federal financial assistance. Failure to comply with this title is penalized by forfeiture of all federal monies. It exempts educational institutions controlled by religious organizations if compliance would interfere with their beliefs.
- **The Education for All Handicapped Children Act of 1975** (P.L. 94–142). This statute requires states to cease placing the burden for educating handicapped children primarily on the family. It compels them to adopt policies assuring that **all** handicapped children, including those who are severely and profoundly handicapped, are provided a "free appropriate public education." It stipulates that these services will be provided in the "least restrictive environment." It also provides federal funds for special education programs if states meet federal requirements.
- **Pregnancy Discrimination Act of 1978** (P.L. 95–555). This legislation includes pregnant women in the protections afforded by the Civil Rights Act of 1964.

Notice how this representative sample of **federal school legislation targets special concerns**, rather than providing day-to-day support of the whole schooling enterprise. The latter is the reponsibility of state and local government.

Case Law

The federal government also participates in school governance through the federal judiciary. Time and again, decisions reached in cases before the federal courts, most particularly the Supreme Court, have proved decisive.

Case law refers to principles of law established by court decisions. It is based largely on legal precedents established in earlier court decisions that were relevantly similar. Barring congressional action to restrict the Court's jurisdiction, they have the force of law. They may be altered only by another Supreme Court decision or an amendment of the Constitution.[14]

Case Law in Action.   The following highlights selected High Court decisions that exemplify different aspects of federal judicial involvement in school governance. It is arranged by categories of interest, and, with one illustrative exception, is confined to case law established by the Supreme Court.

School Desegregation.   Case law has been particularly influential in determining public school policies relative to race. This involvement dates back to 1896 in deciding *Plessy v. Ferguson.*[15] In 1899 in *Cumming v. County Board of Education,*[16] the Court extended the **separate but equal doctrine** to include schooling.

The High Court did not change its position on separate but equal facilities until 1954. Then, in *Brown v. Board of Education, Topeka,*[17] the Justices reversed years of case law precedent by declaring that "**separate is inherently unequal.**" The Court found that schools segregated by race generate in black children ". . . a feeling of inferiority as to their status in the community that may affect their hearts and minds in a way unlikely to ever be undone." They ruled that segregation was an unconstitutional denial of rights guaranteed by the Fourteenth Amendment and ordered southern schools desegregated "with all deliberate speed."

A number of other critically important court cases followed. For instance, in *Green v. County School Board of New Kent County* (1968),[18] the Supreme Court outlawed so-called "freedom of choice plans." Under such plans parents theoretically determined which school their children would attend. In finding that this practice did not eliminate racial segregation as required in *Brown,* the Court declared:

> Rather than further the dismantling of the dual system, the plan has operated to burden children and their parents with a responsibility which (this Court) placed squarely on the School Board. The board must ... fashion steps which promise realistically to convert promptly to a system without a "white" school and a "Negro" school, but just schools.

In *Swann v. Charlotte-Mecklenburg Board of Education* (1971),[19] the High Court further defined the duty of school boards to eliminate dual school

[14]Michael La Morte, *School Law: Cases and Conflicts* (Englewood Cliffs, N. J.: Prentice-Hall, 1987), p. 11.
[15]*Plessy v. Ferguson,* Supreme Court of the United States, 1896, 168 U.S. 537.
[16]*Cumming v. Board of Education,* Supreme Court of the United States, 1899, 175 U.S. 528.
[17]*Brown v. Board of Education,* Supreme Court of the United States, 1954, 347 U.S. 483.
[18]*Green v. County School Board of New Kent County,* Supreme Court of the United States, 1968, 391 U.S. 430.
[19]*Swann v. Charlotte-Mecklenburg Board of Education,* 402 U.S. 1, 1971.

systems. In a detailed attempt to clarify its intent regarding the elimination of racially segregated schooling, the Court declared that the following measures were appropriate:

- Busing to dismantle dual systems.
- Altering attendance zones to counteract past segregation.
- Assigning teachers by race in order to achieve faculty desegregation.
- Evaluation of one-race schools to make sure that they were not a result of present or past discrimination.

This decision had far-reaching practical consequences that are still with us. For example, in big city schools it is routine to assign teachers to schools on the basis of race. Thus, new teachers who are white very frequently end up in inner-city schools while their African-American counterparts are assigned to schools that serve predominantly white neighborhoods.

(Phila.)

De Facto Segregation.   In *Milliken v. Bradley* (1974),[20] the High Court took up the continued "de facto" segregation of nonsouthern schools. **De facto segregation results from customs, housing patterns and racial attitudes rather than segregationist legislation.** Making an important distinction, the Court stressed the importance of not relying purely on the **results** of a school board's actions. Instead, they ruled that there was a compelling necessity to find "**segregative intent**" before a school board action could be determined as unconstitutionally supportive of racial segregation.

Affirmative Action.   With respect to **affirmative action**, the Court has rendered a number of key decisions. For example, in *Wygant v. Jackson Board of Education* (1986)[21] the court ruled that an agreement that laid off white teachers with seniority in order to maintain a certain percentage of black teachers, violated the Equal Protection clause. It also noted, however, that carefully tailored plans creating goals for increased percentages of minority employees would be lawful.

Compulsory Education and Regulation of Private Schools.   Of course, case law applies to a broad spectrum of school-related issues, not just to racial ones. For instance, a U.S. Supreme Court decision was the key determiner in the matter of whether or not it is legal to compel students to attend **public** schools. In *Pierce v. Society of Sisters* (1925),[22] the Court ruled that compelling school attendance was constitutional, but that attendance at parochial or private schools satisfied this state requirement.

Once Pierce established that private school attendance satisfied state compulsory attendance requirements, the question arose as to whether or not

---

[20]*Milliken v. Bradley,* Supreme Court of the United States, 1974, 418 U.S. 267.
[21]*Wygant v. Jackson Board of Education,* Supreme Court of the United States, 1986, 106 S. Ct. 1842.
[22]*Pierce v. Society of Sisters*, Supreme Court of the United States, 1925, 268 U.S. 510.

state authorities had the right to regulate private schools. In *Farrington v. Tokushige* (1926),[23] the Court ruled on the state of Hawaii's attempt to regulate Japanese language private schools. In an attempt to "Americanize" youngsters attending such schools, Hawaiian authorities required them to teach the "ideals of democracy," American history, and English. They also sought to prescribe textbooks, set the hours of operation, and establish entrance requirements. The Supreme Court found that the Hawaiian government's actions served no demonstrable public interest and infringed on the rights of both parents and the school owners.

Farrington did not totally rule out state regulation of private schools. But it did establish that such **state regulation had to serve a demonstrable public interest**. Today, some states have established fairly strict regulations within that general guideline. They require that all schools, public and private, employ only certified teachers and that certain courses must be offered. Other states regulate only health, safety, and sanitation, leaving the rest to market forces. All require attendance information.[24]

The *Pierce* and *Farrington* decisions support parental choice in the fulfillment of state compulsory school attendance requirements.

Religion and the Schools.   Religion and the public schools has been another key area for High Court action. For example, in *Engel v. Vitale* (1962),[25] the Court declared that compulsory recitation of the prayer, "Almighty God, we acknowledge our dependence upon Thee, and we beg Thy blessings upon us, our parents, our teachers, and our Country" composed by the New York State Board of Regents, was unconstitutional. The Court ruled that such prayers violated the First Amendment of the Constitution, which states in part, "Congress shall make no law respecting the establishment of religion."

In *School District of Abington Township v. Schempp* (1963),[26] the High Court dealt with schooling and the separation of church and state. The Court ruled that a Pennsylvania law requiring that the school day begin with the recitation of the Lord's Prayer and the reading of ten verses from the Bible was a violation of the Establishment Clause. Mr. Justice Clark delivered the opinion of the Court, which stated, in part:

> The place of religion in our society is an exalted one, achieved though a long tradition of reliance on the home the church and the inviolable citadel of the individual heart and mind. We have come to recognize through bitter experience that it is not within the power of government to invade that citadel, whether its purpose or effect be to aid or oppose, to advance or retard.

---

[23]*Farrington v. Tokushige*, 1926, 273 U.S. 284.
[24]La Morte, op. cit., p. 26.
[25]*Engle v. Vitale*, Supreme Court of the United States, 1962, 370 U.S. 421.
[26]*School District of Abington Township v. Schempp*, Supreme Court of the United States, 1963, 374 U.S. 203.

Pennsylvania legislators sidestep "excessive entanglement" with religion by providing publicly financed services to parochial school students in a trailer located next to the school.

The Court made it clear that the Bible could be read as literature and that comparative religion could also be taught. This decision was highly unpopular, particularly in conservative areas of the country. It provoked a movement to amend the Constitution so that school prayer would be constitutional.

In *Lemon v. Kurtzman* (1971),[27] the High Court declared unconstitutional an attempt by Rhode Island to provide a 15 percent supplement to the salaries of teachers of secular subjects in nonpublic schools. In this and subsequent decisions the High Court established a set of guidelines that are now used to determine if state aid to nonpublic schools violates the Establishment Clause. These are:

- Does the law have a clearly secular purpose?
- Does it neither enhance nor inhibit religion?
- Does it foster excessive government entanglement with religion?

Using these guidelines, the Court has established that states **may**:

- provide textbooks
- authorize funds for testing and scoring
- provide diagnostic services on public school premises
- provide therapeutic and remedial services in public schools, public centers, or mobile units located off the nonpublic school premises
- loan instructional materials and equipment to nonpublic school students provided it cannot be converted for religious use
- provide money for field trips that enrich secular studies

In *Wallace v. Jaffree* (1985),[28] a federal circuit court further defined church/state relations. It struck down two Alabama statutes when it found that

---

[27]*Lemon v. Kurtzman*, Supreme Court of the United States, 1971, 403 U.S. 602.
[28]*Wallace v. Jaffree*, 105 S. Ct, 2479.

their requirements for silent prayer, meditation, and voluntary prayer in schools constituted "Alabama's attempt to establish a state religion."

Other Sources of Federal Authority

The executive branch of the federal government is also involved in school governance. The president of the United States may issue an executive order that applies to schooling. Once issued, it would be another federal source of educational law.[29] Thus far, such orders have not been a major consideration.

The attorney general of the United States, the nation's chief law enforcement officer, may also be influential in providing official opinions regarding the enforcement of constitutional or statutory educational practice. During the Reagan years, for example, the attorney general chose not to pursue school integration cases with the same vigor as his Democratic predecessors. This stance had a considerable impact.

The Secretary of Education of the United States can also exert federal influence—primarily by using the office to express views and urge actions. Secretary Bennett, who resigned in 1988, was the first to use this power extensively. Unless they are backed by an act of Congress or the federal judiciary, however, the Secretary's publicly expressed opinions do not have the force of law.

State Level

In every case, the respective state governments have taken up the authority to operate public schools offered by the Tenth Amendment. Indeed, their involvement in schooling has become so extensive that, if state government ceased to exist, there would be no public schools nor any right to a free and appropriate education.

State laws and related regulations provide the basic structure for school governance in the United States. In addition to much of the financing, the states are the source of the laws that spell out requirements for graduation, teacher certification, the length of the school year, and a host of similar details.

Ultimately, state government even has the authority to take over local school districts. In 1988, for example, New Jersey education officials became the first in the nation to set out to actually seize control of a large urban school district. As a part of their general school reform efforts, education officials of the Kean administration declared their intention to impose a five-year takeover of the Jersey City schools. The action was initiated after an independent consulting firm retained to evaluate the district reported that, "The Jersey City School District can be characterized as a public enterprise that has reached a state of managerial bankruptcy."

The Jersey City District is one of ten among the state's 600 public school districts being scrutinized for possible takeover. New Jersey is the sixth state

---

[29]La Morte, op. cit., p. 11.

Figure 14.5 **TYPICAL STRUCTURE OF A STATE SCHOOL SYSTEM**

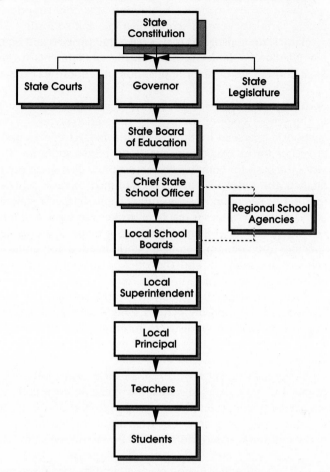

to authorize such actions. The first statute of this type was passed by Arkansas in 1983, and similar statutes have become law in Georgia, Kentucky, South Carolina, and Texas.[30]

State Constitutions. If a state is considering laws permitting its takeover of educationally bankrupt school districts, it is the state constitution, as interpreted by state courts, that determines if this is permissible—because state constitutions are the primary source of legal authority for any school-related action by state government.

Although the details vary, these constitutions all contain provisions requiring state legislatures to maintain systems of free and compulsory public

---

[30]Craig McCoy, "New Jersey Proposes Takeover of School District," *Philadelphia Inquirer*, May 25, 1988, p. 1.

schooling. Many also specify the creation of local school districts, define the qualifications and manner of selection of school superintendents, outline the taxing authority of local school districts, and so forth.

Many state constitutions also have due process and equal protection of the law guarantees similar to those in the amendments to the U.S. Constitution. State courts rule on their application in school-related matters.[31]

State Statutes. The legislative basis of schooling in America can be found in the school code of each of the respective states.[32] This body of state legislation is overseen by both state and federal courts, and depends upon the governor for its execution; but it still reigns supreme. The school code provides the basis for compulsory education. It also spells out the details of school finance, the taxes that may be employed to raise school revenues, and the method of selection, responsibilities, and terms of state and local education officials. It determines if teachers' strikes are legal and, if so, sometimes spells out the details of collective bargaining or professional negotiations. Often it specifies the minimum course work needed for graduation, length of the school day and year, and the rules regarding suspension and expulsion of students, and the dismissal of teachers.[33]

There are broad variations in control among the states. In some states legislators spell out only general guidelines for the state department of education and local school districts. In other states they are highly specific, specifying what may and may not be taught, to whom, and under what circumstances.

Oklahoma's recent mandate of an AIDS education program for school children shows how detailed state control can be. Impelled by a sense of urgency, state legislators resisted the temptation to deal in slogans. Instead, they drafted a statute specifying precisely what they wanted taught. They required that every child in a state public school be instructed as follows:

> 1. ... engaging in homosexual activity, promiscuous sexual activity, intravenous drug use or contact with contaminated blood products is now known to be primarily responsible for contact with the AIDS virus;
>
> 2. avoiding (these) activities is the only method of preventing the spread of the virus;
>
> 3. sexual intercourse, with or without condoms, with any person testing positive for human immunodeficiency virus (HIV) antibodies, or any other person infected with HIV, places that individual in a high risk category for developing AIDS.

---

[31]La Morte, op. cit., p. 12.
[32]Ben Brodzinsky, *How A School Board Operates* (Bloomington, Ind.: Phi Delta Kappa, 1977), p. 12.
[33]Ibid.

The state lawmakers also required that each program

> shall teach that abstinence from sexual activity is the only certain
> means for the prevention of the spread or contraction of the AIDS
> virus through sexual contact. . . .

Anxious that timid school districts would postpone this instruction until it
was of little value, they also stipulated that AIDS prevention programs, ". . . be
presented at least once during grades five through six, at least once in grades
seven through nine, and at least once during grades ten through twelve."[34]
Whether such instruction will actually reduce student risk of AIDS is problematic. Perhaps the prescription goes too far. One can imagine teachers reading this information to students as the police read a suspect his or her rights.
In any case, it does demonstrate that when they choose to use it state legislators have considerable authority over our public schools.

Case Law.   As mentioned previously, State Courts determine whether school
legislation satisfies the state constitution. They decide educational controversies that cannot be resolved in any other way. State courts render decisions
regarding questions of student dress or punishment, busing, use of controversial textbooks and so forth. They also settle disputes concerning who may
or may not be fired, curriculum, finance, and administration.[35]
We should remember that the most striking characteristic of the U.S. court
system is its duality. One federal court system and 50 state court systems
coexist. In practice, this has proved to mean that, despite the importance of
the federal judiciary to education, it is state courts that adjudicate most of the
disputes that affect the day-to-day functioning of our schools.
We should remember, too, that the supremacy clause of the 14th Amendment establishes the supremacy of the rights guaranteed in the Constitution
of the United States. No state court decision, or state legislation, may violate
these rights.

State Boards of Education.   Only Wisconsin has no state board of education.[36] Every other state incorporates such a board in its governance of
schools.
In most states, board members are selected by the governor. However,
there has been a recent trend in favor of direct election. State boards of
education are created by an act of the state legislature. Although the scope of
their authority varies, they are generally charged with writing regulations that
give specificity to the general mandates of state legislation. These regulations
govern the daily conduct of schools.

---

[34] *1987 Oklahoma Laws*, Ch. 46 (Oklahoma State title 70, 11–103.3).
[35] Ibid, p. 13.
[36] P. W. Krohne, *An Analysis of the State Board of Education in Indiana—Its Composition,
Organization, Operation and Areas of Jurisdiction* (Bloomington, Ind.: Indiana University unpublished doctoral dissertation, 1982), p. 28.

Figure 14.6 **THE SELECTION OF STATE SCHOOL BOARD MEMBERS**

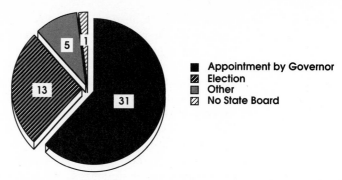

When these new regulations are formulated, they are typically put through an exhaustive process of review and refinement. In Pennsylvania, for example, new regulations are first drafted by special committees of the state board. Often this special committee includes non-board members and invites testimony from interested parties. When the special committee submits its recommendations, the entire school board reviews them. If they are satisfied, a special Governor's Task Force reviews the resulting proposed regulations. The state attorney general also reviews them for their legal ramifications. The Pennsylvania House and Senate Education Committees also have their turn, as does a special Review Commission. If all goes well, the proposed regulations are published for comment by the citizens of the Commonwealth. Only after all these steps have been satisfactorily completed are the new regulations put into effect.

This process, essentially similar to that which goes on in other states, reveals an essential element of school governance in our pluralistic democracy. In order that a variety of interested parties may be heard, we have developed a multistaged process of review and evaluation that encourages a wide variety of input.

School governance is perpetually involved in the give and take of debate and negotiation. Often the painfully slow progress required by such a process seems to stand in the way of progress or reform. But any alternative requires tyranny.

Chief State School Officers. All states also have a chief state school officer—often called the state superintendent of education. Like state boards of education, their scope of authority varies from state to state, but their primary responsibility is to head the state department of education.

Notice that in the majority of the states the chief state school officer is appointed by the state board of education. Unlike those elected or appointed by the governor, this procedure makes them employees of the board, rather than state officers.

State Departments of Education. The chief state school officer is the chief executive of the state department of education. State departments of education

Figure 14.7 **THE SELECTION OF CHIEF STATE SCHOOL OFFICERS**

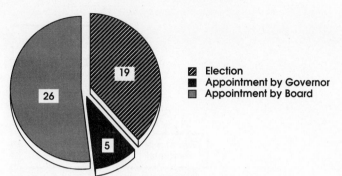

Election
Appointment by Governor
Appointment by Board

are staffed by career professionals. These are the individuals who translate the regulations of the state boards of education into policies, practices, and standards. Should state legislators choose to write a new school code, for example, state department of education staffers advise them as the bill is written. Once it becomes law, they also assist the state board of education in writing regulations that implement the law. When it is time to put these regulations into daily practice, the staffers also compose the actual forms that must be completed and specify the reports that must be filed—often dealing directly with hundreds of local school districts.

The professionals in any state department of education see many governors, chief state school officers, and state legislators come and go. They provide much of the continuity, and serve to damp the oscillations to which the system is prone when administrations and thus political appointees change.

Regional School Agencies.   In many states regional school agencies function between the state department of education and the local school districts. Often called "intermediate units," their major purpose is to unite two or more school districts for the purpose of providing services that on their own they could not provide economically. For example, they may cooperate to provide more comprehensive special education programs, or to develop more ambitious vocational education efforts. Often they also serve as a central clearinghouse for instructional materials, offer in-service training to teachers, and provide a variety of other specialized services.

In some states chief executive officers are elected; in others they are appointed. They commonly have the equivalent rank of a superintendent of schools. Funds come from a combination of sources. State monies are usually augmented by payments from local school district budgets.

Local Level

Schooling was once a much more local matter. In the late 1930s, for example, states exercised broad regulatory powers and contributed some funding, but the day-to-day business of running and paying for the nation's schools was the chief responsibility of some 127,000 local school districts. Today, largely un-

Figure 14.8   AN EXAMPLE OF SCHOOL DISTRICT ORGANIZATION

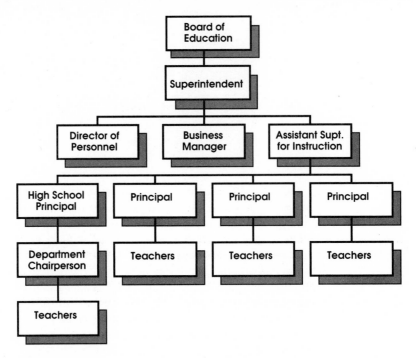

der the pressure of state-required consolidation, the number of districts has shrunk to just 15,427. Both state and federal power has increased at school districts' expense. Despite this trend, however, America's vast public school system is still conducted with a great deal of local control. The administrative heart of this enterprise is the local school district.

The Local School District.   The local school district is the basic administrative unit of American public schooling. Here billions upon billions of federal, state, and local dollars are disbursed as schools are built or closed, instructional programs inaugurated or folded, teachers hired or fired.

The School Board

Much of the daily business of running the nation's public schools is accomplished part-time, in the evenings, by local citizens who are not paid for their services. They staff the more than 15,000 boards of education that direct our local school districts.

Eighty-six percent of school board members are selected by the ballot box. Only 14 percent are appointed, usually to the boards of large, urban school districts. Thus, much of what schools do is determined democratically in the spotlight of local publicity. A few local citizens set the tax rates for their neighbors, decide which programs are to be funded and which dropped, set limits on class size, and make hundreds of other potentially controversial decisions.

Local school boards carry out much of the daily business of running the nation's public schools.

A national survey conducted in 1988 by the *School Board Journal* indicated that school board members have the following typical characteristics:

- **Sex**   male
- **Age**   41 to 50
- **Marital Status**   married
- **Race**   white
- **Children in School**   one or two
- **Education**   college graduate
- **Occupation**   professional or managerial
- **Housing**   owns home
- **Family Income** $40,000–$49,999
- **Years on School Board**   one to four
- **Number of Board Members**   seven or eight
- **Method of Selection**   election[37]

Dr. Tom Davis, Superintendent of the Springfield Township School District in Pennsylvania, interviewed during the writing of this text, made the following observation about some of the consequences of relying so heavily on local boards:

> America's public schools are the most purely democratic institutions that we have. As a consequence, they are inevitably involved with controversy and politics. Within any community there are people with competing interests. Often they form coalitions and seek to influence school policy. Naturally, each coalition wants decisions favorable to their needs. Often, however, this is impossible because the needs of one coalition conflict with those of another. For example, taxpayers with children in the public schools want smaller classes and more services, while those without children in the schools want reductions in school spending. All of these competing coalitions come together at meetings of the local

---

[37]*American School Board Journal*, Vol. 198, No. 1, January 1989, p. 26.

schoolboard—particularly at budget time. Here, where people often know one another on a personal basis, their elected representatives attempt to arrive at some sort of workable consensus.[38]

School board members are the state's legal agent. Acting as a board, they are the only legal entity that can make contracts on behalf of the school district, employ staff, purchase real estate and other property, accept federal and state funds, and (where authorized by law) levy taxes.[39]

The board also develops policy. Regulations governing hiring and firing, pay, business management, construction and maintenance of schools, and dozens of other similar matters all fall within their jurisdiction. These school district regulations are a rough equivalent of state or federal legislation.

The school board also passes judgment on educational programs and practices. Shall the district offer sex education next year, and, if so, what will it cover? Shall it offer driver education or drop the fourth year of German? Unless the state has already spoken on these matters, they are for the school board to decide.

Recently school board members have become increasingly concerned about what they claim are state encroachments on their responsibilities. A 1987 survey conducted by the *School Board Journal* reveals that this issue has now reached second place on their list of the three biggest problems facing the schools. (Lack of financial support is their biggest concern; declining enrollments is third.) Significantly, state mandates usually target smaller classes, more rigorous academics, and teacher training and recognition efforts. Board priorities favor renovation of existing buildings or new construction.[40]

All of these matters are determined at the evening meetings of the board. When members sit down at the table, they do so as a legal body. Under law, they usually do their work in public. The process can be routine and uncontroversial. At times, however, it becomes a public stage for basic conflicts as Americans seek some form of workable consensus regarding the proper ends and means of schooling.

School Administrators

The day-to-day administration of the nation's public schools is not the responsibility of local school boards. They hire a chief administrator, the **Superintendent of Schools**, who advises them and acts on their behalf.

The superintendent is the chief executive of a school district. He or she is an employee of the local board, and theoretically administers board policy. In actual fact, the legal and technical complexities of modern school district

---

[38]Personal interview with Dr. Tom Davis, Superintendent, Springfield School District (Montgomery County), July 29, 1988.

[39]Brodzinsky, op. cit., p. 16.

[40]"State Mandates Are Your Most Serious New Concern," *School Board Journal*, Vol. 174, No. 1, p. 27.

management have encouraged the untrained members of the board to rely more and more on their chief executive.

The specific duties of the local superintendent are spelled out in state law. Some states are quite specific; others provide only general guidelines. In any case, in most communities the school superintendent is the most visible symbol of the public schools. School board meetings, football and basketball games, senior citizens meetings concerning the burden of school taxes, luncheons, all require the presence of the superintendent.

The absence of a deep consensus concerning the proper role of our public schools means that superintendents live with conflict. In fact, a study done by Blumberg in 1985 revealed that most of the superintendents interviewed saw conflict as the very nature of the superintendency.[41] This conflict is not only a function of community disagreements. State and federal legislation, as well as state and federal court decisions, also has an impact on local districts in ways that upset their balance.

The building administrator, usually called a **principal**, is in the front lines of school administration. He or she is responsible for the daily functioning of a particular school.

The traditional role of the building principal is much like that of the captain of a naval vessel. Acting as program administrator, disciplinarian, teacher evaluator, public services coordinator, instructional supervisor, public relations facilitator, morale builder, curriculum supervisor, and staff selector, the traditional principal enjoys the authority to make a real difference in the climate of a school. Of course, he or she also shoulders major responsibilities in so doing.

No other educational administrator enjoys the autonomy that is given to many principals—partly a reflection of the fact that differences in individual schools require different styles of leadership. It also is a function of our basic inability to reach a deep consensus on the means and ends of schooling. The principal moves into the vacuum created by disagreement and sets his or her own agenda.[42]

The emerging role of the principal has to do less with command than it does with facilitating the professional judgments of teachers. The professionalization of teaching, encouraged by national reform initiatives covered elsewhere, is causing a major reconsideration of the proper role of the building administrator. As we learned in Chapter 3, this is not being accomplished without controversy.

The Teacher's Role in Governance

In many school districts the contract negotiated between the teachers and the board defines nearly every aspect of their respective responsibilities. Until

---

[41]Arthur Blumberg, *The School Superintendent: Dealing With Conflict* (New York: Teachers College Press, 1985).
[42]Thomas Sergiovanni, op. cit., p. 286.

recently, this was the extent of teacher involvement in school governance. However, their role has begun to change. In the wake of a national movement to hold teachers more accountable for student progress, there has been a related movement to give them more real say over what is taught, how materials are used, and how the budget of their school is spent. Such changes require a major revision of the role of the principal.

Highly influential reform proposals such as the landmark report of the Carnegie Forum on Education and the Economy, *A Nation Prepared: Teachers for the 21st Century,* back a strong voice for teachers in school decision making. Some districts have already given teachers major new responsibilities, and many others are currently considering similar moves.

According to pollster Louis Harris, such a change enjoys the enthusiastic backing of the general public and the nation's business leaders. Harris reports:

> It is clear from the results that both groups surveyed are firmly in support of giving teachers greater voice and participation in the determination of how students are taught, what materials are used and in budget priorities that should be followed in their schools.[43]

The Dade County Experiment

The Dade County, Florida Schools—the fourth largest district in the nation—have developed a pilot program that is part of a district wide effort to restructure schools by reducing regulatory control and encouraging teachers to assume more authority. Thirty-two schools have been given permission to set up new school governance procedures in which principals and teachers will run the school together. They also have been given unprecedented control over how their schools spend money, allocate staff, and organize instruction.

Both the teachers' union and the school board have agreed to set aside normal contract provisions and school regulations. Thus, teachers can choose to give up their planning periods, work longer hours for no additional pay, and evaluate their peers. In return the school board has waived its restrictions on class size, the length of the school day, the number of minutes per subject, the dates when report cards are handed out, and dozens of other matters.

The board's biggest concession concerns budgeting. Typically, each school's budget is allocated at the district level. Discretionary funds are only for materials and supplies. Dade County's pilot schools enjoy total control of their budget of $3,411 per child. Provided they do not violate state or federal mandates, the teachers and principal are free to cooperatively determine how to spend the entire amount.

In 1988 the pilot project was in its second year. There is national interest in the outcome.[44]

---

[43]Louis Harris Poll, July 1986.

[44]Lynn Olson, "The Sky's the Limit: Dade Ventures Self-Government," *Education Week,* December 2, 1987, p. 1.

SUMMARY

1. Schooling is a federal concern, is a state res[...]
at the local level. Overlapping controls provok[...]
balance of school governance has shifted over ti[...]
and federal levels. State and federal commissior[...]
branch of government," exercising considerabl[...]
ernance. There are many informal aspects of [...]
greater impact than official regulations.

2. There are three sources for the legal foundations of education, the federal
and state constitutions, statutes, and case law. Federal school law is determined by the U.S. Constitution, federal statutes and case law determined by
federal court decisions. State school law is determined by state constitutions,
state statutes and case law determined by state court decisions.

3. There is a growing sentiment to greatly expand the involvement of teachers in school governance which could transform teaching, making it a very
different occupation from what it is today.

QUESTIONS

1. Recalling some of the conflicts mentioned in Chapter 8, what consequences do you see as a result of overlapping authority?
2. Who were the stakeholders in *Brown v. Board of Education*? Who were
the powerholders?
3. What are the costs and benefits of overlapping jurisdiction and blurred
lines of authority? Delineate these costs and benefits in terms of powerholders, implementers, and others. (See Chapter 8.)
4. What effects on the nature of school consensus might the reduction of
the number of school districts have had? Do you think there might be a
relationship between this consolidation movement and the perception
that school problems have increased?
5. What effect do you think court decisions on schooling might have had
on school consensus?
6. What are the costs and benefits (and for whom) of allowing commissions
to make quasi-judicial decisions?
7. What is the legal basis for federal involvement in schooling?
8. Consider some case law examples involving schooling and how their
decisions are justified. Is an attempt made to balance competing interests?
9. How would you sketch in lines of informal authority in Figure 14.5?
10. With respect to the Dade County experiment, who are the stakeholders
outside the school system?

GAL
BASICS for
TEACHERS

Chapter 15

PREVIEW

Teachers cannot afford to go about their business ignorant of the legal basics that help shape school practice. A basic understanding of legal concepts and principles is now essential—particularly if teachers are to rise to the demands generated by their emerging professionalism.

Teachers who participate in the making of school policy should be able to intelligently anticipate and assess the legal risks of their choices. They should know if a given policy will result in violations of the Constitution, illegal discrimination, or a lawsuit alleging negligence. They should also be able to plan strategies for preventive action.[1] Additionally, in recent years more and more Americans have demonstrated a willingness to turn to the courts to resolve school disputes. For this reason legal principles have taken on additional significance.

This chapter presents, in nontechnical language, some basic legal guidelines for teachers. It highlights three topics:

- The rights of teachers.

- The rights of parents and students.

- The issue of legal liability resulting from school-related incidents.

TEACHERS AND THE LAW:

In this section we address teachers' rights. These rights are defined by the federal and state constitutions, legislation, principally state legislation, and case law. Also since much of the day-to-day operation of public schools has been delegated to the local board of education, board policy also defines some of the rights of teachers. However, school board policy may not violate rights guaranteed by the Constitution of the United States or state constitutions, nor may it exceed the board's delegated authority as agents of state government. Board policy must also comply with all federal legislation, such as the Civil Rights Act of 1964, and honor the terms of any legal contracts with teachers.

In the following section we detail the rights of teachers with respect to specific issues. Statutory law is always relevant in that state laws and local regulations define many details. Consequently, we do touch on statutory provisions. Our emphasis, however, is on federal case law because it has universal applicability and supplies the basic constitutional ground rules that no state law or local regulation may violate.

---

[1]Richard Strahan and L. Charles Turner, *The Courts and the Schools* (White Plains, N.Y.: Longman, 1987). Strahan and Turner stress that school administrators should master these skills. We think them equally necessary for teachers.

Figure 15.1

**GROUNDS FOR LEGALLY CHALLENGING
A LOCAL SCHOOL BOARD REGULATION:**

It exceeds the authority
given to the board by
the state legislature.

It violates the rights of
an individual or group.

It violates the terms
of the contract.

Nonrenewal and Dismissal

It used to be that teachers were often fired for things like expressing unpopular views, or joining the "wrong" church. It was also common to lose one's position to a less expensive younger teacher, or to be dismissed so that there was room on the staff for the local committeeman's wife or cousin.

Today, hard-won state tenure statutes provide most teachers with safeguards against such dismissals. One court explained:

> The broad purpose of teacher tenure is to protect worthy instructors from enforced yielding to political preferences and to guarantee to such teachers employment after a long period of satisfactory service regardless of the vicissitudes of politics or the likes or dislikes of those charged with the administration of school affairs.[2]

Though they vary from state to state, tenure laws generally provide that teachers may not be dismissed without due process that proves that they are guilty of specific offenses. These commonly include:

- nonperformance of duties
- incompetence
- insubordination
- commission of crimes involving moral turpitude
- violation of contract provisions
- revocation of the teaching certificate.[3]

Of course, some of these conditions are sloganistic. And even though case law often defines them with some exactitude, a competent attorney can be helpful in defending against abuse. He or she might be able to establish, for

---

[2]Quoted in Daniel and Richard Gatti, *The Teacher and the Law* (West Nyack, N. Y.: Parker, 1972), p. 115.
[3]La Morte, op. cit., p. 189.

example, that what the superintendent of schools sees as insubordination is really a teacher's acting on ethical principle.

Tenure laws do *not* apply to layoffs that are the result of declining enrollments or the elimination of programs. In this regard, teaching is no different from any other occupation; no work, no job. Also, teachers are *not* tenured until they have been employed by a school district for a period of time specified in state law—usually two or three years. This means that a teacher with less experience is not afforded the protection of tenure. However, beginning teachers are *not* totally vulnerable to capricious nonrenewals of their contract.

Even though they lack tenure, beginning teachers in the public schools are afforded legal protection by the federal and state constitutions. If dismissal because of discrimination is the issue, federal and state antidiscrimination statutes also offer protection. In addition, if the nonrenewal can be shown to be patently arbitrary, wholly unsupported in fact, or based on a violation of policy, even if that policy is unannounced, the nonrenewal is invalid.[4]

A few states, California and Alaska are examples, provide statute protection for nontenured teachers. These laws provide that a teacher may request a hearing that will provide due process protection. Unlike a criminal proceeding, however, the burden of proof falls on the dismissed untenured teacher.[5]

The general principle is that public school employees have no right to keep their government job, but the Constitution does not allow the government to condition continued employment upon the person's willingness to give up any of the rights of American citizenship. There is the qualification that the exercise of these rights may not disrupt the proper functioning of the school, nor disrupt the proper performance of the teacher's duties.[6] We can imagine that this qualification could be problematic.

In *Board of Regents of State Colleges v. Roth* (1972)[7] the Supreme Court helped clarify some of these issues. David Roth was hired for his first teaching job at Wisconsin State University on a one-year contract. At the end of the year he was informed that he would not be rehired. No reason was given. Roth alleged that this was due to comments he had made which were critical of the university. The High Court found that there was no evidence that this was the case. Consequently, his right of free speech had not been violated. Further, the lack of a hearing was not problematic because the Court found that University officials had not accused Roth of incompetence or anything else that might damage his chances for future employment. A key element of the case was that his contract had been for one year only. In consideration of all these factors, the Court found that Roth's dismissal was constitutional.

We might note that teachers who are employees of private schools are protected from arbitrary dismissal only if they are union members, minority

---

[4]Gatti and Gatti, op. cit., p. 125.
[5]Ibid.
[6]Robert O'Neil, *Classrooms in the Crossfire* (Bloomington: Indiana U. Press, 1981), p. 108.
[7]*Marvin L. Pickering v. Board of Education of Township High School District 205,* 1968, Supreme Court of the United States, 391 U.S. 563.

group members, women, or handicapped. All other individuals fall under the common-law "at will" doctrine that allows dismissal without cause.[8]

Freedom of Expression

As we noted earlier, public employment is considered a privilege rather than a right. In addition, governmental employees have often had their political activities restricted by federal or state statute. These two factors have contributed to the traditional view that teachers had limited rights of freedom of expression.[9]

In *Pickering v. Board of Education of Township High School District 205* (1968)[10] the Supreme Court established new guidelines for the rights of expression of public school teachers. The Court found that regardless of the fact that they are government employees, teachers have the same First Amendment rights to freedom of expression as any other American.

Marvin Pickering had been dismissed for publicly criticizing the local school board's distribution of school funds in a letter to the local newspaper. After a full hearing Pickering was fired. He appealed this decision all the way to the Supreme Court.

The High Court overruled Pickering's dismissal on the grounds that it trespassed on his First Amendment right to freedom of speech. In its decision the Court noted:

> Teachers are, as a class, the members of the community most likely to have informed and definite opinions as to how funds allotted to the operation of the schools should be spent. Accordingly, it is essential that they be able to speak out freely on such questions without fear of retaliatory dismissal.

The Court went on to note reservations about a teacher's rights to speak out freely on school policy. First, they noted that Pickering's action had not contributed to disharmonious working relationships in the school. It might have been different had he publicly criticized his principal or department head. Second, he had not made knowingly or recklessly false statements. Had he done so, it is doubtful that the Court would have decided in his favor. Finally, the Court noted that Pickering was dealing with an issue of "public importance," not with idle gossip. This also worked to his advantage.

Thus, Pickering established a qualified rather than an absolute right for teachers to speak out in public on school-related matters.

Because Pickering's comments took place outside the classroom, the Court's decision did not help settle another question. It is, can teachers be fired for something they say or do **in** class?

---

[8]La Morte, p. 195.
[9]Ibid., p. 196.
[10]*Pickering,* op. cit.

Figure 15.2

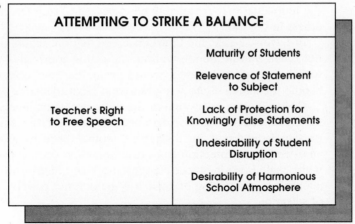

ATTEMPTING TO STRIKE A BALANCE

Teacher's Right to Free Speech	Maturity of Students
	Relevence of Statement to Subject
	Lack of Protection for Knowingly False Statements
	Undesirability of Student Disruption
	Desirability of Harmonious School Atmosphere

The answer to that is a conditional yes. No citizen's freedom of speech is absolute. It is illegal, for instance, to shout "Fire!" in a crowded theater if there is no fire. Similarly, teachers do not have unbridled liberty to say whatever they wish in class. Speaking generally, the courts have established that the age of the students is a key consideration. So is the relevancy of the teacher's expression to the subject being taught, whether or not the statements are knowingly or recklessly false, the existence and definitiveness of school policies and regulations concerning what teachers may or may not say, and finally, whether or not the teacher's utterance creates a disruption among the students. These points are summarized in Figure 15.2.

We can realize from these considerations that there are instances where a teacher can be lawfully fired for something that he or she has said in class. However, the courts are very reluctant to sanction the suppression of free speech, even if it takes place in a special setting like a school where the immaturity of the students requires special considerations.[11]

Discrimination

We have already learned that federal and state antidiscrimination statutes afford considerable protection to particular groups. Discrimination based on age, union membership, race, religion, national origin, sex, pregnancy, or handicap is forbidden under various state and/or federal laws.

In certain cases, however, the courts have been called upon to clarify the rights of individuals whose situation is not specifically covered by state or federal antidiscrimination statutes. For example, in *Gaylord v. Tacoma School District No. 10* (1977), the supreme court of the State of Washington upheld the firing of a high school teacher who was a "publicly known homosexual." The Court ruled that the key issue was whether or not "... the conduct of

---

[11]Flygare, op. cit., pp. 9–12.

the individual may reasonably be expected to interfere with … the person's fitness in the job … "

In Gaylord's case, the Court observed that the school district officials could not retain him in the job without indicating approval of his active homosexuality. This, they declared, would prejudice their obligation to responsibly handle the affairs of the school district. Gaylord's firing was upheld.

Gaylord's case raises one of the most problematic aspects of antidiscrimination statutes. It concerns **the criteria of selection for protection**. Under present federal law, for instance, a woman born to wealth and privilege is afforded legal protection from discrimination on the basis of her gender. A white male born in abject circumstances and deprived of every advantage is afforded no protection because it is gender, not poverty, that is the criterion of selection.

Immorality

Many times teacher dismissals or revocations of certification involve allegations of immorality. These reflect the well-founded, though often abused, concern that teachers provide an appropriate example. This bit of verse captures the essence of the matter:

> No printed word nor spoken plea
> can teach young minds what they should be.
> Not all the books on all the shelves,
> but what the teachers are themselves.
>
> *Mark Twain*[12]

Of course, it is not always easy to decide where to draw the line. An Iowa Supreme Court case, *Erb v. Iowa State Board of Public Instruction* (1974), provides an instance. Richard Erb, married with two children, taught art in Iowa. By hiding in the trunk of his wife Margaret's car, Robert Johnson, a local farmer, confirmed that Erb was having an affair with her. Not knowing that her husband had hidden himself there, the farmer's wife picked up Erb, drove to a secluded rendezvous, and had intercourse in the back seat. Johnson did not disclose his presence.

Johnson subsequently consulted a lawyer about a divorce. He was informed that it would be helpful if he had witnesses to his wife's infidelity. Organizing a group of friends into a "raiding party," Johnson managed to sneak up on Erb

---

[12]Quoted in James Leary, *Education on Trial* (Pymouth, Mich.: Teachers Central Clearing House, 1981), p. 87.

and Margaret as they were having intercourse in her car on a remote lover's lane. Johnson and the others swooped down on the car and took photos as the lovers cowered half naked in the back seat.

Armed with the photos, Johnson sued for divorce. The matter became a public scandal when he also demanded Erb's removal from his teaching position. Erb offered to resign, but by then his wife had forgiven him and he had regained the respect of the community. The school board therefore refused Erb's resignation. Nevertheless, the Iowa Board of Educational Examiners revoked his license to teach on the grounds that he was morally unfit.

Upon Erb's appeal, the Iowa Supreme Court overruled the Board of Examiners. Adhering to a more technical concept of teaching, they found that the Iowa School Code stated that a certificate can be revoked for moral unfitness only if there is a reasonable likelihood that the teacher's retention will adversely affect the school community. There was, said the Court, no evidence that this was the case.

The Erb decision was not definitive. Teacher firings that result from charges of immorality continue to produce mixed results in the courts. In a somewhat similar case, for example, the dismissal of a single female elementary teacher for openly living with a man was upheld in federal court.[13] In another federal case, however, an unwed pregnant teacher was ordered restored to her job.[14] Other court decisions concerning sex change operations, sexual advances of teachers to students, and similar matters have been equally inconsistent.

These mixed results suggest that teachers run the risk of dismissal by engaging in activities that are likely to bring charges of immorality or failing to act as a proper example. They cannot count on rescue in the courts. In general, however, judges seem to be moving toward the position that teachers do not necessarily have to be exemplars, provided that their behavior does not hamper or disrupt the educational process.[15]

As a practical matter, charges of disruptive immorality are far more likely in a small community than in a big city school system. Behavior guaranteed to create a scandal in Iowa or South Dakota might attract little or no attention in San Francisco or New York City.

Teacher Bargaining and the Right to Strike

Traditionally, school boards controlled virtually every aspect of school policy without input from teachers. This practice began to change in the early 1960s when the American Federation of Teachers won the right to bargain collectively in several key big city school districts. Today, most teachers engage in some sort of bargaining with their local school boards. In addition, all teachers have the right to hold membership in unions.[16]

---

[13]*Sullivan v. Meade Independent School District No. 101*, U.S. Court of Appeals (8th Cir. 1976).
[14]*Avery v. Homewood City Board of Education*, U.S. Court of Appeals (5th Circuit, 1982).
[15]La Morte, op. cit., p. 230.
[16]Strahan and Turner, op. cit., p. 156.

Teachers often strike in
defiance of state law.

Collective bargaining is the negotiating process that develops the content of school district/teacher contracts. It usually governs wages, hours, and conditions of employment. In some states the law mandates that school boards must engage in collective bargaining with teachers. In others it requires only that they meet and confer with teacher representatives. Approximately half of all the states provide for some sort of good faith negotiation. In a few states collective bargaining is prohibited. Forty percent have no statutory provisions at all regarding the matter.

The situation is equally mixed so far as teacher strikes are concerned. Very generally, it is usually illegal for public employees of any kind to strike. Approximately half the states explicitly forbid them, and this prohibition has been upheld by the courts. Nevertheless, seven states (Hawaii, Montana, Maine, New Hampshire, Oregon, Pennsylvania, and Vermont) have made it legal for teachers to strike under certain circumstances.

Such laws have not been successful in actually eliminating teacher strikes. Believing that meaningful benefits cannot be secured from school boards who think themselves invulnerable to the costs of a work stoppage, teachers often walk out in defiance of the law—even though they risk loss of pay, firing, fines, and jail. When teachers have lost their jobs as a result of participating in an illegal strike, the courts have upheld the local school board's right to take such an action.

Teacher strikes have diminished in recent years. As of October 31, 1986, teachers in fifty-five school districts were on strike. This figure accounts for 3.5 percent of the 15,681 school districts in the United States.[17]

Political Activities

In some states teachers are prohibited from engaging in partisan political activity such as electioneering. They may speak their minds on political issues

---

[17]Sherwood and Lorna Harris, *The Teacher's Almanac, 1987–88* (New York: Facts on File, 1987), p. 88.

and are free to vote, but they may not engage in active political advocacy. These prohibitions have their roots in an act of Congress.

This measure, popularly known as the Hatch Act, was passed in 1939. Among its provisions is a prohibition against interfering with or affecting the election of any candidate for federal office by any person employed in an administrative position of the government. Many states subsequently passed so-called "mini-Hatch Acts" prohibiting state employees from participating in electioneering. Teachers were sometimes included.

The Supreme Court has upheld a mini-Hatch act in the state of Oklahoma. In *Broderick v. Oklahoma* (1973),[18] the Court declared that such laws can forbid state employees from participating in a wide variety of political activity. It follows from this that such restrictions can be placed on public school teachers.

However, most teachers are not affected by mini-Hatch Acts. They may engage in any form of political advocacy without penalty or restriction. But in the final analysis, if a local law forbids teacher candidacy for public office, for example, they have the right to run, but they do not have the right to keep their jobs as teachers if they win.

PARENTS, STUDENTS, AND THE LAW

Parental and student rights have become increasingly well defined. As is the case with teachers, these rights have two legal bases — statutes and case law. We will review the role of both through selected examples.

Compulsory Education

As we learned in the section on the history of education, there was a time when parents had nearly absolute control of the person and property of minor children.[19] In the seventeenth and eighteenth centuries, however, state and church officials assumed the authority to remove neglected children from their natural parents.[20]

In the late nineteenth century a far more fundamental assumption of governmental authority took place. State lawmakers began passing statutes compelling parents to send their children to school, and backing them up with mechanisms of enforcement and meaningful penalties. This assumption of the authority to compel children to attend school, regardless of their parents' wishes, represented an enormous inroad on the traditional prerogatives of parents.

Predictably, this step was challenged in the courts. The judiciary, however, sided with the lawmakers. In 1922 the voters of Oregon, by means of a state

---

[18]*Broderick v. Oklahoma*, U.S. Supreme Court, 1973, 413 U.S. 601.
[19]Note, for example, that in the history of education section we explained that the Roman *pater familias* had the power of life and death over his children.
[20]David Nassaw, *Schooled to Order: A Social History of Schooling in America* (Oxford, England: Oxford U. Press, 1979), p. 10.

petition passed in an atmosphere of antiforeign and anti-Catholic sentiment, went one step farther. They virtually eliminated all but public schooling as a way of satisfying the state's school attendance laws.

This petition went too far for the Supreme Court. As we know, in *Pierce v. Society of Sisters* (1925)[21] the Supreme Court overturned the Oregon statute. In doing so the High Court declared:

> ... we think it is entirely plain that the Act of 1922 unreasonably interferes with the liberty of parents and guardians to direct the upbringing and education of children under their control. ... The fundamental theory of liberty upon which all the governments of this Union repose excludes any general power of the State to standardize its children by forcing them to accept instruction from public teachers only. The child is not the mere creature of the state; those who nurture him and direct his destiny have the right, coupled with the high duty, to recognize and prepare him for additional obligations.

Since Pierce the agreed-upon legal convention has been that the state may compel school attendance, but parents may determine whether the school attended is private, parochial, or public.

Significantly, in winning the Pierce case, the attorneys representing the Society of Sisters argued that "It is not seriously debatable that the parental right to guide one's child intellectually and religiously is a most substantial part of the liberty and freedom of the parent." The Court made no mention of the rights of children. Indeed, the prevailing assumption in children's law is that "a child's interests are identical with those of his parents." As a matter of fact, in *Wisconsin v. Yoder*, covered next, the High Court ruled that "(The)

---

[21]*Pierce v. Society of Sisters*, U. S. Supreme Court (1925), 268 U.S. 510.

Figure 15.3

ATTEMPTING TO STRIKE A BALANCE (COMPULSORY SCHOOLING)	
Liberty of Parents to Direct the Upbringing of Their Child Freedom of Religion	Public Authorities' Responsibility to the General Population

The Supreme Court found that Amish religious beliefs outweigh the state's strong interest in compulsory education.

primary role of the parents in the upbringing of their children is now established beyond debate as an enduring American tradition."[22] David Owen questions the wisdom of such a position and asks if our changing idea of childhood may not require a review of relations between parent and child. He wonders if "... the exercise of power of one individual over another is justified if the latter is able to reflectively express for herself or himself a serious choice in life, based on exposure to a variety of ideas, actions and values?"[23]

The issue of state authority to compel school attendance was further defined in the case *Wisconsin v. Yoder* (1972).[24] Maintaining that they had the authority to extend the benefits of secondary schooling to all the children of the state, educational authorities in Wisconsin brought charges against Jonus Yoder, an old order Amish, who refused to send his children to high school because of the historical and religious traditions of his faith.

Yoder was convicted, but appealed all the way to the Supreme Court. Citing the nearly three hundred years of the group's existence, and their unconventional but highly successful social traditions, the High Court reversed the Wisconsin conviction. Finding that the state law gravely endangered the free

[22]*Wisconsin v. Yoder*, U. S. Supreme Court (1972), 406 U.S. 205.
[23]David B. Owen, "Recent Textbook Cases and Children's Rights," *Religion and Public Education*, Vol. 15, No. 3 (Summer 1988).
[24]Ibid.

exercise of Amish religious beliefs, the Court declared that this outweighed the state's strong interest in compulsory education.[25]

The Right? to Schooling

The U.S. Supreme Court has made several decisions dealing with the question of whether or not students have the right to an education. In Chapter 11 we referred to the fact that the absence of any specific mention of schooling means that it is not a fundamental enumerated right guaranteed in the U.S. Constitution. This, however, still left open the question of whether or not it was an implied right.

In *San Antonio Independent School District v. Rodriguez* (1973)[26] the High Court, in a five to four decision, ruled against parents in a relatively poor school district who filed suit against the Texas system of funding schools. The parents complained that their son was being deprived of an equal education simply because he resided in a relatively poor school district. In ruling against the Rodriguez family, the Court noted that education is **not** among the rights afforded explicit protection under the Constitution. Significantly, they added, "... nor do we find any basis for saying it is implicitly so protected."

In 1988 the Supreme Court further defined the lack of constitutional protection of a child's right to schooling. In *Kadrmas v. Dickenson Public Schools* (1988)[27] the justices ruled that schooling is not "... a 'fundamental right' that triggers strict scrutiny when government interferes with an individual's access to it." Thus, a citizen's right to a public education depends solely on state statutes and state constitutional guarantees. The only other alternative is to amend the Constitution of the United States.

Corporal Punishment

Corporal punishment involves the use of physical contact, such as paddling or spanking, for disciplinary purposes. There was a time when such punishments were virtually universal. Often they were administered for poor schoolwork as well as for misbehavior.

Experts are fairly unanimous in their agreement that corporal punishment is ineffective and counterproductive. Indeed, in 1975 the American Psychological Association passed a resolution opposing its use because "... it lowers self-esteem, encourages children to resolve difficulties with violence, and instills rage and a sense of powerlessness without reducing undesirable behavior."[28]

Despite its lack of popularity with the experts, corporal punishment is still widely practiced in the nation's schools. Some states and local school districts

---

[25]See *Wisconsin v. Yoder*, op. cit.
[26]*San Antonio I.S.D. v. Rodriguez*, U.S. Supreme Court (1973), 411 U.S. I.
[27]*Kadrmas v. Dickenson Public Schools*, U.S. Supreme Court (1988), 108 S. Ct. 2481
[28]Proceedings of the American Psychological Association for the Year 1975, *American Psychologist*, Vol. 30, No. 620, pp. 605–606.

Although corporal punishment is less honored now than in the past, nevertheless, the Supreme Court has ruled that it is constitutional.

forbid it, more require that the parent sign a consent form before it can be used, but most permit it and allow it to be administered without parental consent.

The Constitution of the United States forbids cruel and unusual punishment and some think that this prohibition should include the corporal punishment of children. In *Ingraham v. Wright* (1977)[29] the Supreme Court ruled that corporal punishment is constitutional. In declaring that it did not constitute cruel and unusual punishment, the High Court stated:

> At common law a single principle has governed the use of corporal punishment since before the American Revolution: teachers may impose reasonable but not excessive force to discipline a child. . . . The prevalent rule in this country today privileges such force as a teacher or administrator reasonably believes necessary for [the child's] proper control, training or education.

---

[29]*Ingraham v. Wright*, U.S. Supreme Court (1977), 430 U.S. 651.

Figure 15.4   **OVERLAPPING CONSIDERATIONS RELATIVE TO THE USE OF CORPORAL PUNISHMENT**

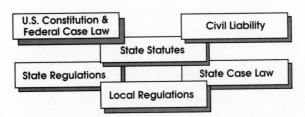

The Court went on to say that a hearing prior to such punishment was not necessary.

The Court's decision does not stop states or local school districts from forbidding or regulating corporal punishment. State statutory and case law are still relevant, and local regulations against the practice are also unaffected.[30] There is one other consideration. Civil suits for damages are also a possibility. The liability section of this chapter gives us more details.

Freedom of Expression

At one time school authorities had little regard for the freedom of expression guaranteed in the Constitution of the United States. Operating on the time-honored principle that they were *in loco parentis*, literally in place of the parent, educators seldom gave much thought to the place of the Constitution in determining student rights. They assumed that possessing a portion of the parent's rights, duties, and responsibilities included the right to control the expression of opinion.

The landmark case of *Tinker v. Des Moines Independent School District* (1969)[31] changed this assumption. The decision did not address the question of "pure speech," but it did address a symbolic act closely akin to it, the wearing of black armbands.

In 1965 a group of students attending high schools in Des Moines determined to publicize their objections to the war in Vietnam by wearing black armbands during the Christmas season. The principals of the Des Moines high schools learned of the plan and adopted a policy that any students wearing such a band would be asked to remove it. If they refused, they would be suspended until they returned without it.

John Tinker and two others refused to remove the armbands and were sent home. They filed a complaint in federal court which eventually ended in the Supreme Court. Finding in favor of the students, the Court noted that their symbolic act had not intruded on the work of the schools or the rights of other students. This was a key consideration.

The Court also observed that school officials had not forbidden the wearing of other symbols, including the Iron Cross, a Nazi symbol. Apparently, they noted, only symbols opposing the nation's involvement in Vietnam were prohibited.

Following these preliminary observations, the Court criticized the principals' action, saying:

> In our system, state-operated schools may not be enclaves of totalitarianism. School officials do not possess absolute authority over their students. Students in school as well as out of school are "per-

---

[30]Strahan and Turner, op. cit., p. 132.
[31]*Tinker v. Des Moines Independent Community School District*, U.S. Supreme Court (1969), 393 U.S. 503.

Figure 15.5

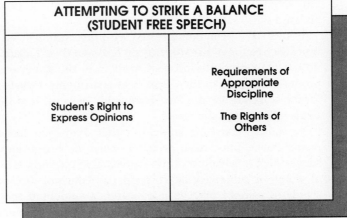

**ATTEMPTING TO STRIKE A BALANCE
(STUDENT FREE SPEECH)**

Student's Right to
Express Opinions

Requirements of
Appropriate
Discipline

The Rights of
Others

sons" under our Constitution. They are possessed of fundamental rights which the state must respect. In our system students may not be regarded as closed-circuit recipients of only that which the State chooses to communicate. They may not be confined to the expression of those sentiments that are officially approved. In the absence of a specific showing of constitutionally valid reasons to regulate their speech, students are entitled to freedom of expression of their views.

The High Court went on to make it clear that the student's right to express him- or herself extended to all parts of the school day, noting: "We do not confine the permissible exercise of First Amendment rights to a telephone booth or the four corners of a pamphlet, or to supervised and ordained discussion in a school classroom." But they added an important qualification:

> ... he may express his opinion, even on controversial subjects ... if he does so without materially and substantially interfering with the requirements of appropriate discipline in the operation of the school and without colliding with the rights of others. ... But conduct by the student, in class or out of it, which for any reason— whether it stems from time, place, or type of behavior—materially disrupts classwork or involves substantial disorder or invasion of the rights of others is, of course, not immunized by the constitutional guarantee of freedom of speech.

Searches of Lockers and Students

American citizens are protected from warrantless searches of their homes by the Fourth Amendment's ban on unreasonable searches and seizures. Students arrested as a result of material found during warrantless locker searches have attempted to have the evidence suppressed on the grounds that the search violated these same Constitutional rights.

Courts have been unimpressed with this argument for a variety of reasons. A primary factor is that students do not own their lockers. Consequently, they do not have property interests in them in the same sense that citizens have property interests in their homes or apartments. Courts have also found that locker searches are not "unreasonable" because it is likely that contraband items will be stored there.[32]

Personally searching students rather than their lockers, is more problematic. Police must have probable cause to search anyone. Evidence must suggest that it is likely that the individual in question is in personal possession of stolen or otherwise illegal property. Educators are held to less stringent standards. School officials may search a student if they have a reasonable suspicion that the student has stolen something or is in possession of something illegal.[33] A reasonable suspicion is more vague than probable cause and requires less evidence of guilt.

A recent Supreme Court case illustrates the issues involved and recounts how this new standard was established. *New Jersey v. T.L.O.* (1985)[34] concerned a girl discovered smoking in a school lavatory. Taken to the principal's office, she denied that she had been smoking, claiming that she did not even smoke. The principal asked to see her purse. Opening it he found a pack of cigarettes. Taking them out of the purse he also noticed cigarette rolling papers. Believing that these suggested marijuana use, the principal then searched the purse carefully. He discovered marijuana, a pipe, quite a bit of money in one-dollar bills, what appeared to be a list of students owing money to T.L.O., and letters implicating her in drug sales. On the basis of these and a subsequent confession, T.L.O. was convicted of delinquency in Juvenile Court.

T.L.O. sought to have her conviction overturned on the basis that she had been subjected to an unreasonable warrantless search in violation of her Fourth Amendment rights. The matter was appealed all the way to the Supreme Court. In its finding, the High Court observed that the Fourth Amendment did in fact safeguard the privacy and security of students against arbitrary invasions by governmental officials—principals included. It also dismissed the notion that such searches were automatically constitutional because of the *in loco parentis* status of educators, noting that contemporary reality and the teachings of the court have established that school authorities are state actors, not parents, when it comes to constitutional guarantees.

Having made these observations, the High Court went on to note that modern schools face a real problem in maintaining an environment in which learning can take place. Thus, they commented, there was a need to balance the student's legitimate expectations of privacy with the school's need for an orderly environment.

---

[32]Flygare, op. cit., p. 18.
[33]La Morte, op. cit., p. 134.
[34]*New Jersey v. T.L.O.*, U.S. Supreme Court (1985), 105 S. Ct 733.

In *Goss v. Lopez* (1975)[36] nine students who were susppating in school disturbances, the record of same removed

The Ohio law under which be given a hearing. Some tho The Supreme Court agreed to

In reviewing the case the Su that a student's entitlement t tected by the Due Process C have the right to determine misconduct has occurred.

> … Many school autho power to act unilaterall hearing. But it would b cational institution if n plinarian with the stude liction and to let him t sure that an injustice is by secret, one-sided de "Secrecy is not congen gives too slender an ass has been devised for ar jeopardy of serious loss tunity to meet it."

The Court specifically dis pending students for brief pe to counsel, to confront and witnesses. But it did make it alleged misconduct with stu their version of the facts.

The Court went on to say more formal procedures.

Inspecting and Reviewi

When Congress passed the 1974 (P.L. 93–380), it defin students eighteen years of ag have the right to inspect and also not be disclosed withou dents. Parents or eligible stu

inaccurate information is on file. Schools are required f these rights.

e authors was involved in an incident concerning her llustrates why this act was passed. An education major young woman asked a number of professors to write ion to be put in her file at the school's job placement ividuals, such as the student's college adviser, had to

hough this was a time of great teacher shortage, she calling her for an interview. At her request, her file zens of school districts who had expressed tentative ffers.

f schools trying to find out if there was some problem. polite evasiveness. Finally, she phoned someone who omething was seriously wrong with one of her letters ortunately, she could not determine the nature of the cords were closed to her.

s father was a college official, it was ultimately possible ature of the problem. One of her advisers, who had italized for psychiatric problems, had made untrue er sexual behavior in his letter of recommendation. w what the problem was, she had no means of de tting a retraction. The letter continued to dog her. t difficulty, she got a teaching job in a distant state. ciation of a subsequently hospitalized mental patient years.

od, and Marriage

utinely exclude students who were pregnant, mar and statute law have combined to effectively end icies have been successfully attacked in the courts.

that **Title IX of the Education Amendments of** ds sex discrimination and the *Pregnancy Discrimi-* 5–555) includes pregnant women in the protections ts Act of 1964. In short, students who are either not be excluded from public schooling.

e for coming to school sporting multiple earrings, ts, and a sleeveless T-shirt emblazoned with a Nazi braless? May the principal then send her home? vided consistent guidelines regarding this matter. rted dress codes that prohibit immodest or sugges-

---

[36]*Goss v. Lopez*, U.S. Supreme Court

Legal guidelines on grooming are inconsistent.

tive clothing. Dress that creates a disturbance or distraction may also be prohibited, as may unsanitary clothing that creates a health hazard. If a school tries banning blue jeans, however, the courts are unlikely to be sympathetic.[37]

Guidelines on grooming are a bit less consistent. For example, one attorney has counted 131 different decisions on the issue of male hair length in the period 1969–1975. Seventy-four were in favor of the board; fifty-seven supported the student.[38] Apparently local tastes have a great deal to do with what aspects of grooming schools may limit and be supported in court.

THE ISSUE OF LIABILITY

It is a fundamental legal premise that all individuals are responsible for the consequences of their action. This is the basis of **tort liability** laws that provide that an individual is entitled to compensation for harm caused them by the unreasonable conduct of another. Distinct from criminal suits brought by the state to redress public wrongs, civil suits are brought by individuals seeking damages. Such cases are usually handled on the basis of state laws.[39]

School District Immunity

Recently, the Supreme Court limited the immunity of local government, including school districts, by ruling that they can be sued for damages if official

[37]See *Bannister v. Paradis*, 316 F. Supp. 185. (D.N.H. 1970).
[38]Flygare, op. cit., p. 45.
[39]Mary McCarthy and Nelda Cambron, *Public School Law: Teachers' and Students' Rights* (Boston: Allyn & Bacon, 1981), p. 167.

policy inflicts injury. Nevertheless, in approximately half of the states surviving statutes confer at least some measure of **sovereign immunity** on local school districts.[40] "Sovereign immunity," a legal precedent based on the ancient common law legal notion that "the King can do no wrong," is used to grant immunity to government agencies from tort liability.

Government officials are not always so invulnerable. A section of the Civil Rights Act of 1871 provides for liability if a person operating under state authority violates another person's civil rights. In *Wood v. Strickland* (1975)[41] the Supreme Court determined that school officials may be held personally liable for damages under this act if they intentionally violate or disregard a student's clearly established constitutional rights. The Court did not clarify whether similar considerations would apply to school administrators or teachers.

A few states, Georgia being the most notable example, have attempted to exempt school administrators and classroom teachers from tort liability.[42] In the majority of states, however, the best protection for teachers is afforded by a knowledge of their legal responsibilities, care commensurate with their obligations to the students in their charge, and the ready availability of relatively inexpensive malpractice insurance.

Teacher Liability

Generally if teachers are found liable it is the result of negligence. **Negligence** involves conduct that falls below an acceptable standard of care and results in an injury.[43] There also are occasions where teachers are found liable for intentional injuries they have inflicted. We will review those as well.

Negligence

Most school injuries are **pure accidents**. These are the sorts of incidents that can occur with the best of supervision. Teachers are not liable in such cases.

Sometimes students contribute to their own injury by ignoring instructions or failing to use the safety equipment provided. If it can be established that the student has been injured as a result of such **contributory negligence**, the teacher is not liable.

If a teacher fails to lock up hazardous chemicals, leaves climbing ropes dangling in the gym, or fails to safeguard children from any similar **attractive nuisance**, he or she is a likely candidate for a successful negligence suit.

The general standard followed in determining negligence is to look at the teacher's role in the incident and ask if a "reasonable and prudent" person

---

[40]See *Monell v. Department of Social Services of City of New York*, 436 U.S. 658 (1978).
[41]*Wood v. Strickland*, U.S. Supreme Court (1975), 420 U.S. 308.
[42]La Morte, op. cit., p. 370.
[43]McCarthy and Cambron, op. cit., p. 167.

would have behaved similarly in like circumstances. If not, the teacher was negligent.[44]

Teachers are not expected to keep each student under constant surveillance. But they are required to provide adequate supervision, to make certain that equipment is in good working condition, and to warn students of any known dangers.[45]

We should also understand that a successful suit against a teacher requires that he or she must be the **proximate cause** of the injury; that is, the teacher's conduct must have a causal connection to the injury incurred. In addition, an **actual loss** or injury must have been sustained. Close calls do not count.[46]

Negligence always depends on individual facts and circumstances, but these general guidelines prove helpful:

- Teachers have a legal obligation to take reasonable care, the same care an "ordinary teacher" would take, to ensure the safety of their students.
- Teachers need to establish carefully explained rules and procedures concerning playground conduct, science lab procedures, and so forth, which are enforced at all times.
- Teachers have a legal obligation to eliminate dangerous conditions or activities that could easily lead to an accident.
- Teachers are not necessarily protected if the student has been careless and has contributed to an injury.[47]

Medication

Negligence suits sometimes involve teacher administration of medication. The general guideline is, the teacher should give no medication to students. If in the absence of a school nurse the student must take medication, the teacher should ask to see the doctor's prescription. A note from home or a phone call is unacceptable because it could easily be inaccurate. In addition, teachers should not give students nonprescription medication such as aspirin or cough drops. Allergic reactions can be problematic.[48]

Field Trips

Field trips are particularly troublesome when it comes to teacher liability. Prior to any such event, the teacher must be sure to obtain parental permis-

---

[44]Robert Monks and Ernest Prouix, *Legal Basics for Teachers* (Bloomington, Ind.: Phi Delta Kappa Educational Foundation, 1986), pp. 8–9. This inexpensive pamphlet provides an excellent introduction to teacher liability issues.
[45]McCarthy and Cambron, op. cit., p. 168.
[46]Strahan and Turner, op. cit., p. 92.
[47]Adapted from Gatti and Gatti, p. 51.
[48]Monks and Prouix, op. cit., p. 20.

sion. This is best accomplished with a form indicating parental knowledge of the date of the trip, the mode of transportation, and the location. Any student lacking this permission should not go.

The use of private autos is problematic. Because the teacher or the school district may be held liable for the acts of any of the drivers, it is desirable to have the school provide transportation. An adequate number of adult supervisors is also essential, as are rules defining acceptable conduct and instructions in what to do should a student become separated from the group.[49]

Intentional Torts

Civil suits against teachers are often a consequence of an attempt to discipline students.[50] Teachers are given fairly wide authority with respect to discipline. We have, for example, already discussed the Supreme Court's ruling supporting corporal punishment. Wide authority or not, however, teachers may be sued for damages they have allegedly inflicted on a child.

These suits are termed intentional tort actions. An **intentional tort** is committed if a person intentionally impairs the rights of another. This usually involves the charge of assault and battery. An **assault** takes place when there is an overt attempt to put another in fear of bodily harm. **Battery** requires actual physical contact.

Courts have been reluctant to interfere with a teacher's authority to discipline students. This does not mean, however, that a teacher can never be held liable for the commission of an intentional tort.

The following are key considerations relative to teacher liability:

- The child's age
- The child's mental capacity
- The child's offense
- Where the child was struck
- Whether the punishment was cruel or excessive (If so the teacher may find him- or herself also facing a criminal charge)
- Whether the teacher was angry while administering punishment[51]

Self-defense is a related consideration. Speaking generally, a teacher has the right to use reasonable force to discipline a student, to protect him- or herself, or to prevent a student from injuring others. The key consideration is whether or not the employed force was excessive or brutal.[52]

---

[49]Ibid., pp. 22–24.
[50]La Morte, op. cit., p. 382.
[51]Ibid.
[52]McCarthy and Cambron, op. cit., p. 178.

SUMMARY

1. For self-protection, if for no other reason, teachers need to be knowledgeable about the leading legal developments affecting their occupation.

2. The rights of teachers are defined in statute and case law.

3. School teachers enjoy the same constitutional protections guaranteed to all Americans. State tenure laws further define these rights.

4. Statutes and case law also define parental and student rights.

5. The state has a well-defined right to compel school attendance, but children do not have a federal constitutional right to a public education.

6. Public school students do not leave their constitutional rights at the schoolhouse door.

7. Concerning teacher negligence liability, teachers are responsible for the harmful consequences if they behaved unreasonably, failed to warn of hazards, provide proper instructions, or maintain adequate supervision.

8. Regarding intentional torts, teachers can be held personally liable for assault and battery if they use excessive or brutal force. Teachers might also be held liable for intentional violations of student rights.

9. The courts require that teachers make reasonable efforts to stay abreast of their student's rights.

10. Liability insurance and access to a competent attorney are desirable. Often these can be obtained through membership in a teacher's union or professional association.

QUESTIONS:

1. What sorts of difficulties could a teacher blunder into if he or she is ignorant of the legal basics of schooling?
2. Which of the following decisions, if made by a school board, might face reversal in a court of law: the decision
   a. to prevent Asian students from taking calculus
   b. to require all third-grade students to study calculus
   c. to require teachers to stay in the school building until 4:00 P.M.
3. What are the costs and benefits of tenure laws? For whom?
4. What are the costs and benefits of permitting teachers the right of free speech? For whom?

5. How do you suppose ideas of morality vary with different images of the school? Which image does the *Erb* decision support?

6. What are the costs and benefits of permitting or forbidding teachers' strikes? For whom? Are these benefits and costs divisible or indivisible?

7. Can you imagine a society in which the child is a "mere creature of the state"? What differences in rights and responsibilities do you think this status would imply?

8. How would arguments **pro** and **con** corporal punishment vary with the image of the school invoked?

9. Which image of the school do the *Tinker* and *Goss* decisions support?

10. In *New Jersey v. T.L.O.* two values are seen to be in conflict: privacy versus learning environment. Are these the same kinds of values, e.g., both intrinsic or both instrumental? Both divisible or both indivisible? If not, how can we weigh one against the other in a reasonable way? What does this tell you about the resolution of conflicts?

Chapter 16

STOP

TAX HIKE

BUDGET

MEETING

NOV. 9TH 7:30 P.M.

TOWN HALL, NEW CITY

PREVIEW

In 1989, for the seventh straight year school board members—the individuals responsible for the crucial work of local school governance—said lack of proper financial support was their biggest worry.[1] And when the "20th Annual Gallup Poll of the Public's Attitudes Toward the Public Schools" asked, "What do you think are the biggest problems with which the public school in this community must deal?" the public identified lack of proper financial support as subordinate only to use of drugs and lack of discipline.[2]

In this chapter we learn where funding for public elementary and secondary schools comes from. We also outline what levels of government pay these costs and what sorts of taxes are used to generate the revenue. We explore why, despite billions in expenditures, public schools in some communities remain chronically underfunded. We also examine the extent of the "Taxpayer's Revolt," and how it has affected schools. Finally, we summarize the efforts of federal, state, and local school officials to use school finance as a goad for school reform.

FEDERAL, STATE, AND LOCAL SCHOOL FINANCE

There is little agreement about what the relative roles of each level of government should be with respect to school finance. Nevertheless, we can come up with figures that represent the average of fifty different funding schemes. Currently, state governments take up most of the burden in a majority of states. In 1987 state governments paid an average 49.9 percent of America's public elementary and secondary school costs, while local school districts paid 43.8 percent. The federal government contributed only 6.1 percent of the total.

Figure 16.1 shows a graphic representation of the school finance pie. These percentages do not remain constant. Throughout this century, for example, the local share of school funding has declined steadily, with state government taking up most of the slack. In the 1960s the federal contribution expanded dramatically; then the Reagan administration reversed this process. Figure 16.2 summarizes the shifts in school funding since 1930.

The Federal Role in Public School Finance

Despite growing public concern about the quality of American public schooling, the Reagan administration cut the federal government's contribution to

[1]"Our Eleventh Annual Survey," *The American School Board Journal*, January 1989, Vol. 176, No. 1, pp. 19–24.
[2]Alec Gallup and David Clark, "The 20th Annual Gallup Poll of the Public's Attitudes Toward the Public Schools," *Phi Delta Kappan*, Vol. 70, No. 1 (September 1988), p. 33–46.

Figure 16.1 **SOURCES OF PUBLIC ELEMENTARY AND SECONDARY SCHOOL FUNDING, 1987**

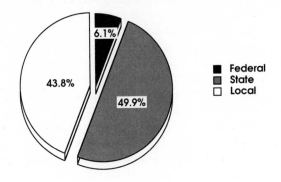

Figure 16.2   **CHANGING PATTERNS OF SCHOOL FINANCE**

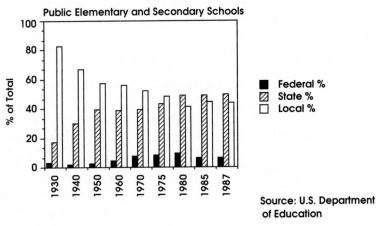

Source: U.S. Department of Education

school finance by nearly 66 percent from 1980 to 1987. Administration officials argued that more spending would not necessarily promote school improvements, and that schooling was the responsibility of state and local government. They also maintained that the federal government should emphasize its role as an information clearinghouse and promoter of change through persuasion.[3]

Of course, collecting and dispensing information is relatively inexpensive, and persuasion is even cheaper. And these economies matched the Reagan administration's decision to cut costs in some budget areas in order to pay for an enormously expensive military buildup.

Certainly it is true that increased expenditures do not guarantee school

---

[3]Ibid. p. 182.

improvements. But all tasks, including schooling, require resources for their accomplishment.

As of this writing the Bush administration is recommending an additional $441 million for the federal education budget. Most of this 2.7 percent increase over 1989 is for a series of new initiatives targeting the disadvantaged. The Bush plan calls for a child-care tax credit, increased funding for the Head Start program, an increase in funds for the National Science Foundation, a youth service program, antidrug initiatives, alternative teacher certification grants, and support for historically black colleges. It also cuts twenty-five existing programs and reallocates $750 million to other initiatives.[4]

Federal funding has traditionally been divided between **categorical grants**, intergovernmental fund transfers designated for specific purposes, and **block grants** which can be used for broadly defined school purposes. In the 1960s and 1970s categorical grants were held out as financial carrots before the hungry gaze of state and local officials to encourage them to pursue federal priorities. However, there were considerable differences in federal, state, and local priorities. And even when state and local officials shared federal goals, it was often difficult to integrate the federal categorical funds into their own educational efforts.[5] These realities, as well as complaints about excessive paperwork, unnecessary administrative costs, and unfair competition for funds among states and districts, led in 1981 to the **Federal Education Consolidation and Improvement Act**. It replaced many categorical grants with single block grants that state and local education agencies could use with broad discretion.

The State Role in Public School Finance

State governments have been paying an ever larger share of the public elementary and secondary school bill. In 1930, for example, state contributions to total elementary and secondary school funding stood at only 17 percent. These then increased steadily until state government was paying about 50 percent of the total in 1987.

This average state contribution figure can be misleading, however, because state by state the school funding percentages of state and local government vary widely. For instance, in 1987 Hawaii's state government contributed 92 percent of all public elementary and secondary school expenditures. In contrast, New Hampshire legislators funded only 6 percent of that state's total.[6]

State school expenditures flow through the local school districts, being distributed in a number of ways. **Flat Grant Plans** are the simplest and most inequitable of state fund distribution plans. For these, state aid is simply based on the number of students in attendance in each local school district.

---

[4]Julie A. Miller, "Bush Proposes $441 Million Boost for E.D.," *Education Week*, February 15, 1989, p. 1.
[5]Ibid., p. xix.
[6]National Center for Education Statistics, *The Conditions of Education* (Washington, D.C.: Government Printing Office, 1985), p. 27.

Such flat grant plans do nothing to overcome local school district financial inequalities. For that reason most state governments have authorized a variety of equalization plans. **Foundation Plans** are among the most common. They are intended to guarantee each district a minimum amount of funding per pupil (the foundation level) based on the local district's property tax rate. The idea is to use state tax revenue to help equalize local funding, but to base the amount of that aid on local willingness to tax for schools.[7]

District Power Equalizing Plans go one step further. They are designed to insure that each district has an equal opportunity to obtain funds for schooling provided they make the same effort. Thus, if a property-wealthy district taxes properties at the same rate as a property poor district, the state power equalizing plan makes up the difference for the poor district.

Weighted Student Plans are another common method of distributing state funds to local districts. Here, state revenues to the local district are quitbased on the special characteristics of the children attending school in that district. Children from impoverished homes, those with handicaps, those who require bilingual services, or those enrolled in vocational education programs, for example, are worth more in state funds.

Despite these equalization schemes for state school funding, however, problems remain. Local school tax burdens and per-pupil expenditures continue to be unequal and inequitable.[8]

State government also reimburses local school districts for specific expenses. In Kansas, for instance, state regulations provide local school districts with transportation-cost reimbursements if students live at least 2.5 miles from the front door of the school.

Because of local desire for state aid, these various state plans and regulations can have unwanted side effects. For example, school officials in Liberal, Kansas, recently found an inexpensive way to pick up an additional $6,000 to $8,000 in state transportation cost reimbursements when they paid $500 to move the flagpole outside Liberal High School from one side of the building to the other. It seems that the flagpole has traditionally identified the fronts of schools, and the old front was 100 feet short of the 2.5 miles needed to qualify for state transportation reimbursement of children living in a mobile home park. By moving the pole from the school's south to the identical north entrance, a distance greater than the 100 feet needed to put the park outside the 2.5-mile limit, school officials were able to qualify for the additional funding.[9]

Unfortunately, all local distortions are not as harmless as this one. If there are extra state funds for children with special needs, for instance, local authorities might be more liberal in deciding which children require special education. Similarly, districts compensated for the number of children in at-

---

[7]Steven J. Carrol, "The Search for Equity in School Finance," in Walter McMahon and Terry Geske (eds.), *Financing Education: Overcoming Inefficiency and Inequity* (Urbana, Ill.: U. of Illinois Press, 1982), pp. 238–239.

[8]Carrol, op. cit., p. 256.

[9]"It's a (6 to 8) Grand Old Flag," *Education Week*, February, 10, 1988, p. 3.

Liberal High School

tendance might decide not to suspend many discipline problems because each such suspension costs the district state funding. These examples illustrate that *finance policies can encourage fundamental distortions in the process of schooling*.

In the late 1970s the focus of state school support shifted to a new emphasis on **efficiency criteria**. Many states mandated minimum competency testing, and there were other efforts to link state aid to greater school efficiency through tax and expenditure limitation provisions.[10] Issues like school productivity—the relationship between school resources and student achievement—are becoming more and more important as efforts to relate data about student level performance over time to resource allocation are being used to draw both effectiveness and efficiency conclusions.[11]

Efficiency concerns involve attempts to balance the cost of government programs against their benefits. They also involve how these benefits are distributed. Efficiency concerns are particularly important because schooling is what economists call a **merit good**. Merit goods are services, like low income housing, considered so socially desirable that the government intervenes in the marketplace, makes a certain amount of it available, and then passes the costs on to taxpayers.[12] With this sort of arrangement, the marketplace does not penalize inefficiency in the normal manner.

A typical result of the various state efforts to equalize educational spending is illustrated in the graphs of Figures 16.3 and 16.4. The first shows the revenue sources of a middle income Philadelphia, Pennsylvania, suburban school dis-

---

[10]Terry Geske, "Educational Finance: Research Findings and Policy Implications," in Walter McMahon and Terry Geske (eds.), *Financing Education: Overcoming Inefficiency and Inequity* (Urbana, Ill.: U. of Illinois Press, 1982), pp. 324–325.
[11]Allen Odden, "State and Federal Pressures for Equity and Efficiency in Education Financing," in McMahon and Geske, op. cit., p. 319.
[12]Ralph T. Byrns and Gerald Stone, *Economics* (Glenview, Ill.: Scott, Foresman and Company, 1987), p. 627.

Figure 16.3 **A SUBURBAN SCHOOL DISTRICT'S REVENUE SOURCES**

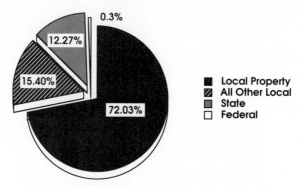

Source: Springfield School District Budget, 1988-1989

Figure 16.4 **AN URBAN SCHOOL DISTRICT'S REVENUE SOURCES**

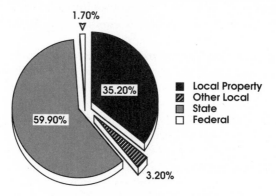

Source: School District of Philadelphia

POINT/COUNTERPOINT

Although there presently is a fairly broad consensus that schooling should be placed in the merit good category, the matter is by no means settled. Those who feel that parents may be too ignorant or selfish to adequately value schooling generally agree that merit good classification is a good idea because children will suffer otherwise. Because educational choices have very broad social consequences, if taxpayers fail to pay for it up front, they will end up paying even more in the end.

Advocates of consumer sovereignty, on the other hand, believe that neither of these considerations is sufficient to interfere with free market choice. They contend that schools should be paid for by those whose children use them in much the same way people buy homes or cars because exposure to market forces will force schools to be more efficient.

trict (Springfield, Montgomery County); the second shows the revenue sources of the urban School District of Philadelphia. We should note the suburban district's heavy reliance on local taxes, while the less affluent Philadelphia school district qualifies for more of Pennsylvania's equalizing plan money. We should also note the larger federal contribution to Philadelphia, and the great importance of the property tax in raising local school revenues in both communities.

Shifts in the economy, financial cycles, inflation, or natural disasters can imperil state school funds. In 1988, for example, a report released by the National Governor's Association and the National Association of State Budget Officers noted that states in the Northeast and Far West were enjoying steady growth in state revenues, but states in other regions of the country had been hurt by poor farm economies, and a downturn in energy prices.[13] The effects of the record-breaking drought of 1988 also affected the nation's midwestern states in fiscal 1989. In most cases these hard times influenced school funding. In North Dakota, for example, state school aid was reduced $55 per pupil after farmers there lost much of their wheat crop. Meanwhile, North Dakota school districts serving agricultural areas struggled for survival when many local farmers found it impossible to pay their school taxes because their crops had failed.[14]

The Local District's Role in Public School Finance

Local school districts still provide an average of almost 44 percent of the moneys spent on public elementary and secondary schools. Moreover, local school officials, working within fairly strict guidelines, are responsible for spending most federal and state, as well as all local, revenues. However, control follows money, and federal and state officials have established a whole host of regulations that local school officials must abide by. Judicial decisions at the state and local level add still other constraints on the fiscal actions of local boards.[15]

Many fear that the tradition of local control is being undermined by increases in state funding. Their opponents respond that schools have always been the legal responsibility of state government, and that there is no evidence to show that increases in state funding undermine the local district's autonomy.[16]

Whatever their autonomy, however, local school districts vary dramatically

---

[13]"Economic Shifts, Federal Aid Cuts Could Imperil States, Study Finds," *Education Week*, October 19, 1988.

[14]Nancy Mathis, "Farm States Begin to Feel Drought's Fiscal Impact," *Education Week*, October 5, 1988, p. 10.

[15]Lewis Guthrie, Walter Garms, and Lawrence Pierce, *School Finance and Education Policy: Enhancing Educational Efficiency, Equality and Choice*, 2nd ed. (Englewood Cliffs, N. J.: Prentice-Hall, 1988), pp. 187–189.

[16]Ibid., pp. 207–208.

in their ability to support public schooling. We have already noted the problems of big city schools. Rural areas like Appalachia are also chronically short of resources while long on problems. On the other hand, wealthy suburban districts have an abundance of resources and the fewest problems. In an upcoming section we explore these dimensions in detail.

The Particular Problems of the Cities

Although America's cities contain financial and banking institutions, museums and symphony orchestras, educational research and engineering facilities, and the world's finest medical centers, they also have a disproportionate number of the poor, many of whom live in acutely deteriorating neighborhoods and attend the nation's most troubled public schools. This situation has made urban life less attractive and encouraged millions of affluent Americans to move to the suburbs. Many of the more profitable businesses have fled there too. In the suburbs both individuals and corporations can enjoy the advantages and opportunities of urban living while simultaneously avoiding the problems.

We must remember that this process is self-reinforcing and cumulative. The migration of wealthier people and businesses to the suburbs seriously diminishes the city property tax base. This erosion, in turn, requires tax increases if services are to be maintained. These increases, or the deteriorating services that accompany their absence, encourage even more people to flee to the suburbs and the cycle repeats itself.

The net effect of all this, as far as schooling is concerned, is that big city school districts are presented with more and more impoverished students having ever more expensive educational needs, at the same time that their revenue sources are drying up. Thus, urban schools deteriorate while simultaneously becoming more and more dependent on federal and state aid.[17] In the meantime, suburban schools enjoy far more abundant financial resources.

THE SCHOOL REVENUE TAX BASE

In their early days public schools were supported, primarily at the local level, by all sorts of revenue-raising schemes. There were "rate-bills" or tuition taxes, state permanent funds that paid interest to the schools, and attempts to support schools through lotteries.[18] Today the mix of federal, state, and local taxes used to generate school revenues are more standardized. In what follows we will outline the major sources of school revenues. First, however, in order to provide a framework for intelligently appraising these sources, we summarize some general principles of taxation.

---

[17]Benjamin Chinitz (ed.), *City and Suburb* (Englewood Cliffs, N.J.: Prentice-Hall, 1964), pp. 23–27.

[18]H. Warren Button and Eugene Provenzo, Jr., *History of Education and Culture in America* (Englewood Cliffs, N.J.: Prentice-Hall, 1989), p. 79.

Some General Considerations Concerning Taxes

Some taxes are more effective than others.

Economists suggest four basic principles for measuring tax effectiveness. These are:

- **Certainty**—a tax should be unavoidable.
- **Convenience**—a tax should be easy to pay.
- **Economy**—a tax should be easy to collect.
- **Neutrality**—taxes should cause only income effects, not substitution effects. In other words, individuals should not change their behavior to avoid the tax; the only behavior change should be loss of spending power.

Two other principles also require consideration. Unlike certainty, convenience, economy, and neutrality, however, there is little consensus as to which of these principles should prevail.

- **Ability to Pay**—taxes should fall equally on those in equal circumstances.
- **Benefits Received**—taxes should be in proportion to the benefits people receive from government.

The **ability-to-pay principle** assumes that one's tax burden should be based on ability to support government activities. Two aspects of equity are involved in the ability-to-pay principle. First, there is **vertical equity**, which holds that a wealthy individual should pay more taxes than a poor one if each is to bear a fair portion of public costs. Such a tax is called **progressive**. Second, there is **horizontal equity**, which requires that equals be treated equally. For example, two individuals who live in homes of equal value should pay the same property tax.[19]

The alternative to the ability-to-pay principle of taxation is the **benefit principle of taxation**. This holds that taxes should be in proportion to the benefits people receive from government. In other words, individuals should pay for what they get.[20]

Which of these two principles should govern American tax policy is a function of values that go far beyond economics. Certainly, they suggest interesting alternatives for funding schools. If we advocate the benefit principle of taxation, for example, we might adopt something like the old New England rate fees. We could relate taxes to personal benefits by charging public school users fees that would operate in the same way that government charges bus fares and entry fees for public museums, zoos, or toll roads. We could even attempt to make this user tax roughly proportional to benefits in the same

---

[19]Ibid., p. 79.
[20]Byrns and Stone, op. cit., p. 629.

way that the fuel tax imposes a greater burden on owners of heavy trucks that wear out the roads more quickly than do fuel-efficient compact cars. If a child were particularly disruptive, for example, we could charge his or her parents extra for the same reason that big trucks pay high fuel taxes. If, on the other hand, a child practically taught himself or herself, the parental tax burden could be reduced to a level roughly equivalent to the fuel tax paid by the owner of a compact car.

Such user fees would eliminate the **free rider** problem where people enjoy the benefits of public schooling whether they pay school taxes or not. It would be a way to save elderly home owners on a fixed income from high property taxes. It might also be the best way to deal with the complaint of the millions of Americans who have their children in private schools that they are being forced to pay twice for their children's education.

Of course, user fees violate the ability-to-pay principle. They also fail to consider that the benefits derived from public schooling are not all highly divisible and do not go just to the student and his or her parents. It is evident, for example, that the retired couple living on a fixed income do receive benefits from the operation of the public schools. So do the parents who send their children to private schools. These benefits include a more durable democracy, a more vital national economy, fewer people on the dole, a more effective national defense, improved goods and services, reduced crime and social disruption, the use of school facilities for public functions, increased property values if the public schools in the community are good, and so forth. **The importance of these indivisible benefits demonstrates that even under the benefit principle of taxation, it makes sense to tax those who do not have any children in public schools.**

In point of fact, the American way of funding schooling is a pragmatic mixture of both the ability-to-pay principle and the benefits received principle. And, more than anything else, which way applies in any specific situation seems to be a function of which choice makes the fewest enemies.

The Public School Tax Base

Different taxes are used for public school finance by the three levels of government. These sources of tax revenue are critical because they determine the resources potentially available, and are either more or less vulnerable to public opinion, economic changes, and so forth.

Federal Taxes

The federal government relies heavily on personal and corporate income taxes for most of its revenue, including that spent on schools. The federal personal income tax produces more tax revenue than any other U.S. tax, and is also the most progressive.

The federal government is permitted to pass a budget that exceeds revenues rather than being required to raise taxes. Most states do not have this option.

Figure 16.5

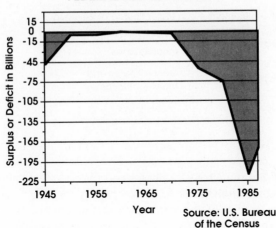

FEDERAL BUDGET DEFICIT

Source: U.S. Bureau
of the Census

Predictably, federal officials have taken advantage of this. Figure 16.5 illustrates
the trend.

State Taxes

State school revenues come from general state revenues. Recently, there has
been a shift in the origin of these revenues. In the 1920s state governments
depended upon motor fuel and vehicle licenses and property taxes for the
majority of their tax dollars. In the 1940s state sales taxes began to supplant
those sources. In more recent years, generally from the 1960s onward, there
has been a gradual shift to greater and greater reliance on state individual and
corporate income taxes. Nine states also earmark state lottery profits for
education. But they contribute only 3 percent to 7 percent of total school
revenues.[21]

Local Taxes

Local school districts depend on property taxes for an average 90 percent of
the revenue they raise.

The **personal income tax**, the chief source of federal school revenues and
much state school revenue, is relatively easy to avoid, particularly if an individual's income is not salaried. It is also inconvenient to pay, and expensive
to collect. In addition, it lacks neutrality, for individuals often change their
behavior to avoid the tax. It tends to discourage investment, work effort, and
other attempts to make income. It is designed with the ability-to-pay principle

[21]John F. Due, "Shifting Sources of Financing Education and the Taxpayer Revolt," in McMahon
and Geske, op. cit., p. 272.

Figure 16.6   **TAX REVENUES FOR SCHOOL FINANCE**

Branch of Government	Major Source of Revenue
Federal	Individual and Corporate Income Taxes
State	General Sales and Individual Income
Local	Property Tax

in mind, but numerous loopholes and the so-called "underground economy" permit some individuals to evade paying their fair share. There is one redeeming feature of the tax, however, which makes it an elected official's dream. The tax is **elastic**—that is, it provides ever-increasing revenues without increasing taxes. Not since World War II has there been a meaningful increase in federal income tax rates, yet the tax revenues continue to mount as incomes rise and put everyone in a higher tax bracket.[22]

The **sales tax**, another major source of state school revenue, is nearly unavoidable: easy to pay, easy to collect, and neutral. Its primary weakness is that it is *regressive*. Since the wealthy generally spend a smaller percentage of their income than do the poor, they end up paying a smaller percentage of their income in taxes than those who can least afford it. This violates the ability-to-pay principle.

The **property tax**, a principal source of public school revenues in almost every state (Hawaii and New Mexico are exceptions), has many shortcomings. Its full collection is not sure because of outdated, faulty or corrupt assessments. It is neither convenient to pay, nor economical to collect, since it requires an assessment process. The tax is not neutral, because it discourages property development or repair. It also violates the ability-to-pay principle because people in equivalent circumstances often do not pay the same taxes.

The poor and the retired can be particularly troubled by real estate taxes. The poor are penalized because they pay a larger share of their income in housing costs than do the wealthy. The retired are penalized because they often live on fixed incomes, but the assessed value of their homes often keeps rising. Although the poor usually suffer in silence, the retired are among the most vocal opponents of any increase in local school taxes. Their position often results in pitched school board election battles between enraged retirees and indignant parents of school age children. The central theme of the controversy concerns costs and benefits. The retirees, with no children of school age, complain that they are being taxed out of their homes. The parents countercharge that their children are being shortchanged by penny-pinchers who no longer care about schools because their children are grown.

---

[22]Guthrie, Garms, and Pierce, op. cit., pp. 186–189.

All of these disadvantages must be weighed against two major advantages. First, the tax generates large amounts of revenues. Second, it tends to be elastic in periods of prosperity, increasing in yield faster than the economy, but inelastic during a recession, decreasing in yield little if at all even if the recession is severe. Such **revenue resilience** makes it a very stable source of school finance.[23]

Considering One Alternative

The shortcomings of our present methods of funding schools suggests the need for reform. Fortunately, there are other ways of paying for public schools that might be more in accord with the principles of taxation just outlined.

The **value-added tax** (VAT) is one possibility that we will use as an example. Similar to the retail sales tax, the VAT is applied only to the difference between a firm's sales and the cost of materials and supplies used to produce the item. If, for example, a $1.00 loaf of bread requires $0.60 worth of wheat, yeast, and so forth, the value added by wages, interest, and profit is $0.40.[24] Only this amount would be taxed.

VATs are reasonably neutral and have a high degree of certainty. They are not, however, very convenient or economical because they require cumbersome accounting procedures. The tax is also largely hidden, the final customer usually being unaware of how much he or she is paying. Nevertheless, economists think that VATs are probably more efficient and less inequitable than a number of other taxes.[25]

A VAT could be used to replace all present methods for generating public school revenues. Public education would then be assured of its own independent revenue source and would no longer have to compete for funds with other public priorities such as national defense and road building. Now, particularly at the federal and state level, schools compete with other priorities for a share of general revenues.

Such a VAT would probably be collected at the national level. But we can imagine an equalizing plan whereby the federal government would not only collect it, but also share it with state and local government. Although such a procedure would worry those state and local officials who believe that control follows funding, it could be one way to reduce the present inequitable fragmentation of school finance.

Public Schooling and the Tragedy of the Commons

In England, everyone in a town or village could use a property held in common. But because it belonged to everyone, the "commons" was often treated

---

[23]Ibid., p. 122.

[24]Paul A. Samuelson and William D. Nordhaus, *Economics* (New York: McGraw-Hill, 1989), p. 984.

[25]Byrns, op. cit., p. 639.

as if no one owned it. With little personal incentive to maintain it and a great deal of rivalry for its use, it was overgrazed and generally neglected.

In some ways public schools are like the commons. Nonexclusion and rivalry for resources apply here too. These encourage a curious combination of overuse (all sorts of people want the public schools to do *their* thing), neglect, and abuse. And the abuser's costs are trivial unless and until they are caught. We should also not forget to consider that the farmer who abused the commons wanted to use it. The youngsters who abuse the educational commons would sometimes rather be almost anywhere else.

School Finance Inequalities

> The method of financing public schools in Texas, as in almost every other State, has resulted in a system of public education that can be fairly described as chaotic and unjust.
>
> —————— *Justice Potter Stewart,* San Antonio
> Independent School District v. Rodriguez, *1973*

Reliance on state and local revenue to support most of the public school budget results in inequality of educational opportunity throughout America. It discriminates against individuals who, irrespective of their personal incomes, happen to reside in relatively poor states or school districts and send their children to public school. It also tends to discriminate against the poor and minorities, because both are concentrated in revenue-poor areas.

The children of poor families are more likely to require expensive school services, such as special education or remedial reading; but they are likely to

Figure 16.7   **EXPLORING INTERSTATE SCHOOL INEQUALITIES**
(Comparing Selected States)

	Alabama	Connecticut	Mississippi	New York
Average Income (1987)	$11,780	$20,980	$10,204	$18,055
Retail Sales Per Capita (1986)	$4,726	$7,680	$4,657	$6,022
Tax Revenue Per Capita (1985)	$990	$1,816	$918	$2,334
Expenditures Per Student (1987)	$2,610	$5,552	$2,534	$6,229
% of State Budget Spent on Schooling (1985)	39%	24%	36%	24%

Different types of communities have different tax resources to pay for schools.

live in areas where school resources are meager. The children of more affluent families, on the other hand, require fewer of these expensive services; but they tend to live in areas that are resource rich. The net result of these differences is that the children who most need expensive educational services are often the least likely to get them.

Of course, it is an open question whether increasing expenditures in poor school districts is a cost-effective way of dealing with the effects of poverty, discrimination, and the like. As we learned in an earlier chapter, the educational deficits of this type of child may not be the result of putting them in school districts with lower per pupil expenditures. In fact, they do not reach the level of achievement obtained in other neighborhoods even when more money is spent on them.[26]

State to State Funding Inequalities

Great differences exist among the states in expenditures per public school pupil. There are also considerable differences among the states in their commitment to schooling as measured by per capita spending These are mapped in Figure 16.8.

"Wealthy" states—that is, states with high retail sales and high individual income—can raise large amounts of money for schools even if they have

---

[26]Thomas Sowell, *Race and Economics* (New York: Longman, 1975), p. 229.

Figure 16.8

1987 PER CAPITA SPENDING
PUBLIC ELEMENTARY
& SECONDARY SCHOOLS

$480 to $746
$746 to $1012
$1012 to $1277
$1277 to $1543
$1543 to $1809

comparatively low retail sales and individual income tax rates. However, "poor" states like Mississippi can charge higher sales and individual income tax rates and still not generate the same resources per pupil.

District to District Funding Inequalities

Expenditures per pupil vary widely from district to district within states just as they do from state to state. Since local school districts rely heavily on the property tax, enormous district to district differences in the value of real property generate fundamental inequalities. In many states the top 20 percent of property-wealthy school districts have a four to five times greater tax base per child than the bottom 20 percent. In 1974, for example, Joel Berke, an expert witness in a New York suit concerning school funding inequalities, testified that average real property wealth among New York State's school districts ranged from $8,884 to $412,370—a difference of over 4,600 percent![27] Such vast differences mean that property-wealthy districts end up with much greater school revenues per child, even when they tax at a lesser rate. Property-poor districts, by contrast, can tax property at much higher rates and still not make up the difference.[28]

"Wealthy" school districts contain valuable taxable properties, such as shopping centers, corporate headquarters, and highly valued residential properties. For instance, a school district may encompass an enormous shopping mall or the national headquarters of a Fortune 500 company. It might also

[27]Guthrie, op. cit., pp. 262–263.
[28]Ibid., p. 81.

incorporate swank suburbs like Greenwich, Connecticut, Mill Neck, New York, Alpine, New Jersey, or Saddle River, New Jersey, where average home prices are well over the one million dollar mark.[29] Such happy circumstances generate a great deal of school revenue at comparatively low tax rates. In contrast, a "poor" district, such as Newark, or Jersey City, New Jersey, filled with abandoned factories and vast expanses of deteriorating slums, can impose high property tax rates and still never hope to match the "wealthy" district's income.

As a further complication, in comparison to students in "poor" districts, students attending schools in "wealthy" districts tend to have less interest in highly expensive vocational education and require fewer special services. Thus the districts in most urgent need of extra school revenue are the least likely to have it.

This sort of inequity resulted in the famous California supreme court decision in *Serrano v. Priest*, (1967). When John Serrano, the father of a Los Angeles area public school student, complained about the lack of instructional services in his son's school, the principal told him that he should consider moving to an adjacent property-rich school district because they could afford better services. Citing the dramatic disparities existing in the California school finance system, Serrano brought suit against state education officials, arguing that schooling is a "fundamental interest" that cannot be conditioned on wealth.

California school-funding inequalities were outlined for the court. Differences in district tax bases were shown to yield differences on the order of 10,000 to 1 in ability to support local school programs.[30] For example, in 1968–1969, Beverly Hills School District, with property wealth of more than $50,000 per pupil, was able to spend $1,232 per pupil even though they taxed real estate at only $2.38 per thousand dollars of assessed value. Nearby Baldwin Park had a property wealth of only $3,706 per pupil; even though it taxed real estate at the rate of $5.48 per thousand, the district was able to spend only $577 per pupil. State aid canceled out some of this difference. Nevertheless, Beverly Hills was still able to spend over one-third more per child.[31]

The California supreme court held in Serrano's favor. They ruled that the California constitution forbade such discrimination in the delivery of school services, and ordered state officials to reform California's school financing arrangements.

Following Serrano, cases filed in many states challenged the state constitutionality of local funding arrangements. They met with a variety of results that only partially changed the basic situation.[32] In some states, particularly those whose constitutions clearly indicated schooling as a fundamental inter-

---

[29]Source: Relo Broker Network.
[30]Richard Strahan and L. Charles Turner, *The Courts and the Schools* (White Plains, N.Y.: Longman, 1987), p. 254.
[31]Ibid., pp. 40–41.
[32]Ibid.

est, state courts held that equal protection required equal funding. In other states, the courts ruled that the state legislature had authority to use local schemes for funding schools even if this practice did result in school finance inequalities.[33]

The U.S. court system also became involved in a dispute about finance inequalities. Recall from Chapter 15 that in *San Antonio Independent School District v. Rodriguez* (1973), the U.S. Supreme Court overturned a federal district court ruling that school finance inequalities violated the U.S. Constitution's equal protection clause. The Court ruled that in the absence of a specific constitutional reference, schooling did not constitute a "fundamental right."[34] Also, in *Kadrmas v. Dickenson Public Schools* (1988), the justices ruled that schooling is not ". . . a 'fundamental right' that triggers strict scrutiny when government interferes with an individual's access to it." These decisions effectively ruled out using the U.S. Constitution to enforce the equalization of school financing.

State governments have considerable unused intrastate school finance equalization power, even at current funding levels. The various plans intended to promote intrastate equality are unsuccessful primarily because state funds are not a sufficiently large percentage of total funds. If state revenues provide a large percentage of total funds, as they tend to in the South, there is a greater equalizing effect even if the funds are distributed in flat grants keyed only to the number of children enrolled.[35]

Is Equality of School Funding Possible?

It is possible to equalize per pupil public school funding, but because of great intrastate differences in income and the value of real property, the present delegation of school taxing authority to local school districts virtually ensures major school funding inequalities. Even if finance were shifted entirely to the states, differences in their resources would still ensure that nationally some students would have more spent on their education than would others.

Probably the only way to equalize the public school finance base involves massive funding at the national level. Only the federal government has a sufficiently broad tax base to cancel out differences in state or local taxable wealth. The current small percentage of school funds derived from federal programs helps minimize school funding inequalities. But present federal school legislation is not designed to do this directly, even though it often does it indirectly. A good example is Title I of the Elementary and Secondary Education Act of 1965. Though the direct intent of Title I is to systematically aid poor children, relatively poor states or school districts still end up with more federal dollars. For instance, Mississippi, a poor state, gets 16 percent

---

[33]Strahan, op. cit., p. 259.
[34]Ibid., pp. 197–198.
[35]Steven Michelson, "The Political Economy of Public School Finance," in Martin Carnoy, *Schooling in a Corporate Society* (New York: David McKay, 1972), pp. 162–163.

of all its school revenues from the federal government, while comparatively wealthy Connecticut gets only 4 percent.[36]

Numerous plans for equalization of school financing have been proposed. All presuppose that roughly similar amounts per pupil should be expended by each state and that the federal treasury would be used to balance accounts. However, given the present federal deficit and the priorities of the Bush administration, it seems unlikely that any school finance equalization legislation will be enacted in the foreseeable future. The likely appointment of more strict constructionists to the Supreme Court also suggests that federal suits alleging that school finance inequities violate the equal protection clause of the Federal Constitution will continue to be unsuccessful.

Is Equality of School Funding Desirable?

In *Brown v. Board of Education, Topeka,* Chief Justice Warren commented:

> In these days it is doubtful that any child may be reasonably expected to succeed in life if he is denied the opportunity of an education. Such an opportunity, where the state has undertaken to provide it, is a right which must be made available to all on equal terms.

Although in *Rodriguez* the Court did not find schooling a "fundamental right" protected by the federal Constitution, if Justice Warren's observation is correct, it certainly makes a compelling case for equal school funding. There are, however, those who argue that differences in school funding are as much a function of state and local officials' willingness to pay, as it is the availability of tax resources. For instance, when researcher William Hartman studied the inequality of per pupil spending in Pennsylvania he discovered that although high-spending districts had a better tax base than did low-spending districts, they also averaged higher tax rates for schools. Hartman concluded that "People in these [high spending] districts place a higher value on education and are willing to tax themselves at a higher rate for their children."[37] The question arises as to whether present differences in school support may be as much a function of choice as of necessity.

THE TAXPAYER'S REVOLT

There is evidence that taxpayers in some areas are becoming increasingly dissatisfied with the cost of government. And, although polls show that public schools are often among the last services that voters want cut, antitax

---

[36]U.S. Department of Commerce, Bureau of the Census, *Statistical Abstract of the United States, 1988* (Washington, D.C.: U.S. Government Printing Office, 1988), p. 132.

[37]David Martin, "Study Links Wealth, School Spending," *Philadelphia Daily News,* June 22, 1988, p. 7B.

measures often hit them hardest.[38] For example, the tax and expenditure limitation measures approved in a number of states have proved to be particularly tough on public schooling. The most famous instance is California's Proposition 13. Its approval in 1978 drastically reduced property taxes and made state and local tax increases far more difficult. These changes, in turn, substantially reduced school revenues.[39]

The taxpayer's revolt hits public schooling particularly hard in those states that require local school levies and/or bond issues to be approved by the voters. Ohio is a case in point. That state's 738 school districts submit their operating levies to the voters every year. And, in the current antitax climate, about half of them fail. Indeed, during a special election in the summer of 1988 only fourteen of seventy levy proposals were passed, the lowest approval rate in thirteen years.[40]

Voter rejection of these levies, coupled with small increases in state aid, subsequently forced a record number of Ohio school districts to seek help from the state's emergency "bail out" loan fund. In the meantime, districts are forced to lay off teachers, eliminate athletics as well as other extracurricular activities, and shelve plans for badly needed school repairs.[41]

Some claim that taxpayer revolts of this type signify a major turning point in the public's support for schooling. Certainly taxpayer revolts in a number of states have had a great impact on local school districts. But it does not necessarily follow that the nation's broad, if shallow, consensus in support of public schooling is collapsing. Indeed, there is evidence that taxpayer support for school spending is on the rise. In late 1988, for example, California voters approved Proposition 98, a measure giving public schools and community colleges hundreds of millions of dollars in additional state revenues and modifying the state's constitution in order to guarantee that a fixed percentage of all future state budgets will be set aside for schools.[42]

Similarly, in 1989, voters in the state of Washington handed their lawmakers a petition demanding that they come up with the revenues necessary to *increase* school funding and social programs for children. Known as the Children's Initiative, the petition was signed by more than 219,000 voters—far more than the 151,000 needed to put the measure before state legislators. The state's superintendent of public instruction supports the measure, and its enthusiastic endorsement by so many citizens puts strong pressure on legislators to pass it.[43]

---

[38]John F. Due, "Shifting Sources of Financing Education," in Walter McMahon and Terry Geske (eds.), *Financing Education: Overcoming Inefficiency and Inequity* (Urbana, Ill.: U. of Illinois Press, 1982), pp. 283.

[39]Ibid.

[40]Nancy Mathis, "Lottery Misconceptions Making Long Odds on School Tax Votes," *Education Week*, October 19, 1988, p. 1.

[41]Lisa Jennings, "38 Ohio Districts Seek Help From State 'Bail Out' Funds," *Education Week*, October 19, 1988, p. 12.

[42]Richard Colvin, "California Voters Back 'Guarantee' for School Funding in Constitution," *Education Week*, November 16, 1988, p. 1.

[43]Lisa Jennings, "Washington State Petitioners Demand 'Children's Initiative'," *Education Week*, February 8, 1989, p. 10.

This sort of support explains why in the late 1980s, many candidates for political office discovered that good education can be good politics. George Bush, who wants to be remembered as the "Education President," is the most obvious example. But the governors of a number of states, individuals such as James Hunt of North Carolina, Tom Kean of New Jersey, Bill Clinton of Arkansas, Madeleine Kunin of Vermont, Rudy Perpich of Minnesota, and Lamar Alexander of Tennessee were able to raise political capital through their support for schooling.

The "taxpayer's revolt" is at least partially provoked by unfair methods of public school finance. Returning to the Ohio example, the governor's special tax reform panel describes that state's system of school funding as "archaic and inequitable." The panel and three different state legislative committees are attempting to hammer out reforms. In the meantime, spending per pupil among Ohio school districts ranges from a low of $2,280 to more than $10,000.[44]

The widespread rejection of school levies and bond issues also reflects the shortcomings of simple majority rule in deciding such matters. Unlike shopping, where intensities of preference are easily registered in the marketplace, such referenda permit only a simple "Yes" or "No" vote. You can buy many more pairs of a particular brand of socks if you really liked the first pair, but even if you really want your local school bond issue to be approved, you can vote "Yes" only once. In fact, your vote can very well be offset by someone who votes "No" just because the city keeps failing to pick up his trash. For this reason, tax or bond referenda are inefficient and often result in higher costs to the losers than benefits to the winners.[45]

Escalating "Bricks-and-Mortar" Costs

One consequence of the taxpayer's revolt and the new emphasis on instructional priorities is that many of the nation's school buildings are in bad shape. Asbestos abatement, new roofs, upgraded electrical systems and other physical improvements have often been put off, and then put off again. For example, a national survey completed in 1989 revealed that rural and small schools enrolling fewer than 800 students had an average $300,000 in deferred-maintenance needs. In Wisconsin deferred school maintenance resulted in a series of newspaper articles highlighting unsafe conditions. This sparked state safety inspections and calls for more state aid.[46]

Similarly, many districts have also delayed new construction to the point where schools have become badly overcrowded. School finance experts observe that capital construction projects have traditionally been paid for by local districts—usually by having them underwritten by local bond issues approved by voters. Predictably, voters angry about high taxes have been

---

[44]Ibid.

[45]Byrns, op. cit., pp. 646–647.

[46]Nancy Mathis, "Escalating 'Bricks-and-Mortar' Cost: The Problem Nobody Wants," *Education Week*, March 1, 1989, p. 1.

Weeds and graffiti mar the entrance to Philadelphia's prestigious Central High School. Scenes such as this are all too common across the nation.

downing these bond issues with increasing frequency. Property-poor local districts are particularly hard-hit.[47]

Presently, only three states—Alaska, California, and Hawaii—fully fund school construction projects. Seven others have loan programs. Recent court cases concerning school finance promise more state involvement. But in the meantime a lot of local districts still have to cope with severe overcrowding. Many have been turning to alternative methods of financing construction. Lease-purchase arrangements are particularly popular: under this arrangement private investors construct the building and equip it. The school district then leases back the facility under a long-term contract. The arrangement permits paying for the lease directly out of general funds, and eliminates the necessity of going to the voters for approval to sell bonds.[48]

FINANCE AS A GOAD FOR REFORM

In recent years there has been a growing effort to use school finance measures as a way of encouraging reform. These efforts take two forms. First, there are **direct efforts** to use funding, usually state funding, as the reward for school improvements. Second, there are numerous proposals to allow parents the opportunity to shop for their children's schooling. These proposals include **choice plans**, whereby parents can select from the public schools of their

---

[47]Ibid.
[48]Ibid.

district or state, and **voucher plans**, which permit the inclusion of private schools in the choice pool. Both of these rely on linking school finance to market forces in order to encourage reform.

Direct Efforts

For quite some time, the federal government has used school finance, in the form of categorical grants, to encourage state and local school reforms. In the Reagan years, federal initiatives of this type gave way to block grants. However, there are signs that the Bush administration may give considerable emphasis to using school finance to hold schools and districts accountable for student performance. For instance, President Bush's 1990 education budget proposal included $250 million for a new Merit Schools program. Intended to reward schools that demonstrate educational improvement, the program, whose funding would gradually increase to half a billion dollars each year, places a special emphasis on schools enrolling many disadvantaged students.[49]

Accountability has become a hot issue in state legislatures. Frequently, state officials will approve proposed increases in school spending only if they are assured that the state will get a good return on its investment.[50] A number of states have also announced plans to financially reward school districts that meet certain state-specified reform objectives. For instance, Texas Governor William Clements recently announced a plan to reward school districts that improve pupil performance, combat drug and alcohol abuse, and reduce their dropout rate. The plan would also reduce state funds for districts that did not cut their dropout rate. The Governor's proposed "Educational Excellence Program for Texas," would have an initial $30 million to hand out for school improvement—a small fraction of the $13.8 billion state-spending level proposed for Texas schools for fiscal years 1990 and 1991.[51]

Given this new climate that links performance to finance, school districts can even end up being graded locally by their own constituents before they get needed cash. In Detroit, for example, where the public schools are facing a large deficit, school officials are asking the public to approve a $160 million bond issue to eliminate the shortfall. But poor student achievement has eroded public support for such an initiative. Therefore, the school board has agreed to have Detroit's schools graded once a month by an independent citizen's education committee in return for that committee's support for the bond referendum. They hope that the monthly "report cards" will allay concerns that the school system is wasting the money it now receives.[52]

---

[49]Robert Rothman, "E.D. Creates a 'CAT Scan' to Help States Assess Schools," *Education Week*, October 5, 1988.
[50]Ibid.
[51]William Snider, "Texas: 39 Million Sought for Reform Efforts," *Education Week*, February 8, 1988, p. 10.
[52]"Citizens to 'Grade' Detroit Schools in Return for Bond-Issue Support," *Education Week*, November 2, 1988, p. 2.

Choice Plans

Parental opportunity to choose schools within their home school districts has been gaining in popularity for a number of years. During the Reagan years, Secretary of Education William Bennett repeatedly hammered at the idea of choice as a key issue in school reform. School districts in at least 15 states now permit local districts to offer choices among their schools.[53] Historically, many districts have offered parents and students options, in the form of magnet, alternative, or special purpose schools, as a part of their voluntary desegregation plans. Today the concept is being expanded to encourage better school performance through a free public school market mechanism. The idea is to apply the principles of the marketplace to public elementary and secondary schools. Just as businesses compete for customers, so schools compete for students and their tuition.

Districtwide open enrollment programs have thus far met with mixed success. A number of school districts in Massachusetts have adopted "controlled choice" plans that seem to be working. Other districts, such as that of Little Rock, Arkansas, have adopted plans which turned out to be disastrous. A chief stumbling block appears to be the reluctance of white parents to have their children bused from the suburbs to city schools.[54]

Despite the uneven success of districtwide open enrollment, Minnesota recently applied this concept of finance-based school reform statewide. State legislators adopted a school finance pilot program allowing parents to send their children to any school they choose within the state. By 1990 all Minnesota students will have the option of either remaining in their neighborhood school, or transferring to any other public school in the state. Students may apply to attend school in any other district and up to $4,000 in state-provided tuition money goes with them. And if a school finds itself without students, Minnesota Governor Rudy Perpich states, "... it will file for 'bankruptcy' like any other business."[55]

This radical expansion of educational consumerism wins the plaudits of many. The top members of America's corporate community are particularly enthusiastic. For instance, David Kearns, chairman of Xerox Corporation, believes that "Public schools acting as monopolies are failing. Providing choice means allowing schools to compete with one another for the most valuable of assets: students."[56]

Critics are less optimistic. They point out that some students might be considered liabilities rather than assets, and claim that choice plans may only make strong schools stronger while totally enfeebling weaker ones. There is also a concern that the plan would be unfair to inner city schools. (Governor Michael Dukakis vetoed Massachusetts' prototype choice plan for that reason.)

---

[53]Connie Leslie, "Giving Parents a Choice," *Newsweek*, September 19, 1988, p. 77.
[54]Ibid., p. 78.
[55]Jill Rachlin, "When Parents and Students Give the Grades," *U.S. News and World Report*, September 12, 1988, pp. 60–61.
[56]Quoted in Leslie, op. cit., p. 77.

There are, in addition, practical questions relating to administration. How are school boards to engage in long-range planning without knowing how many students the district will serve in a given year? Would popular schools be able to pick and choose only those students they wanted? Would transportation become prohibitively expensive? If parents were forced to pick up transportation expenses, would only affluent parents really have a choice?

Minnesota's plan addresses some of these concerns. School districts must select students solely on a space available basis. Students can be rejected only because of overcrowding, and out-of-district transportation costs are picked up by the state if the income of the child's parents is below the poverty line.

Voucher Plans

In their purest form voucher plans would completely dismantle the present system of publicly operated schools. Instead, governments would require a minimum level of schooling which would be financed by providing parents with vouchers redeemable for a specific sum at any "approved" school.

Parents would use these vouchers to shop for schools. If they were able, they could "spend" not only the voucher, but whatever additional sum they could afford, to purchase educational services. These services would be provided by for-profit businesses, or by nonprofit institutions. The role of the government would be limited to establishing minimal standards, such as the inclusion of certain content, and ensuring acceptable sanitary standards.[57]

Proponents of the voucher plan argue that it would be even better than choice plans in opening schooling to the efficiency-inducing breezes of the marketplace. Teachers' salaries, for example, would become more responsive to these forces. A healthier variety of educational services would also become available.

Critics respond that vouchers would encourage even greater class and racial segregation of America than presently exists. And their greatest concern is that Horace Mann's partially unfulfilled vision of a common school/common experience uniting all Americans will be replaced by a free market economy that encourages destructive levels of dissensus. There is also a question about using vouchers for tuition at schools sponsored by religious organizations. It is possible that this application would be regarded by the Supreme Court as a violation of the U.S. Constitution.

The G.I. Bill, versions of which have provided education and vocational training to hundreds of thousands of veterans, is the equivalent of a voucher plan for postsecondary education. In general, this plan has worked well, though there have been serious problems with the private for-profit schools that spring up just to educate veterans.[58]

The voucher plan has never actually been tried at the secondary or ele-

---

[57]Milton Friedman, "The Role of Government in Education," in *Economics and the Public Interest* (New Brunswick, N.J.: Rutgers U. Press, 1955), Robert A. Solo, ed., p. 200.
[58]Lewis Guthrie, op cit., p. 156.

mentary school level. The U.S. Office of Economic Opportunity and the U.S. Office of Education did attempt a limited experiment in Alum Rock School District in California which involved no private schools. It ended inconclusively.[59] Former President Reagan and his Secretary of Education William Bennett also failed in their attempt to implement a voucher plan that would have resulted in a substantial shift of educational services to the private, nonprofit sector. And while George Bush pledges full support for choice, he has carefully avoided any mention of extending choice to private schools.

Tuition Tax Credits

The idea has also been advanced that parents should be given a tuition tax credit equal to either all or a portion of their children's private school tuition. The idea is to expand parental choice and simultaneously encourage greater school efficiency through competition. As an example of a hypothetical federal full tuition tax credit, if a family owed $15,000 in federal income tax and also paid $10,000 tuition to send their children to private school, their tax bill would be lowered to just $5,000. Of course, plans giving families half credit, one-third credit, and so forth could also be devised.

The Reagan administration proposed a federal tuition tax credit plan for the nation. However, enormous federal deficits made the plan unattractive. Previously, in 1979, the House of Representatives actually passed a tuition tax credit bill. But Jimmy Carter's threatened veto was sufficient to kill the proposal in the Senate.[60]

---

[59]Ibid.
[60]Ibid., p. 174.

Would tuition tax credit plans that included religious schools be seen by federal courts as unconstitutional?

Would tuition tax credit plans that included religious schools be seen by federal courts as unconstitutional? Probably not. Although it is unconstitutional to directly support religious instruction, the Supreme Court's five-to-four decision in *Mueller v. Allen* (1983), upheld a Minnesota law providing for a **tax deduction** of up to $700 per student for "tuition, textbooks and transportation," which applied to all parents of school children even if they attended public school. In the majority opinion Justice Rehnquist found that Minnesota's legislation supported legitimate secular purposes including:

■ **ensuring that the state's citizenry is well educated**
■ **assuring the continued financial health of private schools**
■ **encouraging wholesome competition with our public schools**

A majority of the High Court concluded that because the Minnesota law includes parents whose children attend public schools, it does not have "the primary effect of advancing the sectarian aims of the nonpublic schools."[61]

SUMMARY

1. State government bears the chief financial burden for public school finance using sales tax and personal income taxes as the chief sources of revenue. However, local school districts come in a close second, and their chief source of income is the property tax. The federal government comes in a distant third, and the revenue for this comes primarily out of individual and corporate income taxes.

2. There are basic principles of taxation that can help us examine public school revenue sources. The Value Added Tax is one alternative tax base for schools. "Tragedy of the Commons" is useful in understanding issues relating to public school finance.

3. There are interstate and intrastate inequalities in school funding. Recently there has been a "Taxpayers Revolt," that is having an impact on school finance. School reforms could be accomplished through school finance by, among other things, encouraging choice.

QUESTIONS

1. What level of government pays most of America's school bill today? What level of government paid it in 1930?
2. How did the federal share of the school finance burden change during the Reagan years?

---

[61]Michael La Morte, *School Law: Cases and Concepts* (Englewood Cliffs, N. J.: Prentice Hall, 1987), p. 71.

3. What is the difference between categorical grants and block grants, and which was encouraged by the Federal Education Consolidation and Improvement Act of 1981?

4. Compare the income tax and the property tax as a source of school funds using the principles of taxation. Which is better and why?

5. Economists consider schooling to be a "merit good," that is, it is so socially desirable that the government makes a certain amount of it compulsory. List three other examples of services or goods that you consider merit goods. Would you rank any of these above schooling? If so, why? If not, why not?

6. Some economists hold that the ability-to-pay and benefit principles of taxation are not totally incompatible. Suggest a way of at least partially reconciling them?

7. The property tax enjoys "revenue resilience." Explain what this means.

8. Use the "powerholder"/"stakeholder" distinction to explain the persistence of school finance inequalities. How does William Hartman's research, cited in this chapter, affect your conclusions?

9. Consider the socioeducational system described in Chapter 6. Do you think that proposals to use finance as a goad for reform are realistic?

10. How does a voucher plan differ from a tuition tax credit? Does that difference mean the voucher plan is more or less likely to run into problems with the First Amendment? Why?

Section VI

Schooling Practice

Curriculum, Learning, and Teaching

The reconstruction of perception is the goal of criticism.
—————————————— *Elliot Eisner,* The Educational Imagination.[1]

The curriculum determines learning and teaching. What should be taught has historically determined what was to be learned and how it was to be taught. Our analysis of consensus, given in Chapter 2, would hardly have us expect differently. It is far easier to agree on the general, overarching goals of schooling, than to come to a consensus on the specifics of the nature of learning and the modes of teaching. These are, at best, afterthoughts in the practice of schooling.

What should be taught? An overwhelming variety of possible curricular items is found to be very differentially selected according to a variety of concerns. Stakeholders in the curriculum invoke different structures of knowledge, as well as different concerns for outcomes in the attempt to establish their authority over the curriculum. The nature of the curriculum depends upon the expectation models of the school: Temple, Factory, Town Meeting.

---

[1]Elliot Eisner, *The Educational Imagination,* p. 191.

THE FOUNDATIONS of CURRICULUM

Chapter 17

... Whether they attempt to preserve or reshape society, curriculum policymakers are inescapably involved in a political act, for their positions will have some bearing upon who gets what, when and how now and in the future.

_____ William Lowe Boyd[1]

PREVIEW

In this chapter we will address the critical question "What should be taught?" We will see that our answers depend on our image of the school. A variety of interests have brought about the scope and sequence of subject matter that is the present school curriculum. The medieval trivium, rhetoric, logic, and grammar, once vocational training for the few, has evolved into today's academics for the many. Conceptions of human nature, of society and of the good have contributed to this curriculum. So, too, have the very practical concerns of many interested parties.

We will learn that curricula of different kinds represent different value choices. Just as policy and implementation can vary widely, so, too, can the subject matter actually taught vary from that proposed. We will also look at the way knowledge is transformed into a commodity, a "thing" that can be parceled out and exchanged in a market. The commodification of knowledge, the disciplines as we recognize them, and the nature of the curriculum are intimately related.

WHAT SHOULD BE TAUGHT?

As things are, there is disagreement about the subjects. For mankind are by no means agreed about the things to be taught, whether we look to virtue or the best life.

_____ Aristotle

Surely, some progress has been made since the time of Aristotle. It seems there is broad agreement about which subjects schools should teach. Anyone examining the curriculum documents of the different U. S. states will see that they are amazingly uniform. In many places the curriculum of private schools is hardly distinguishable from that of the public schools. Certainly, that lack of consensus that Aristotle bemoaned has been remedied. Or has it?

_____

[1]William Lowe Boyd "The Politics of Curriculum Change and Stability," *Educational Research,* Vol. 8, No. 2 (February 1979), pp. 12–18, in Baldridge and Deal.

We might wonder about the great classroom-to-classroom variation in subject matter that John Goodlad reports.[2] History in one classroom may not be History in another. Course titles may have as little to say about course content as reform slogans have to say about results. Perhaps this is the reason for recurring concern about the lack of knowledge of American students. In 1985, for example, a panel of nine prominent educators[3] was concerned enough to advise the National Institute of Education to cut back on research on the cognitive development of students so that it should devote a greater percentage of its dollars to define a common core of knowledge for American students. If there really were broad agreement on what is to be taught, such a recommendation would make no sense.

We see that the curriculum which, at first glance, looks so standard actually lacks uniformity and is the source of much educational controversy. And the nature of that controversy is greatly illuminated when the concerns and choices underlying it are brought to the surface.

To get an idea of the breadth of choices we face, let's look at the following categories of possible curriculum items. In going over these categories, we should ask why the different items are where they are. By what process did they end up in one category rather than another?

- **things previously, but no longer, generally taught in public schools**: Bible; computation of cube roots; Grimm's fairy tales; Aesop's fables; solid geometry; Rudyard Kipling's poems; Longfellow's poetry; the Iliad; the Odyssey; use of the slide rule; Robert's Rules of order; Latin; Greek; Greek mythology; rhetoric; geography; logic; logarithmic extrapolation
- **things not previously taught but now taught in public schools**: laws of association, commutation, and distribution; computer literacy; space science; plate tectonics; elementary functions, "pre-calculus"; World Cultures; substance abuse education; human sexuality; AIDS prevention
- **things still taught but rarely used outside of school**: long division; computation of square roots; synthetic division; formal grammar
- **things generally useful but not taught in "status", e.g., college preparatory, curricula**: auto maintenance; child care; cooking; woodwork; stenography and typing; filing; bookkeeping
- **things not generally taught in the public schools, but useful**: basic law; home maintenance; stock market analysis; basic organizational skills; political activism; income tax preparation; gardening; and library science

How can we explain why some things are taught; others, not? We will see that a great variety of factors influenced this arrangement of curricular items.

---

[2] Cf. John Goodlad, *A Place Called School*, pp. 132–138.
[3] "Researchers Urge E.D. Effort to Define 'Common Core,'" *Education Week*, April 24, 1985, p. 9.

A few of these factors are technical obsolescence, status concerns, the power of special interest groups, beliefs about child development, moral concerns, and organizational priorities.

What's the Situation? An Overwhelming Variety

There are many things that can be taught but only so much time, energy, and money to teach them. How can we work at a consensus on what should be taught?

This question refers us to what many consider the basis of curricular choice, that is, **goals**. Because goals can help us restrict our choices, it seems reasonable to hope that whatever curriculum develops, it would be a means to specific ends.

Perceived and Preferred Goals of the Public

In *A Place Called School* John Goodlad makes an intensive study of existing school goals. He identifies four kinds found in documents from different sources.[4] These goals, which we will call **public goals**, could each be a source of elements in the school curriculum. They include:

- **social, civic, and cultural goals**: for example, interpersonal understandings and citizenship participation;
- **intellectual goals**: academic knowledge and intellectual skills;
- **personal goals**: emotional and physical well-being, creativity and aesthetic expression, and self-realization; and
- **vocational goals**: preparation for an occupation.

Should the school emphasize the four kinds of goals—social, intellectual, personal and vocational—equally? How would we determine this equality of emphasis? And in case of conflict, what takes priority, personal over intellectual, vocational over social? Or the reverse?

Goals can help us restrict our choices. What we find, however, is that there is a substantial difference between the mix of goals that students, teachers, and parents perceive in their schools and the mix of goals each would prefer. In general, the Goodlad study found that perceived intellectual goals far exceed preferences; whereas, perceived personal goals do not meet preferred levels.[5]

Why is it that the perceived goals in Goodlad's study do not express the preferences, not even in some consensual way, of the major stakeholders? The obvious answer is that the people we want to consider to be the primary

---

[4]Goodlad, op. cit., pp. 50–56. Goodlad does not address the issue as to what kind of consensus exists to support the implementation of these goals.
[5]Ibid., pp. 62–69.

stakeholders—the students, parents, and teachers—are not the powerholders in the process of formulating public goals for the schools.

Organizational Structure and Goal Incongruity

There is in addition to goals the matter of curricular implementation within the school organization. We have to translate our goals into tasks backed up by necessary resources. Failure to do so means that school outcomes will not match goals.

Chapters 8 and 9 showed that in all organizations discrepancies frequently arise between goals and outcomes. We should recall that these can be explained in a variety of ways, depending on the implementation model of the school invoked:

- **systems management model:** a lapse in planning, specification or control; for example, curricular goal incongruence reflects bad administration.
- **bureaucratic model:** failure to change routines to reflect goals; or the existence of lower level delivery problems; for example, curricular goal incongruence is a matter of poor or off-target teaching, or lack of supplies.
- **organizational development model:** lack of consensus and commitment among implementers; for example, curricular goal incongruence occurs because people are not committed to certain goals.
- **conflict and bargaining model:** no unit has the power to impose its goals on the others; for example, curricular goal incongruence results when strong and different interests vie for instructional time.

We can also refer to the basic organizational conflicts discussed in Chapter 8, for a curricular counterpart. Chart 17.1 recasts these conflicts with relevant curriculum examples.

Chart 17.1

BASIC CURRICULAR CONFLICTS

conflict	curriculum—relevant examples
following policy vs. sensitivity	Teaching a Standard Curriculum vs. Meeting the Pupils at Their Level
delegating authority vs. authorized goals	Teacher Variation vs. Strict Adherence to Curriculum
process vs. product	Teaching for the Experience vs. Teaching to the Test
power vs. morale	Teacher—Proof Curriculum vs. Teacher-Generated Curriculum

Whom Does It Concern? Stakeholders in the Curriculum

Even if goals are matched to curriculum, the concerns of the stakeholders turn out to be a major determinant of what is taught. Let's look at this more closely. In the sections to follow we will identify groups of stakeholders and consider what kinds of concerns motivate them to lay claim to the curriculum.

What are the concerns of the different stakeholders? We can expect to find a variety of concerns for each stakeholder group. We can also expect that there will be conflicts among these concerns that may not be perceived by those who desire them.

- **Students** want interesting classes; as they get older they want to deal with things they feel are relevant to a future free of the major problems of life, such as poverty and ill-health. For example, they may wish to study things that get them into the university, if they see this as a stepping stone to future success. They may also want to develop relationships with others that help address concerns about their identity and the value of living. Some simply want any kind of curriculum that will allow them to pursue their own private agendas.

- **Parents** want their children to be well cared for and taught things they, the parents, esteem. They want the school to teach the students what they, the parents, believe prepares them for the future. Most prefer this to be done in a stimulating and congenial atmosphere. Parents would also like to be esteemed for what their children do and become.

- **Teachers** want to enjoy teaching and watching their students develop interests and skills in and esteem for what they, as teachers, esteem. Teachers also want to work at discovering and codifying the effective practices of their profession. They want to enjoy the esteem of their peers. Teachers often belong to subject matter interest groups that pursue their own goals of securing and enhancing their particular disciplines within the curriculum.

- **Administrators** want to believe they have been instrumental in bringing about school outcomes they esteem. (Recall Chapter 2.) Although their relationship with students is often indirect, their concern is nonetheless real. Administrators tend to have a bigger stake in public and peer esteem: unlike parents, students, and teachers, their professional future is more dependent upon such esteem. Administrators tend to be more career-oriented than teachers because they are generally not protected by tenure rules and are more removed from the substantial interpersonal rewards—and pains—that close interaction with students provides.

- **School board members**, because they are not paid for their efforts, tend either to represent outside interest groups, or to pursue **rela-**

Stakeholders in the
curriculum.

tively indivisible benefits through their participation. There is often a sense of *noblesse oblige* in that board members come from more comfortable backgrounds than other members of their districts and see their board membership as a kind of public service. Board membership can also encompass a great deal of personal satisfaction and community esteem.

■ **Outside interest groups** may have concerns that vary in the pursuit from divisible to indivisible, from positional to absolute benefits. The most important of these for understanding the curriculum of the public schools, are the colleges and universities and interest groups within them, the subject-matter interest groups, and certain political and moral movements in our society. In the average American community, many different groups will be found to have a curricular agenda for the schools. They include: The American Legion, The League of Women Voters, The National Association of Manufacturers, The National Rifle Association, The Boy Scouts of America, local religious organizations, and many others.

By this time we should know better than to expect an easy harmony, if harmony at all, among the various stakeholders in the school curriculum. We can already discern within each group of stakeholders both individual and social interests. These often conflict.

In the attempt to reconcile personal and social interests within groups, as well as conflicts among groups, we will discover the dynamics of the formation of the curriculum. Curriculum is conceived, nurtured, and comes to maturity in a conflictual environment.

How Do They Perceive It? The Structure of Knowledge

A multiplicity of perspectives is important when we recognize intellectual traditions as socially constructed and containing interest. Each provides a vantage point for considering the complexities of our human conditions. When practiced well, the different intellectual paradigms can enable us to "see" and think about various elements of our social world in ways that can increase our understanding of the whole.

——————— *Thomas S. Popkewitz*[6]

Even if we are utterly clear on the goals the curriculum is to serve, we must still solve the question of how to organize it. What criteria should we use to give it structure? The interests of certain stakeholders in competition with others will be supported or undercut depending upon the criteria we use.

Curricular Structure

We can organize our instructional program in at least four different ways. The structure of curriculum can be:

- **logical**, built up from simple elements to complex ones by some rules of combination;
- **pedagogical**, organized so as to make teaching them more efficient;
- **disciplinary**, organized according to the claims of different interest groups as having expertise about them; and
- **institutional**, structured so as to serve the functioning of a social organization.

Remember, different people have a substantial stake in which one of these we use. The kinds of changes we expect from the schools and who has authority to direct them will depend upon it.

POINT/COUNTERPOINT

There is a long-standing debate whether knowledge is structured by a unique relationship to "reality" or whether knowledge is "socially constructed."[7] This argument is whether there is an "objective" organization of the facts of the world, or whether that organization depends upon the interests of the organizers.

The social constructionist view is, for our purposes, more useful because it helps us identify potential stakeholders. What the other view offers, that is, that the structure of knowledge is independent of human interests, does not advance this objective. Besides, the claim to "real knowledge" is made by many competing groups. We would have to deal with questions of consensus and authority that, at this point would only distract.

---

[6]Thomas S. Popkewitz, "Knowledge and Interest in Curriculum Studies," in Thomas S. Popkewitz (ed.), *Critical Studies in Teacher Education* (London: The Falmer Press, 1987), p. 352.
[7]Cf. Peter L. Berger and Thomas Luckmann, *The Social Construction of Reality* (Garden City, N.Y.: Anchor Books, 1967).

Logical Structure

Many people believe that there is a way of organizing knowledge that is independent of human interests. B. Othaniel Smith writes

> ... teaching will be more effective if it incorporates the ways the
> elements of knowledge are related logically.[8]

The belief that there are "basic skills" rests on belief about logical structure.
"Back-to-Basics" is a reform movement that makes sense only if there is a
general consensus about the logical relations among elements in the curriculum. For example, many people believe you have to learn how to add before
you can learn how to multiply. This simply isn't true.[9] The way items relate
is a matter that still requires a lot of investigation.

Are there unique elements of knowledge? And are logical relations unique?
Mathematicians, logicians, and philosophers are far from agreed on these questions.[10]

Mathematics is perhaps most familiar to us as a logically structured body
of knowledge. In fact, geometry is taught to introduce students to a particular
traditional approach to reasoning. One of the things that makes mathematics
hard for many people is that they do not learn in the manner that mathematics
is often taught. In fact, mathematicians do not do mathematics the way it is
taught. They rely heavily on intuition, big jumps from hypothesis to hypothesis
and "backward" reasoning, reconstructing proofs from premises and conclusion.[11] And even intuition is problematic. Mathematician Hans Hahn
comments,

> ... it is not true, as Kant urged, that intuition is a pure *a priori*
> means of knowledge, but rather that it is a force of habit rooted in
> psychological inertia.[12]

Hahn is saying that mathematics, generally viewed as the most logical and
disinterested of disciplines, is founded on habit and custom rather than on
some "logic" that is part of the very essence of mathematical knowledge.

Even more important for our considerations, it has been proved to the
satisfaction of mathematicians that mathematical knowledge cannot be organized on the logical model. There is no unique way to find the simplest
mathematical elements and build them up consistently so that more complex

[8]B. Othaniel Smith, "Introduction" to *Education and the Structure of Knowledge*, Fifth Annual
Phi Delta Kappa Symposium on Educational Research (Chicago: Rand McNally, 1964), p. 3.
[9]But see Gerald W. Bracey, "Advocates of Basic Skills 'Know What Ain't So,'" *Education Week*,
April 5, 1989, p. 32.
[10]Cf. Stephen Koerner, *The Philosophy of Mathematics: An Introduction* (New York: Harper &
Row, 1960), esp. pp. 98–118.
[11]See George Polya, "How to Solve it," in James R. Newman (ed.), *The World of Mathematics*,
Vol. III (New York: Simon & Schuster, 1956), pp. 1980–1992.
[12]Hans Hahn, "The Crisis in Intuition," in Newman, op. cit., p. 1976.

and interesting mathematical statements can be shown to be derived from them.[13]

Why then is mathematics usually taught as though logical structure were the most important part of it? And why do people in other disciplines attempt to mimic mathematics in its logical form? For two basic reasons. First, it is ancient and elegant; it appeals to people brought up in certain traditions. Second, many people believe that it is pedagogically efficient to use some logical organization in subject matter. But what is "logical" may be very much a matter of culture or tradition.[14]

Because they are recognized as most expert in the field, the stakeholders whose claims on the curriculum are best served by the logical organization of subject matter tend to be university professors of all kinds—more specifically, professors involved in disciplines where measurement or logic is a major concern, for example, the sciences, certain kinds of psychology, mathematics, philosophy. It is primarily the belief that logical organization is necessarily pedagogically relevant that lends credibility to the pronouncements of representatives from these fields on the school curriculum.

Once we admit that pedagogical structure may be different from logical structure we complicate things enormously. Teaching becomes an enterprise of discovery. How kids **do** learn takes precedence over ideas about how they **should** learn. The stakeholders whose interests are considered central tend to be those most directly concerned with the schooling process: teachers, researchers, building administrators, parents, and students. Formal degrees alone do not guarantee expertise in schooling and pedagogy.

Pedagogical Structure

Smith also relates pedagogy to cognitive structures:

> . . . what is learned will be retained longer if it is tied into a meaningful cognitive structure.[15]

Pedagogical structure is that organization imposed on curriculum according to some beliefs about how people learn. As we discovered in a previous chapter, the ancient Greeks believed reading was best learned by memorizing combinations of letter sounds. All simple combinations of letters had to be memorized forward and backward. Thus it took years for students to learn to read a simple sentence in school.[16] (What this historical example shows is

---

[13]See Ernest Nagel and James R. Newman, "Goedel's Proof," in Newman, op. cit., pp. 1668–1695.
[14]Piagetian theory postulates an invariant universal human logical development. It does not meet the empirical test. See Patricia Teague Ashton, "Cross-Cultural Piagetian Research: An Experimental Perspective," *Harvard Educational Review,* Vol. 45, No. 4 (November 1975), pp. 475–506.
[15]Smith, op. cit.
[16]See Robert M.W. Travers, "Unresolved Issues in Defining Educational Goals," *Educational Theory,* Vol. 37, No. 1 (Winter 1987), p. 30.

that students do not necessarily learn more efficiently by having things broken down into small pieces.)

Didaxis—the name of an ancient Greek method of presentation, memorization, and recitation—was supported by a good deal of physical punishment. Socrates argued that certain things are known which are not acquired through didaxis. In his *Meno* the elicitation from the slave boy about the construction of the doubled square masterfully demonstrates this point. The Socratic dialogue became the ideal pedagogy. So it came to be that the Platonic tradition identified pedagogical organization with logical organization.[17] It is still a very strong belief despite the fact that mathematics, that most "logical" of disciplines, can no longer be casually invoked as an ideal of logical organization.

Modern linguistics, for example, has developed varieties of logical structures called "phrase grammar" and "generative grammar." These have been investigated with the goal of structuring the teaching of reading and writing in the schools. Traditional grammar is relatively unstructured, but is accorded ceremonial respect as an unchanging standard. Generative grammar sees language as a systematic whole. It starts with basic elements, or "kernel sentences," and attempts to develop rules that combine them into more complex structures in a consistent way.[18] Generative grammar is logical in its structure. But it fails in its program to provide a comprehensive logical structure for language.[19] An even newer approach conceives of language as an inconsistent complex of speech activities for "negotiating meaning" and sees so-called standards as political impositions of powerful groups' own communication preferences.[20] Although modern linguists have departed from the tradition, the original impulse in language studies was to identify pedagogical organization with logical organization: learning language meant learning grammar.

Disciplinary Structure

Curriculum can be structured along disciplinary lines. Academic disciplines are social organizations. They consist of people who have been taught in a certain tradition and who recognize certain items of knowledge and approaches to them as "belonging to their discipline." Disciplines put limits on inquiry. Facts discovered in one discipline may be ignored in pursuing investigation in another.

The primary source of disciplinary divisions comes through the universities. By setting college entrance requirements, and by appealing to the concerns of secondary teachers for professional identity, university personnel have the

---

[17]See Joseph J. Schwab, "Problems, Topics and Issues," Chapter 1 in Smith, op. cit.
[18]See Roderick A. Jacobs and Peter S. Rosenbaum, *English Transformational Grammar* (Waltham, Mass.: Blaisdell, 1968).
[19]See Douglas Frank Stalker, *Deep Structure* (Philadelphia: Philosophical Monographs, 1976).
[20]See Linda M. Phillips and Laurence Walker, "Three Views of Language and Their Influence on Instruction in Reading and Writing," *Educational Theory*, Vol. 37, No. 2, pp. 135–144.

power to determine much of the curricular organization of the secondary schools.[21]

Disciplinary structure manifests itself as subject matter at the secondary and primary levels of schooling. History, English, Mathematics, Science, and so forth are ways of organizing knowledge that may have little to do with logic or pedagogy. But they have a lot to do with the recognition and continuance of specialist roles, certificates, and degrees at all levels of schooling.[22]

Identifying disciplinary structure as being pedagogically necessary biases the competition among various stakeholders in favor of the university. It is here that disciplinary structures are most developed.[23] Secondly, disciplinary divisions protect against "intruders" who don't share the relevant credentials. Pedagogical criticism is taken seriously only from one's own disciplinary peers. Disciplinary organization also protects against a perception that has long been part of teacher folklore: pedagogical skill varies inversely with the level taught.

Institutional Structure

The way we organize schools often acts to determine curriculum. Institutional structure is revealed in the organization of knowledge as curricula, grade levels, courses, units of study, texts, chapters, and the like. One way of understanding curriculum is that it is an institutional construct. No experienced teacher, for his or her own purposes, needs a formal curriculum. But in the context of schooling, where coordination and control become concerns, we use curriculum documents to give the appearance of order.

In large school systems bureaucratic conveniences become pedagogical necessities. To monitor classroom activities, teachers are often required to make formulaic lesson plans, to pace their teaching in accord with a standard curriculum, to avoid deviating from such a curriculum, and to use textbooks picked out by committee. Their teaching must be timed to bells, and adjusted to interruptions from the public address system. Students must be evaluated on a preset schedule. Most teachers do not believe such administrative organization helps their pedagogy. They seldom suggest too loudly, however, that it has a definitely negative effect on learning.

There are stakeholders in the schooling process whose credibility depends most on the belief that the administrative organization of knowledge is pedagogically efficient—or, at least, not harmful. They are those people who bene-

---

[21]See Ivor Goodson, *School Subjects and Curriculum Change* (Philadelphia: Falmer Press, 1987) esp. pp. 24–37.
[22]See Bob Moon, *The "New Maths" Curriculum Controversy: An International Story* (Philadelphia: Falmer Press, 1986), "The Power of the Lobby," esp. pp. 312–233.
[23]See J. Hullett, "Which Structure?" *Educational Theory*, Vol. 24, No. 1 (Winter 1974), pp. 68–72. So strong is the disciplinary bias that teacher lesson planning is invariably done in terms of content rather than objectives. See Richard Kindsvatter, William Wilen, and Margaret Ishler, *The Dynamics of Effective Teaching* (New York: Longman, 1988), p. 56.

fit from the traditional role structure of school administration: principals, upper administrators, school boards, and state boards of education.

Stakeholder Status

We should realize that the four ways of organizing the curriculum—logical, pedagogical, disciplinary and institutional—are not necessarily related. To structure knowledge one way does not ensure that it will be structured according to another. Logic, learnability, tradition, and administrative convenience may have nothing to do with one another. But assumptions that they are logically related support the predominance of one group of stakeholders over others in the schooling enterprise.

Different groups of stakeholders are accorded more or less credibility depending upon the assumed relations among the logical, pedagogical, disciplinary, and institutional organization of the curriculum. If we assume that logical and disciplinary organization is the most pedagogically effective way to structure the curriculum, we concede ultimate authority over the curriculum to university professors. If we assume that institutional organization is pedagogically most effective, we concede ultimate authority to administrators. However, if we hold back from such assumptions and allow that a pedagogically effective structure may be different from either the logical, disciplinary, or institutional structure of the curriculum, we retain ultimate authority for those who work on-site in the schools. These are building staff, researchers, and even parents and students. Chart 17.2 summarizes these relations.

Curricular Evolution

As items are introduced and then become permanent subject matter in the curriculum, the dominant stakeholders change. Layton proposes that curricular items go through the following stages of evolution:

- **Stage One**: justified by pertinence and utility, the new curricular item attracts students who feel it bears on matters that concern them. The teachers are rarely trained specialists of this item, but bring pioneering zeal to their task. Relevance to the needs and interests of the learners is the dominant criterion for inclusion in the curriculum.
- **Stage Two**: a tradition of scholarly work along with a corps of trained specialists is developing. Students are attracted to its study not only because of its relevance to their problems, but also because of its growing academic status. The organization of the subject matter is increasingly influenced by the internal logic and discipline of the subject.
- **Stage Three**: the teachers are now a professional subject matter body. Students are initiated into a tradition. Rules and values have been

Chart 17.2

	Supports These Stakeholders		
ASSUMED STRUCTURAL RELATIONS SUPPORT CLAIMS ON THE CURRICULUM OF THE SCHOOLS			
Assumed Related to Pedagogical Structure	University Professors in Certain Disciplines	University Professors in Certain Disciplines	Persons in Traditional Administrative Roles
STRUCTURES	LOGICAL	DISCIPLINARY	INSTITUTIONAL
Not Assumed Related to Pedagogical Structure	Researchers, Building Staff, Parents, Students	Researchers, Building Staff, Parents, Students	Researchers, Building Staff, Parents, Students

established and the selection of subject matter is determined primarily by specialists in the field.[24]

Layton's theory supports our idea that the relationships among different ways of organizing knowledge determine who are the primary stakeholders in the selection of curricular items.

Why Does It Concern Them? Curricular Aims

Our original question, "What should be taught?" yielded us the difficulty that there are many possible things that can be taught, yet insufficient time and resources to teach them all; a selection must be made.

We then looked to identify stakeholders and found that the actual curriculum in some U.S. schools did not agree with what students, parents, and teachers want. This discovery led us to look elsewhere for stakeholders who might also be powerholders. We found other stakeholders. Their claims on the curriculum depended upon our beliefs as to how knowledge should be organized: logically, pedagogically, by discipline, or for organizational convenience.

We will now look at another dimension of curriculum. What general purposes or functions does a curricular item support? Is music taught in the schools because it has substantial value? Or are its benefits symbolic? What about geometry, or French? We will see that the hodgepodge of subject matters that constitutes the curriculum of today's school does have a rational basis.

---

[24]From D. Layton, "Science as General Education," *Trends in Education*, January 1972, cited in Goodson, op. cit., p. 10.

Status, Vocation, and Social Control Interests

The differences among the main types of educational structures in the modern world can be explained by differences among lineups of contending interests.

_____ *Randall Collins*[25]

Stakeholders in the curriculum not only have different notions of how knowledge should be organized, but also value different kinds of schooling outcomes. The traditionally sought products of schooling such as character, skill, and citizenship represent different kinds of curricular interest. We will look at these interests in a more generalized form.

Status Interests

Status is a **divisible** benefit: some may have a certain degree of it; others, not. Moreover, it is a **positional benefit**: if some have more, others necessarily have less.[26] For these reasons questions of status inevitably raise questions of equity.

Randall Collins argues that the curriculum of the modern comprehensive high school is a mix of three historical interests: status, vocation, and social (primarily bureaucratic) control. We have used these distinctions earlier in the book. Now we can use them to understand curriculum.

- **Status Interests** pursue a curriculum perceived by members of a cultural group to support its particular values and maintain or enhance its status relative to other competing groups.

Status concerns need not be narrow, divisible items. They may be as broad as the desire to maintain a democratic society, or to extend freedom of choice to all people. But partisans of a democratic society do not merely see democracy as an option of equal status with monarchy or dictatorship; rather, they believe that democracy is of greater worth. Other value systems are competitors of lower status.

The items of a status curriculum provide what we have called in this book *symbolic benefits*. They support and enhance the formal culture of a group. If we were to ask why such an item is studied, the likely answer would be "Because to be educated, one has to know something about it." Other answers might be that it is enlightening, develops the mind, supports morality, or

---

[25]Randall Collins, "Some Comparative Principles of Educational Stratification," *Harvard Educational Review*, Vol. 47, No. 1 (1977), pp. 1–27.

[26]Cf. Fred Hirsch, *The Social Limits to Growth* (Cambridge: Harvard U. Press, 1976), pp. 27–31.

strengthens character or democracy. Examples might be religious education of all kinds, ethnic studies, English grammar, literature, higher mathematics, history, art, music, high school sciences. In short, anything seen as having intrinsic value, apart from its being required to pursue an occupation.

Status interests can be divided into two subgroups that are important for distinguishing among actual curriculum proposals. They can be concerned with **group status** or **individual status**, as are curricula that pursue developmental goals such as character, self-realization, self-esteem, self-concept, independence, and critical thinking.[27] These are not pursued solely or primarily for their economic promise, but because they are thought to turn out a better human being.

Status interests can be **traditional** or **reconstructionist**. That is, they can aim at social distinctions traditionally found in society, or they can pursue the revitalization of lost values or the promotion of new ones. Creationism is a traditionalist movement with a curricular agenda for the schools. Peace curricula and World Government curricula, promoted by organizations like The Society of Friends, are examples of reconstructionist status concerns.

Vocational Interests

As we have learned in Chapter 10, the most ancient purpose of schooling was vocational, aimed at transmitting particular skills, primarily literacy. Collins sees such interests as the second determinant in the modern curriculum.

> ▬ **Vocational Interests** pursue a curriculum designed to pay off in substantial benefits.

"Why study that?" is answered, "Because it leads to a good job." However, the division between status and vocational curriculum is often blurred. The expansion of schooling transforms the nature of its costs and benefits.[28] Previously optional costs become necessary evils. Previously symbolic benefits become substantial. Schooling becomes the prerequisite for more schooling. A doctor may never use trigonometry, but it is unlikely that a student who fails it will get into medical school.

An extremely important point to keep in mind is this: *there need be no scientifically recognized causal relationship between what is required for vocational purposes and the subject matter studied.* Christopher J. Hurn comments:

> A large part of the explanation for the well-known correlation between educational qualifications and occupational status should be that such educational qualifications reflect the possession of cog-

---

[27]Cf. Goodson, who distinguishes between Academic and Pedagogic curricular traditions, op. cit., p. 25.
[28]See Thomas F. Green, *Predicting the Behavior of the Educational System* (Syracuse, N.Y.: Syracuse U. Press, 1980), esp. pp. 90–113.

nitive skills necessary or useful for effect role performance. But the evidence that we have suggests that it is educational *credentials* rather than cognitive skills that predict future status and earnings. We know that employers prefer to employ college graduates, but there is no solid evidence that they make great efforts to hire people with the highest levels of cognitive skills. Nor is there evidence that once on the job those who have the highest skills perform better than those with lower skills.[29]

Social Control Interests

Collins sees the curriculum as shaped by the bureaucratic structure of the modern school. Administrational convenience determines much of the process of modern schooling, often in conflict with other values. Here we broaden Collins' concept somewhat to recognize that every stakeholder has a social control interest.

- **Social control interests** pursue a curriculum that maintains or enhances the allocation of costs and benefits, both symbolic and substantial, enjoyed by present powerholders. Because these interests might provoke controversy if declared openly, they are generally covert, often part of the informal culture of the school.

If students were in charge, they would support curricular items that incorporate field activities, trips, and hands-on experiences.[30] Parents support highly supervised activities for students and ones that permit them, the parents, to come into the school at will. (See Chapter 2.) Teachers support curricular items that enhance their control over the costs and benefits of their position as do administrators, school board members, community groups, and so on up.

There are two kinds of social control interests: **domination** interests and **market control** interests. What items in the curriculum support domination interests? Mass calisthenics in gym class. School assemblies and the rites associated with them. Tests and examinations and the training preparatory to their administration. Late bells and division of the day into class periods. Standing in line and raising one's hand. Getting a note to go to the nurse or the bathroom. All of these practices restrict individual decision on items often of a very personal nature. These restrictions may be justified, for example, on grounds of immaturity or crowding, but often the practices outlive their rationales.

Market control interests are more indirect. The very division of knowledge

---

[29]Christopher J. Hurn, *The Limits and Possibilities of Schooling* (Boston: Allyn & Bacon, 1978), p. 39.
[30]There are long-established traditions that support this approach to education. Rousseau, Pestalozzi, Dewey, and Kilpatrick among many others promoted it.

Status and control concerns.

into disciplines is supported by them. Their purpose is to restrict schooling benefits in certain traditional ways. We will look at them more closely below when we consider knowledge as a commodity.

The three kinds of interest—status, vocational, and social control—do not divide curricular items into mutually exclusive classes. One and the same item may support status, vocational, and social control interests. In fact, we might define the "strength" of an item in the curriculum relative to another item depending upon the degree to which it satisfies all three interests. Items that are strong in this way are supported by resources. Teachers who teach them risk fewer layoffs and less controversy about their subject matter (although specific parts of items may be controversial). We might also expect that symbolic items will be weaker than substantial items unless there are strong professional or community groups who support them and who can affect the budgeting process.

Knowledge as a Commodity

Preparing for the SATs (Scholastic Aptitude Tests) is big business. One in nine U.S. high school students pays for private coaching while an estimated 47 percent of high schools offer some kind of SAT preparation class.[31] What is this market? What is being offered?

In order to be sold, knowledge has to be substantially transformed in ways that violate traditional notions of what knowledge is and how it benefits a community. To be an item of exchange, knowledge must be turned into a commodity, like gold, soybeans, and concentrated frozen orange juice. What is knowledge and how must it be transformed?

If we know something and tell someone else, we do not know it less.

---

[31]Mark Walsh, "1 in 9 Said To Use Private Coaching For S.A.T.," *Education Week*, October 12, 1988, p. 6.

Indeed, knowledge increases the more it is given away. Knowledge, valued intrinsically, is an **absolute** benefit. On the other hand, if we have a commodity and give another person some, we have less. A commodity is divisible and consumable. It is a **positional** benefit.

How can we change knowledge into a commodity? By valuing it not for itself, but as an instrument to something else. Instrumentally valued knowledge can be made into a commodity through secrecy or monopoly. Students do not pay for SAT preparation courses because they value the knowledge they get from them intrinsically.

People are willing to pay for intrinsically valued knowledge. Traditionally, however, the clergy and the university and elite secondary schools have been the only groups to receive that kind of support.

Schools historically have always taught a mixture of intrinsically valued and extrinsically valued knowledge. But a prolonged emphasis on knowledge as substantial, a commodity, both undercuts their esteem and greatly affects the curriculum.

The important thing about SAT preparation is that it is believed to provide its buyers with a **positional benefit**, one that gives them advantage over someone who lacks it. Knowledge transformed from an absolute benefit into an instrument of positional benefits becomes much like wealth. And it suffers from many of the same economic illnesses that wealth can.

Commodification

The first step for selling knowledge is to give it a medium of exchange. It must be made divisible and transferable. Knowledge does not mark one's forehead to indicate its presence. Rather, certificates must provide a guarantee of that knowledge. But because guarantee is a matter of trust and belief, certificates are only as good as the esteem held for their issuer. Diplomas from a new school are seen as inferior to those of an established school, independently of any investigation of the actual knowledge of its graduates.

The second step for selling knowledge is to restrict access to the process culminating in a diploma. This is normally done through curriculum prerequisites. If knowledge were the only thing at issue, then university degrees and professional certificates might be got solely by test, without attendance requirements. That no one can practice surgery on the basis of tests alone indicates something important. Tests results are not trusted to catch everything important in the training toward a diploma. Also, important stakeholders in the process control it for considerations other than those of efficiency. Their livelihoods or their disciplines may be at stake.

The Systemics of Commodification

When knowledge becomes a commodity, the curriculum itself suffers modification. Let's see how.

Suppose schools were so effective in teaching traditional academics that every child graduated with a high degree of competence. Can you imagine what an impact this situation would have on society? What would be its costs and benefits? For whom? In this section, we consider such effects. We will be looking at some reasonable conjectures about the consequences of an overly successful system of schooling, particularly if knowledge has been transformed into a commodity that pursues other positional goods, for example, wealth and status. Thomas Green[32] proposes wider effects that any system of schooling will have under these circumstances.

The Law of Zero-Correlation

If we pursue a high school diploma so that it gets us better jobs because employers prefer to hire people with such diplomas, then we can reasonably conclude the following things:

- If *no one* has a high school diploma, no one has *that* advantage when seeking employment.
- If *everyone* has a high school diploma, no one has *that* advantage when seeking employment.
- So, for some people to get an advantage from having a high school diploma, others cannot have that diploma.

Figure 17.1 illustrates these points.

Thus the goal of trying to bring all students to the point of getting a high school diploma undercuts the **instrumental value** of that diploma. Equity conflicts with efficiency.

[32]Thomas F. Green, *Predicting the Behavior of the Educational System* (Syracuse, N.Y.: Syracuse U. Press, 1980). Also, Michael A. Oliker,"Review of *Predicting the Behavior of the Educational System*," by Thomas F. Green, *Journal of Thought*, Vol. 18 (Spring 1983), pp. 118–124.

Figure 17.1

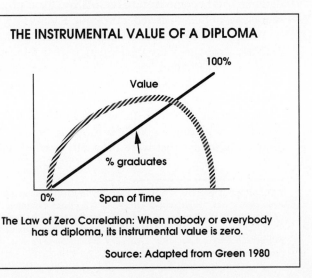

THE INSTRUMENTAL VALUE OF A DIPLOMA

The Law of Zero Correlation: When nobody or everybody has a diploma, its instrumental value is zero.

Source: Adapted from Green 1980

Shifting Costs and Benefits

The effect of this conflict, says Green, is that the benefits and costs of a high school diploma change. At first to offset the general devaluation of diplomas, the curriculum becomes tracked. No longer are students given a single general diploma. Rather, different kinds of diplomas, for example, academic and vocational, will be given. And the value of some kinds of diplomas will be maintained at the cost of devaluing others, depending upon the power of the involved stakeholders. Thus, academic diplomas may be held in higher esteem than general or vocational diplomas.

Transformation of Costs

Secondly, the costs to the individual of not getting a diploma will change. In 1910 about 20 percent of the appropriate age-level students earned a high school diploma. But there were plenty of opportunities for employment for nongraduates. Not having a diploma could be seen as a rational choice to investing one's time and energies in earning money and gaining on-the-job experience, rather than continuing in school and pursuing future possibilities. Besides, economic pressures often forced the choice.

As more students got diplomas—over 60 percent of appropriate students in the 1950s—nongraduation became a problem. Not having a diploma became an increasing liability, as Figure 17.2 illustrates. At this point "dropouts" were discovered.[33] But there had always been dropouts. Why had circumstances changed? Because society had changed. The perception had become that leaving school indicated a deficiency, rather than a rational choice. In addition, because there were more high school graduates, employers could raise their requirements for the level of education.

Thus the motivation to stay in school changed. One stayed in school to avoid the costs of being identified as a dropout. The instrumental utility of a diploma had become **defensive utility,** for it protected you against the consequences of being labeled a dropout. Figure 17.3 illustrates defensive utility.

The effect on the curriculum was that special programs for identifying potential dropouts were developed. Career Education, for example, was conceived as a curriculum focus.[34] The most recent of such programs are those for "At-Risk" students. Whether such innovations can offset the dynamics of commodification is another question.

The second effect on the curriculum was that the benefits of a diploma shifted from getting a good job to going on to college. This emphasis transformed disciplines that were originally born of status interests into, in effect,

---

[33]The dropout picture is complicated by the fact that many students return or complete an equivalency. See "High School Dropouts Who Later Complete Their Education," *The Condition of Education* (Washington, D.C.: Center for Education Statistics, 1987), pp. 28–29.

[34]See W. Norton Grubb and Marvin Lazerson, "Rally 'Round the Workplace: Continuities and Fallacies in Career Education," *Harvard Educational Review,* Vol. 45, No. 4 (November 1975), pp. 451–474.

Figure 17.2

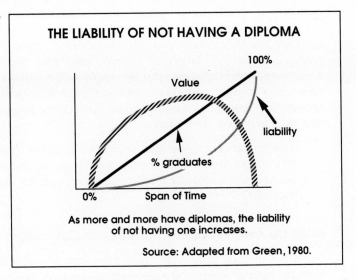

THE LIABILITY OF NOT HAVING A DIPLOMA

As more and more have diplomas, the liability
of not having one increases.

Source: Adapted from Green, 1980.

Figure 17.3

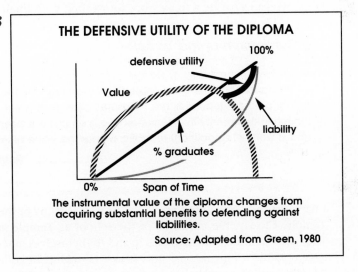

THE DEFENSIVE UTILITY OF THE DIPLOMA

The instrumental value of the diploma changes from
acquiring substantial benefits to defending against
liabilities.

Source: Adapted from Green, 1980

vocational ones. Students who may have never taken certain courses were now confronted by teachers unprepared to meet their special needs. These then generated special curricula and laid the foundation for the identification of "special needs."

Last Entry

In an expanding school system some groups will enter it after others. Green's insight is that the benefits of the system will be enjoyed by the early-comers. Those entering last, generally of lesser status in society, will be faced with a market glutted with diplomas. Early entrants to the U.S. educational system—

up to 1950—found that a high school diploma helped and dropping out did not severely handicap one in the economic race. Within the last forty years, however, the high school diploma has become a floor, so to speak, and advantages can nearly always be pursued only with higher degrees. Green's conclusion is that diplomas must inevitably suffer deflation as long as they are valued only instrumentally *and* we pursue a public policy of equal educational opportunity. Since such a policy is only just, Green suggests that the diploma race be abandoned. He remarks,

> As a matter of political choice and public policy, perhaps it is time to consider whether it is easier, more humane, and more desirable to make the world safe for illiterates than to make the whole world literate.[35]

What Do They Propose? Varieties of Curriculum

There are literally thousands upon thousands of curriculum proposals. But with the help of some of the distinctions we have reviewed throughout the book, we can provide a framework for dealing with them in an efficient way.

The Curriculum of the Temple

> ... the ideal republic is the republic of learning. It is the utopia by which actual political republics are measured. The goal which was started with the Athenians twenty-five centuries ago is an unlimited republic of learning and a worldwide political republic supporting each other.
>
> ———— *Robert M. Hutchins*[36]

Character and community are the educational focus of the curriculum of the Temple. Clearly, the concerns of the school as Temple are status concerns. They are commitments to values in and of themselves, uncompromised wherever possible with practical necessities. Hutchins finds those values in what he perceives as an unbroken tradition from ancient Greece to modern America. He is certainly not concerned with any issues of consensus about those values.

We might note that different cultures at different times have chosen different items of knowledge to support their status interests. We think of the liberal arts as serving status concerns, and the dons at Cambridge University during the nineteenth century deliberately refused to recognize any subject as appropriate for university study which could be put to use in commerce

---

[35]Thomas F. Green, "Weighing the Justice of Inequality," *Change*, Vol. 12, No. 5 (July/August 1980), pp. 26–32.
[36]Robert M. Hutchins, "The Basis of Education," reprinted in James Wm. Noll, *Taking Sides: Clashing Views on Controversial Educational Issues* (Guilford, Conn.: Dushkin, 1987), p. 26.

Is this vocational preparation?

and industry.[37] But the rhetoric, logic, and grammar they undoubtedly revered were once part of the vocational training for positions in the medieval Christian Church. Similarly, calligraphy strikes us as primarily a status pursuit, but it was required preparation for the civil service of the Chinese emperor.

Fixed and Emerging Interests

The curriculum of the Temple is founded on traditions and preformed goals. On the other hand, certain processes may be thought to be of intrinsic value and generate new goals for the schools. Elliot Eisner comments:

> I believe that it is perfectly appropriate for teachers and others involved in curriculum development to plan activities that have no explicit or precise objectives. In an age of accountability, this sounds like heresy. Yet surely there must be room in school for activities that promise to be fruitful, even though the teacher may not be able to say what specifically the students will learn or experience. Parents do this all the time. The trip to the zoo, weekends spent camping in the woods, the bicycle ride after dinner; no specific objectives or problems are posed prior to setting out on such activities, yet we feel that they will be enjoyable and that some "good" will come from them.[38]

It is the Temple, rather than the Factory or Town Meeting, that permits such undirected experimenting. In the Temple, the character and concern of the teachers guarantee that the mere participation in the activity will be of value. The Factory tends to be too cost-conscious and often overestimates the risks of failure. In the Town Meeting generating new values threatens the old if only by dissipating energies focused for the conflict. Novel ideas create new competitors.

---

[37]S. Rothblatt, *The Revolution of the Dons* (London: Faber and Faber, 1969), cited in Goodson, op. cit., p. 8.
[38]Elliot W. Eisner, *The Educational Imagination: On the Design and Evaluation of School Programs* (New York: Macmillan, 1979).

Exegetical Curriculum

Metaphoric precision is the central vehicle for revealing the qualitative aspects of life.

——————— *Elliot Eisner*[39]

How does one write curriculum for the Temple? Assuming certain basic values, how can we proceed with the selection? The technique is primarily **exegetical**—that is, items are chosen on the basis of an interpretation of what the goal "means."[40] If "Basic Knowledge" is the goal pursued, choices for the curriculum will be explained as being "Basic Knowledge." It is a matter of persuasion and consensus building. Robert M. Travers calls this approach to curriculum theory, the "literary" approach. He comments:

> . . . a major and overwhelming advantage of the literary approach is that with literary talent, one can make educational goals attractive, and they must be attractive if they are to appeal to all those involved in achieving them. . . . They need to be attractive for very much the same reason that political goals do. Goals should motivate, and appealing goals have energizing properties.[41]

Unlike the Factory, the Temple treats casually the determination of causation from curricular item to goal. If someone can convince the proponents of Basic Knowledge that he or she knows "what Basic Knowledge is" and that Sex Education is Basic Knowledge, then Sex Education—whatever it is—will be part of the Basic Knowledge curriculum. (In reality, this persuasive process will be supported with Factory-like claims for causal effectiveness. We will review this approach below.)

The problem with the exegetical approach is that mere expressions of hope often serve as justifications for curricular choices. The assumption is made that if the ends can be stated, the means are made somehow more determinate.[42] Thus schools announce a Substance Abuse Education Curriculum and many assume (hope?) that a significant step has been taken to control drugs. But does a school program prevent distribution? Does it cut off the sources of supply? Does it even limit demand? A critical thinker may well find fault with the program on such technical grounds.

---

[39]Ibid., p. 200.
[40]See Deal and Wiske on research as Scripture, op. cit., p. 459.
[41]Travers, op. cit., p. 37.
[42]Cf. Edward G. Rozycki, "Hope as Educational Theory: Rejoinder to Wain," *Educational Theory*, Vol. 39, No. 2 (Spring 1989), pp. 163–165.

The Factory Curriculum

The fact that many educators now equate "goals" with "intended student outcomes" is to the credit of the behaviorists, particularly the advocates of programmed instruction. They have brought about a small reform in teaching by emphasizing those specific classroom acts and work exercises which contribute to the refinement of student responses.[43]

Science sells. It has been selling curriculum since about 1913 when Franklin Bobbitt adopted "science" as the slogan for restructuring the curriculum.[44] Advertising has long taken advantage of the word. It implies objectivity, lack of ulterior purpose, trustworthiness. Downplayed are the special attributes of real science: self-criticism, intellectual rigor, standards of evaluation not distorted for personal ends.

The "Science" of Curriculum and the School as Factory are intimately related. In fact, a new group of stakeholders lays claim to the curriculum under the image of the school as Factory. They are the test makers, the Scientific Curriculum Theorists and certain groups of academic psychologists—that is, those who see themselves in the tradition of, for example, Thorndike, Terman, and Skinner—generally called Behaviorist.

Skinner's formulations became a very popular basis for scientific curriculum making. Yet Wilbert J. McKeatchie, in his 1974 presidential address to the Division of General Psychology of the American Psychological Association, reviewed the literature on the application of Skinner's theories and concluded "the research evidence demonstrates . . . that each point enunciated by Skinner is untrue—at least in as general a sense as he believed."[45]

McKeatchie offers an explanation for the popularity of Skinnerian psychology despite its inadequacy: it is simple, educators are looking for magic, and Skinner is, at least, persuasive.

> Those who by his approach find that the basic ideas are simple to apply and work often enough to maintain their enthusiasm. This is no small matter. Anyone who can take discouraged, dispirited teachers, mental health aides or prison officials and revive their hope and vigor has done a great deal. Probably no one thing is more important in education than the teacher's enthusiasm and energy.[46]

The Factory Model is attractive because it portrays status interests as scientific, it offers efficiency in pursuing vocational interests, and it rationalizes

[43]Robert E. Stake, "The Countenance of Educational Evaluation," in Taylor and Cowley, op. cit., p. 97.

[44] Herbert M. Kliebard, "The Rise of the Scientific Curriculum and its Aftermath" *Curriculum Theory Network*, Vol. 5, No. 1 (1975), pp. 27–38.

[45]Wilbert J. McKeatchie, "The Decline and Fall of the Laws of Learning," *Educational Researcher*, March 1974, pp. 7–10.

[46]McKeatchie, op. cit., p. 10.

social control. But in general and in specific, the Factory still generates major controversy at all levels of schooling.[47]

For the Factory the relationship between curricular concerns and choices is simple. The items chosen for curriculum are supposed to *produce* outcomes that satisfy the concerns. The only justification for selection is causation. In the Factory, curriculum development is supposed to be science.[48]

The problem is, goals that are slogans do not become less so just because one is prepared to measure their possible causes. Thus curriculum developers with an empirical bent invent an intermediate category called **objectives**. Objectives have measurable, controllable processes that are causally related to them. But an important problem still remains. How are the objectives related to the goals?

The relationship of goals to the objectives is just as dependent upon persuasive, noncausal argument of the kind found in the Temple. Whether or not certain objectives serve even generally recognized goals is often a matter of great controversy. Good tests may be developed for objectives, but if the objectives are not related to the goals, the tests are pointless. Even worse, the tests, being substantial, may come to stand in for the goals, which are often not. This concern has bothered educators for many years.[49]

The Curriculum of the Town Meeting

The curriculum of the Town Meeting is the result of bargaining. Objectives may or may not be brought up to help persuade someone to accept an item, but in this setting goals are generally nonfunctional. The fundamental difference between the Town Meeting and the Factory is that in the Town Meeting causation provides just one more argument not necessarily more convincing than "I'll make you a deal." (We might recall the quote from Fisher and Ury in Chapter 3 that Truth is simply one more argument.)

The fundamental difference between the Town Meeting and the Temple is that in the Temple we assume that a consensus about what goals mean exists upon which exegetical arguments could be made. In the Town Meeting no such consensus is assumed to exist. Figure 17.4 illustrates the relation of curricular items to goals for the three expectation models of the school.

The goal we pursue may be to turn out good citizens. Under the Temple

---

[47]See Hugh G. Petrie, "Can Education Find Its Lost Objectives Under the Street Lamp of Behaviorism?" in Ralph A. Smith (ed.), *Regaining Educational Leadership* (New York: Wiley, 1975), pp. 64–74. Also, see Edward G. Rozycki, "Rewards, Reinforcers and Voluntary Behavior," *Ethics*, October 1973, pp. 38–47; "More on Rewards and Reinforcers," *Ethics*, July 1974, pp. 354–358; "Measurability and Educational Concerns," *Educational Theory*, Winter 1974, pp. 52–60.

[48]Kliebard, op. cit.

[49]See Millie Waterman, "The Risks of Comparing NAEP Results," *Education Week*, October 12, 1988, p. 24. Also, see David Owen, *None of the Above: Behind the Myth of Scholastic Aptitude* (Boston: Houghton Mifflin, 1985); Jane S. Stallings, "Are We Evaluating What We Value?" *Action in Teacher Education*, Vol. IX, No. 3 (Fall 1987), pp. 1–3; Samuel Messick, "The Criterion Problem in the Evaluation of Instruction: Assessing Possible, Not Just Intended Outcomes," in Peter A. Taylor and Doris M. Cowley, *Readings in Curriculum Evaluation* (Dubuque, Iowa: Brown, 1972), pp. 49–58.

Figure 17.4

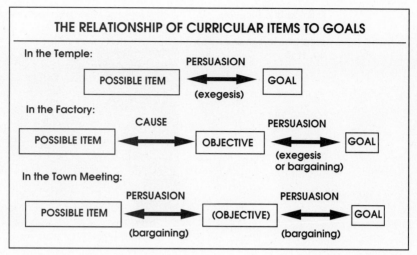

THE RELATIONSHIP OF CURRICULAR ITEMS TO GOALS

In the Temple:

PERSUASION

POSSIBLE ITEM ⟷ GOAL

(exegesis)

In the Factory:

CAUSE   PERSUASION

POSSIBLE ITEM ⟷ OBJECTIVE ⟷ GOAL

(exegesis or bargaining)

In the Town Meeting:

PERSUASION   PERSUASION

POSSIBLE ITEM ⟷ (OBJECTIVE) ⟷ GOAL

(bargaining)   (bargaining)

model, someone might argue that knowing American History is part of being a good citizen. In the Factory, the argument can become complex in two ways:

- the claim may be made that it is a causal necessity to know American History to bring about being a good citizen; or
- an objective will be constructed to view specific teaching as causing that objective, that is—Objective: the student will recite the names of the presidents of the United States. How that objective relates to the goal is left to the same kind of argument found in the Temple

Claims of causal necessity are difficult to establish. Indeed, we know from Chapter 9 that the very functioning of the school as an institution would impede investigation into causal relationships of any kind.

In the course of developing our discussion on curriculum, we have used the Analysis Questions from Chapter 3 to guide our inquiry. Two remain to be asked and responded to:

Q6: Can and Will Anything Be Done? That is, will proposed curricular changes be acted upon? Whose, specifically?

Q7: Who gains and who loses from the changes?

Q6 asks whether the stakeholders can and will do anything to implement their proposals. It brings up the issue of who exactly are the powerholders. (See Chapter 3.) We can assume that the curriculum as it exists is a manifestation not only of the efforts of powerholders but of the organizational interactions depicted in Chapters 8 and 9. Q7 asks what the costs and benefits of the changes are. Answering that question would be the enterprise of a whole book

Citizenship education. Students in a patriotic program, Fowler, Colorado, ca. 1918.

in itself. This chapter—indeed, this book—is only a step toward that undertaking.

SUMMARY

1. From a wide variety of possible things to teach, only a relatively few are chosen. These choices do not reflect the interests of primary stakeholders: the students, the parents, and the teachers. Thus we must consider other stakeholders who are also powerholders.

2. The organization of knowledge according to logic, teachability, discipline, and administrative interests gives the advantage of credibility to different stakeholders' claims to authority on the curriculum.

3. Outcome concerns about status, vocation, and social control exert a formative influence on the curriculum. Treating knowledge as a commodity tends to bring equity and efficiency into conflict.

4. The three images of the school support different curricular choices and different approaches to curriculum theorizing.

QUESTIONS

1. What are the costs and benefits of (a) teaching to the test, (b) not testing at all? For whom are these costs and benefits?

2. One popular curricular reform proposes a production model: more subject matter specified in the curriculum yields more informed students. Do you think this model is realistic?

3. In the business world, even simple mathematical calculations are done with the help of machines. Yet, students are still taught—with greater or less degree of success—to do these calculations in their heads. Why do you think this is? What are the costs and benefits of keeping calculating skills in the curriculum?

4. Create a scale that goes from 0 percent to 100 percent that indicates the probability of use in an adult occupation. Arrange different curricular items along this scale—you may add to those already mentioned above. What reasons could there be for including low probability items in the curriculum? What reasons could there be for excluding high probability items from the curriculum?

5. In Renaissance Italy bankers used addition tables to compute sums on the job. Today addition "facts" are taught in elementary schools. Why? Why not teach calculus in the elementary schools?

6. Some researchers believe that reading problems are mainly caused because we try to get most children to read at too early an age. What are the costs and benefits of early literacy? For whom?

7. Consider the basic curricular conflicts. Are they different for students or parents from those for teachers?

8. There are two major explanations for consensus: natural congruence of sympathies on means and ends; and social conditions exist which make agreement on conflict handling methods seem reasonable to all parties.
   a. Which image of the school would support which explanation?
   b. How might either theory affect curricular choice?

9. Edward B. Fiske and Joseph M Michaluk, in their book, *Best Buys in College Education* (New York: Times Books, 1987, p. 4), use the following criteria in defining the quality of colleges: entering Freshman SAT scores; at least 60% Ph.D. holders on faculty; good acceptance rate into graduate school; admissions selectivity, that is, percent accepted/percent applied. Additional but minor criteria are faculty interest in students, quality of library, counseling services, class size, coherent curriculum, and academic opportunities, for example, study abroad.
   a. How might such criteria affect curriculum at both the high school and college levels?
   b. What structures of knowledge do they tend to support?

10. Sort out curricular items and school practices into three classes: those that support status interests, those that support vocational interests, and those that support social control interests.

11. Discuss grade inflation and diploma devaluation in terms of commodification.

12. Find a document that states some learning objectives. What goals do they relate to? How can you explain this relation? Is the relation causal, exegetical or mostly supposition?

LEARNING and TEACHING

Chapter 18

Cognitive research demonstrates that people work best with and within a complex system if they have a "mental model" of the system—that is, an idea of all of its parts, what each does and how they work together, how changes in one part of the system cause changes in other parts. This mental model permits flexibility in responding to unexpected situations. . . . One important function of schooling is to develop the knowledge and mental skills students will need to construct appropriate mental models of systems with which they will eventually work.

——————— *Lauren B. Resnick*[1]

PREVIEW

How does what teachers do connect with what students learn? Bad teaching, so we are told in the mass media, has helped bring about the trade deficit. But why not blame someone or something else? Why should educators bear such responsibility? In this chapter we will examine different models of learning and teaching and different conceptions of causation that might connect them. Our review will help us clarify what it is reasonable to hold teachers accountable for.

We will discover that there are competing traditions in terms of which causation, learning, and teaching are identified and assumed to be related. We will see that the relationships between teaching and learning, and the kind of causal connections believed to link them, depend very much on the image of the school that has been invoked.

INTRODUCTION

Teachers face at least two problems. The first is where to get knowledge about learning and teaching. The second is whether or not they can put that knowledge to use.

Consider the following scenario: it is discovered that reduction of class size to nine pupils per teacher produces substantial increase on all measures of student achievement. Can this knowledge be put to use? Who will rush to triple the size of the school budget to take advantage of this discovery?

Concerns about the nature of learning and teaching are not merely theoretical exercises, but bear heavily on who enjoys what benefits and who pays what costs in the socioeducational system.

———————————————
[1]Lauren B. Resnick "Learning in School and Out," *Educational Researcher*, December 1987.

Is Learning A Generic Process?

In her 1987 Presidential Address to the American Educational Research Association, Lauren B. Resnick summarized the research on learning in and out of school. She described how very different learning is in school from what it is on the job.[2]

School learning, Resnick pointed out, demands individual cognitive effort, generally unaided by tools. However, individuals in the work world are generally involved in cooperative thinking and use a variety of tools and artifacts to support their learning process. Reasoning in school is generally a matter of the manipulation of abstract symbols, whereas reasoning at work is contextualized and concrete. Learning in school tends to be of a general nature. At work it is specific to the job situation. Thus the idea that school prepares students for the world of work does not seem supported by research. Does this mean that schooling is irrelevant?

No. According to Resnick's research, schooling affects trouble-shooting ability. When the specific, concrete situations of the workaday world become snarled, when the normalcy that supports job skills falls apart, then people with more schooling adapt more readily to the emergency situation. But how often do such emergencies arise? Should every student be prepared to deal with such irregularities? The differences between in-school and on-the-job learning seem to indicate that substantial reform in the school curriculum may be called for. Chart 18.1 summarizes Resnick's findings.

Resnick's distinctions point to an important consideration: *Learning may not be a uniform process.* That is, learning English may not be the same as learning math or music. Indeed, the casual term "learning" may be not much

---

[2]Resnick, op. cit., p. 18.

Chart 18.1

LEARNING IN SCHOOL AND OUT

from Resnick, 1987

Differences In	In School	On the Job
Cognition	Individual, Isolated	Cooperative, Teamwork
Use of Tools	No tools, "pure mentation"	Tools for thinking, manipulation of media
Reasoning	Manipulation of Symbols	Contextualized Reasoning
Specificity of Learning	Highly Generalized	Situation Specific
Reaction to Breakdown	Adaptive	Unadaptive, Stymied

more than a slogan that is traditionally applied to a variety of processes or outcomes with little concern for their actual similarity.

On the other hand, many theorists presume that "learning" indicates some sort of **generic** process so that different kinds of learning can all be understood as variations of the same thing. Hilgard's classic textbook in introductory psychology defines learning in this manner: learning is *the* process by which an activity originates or is changed when someone responds to a situation.[3]

So important is it for some theorists to insist on a generic process, that they are willing to ignore contradictions. Hilgard defines "latent learning" as that occurring even if the learner does not respond to a situation. We could just as easily say that nothing acquired "latently" is learning, for by Hilgard's own definition it did not involve a response to a situation.

Are we quibbling? What conceivable practical difference could a matter of definition make? We will see shortly.

These issues are not mere abstractions. In considering the controversy about whether learning is multiplex or generic, we should note that **a decision on this issue is likely to affect the authority of different stakeholders in the curriculum controversy**. If learning a language is a substantially different process from that used learning to shoot a basketball, then research in one area may not be relevant to another. People on the "front line" of schooling may well know things that university study alone cannot give them.

Thus what appears at one level to be a theoretical dispute, may at another have substantial consequences in terms of who benefits and who loses in the competition for school resources.

Wittgenstein's Elephants

Philosopher Ludwig Wittgenstein asks us to consider two bushes both trimmed into the same shape; let's say, an elephant. We look and see the same two floppy ears and curled trunk on both of them. There, too, the curled tail and raised foreleg. The bushes have been expertly trimmed into the same configuration.

But would we then expect to find the same pattern of branches, twigs, and leaves, the same root structure, in both bushes? Of course not! We recognize that even substantial surface regularities may have very different underlying structure. (See Figure 18.1.) Why should we then assume that learning to play the piano is the same thing as learning to do quadratic equations, or even that learning to play the piano is the same thing for different people? Why should we imagine that learners are alike? Why should we expect teaching to have the same effects even when motivation may be the same?

Do dissimilar appearances indicate dissimilarities? How do we judge these matters? Again, these may seem to be esoteric theoretical questions. But every

---

[3]Ernest R. Hilgard, *Introduction to Psychology*, 3rd Ed. (New York: Harcourt, Brace & World, 1962), p. 252.

Figure 18.1   **WITTGENSTEIN'S ELEPHANTS**

teacher is faced with these "abstract" questions every day in the classroom. All the students have successfully completed a lesson in a workbook. Have they all learned the same? Not necessarily.

Couldn't some students skip that lesson or do something different and still learn the topic? It is possible. Yet, for organizational reasons, we often plan the same lessons for all the students in a class. How are such plans connected to the results we are looking for? How is what we do connected to what we look for? And how is what we see connected to what we plan to do?

In the next section we will look more closely at the notions of cause and effect in learning and teaching. They are indeed not simple.

CAUSATION IN LEARNING AND TEACHING

It is perplexing, even annoying to teachers to hear would-be reformers tell them that their efforts at teaching affect the balance of international trade, the alcoholism rate among teenagers, or the prospects for American democracy in the twenty-first century. Yet, when teachers ask in return, "How should I deal with children from broken homes, with alcoholic parents, with high needs for attention, or with low level reading skills?" the answers they receive are seldom explicit or pertinent. Many people seem to be able to discern all sorts of connections between the schools and social evils, yet far simpler connections between teacher treatments and student learning remain deepest mysteries.

Criteria and Authority

What connects with what? That is the general question of causation, posed in its most informal guise. More practical minded people might put it, "We want some results. So how do we get them?" Fancy theories of causation will amount to little if they do not help us with everyday questions like these.

But there are problems with finding causes, not the least of which is that the word "cause" is ambiguous. It has at least the following meanings:

- reason or justification, for example, "What's the cause of your sarcasm?"
- legally or morally accountable person, for example, "Your negligence caused this accident!"[4]
- productive agent, for example, "More fertilizer made the corn grow taller."
- item of interest in a complex productive system, for example, "By letting the water splash on the floor you shorted out the school transformer which caused a brownout in the neighborhood."

These rather informal, nonscientific senses contrast with the technical notion of cause generally used by scientific researchers:

- A is the cause of B if A and B are distinct, highly correlative variables and A can be manipulated, for example, "Turning the knob to the right makes the gas flame higher."[5]

It is a matter of dispute how this technical notion of cause relates to our traditional ones. Are sarcasm and negligence variables? What about persons? It is unclear.[6]

The technical concept of causation is **summative**. It requires that if all of certain conditions are met—that is, if the "cause" is present—certain results must occur—that is, the "effect" must follow. If not, there is no causal relation. So if we manipulate A and there is no change in B, or if B changes independently of our manipulations of A, there is no causal relation between A and B. We will understand the point of this apparent technicality when below we consider hoped-for learning outcomes that are not summative.

Controversies in education often rest on confusing different senses of cause. It is easy to find two items of interest and discover they co-vary, that is, changes in one appear to relate to changes in the other. It is quite another thing to establish a causal relationship between them. For example, the following things have all increased over the past ten years:

---

[4]Cf. H. L. A. Hart, "The Ascription of Responsibility and Rights" in Anthony Flew (ed.), *Logic and Language* (Garden City, N. Y.: Doubleday Anchor, 1965), pp. 151–174.
[5]The literature on the concept of cause is immense and its application to education problematic. See Edward. G. Rozycki, "The Functional Analysis of Behavior," *Educational Theory*, Vol. 26, No. 3 (Summer 1975), pp. 278–302. Also, the classics: Donald T. Campbell and Julian C. Stanley, *Experimental and Quasi-experimental Designs for Research* (Chicago: Rand-McNally, 1963); Mario Bunge, *Causality* (Cleveland: World Publishing, 1963); and Arthur L. Stinchcombe, *Constructing Social Theories* (New York: Harcourt, Brace & World, 1968).
[6]Edward G. Rozycki, *Human Behavior: Measurement and Cause. Can There Be a Science of Education?* Ed.D. dissertation, Temple University (Ann Arbor, Mich.: Xerox University Microfilms, 1974), Chap. IV, "The Causes of Behavior."

1. the national debt
2. the average age of Americans
3. the age of the moon
4. SAT scores
5. the deterioration of urban public school facilities
6. the number of Jeanne Dixon prophecies
7. general interest in public schooling
8. public recognition of Bill Cosby

Would anyone want to claim any item in the list has caused any other? What connection, if any, could we claim between them?

We recall from Chapter 3 that a major concern in dealing with educational problems is the extent to which stakeholders in a situation share the same perception of it. Those perceptions depended upon their sharing criteria and authorities in case of dissensus. Exactly the same problems exist when we seek a connection between items of interest. Understanding a causal relationship depends upon

- shared criteria about the items under consideration; and
- shared authorities for determining their connection.

People who believe in astrology see connections that others reject as "unreal." Teachers who believe in Freudian theory see connections that Behaviorists don't, and vice versa.

Most Americans, having absorbed one lesson of our pluralistic society, readily recognize that different beliefs affect a person's notions of cause. What is harder to see, however, is that our everyday language mixes concepts from different traditions so that they cannot be translated into the simple, uniform concepts required for precise measurement.[7] Many terms are taken from experimental contexts and used in schools applying traditional, rather than the experimental criteria that were their original context. Thus teachers talk about "reinforcing behavior" and mistakenly think they are doing the same thing with kids that Skinner did with the rats in his "Skinner boxes."

Causal Fallacies in Education

Educators often find themselves in a dilemma. The schools are relied upon to make up for all kinds of social ills but teachers are seldom trained to look for causal linkages between what they might do and the benefits expected of their actions. Nor are they trained to be critical of those who claim to see a connection between changes they want in the schools and some imminent calamity.

Because it is important that school people have some idea about expectations that might be based on ill-established causal claims, we will review

---

[7]Edward G. Rozycki, "Rewards, Reinforcers and Voluntary Behavior," *Ethics*, Vol. 84 (October 1973), pp. 38–47.

quickly errors they might meet where a connection is claimed between school practice and some other kind of event. These errors are

- Spurious Correlation,
- Nonsystemic Thinking,
- Developmental Misperceptions, and
- Assumptions of Passivity.

We will look at each of these in turn.

Spurious Correlation

Two kinds of events may correlate yet be unrelated causally. The national debt has recently risen along with SAT scores. Does this mere correlation establish a connection? Not at all.

Mere change is often accompanied by an increase in another variable. A teacher, for example, may find an increase in student motivation when new materials are handed out. This increase may have to do with the novelty rather than the nature of the materials. Also, the special attention paid persons in experimental groups tends to bring about changes even though the special treatment itself has no effect. This is called the *Hawthorne effect*.[8]

Sometimes two items correlate because they have a common cause. Thus, reduction of pre-school activities may correlate with reduction of after-school activities because of a generally reduced school budget, not because pre-school and after-school activities are causally related.

There is an extensive professional literature on "effective schools." Very often such articles give a list of characteristics that correlate with measures of school effectiveness. For example, George and Oldaker[9] mention such a correlation between "learning climate," "student behavior," and "student achievement." What are we to make of this? First of all, we must know that the measures of the three variables, "learning climate," "student behavior," and "student achievement" are independent. That is, one is not measured by the other. Otherwise, we are not talking about three distinct variables. Secondly, and most importantly, the correlations may not be causal. They may be the result of a common cause, for example, parental support. Thus, attempts to make a school more effective by directly improving "learning climate," "student behavior," and "student achievement" may not work.

Nonsystemic Thinking

Perceptions of straightforward cause and effect are invariably the result of a stable underlying system. We turn the knob on the stove and the flame shoots

---

[8] See literature on the "Hawthorne effect," for example, Perrow, pp. 90–92.

[9] Paul S. George and Lynn I. Oldaker, "A National Survey of Middle School Effectiveness," *Educational Leadership*, December 1985/January 1986, pp. 79–85. See also M. Donald Thomas, "What is an effective school?" *The Effective School Report*, Vol.17, No.1 (January/February 1989) (New York: Kelwyn Press, 1989), p. 5, for criteria that conflict along the dimensions divisible-indivisible and absolute-positional.

Lecture: causation or ceremony?

up in direct relation to the angle of the turn. We have here a direct, unilinear correlation: the paradigm of efficient causation—but only because the rest of the system is stable. If the gas coming into the house varied in its pressure, or if the pipes leaked, our simple causal relationship would disappear. Most causes are multiple. We tend to focus on those that we can manipulate while maintaining the rest constant.

Lecture is by far the most widely used method of instruction from seventh grade onward. But how effective is the lecture method? Do better lecturers get more taught? That is not clear. Are students learning **because of** the lectures? That is not clear either. Suppose now we transfer a competent lecturer to a situation where either motivation or IQ varies. Should we be surprised if test grades fall? Successful teachers who are wise will recognize the contribution that both their students and their schools make to their success.

Developmental Misperceptions

Organizations are systems. But in many ways so are people. Systems change and develop through time. So do the causal relations within them. Readiness

Is this developmentally
appropriate?

is an educational concept that recognizes that a technique may be appropriate at one time in the development of a learner and inappropriate at another. Some researchers believe, for example, that reading problems are almost invariably a result of trying to push early literacy. Teachers used to working with kids within a certain age range often find their expertise reduced when they have to deal outside it.

It is here that curriculum material organized along logical, disciplinary, or organizational lines conflicts with what is pedagogically effective. (See Chapter 17.) Keeping the possibility of developmental difference in mind can help us through our failures. A technique may test as ineffective, when in fact it is only inappropriate to the developmental level of the student. The notion of development leavens our judgment against rash decision.

Assumptions of Passivity

Some reforms are not worth the pain. Expecting to make substantial changes to a system assuming that the stakeholders will remain passive while these changes are effected, is no small mistake in judgment. The systems management model we discussed in Chapter 8 rests on substantial assumptions of passivity within the system. So do the great majority of reform proposals that receive airing in the press. We begin to understand the recurrent call for educational reform in the United States. It is based on false assumptions of passivity. Less obvious is why such assumptions persist in the face of bitter experience. Perhaps it requires some investigation into the possibility of perceptual encasements (see Chapter 8) to find this out.

MODELS OF LEARNING

Most people who have ever been to school have firm expectations about what teaching and learning should be. These expectations, founded in long-standing traditions, often make it difficult for us to examine teaching and learning to assess what, if any, causal connections there might be between them.

What we try to teach students is often less determined by what we think they *can* learn, than by what we think they *should* learn. Since ancient times, the curriculum has guided learning. It is only with the development of pedagogical focus that learning has been addressed in its own right.

"Learning" is at best a vague and ambiguous term.[10] We saw above that there is a dispute over whether it should be considered a **generic** or **multiplex** term, that is, whether we should look to find a *common* process in every situation where we would want to say someone has learned something, or whether we are willing to allow for the possibility that our everyday use of the term is sloganistic and that different processes may be discovered depending upon the kind of learning we are considering.

---

[10]B. Paul Komisar, "More on the Concept of Learning," *Educational Theory*, Vol. XV, No. 3 (July 1965).

A second ambiguity occurs when people confuse **process** with **product**. If our interest is in what is going on while someone learns and whether that going-on can be enhanced, then we are concerned about process. If, however, our focus is on outcomes, we are concerned about product.

This ambiguity between learning as process and learning as product tends to intensify the dispute over whether learning is generic or multiplex. For example, we might agree that students exhibit learning (products) in a variety of classes without committing ourselves to the theory that a single kind of learning (process) has occurred in each classroom.

In this chapter we will restrict our attention to learning **products**. Historically, people have been able to identify these without having much conception of the learning process. More important, they can often agree on what the products are even if they disagree on the underlying process. Indeed, in many areas of schooling, the relationship of teaching to learning has a somewhat mystical, even magical character. We will discuss this below.

What Can be Learned?

We have inherited a broad and conflicting set of traditions as to what can be learned. However, there is widespread consensus on the way teaching and learning relate to one another. We can identify some principles upon which our beliefs in learnability rest. By "principles" we mean slogans that link ideas in a way that makes them widely acceptable to people from different communities. Despite our society's being very pluralistic in some ways, there are conceptual linkages we all share. Let's look at some of these.

What can be learned? A wide variety of things. Let's use **X** as a variable that represents a possible curricular item and state what we can call here the curricular principle of learnability:

- **The curricular principle of learnability**: if **X** is in the curriculum, **X** can be learned.

It is unlikely that anyone would find this "principle" acceptable. The problem here is that it does not help us decide whether something should be added to the curriculum. Secondly, it overlooks that possibility that **X** has been mistakenly put there. What we have here is an item for which a broad negative consensus likely exists. Can you imagine trying to teach in a community where a principle like this one is generally accepted?

Certainly, physical impossibility rules out learnability. We can formulate the following principle:

- **The physical impossibility principle of learnability**: if it is physically impossible to (do) **X**, **X** cannot be learned.

We might suspect that a broad consensus exists on this principle, even if there is dispute about specifics. Consider the contrary. What if someone were to say, "This can be learned but it is physically impossible to do"? It would probably strike us as nonsense.

Of course, our ideas of what is physically possible can change. But so then would our ideas about what is learnable. Before the development of biofeedback devices, most experts would have thought it physically impossible for people to consciously control their pulse rate or their blood pressure.[11] But they *can* learn to do so, and this fact expands our notions of the physically possible. Some people believe in mental telepathy; others do not. The latter would deny that one could learn to perform feats of mental telepathy. The former might not. "Might not" is a crucial phrase, because the principle is very broad. It tells us that physically *impossible* things *cannot* be learned, but it does not say that all physically *possible* things *can* be learned. Certainly, some physically possible things may be unlearnable for other reasons.

Most of us have some belief that learning depends upon developmental appropriateness; that is, if a person is intellectually or emotionally unready, certain things cannot be learned by that person, even though they might be learned at some later, more developed stage of life. We can formulate this belief as:

> ▬ **The developmental appropriateness principle of learnability**: if it is developmentally inappropriate for a certain person, **P**, to (do) **X**, **X** cannot be learned by **P**.

Different cultures vary widely in how they believe children are capable of behaving. In one culture, table manners may be expected of two-year-olds; in another, children are not expected to learn table manners until they are eight or nine. Again, we have a principle of likely broad although shallow consensus.

If we put the two principles together, we come up with the following:

> ▬ If *X* is physically possible and developmentally appropriate for *P*, then *P* can learn *X*.

For example, it is physically possible to broadjump 20 feet. John is an athletic person. Therefore, John can learn to broadjump 20 feet. However, we might well consider that bad coaching, bad weather, or tight pants could frustrate John's learning. Perhaps we need a supportive principle along these lines, for example,

> ▬ **The nonimpediment principle of learnability**: if certain circumstances impede learning to (do) **X** for person **P**, **X** cannot be learned by **P** under those circumstances.

---

[11]Cf. John Paul Brady, Lester Luborsky, and Reuben E. Kron, "Blood Pressure Reduction in Patients with Essential Hypertension Through Metronome-Conditioned Relaxation: A Preliminary Report," in Leo V. Dicara et al. (eds.), *Bio-Feedback and Self-Control 1974* (Chicago: Aldine, 1975), pp. 256–262.

This "principle" seems even more obvious than the rest because it merely states that some things impede learning. It is useful only if it allows that other things beside physical impossibility and developmental inappropriateness impede learning.

One more principle is necessary to identify the structures of belief that connect with widely held notions of learning. Many people believe that "natural gifts" or "talents" are not learnable, although they may be developed or "sharpened" through learning. We could formulate this as:

- **The talent principle of learnability**: if talent is necessary for **X**, **X** cannot be learned without that talent.

Playing the piano probably does not require talent. Playing Mozart's Turkish March well probably does. Thus, while we may place "piano studies" in the school curriculum, we should not place "brilliant playing of Mozart's Turkish March" in the curriculum, unless we believe that we can control the bestowal of talent. We can indeed wonder if those who make recurrent calls for "excellence" in our schools might be neglecting the talent principle of learnability.

What we are trying to do in laying out these "principles" is to spell out a consensus of beliefs that underlie our notions of learning. So far we have discovered that learning connects with our beliefs about physical and developmental possibility, with the belief that some circumstances are impediments to learning and to a concept of talent. We might want to argue as follows:

- Everything in the curriculum must be learnable by any normal child. Therefore we must exclude things that
    a. are physically impossible;
    b. are developmentally inappropriate;
    c. require talent to be done.
  Furthermore, we must take care to remove other impediments to learning as we discover them.

This all seems obvious because it is highly sloganistic. No specifics are given. But the slogans in effect tells us much about our "conceptual map" in the area of learning; that is, our concept of learning is related to our concept of physical and developmental possibility, and to our notions of talent and impediment.

This "conceptual map" can be a practical tool. If we expect learning to take place under certain circumstances and it doesn't, we use the "map" to look for specific impediments, to reconsider the physical and developmental possibilities, and to rule out the possibility that we are trying to get someone to learn what we believe only those with special talent can do. Perhaps academic excellence requires rare talent. That would explain its scarcity.

The specifics that underlie our "principles" will depend upon the authorities we accept for determining such specifics. Chart 18.2 illustrates how the

Chart 18.2

CAN IT BE LEARNED?

TO BE LEARNED	Group A	Group B	Group C
	Curing illness by the laying on of hands		
Physically Possible?	No	Yes	Yes
Developmentally Appropriate?	Not Applicable	Not for kids. For adults trained in certain therapeutic procedures	Yes, for all understanding believers
Talent Necessary?	Not Applicable	Yes, certain personality types	No
Other Impediments?	Not Applicable	No organic damage can exist	Inner lack of Faith. Sinful soul.
Can It Be Learned?	No	Yes	Yes

same conceptual map may be used differently by people from different and disagreeing cultural subgroups. According to the beliefs held by each of the groups, they might come to different conclusions as to whether a particular item is learnable.

In Chart 18.2 we might assume that group A are members of the American Medical Association, group B would be psychiatrists of a certain type, and group C would be certain Fundamentalist Christians. The figure demonstrates that all groups share a common conceptual map of learning as it relates to physical possibility, developmental appropriateness, talent, and impediments. However, they differ in the specifics of each category.

Character, skills, and citizenship are often given as major curricular goals. Let's investigate conceptions of learning in each of these major types. These conceptions will be:

■ learning as forming character,
■ learning as gaining understanding, and
■ learning as skills acquisition.

Learning as Forming Character

It is not then how much a man may know, that is of importance, but the end and purpose for which he knows it. The object of knowledge should be to mature wisdom and improve character, to render us better, happier, and more useful; more benevolent, more energetic and more efficient in the pursuit of every high purpose in life.

———————— *Samuel Smiles*[12]

The most ancient concept of learning is that it is the formation of character. This is the primary thrust of the Temple image of the school. Morality, propriety, a sense of social fitness, all of these take precedence over "mere" knowledge, for example, book learning and skills. Samuel Smiles, a widely read author of popular self-help and motivation books of the late nineteenth century, restates this ancient idea in the quote above in terms of what a newly industrialized America would recognize as virtues—happiness, usefulness, energy, and efficiency.

Thus we move from the Temple to the Town Meeting. Character is a sufficiently vague notion that not only traditional communities but national governments can define it to their own purposes. Nothing guarantees that learning that "forms character" will produce something good. Spartan parents no doubt believed that their sons' experiences in slaughtering helpless helots strengthened their character.

Character is not merely a matter of intellect, but also of emotions and values. To the extent that modern schooling does not address the issues of educating the emotions[13] and lacks consensus on the values to be emphasized, to that extent do some contemporary theorists believe schooling cannot be educational.

In terms of the curricular interests formulated in Chapter 17, learning as character is a status interest. It serves to maintain a system of values of particular social groups. Thus, "character" is also a slogan-term. We could no doubt find wide agreement that schools should develop the student's char-

---

[12]Samuel Smiles, *Happy Homes and the Hearts That Make Them* (Chicago: U.S. Publishing House, 1882), p. 302.

[13]Daniel R. DiNicola, "The Education of the Emotions," *Philosophy of Education*, Vol. 19.

What can he teach them?

acter, and yet, when we press for depth, we discover that the exact meaning of "character" to different people might vary from community to community or even person to person.

Learning as Gaining Understanding

In many cultures learning is defined as gaining understanding. But it is the understanding of tradition, authority, and passed-down wisdom. A more modern status concept of learning is that learning is understanding, even understanding to the point of self-actualization, where individual values oppose those of the community. We must not assume that understanding formulated in terms of long-standing traditions is the same as understanding pursued by individualist theorists. People in many traditions do not worry, for example, about indoctrination. To them, reason that conflicts with tradition is false reason.

To believe that reason can lead one into conflict with tradition requires commitment to one of the many variants of Socratic theory that exist in our culture. In the Socratic tradition, status learning, the pursuit of Truth, struggles with social control interests, the recognized authorities of the community. Understanding becomes the possession of an elite who hold a method, an intuition, whatever it is, that is justified within the tradition as a legitimate alternative to received wisdom.

Skills Acquisition

The oldest explicit focus of schooling has been to develop skills. We take the demonstration of new skill to be an undeniable sign of learning. Unless, of course, we believe it to be a matter of natural development, in which case we are less likely to call it a skill and more likely to call it a new "ability." We should note that careful appraisal of our linguistic traditions can give us insight into the conceptual structures that incline us to find such ways of thinking to be more "reasonable" than others.[14] These cultural traditions are not ephemeral verbalizations but are deeply rooted in time-tested practice.

For example, animals show many different complex **abilities** as they mature, web-weaving, nest-building, and so forth. We tend to relate "skill" to learning. No matter how complex behavior is, if we believe it to be unlearned, we tend not to call it a skill.[15] Birds build nests better than spiders do, not because of greater skill, but, perhaps, because of better "adaptation." Similarly, spiders build webs better than birds do, not because of greater skill, either.

---

[14]Some classic investigations in this vein can be found in B. Paul Komisar and C.B.J. MacMillan (eds.), *Psychological Concepts in Education* (Chicago: Rand McNally, 1967); R. S. Peters (ed.), *The Concept of Education* (London: Routledge & Kegan Paul, 1967); Israel Scheffler, *The Language of Education* (Springfield, Ill.: Charles C. Thomas, 1960); B. Othaniel Smith and Robert Ennis (eds.), *Language and Concepts in Education* (Chicago: Rand McNally, 1961).

[15]Cf. Noam Chomsky, "Review of B.F. Skinner, *Verbal Behavior*" in *Language*, Vol. 35 (1959), pp. 26–59, for his criticism of Skinner's theory that language is built up from elements to reach higher and higher levels of skill.

Birds and spiders do what they do because their bodies work the way they work. "Adaptation" is not a skill-concept; rather it is an evolutionary notion of talent, talent that comes to be.

In general, what develops naturally we tend to distinguish from what may be developed through teaching interactions. If coming to know, or to do, or to be is traditionally recognized as a kind of learning, then not all learning is a matter of acquiring skills.

Let's look at an interesting problem that serves as the focus of much concern in schooling today—the teaching of values.

Can Morality Be Learned?

Can you tell me, Socrates, whether virtue is acquired by teaching or by practice, or if neither by teaching nor practice, then whether it comes to man by nature, or in what other way?

_____*Meno*[16]

The debate as to whether morality can be taught is an ancient one. Today, educators are becoming more and more involved with explicit instruction in "values." By observing the distinctions we have made in this and earlier chapters, we can shed some light on the question whether morality can be taught. More importantly, we will see that many kinds of learning are similar to what we might call moral learnings and can be dealt with in a similar fashion.

Let's begin by narrowing down the question, "Can morality be taught?" This is an ambiguous question. It could mean

a.   Can a someone, for example, a teacher or parent, be held responsible for the formation of character in a child? or,

b.   Can there be a scientific process (a summative cause) that a teacher could set in motion which would result in a student's becoming honest?

The answer to **a** is a clear yes. We often hold people responsible for things that they have little causal control over, in the scientific sense. One informal meaning of cause, as we have seen earlier in the chapter, is a legally or morally accountable person.

To the second question, **b**, we will argue no. The reasons for this will be given shortly by way of analogy rather than argument. This is a difficult topic and the technically adventurous reader interested in additional argument might refer to Item A in the Technical Appendix for Chapter 18.

We might reformulate the question of whether morality can be taught as

---

[16]*Plato's* Meno, Alexander Sesonske and Noel Fleming (eds.) (Belmont, Calif.: Wadsworth, 1965), p. 5.

"What (or how) does one teach to cause (summative sense) a person to become an honest person?" This question is much like the question, "How much power do you need to become an authority?" Such a question indicates a failure to understand that the relationship of power to authority is not a causal one.

In Chapter 9 we carefully defined the distinction between power and authority. Someone's power depends upon his or her control of resources but authority depends upon other people's assenting to recognize it as such. Power is a summative concept but authority is a matter of assent. If a person has enough power, we may feel coerced to concede to their demands. But, as we have seen, this power of compulsion is not authority. Only when we defer freely to the judgment of another is this the recognition of authority.

In a parallel fashion we might argue that certain kinds of training and behavior give us reason to bestow moral titles, such as "honest" or "trustworthy." It may be reasonable or traditional or even moral to show people such respect. But it is not necessary. For example, racism denies titles of respect to people on the basis of their skin color, even though they may show all the qualities that other people have that racists respect. Racists are making a moral error, however; not a logical one.

Let's contrast learning as character development with learning skills. We normally evaluate skills incrementally; character tends to be an all or nothing thing. We can make judgments of more or less skill, say, at basketball, by seeing how accurately a player shoots, whether he or she defends well or works well in the offense. But judgments of honesty are a different matter. A person who steals once a month does not merely have less character than someone who doesn't steal at all, or more than someone who steals twice a month. He or she is dishonest, of "no character," or of "bad character." Positive evaluations of character, once disconfirmed, tend to be lost—unless "forgiven" as "out of character." A clever thief may do acts characteristic of honest people to gain our confidence. These do not suffice to make him or her honest. Rehabilitation is not merely a matter of doing good and refraining from evil. There is another aspect to be considered.

Once lost, character can be reestablished only within certain traditions of redemption. One purpose of traditional religious rituals of atonement is to reestablish an individual's status as trustworthy. This is the point of the saying, "Forgive and forget!" Moral status is granted totally, so to speak, rather than incrementally. No specific tests of honesty can establish a person's honesty. That person, may, after all, be trying to deceive us. But specific individual acts of dishonesty may invalidate that ascription.

This is an important point. Certain characterizations of learning are not so much **summative descriptions** of a learner as **ascriptions**, acts of acknowledgment on our part that a learner is entitled to be recognized in a certain way. These ascriptions are conceded to someone because he or she has participated in a socially valued (or despised) process, or because a recognized authority has bestowed them. (See also Item A in the Technical Appendix to Chapter 18.)

What then can "moral education" amount to? Moral education *depends upon a consensus* that children (people) who have been trained in a particular way, or have been exposed to example and preachment of a certain kind, are worthy of trust, i.e., they should be recognized and dealt with as morally upstanding persons. (Such recognition is not the same as a prediction that morally upstanding persons will not commit offenses, although we normally concede such recognition only with the expectation that offenses will not, at least, be actively pursued.)

Learning and School Image

Learning outcomes in the Temple tend to be ascriptive. They emphasize the role of authority in certifying the attainment of broad, vague goals supported by an assumed depth of consensus. Let's consider, for example, that education for the Imperial Chinese civil service required the study of calligraphy and Confucian philosophy. British elite schools emphasized Greek and Latin classics. Japanese elite education required calligraphy, tea ceremonies, and poetry writing. Certainly, it was not skills for political administration that were sought after with such curricula.[17]

Unless such schooling was bureaucratized, as in the Chinese case, examinations were not a major factor, at least not in the sense that we understand them. It was the pronouncement of acceptance by a recognized master that counted, rather than some "objective" test based on well-articulated, public criteria.

Even traditional vocational training based on apprenticeship relies on the pronouncements of a master that the novice has reached certain levels of skill. In order to advance in the ranks, very often it is time spent in service that counts as much as presumed increments in skill.

The Factory image of the school invokes criteria that are (theoretically, at least) public and understandable by those indifferent to the outcomes sought. Under the Factory image curricular items tend to be less ascriptive. The Behavioral Objectives movement,[18] popular in the 1970s, attempted to replace all ascriptive learnings with descriptive ones. The major complaints about these efforts were that such objectives were pale shadows of the rich goals they were derived from and it was not obvious why certain objectives related to any particular goals. (See Chapter 17 on the curriculum of the Factory.) The Behavioral Objectives movement thus transformed itself into a **competencies** movement. But competencies are certainly more ascriptive than behaviors. Let's compare, for example, the difference between "John speaks *some* Spanish" and "John speaks Spanish." That John can say *Buenos dias* proves the former, not the latter—for the latter is an ascription based on no particular summative set of behaviors. (See also Item B in the Technical Appendix to Chapter 18.)

---

[17]Cf. Randall Collins, "Some Comparative Principles of Educational Stratification."
[18]See Mager, op. cit.

When the power-holding constituencies of the school become broad enough, the school becomes a Town Meeting. The objectivity that the Factory orientation attempted to impose on the school becomes the device that threatens the legitimacy of school authority now exposed to a wider community of concern. Insulating this authority from the possible disappointments of Factory evaluation encourages the institutionalization of the school. (See Chapter 9 on institutionalization.) The compromise reached is that certification, not "objective" evaluation, will be the touchstone of achievement. It tends to make learning more ascriptive and teachers more vulnerable to a variety of criticism that specific skills are not being mastered by the students.

In the next section we will look at models of teaching. They will be:

- teaching as telling,
- teaching as initiating,
- teaching as training, and
- teaching as nurturing.

We can expect that our conceptions of learning and the images of the school will, to some extent, determine these models. Does teaching connect to learning as cause to effect? This will be one of the concerns supporting our inquiry.

MODELS OF TEACHING

> To suppose that you can properly regulate (the) process of forming and accumulating ideas, without understanding the nature of the process, is absurd.
>
> —————*Herbert Spencer,* On Education[19]

In November 1988 Arnold Rich of Louisville, Kentucky, in behalf of his son, John, filed suit against the Kentucky Day School, a private school his son had attended for nine years. His charge was that the school had failed to give the boy the superior education that the family had contracted for.[20]

From the second through the fifth grades, John Rich was a good student. Then his grades began to fall. The boy, according to Mr. Rich, would do his assignments but leave them in his locker. Thomas G. Monaco, the director of the school, admitted that John had been rebuked as lazy and irresponsible in order to "motivate" him. Finally, the school refused to admit him into the tenth grade.

---

[19]Herbert Spencer, *Essays on Education* (New York: Dutton, Everyman's Library, 1963), p. 23.
[20]Kirsten Goldberg, "School in Kentucky Faces 'Malpractice' Charge," *Education Week*, November 16, 1988, p. 6.

John Rich's IQ is 135. An evaluation by a psychologist found the boy to be suffering from "attention-deficit disorder," a learning disability that "causes children to be distracted and slow to follow directions." Although using Ritalin, a drug often prescribed to increase attention span, and being specially tutored, the improvement in John's grades was not considered sufficient by school authorities to retain him in tenth grade. They do not believe John has a learning disability.

Rich, in a court deposition, commented, "If they're the educational specialists that they say they are, they should have the ability to recognize that a problem other than just laziness and irresponsibility exists."

We can see from the example of John Rich that considerations of causation and the relationship of teaching to learning are not just idle speculation. There may be substantial consequences to be faced when disagreement on these issues is met. As we learned in Chapter 15, the accusation of negligence in teaching is the accusation that care has fallen below a certain accepted level and resulted in an injury. Lawyers for the Kentucky Day School do not believe their clients are in trouble and have asked for dismissal of the suit.

From our previous discussion we can discern certain difficulties in Rich's establishing his complaint:

- Theories about learning disability are controversial.[21] Many experts believe the terms such as "attention-deficit disorder" are nothing more than a slogan to give a name to our ignorance.
- Even if there were agreement on the nature of the learning disability, we might not know how to deal with it.
- "Accepted level of care" is vague. That a failure has occurred is no reason to suppose that negligence has, also. There must be a broad consensus on the kind of causal relation, if any, that exists between normal traditional schooling procedures and the failures of individuals in a given school.
- "Laziness" and "irresponsibility" are a kind of causal explanation. But they are ascriptive terms, not summative ones. Thus they do not indicate conditions that can be manipulated to change an outcome.
- "Laziness" and "irresponsibility" are also terms that deny concerns and interest (see Chapter 3). This may be the underlying motive of Mr. Rich's suit. Calling a student "lazy" or "irresponsible" is too easy a way to shift responsibility from the school staff to the student.

The courts may determine that private schools, unlike public schools, are in a unique contractual relationship with parents that permits learning failure to be interpreted as a fault. If so, the nature of cause in teaching and learning will become an even more cogent issue.

---

[21]Cf. Diane McGuinness, "Facing the 'Learning Disabilities' Crises," *Education Week*, February 5, 1986, p. 28; See also, Mary Saily, "Learning Remains Elusive for Handicapped Children," *Educational R&D Report*, Vol. 4, No.4 (Winter 1981–1982).

What Can Be Taught?

> When a superior man knows the causes which make instruction successful, and those which make it of no effect, he can become a teacher of others. Thus in his teaching, he leads and does not drag; he strengthens and does not discourage; he opens the way but does not conduct to the end without the learner's own efforts. Leading and not dragging produces harmony. Strengthening and not discouraging makes attainment easy. Opening the way and not conducting to the end makes the learner thoughtful. He who produces such harmony, easy attainment and thoughtfulness may be pronounced a skillful teacher.
>
> ——————— *Confucius*[22]

Confucius' advice looks sound to those who know what to make of it and how to specifically apply it in a real teaching situation. We should notice, however, that he mentions successful instruction, not learning. He may have meant by "successful instruction" to indicate "learning," but we should not jump to that conclusion. Teaching, even good teaching, does not, in and of itself, guarantee a specific kind of learning. If it could, then "Teach them!" would be a no-fail prescription to cure all ignorance. (See Chapter 3 and the "can-it-fail?" rule.)

Teaching is an occupation as well as an activity. Provided we're not merely referring to an occupation, it does no great injustice to our traditional notions of teaching to say that teaching is an *attempt* to get someone to learn something.[23] Like running in the Olympics, teaching may be done extremely well,[24] even if a medal is not won, that is, even if some circumstance impedes the desired learning. What can we say about teaching and its connection with learning?

We have to be careful not to confuse process with product. "Can **X** be taught?" is an ambiguous question. It may mean either

a. Can a **good faith attempt** be made to get someone to learn **X**? (a process notion) or
b. Is there some way of **successfully** bringing someone to learn **X**? (a product notion)

As with learning, a **generic** concept competes with a **multiplex** concept. Advocates of the generic concept hold that some common set of teacher behavior is found in every instance of teaching. They have yet to make their

---

[22]Confucius, *HSIO KI (Record on the Subject of Education)*, Book XVI.
[23]Cf. B. Paul Komisar, "Conceptual Analysis of Teaching," *The High School Journal*, Vol. 50, No. 1 (October 1966), pp. 14–21.
[24]Harry S. Broudy, "Can We Define Good Teaching?" *The Record—Teachers' College*, Vol. 70, No. 7 (April 1969), pp. 583–592.

case empirically. A multiplex approach would expect no more commonality than with any slogan-like term deriving from a variety of traditions. As with learning, the generic-multiplex dispute is not merely one of theoretical interest. The authority of different stakeholders in the schooling enterprise depends on the way the battle goes.

Again, as with learning, no curricular principle can help us determine what can be taught. That **X** is in the curriculum does not mean it can be taught, although we can expect that someone with the authority to direct the teaching will call anything in the curriculum teachable. Perhaps what can be learned can help us determine what can be taught.

It does not follow that because something can be learned, it can be taught. Plato did not believe that virtue could be taught, but that it came of a self-discovery process, philosophical inquiry. By "could not be taught" he meant that virtue was not brought about by the attempts of others to get someone to be virtuous. The discussion above on ascriptive learnings lends some credibility to his claim.[25]

For purposes of shorthand, let us use **X** to mean our curricular item; **S**, to designate a student; and **T**, the teacher. The ambiguity of the phrase "**X** has been taught to **S** by **T**" can indicate either:

a. process: "a good faith attempt has been made by **T** to get **S** to learn **X**" or

b. product: "**T** has succeeded in getting **S** to learn **X**"

These permit those who are unobservant of the ambiguity to accuse every unsuccessful teacher of dereliction. Recall that **X** is learnable if no talent is necessary to do **X**, if **X** is physically and developmentally possible, and if no other impediments stand in the way. But the problem with what is teachable is whether one can make a good faith attempt to get someone to learn **X**.

"Teach the children" is a fair demand only if we think of teaching as a fallible process. The teacher may strive mightily indeed and still fail. The critic, switching to the product sense of "having taught," then unfairly accuses the teacher, "You haven't been teaching!" This is the basic maneuver in all criticism which goes directly from poor test results to clamoring for the reform of teaching.

Let us consider now the traditional notions of teaching as telling, initiating, training, and nurturing. We will see that how they relate to learning and the notion of causation involved can vary surprisingly from case to case.

Teaching as Telling

. . . but speak the word only, and my servant shall be healed.

——————— *St. Matthew, 9:8*

---

[25]See Edmund L. Pincoffs, "What Can Be Taught?" *Philosophy of Education*, 1967, pp. 44–54.

... the Word was God.

——————— *St. John, 1:1*

Lecturing and explaining are the predominant teacher activities at the junior high and senior high level.[26] Indeed, in the public mind, teaching is telling. When William J. Bennett, Secretary of Education during the Reagan administration, visited schools and talked to classes, reporters would rush in afterward to ask students whether Bennett was a good teacher. The answers they got were not surprising.

Telling, exhorting, and preaching are believed to be a primary, if not the primary method of teaching in our culture. This faith in the power of the word supports teaching traditions in which the teacher alone is the source of knowledge and authority in the classroom. It also reinforces the "magic" of speech.[27]

No less important than the contribution of religious traditions to belief in the power of the Word is our everyday experience with swearwords and curses. These may evoke strong emotional responses and they work to maintain general belief in the effectiveness of command. Forgotten is the training that went into producing such responses. The sounds themselves take on the power.

If we add to these traditions the economic reality that lecture is the least expensive form of instruction, that it is the honored form of professorial performance, and that it supports our beliefs in the value of IQ as a measure of personal quality, we begin to comprehend why telling plays such a central role in instruction. If people are told and they still don't learn, we can blame *them* for not really listening. That is, we then *tell* them it's their fault. This is the cheapest of remedial services.

Initiation

Closely related to teaching as telling is the idea that the teacher is a kind of priest who initiates the student into a discipline. Typical initiation processes involve rituals of submission to authority, ranking, testing, enlightenment, and certification usually enhanced with a substantial dose of mystery and pomp.

---

[26]Goodlad, op. cit., p. 107.

[27]A sophisticated version of the "teaching is telling" theory is the "erotetic concept" of teaching. This theory requires that the teacher conduct his or her teaching as though he or she were answering the questions students would ask about a subject matter if they were clear about how what they needed to know related to what they actually know. This theory presumes that the logical structure of knowledge is the pedagogical structure. (See Chapter 17.) For presentation and discussion of this theory, refer to the following: C. J. B. MacMillan and James W. Garrison, "An Erotetic Concept of Teaching," *Educational Theory*, Vol. 33, Nos. 3 & 4 (Summer-Fall 1983), pp. 157–167; Robert H. Ennis, "Is Answering Questions Teaching?" *Educational Theory*, Vol. 36, No. 4 (Fall 1986), pp. 343–347; Shirley Pendlebury, "Teaching: Response and Responsibility," *Educational Theory*, Vol. 36, No. 4 (Fall 1986), pp. 349–354; C. J. B. MacMillan and James W. Garrison, "Erotetics Revisited," *Educational Theory*, Vol. 36, No. 4 (Fall 1986), pp. 355–361.

Subject matter traditions, rather than occupational concerns, heavily influence instructional decisions. We saw in Chapter 17, for example, that lesson planning is rarely done in terms of student outcome objectives, but rather in terms of content. Research results are perplexing. On the one hand, high school teachers see the curriculum as more intellectually focused than they would prefer, while high school parents find it less intellectual than they desire.[28] On the other hand, teachers show remarkably little interest in their students' concerns for making a living or learning about careers, while the public thinks much more should be done.[29] Teachers in a specialty are often biased. They are successful students in that specialty and they tend to want to make their students have the same kind of success.

Initiation is an ancient rite in all cultures. We know from Chapter 17 that in an expanding system of schooling pursuing equity, the diploma loses its instrumental value. Nonetheless, it marks an important rite of passage in our culture.

Training and Nurturing

The point of training is to meet certain external demands imposed on the individual. The point of nurturance is to respond to the developmental needs of the individual. We can conceive of nurturance and training as being on a continuum from low to high imposition of external demands. (See Figure 18.2.)

The labeled points indicate different locations along the continuum with different levels of concern about nurturance and training. Point A permits growth undirected by external demands. We can picture this as raising to-

[28]Goodlad, op. cit., p. 64.
[29]Joyce D. Stern (ed.), *The Condition of Education 1987 Edition*. Statistical Report, Center for Education Statistics (Washington, D.C.: Office of Educational Research and Improvement, U.S. Department of Education, 1987), pp. 78–79.

Training or nurturance?

Figure 18.2

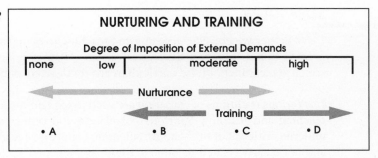

Chart 18.3　　　　　**LEVELS OF NURTURANCE AND TRAINING**

Reference Point	TOMATO PLANTS	SOME CHILDREN	SOCIAL INSTITUTIONS
Point A	Unstaked	Feral Children	free play, frat parties, charismatic religion
Point B	Caged	American Children	"progressive" schools, summer camps, sports
Point C	Espaliered	Spartan Boys	"traditional" schools, military training, ballet
Point D	Winter Forced	Maimed Beggars	forced labor camps, war

matoes that are given water, sunshine, and fertilizer but allowed to lie on the ground and grow like a weed.

Point B shows some concern for external demands. Here we cage our tomatoes to keep the fruit off the ground, perhaps pinching off tertiary shoots or suckers. Point C indicates heavier external demands. At this point, for example, we might **espalier** our tomatoes, pruning them to a single main stem and supporting three or four secondary bearing shoots horizontally with wires. This procedure tends to reduce the amount of crop, but to make individual tomatoes very big.

Point D shows the sacrifice of the developmental needs of the plant (or individual) to the external demands of the training. Nurturance is forgone. This is exemplified by forcing tomatoes in winter to get fruit. The fruit will be inferior and the plant will die sooner.

We can locate a variety of social and schooling practices and products along such a continuum. Chart 18.3 uses reference points A through D from Figure 18.2, along with the example of the tomato plants, to locate some of these practices.[30]

---

[30]The phrase "maimed beggars" refers to the practice in some countries of maiming children to make them more pitiable and therefore better beggars.

SUMMARY

1.   Whether we consider learning and teaching to be a generic or a multiplex process is not merely a theoretical dispute. Rather it bears importantly on which stakeholders in the curriculum are recognized as having authority.

2.   Various traditions of causation are used to explain the connection between teaching and learning. Spurious correlation and other causal fallacies often underlie.criticism of the schools. Scientific concepts of learning are summative and not clearly related to other traditional concepts.

3.   Learning can be conceived of as forming character, gaining understanding, and acquiring skills. Learning can be summative or ascriptive. Ascriptive learning such as learning to be honest is not compatible with summative causal concepts.

4.   Teaching can be conceived of as telling, initiation, training, or nurturing. Telling is considered to be effective on the basis of ancient beliefs in the power of the word. Nurturing and training distinguish themselves in terms of external demands placed on the learner. Commitments to a specific expectation model create differences in understanding "Teaching A causes learning B."

QUESTIONS

1.   Can you select items of the curriculum and rank them as involving thinking and problem-solving skills more or less like out-of-school activities?
2.   Consider the possibilities that teaching and learning are either generic or multiplex concepts. Who gains and who loses if a school decides to treat them as either generic or multiplex?
3.   The image of Wittgenstein's elephants can be used to address the following question: How do I know if what I mean when I say "learning" is what you mean when you say "learning"?
4.   Make a list of ten common causal connection, for example, "Cold freezes water," or "Rainy days make kids jumpy." Sort them out among the various conception of cause cited in this chapter. Do some fit in more than one category?
5.   Consider some common criticisms of the schools. Do they rest on causal fallacies?
6.   Can you make a list of talents necessary for some kinds of learning? How about some known impediments to learning?
7.   Consider Chart 18.2. Can you reconstruct it for the following items to be learned: winning at roulette, being a good teacher, telling the future?
8.   Write down ten common learning objectives. Rank them from summative to ascriptive. Can you rewrite the most ascriptive objective as something

or somethings less ascriptive? (See Item B, the Technical Appendix to Chapter 18.)

9. Think of the different kinds of educational institutions we have in our society, for example, church, Boy Scouts, schools, and so forth. Do some favor certain conceptions of teaching over others?

10. Can you delineate the relationship between different expectation models of the school, associated conceptions of teaching, causation and learning, and the curricular structures discussed in Chapter 17?

Section VII

The Role of Philosophy in Schooling

In this section we will examine the relationship between the school and a wide variety of traditions of authority. These many, often conflicting traditions of wisdom, ideology, and criticism we will accept under the title, "philosophy," unprejudiced by whether these traditions have been founded by prophets or professors.

Philosophy is often seen as fundamental to school activity. One often encounters the opinion that from philosophy—however one defines it—flows the rest of the activity of the school. School people are expected to be ready at all times to answer, "What is the philosophy behind that?" for almost any action they take on the job.

The authors are of a different opinion, and the position of this section in the book will reflect it. Our common experience as learners is that we encounter philosophy—in any form—quite late in our intellectual development. Philosophy derives from, even though it may illuminate, activity. Students have to know a lot about the world, be this knowing ever so tentative, before that reflective activity known as critical philosophy is of use. Wittgenstein makes a pertinent point here: one must first believe in order to criticize.

We will see that different conceptions of what philosophy is support different models of the school. Indeed, the structure of the school determines to a great extent what function philosophy will serve within it. That there is anything at all in the schools called philosophy is interesting. That the most mundanely oriented school bothers to expend resources to develop and publicize what it calls its philosophy, attests to the strength and authority of these traditions.

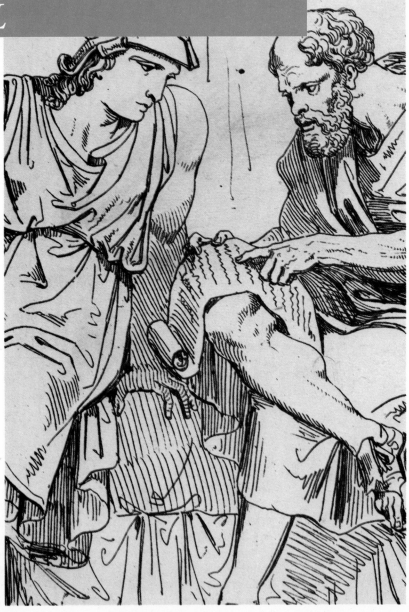

PHILOSOPHY
and the
SCHOOL

Chapter 19

We cannot act on information alone; the information must first be understood, then interpreted for relevance, and finally command belief and commitment. But what if the citizen cannot assess the truth of the available information or its import for action? Science has given us the criteria for warranted assertion about matters of fact, but where do we find the criteria for warranted acceptance of their import?

—*Harry S. Broudy*[1]

PREVIEW

The image we hold of the school as Temple, Factory, or Town Meeting affects our conception of philosophy and its role in schooling. We will see that the way many teachers are introduced to philosophy is influenced greatly by commitments to the Temple and Factory models. Also, we will examine what rational schooling practice might be and how theory can influence it. In that process, we will learn how organizations "set premises" to foreclose on inquiry. Finally, we will address the question of identifying a fundamental authority for settling conflicts among moral communities.

INTRODUCTION

Come then, and let us pass a leisure hour in story telling, and our story shall be the education of our heroes.

———— *Plato*, Republic, Book II

A long and intimate relationship has existed between philosophy and educational theory. Philosophers of all stripes have pronounced on the way we ought to go about educating the young. In earlier times those who claimed the title "educator" believed a substantial philosophical background to be essential to their calling.[2] For example, William Torey Harris, U.S. Commissioner of Education from 1889 to 1906, was an ardent and influential disciple

---

[1]Harry S. Broudy, *Truth and Credibility. The Citizen's Dilemma* (New York: Longman, 1981), p. 13.
[2]Cf. Kingsley Price, "Philosophy of Education, History of" in Paul Edwards (ed.), *The Encyclopedia of Philosophy* (New York: Collier MacMillan, 1967), Vol. 6, pp. 230–242. See also Jonas F. Soltis, "Philosophy of Education: Retrospect and Prospect," *Philosophy of Education 1975* (Champaign, Ill.: Philosophy of Education Society, 1975), pp. 7–24.

of the German philosopher Hegel.[3] John Dewey, initially Hegelian, too, but later a world-renowned proponent of Pragmatism in education, exercised wide influence on educational thought in the first half of the twentieth century.[4]

But we have learned that education is not necessarily schooling and institutions of schooling constrict philosophical inquiry in a variety of ways. Nonetheless, philosophy of education is a discipline pursued in many universities, and, to this day, substantial numbers of people feel that philosophy should play a central role in schooling.

WHAT IS PHILOSOPHY?

Ich möchte wissen, was die Welt
Im Innersten zusammenhält.

I would like to know what, in its deepest core, holds the World together.

——————— *Goethe,* Faust

When uninformed people think of philosophy, they think only of the sort of speculation in this quote from Goethe: deep stuff, but hard to relate to the concerns of everyday life. In fact, we will see that there are philosophical traditions that attempt to bypass the "deep stuff" and others that look to inform day-to-day practice. Nevertheless, we can understand philosophy broadly to

---

[3]See Loyd D. Easton, "Harris, William Torey" in Edwards (ed.) op. cit., Vol. 3, pp. 416–417.
[4]See George Dykhuizen, *The Life and Mind of John Dewey* (Carbondale, Ill.: Southern Illinois U. Press, 1973), pp. 44–50. See also Anthony Quinton, "Inquiry, Thought and Action: John Dewey's Theory of Knowledge," in R. S. Peters (ed.), *John Dewey Reconsidered* (London: Routledge and Kegan Paul, 1977), pp. 1–17.

What holds the world together?

be a search for consensus on general, even cosmic issues, for example, questions about what is real, true, or good. This search often takes the form of a search for an "ultimate" or "fundamental authority," be it a system or a process, that might compel all thoughtful people to its adoption. The nature of this search has varied with the specific traditions followed. Let us look at some of these.

The term "philosophy" covers a complex and varied group of traditions. We can discern at least three different kinds of activity or tradition which are commonly called philosophical:[5]

- ■ **Wisdoms**: broad pronouncements taken as authoritative, These can range from isolated statements of "crackerbarrel" philosophers, to complex and revered doctrines. Our examples will range broadly and indiscriminately over the teachings of Confucius, Moses, Jesus, Mohammed, Zoroaster, Buddha, Joseph Smith, Nikolai Lenin, Jim Jones, Madame Blavatsky.
- ■ **Institutional philosophies** or **ideologies**: rationalizations, often theoretically intricate, of practices and social institutions; for example, Confucianism, Christianity, Islam, Bahai, Mormonism, Leninism, Theosophy.[6] School and curricular philosophies tend to be of this nature.
- ■ **Critical philosophy**: critical analysis or discussion done in any of the Western traditions widely accepted as Socratic. These approaches tend to be self-critical in ways the other two avoid because the critical philosophies assume the capacity of the individual to discern truth, even when in conflict with traditions or institutions.

Within each strand there is conflict and disagreement; and among them, overlap. Many social institutions have borrowed from the wisdom of sages to

---

[5]Cf. John Passmore, "Philosophy" in Edwards, *The Encyclopedia of Philosophy, Vol. 6* pp. 216–226.
[6]Cf. John B. Thompson, *Studies in the Theory of Ideology* (Berkeley: U. of California Press, 1984), pp. 3–6.

Figure 19.1

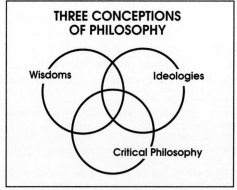

THREE CONCEPTIONS OF PHILOSOPHY

Wisdoms Ideologies

Critical Philosophy

complement philosophies that support their aims and policies. Also, critical philosophy has been used to construct and rationalize institutional philosophies.

We saw in Chapter 3 that analyzing educational problems and reaching consensus on them depended upon common recognition of authority. In this chapter, we will discover that philosophy, long relied upon to determine such authority, will provide different answers depending upon whether we are willing to settle for wisdom, ideology, or critical philosophy.

Philosophy and Authority

> *Sapere aude!*
> Dare to know
>
> ———————— *Immanuel Kant*[7]

For those involved in schooling, the search for fundamental authority is not an idle pastime. Controversy rages around issues that have occupied philosophers for milennia. The conflicts among the different traditions of philosophy (wisdoms, ideologies, and critical philosophy) are mirrored in the conflicts that make schooling so interesting.

Breadth in philosophical perspective requires exploring alternatives. But, in the very first citation of this book,[8] Stanley I. Benn has cautioned us that exploring alternative ways of structuring the world may bring us to question some of our most valued beliefs.

In our pluralistic society, philosophical issues about schooling are very far from being "merely theoretical." To the extent that schools invite reconceptualizations of traditional understandings, they risk conflict. Indeed, conflict may arise wherever an object of reverence for a community becomes an object of knowledge in the schools. Sex education disputes are examples of this. The demystification that the pursuit of knowledge may bring about is seen to threaten the attitudes of respect for authority that the object of reverence supports.

The authority of critical inquiry is seen to undermine the authority of particular wisdoms. For example, those who interpret the Bible literally find evolutionary theory particularly disturbing.and have challenged the curriculum in the public schools.[9] Many people believe that scientific approaches to the origins of life contradict the teachings of their own religious authorities.[10]

---

[7]Will and Ariel Durant, "Kant," *Rousseau and Revolution,* in *The Story of Civilization,* Book 10 (New York: Simon and Schuster, 1967), Chap. XXI, p. 540.

[8]See the Introduction to Section I.

[9]Tom Mirga, "Textbooks Do Not Imperil Christians' Beliefs, 2 Courts Rule," *Education Week* September 9, 1987, p. 10.

[10]M. Sandra Reeves, "On Trial: Secular Humanism in the Schools. A Nebulous Concept Provokes Bitter National Dispute," *Education Week,* October 15, 1986, p. 1.

As a consequence, the Louisiana State Legislature enacted a law in 1981 mandating a "balanced treatment" be given to "creation science" and "evolution science" in the schools. In 1987 the Supreme Court, invoking the authority of the Constitution, struck down the law as having an unconstitutional religious intent.[11]

The Court's ruling is an abstract solution to an abstract problem (see Chapter 3). But it is not clear that the concerns which Fundamentalist parents express have even been addressed. Nor is it clear how to address them within the framework of the public school, because the issue is fundamentally one of authority. Let us review different conceptions of philosophy and see how they address the issue of authority.

Wisdoms

> In all cultures before our own, the competing symbols took the form of languages of faith. A language of faith is always revelatory, communicating through some mouthpiece of the god-term a system of interdicts—a pattern of "thou shalt nots," or taboos. The language of science is not revelatory but analytic; for this reason, the scientist can never claim that his own terms have a prophetic function.
>
> *Phillip Rieff*[12]

Wisdoms, according to their specific tradition, pronounce on what is Goodness, Beauty, and Truth. They are generally associated with a charismatic individual who, in the Western traditions, tends to speak in a prophetic tone.

Particular kinds of wisdom are sometimes called doctrine, dogma, or common sense, depending upon the commitments and attitudes of the person referring to it. In any case, the traditions of wisdom pronounce; they do not inquire. They posit the authority for fundamental decisions in a tradition or in its leaders. And they warn the individual about conflict that can only be heresy.

In Western literature, Faust symbolizes the plight of the inquiring mind torn between the pursuit of Truth and the demands of the world. Goethe's question about what it is that holds the World together is answered in various ways within different traditions of wisdom. The World may be seen as ultimately a unity, only apparently fragmented to the finite mind. Or, God may be invoked to sustain His Creation. Goethe himself has Faust opt to reject the wisdoms of his time, philosophy, and theology, and seek redemption through physical love and worldly works. That is, he abandons the question.

---

[11]Tom Mirga, "Creationism Law In La. Is Rejected By Supreme Court," *Education Week*, June 24, 1987, p. 1.

[12]Phillip Rieff, *The Triumph of the Therapeutic: Uses of Faith After Freud* (New York: Harper & Row, 1966), p. 234.

Often, when people ask, "What is your philosophy of education?" they seek some vague generalization that indicates to them what we consider to be ultimately authoritative in making educational decisions. So, if we say, "I teach children, not subject matter," they will understand this to mean that our primary concern is the developmental needs of children and that we would adjust curriculum to the kids, rather than vice versa.

Such philosophy is much like policy. From what we have learned about organizations (see Chapters 8 and 9) we might expect that at best it represents good intentions. Most often, the particular circumstances of the school have more to do with how teachers behave than do their philosophical theories.

Institutional Philosophy: Ideology

The ideological conception of philosophy is defined by doctrines that are politically or institutionally inspired and officially sanctioned. Unlike wisdoms, which often have the informal and un-self-conscious quality of the prophetic, ideology is a conscious, official statement of ideas and commitments.[13]

School accreditation procedures in the United States often require the declaration of ideology. Accreditation is valued because it is taken to be a guarantee to parents that schools are what they claim to be, that they meet "minimum standards." It also assures the market value of degrees and the transferability of credits among schools.

Accredited schools may vary widely in philosophy. Their accreditation has much to do with how they are believed to live up to the philosophy they espouse. Schools often have philosophies that are not those of its administration or teachers or board members. This philosophy is often arrived at by some consensual process involving compromise and sloganeering. Samples of school philosophies based on various kinds of wisdom or technical philosophy can be gotten from school accrediting organizations.[14] They serve a ritual function in legitimating the school as an educational institution.

Ask for the philosophy of a school and you will be, very likely, handed a document entitled, "School Philosophy." Ask whether a given school activity is a consequence of that philosophy and you will be asking a question that indicates that a rereading of Chapters 8 and 9 is in order. It is widely believed that school philosophy ties directly into school activity. The very possibility of "garbage can" decisions (recall Chapter 8) should caution you, however, to the consideration that school philosophy might be a rationalization of activities first accepted as tradition and only later thought about. It might even serve to conceal the real motives of power holders.

---

[13]For broader conceptions of ideology—not as well suited to our purposes, however—see Henry D. Aiken, *The Age of Ideology* (New York: Mentor, 1956), Chap. 1.

[14]Cf. *The Preferred Wisdom of Elementary Schools: An Anthology of School Philosophies* (Philadelphia: Assembly of Elementary Schools, 1980). Middle States Association of Colleges and Schools, 3624 Market Street, Philadelphia, PA 19104.

Here is a partial example of a school philosophy:

> The social development of elementary school students proceeds as the child becomes aware of the various authority structures that operate throughout the school, the community, the region, and the nation. We believe the school must help the child establish a perspective on the responsibilities and opportunities inherent in the multitude of authority systems in a democratic social order.[15]

These statements are not intended as the starting points for inquiry. Rather they provide the conceptual framework for the rationalization of practice. An organizationally adept teacher or administrator knows how to use exegetical processes (see Chapter 17) to support a proposal as "deriving" from school philosophy. Similarly, unwelcome proposals can be argued against as "in violation" of that fundamental document.

Authority in the school is legal and traditional and school philosophy rationalizes it so that it cannot be criticized as "merely legal" or "merely traditional." Vague statements of philosophy are particularly useful to powerholders, for it is they who will inevitably decide to suit themselves what the particulars mean. In practice, school philosophy gives no one authority not already delegated to specific roles in the organization.

Critical Philosophy

> . . . as long as the myths we use remain unconscious, they are constraints on our freedom; they determine our choices and actions without our knowing. So the first step towards making myths truly servants instead of masters is to make them explicit and show generally what their function is.
>
> —————— *Kieran Egan*[16]

It has been the tradition in much of Western philosophy to raise the unconscious, informal concessions of authority to the technical level where they can be examined. Habits of deference and inference, so often part of our transparent informal culture, are raised to consciousness for evaluation. For example, a technical treatment of Goethe's question might point out that to ask what holds the World together is to assume that the World is made of parts that would normally fly apart unless constrained. Critical philosophy often undertakes to explicitly lay out the the conceptual connections, the models, that underlie the approaches that our very questioning assumes.

---

[15]Ibid., p. 16.
[16]Kieran Egan, "The Necessary Role of Myths in Education," *Philosophy of Education 1972*, p. 367.

Dare to know!

Psychology is sometimes thought of as the modern replacement for philosophy in schooling[17]; it is the guise some philosophies take when the Temple becomes a Factory.[18] Sometimes this replacement process is quite visible. For example, Resnick claims (see Chapter 18) that the function of schooling should be to develop model-building abilities in students. Thus, a psychological researcher promotes as the primary function of the school what has long been a major interest of critical philosophy.[19]

Let's refocus on some excerpts of school philosophies from a technical perspective and ask critical questions of each ideological statement:

■ **Ideology on Developing a Conception of Authority:** The social development of elementary school students proceeds as the child becomes aware of the various authority structures that operate throughout the school, the community, the region, and the nation. ... We believe the school ... must help the child establish a perspective on the responsibilities and opportunities inherent in the multitude of authority systems in a democratic social order.

Related critical questions: Are there dimensions other than the awareness of authority by which the social development of the child proceeds? Which perspectives on responsibilities and opportunities are to be selected to be taught? What does it mean to say that these are "inherent in" the authority systems? How do we teach students to deal with conflicts among authorities?

---

[17]See R. S. Peters and C. A. Mace, "Psychology," in Edwards (ed.), op. cit., Vol. 7, pp. 1–27. See also Geraldine M. Joncich, *Psychology and the Science of Education: Selected Writings of Edward L. Thorndike* (New York: Teachers' College Press, 1962), pp. 6–7.

[18]Cf. Jerry Fodor, *Psychological Explanation: An Introduction to the Philosophy of Psychology* (New York: Random House, 1968), pp. 5–48.

[19]See also Walter B. Weimer, "Psycholinguistics and Plato's Paradoxes of the *Meno*," *American Psychologist*, January 1973, pp. 15–33.

- **Ideology on the Learner as a Self-actualized Knower**[20]: The only learning that significantly influences behavior is personal, self-discovered, self-appropriated learning. This kind of learning cannot be communicated through conventional forms of teaching where the school approaches students with preset curricula and methods. . . . Although the school experiences are social, each student follows his or her own path in the acquisition of knowledge.

  Related critical questions: What forms of learning are not personal, self-discovered, or self-appropriated? What counts as a significant influence on behavior? Is the claim that only self-discovered learning significantly influences behavior a research discovery? Or is it a matter of definition? Why can't traditional curricula serve the self-actualized knower? What grounds are there for this assertion?

- **Ideology on Affective Education for Religious Community**[21]: The affectivity of our school leads to acceptance of Christ as personal savior. Our school is part of a community of faith. It is a spiritual environment. . . . It is an environment that arouses a student to faith.

  Related critical questions: If Faith is the end, does it justify any means? Why choose this affective approach and not another? Is this approach uniquely Christian? Can the affective needs of the individual come into conflict with those of the community?

We should not suppose that people who accept ideology are capable of technical argument in its support. Some communities frown on the inquiry that the critical approach undertakes, fearing it will undermine the mystery and authority that defines the community. That is why church authorities had early problems with Thomas Aquinas' efforts to reconcile faith and logic. Such communities may relegate critical inquiry to a special study, usually restricted in scope. In religious communities this is often known as theology.

Pythagoras, first to have described himself as a philosopher, contrasted philosophy as a reflective activity in distinction to activities that pursue fame and profit. The "best people," thought Pythagoras, a member of a leisured class of free men, acquired Truth through contemplation.[22] For Plato, the test of philosophical wisdom was that it could stand up to critical discussion. The process of philosophical inquiry was "dialectic," from the Greek words for "the art of conversation." The traditional basis of technical philosophy is thus critical inquiry, an art form almost unconcerned with (one might say, "undisciplined by") considerations of cost and benefit.

To reiterate: the image one holds of the school as Temple, Factory, or Town Meeting affects one's conception of philosophy and its role in schooling. The Temple image of the school sees philosophy as a set of fundamental principles that direct and justify the activities of the school. Philosophy is also conceived as external principles that set the goals guiding the productive activities of

---

[20]*The Preferred Wisdom of Elementary Schools*, p. 17.
[21]Ibid., p. 23.
[22]Passmore, in Edwards (ed.), op. cit., Vol. 6, p. 216.

the Factory. There is room, however, for a critical component of philosophy inasmuch as it helps production. In the Town Meeting, where consensus on wisdom or ideology may be lacking, skills in critical philosophy become of greater importance.

The Role of Philosophy in Schooling Practice

In the Temple, philosophy provides fundamental authority in the form of wisdom and ideology. The critical question, "On what basis ought we choose among competing wisdoms or ideologies?" is ignored or bypassed through tradition or "premise setting," which we will discuss below.

In the Factory, wisdoms and ideologies specify goals and, often, procedures. Critical philosophy is a technical tool most often serving, rather than examining, them.

It is in the Town Meeting, a "marketplace of ideas," that critical philosophy comes into its own. It provides a commonly acceptable critical procedure for sorting out competing wisdoms and ideologies, even though such critical examination may not be generally recognized as a form of dialectic by those unfamiliar with the tradition. Unfortunately, school people are usually less than adequately trained to take full advantage of it.

Chart 19.1 compares and contrasts conceptions of philosophy under the different images of the school.

What Philosophy of Education is conceived to be, depends, too, upon the aspect of schooling stressed for some particular purpose. We will consider three general conceptions of the relation of philosophy to schooling practice: foundationalism, rationalization, and criticism.

Philosophy of Education as Foundationalism

... How does change occur in *any* complicated, highly organized setting?
... those fields (political science, sociology, anthropology, history) that have been most interested in the general issue have concerned themselves only minimally, if at all, with the school setting.... it is by no means

Chart 19.1   **SCHOOL IMAGE AND PHILOSOPHY**

	Temple	Factory	Town Meeting
Wisdoms / **Ideologies**	Provide Fundamental Authority	Provide Goals and Procedures	Provide Competition
Critical Philosophy	Provides Technical Assistance	Provides Technical Assistance	Provides a Common Procedure

clear that what these fields have come up with is applicable to the problem of change and the school culture.

——————— *Seymour B. Sarason*[23]

Foundationalism is very much an academic concern. It involves a general belief that:

a.   schooling practice and educational practice are derivative; they do not have unique problems and practices which warrant study in their own right;

b.   "parent" disciplines are logically more fundamental and thus more authoritative. Therefore, they should set the agenda when it comes to studying the schools.[24]

Consequently, other academic and scientific disciplines are looked to to find models that will inform schooling practice. History of education is thus seen as a subspecialty of history. Likewise, sociology of education is a subfield of sociology, and philosophy of education is a special focus of philosophy. Furthermore, these "foundational" fields are thought somehow to be more "basic" or "fundamental" and their educational "applications" not central to their disciplinary inquiry. However, like Sarason above, some educational philosophers[25] question the adequacy of foundationalism. James Giarelli comments,

> Philosophy . . . is rooted neither in some privileged access to reality nor in some neutral procedure, but rather in an analysis of those practices by which human communities maintain, extend and renew their continued existence. In short, philosophy is rooted in an analysis of educational practices . . . education is not dependent upon philosophy for a justification and explanation of its theories, methods and practices. It is not the philosopher as midwife delivering a grounding to education, but rather practice, educational practice, which delivers to philosophy a point and purpose for its existence and identity.[26]

---

[23]Seymour B. Sarason, *The Culture of the School and the Problem of Change* (Boston: Allyn & Bacon, 1971), p. 10.
[24]Cf. Foster McMurray, "Retrospective Two," pp. 253–287, and Clarence J. Karier "Retrospective One," pp. 233–251 in Arthur Bestor, *Educational Wastelands*, 2nd Ed. (Urbana, Ill.: U. of Illinois Press, 1985), for opposing considerations.
[25]Cf. Ralph C. Page, "Educational Inquiry Supports Its Own Foundations," *Philosophy of Education 1978* (Champaign, Ill.: Philosophy of Education Society, 1978).
[26]James M. Giarelli, "Philosophy, Education and Public Practice," Presidential Address, Middle Atlantic States Philosophy of Education Society. Manuscript (Rutgers, N.J.: Graduate School of Education, unpublished, May 2, 1987).

Figure 19.2

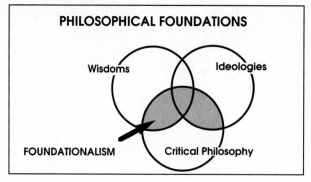

Thus, the relationship of philosophy and other disciplines to education is a matter of controversy.

We can locate Foundationalism in Philosophy by shading the intersections of the three aspects of Philosophy shown in Figure 19.1. This gives us Figure 19.2.

Advocates of foundationalism see critical philosophy both as a supporting and as a limiting process. Conceiving of the school under the Factory image, they tend to reject wisdom or ideology unsupported with technical philosophy as extraneous. On the other hand, they do not go so far as to allow critical philosophy free rein to attack the restrictions that serve disciplinary interests.

Philosophy of Education as Rationalization

John Martin Rich argues against the notion that there is a simple correspondence between philosophy and education:

> It is well known among educational philosophers that philosophy is not a deductive system like geometry and, therefore, no one-to-one correspondence exists between philosophy and policy.... by examining educational history it can be seen that a variety of educational policies have been espoused by a philosophy. Idealists, realists and pragmatists, for instance, have usually supported democratic policies; and though differences may exist in interpretation, these differences may stem more from disagreements over educational aims than from divergences in metaphysical systems.[27]

Rich's argument can be extended to any attempt to simply relate philosophy to a school practice. This is a matter of some controversy. But it is important to distinguish between *deriving* a practice from an abstract philosophy applied

---

[27]John Martin Rich, "The Role of Philosophy of Education in Educational Policy Studies," *Philosophy of Education 1973*, pp. 151–152.

Figure 19.3

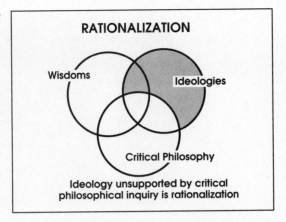

RATIONALIZATION

Wisdoms

Ideologies

Critical Philosophy

Ideology unsupported by critical
philosophical inquiry is rationalization

to a concrete situation, as opposed to *rationalizing* an already adopted practice by invoking a philosophy to justify it.

Rationalization sacrifices means to ends. Such philosophy has no independent goals; its purpose is to support the institution. Critical philosophy,
committed to inquiry, is, at best, mimicked, but not taken seriously. Wisdom
is selected to support ideology. Conflicting wisdom is filtered out. Figure 19.3
illustrates the realm of rationalization. In politically sensitive or otherwise
turbulent environments (see Chapter 9), school philosophy tends to be rationalization.

Ideologies developed to meet institutional needs may have historical links
with critical philosophical theories. Whether the ideologies remain logically
consistent with their "parent" theories is a question seldom considered. For
example, we will see below that "Idealism" is an ideology presented in many
texts as derivative of one of the idealist traditions in critical philosophy.
Whether such "Idealism" retains its historical sense in an institutional environment is seldom examined.[28]

Philosophy of Education as Criticism

Pilate saith unto him, what is truth?

———————————— St. John, 18:38

Critical philosophy pursues the answer to the question we posed in Chapter
3 and have been putting off throughout the book: how do we reach consensus

---

[28]John Paul Strain, "Idealism: Clarification of an Educational Philosophy," *Educational Theory*,
Vol. 25, No. 3, pp. 263–271. Strain does not believe there are practicing Idealist philosophers
but perceives "Idealist thought patterns" in many educational concerns. But what makes a person
an unconscious Idealist rather than a misinformed Realist, or something else?

What is the truth?

when authorities conflict? However, many critical philosophers have disclaimed an interest in consensus by saying something more or less like, "It doesn't matter whether people agree. What matters is who is right! A thousand people may believe the moon is made of green cheese. The one who doesn't is right." But what if two people who are "right" disagree? How do we decide whom to agree with? Shouldn't there be a consensus among the knowledgeable?

Many people would reply that this is absurd. If two people disagree about matters of fact, it cannot be that both are right. However, to say this is to make a very broad philosophical generalization (or maybe to emphasize what we mean by the phrase "matter of fact"). About this generalization we can ask: Why should we accept it? What difference does it make if we do not? We will look at these questions again below when we consider the relation of knowing to reality.

Critical philosophy has historically tried to uncover the basis of consensus of the knowledgeable without relying on Wisdom or Ideology. Figure 19.4

Figure 19.4

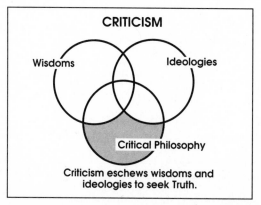

CRITICISM

Wisdoms   Ideologies

Critical Philosophy

Criticism eschews wisdoms and
ideologies to seek Truth.

illustrates this. In the process of searching for Truth or Reality, a number of distinct positions have developed. We will look at some of these in the next section.

Teaching Philosophy to Teachers

> . . . fundamental differences in conceptions of the basic values which are to shape and direct our educational institutions are grounded in differing and incompatible myths, stories, symbols, and rituals, that is, in differing and incompatible senses of reality.
>
> ———— *William Vaughan*[29]

How do philosophical traditions come to bear on schooling practice? Through the professional preparation of teachers and administrators. We will see that how the school is conceived has a lot to do with what philosophy is thought to be proper to such preparation.

Because the Temple and Factory images of the school dominate in our culture, the role of philosophy in teacher preparation has been to offer prospective teachers "philosophical systems" rather than training in pertinent critical thinking skills.[30] Even philosophers of education who stress the critical training aspect of philosophy tend to do so from the perspective of their particular commitments to an ideology.[31]

We should hold open the questions as to whether and to what extent the theories sketched below bear on decisions in the school context. Philosophy can bear on school decisions, but it is likely that the "philosophies" commonly discussed in textbooks are not, as a researcher would say, "the relevant variables." That is, they may not bear on the distinctions upon which the decision is based.

---

[29]William Vaughan, "Fundamental Value Conflicts in Education: Towards Reconciliation," *Philosophy of Education 1974*, pp. 127–136.

[30]Those interested in critical thinking should see John Stuart Mill, "Logic," or Charles Sanders Pierce, "How to Make Our Ideas Clear," excerpted in Morton White, *The Age of Analysis* (New York: Mentor, 1955). See also, John Dewey, *How We Think* (Boston: D. C. Heath, 1933), and R. Bruce Raup, George Axtelle, Kenneth Benne, and B. Othaniel Smith, *The Improvement of Practical Intelligence* (New York: Harper, 1950). See also Richard A. Gibboney, *Toward Intellectual Excellence: Some Things to Look for in Classrooms and Schools*. Manuscript (Graduate School of Education, 3700 Walnut Street, Phila. PA, 19107). See also, D. J. O'Conner, *An Introduction to the Philosophy of Education* (London: Routledge and Kegan Paul, 1967), and Matthew Lipman, Ann Margaret Sharp, and Frederick S. Oscanyan, *Philosophy in the Classroom* (Upper Montclair, N. J.: Institute for the Advancement of Philosophy for Children, 1977).

[31]Cf. James Bowen and Peter R. Hobson, *Theories of Education* (New York: Wiley, 1974); Steven M. Cahn, *The Philosophical Foundations of Education* (New York: Harper & Row, 1970); George F. Kneller, *Movements of Thought in Modern Education* (New York: Wiley, 1984).

POINT/COUNTERPOINT: THE ISMs

Philosophers of Education disagree often vehemently among themselves whether the tradition of presenting philosophies of education, Idealism, Realism, Pragmatism, Existentialism, Perennialism, Essentialism, Progressivism, Naturalism, and so forth, is a legitimate pedagogical and philosophical enterprise.

The ISMs approach, as it is often called, is championed as a useful introduction to a long and complex history of educational thought. The ISMs illustrate how very central a role abstract philosophical theories have played in the educational thinking of people of historical importance. Also, several informative books expound these theories in a pedagogically effective way, a useful *first* step into philosophy.

Critics rejoin that such a smorgasbord approach tends to emphasize information about philosophies rather than to develop critical thinking skills in the student. In the absence of detailed study, a "school" of philosophical thought often becomes a system of slogans.

Furthermore, that these philosophies have often been the foci of social conflict is overlooked. The ISMs approach tends to treat it as a matter of personal taste which philosophy one chooses, if any. By treating all the ISMs on an equal footing, they overlook the fact that some of them are considered to be outmoded. Also, offering philosophical theories as living options obscures the powerful role of school organizations in controlling behavior despite philosophical diversity.

Textbooks and ISMs

Just as high school textbooks have been criticized in a variety of subject matter areas (see Chapter 9), so have college texts been in regard to the preparation of teachers. Tozer and McAninch,[32] reviewing texts used for teacher preparation, criticize them for the following reasons:

- they fail to stimulate critical inquiry
- they present unexamined surface realities
- they fail to provide competing explanations of school and social realities
- they make authoritative declarations that lack supporting evidence or argument

From the perspective of the Temple, these are hardly criticisms. However, the fact that in our society there are many "Temples" is reason for concern. From the standpoint of a community of critical practice, this hodgepodge can create only confusion.

Chart 19.2 presents a synopsis of similar charts from a variety of sources. It shows what are conceived as philosophical schools and their proponents, together with a brief—and sloganistic—characterization of the tenets of that

---

[32]Steve Tozer and Stuart McAninch, "Four Texts in Social Foundations of Education in Historical Perspective," *Educational Studies*, Fall 1987.

Chart 19.2   ### A SYNOPSIS OF "SCHOOLS OF PHILOSOPHY" CHARTS
WITH COMPARISONS FROM OTHER SOURCES

Schools	Proponents	Characterizations
Idealism (RC)	Plato (RC) Kant—OC, P, AK Hegel—(SS) Berkeley—OL (G) J? (SS)	Reality is spiritual or mental. Knowing is recalling; values, absolute. We construct World. (Kant—OC, AC, P)
Realism (RC)	Aristotle James—HW Aquinas Kant—D Spencer—OC Locke—HW (J, SS, OL)	Reality exists unperceived. Values are natural and absolute. Knowledge comes through the senses.
Naturalism HW, RC (OL)	Rousseau Hobbes—(J) Spencer—A, G (J)	Only Nature exists—HW Nature is better than Civilization
Empiricism (RC)	Spencer—A, (J) Locke (J) Berkeley—T (G), AC	Knowledge comes through the senses.
Pragmatism (RC)	Rousseau—OC Kant—D James Pierce Dewey Wittgenstein—W (G)	Knowledge is what works. Truth is warranted assertion. Values are relative.
Existentialism	Hegel—D Kierkegaard Sartre Jaspers—SS A.S. Neill—SS (G), HW, J	Individuals construct their reality. We are what we do. Deciding precedes knowing.
Philosophical Analysis (HW, J, SS)	Russell Moore Wittgenstein—OC, G	Reality is what is verifiable. Truth corresponds to reality. Usage determines meaning—W
Perennialism	Hutchins Adler Maritain—OL	Some knowledge is eternally valid. Education cultivates intellect.
Essentialism	Plato (RC) Aristotle Bestor Conant—OL	Certain skills and knowledge are essential for rational living.
Progressivism	Dewey Kilpatrick—(J, SS)	Children are naturally good.—RC The child's needs and interests are relevant to the curriculum.
Reconstructionism (RC)	Counts—(SS)	The school should help rebuild the social order.
Behaviorism OC, RC, SS (OL)	Skinner—(HW) Hobbes—OC	Only the physical world is real. Learning is changing behavior.

Sources: (for fuller commentary, see text)

AC = Acton AK = Aiken	OL = Ornstein & Levine
D = Durant	P = Price
G = Gutek	RC = Ryan & Cooper
HW = Hessong & Weeks	SS = Sadker & Sadker
J = Johnson et al.	T = Taylor
OC = Ozmon & Craver	W = White

> **LEGEND**
> XX = source (sole, if alone)
> (XX) = omitted by source
> XX? = problematic treatment
>
> Uncoded items enjoy a
> general consensus.

school. The chart demonstrates that on certain items there is lack of consensus as to

a. who belongs to which school;
b. which tenets are espoused by that school; and
c. which philosophical thought is relevant for teachers.

The chart was prepared from texts that ranged from general education texts, through texts on foundations of education, philosophy of education, to books and articles by philosophers and historians. The sources were the following (the chart code for each is given initially):

■ general education and foundations texts:

HW, Hessong and Weeks, *Introduction to Education*[33]
J, Johnson et al., *Introduction to the Foundations of American Education*[34]
OL, Ornstein and Levine, *An Introduction to the Foundations of Education*[35]
RC, Ryan and Cooper, *Those Who Can, Teach*[36]
SS, Sadker and Sadker, *Teachers, Schools and Society*[37]

■ texts dealing specifically with philosophy of education:

G, Gutek, *Philosophical and Ideological Perspectives on Education*[38]
OC, Ozmon and Craver, *Philosophical Foundations of Education*[39]

■ general philosophical texts or articles:

AK, Aiken, *The Age of Ideology*[40]
AC, Acton, "Berkeley, George" and "Idealism" in Edwards, *The Encyclopedia of Philosophy*[41]

---

[33]Robert F. Hessong and Thomas H. Weeks, *Introduction to Education* (New York: Macmillan, 1987).
[34]James A. Johnson, Harold W. Collins, Victor L. Dupuis, and John H. Johansen, *Introduction to the Foundations of American Education*, 6th Ed. (Boston: Allyn & Bacon, 1985).
[35]Allan C. Ornstein and Daniel U. Levine, *An Introduction to the Foundations of Education*, 3rd Ed. (Boston: Houghton Mifflin, 1984).
[36]Kevin Ryan and James M. Cooper, *Those Who Can, Teach,* 4th Ed. (Boston: Houghton Mifflin, 1984).
[37]Myra Pollack Sadker and David Miller Sadker, *Teachers, Schools, and Society* (New York: Random House, 1988).
[38]Gerald L. Gutek, *Philosophical and Ideological Perspectives on Education* (Englewood Cliffs, N. J.: Prentice Hall, 1988).
[39]Howard A. Ozmon and Samuel M. Craver, *Philosophical Foundations of Education* (Columbus: Merrill, 1981).
[40]Henry D. Aiken, op. cit.
[41]H. B. Acton, "Berkeley, George," Vol. 1, pp. 295–304, and "Idealism," Vol. 4, pp. 110–118, of Edwards (ed.), op. cit.

D, Durant, "Immanuel Kant" and "Hegel" in *The Story of Civilization*[42]
P, Price, "Philosophy of Education, History of" in Edwards[43]
T, Taylor, *The Empiricists*[44]
W, White, *The Age of Analysis*[45]

In Chart 19.2, items for which consensus exists are given without source citations. Items championed by a minority are cited by code. Items omitted by a minority are cited by a code in parentheses. The chart indicates some disagreement. Note that Plato, Berkeley, Kant, and Hegel are all listed as idealists. The chart fails to note that the term, "idealism" means different things at different times in the history of philosophy. Plato believed that universals, designated with terms like "greenness" or "goodness," were more "real" than physical objects because they did not come in and out of existence. Berkeley believed that objects of sensation were real, but that we could not know through sensation that something called "material" exists. Kant—strangely missing from many of the texts reviewed above—agreed, saying that things like space, time, and causation were basic ways in which the human mind organized its experience, not realities as Plato thought they were. Thus Kant would be a "Realist."

Furthermore, asserted Kant, reason is not capable of bringing us knowledge of things beyond the basic categories of human experience, for example, space, time, and causality. His theories of practical reason would allow him to be categorized as a "Pragmatist," as well. Hegel, following Kant, believed that absolutes manifested themselves within human experience, not in some other world beyond it. However, the major exponents of Existentialism saw in Hegel's *Phenomenology of the Spirit* the foundations of their own philosophy. Chart 19.2 obviously oversimplifies.

We should observe two points:

■ Criticisms of the kind offered in the previous paragraph undermine the usefulness of simple slogan-terms like Idealist, Existentialist, and so forth, for supporting the authority of the Temple or Factory. The consensus such terms insinuate is illusory.

■ The disputes between "Realists" and "Idealists" about some "ultimate reality" need not bear on school practice any more than theoretical disputes among physicists about the ultimate nature of matter need bear on bridge construction. What, then, could be the point in introducing prospective teachers to them?

---

[42]Will and Ariel Durant, "Kant" *Rousseau and Revolution*, Book 10, pp. 531–551, and "Hegel," in "German Philosophy," in *The Age of Napoleon* Book 11, Chap. XXXII, pp. 645–658, in *The Story of Civilization*.
[43]Kingsley Price, "Philosophy of Education, History of," Vol. 6 in Edwards, op. cit., pp. 230–243.
[44]Richard Taylor *The Empiricists Locke, Berkeley, Hume* (Garden City, N.Y.: Doubleday, undated).
[45]Morton White, *The Age of Analysis* (New York: Mentor, 1961).

Both empiricists?

George Berkeley   John Locke

One explanation to consider is that some philosophies are, in fact, dangerous to some kinds of organizational authority. Introducing prospective teachers to apparently irrelevant philosophical "schools" may "inoculate" them against further philosophical inquiry and thus render them more accepting of organizational authority as it is. This does not mean that those who teach about philosophical schools intend to intellectually hamstring their students. Rather, we can understand the development of this approach to philosophical studies as most "adaptive" to the organizational structures in which it is found. Philosophers are no more likely than other people to bite the hand that feeds them.

A philosophically knowledgeable person could offer similar criticism of any of the classifications in Chart 19.2. What is the use of such distinctions in the training of teachers? They can be a useful first step into philosophy. But they may, for example, serve to reinforce the Temple and Factory images of the school, placing authority beyond the scope of critical inquiry. Is it just coincidence that Immanuel Kant, known in his own day as the great destroyer of systems,[46] who hated all "dogmatism," that is, philosophical systems accepted without critical thought, should be absent from so many of the books purporting to deal with systems of philosophy?

By having students study systems, rather than examining how and why a choice among them might be made, authority of one kind or another gets "premised" into their thinking. But accepting authority is not necessarily a philosophical activity. We believe that philosophy is well worth studying—not for pat systems of answers, but to develop techniques and strategies for inquiry.[47] Osmond and Craver consider the conflict between those who ad-

---

[46]See Michael Harrington, *The Politics at God's Funeral* (New York: Penguin, 1983), pp. 15–25.
[47]Cf. Carl Knape and Paul T. Rosewell, "The Philosophically Discerning Classroom Teacher," *Educational Studies*, Vol. 2 (1980), pp. 37–47. See also John W. Friesen, Evelina Ortega y Miranda, and Henry C. Lu, "Philosophy of Education: A Description of the Field," *Philosophy of Education 1972*, pp. 197–220; Jerome A. Popp, "Philosophy of Education and the Education of Teachers," *Philosophy of Education 1972*, pp. 222–229.

vocate and those who spurn an "isms" approach to philosophy of education and, echoing Resnick's earlier point, comment,

> Perhaps, after all, the major role of philosophy in education is not to formulate some system or school of thought, but to help develop the educator's thinking capacities.[48]

Critical Questions

How can we determine if and to what extent philosophy bears on schooling practice? Our strategy will be the following: simplistic, but useful characterizations of philosophies can be distinguished by their answers to what we will call here "critical questions." Reasonable schooling practice, we will argue later, is also based on a set of critical questions. To the extent that the philosophically critical questions bear on the practically critical questions, to that extent can philosophy bear on schooling practice.

Rather than trying to categorize philosophers into predetermined groups, another way we can go about relating them is to identify philosophers or philosophies in terms of the questions they were concerned with and the answers they gave to them. For our purposes, these philosophically critical questions will be:

- Who has authority to question?
- What exists?
- How do we know?
- What is the nature of value?

These will help us distinguish among some of the traditionally studied philosophies of education. Will these questions be relevant to schooling practice? If so, then schools of philosophy will have a direct bearing on schooling decisions.

Let's now run through the critical questions, recapitulating some of the characteristics of philosophical "schools."

Authority: Who Dares to Question?

The Socratic tradition in Western philosophy, in contrast with Eastern philosophies and religious traditions of many kinds, treats the search for Truth as an inquiry and authorizes each person, to the extent he or she is capable, of pursuing that inquiry. Everyone has the authority to question.

Ontology: What Exists?

The world is not always what it seems. Plato bestows upon philosophers the role of bringing knowledge of Being to those entranced by the shadows of

---

[48]Osmond and Craver, op. cit., p. 274.

Seeming. Relatives of his Idealism are found today in religious traditions around the world. Late nineteenth-century Americans, like W. T. Harris, troubled with a growing American pluralism, found German Idealism, with its conception of an all-embracing supermind, to be a congenial philosophy to support their conceptions of public education as the great homogenizer.[49]

Idealists hold that to be is to be perceived, that we can't know there is anything independent of our minds. Therefore what exists is minds and their contents. Philosophers traditionally identified as idealists are Plato, Berkeley,[50] Froebel, and Hegel. The literature, we have learned, is ambivalent about Kant. **Realists** hold that objects can exist independently of their being perceived. Aristotle is identified as a realist, but one who posited that humankind had a dualistic nature of immaterial soul and material body.

Would the distinction between Idealist and Realist ontology offer a live option to a practicing teacher or administrator? Doesn't the very practice of schooling presume a decision in favor of one side of the dispute? We will consider these questions below when we look at a conception of rational schooling practice.

Epistemology: How Do We Know?

Many philosophical positions treat knowing as perceiving or somehow apprehending Reality. A common conception of knowing has it that when a person's thoughts **correspond** in some sense to the structure of reality, then that person has knowledge. Knowing is being in some relation of correspondence to reality. Truth is a matter of language that reflects a correspondence with reality: that is, true statements are those whose structure and meaning correspond in some sense to reality. Kant rejected this notion and caused a reconceptualization of the role of reason in philosophy. Consensus and consistency became, respectively, the Empiricist and Idealist criteria for Truth. However, the correspondence theory appeared later among people such as Bertrand Russell (1872–1970) and G. E. Moore (1873–1958).[51] Thus the tradition on Truth is controversial.

Today, researchers often assume some kind of correspondence theory to explain their enterprise:

> The ultimate test of the truth or falsity of an empirical statement
> is the **test of observation**, for what we **mean** by a true empirical
> statement is one that corresponds with observed reality.[52]

This Correspondence Theory of Truth, as it is called, is problematic. How does someone determine if his or her statements or thoughts correspond to reality?

---

[49]See Price, op. cit.
[50]But see H. B. Acton, "Berkeley, George" in Edwards (ed.), Vol. 1, op. cit., pp. 295–304, who suggests the characterization "idealist" for Berkeley is inadequate.
[51]See White, op. cit.
[52]Barry F. Anderson, *The Psychology Experiment* (Belmont, Calif.: Brooks-Cole, 1971), p. 25.

Figure 19.5

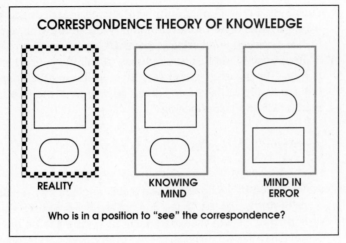

CORRESPONDENCE THEORY OF KNOWLEDGE

REALITY

KNOWING
MIND

MIND IN
ERROR

Who is in a position to "see" the correspondence?

How can either one's thoughts or reality be approached *independently* to make the comparison? The Correspondence Theory of Knowledge (Figure 19.5) is found in the school in several guises, the most common being the Decoding Theory of Reading.[53] According to this theory, communication between writer and reader is accomplished when the writer's thoughts, encoded into written language, are decoded so as to cause corresponding thoughts in the mind of the reader.

Because of the problem with ascertaining correspondences, **Pragmatists,** like James, Pierce, and Dewey (see Chapter 13), propose that knowledge is whatever works to help us pursue our goals.[54] What we often do if we are concerned about our perceptions is to ask other people. **Our confidence that we know increases as consensus increases.**[55]

But notice we are not investigating correspondences with reality anymore. We are attempting to build up our confidence. If we really doubted our perceptions, we would doubt our perceptions of other people, too. If the World is an illusion, so, too, are those people in it we might seek consensus with. This is what bothers Existentialists.

Existentialists worry about our inability to have independent access to a reality external to us and thus see the primary task of knowing to be defining the self from the welter of perceptions that confront each one of us.

By acting as Realists and looking for consensus, we escape from one dilemma. But we know that consensus is no absolute. A broad and deep consensus can exist because a group of people share a common way of life. They

---

[53]See Frank Smith, *Understanding Reading* (New York: Holt, Rinehart & Winston, 1971), on decoding.
[54]See Brody on Dewey's *Complete Act of Thought,* op. cit., pp. 4–9. See also Michael Levin, "Why Not Pragmatism?" *Commentary,* January 1983, pp. 43–47.
[55]Anderson, op. cit., concedes that correspondence depends ultimately on consensus, p. 25.

constitute a moral community with shared practices and traditions. But what happens when one moral community disagrees with another. How can we decide between conflicting consensus?

Both Idealist and Realist would say, "By finding out which moral community is right." Pragmatists would say, "By considering the costs and benefits, symbolic and substantial, of deciding one way over the other." The Existentialist would say, "By just choosing."

Axiology: What Is the Nature of Value?

The Platonists would like to see a culture guided by something eternal. The positivists would like to see one guided by something temporal—the brute impact of the way the world is. But both want it to be guided, constrained, not left to its own devices. For both, decadence is a matter of unwillingness to submit oneself to something "out there" . . .

—————— *Richard Rorty*[56]

Do values change? Or do they stay the same? Are they objective, a matter of the structure of the World? Or are they based on human sentiment and changing with it? Idealists and some Realists hold that values persist. They are

---

[56]Richard Rorty, "Pragmatism and Philosophy," p. 57, in Kenneth Baynes, James Bohman, and Thomas McCarthy (eds.), *After Philosophy: End or Transformation?* (Cambridge, Mass.: MIT Press, 1987), pp. 26–66.

All existentialists?

Friedrich Nietzsche   Soren Kierkegaard   Jean Paul Sartre

Chart 19.3

TWO "WORLD VIEWS"	
Normative Absolutism	Sociological Relativism
Social norms are realities given by divine forces, or by nature.	Values develop in human experience through time. They are man-made.
There are no alternative moral rules. A given set of rules is valid for all and for all time.	Different people have different norms valid for themselves.
Rules are as real as the earth we walk on. They are discovered, not created.	Change in social norms is inevitable and often desirable. Rules are conventions.

independent of human desires. What changes is people's perception or acknowledgment of them.

Pragmatists see values as based on people's attitudes. These change. Existentialists, in particular, are concerned that individuals define themselves and their values by the choices they make. Traditionally, Kierkegaard, Nietzsche, and Sartre are identified as Existentialists, although none of them claimed to belong to a school or movement.

In the Spring of 1975, 445 students at a midwestern university were questioned about their attitudes toward the nature of values. Westie and Hummel[57] defined two perspectives, Normative Absolutism and Sociological Relativism, in the manner indicated in Chart 19.3 Normative Absolutism parallels the axiological theory of either Idealism or Realism. It is the basis for the schooling ideologies called Perennialism and Essentialism. Twenty to thirty percent[58] of the respondents were in this group. Sociological Relativism is either Pragmatist or Existentialist. Seventy to eighty percent of the students placed themselves in this category.

A Chart of Comparisons

Chart 19.4 contrasts and compares the different philosophical positions as they are commonly expounded in the literature. The critical questions provide an easy although superficial sorting device. In the sections below we will investigate to what extent these critical questions bear on problems of practice in the school.

---

[57]Frank R. Westie and Richard Hummel, "Normative Absolutism vs. Sociological Relativism: An Investigation of Two World Views," *Educational Studies*, Vol. 11, 1980, pp. 25–36.
[58]The spread in response percentages exists because questions were posed in two forms, absolutistic and relativistic, for example, "We should support our country, right or wrong," vs. "Disobedience to government is sometimes justified." op. cit., p. 29.

Chart 19.4

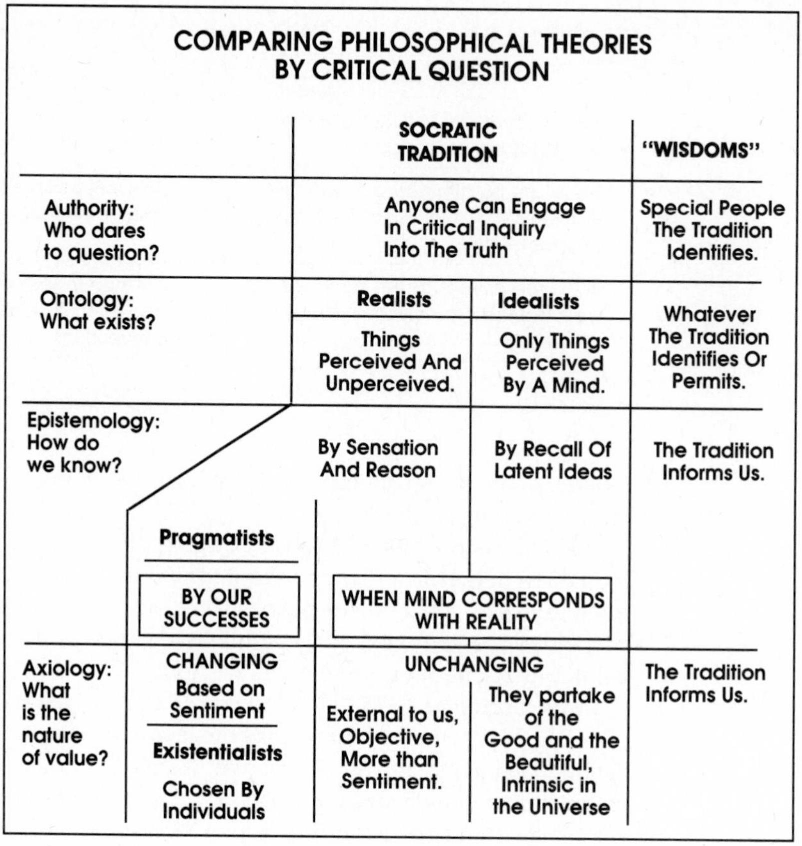

COMPARING PHILOSOPHICAL THEORIES BY CRITICAL QUESTION

	SOCRATIC TRADITION		"WISDOMS"
Authority: Who dares to question?	Anyone Can Engage In Critical Inquiry Into The Truth		Special People The Tradition Identifies.
Ontology: What exists?	**Realists**	**Idealists**	Whatever The Tradition Identifies Or Permits.
	Things Perceived And Unperceived.	Only Things Perceived By A Mind.	
Epistemology: How do we know?	By Sensation And Reason	By Recall Of Latent Ideas	The Tradition Informs Us.
Pragmatists	BY OUR SUCCESSES	WHEN MIND CORRESPONDS WITH REALITY	
Axiology: What is the nature of value?	CHANGING Based on Sentiment / **Existentialists** / Chosen By Individuals	UNCHANGING — External to us, Objective, More than Sentiment. / They partake of the Good and the Beautiful, Intrinsic in the Universe	The Tradition Informs Us.

MAKING DECISIONS IN THE SCHOOL

> The primary and pervasive significance of knowledge lies in its guidance of action: knowing is for the sake of doing. And action, obviously, is rooted in evaluation. For a being which did not assign comparative values, deliberate action would be pointless. . .
>
> —————— *C.I. Lewis*[59]

In trying to relate philosophical theories to school practice, we should keep in mind the following points:

---

[59]C.I. Lewis, *An Analysis of Knowledge and Valuation* (LaSalle, Ill.: Open Court, 1946), p. 1.

a. Philosophy derives historically from the pastimes of a leisured class of men who thought being a spectator and contemplating action were preferable to direct participation in the action.[60]

b. Philosophy's important test of wisdom is that it be able to survive critical discussion.[61] But this tends to overlook knowledge that is **tacit**, that is, embedded in or presupposed by action,[62] because those who know how, often do not have the skills to articulate what it is that they know.

c. Because ancient philosophers believed that the pursuit of fame and fortune sullied knowledge, the costs and benefits of different stages in the process of critical inquiry are to this day overlooked.

In order to see whether the commitments of philosophical theorists bear on school decisions we have to sketch a theory of rational action. We will see at what points in the decision to take action (or refrain from such) philosophical theories can be brought to bear.

Let's begin by analyzing all decisions in terms of three components: cue, concern, and control. What we will say is that a decision to intervene will be understood to be rational only if

a. it was occasioned by something (the **cue**)

b. the person who intervened had an appropriate **concern**; and

c. the person who intervened believed he or she could exercise some **control** over the situation.

We can look at these conditions not only as a set of criteria for rational intervention, but as the acceptable narrative form for rationalizing an action that has been taken. That is to say, a person will invariably rationalize his or her action, if questioned, by calling our attention to a cue, in the context of a concern and his or her belief that he or she could control the situation. This may, of course, be fabrication and no more than a feeble attempt to dress an impulsive act in the mantle of reason. But cue, concern, and control constitute that mantle.

Let's consider three very different actors in different cultural contexts to see how the analysis can be applied to them (Chart 19.5). Note that in each case, we would not understand the intervention as being a rational decision

---

[60]John Dewey in *Democracy and Education* (New York: Macmillan, 1965), p. 161, comments, "It may be seriously questioned whether the philosophies which isolate mind and set it over against the world did not have their origin in the fact that the reflective or theoretical class of men elaborated a large stock of ideas which social conditions did not allow them to act upon and test. Consequently men were thrown back into their own thoughts as ends in themselves."

[61]Cf. Harvey Siegel, "How 'Practical' Should Philosophy of Education Be," *Educational Studies*, Vol. 12, 1981, pp. 125–134.

[62]Cf. Walter B. Weimer, "Science as Rhetorical Transaction: Toward a Nonjustificational Conception of Rhetoric," *Philosophy and Rhetoric*, Vol.10, No. 1 (Winter 1977), on Justificationism and the nature of knowledge.

Chart 19.5

ANALYZING A DECISION TO ACT: CUE, CONCERN AND CONTROL			
	Physician	**Shaman**	**Religious Leader**
Cue	A patient complains of soreness in joints.	A tribal member falls to the ground shaking and moaning.	A church member is overcome with grief at the death of a loved one.
Concern	Worry about unnecessary suffering and damage from continued inflammation.	Worry that evil spirits will cause death.	Desire to console, stave off pessimism, and strengthen religious beliefs.
Control	Believes aspirin will treat inflammation and that patient will follow directions.	Believes in power of amulets to placate or ward off evil influences.	Believes that his expressions of concern and spiritual authority will console.
Intervention	Prescribes aspirin therapy.	Places amulets on victim.	Counsels member with Scriptural citations.

if either cue, concern, or control beliefs were lacking. It is the *sincerity* rather than the truth or falsity of the beliefs that bears on the rationality of the decision. Many parents restrict their children's TV viewing in the belief that it affects cognitive development or has negative effects on schoolwork. Little evidence bears out these beliefs.[63] They may well be false. Yet the parents' good-faith decisions are nonetheless rational if they are based on cue, concern, and control.

Rational behavior is behavior understandable as human agency: the person is the actor, or cause, rather than the pawn of an external power, or effect. Lacking a rationale in terms of cue, concern, and control, we look for some other kinds of explanation to account for someone's decision to intervene. When we invoke psychological, sociological, or anthropological theories, we are going beyond what we think the actor understood himself or herself to be doing in making the decision.

Chart 19.6 gives three different analyses of the same intervention by three different teachers. What do you make of them?

Clearly, teacher A's intervention is rational. It may in fact be counterproductive if Charlie gets so upset about the detention that he refuses to study for the test. But rationality is one thing, actual effectiveness is another.

Teacher B's intervention we are likely to write off as a mistake: is it a new class? Do Charlie and John look that much alike?. Teacher C's intervention

---

[63]Mark Walsh, "Key Beliefs About TV's Ill Effects Remain Unproven, Study Finds," *Education Week*, December 17, 1988, p. 1.

Chart 19.6

WHICH IS THE RATIONAL INTERVENTION?		
	Teacher A	**Teacher B**	**Teacher C**
Cue?	A student, Charlie Jones, has not turned in homework again.	A student, Charlie Jones, has not turned in homework again.	A student, Charlie Jones, has not turned in homework again.
Concern?	Teacher A is concerned that Charlie will fail the upcoming test.	Teacher B is concerned that Charlie will fail the upcoming test.	Teacher C is concerned that Charlie will fail the upcoming test.
Control?	Teacher A believes Charlie needs to do some quiet study uninterrupted by his friends or TV.	Teacher B believes Charlie needs to do some quiet study uninterrupted by his friends or TV.	Teacher C believes that no matter what he tries, Charlie is a lost cause.
Intervention	Keeps Charlie after school to do homework.	Keeps John Smith after school to do homework.	Keeps Charlie after school to do homework.

looks like a punitive emotional reaction. It is possible, however, for an ingenious person to expand the stories about teachers B and C so that we can see their interventions as rational. But this narrative expansion will involve reinterpreting Cue, Concern, and Control in a different, and perhaps complex manner.

Philosophical Theories and Rational Decision

How might a difference in philosophical outlook bear on the way one makes decisions? Would a Realist interpret Cue, Concern, and Control differently from an Idealist, a Pragmatist, or an Existentialist? Would a teacher or administrator who adopted one of these philosophies find in the daily activities of the school any opportunities to exercise commitment?

To develop a plausible answer to such questions, we have to expand somewhat the concepts of cue, concern, and control to see whether the distinctions we have made among philosophies in terms of authority, ontology, epistemology, and axiology find any role in school decision making.

Cue

What is a cue? It is a significant change in a trustworthy indicator.[64] In schooling, **tests** are commonly taken to be cues. If Johnny gets a 75 on a biology

---

[64]Cf. Edward G. Rozycki, "From Test to Treatment: Rationales for Intervention," *Foundational Studies*, Vol. 9, Nos. 1 and 2 (Cortland, N. Y.: New York State Foundations of Education Association, 1981), pp. 33–47.

retest where he formerly got a 60 we may take that to be an improvement in Johnny's knowledge of biology only if the following conditions hold:

a. **change** : we believe 75 is different from a 60 (not too difficult);
b. **significance**: we believe 75 is **significantly** different from a 60 (this may require a statistical analysis to verify);
c. **externality**: we believe the test scores relate to his knowledge of biology rather than, say, to his test-savviness (this may be difficult to establish); and
d. **trustworthiness**: we believe he has not cheated on the test, or somehow manipulated the results.

Perhaps one's philosophical commitments will bear on what one believes constitutes change, significance, externality, and trustworthiness. But these commitments may not fit neatly in a single philosophical system of the sort we have been discussing here. For example, teachers sometimes believe that student performance would improve if the students changed their "attitude." How do we determine if an attitude has changed? Is that change significant? What does it indicate? Can it be trusted?

Let's look as the conditions presumed by cue from the perspective of the dispute between Idealism and Realism. For an Idealist, change is illusory, externality not possible. Does this mean that Idealists don't examine their paychecks for errors but Realists do? But the dispute is about the nature of ultimate reality, you suggest. The question that has to be attended to is what aspects of schooling practice touch on "ultimate reality." Perhaps, for an Idealist, tests can be neither significant nor trustworthy. Then it is no mere accident that many people who profess Idealist philosophies have historically advocated the Temple image of the school and resisted testing as really getting at the heart of the matter of education. Perhaps.

On the other hand, how is it possible to work in a school and be a practicing Idealist? Could you imagine interrupting a faculty meeting with the observation, "I don't think the proposal made by the textbook review committee fully comprehends the nature of ultimate reality!" (We are not picking on Idealists here. Certainly no proponent of any school of philosophy could make that kind of objection.) The very organization of the school, we will discover below, has "premised away" Idealism—and many another philosophical tradition—as a viable option.

Concern

School people have many concerns: for example, their students should advance in the system; they, themselves, should continue to enjoy the benefits of the system; students in trouble should get help; stagnation and burnout have to be avoided.

These concerns tend to be of a variety of types. They may be roughly sorted out as

a. interests: maintaining or enhancing one's own or another's perceived benefits, for example, concerns for esteem, general welfare, and power;

b. obligations: moral constraints and duties believed operative upon someone in the given situation; and

c. liabilities: potential costs perceived as likely in the situation.

Again, philosophical commitments will very likely bear on conceptions of interest, obligation, and liability. A great deal rides on whether one believes that a student can be at fault in certain situations. Did Johnny do his homework? No. Do we let him suffer the consequences or do we take it upon ourselves to motivate him to do homework? It all depends. On what?

In terms of traditional categories, we can draw on some rough generalizations found in many books about schools of philosophy. Idealistic theorists tend to stress social obligation; Realists, individual rights. Both see obligation as part of the structure of reality, whereas Pragmatists and Existentialists see it as a matter, respectively, of getting along, or living authentically.

However, school organizations define interests, obligations and liabilities for their participants. Those with philosophical training can easily determine when organizational rhetoric is no more than a thin veneer hiding confusion or special interest. Such "debunking" skills are not peculiar to any particular philosophical school but are the common heritage of critical philosophy. The value of such insights is not that their impassioned proclamation will win converts to the Truth. Rather they provide one with tools often most effective when least publicized.

Control

Many teachers wouldn't try to teach calculus to the mentally retarded. Not that this is impossible to achieve, but beliefs about control affect their efforts. We can analyze control into three primary considerations:

a. nonnaturalness: the belief that we can change, and maintain a change in, a situation—that is, what we want changed is not the "natural" way of things;

b. practicality: the benefits of pursuing change outweigh its costs;

c. optimality: the choice made among competing practical choices to pursue change is the best one.

Again, these conditions may be influenced by the philosophy one comes to them with. Recall from Chapter 18 that we would not attempt to get someone to learn something if we thought it either was physically impossible, was developmentally inappropriate, or required special talent. Certainly, conceptions of possibility, appropriateness, and human capacity—for example, talent—can be interpreted as deep philosophical notions. But they may also be seen as superficial conventions that serve a narrow purpose in the workplace of the school but otherwise offer no food for thought.

Premise Setting

Premise setting is a process by which groups control the behavior of their members in an indirect, often unconscious manner. It is the process of developing an informal culture upon which to base decisions. Premise setting occurs when members of a group accept and build up a tradition of rationales for action. (See Chapter 9, Control as Rationale.) Let's look at how this happens.

The conditions for the narrative unity of rational action are **cue**, **concern**, and **control**. Questions about them provide us with critical questions for reasonable practice which will ask more or less the following:

- CUE: What happened that prompted you do that?
- CONCERN: What was the underlying concern that supported your involvement?
- CONTROL: What makes you think you can do anything about it?

Only to the extent that the philosophically critical questions about authority, ontology, epistemology, and axiology bear on the answers to the questions of cue, concern, and control, will philosophical theories bear on the practice of schooling.

Underlying cue, concern, and control are supporting assumptions of some complexity. Chart 19.7 diagrams these. (In Chapter 20 this chart provides a

Chart 19.7 **THE CONDITIONS OF THE NARRATIVE UNITY OF RATIONAL ACTION AND THEIR UNDERLYING ASSUMPTIONS**

The Conditions of Narrative Unity	Their Underlying Assumptions
Cue:	Change Significance Externality Trustworthiness
Concern:	Interests Obligations Liabilities
Control:	Nonnaturalness Practicality Optimality

framework for us to sort out and address commonly recognized school problems.)

Premise setting occurs when explanations for a decision are accepted as rationales and become part of the traditions of a group or organization. If Teacher A in Chart 19.6 explains his keeping Charlie Jones after school to do homework on the grounds that

- Charlie failed to do homework again, and that
- Teacher A was concerned for Charlie's success, and that
- he could offer Charlie a quiet place for study,

Teacher A sets as premises all the assumptions that support his explanation in terms of cue, concern and control. Chart 19.8 illustrates these. If Charlie begins to get better grades in biology, the assumptions underlying Teacher A's rationale become set as premises for the group as this tale is told and repeated as an example of effective teacher behavior. In fact, Charlie's grades in biology may have improved for quite different reasons, unknown to Teacher A. However, Teacher A's procedure and rationale become part of the folklore of the school: homework detentions may be uncritically accepted as effective.

Because every inquiry has a cost, only failures tend to provoke inquiry. Successes are accepted at face value. We may call this the Principle of Complacent Optimization. (See Chapter 8, The Bureaucratic Model) **Success,**

Chart 19.8

PREMISE SETTING BY TEACHER A		
Conditions of Narrative Unity	**Underlying Assumptions**	**Specifics of Case**
Cue: A student, Charlie Jones, has not turned in homework again.	Change: Significance: Externality: Trustworthiness:	Expected homework missing He has done it in the past This points to something Not considered
Concern: Teacher A is concerned that Charlie will fail the upcoming test.	Interests: Obligations: Liabilities:	Charlie wants to pass Teacher A should help Possibility of failure
Control Teacher A believes Charlie needs to do some quiet study uninterrupted by his friends or TV	Nonnaturalness: Practicality: Optimality:	Charlie can learn Biology Detentions are easy to give Not considered
Intervention:	Keeps Charlie after school to do homework	

whatever its cause, tends to set premises, independent of their truth or falsity.

How Does an Existentialist Peel an Orange?

The section heading is a facetious way to ask what real practical difference a philosophy makes. Whether we can expect a philosophical commitment to bear upon a specific action depends upon the philosophy and the action we are considering. Certainly, we should not overlook institutional constraints on decision. Would a person who seriously doubted his or her perceptions look for a job in a school? Would we want such a person to take care of children?

In the example given above, the rationale for Teacher A's detaining Charlie Jones makes pointless the critical questions which define some of the philosophical positions we have been considering. Schooling is, after all, a practice, not just contemplation. This may make many "schools of philosophy" pointless to schooling practice. If we review the critical questions of authority, ontology, epistemology, and axiology, we find that in most areas of schooling, authority is well defined; the option to question is not open. Ontological disputes may be "premised away." How we know may be of some interest where conflict is present; but, it, too, is often not an open question. (We will learn in the next chapter that axiological questions do bear on schooling practice.) Michael Levin cautions against expecting too much from philosophical theory, even from as congenial a schooling philosophy as Pragmatism:

> Telling people to balance principle against consequence offers little in the way of concrete guidance. But a philosophical overview is supposed to offer insight, not marching orders. Anyone who wants more is really looking for a magic formula to dispel moral quandary. It is a hard truth, existence will be morally perplexing as long as confusing, indeterminate situations demand action.[65]

How, then, can philosophy influence schooling? It may influence schooling not as an ideology but as wisdom or critical practice. We saw in Chapter 17 how those influenced the curriculum. Another way, we will see in Chapter 20, is through various conceptions of human nature and of value. For example, Behaviorism recommends that only "directly observable" behavior be pursued as a schooling outcome. Yet another way is through the practices of testing and evaluation. The assumptions made in constructing a test often reveal commitments to particular philosophical theories. We will also examine these in Chapter 20.

Many scholars believe that philosophy can directly influence research on

---

[65]Levin, op. cit., p. 47.

teaching and learning.[66] The authors of this book agree and would hasten to add that vital organizational conflicts and educational issues often yield to philosophical analysis. We should reread Section I, "Framing the Inquiry." Is it useful? We must realize that it is informed by the traditions of critical philosophy. What these traditions tend to emphasize is laying out all the options of a problematic situation prior to judging them. The skills involved in doing this are often very useful in dealing with the day-to-day problems of the school.

In the next section we will reconsider the problem of identifying fundamental authority, that is, the problem of dealing with disputes among moral communities, where each one claims to know what is right or to have knowledge.

The Search for Fundamental Authority

Ein Reich. Ein Volk. Ein Führer.
One Realm. One People. One Leader.

——————— *Nazi Slogan*

In the search for consensus, humankind has long looked to find a common fundamental authority. Lacking such consensus, it has used power to extort recognition, in public practice, at least, of the authorities recognized as fundamental by powerholders. What we must ask, however, is what the function of a fundamental authority might be. What purpose would such a consensus on fundamental authority serve?

There are, of course, psychological benefits to be gained for some people: a sense of rest, of finality, of being able to give up the critical struggle, of finding safe harbor from unquiet seas of tentativeness. But for others, this same finality means intellectual lobotomy, the blinding of reason, the smothering security that may, in the long run, be nothing more than another disappointment in humankind's long history of disappointments with would-be ultimates.

The basic function of any authority is to bring an end to the process of inquiry. Authority is an inquiry stopper. If we could recognize something as a "fundamental authority" it would save us the costs of worrying out our problems for ourselves.

Clearly, the role of philosophy in schooling, where it is thought of as either foundationalism or ideology, offers authorities as fundamental. And where the

---

[66]Cf., for example, Robin Barrow, "Teacher Education and Research: The Place of Philosophy," *Philosophy of Education 1984*, pp. 183–192. See also B. Paul Komisar and C. J. B. Macmillan (eds.), *Psychological Concepts in Education* (Chicago: Rand McNally, 1967); or Theodore Mischel (ed.), *Human Action: Conceptual and Empirical Issues* (New York: Academic Press, 1969).

power of a tradition or an institution is strong enough, public consensus is compelled. But what happens in the critical tradition?

Inquiry-Stoppers in Critical Philosophy

> In every philosophy there comes the point where the philosopher's "conviction" enters the scene—or, in the words of the ancient mystery,
> > *adventavit asinus,*
> > *pulcher et fortissimus*
> (Enter now the ass, Beautiful and most strong.)
>
> —————— *Friedrich Nietzsche*[67]

To invoke authority is to put an end to inquiry. Philosophers in the critical tradition are thus loathe to admit anything as authority. To concede some person or some system authority makes them vulnerable to the very same critical activity they are engaged in. "Why should we accept *that* as authority?" other philosophers might ask.

Therefore, otherwise critical philosophers who need, for whatever reason, to prevent challenge to a belief or system, have come up with other kinds of technical "inquiry-stoppers." Rather than risk invoking authority, some invoke "clear and distinct ideas" or "human nature" or "a priori judgments" or "intuition" or "empathy."[68] Many of these concepts have passed over into educational discourse to serve as theoretical foundations for various approaches to schooling.

If we ask many people how they know God exists and is good, they may say that the Bible says so or that the Church teaches us that it is so. They invoke something they recognize as authority to justify their beliefs. Philosophers who believe in a good God, on the other hand, tend to say things like, "We can know that by intuition." Or they may give logical arguments, or invoke "clear and distinct ideas." In the case of philosophers, the "inquiry-stoppers" they bring up in lieu of citing authority tend to be "democratic" in a way that invoking traditional religious authority may not be. Traditions of wisdom tend to reserve access to special knowledge to a special class of people. Philosophical traditions tend to concede everyone the possibility of

---

[67]Friedrich Nietzsche, *Beyond Good and Evil*, trans. Marianne Cowan (Chicago: Gateway, 1955), p. 8.

[68]See Alasdair MacIntyre, *After Virtue* (Notre Dame, Ind.: Notre Dame U. Press, 1981), p.15, quoting Keynes on G. E. Moore and the Bloomsbury Group, "In practice, victory was with those who could speak with the greatest appearance of clear, undoubting conviction. . ." Also see Madhu Suri Prakash and Mark Weinstein, "After Virtue: A Quest for Moral Objectivity," *Educational Theory*, Vol. 32, No.1 (Winter 1982), book review, pp. 35–44.

access to knowledge, through contemplation, critical inquiry, intuition, "clear and distinct ideas," and so forth. In a sense, the Protestant Reformation and the Socratic tradition of critical philosophy reinforce each other's fundamental individualism.

Thus, critical philosophy does not easily concede authority, even if it pursues it. There is no fundamental authority on matters of knowledge and morals which is commonly accepted by philosophers in the critical Socratic tradition. Of course, philosophers concede each other authority on the basis of their knowledge of a tradition or literature or their skill in argumentation. But this is not recognition of authority in some foundational sense. Rather, it is very much like the admiration soldiers of opposing armies might show for one another as regards their bravery or tactical skill.

The Practice of Tentative Finality

President Reagan cautioned that, despite optimism about Gorbachev's visit, fundamental differences still exist between the U.S. and the Soviet Union.

———————— *anonymous attribution, December 7, 1988*

What are fundamental differences and why should they be worrisome? Is it because they threaten conflict? But conflict is always possible and not necessarily seen as undesirable. Among sociological relativists fundamental differences should be expected. Indeed, if we recall the metaphor of Wittgenstein's elephants (Chapter 18), even the appearance of agreement might obscure deeper differences. The belief that between two people there are **no** differences is not something that can be confirmed by evidence.[69] So sociological relativists must accept differences as unavoidable.

But normative absolutists see things differently. If values are part of a unique reality, and people disagree on values, then somebody is denying reality. Thus the worry about fundamental differences. In addition, some of the people who know what is Right may feel the need to compel those who are wrong to correct their views, if only to defend the Right against possible attempts to impose the Wrong.

But even normative absolutists need not believe that conflict is irreconcilable. We touched briefly in Chapter 3 (Sources of Authority) on the possibility of a pluralism's working like a moral community. That the great majority of people obey the law most of the time does not mean that they do it for the

---

[69]This is an example of what logicians call a universal negative. No finite number of examples of agreement can prove there is no disagreement.

same reasons. Indeed, for some it may be a matter of morality; for others, a commitment to the governing process; for some, habit; for others, fear of punishment; and for others, finally, a case that the benefits of obedience outweigh the costs. If people agree to accept a procedure or authority as *tentatively* final so that they can work together—even though such acceptance may be for different reasons—there is no need to fear that fundamental differences, whatever they may be, will necessarily lead to irreconcilable conflict. Pursuit of the benefits of conflict are more often its cause, than is some presumed fundamental difference between the antagonists.

SUMMARY

1. The preferred image of the school influences the perception of the role of philosophy in schooling. Critical philosophy threatens the authorities of Temple and Factory.

2. Two traditions of introducing teachers to philosophy compete: the ISMs vs. critical philosophy. Although of historical interest, the ISMs tend to create an illusion of consensus that supports the Temple and Factory images of the school.

3. Critical questions used to sort out commonly accepted philosophical schools have little application to the rationalization of decision in schooling.

4. Unless one is an absolute moralist, the search for fundamental authority is pointless. Even then, irreconcilable conflict need not be inevitable.

QUESTIONS

1. What kind of consensus exists, evaluated in breadth and depth, for the various traditions of wisdom mentioned in this chapter?

2. Many religious denominations do not find the Theory of Evolution threatening. Why not?

3. How does critical philosophy threaten the Temple image of the school?

4. If two people believe that values are absolute, but disagree on them, how can they avoid conflict?

5. If values are relative, what are they relative to? What, then, is the force of telling someone they should do something?

6. What does 100 on a spelling test indicate? Suppose the words are in French.

7. Suppose Johnny refuses to study and fails a test. How does our belief that he is at fault affect our concern to help him?

8. Using the conditions of Cue, Concern, and Control, analyze
    a. the use of IQ tests to place students in tracks, for example, academic, general, vocational.

    b. the practice of giving report cards. What premises are set by such a practice?

9. How do the narrative conditions Cue, Concern, and Control relate to the Analysis Questions introduced in Chapter 3?

10. Recall from Chapter 4 the functions of conflict. Consider the dispute between Pro-Life and Pro-Choice advocates. Is it based on a fundamental difference about authority? What costs and benefits, both symbolic and substantial, does this conflict cause the parties involved? What is to be gained by reconciliation?

CRITICAL PRACTICE in SCHOOLING

Chapter 20

T_{hey} who are to be judges must also be performers.

— *Aristotle*[1]

Pursuing their professional education, school people often feel overwhelmed by theory. "How can that ever help me in teaching?" they react, frustrated with conceptual schemes that seem far removed from immediate concerns. Many of them develop an almost knee-jerk reaction against theory and in favor of the "practical." What they fail to recognize is that they have not rejected theory. They have merely chosen to ignore the theories they have picked up unwittingly and that, having become habit, guide their action uncritically. To accept something as practical is to make a judgment based on theory. And to do it uncritically is no less theoretical, just a good deal less thoughtful.

PREVIEW

Intelligent professional practice requires the ability to connect critical theory with practical schooling issues. In this chapter we will see how critical philosophy can help us do that. We will learn that judgments of practicality involve both philosophical perspectives and moral commitments. We will use action-focused inquiry to look at three crucial components of American schooling practice: testing, providing equity in schooling, and dealing with competing notions of human nature. We will examine the mechanism of testing, because it is around testing that much schooling practice develops. We will see why testing is relied upon to address our cogent concerns about providing what we believe to be the best education for each individual child. Also, we will discover that there is a close and intimate connection between our conceptions of justice and our beliefs about human nature.

FROM PHILOSOPHY TO PRACTICE

... there are value judgments in which the criteria themselves are debatable ... reflect(ing) the fact that important issues are not always easy ones.... It is immature to react to this kind of judgment as if it is contaminated with some disgusting disease; the only proper reaction is to examine the reasons put forward for them and see if and how the matter may be rationally discussed.

— *Michael Scriven*[2]

[1]Aristotle, *Politics*, trans. Benjamin Jowett, 8:6.
[2]Michael Scriven, "The Methodology of Evaluation," in Taylor and Cowley, Chap. 5, p. 32.

School people tend to shrug off certain kinds of inquiry as "too philosophical" or "too theoretical." By the short shrift given many issues, we might think that the driving force in any school was the search for immediate, hands-on practicality. Yet, if we stopped most school people in the midst of practice and asked them the basis for their decisions, they would likely give us reasons of the most theoretical kind.

For example, if we asked, "Why do you insist on students' getting in before the bell?" a principal might answer, "To prepare them for work in later life." Or, if we asked a teacher, "Why do you have your students outline their notes?" the teacher might say, "To help them develop mental organization." But there is a big jump from beating the bell or outlining to getting a job or being mentally organized. To connect them takes a lot of theory, along with many assumptions that may be, at best, fervent hopes.

Schooling practice is awash in theory, but theory that is seldom subject to critical review. What are we to make of this? To begin, we have to give up the idea that there is a great gulf between the theoretical and the practical. The theoretical imaginations of a German patent office clerk, Albert Einstein, have led to consequences of impressive practicality. The practically important social debates over abortion, birth control, and school reform involve ideas that are nothing, if not theoretical.

Identifying the Practical: Constraints and Scope

The distinction between the practical and the theoretical is determined by the presence of two factors: **constraints** and **scope**. By "constraints" we mean **factors that restrict options**. Many reform proposals, for example, tend to be pointlessly theoretical, because they fail to take into consideration important nonschool factors that affect schooling. We can discuss to the point of

Which is more practical?

exhaustion what we want from schools; our deliberations are "theoretical" in the worst sense, however, if we overlook the many real impediments school people have to face on the job.[3]

For example, teachers are constantly admonished to "individualize" their instruction to the specific needs of students. But in *The Real World of the Public Schools*, Harry Broudy points out that teachers have little real possibility of doing this if they are concerned about twenty-five to thirty-five youngsters. In such a context, says Broudy, the refrain, "Treat every pupil as an individual" becomes "blithe idiocy," and "mischievous sentimentalism."[4] In other words, instructional individualization becomes too theoretical if its design does not deal with this vital dimension of the situation.

Attempts to make schools an essential part of the Drug War provide another example. Michael Kitzner, a senior research scientist at the Pacific Institute for Research and Evaluation, observes that if a child in a drug education program lives in a neighborhood where many, possibly including his uncle or brother, are making big money by dealing drugs, this reality "washes out" the effect of the education.[5] In other words, it becomes pointlessly "theoretical" because it fails to deal with this critical nonschool factor.

On the other hand, an action may be so particular to its time and circumstances that it offers us no guide beyond the framework of constraints in which it occurred. Here we would say that the "scope" is too limited, too uniquely practical. Let's suppose, for instance, that Mr. Herodotus has the son of the Superintendent of Schools as a pupil in his American history class. Let's suppose, further, that the boy happens to be a direct descendent of General Andrew Burnside of Civil War fame. We can imagine that Mr. Herodotus would make sure to mention the brilliance of Burnside. But the teacher's reason is so specific to these circumstances that it is unlikely to offer much in the way of general principles. Its scope is simply too specific for that. Figure 20.1 illustrates the relationships of scope and constraint to practicality.

Debates about schooling often center on whether certain factors are or should be constraints on schooling practice. To illustrate, race and sex are factors thought to be important to some schooling decisions and irrelevant to others. At one time both were thought to be critically relevant in making all kinds of educational decisions. Today, however, while they are still considered relevant, they are thought to be so only in a much narrower context. In the past, for instance, race was considered so relevant that it was the primary determiner of who could attend school. Today, such a constraint is illegal. Similarly school officials used to sort students by sex—eliminating females from subjects that were thought unsuitable for their allegedly delicate constitutions. Today, though we often still sort gym classes by sex, we shrink

---

[3]Lynn Olson, "Work Conditions in Some Schools Said 'Intolerable,'" *Education Week*, September 28, 1988, p. 1.
[4]Harry S. Broudy, *The Real World of the Public Schools* (New York: Harcourt Brace Jovanovich, 1972), pp. 44–45.
[5]Ellen Flax, "Anti-Drug Efforts Need Resources, Those in the Trenches Advise 'Czar,'" *Education Week*, March 1, 1989, p. 1.

Figure 20.1

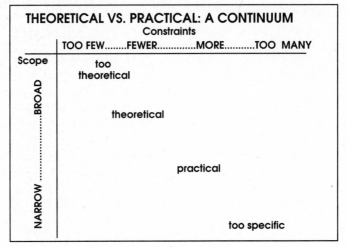

from the very thought of using sexuality to determine who may take academic subjects.

We see, then, that controversies about schooling often are not so much about what factors *are* relevant but about what factors *should be treated as* relevant. And this judgment is as much a matter of morality as it is of practicality. This is quite clear if we recall previous discussion about the usefulness of torture and sexual gratification as school motivators.

Indeed, moral considerations always come into play in deciding which constraints are school relevant.[6] For example, racism can be understood as a theory and practice so overly constrained by factors generally identified as "racial characteristics" that it becomes immoral. Yet, we still have to decide if and when race is ever relevant. Some argue that race should be totally ignored, others argue it is still morally relevant for Affirmative Action purposes. Both positions ultimately rest on a moral foundation.

Consider Figure 20.2. Where would you place race and sex as you understand them to currently constrain school practice? Do you think that race, for instance, still imposes too many constraints? Too few? How about scope? Do you think race counts in too many areas of American life? Too few?

Newer Philosophies of Education

In the last chapter we used five critical questions to sort out different traditional philosophies. We argued that within the school, many of these questions were "premised away" by practices and traditions. In fact, only one of those

---

[6]Cf. Thomas Sowell, in *A Conflict of Visions* (New York: Morrow, 1987), argues that the long-running disputes between conservative and liberal theorists are based not on different values or interests but on different conceptions of feasibility and moral choices as to who should control the relevant factors.

Figure 20.2

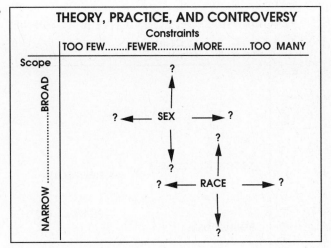

critical questions serves as a point of contention in today's schools: What is the nature of value?

The question of the nature of value is seldom addressed directly. Educators seldom think they have either the time or the inclination to do so. But they still do champion different approaches to the curriculum which make some basic value-related assumptions. We will consider here those most commonly recognized as newer philosophies of education: Perennialism, Essentialism, Pragmatism, Reconstructionism, and Behaviorism. (Of course, all of the warnings of the previous chapter about the shallowness of such easy comparisons still hold.) Chart 20.1 indicates some differences and similarities. Note that

Chart 20.1

FIVE MODERN PHILOSOPHIES OF EDUCATION			
	Nature of Value	Teach What?	Proponents
Perennialism	Objective, eternal.	Things of perennial value.	Hutchins, Maritain
Essentialism	Objective, eternal.	Essentials of Rationality	Adler, Bestor
Pragmatism	Relative, changing.	Things needed for personal and social development.	Dewey, Kilpatrick
Reconstructionism	Relative, changing.	Things to promote social change.	Counts
Behaviorism	Relative, changing.	Changes in overt behavior cued to environment.	Skinner

Figure 20.3

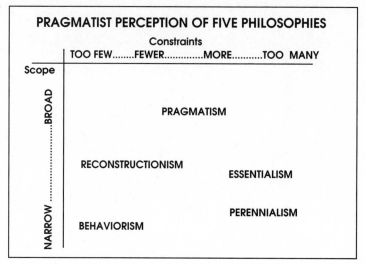

Perennialism and Essentialism begin with the notion that value is objective and eternal. Pragmatism, Reconstructionism, and Behaviorism, on the other hand, assume it to be both relative and changing.

These philosophies compete not only over the issue of the nature of values, but also in their perceived scope and the constraints believed to be recognized by them. A Pragmatist, focusing on what works for students in today's society and dismissing Perennialist and Essentialist concerns for traditions, might perceive their relative positions as in Figure 20.3. The Perennialist would view them quite differently. The different locations for each philosophy in Figures 20.3 and 20.4 are significant. For the Perennialist the vast scope of the tradi-

Figure 20.4

```
┌─────────────────────────────────────────────────┐
│      PERENNIALIST PERCEPTION OF FIVE PHILOSOPHIES │
│                    Constraints                    │
│         TOO FEW.......FEWER.............MORE...........TOO  MANY │
│  Scope                                            │
│              PERENNIALISM                         │
│         ESSENTIALISM                              │
│                                  PRAGMATISM       │
│                            RECONSTRUCTIONISM      │
│  BEHAVIORISM                                      │
└─────────────────────────────────────────────────┘
```

tions of the humanities has to be brought to the student. Perennialist advocates perceive the scope of their concern to be broad. Pragmatists see this as suffering from too many constraints. On the other hand, the Pragmatist's concern that students get along outside of school would be viewed by the Perennialist as overly constraining factors beyond the function of the school. The Pragmatist does not make any claims on very broad philosophical issues, such as the nature of morality, that might interest the Perennialist. Thus, judgments of scope and constraints change accordingly.

What we learn from these comparisons is that how you see things depends on where you stand. That individuals in a pluralistic society take all sorts of stances accounts for a great deal of the controversy and conflict swirling around school-related issues.

What we will attempt to do in the following sections is to look at some considerations that are practical from the point of view of someone working in a school. Certainly, philosophical commitments of one sort or other will tend to flavor the result. But we will try to acknowledge major issues of controversy wherever possible.

Toward A Practical Philosophy of Education

> As a practical discipline, philosophy of education is an attempt to find the most rationally defensible reasons for doing education one way rather than some other. What makes this kind of educational philosophy different from philosophy is that decisions must be reached as preparation for subsequent action, and the actions which follow upon decisions are intended to have consequences—to make a difference—in human lives.
>
> ——————— *Foster McMurray*[7]

McMurray suggests the following criteria for a practical philosophy applicable to schooling:

1. **Action Orientation:** the inquiries of a practical discipline must affect decisions about behaviors to adopt rather than merely clarifying theory.
2. **A Trusted Decision Process:** the process of reaching decisions must have a capacity to generate some degree of conviction in the outcomes that are reached.
3. **Consensus of Stakeholders on Cogency:** what are offered as "good reasons" should be recognizable as such by those concerned.

---

[7]Foster McMurray, "Concepts of Mind and Intelligence in Educational Theory," *Educational Theory*, Vol. 25, No. 3 (Summer 1975), pp. 236.

We are looking for a process that yields results having application to school situations, that is seen as trustworthy by stakeholders, and that justifies itself in terms of reasons recognized by stakeholders to be pertinent.

We can meet McMurray's criteria with a focus on the Rationale for Action developed in the last chapter. It is action oriented and, being based on critical philosophy, it provides a trustworthy decision process. (Sectarian philosophers do not quarrel with the process of critical philosophy, only with its scope. And by introducing the Analysis Questions explained in Chapter 3 at critical junctures, each individual can likely work from concerns he or she finds cogent.)

We recall from the last chapter that, in order to have narrative coherence, school decisions had to have a certain structure: they had to be analyzable in terms of **cue**, **concern** and **control**. In the rest of this chapter we will locate some major schooling concerns within this framework and show how to deal with these sample issues in a way that is useful, trustworthy, and cogent.

APPLICATIONS TO PRACTICE

> There is a kind of idle theory which is antithetical to practice; but genuinely scientific theory falls within practice as the agency of its expansion and its direction to new possibilities.
>
> *John Dewey*[8]

Many people talk as if knowing what is practical were the most obvious thing in the world. But, in fact, there is no broad and deep consensus on this. As

---

[8]John Dewey, *Democracy and Education* (New York: Macmillan, 1965), p. 228.

John Dewey

we have seen, a judgment of practicality is a matter of perspective and commitment. It is based on moral judgment as well as considerations of constraint and scope. In the rest of this chapter we will use some of the techniques of critical philosophy to focus on rationales for action. We will find that we can understand important problems in schooling and more usefully evaluate approaches to their solution through such a focus.

Rationales for actions require an indication of cue, concern and control. There are many problems which can be grouped into one or more of these facets of rational action. For example, questions about testing can be analyzed as a set of assumptions about **cue**. Justice and equality are **concerns** which motivate much schooling activity. Ideas of **control** express themselves in conceptions of goal, human variability, and individual responsibility. We can analyze some of these topics by examining the underlying assumptions of cue, concern, and control that we developed in the last chapter.

The Assumptions of Cue: Testing for Justice

> American schools are going test-crazy. The scores emerging from those sheets full of X's and penciled-in circles are increasingly being used to promote and hold back students, hire and fire teachers, award diplomas, evaluate curriculums, and dole out money to schools and colleges.
>
> ————— *Edward B. Fiske*[9]

An understanding of testing and the assumptions it is based on are indispensable to intelligent schooling practice. The use of tests can be critiqued not only with respect to their technical efficiency, but also as to whether they are fair and whether the very process of testing is little more than an exercise of political power. Because testing affects lives,[10] it deserves careful examination.

There is a story that school people tell in which they express widely shared concerns. We will call this story **The Testing For Justice Rationale.** It usually goes like this:

> For some children and not others to have their needs met by the schools is unfair. Justice therefore dictates that we meet the needs of all the children. How do we determine those needs? By comparing what they can do with what they can learn to do. Any discrepancy between performance and competence, between achievement and potential is an indicator of need. How do we

---

[9]Edward B. Fiske, "America's Test Mania," *New York Times*, April 18, 1988, Education Life Section, p. 16.
[10]See Lynn Olson, "Tests Found Barring Thousands of Minority Teacher Candidates," *Education Week*, Vol. VIII, No. 12 (November 13, 1988), p. 1.

determine such things as performance, competence, achievement, and potential? By adequate testing.

Thus upon testing is loaded the burden of determining not only need, but ultimately, justice.[11]

Why Have Tests?

Why do teachers give tests? For several reasons, two of which are

a. to support the authority of the teacher's judgment, and
b. to substitute for an infeasibly broad examination of student ability.

In a culture where the image of the school shifts from Temple to Factory or Town Meeting, teacher judgment alone loses its validity. The Factory demands a "scientific" basis for evaluation. This basis also serves as a defense in the Town Meeting. Testing serves as a barrier to lawsuit because it is assumed to demonstrate impartiality.

Indeed, modern schooling, which processes large numbers of students, seems inconceivable without testing, given its convenience for sorting students. It can substitute for a long and involved set of social interactions with master teachers which was common to schools before the Factory model became dominant.

This convenience is so important in the mass schooling carried out today that learnings which don't lend themselves to easy examination—for example, with paper and pencil—find it hard to gain status in a curriculum. Ivor Goodson comments,

> For the groups and associations promoting themselves as school subjects, and irresistibly drawn to claiming "academic status," a central criterion has been whether the subjects' content could be tested by written examinations for an "able" clientele.[12]

In testing, however, many crucial assumptions about causal connections are made. Achievement tests, for example, are not in and of themselves the point of instruction; otherwise we would teach, not merely to the tests, but the very tests themselves. Nor is mere participation in course work thought sufficient to make testing unnecessary. Rather, what is sought in achievement tests are certain important residues of the instructional process.

Calling something a test assumes that there is a relatively clear idea of what the test indicates. But when it comes to things as vague and controversial as human abilities, upon which a judgment of educational need might be based,

---

[11]Cf. Nathan Glazer, "IQ on Trial," *Commentary* June 1981, pp. 51–59, for a critique of Larry P. V. Wilson Riles in which the Testing for Justice Rationale plays a prominent part.
[12]Ivor Goodson, *School Subjects and Curriculum Change* (Philadelphia: Falmer Press, 1987), p. 25.

tests come to stand in for controversial and pluralistic conceptions of human ability. "Intelligence," for example, becomes "what IQ tests measure."[13] Institutionalization thus happens not only to organizations, but to activities within them. Let's look at this more closely.

What Makes a Test a Test?

From the student's point of view every test is a task, and usually less than welcome. But not every task is a test, even if it looks like one. What conditions must a task satisfy, if it is to really be a test? This is a question of great practicality. As we learned in Chapter 16, many state governments have begun to allocate funds to school districts on the basis of efficiency. This efficiency is determined by tests provided by state departments of education and imposed on local school districts. But what is necessary if this procedure is to be anything more than a charade? What assumptions justify such a procedure?

To avoid overlooking assumptions built into our conception of testing, let's begin by talking about **rank tasks** rather than about tests. A rank task is a type of activity some outcomes of which we can rank. The question we wish to ask is whether a rank task is a test, or not. If so, what additional assumptions must we make to identify it as a test and not merely a rank task? Let's now consider what a test is.

Tests are at least rank tasks. They can be performed with more or less skill. But the skill demonstrated may not be what we wish to measure. For instance,

---

[13]For a discussion of long-standing controversy on the nature of IQ, compare Arthur R. Jensen, "How Much Can We Boost I.Q. and Scholastic Achievement?" *Harvard Educational Review*, Winter 1969, with J. P. Guilford, *The Nature of Human Intelligence* (New York: McGraw-Hill, 1967).

What makes a test a test?

students take SAT preparation courses to learn **test-taking skills**, not the information the tests are designed to measure. Often these test-taking skills can be as crucial to a good score as actual knowledge of the material covered in the test. For example, Robinson and Katzman have written a popular book suggesting simple test-taking procedures that they claim can raise SAT scores significantly.[14] The SATs are intended to measure scholastic aptitude. But the usefulness of Robinson and Katzman's book suggests that the SATs are also measuring something else, namely the ability to take standardized tests of this type.

This observation illustrates the very practical nature of our seemingly theoretical observations about testing. Among the readers of this text are certain to be individuals who did not get a scholarship, or who failed to get into the college or university of their choice because of the scores they received on the SATs. And there is a fair chance that the reason they did not get higher scores was not because they lacked "scholastic aptitude," but because they lacked certain test-taking skills. We think the reader will agree that this is a very practical issue.

Tests are also cues. And as cues they require that the conditions be met that we developed in Chapter 19.

a. **change:** they must be able to vary in result;
b. **significance:** the variation must be understood to make a difference;
c. **externality:** they must "point to" something other than themselves;
d. **trustworthiness:** we must be able to believe the results were not manipulated for special purposes.

The first two conditions are met by any well-designed rank task; testmakers identify these conditions as conditions of **internal validity**. Externality is the condition testmakers refer to as **external validity**, and trustworthiness is a matter of **test security**.[15]

The important point is that every test is a task for someone, and tasks can be performed with more or less skill, independent of any considerations of externality and trustworthiness. For example, a student may learn to do multiple choice exams efficiently even if those exams do not test anything we can recognize as subject matter. On the other hand, a student may know a great deal about something, yet be very bad at demonstrating that knowledge through the medium of the test prepared for it.

The claim that a rank task is a test depends *solely* upon the belief that it is an **indicator of something beyond itself,** that is, the condition of externality is satisfied. To call a rank task a test is to claim that it correlates with

---

[14]Cf. Adam Robinson and John Katzman, "Cracking the System: the SAT," *The Princeton Review* (New York: Villard Books, 1986).

[15]However, other subversive factors such as cramming are difficult to deal with. See David P. Ausubel, "Crucial Psychological Issues in the Objectives, Organization and Evaluation of Curriculum Reform Movements," in Taylor and Cowley, op. cit., Chap. 22, pp. 191–197, esp. "Evaluation of Learnability and Measurement of Achievement," p. 196.

Figure 20.5

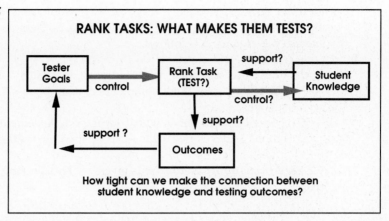

RANK TASKS: WHAT MAKES THEM TESTS?

How tight can we make the connection between
student knowledge and testing outcomes?

something else. And to construct tests we have to use—if unwittingly—some
theory that relates the test we are constructing to the item we are testing for.

We can use the task analysis developed in Chapter 8 to investigate some
crucial assumptions made in testing. If the rank task is a test, then the goals
of the testing control (determine) the kind of test tasks we present to the
student. (See Figure 20.5.) These tasks in turn control the knowledge the
student will bring to support the test task. The causal connections between
student knowledge and the test outcomes used to evaluate it are mediated by
the task itself. This presents two immediate questions:

a. Does an increase in test scores indicate an increase in student knowledge, an increase in test-taking skill, or both?

b. How can we ensure that an increase in knowledge will cause an increase in test scores, even given a constant level of test-taking skill?

It is unwise to try to give general answers to these questions. Rather, they
must be faced up to by each testmaker for each proposed test on each specific
subject matter. The extent to which common assumptions underlie all testing
endeavors, or whether some assumptions are subject-specific is an involved
and interesting inquiry.[16]

From Consensus, Through Testing, to Justice

Let's reiterate an important point: we must have some way of determining
what knowledge a student has that is independent of the test; otherwise the
test becomes problematic. If the test is questionable, evaluations of potential
or achievement are questionable. So then is the determination of need, and

---

[16]See, for example, Daniel R. DiNicola, *Evaluation and Grading: A Philosophical Analysis.* Ph.D.
dissertation. Unpublished. Harvard University. 1973; or Jum C. Nunnaly, *Psychometric Theory*
(New York: McGraw-Hill, 1967), pp. 10–102.

therefore fairness. Thus, in a very real way, problems of consensus bear ultimately, through testing, upon perceptions of fairness in schooling. We can express the argument as follows:

  a. Consensus will affect which ideas of "potential"—for example, native ability, capacity, and competence—can be used for testing in the school.
  b. Consensus will affect which ideas of achievement—for example, acquired or developed skills—can be used for testing in the school.

We then bring in the connections given by **The Testing for Justice Rationale:**

  c. The difference between potential and achievement measures need.
  d. The difference in treatment of need measures justice.

The most immediately practical version of this argument, which we will call **The Status Quo Argument**, is as follows:

> There is a consensus in our community that Group A and Group B differ in potential. We observe that they differ in achievement. Because their achievement reflects merely their potential, there is no disparity in educational need. Therefore, our present treatment of Groups A and B, although they may look different, is not unjust.

It is around such claims of consensus that many of the controversies about the schools cluster.

Concern: Objectivity, Needs, and Justice

We learned in the previous chapter that rationales for action involve considerations of concern, obligation, interest, and liability. One of the assumptions of the Factory is that testing offers us an "objective" way of making decisions that gets around such things, avoiding problems of values and consensus. Let's look at this.

Educationally Relevant Attributes

Numbers impress people; they seem so impartial, so objective. But what can numbers alone tell us? Imagine we have three groups of students, A, B, and C, and we administer a battery of tests to each of them consisting of Test 1, Test 2, and Test 3. Chart 20.2 gives us the results. The numbers represent group averages. Let's assume the differences between groups for each test are significant and that there has been no manipulation of the results. What are we to make of the differences in these scores? Are they any guide to practical decision?

Chart 20.2

TESTING FOR JUSTICE			
	Test 1	Test 2	Test 3
Group A	15	95	50
Group B	50	50	50
Group C	95	15	50

It depends. Our first question should be, "What are these tests supposed to indicate?" Unless we believe them to indicate something, they are merely rank tasks. And if these test results are to be important to making equitable schooling decisions, they must deal with what Green has called "educationally relevant attributes."[17] An attribute is educationally relevant in Green's terms, if it would be fair to distribute schooling benefits on the basis of that attribute. If we believed it was fair, for example, for more males to get diplomas than females just because they were males, then sex would be an educationally relevant attribute.

In the United States, sex is not educationally relevant. In some other cultures, such as Iran, it is considered to be so. In Chart 20.2, let's suppose Test 1 indicates something like "degree of femininity." If Test 2 indicates percentage of high school graduates in the group, we in the United States would find that it indicates an unjust situation, because we reject gender as educationally relevant. But if Test 3 stands for percentage of high school graduates, we would, on the same assumption of the irrelevance of gender, take it to be an indicator of equitable schooling practice.

Chart 20.3 shows attributes in terms of which people might be grouped compared with different kinds of schooling benefits. In each block the word "just" or "unjust" indicates whether there is a general consensus that benefits distributed on the basis of the indicated kinds of grouping are considered just. Question marks indicate controversial practices.

Chart 20.3 indicates that in different situations an attribute may be educationally relevant or it may not. Consider the case of sexual groupings and varsity sports. Sex is generally not considered a relevant attribute so far as any educational benefit is concerned. It is unjust, for example, to distribute high school diplomas on the basis of sex. But participation in varsity sports is another matter. There is sometimes controversy about allowing women to play football, particularly in public high schools. The chart indicates this with a **?**. Ask yourself how this chart would look if it were filled out to reflect the settled opinions of 1790. Also consider how it might look in the future, say in 2090. Do you think it would be dramatically different in either case?

Choice is an important and controversial attribute in our culture. If adults

---

[17]See Thomas F. Green, *Predicting the Behavior of the Educational System* (Syracuse, NY: Syracuse U. Press, 1980), pp. 49–52.

Chart 20.3

SOME EDUCATIONALLY RELEVANT ATTRIBUTES

Attribute \ Benefit	High School Diplomas	Access To Further Schooling	Knowledge Per Se	Playing Varsity Sports	Nurturance	Special Pgms
Sex	unjust	unjust	unjust	?	unjust	just
Race	unjust	unjust	unjust	just	unjust	just
Height	unjust	unjust	unjust	just	unjust	just
Ability	just	just	just	?	unjust	just
Effort	?	?	just	just	unjust	just
Choice	just	just	just	?	?	just
Need	unjust	unjust	unjust	unjust	?	just
Wealth	?	unjust	just	?	unjust	just
Handicap	just	just	?	just	unjust	just
Potential	just	just	just	just	unjust	just
Achievement	just	just	just	just	unjust	just

? = indicates a controversial practice

choose not to participate in certain programs, for example, it is generally not thought to be unjust if they fail to gain the benefits they offer. But if children or mentally incompetent people choose not to participate, it is often taken as a sign of immaturity or incompetence. Truancy is an example of such a case. Significantly, in the case of truancy the lack of consequent benefits is still often argued to be unjust, even though this opinion insinuates that coercion may be justified. (This sense of injustice no doubt supports compulsory schooling statutes.)

Other controversial practices suggested by the chart are:

What are relevant attributes?

- allowing students to play varsity sports on the basis of choice (interest) rather than ability;
- promoting students on the basis of effort rather than knowledge (social promotion);
- providing nurturance, a scarce resource, on the basis of need rather than following traditional practices such as teaching to the middle;
- providing diplomas and sports participation on the basis of wealth (a service of private schooling);
- providing schooling for the severely and profoundly handicapped.

Trying to identify the circumstances under which certain attributes are educationally relevant offers us a systematic way of considering what we want to count as relevant in educational situations. For example, we can use the technique to reconsider whether sexual and racial discrimination should exist with respect to some schooling practices and not others.

Two Conceptions of "Needs"

From each according to his abilities; to each according to his needs.

———— *Karl Marx*[18]

Embedded in the Testing for Justice Rationale is an interesting equation:

Ability − achievement = need

We should read this as "Ability minus achievement equals need" or "The measure of need is indicated by the difference between ability and achievement." On the basis of the "equation," students are often sorted into three types: underachievers, normal achievers, and overachievers. Chart 20.4 shows some hypothetical scores for tests of ability and achievement. By use of the equation given above, need is calculated. On the basis of need, students are typed as overachievers, normal achievers, and underachievers. So it is argued that "underachievers" have greater educational "needs." And numbers make it seem objective.

Vague formulas like the one above guide a surprising amount of daily school practice and we can discern them in the rationales offered for such practice. They express not only accepted generalizations from practice but also conceptions of human nature. Their usefulness is not that they provide exact measures of important pedagogical constructs, but that they can so readily guide practice. (For examples of other formulas, see Item B in the Technical Appendix for Chapter 20.) But do they really identify needs? It depends on what we mean by "needs."

---

[18]Karl Marx, *Criticism of the Gotha Programme*, 1875.

Chart 20.4

	Ability	Achievement	Need	Type
		"KINDS" OF STUDENTS		
Group A	50	95	−45	Overachiever
Group B	50	50	0	Normal
Group C	50	15	35	Underachiever

Needs and Consensus

In schooling "needs" have long been treated as though they were independent of consensus.[19] But critical philosophy suggests that underlying most talk about needs is the assumption that something *should* be desired. We should recall from Chapter 3 that discussing situations as "problems" is a common means of securing commitment by obscuring questions of values. In the same manner, to call something a "need" urges action to address it while begging the crucial question of why we should address it.

We can distinguish between two conceptions of need: a **conditional concept** and an **approval concept**. We can get a clear picture of this distinction by comparing the following situations:

> *Situation 1:* Johnny asks you to borrow a Magic Marker. "I need it to write graffiti on the boys' room wall," he explains.
>
> *Situation 2:* Mark tells you, "I need a Magic Marker to do my school art project."

We would deny that Johnny needs a Magic Marker, but concede that Mark needs one. Why? Because we do not approve of graffiti but we value Mark's art project. If our values were different, our assessment of needs would be different.

The **conditional concept of need** says merely that

> *some item X is necessary to bring about some other item Y.*

Thus, in this relation the Magic Marker is as necessary to put grafitti on the wall as it is to doing the art project. In the conditional sense, both Johnny and Mark have needs, just as cars need fuel or terrorists need explosives. A conditional need indicates, at most, a lack. But lacks do not necessarily beg for remediation.

The **approval concept of need** requires in addition that we *approve* of Y, that is:

---

[19]Cf. Jerry L Patterson and Theodore J. Czajkowski, "District Needs Assessment: One Avenue to Program Improvement," *Phi Delta Kappan*, Vol. 58, No. 4 (December 1976), pp. 327–329.

*some item X is necessary to bring about some other item Y, and we **approve** of Y.*

If we disapprove of graffiti on the wall, we do not grant that Johnny needs a Magic Marker. But if we approve of Mark's art project, we recognize his need for the Marker.[20] Our approval of his aim is the critical element.

Talking about "needs" in schooling is a technique of sloganeering to achieve a broad but shallow consensus. It is an attempt to transform an objective, "take-it-or-leave-it" conditional need into a need that moves us to action without careful consideration.

The common technique is to show that there is a lack of some kind, and then to treat that lack as synonymous with an approval concept of need. A typical instance goes something like this. Researchers working for one or another special interest group announce with alarm that there is a great need to emphasize classical antiquity in the high school curriculum because 97 percent of all five thousand high school seniors surveyed nationwide could not identify Achilles, the Acropolis, Adonis, Aeneas, the *Aeneid*, and several dozen other items. If the research is accurate, it does demonstrate that a lack exists among high school seniors. But it does NOT demonstrate that we should do anything about it. That is an entirely different matter.

We are not disparaging needs-slogans, but merely reiterating the point emphasized in Section I of this text: **needs-slogans assume and obscure value judgments**.[21] If, for example, people do agree on the value of "self-fulfillment" and what it means, then what they believe to be a causal or logical necessity to achieve self-fulfillment will probably be approved of also. But an even more important consideration is this: Where people appear to be unmoved by appeals to needs, this may not be a matter of heartlessness, but rather a disagreement over values or over beliefs in causal or logical necessity.

Fair Play versus Fair Share: Equal Educational Opportunity

Who eat of food after their sacrifice
Are quit of fault, but they that spread a feast
All for themselves, eat sin and drink of sin.

———————— *Krishna*, Bhagavad-Gita, Chapter III[22]

At the root of much schooling controversy lies a dispute over conceptions of justice. It concerns whether justice is a matter of **fair play** or **fair share**. The

---

[20]Cf. Leonard Waks, *Needs and Needs Assessment: A Conceptual Framework* (Philadelphia: Research for Better Schools, 1979). Monograph.
[21]See Debra Viadero, "New Study Documents the Need for 'Culture Sensitive' AIDS Education," *Education Week,* Vol. II, Nos. 15 and 16 (January 13, 1988), p. 1.
[22]"The Bhagavad-Gita or Song Celestial," trans. Sir Edward Arnold, in Charles W. Elliot (ed.), *The Harvard Classics*, Vol. 43 (New York: Collier, 1910), p. 814.

dispute over these two conceptions is far from being settled.[23] Both fair share and fair play are conceptions of justice with long-standing traditions in our culture.

It has long been recognized that the concern over equal educational opportunity is obscured by the ambiguity between the desire for equitable procedures (fair play) and the desire for equitable results (fair share).[24] This concern becomes even more problematic when we recall from Chapter 6 that the meaning of minority is controversial.

Basically the dispute between Fair Share advocates and Fair Play advocates is this:

- **Fair Share Advocacy Claims**: The educational system is just only if educational benefits are distributed among minority groups proportionally, for example, if 3 percent of the population is Cajun, and high school diplomas are an educational benefit, then 3 percent of the high school diplomas should be awarded to Cajuns.
- **Fair Play Advocacy Claims**: The educational system is just if access to educational benefits is open to individuals regardless of their minority membership. If everyone has equal access to the possibility of getting a diploma, and Cajuns end up with fewer than 3 percent, then the system is not unjust.

Central to any practical decisions to be made, irrespective of whether one is a Fair Share or a Fair Play advocate, is some consensus as to what is or is not:

- a relevant minority,
- an educational benefit, and
- a means for controlling both access and distribution.

The advocates of Fair Play argue that the means to realizing Fair Share are unproved and risk the loss of individual freedoms. Fair Share advocates tend to emphasize that there is no real opportunity for fair play, because some people come to the game with handicaps.

A Fair Share advocate might argue, for example, that schools should move beyond Fair Play by establishing a system of affirmative action in which the best schooling is reserved for those disadvantaged in other respects. (This is not a hypothetical example. Christopher Jencks discusses this very possibility in his influential work, *Inequality*.[25]) A Fair Play advocate could well respond that this would require an injustice to more advantaged children and might

---

[23]Cf. William Ryan, *Equality* (New York: Vintage, 1982). See also Thomas Sowell, *A Conflict of Visions* (New York: Morrow, 1987); John Rawls, *A Theory of Justice* (Cambridge, MA: Belknap, 1971); and Robert Nozick, *Anarchy, State and Utopia* (New York: Basic Books, 1974).

[24]Cf. B. Paul Komisar, "The Paradox of Equality in Schooling," *Teachers' College Record*, Vol. 68, No. 3 (December 1966), pp. 251–254.

[25]Christopher Jencks, *Inequality* (New York: Harper & Row, 1972), p. 255.

Chart 20.5

	FAIR PLAY VS. FAIR SHARE: PERCEPTIONS OF COST & BENEFIT	
	Fair Play	**Fair Share**
C O S T S	Does not address certain inequalities. Restricts communal power over the individual. Ignores historically derived disadvantages.	Places undue communal power over the individual. Ignores inadequacy of means. Ignores costs of reforms.
B E N E F I T S	Traditionally, an intrinsic value Restricts communal power over the individual. Permits small-scale adjustments that may bring large changes.	Traditionally, an intrinsic value Attempts to deal with obvious inequities. Makes leaders responsive to needs of group.

not even work. The costs and benefits of each point of view[26] are summarized in Chart 20.5.

Of course, what we *should* do is restricted by what we *can* do. Our ability to exercise control defines the practical limits of our concern. Thus we are advised, "Do not worry about the things you cannot change." We will look at some of these limits in the next section.

Control: What Can We Change?

> ... no human enterprise ... that depends for its effective conduct on the infusion of knowledge can be conducted without an ongoing process of inquiry fed by relevant knowledge.
>
> —————— *John Goodlad*[27]

Change is almost always possible. The hard questions are, What are its costs and benefits? For whom?[28] In this section we will look at three things:

---

[26]Also see James S. Coleman, "Rawls, Nozick, and Educational Equality": Reflections, *The Public Interest*, No. 44 (Summer 1976), pp. 121–128.
[27]John Goodlad, "Studying the Education of Educators: Values-Driven Inquiry," *Phi Delta Kappan*, October 1988, p. 109.
[28]Cf. Lynn Olson, "Questions Raised on Efficacy of Stiffer Math, Science Graduation Requisites," *Education Week*, February 15, 1989, p. 5.

a. how pursuit of competing goals undermines control;

b. how basic differences in the human population might affect the goals we pursue; and

c. how different conceptions of the individual bear on our notions of control.

We should remember from Chapter 19 that our belief that we can and should exercise control over a situation rests upon assumptions we have made about:

- **nonnaturalness**: our attempts to change something are not going "against its nature," that is, we are not dealing with a causal system that will eventually reverse our influence on it;
- **practicality**: the benefits of change outweigh the costs;
- **optimality**: our choice of methods to pursue our goal is the best under the circumstances.

Whenever we find that a situation frustrates one of these conditions, we are well advised to examine whether we want to continue to try to change it. We will see in the next section that these conditions of control are undermined by the pursuit of conflicting goals. To begin, we will review some distinctions made earlier in the kinds of benefits we envision the schools as providing.

Review: Divisible vs. Indivisible; Absolute vs. Positional

Some important distinctions among schooling outcomes perceived as benefits have been made in various places throughout the book. We have distinguished between

a. **divisible vs. indivisible benefits:** those that some persons might enjoy while others might not vs. those that can be said to exist only if all enjoy them—for example, diplomas vs. justice;

b. **absolute vs. positional benefits:** those benefits valued independently of their distribution vs. those valued by virtue of their scarcity—for example, ability to appreciate classical music vs. money.

The practical importance of these distinctions becomes obvious when we consider that schools systems often, at the same time:

1. promote the high school diploma as a positional benefit, for example, "You need a diploma to get a better job!" and

2. adopt policies to promote every student's earning a diploma, for the sake of Fair Share justice, an indivisible benefit the realization of which will largely cancel out the diploma's value as a job-getting tool.

These involve schools in a profound conflict for they set up a situation in which the "natural" tendency of the system is to increase the costs of one option the more the competing option is achieved.

We know from Chapter 17 that positional and indivisible benefits compete with one another. Of course, organizations can and often do pursue incompatible goals. And Fair Play justice requires that competing interests be given their turn. But it takes great political skill to oscillate between competing goals without appearing to be irrational or irresolute.[29] In any case, they must be pursued intermittently rather than simultaneously to minimize conflictual costs and to distribute those costs equitably among stakeholders.

The "swinging pendulum of educational reform" described in Chapter 14 may indeed reflect just such a process. But if so, it is driven by the outcome of competition between special interests rather than the skillful manipulations of some master politician. (See Item C in the Technical Appendix to Chapter 20 for a chart of school benefits structured over the two dimensions.)

Human Differences

> ... the only procedure that could be called unbiased is a completely inaccurate measurement; scores determined wholly by chance exhibit no group differences.[30]

We know that "fair play" is one conception of justice that the school might pursue. But given the variability among human beings, is fair play actually possible?

Being different is not necessarily being worse. But what if those differences maladapt the student for school? Who has the obligation to change? When should school goals or procedures give way before recognition of human differences?[31] We will examine a pertinent issue: psychological differentiation.

Psychological Differentiation

Teachers know "in their bones" that there is a relationship between personality and school success.[32] One long-noted difference among people[33] which has gained currency is that of conceptual style. People gather and evaluate

---

[29]Cf. Edward G. Rozycki, "Policy and Social Contradiction: The Case of Lifelong Learning," *Educational Theory*, Vol. 37, No. 4 (Fall 1987), pp. 433–443.

[30]L. J. Cronbach, G.C. Gileser, and N. Rajaratnam, *The Dependability of Behavioral Measurements: Theory of Generalizability for Scores and Profiles* (New York: Wiley, 1972), p. 385.

[31]Cf. Sandra Salmans, "The Tracking Controversy," *New York Times,* April 10, 1988, Education Life Section, p. 56.

[32]Cf. John F. Hummel, *A Study of Selected Personality Characteristics and Science Related Attitudes of Ninth Grade, Female Students in Urban, Parochial High Schools.* Ed.D. Dissertation. Unpublished. Temple University, 1981.

[33]Cf. H. A. Witkin, "Individual Differences in Ease of Perception of Embedded Figures," *Journal of Personality*, Vol. 19 (1950), pp. 1–15. See also Rosalie Cohen, "Conceptual Styles, Culture Conflict and Non-Verbal Tests of Intelligence," *American Anthropologist*, Vol. 71, No. 5 (1969); Paul L. Wachtel, "Field Dependence and Psychological Differentiation: Reexamination," *Perceptual and Motor Skills*, Vol. 35 (1972), pp. 179–189.

Figure 20.6

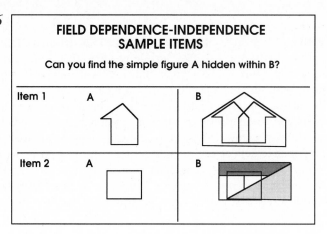

information from their environments in different ways. This difference has been found to affect not only their performance in school, but the rate at which they are socialized to their professional environments.[34]

A trait identified as *Field Dependence-Independence* has been found to relate to a wide variety of other characteristics. Field independence is the ability to discern a simple figure when it is hidden in a complex context. Figure 20.6 gives an example of an item that might be found in a test for Field Dependence-Independence. Field-independent persons tend to do better in school than field-dependent persons. On the contrary, field-dependent persons tend to have higher levels of interpersonal skills. (For additional correlations, see Item D in the Technical Appendix to Chapter 20.) We seem to have something of a tradeoff here: academic skills versus interpersonal skills.

This is a profound conflict because important benefits derive from high levels of interpersonal skills, even if these skills are gained at the cost of academic achievements. If we find that we can change children's field independence in some way, we are then faced with the prospect of increasing their academic achievement at the cost of their interpersonal skills, which, after all, may be more important to their future.

What Should We Try to Change?

We will explore the notion of psychological differentiation because it can be fairly readily tested for and it relates to school performance. Students who are more field independent do better in school. From an action orientation we

[34]Cf. M. J. Hogan, R. A. Sirotkin, and R. E. Gallagher, "Clinical Problem Solving: The Relationship of Cognitive Abilities to PMP Performance," *Proceedings of the 16th Annual Conference on Research in Medical Education, 1977,* pp. 323–328. See also, Paul Cutler, *Problem Solving in Clinical Medicine: From Data to Diagnosis* (Baltimore, Md.: Wilkins & Wilkins, 1979). See also J. M. Scandura, *Problem Solving: A Structural/Process Approach with Instructional Implications* (New York: Academic Press, 1977).

might then ask whether, in the interests of "schooling justice" (equal educational opportunity), we should attempt to change the conceptual styles of students to make them more field independent, or whether we should change schooling practice so that equal demands are placed upon students with both low and high field independence.

Let's formulate the change proposal explicitly as:

Change Option 1: To promote schooling justice either:
a. bring all students to equal levels of field independence, or
b. adjust schooling practice to accommodate students who are both field dependent and field independent

In fact, something encompassing both of these proposals has been attempted. We will look at this below.

The situation with psychological differentiation is certainly not the only area of schooling caught up in the dilemma of where to place the burden of change. Head Start Programs, for example, have emphasized the schooling readiness of students, paying no attention to the possibility of restructuring schools. On the other hand, programs for "At-Risk" students as well as special education and special "motivation" programs like Alternative Schooling have attempted to provide students with equal access to the diploma by offering a restructuring of schooling processes.

Besides trying to adapt the student to the school, or the school to the student, we might try to change what the consequences of school success or failure are. The second fulcrum point for action is the relationship of the school to society. Schools, in issuing diplomas and certificates, serve to restrict access to some of the benefits of society. Thus we are faced with another change option. The following are seen as legitimate practices:

Change Option 2: To promote schooling justice either
a. tighten the connection with social benefits by restricting them to diploma holders, or
b. loosen the connection with social benefits by allowing people other than diploma holders to acquire them.

Both options have been more or less successfully pursued. Tightening the connection with social benefits was attempted in a bill recently defeated in Colorado which would have denied driving privileges to youths under 18 who had dropped out of school, who were chronically truant, or were failing to make "satisfactory progress" toward graduation. But similar legislation has passed both in Wisconsin and West Virginia.[35] Wisconsin, for example, has a "Learnfare" program that links welfare payments to school attendance.

The fact is, however, that there are many routes of access to social benefits

---

[35]News in Brief, *Education Week*, March 1, 1989, p. 12.

Figure 20.7

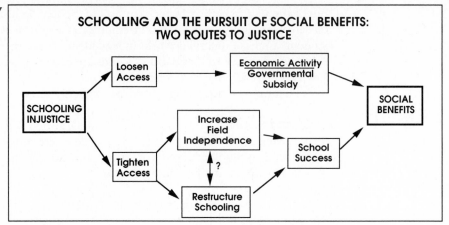

in our pluralistic society. Indeed, if we were to consider the top one-hundred highest paid business entrepreneurs, entertainers, sports players, musicians, plumbers, accountants, airline pilots, and TV evangelists in our society, we would be surprised if we found them consistently high or even moderate academic achievers. Indeed, Resnick's findings on learning in and out of school discussed in Chapter 18 might lead us to expect the opposite. Figure 20.7 shows two ways of proceeding from schooling injustice to social benefits. The upper route loosens access to social benefits, allowing them to be pursued via economic activity or government subsidy, for example. The lower route tightens access to social benefits via school performance. But this is just only if we accommodate either the student to the school or the school to the student.

Reducing the connection between schooling and social benefits is considered by some, however, to be a morally preferable choice. For example, Thomas Green has argued that it is much less socially disruptive to make the world safe for illiterates than to make everybody literate.[36] Knowledge and other schooling benefits should be valued for their own sake, not as commodities.[37]

The route to social benefits which passes through loosening access will be resisted by those who see it as deemphasizing the role of the school and thus threatening traditional public support for its funding. Practical pressures for change that will enjoy broad consensus will probably focus on changing student populations or school structures and practices.

---

[36]Thomas F. Green, "Weighing the Justice of Inequality," *Change*, Vol. 12, No. 5 (July-August 1980).

[37]For another approach to commodification, see Mark Walsh, "Learning or Market Share? Networks see Value in Promoting Big Series as Lessons," *Education Week*, Vol. VIII, No. 12 (November 23, 1988), p. 1.

In Chapter 21 we will look at prospects of changing school structures and practices. Let us cast our gaze now at the possibilities of changing the human factor in schooling practice. Can "human nature" be changed?

Conceptions of Human Nature

> The school-master has really very little to do with the formation of the characters of children. . . . Character and disposition are the result of home training; and if these are, through bad physical and moral conditions, deteriorated and destroyed, the intellectual culture acquired in the school may prove an instrumentality for evil rather than for good.
>
> _____ *Samuel Smiles, 1882*[38]

The theory expounded above by Samuel Smiles is an old one and is today far from extinct. But, even though it places the origins of character outside the school, it still reflects a traditional American optimism about the malleability of human nature. This is a more recent addition to our stockpile of human nature theories than the older, pessimistic one expressed through such rhymes as, "In Adam's fall, we sinned all."

We have hardly enough space to begin to examine a topic that has occupied some of the best minds throughout human history. One benefit of wider study in philosophy is that it exposes one to detailed conceptions of human nature. The reader interested in schooling practice is well advised to pursue such inquiry.

Our concepts of human nature are circumscribed by our beliefs and attitudes about the extent to which permanent changes can be made in people's behavior and attitudes. These beliefs often reflect assumptions that are seldom held up for critical examination. Indeed, a conception of human nature can serve as an inquiry-stopper. Why do people do certain things? Just human nature, that's all.[39]

There is little consensus on what this "human nature" is. Different traditions promote quite different conceptions to support or undermine our expectations of change. And becoming aware of which conception of human nature your schooling organization surreptitiously endorses is necessary to developing a critical practice of schooling.

---

[38]Samuel Smiles, *Happy Homes and the Hearts That Make Them* (Chicago: U.S. Publishing House, 1882), p. 41.
[39]Cf. James E. McClellan, *Toward an Effective Critique of American Education* (Philadelphia: Lippincott, 1968), p. 227. "To say that (a trait) T is a part of human nature adds no information about the human species; it simply signifies the speaker's decision not to entertain further questions about the origin or explanation of T." But, for critical examination of McClellan's claim, see Jon M. B. Fennell, *Rousseau, the Curriculum, and the Standard of Nature*. Unpublished dissertation. (Champaign, Ill.: U. of Illinois, 1976), pp. 232–237.

For example, beliefs about human nature are "premised into" organizational structure. We learned in Chapter 8 what differences exist among Theory X, Theory Y, and Theory Z organizations. Much of what a teacher or principal can do with people is determined by the type of organization he or she finds himself in. Schools are very concerned with the discipline of form, and conceptions of human nature play a big part in what people conceive to be the limits of that discipline. Consideration of three issues that a theory of human nature might bear on will assist us in dealing with such discipline problems:

- **authority**: on what basis do we make the judgment about what is good and bad behavior?
- **causation**: to what extent can individuals be influenced?
- **balancing social and individual interests**: how should costs and benefits be distributed in trying to change behavior?

If the transgression is commonly seen as a moral offense, everyone is believed to gain from its rectification. If it is seen as a technical impediment, questions of competing interests may be raised that bring up other moral issues. For example, if suppressing Johnny's calling out has the effect of stultifying his interest in a given subject matter, is this a proper tradeoff considering that his calling out inhibits others in the class from participating?

An even more interesting example of a tradeoff dilemma is this: corporal punishment is generally frowned upon as a class teaching support technique. Many school districts have policies that either forbid corporal punishment or restrict it to use by the principal. But what if students from a particular social background and culture are most efficiently and least painfully corrected through corporal punishment? (We should realize that severe mental anguish can be inflicted without corporal punishment.) Is it right to sacrifice the learning opportunities of cultural subgroups to preserve a particular institutionalized conception of human nature—for example, a human nature for whose dignity corporal punishment is an inexcusable affront?

On the other hand, many people believe the use of corporal punishment is counterproductive and likely to invite lawsuits and bad public relations. The question again is who benefits and who loses from such a tradeoff.[40] Is it possible that the very conditions that preserve our relatively peaceful pluralistic society undermine the conditions that would motivate certain subgroups to excellence?

Alasdair McIntyre has argued that our present-day judgments of right and wrong are based on remnants of past cultures.[41] These remnants provide us with conceptions of humankind as having a *telos,* a purpose in terms of which judgments of right and wrong could be made. Lacking a common conception of human *telos*, argues McIntyre, our civilization has lost the ability to fun-

---

[40]Cf. Edward G. Rozycki, "Pain and Anguish: The Need for Corporal Punishment," *Philosophy of Education 1978*, pp. 380–392.
[41]McIntyre, *After Virtue*, Chap. 2.

damentally ground moral judgments in a noncontroversial manner. In a similar vein, Michael Harrington[42] points out some of the social consequences of this loss of our traditional notion of human nature, that is, one in the service of a God:

- the loss of the philosophic and "common sense" basis for responsibility before the law as various deterministic theories occupy the territory once held by religious doctrines of free will and/or moral responsibility;
- the decline in the sense of duty toward unborn generations;
- the relativization of all moral values and a resultant crisis of individual conscience.

While Harrington sees the loss of a God-concept as crucial, *telos* does not necessarily involve a concept of mankind serving God. Even the Nietzschean goal for mankind, the attempt to overcome itself and develop into another kind of being, could serve to confound judgments of right and wrong in practice: right is what serves the *telos*; wrong, is what doesn't. But Nietzsche provided no clear concept of what humankind was to become. His concept of the Overman was vague enough to be interpreted by Nazi ideologists to justify their own conceptions of right.

In contrast to a teleological concept of human nature, Existentialists propose a concept of humankind as having no *telos*, as creating itself by its decisions, rather than choosing right in terms of an ultimate purpose. This concept requires according each person a level of individual freedom of choice far beyond what is considered acceptable in the school, focused as it is by concerns for tradition, scholastic achievement, and citizenship. For this reason, Existentialism does not resonate within modern schooling practice.

In Chapter 19, we considered the question of fundamental authority and suggested that we could muddle along with a tentative finality that supported practice yet recognized the essential plurality of our social system. This is a position somewhat intermediate between the teleological and Existential extremes.

Another dimension helping us sort out conceptions of human nature is causation: the extent to which human behavior is externally vs. internally controlled. Here, again, there is a vast literature to explore.[43] At the one extreme we have "empty organism" determinism, which holds that all actions are caused by conditions external to the person. At the other extreme are conceptions of Free Will which imbue all behavior with the spark of intent, so that even infants and the deeply insane are thought to exercise control.

---

[42]Harrington, *The Politics at God's Funeral*, p. 8.
[43]See, for example, Jerry A. Fodor, *Psychological Explanation: an Introduction to the Philosophy of Psychology* (New York: Random House, 1968). See also Theodore Mischel, *Human Action: Conceptual and Empirical Issues* (New York: Academic Press, 1969); Charles Taylor, *The Explanation of Behavior* (London: Routledge & Kegan Paul, 1964).

At what point human decision and certain kinds of causation part company is controversial. Some theorists hold that what has been traditionally called Free Will is a control function that emerges from the complex organization of the brain and transcends the causal processes of the brain.[44] Others hold that the opposite of Determinism is Indeterminism, which would make all choices irrational; therefore, Free Will as a rational faculty is nonexistent in any case.

Somewhere in between are our practical notions of development allowing for external influence, but only when internal circumstances are ready. Recognizing that there are developmental differences in children and adults makes schooling practice difficult. It requires of teachers and administrators more than simpler models of human nature. In effect, to recognize developmental changes is to concede that schooling aims have to be adjusted in a variety of ways likely, no doubt, to frustrate the impatient. Even more important, the complexity of developmental concepts tends to hamper consensus on schooling method. Thus there is always pressure on school people to espouse simplistic, if inadequate, theories of human nature if only to ward off consensual problems.

In regard to the tradeoff between social and individual benefits, strongly deterministic theories can offer no help: the distinction between what a person does and what he or she should do makes no sense. At the other end of

---

[44]E. M. Dewan, "Consciousness as an Emergent Causal Agent in the Context of Control System Theory," in Gordon G. Globus, Grover Maxwell and Irwin Savodnik (eds.), *Consciousness and the Brain. A Scientific and Philosophical Inquiry* (New York: Plenum, 1976), pp. 181–198.

Figure 20.8

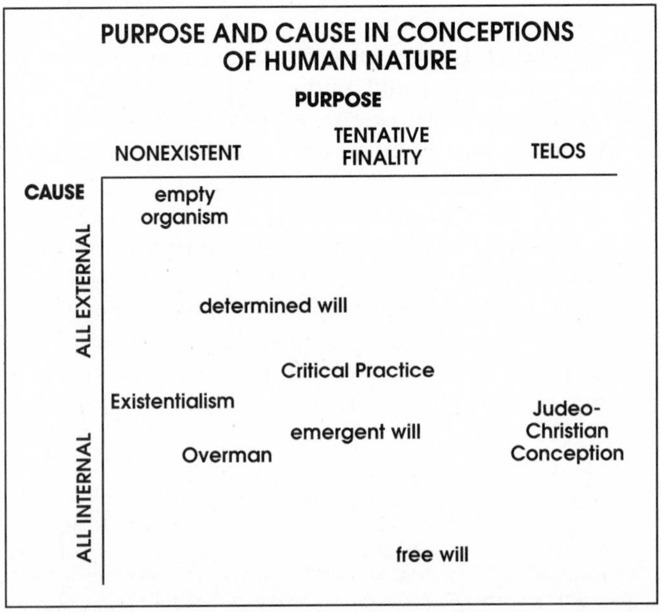

PURPOSE AND CAUSE IN CONCEPTIONS OF HUMAN NATURE

CAUSE	PURPOSE		
	NONEXISTENT	TENTATIVE FINALITY	TELOS
ALL EXTERNAL	empty organism		
		determined will	
		Critical Practice	
ALL INTERNAL	Existentialism	emergent will	Judeo-Christian Conception
	Overman		
		free will	

the spectrum lie a hundred conflicting authorities. We might imagine, at least, that their individual conceptions of *telos* restrict what society can demand of the individual. Our American pluralism survives because so many of them share a common sense of what to render unto Caesar and what, unto God.

If we collapse the dimension of social-individual tradeoff into that of authority, we can create a two-dimensional chart that maps the possible kinds of human nature theories. (See Figure 20.8.)

Pursuing Intelligent Practice

God obligeth no man to more than he hath given him the ability to perform.

——————— *The Koran*[45]

Intelligent action is based on adequate relations among cue, concern, and control. Cue in schooling is usually testing. Testing for differences between what we believe should be—for example, potential—and what is—for example, achievement—identifies the scope of our basic schooling concerns. But no matter how evil a situation appears to us, the call for remedy is pointless unless we can exercise some control over it. The way we conceive of human nature and human behavior, the extent to which we believe them to be changeable, affects both our conceptions and pursuit of justice. The important questions about testing, justice, and human nature have been known for a long time. What is needed is that school practitioners consciously apply themselves in the search for their answers.

The desire to be intelligently practical does not demand that we dispense with theory. We know that this cannot be done. What it does require is that we use theory with critical skill. Our judgments on the scope of applicability, the nature of the constraints we have to deal with, and our moral perspectives determine for us what the connection between theory and practice will be.

What should we ask of those who would work in schools? That their dispositions to nurture be guided by well-developed critical skills. What we desperately need in schooling are many more people who are soft-hearted but clear-headed. We have more than enough of every other combination.

SUMMARY

1. Being intelligently practical demands that truly professional educators use theory with critical skill. Our judgments on the scope of applicability, the

---

[45]*The Koran*, in Rhoda Thomas Tripp (compiler), The International Thesaurus of Quotations (New York: Harper & Row, 1987), 6th and 7th Chapters, 65, p. 168.

nature of the constraints we have to deal with, and our moral perspectives determine for us what the connection between theory and practice will be. Intelligent action is based on developing adequate relations between cue, concern, and control.

2. The "Testing for Justice Rationale" links to schooling needs differences in achievement and equality in potential. Rank tasks become tests only as they are believed to have external validity. One use of tests is to estimate student knowledge on the basis of test performance. The adequacy of tests rests ultimately upon consensus about such things as ability and skills.

3. Educationally relevant attributes are those upon the basis of which it is just to distribute schooling benefits. In our society, for example, sex is generally not educationally relevant, whereas achievement is.

4. Need is generally conceived as a difference between what is and what should be. The conditional concept of need indicates what are, at most, lacks. The approval concept of need presses us to approve a specified goal. Two conceptions of justice, as Fair Play and as Fair Share, compete. Schooling controversies are often disputes about which concept is most desirable.

5. The call for reform is pointless unless we can exercise control. And that is not the end of the matter. We also have to recognize that we must make some very tough choices because we simply cannot have it both ways. There is an inherent conflict in pursuing a positional or an indivisible benefit, for example, diplomas and justice.

6. We can identify a broad class of people who perform well in schools as they are now structured. Should we attempt change the others to be like them? Or should we restructure the school? Perhaps we even need to loosen the connection between school and social benefits.

7. The way we conceive of human nature and human behavior, the extent to which we believe them to be changeable, affects both our conceptions and our pursuit of justice.

QUESTIONS

1. Make explicit some possible theoretical connections between getting into school before the bell and success in the work world. Do this by constructing a narrative that confirms such success to be the result of getting to school on time. Look at the connecting narrative and then propose how its links might in fact be different.

2. It is theoretically possible that a basketball shooting test might predict scores on a French test. Make explicit some theory that would make us

doubt this. For example, construct a narrative that allows us to understand that there is no likely connection between shooting a basketball and knowing French. Look at the connecting narrative and again propose how its links might in fact be different.

3. Alasdair McIntyre[46] writes, "Our evaluations should satisfy two minimal requirements of justice. The first is that everyone involved should have a chance to say what is to count as a cost and what a benefit. The second is that, so far as possible, those who receive benefits should be those who pay the costs, and vice-versa."

   a. Do various kinds of compensatory programs meet these requirements?

   b. Which notion of justice is McIntyre invoking, Fair Play or Fair Share?

4. It has been found that sexual stereotyping reduces conflict in organizations.[47] What might be the costs and benefits of affirmative action? For whom? What kinds of costs and benefits are they, substantial or symbolic? How do McIntyre's criteria (see question 3 above) apply here?

5. Teaching to the middle is a form of triage. Triage is a medical practice applied in emergency situations where medical treatment is not given to those likely to survive without it, or to those who will probably die despite it. Teaching to the middle ignores those students who will do well without instruction as well as those whom no amount of instruction can help. What are the costs and benefits of such practice? To whom?

6. Often without knowing it, teachers restrict access to schooling benefits by demanding "proper respect." These culturally specific rites of deference[48] inadvertently bias schooling in favor of those already acculturated to its norms. Can you think of some examples?

7. Although research results are mixed,[49] it is widely claimed that if teachers expect more from their students, the students will perform better. Teachers should raise their expectations, we are told, to get kids to raise their test scores. But what does raising one's expectations mean? Is it different from making a good faith (though last ditch) attempt to get someone to learn something?

8. **Potential + Learning = Ability**. Thus **Potential = Ability − Learning**. If we think of "potential" as "natural talent," this new "equation" explains how we compare the potential of two individuals who have been exposed to the same amount of instruction: we "subtract" or "factor out" that common instruction and use a test of ability as an indicator of potential.

   If we believe that all humans have the same needs, what does the

---

[46]Alasdair McIntyre, quoted in Harry S. Brody, *Truth and Credibility*, p. 109.
[47]Joan Acker and Donald R. Van Houten, "Differential Recruitment and Control: The Sex Structuring of Organizations," *Administrative Science Quarterly*, Vol. 19, No. 12 (June 1974), pp. 151–163.
[48]Gerald M. Reagan, "Do Institutions Teach?" *Philosophy of Education 1965*, pp. 75–79.
[49]Cf. Hurn, op. cit., pp. 145–154.

equation **Ability − Achievement = Need** tell us about human abilities, given the fact of different levels of achievement?

9. Let's examine the relationship between school success and social benefits. (Recall Figure 20.7) If school success feeds into economic activity or governmental subsidy, there is no certain connection between school success and social benefits: the lowest paid pro football players average more than the most highly educated French professors. In addition, political skill, not schooling success per se, will determine government subsidies.

   Now, if there is a direct route to social benefits, it must be determined. Can you either describe such a direct route, or return to economic activity/governmental subsidy and explain how schooling success might bear strongly on success here?

10. Teacher A asks why Johnny doesn't do his homework. Teacher B replies that he is motivationally impaired. Teacher C replies that he is lazy. What are the practical consequences of accepting Teacher B's explanation rather than Teacher C's explanation?

TEACHING and SCHOOLING: PROSPECTS and OPTIONS

Chapter 21

PREVIEW

In this final chapter we first examine in some detail the occupation of teaching, its background, present status, and prospects. We also review the growth of formal teacher preparation, the teacher education curriculum and the nature of certification.

We offer a brief reconceptualization of the school as a productive organization that is not a Factory as it has been traditionally understood, but that places central emphasis on causal relations between teaching and learning. The research of industrial sociologist Joan Woodward on the structure of productive organizations is reviewed because it is suggestive of school improvement in directions which support technical efficiency. We suggest that scaling down or decentralizing schooling systems will help stave off the pathologies of institutionalization.

Finally, we look to discover where the consensus may exist to support the school. Educators, captives of a Temple image of the school, have traditionally disdained marketing as beneath the dignity of their mission. But marketing research is a useful informational tool. To illustrate we examine marketing research that has defined forty lifestyles based, not on sample expressed opinions, but on actual buying patterns. Using this research we look at the school as a commodity and give some indication as to the kind of American lifestyles that might lend support to the schools.

A CHANGING OCCUPATION

Teaching is enjoying new respect in the U.S.[1] The president, all fifty governors, state legislators, and business leadership have publicly recognized the critical importance of the occupation, and generally agree on the need for higher salaries, stricter college entrance standards for teacher candidates, and improved working conditions.

One consequence of all these changes is that the average pay for teachers—more than $28,000 in 1988—has risen twice as fast as inflation; and the majority of school districts are now paying teachers at the top of the scale more than $50,000 a year.[2] Working conditions are also improving. In a growing number of school districts teachers enjoy new authority, serving as mentors for novice teachers, developing curricula, setting standards for student promotion, evaluating teacher performance, and helping determine school budgets.

These improvements, as well as growing awareness that the nation will need an estimated 1.5 million new teachers by the year 2000, has reversed a

---

[1]See "Teacher Ads Prompt Flood of Calls," News & Trends, *American Teacher*, May 1989, p. 3.
[2]Source: Research Division of the National Education Association, February 27, 1989.

A changing occupation.

twenty-year decline in interest in a teaching career among college freshmen. From an all-time low of 1 in 20 in 1982, the number of first-year college students seriously interested in teaching careers had soared to 1 in 12 by 1988. As a result, applications are rising in schools of education, and the quality of prospective teachers keeps getting better.

Teacher Preparation

Teacher preparation has never enjoyed as much official attention as it has over the past five or six years. State agencies, special commissions, governors' task forces, and various advocacy groups have all subjected teacher preparation to critical examination and made radical recommendations for reform.

The Growth of Formal Teacher Preparation

In the early days of public education teacher preparation was either primitive or nonexistent. It was not until 1839 that the first state-supported school offered a **normal** two-year teacher preparation program in Lexington, Massachusetts.[3]

At the end of the Civil War the idea that teachers should be provided with pedagogical training began making rapid progress. Child-centered and developmentally oriented Pestalozzianism provided much of the groundwork for their philosophy and methodology (see Chapter 13). Ironically, however, this humanistic influence began at the very same time that public schools began to cope with ever growing numbers of youngsters by adopting a Factory model of instruction involving specialization, bureaucratization, and large-scale grading of children by chronological age. The paradoxical result was an assembly-line process staffed by teachers trained in a profoundly developmental and humanistic tradition.[4]

In the 1930s the normal schools began to evolve into teachers colleges— four-year institutions that tended to be similar to liberal arts colleges in their general education requirements and their academic education of secondary school teachers. In time, these state teachers colleges were transformed into state colleges that went beyond the single purpose of teacher preparation. These transformations eliminated all special-purpose institutions devoted exclusively to teacher preparation.

In the meantime, ordinary four-year colleges and universities had been slow to accept teacher preparation as one of their functions—the first programs eventually appearing in the 1870s. Generally, these schools first specialized in the training of secondary teachers because this dovetailed handily with preexisting academic departments. Over time the universities added more and more programs until many had established entire schools or colleges of education. Today, teachers are prepared in a mix of public and private colleges and universities.

The Teacher Education Curriculum

Throughout the history of formal teacher preparation there has been a constant tension between three different aspects of the curricula. These are:

1. **Subject matter knowledge**
2. **Knowledge of the liberal arts**
3. **Knowledge about teaching and the capacity to teach**[5]

The tension reflects the problem of attempting to deal adequately with all three within the limits of a four-year undergraduate program of study. In a

---

[3]H. Warren Button and Eugene Provenzo, Jr., *History of Education and Culture in America* (Englewood Cliffs, N. J.: Prentice-Hall, 1989), p. 128.

[4]Preston D. Feden and Gary K. Clabaugh, "The New Breed Educator: A Rationale and Program for Combining Elementary and Special Education Teacher Certification," *Teacher Education and Special Education*, Spring 1987.

[5]Carolyn Evertson, Willis Hawley and Marilyn Zlotnik, "Making a Difference in Educational Quality Through Teacher Education," *Journal of Teacher Education*, May-June 1985, p. 4.

few states, like California and Texas, state legislators and regulators have dealt with this by strictly limiting the number of credits that can be devoted to developing knowledge about teaching and the capacity to teach. They claim that this restriction is intended to ensure that prospective teachers develop adequate subject matter knowledge while also gaining some experience with the liberal arts. As we will see later, however, there are other less altruistic "benefits."

The move to limit the pedagogical aspects of teacher preparation was encouraged by *A Nation at Risk,* the report of the Presidential Commission on Excellence in Education. This Commission expressed their disapproval of prospective teachers spending much time in "educational methods" courses. They did this despite the fact that undergraduate requirements in pedagogy are strikingly weak when contrasted with the graduate level "methods" preparation necessary to qualify for membership in most professions. The state of New Jersey, for example, whose Governor Kean agreed with reducing the time devoted to developing knowledge about teaching and the capacity to teach, requires that podiatrists (they investigate and treat foot disorders) take about 258 semester hours of professional studies and a one-year internship before they are permitted to practice. We wonder if there is five or ten times as much to know about investigating and treating foot disorders as there is about teaching children.

Clearly, knowledge of subject matter is *necessary* if teachers are to have anything to teach. Everyone agrees on that. But the crucial question is, is such knowledge also *sufficient*? Research suggests otherwise. When Evertson, Hawley, and Zlotnik reviewed a wide variety of research studies on this matter they found that, "... the research suggests that knowing the subject matter does not necessarily make a person a good teacher of that subject." They also concluded, "The research ... provides little reason to believe that increasing teacher's knowledge of their subjects beyond what is required for certification will significantly increase teacher effectiveness."[6]

Despite such research, many continue to maintain that added expertise in an academic subject will make a better teacher. Llynne Cheney, chairman of the National Endowment for the Humanities, provides an example. Cheney complains that "We still spend too much time teaching teachers how to teach and, in the process, deny them opportunities to become experts in their subjects."[7] Cheney, of course, is a stakeholder in this process by virtue of his position. But is he perceived as one?

Evertson, Hawley, and Zlotnik also looked for research evidence that a broad liberal arts education promotes the development of more effective teachers. They could not find *any* evidence in research on either teacher education or undergraduate education in general that would support such a

---

[6]Ibid., p. 6.
[7]Huntly Collins, "Colleges Ponder Better Way to Instruct Teachers-to-be," *Philadelphia Inquirer*, February 23, 1988, p. 18.

claim.[8] On the other hand, they did find that formally developing knowledge about teaching and the capacity to teach in teacher preparation programs does make a positive difference in classroom performance. Teachers who participate in preservice teacher preparation programs are likely to be more effective than teachers who have little or no formal training.[9]

Given this research, it is reasonable to speculate about what other agendas might be served by reducing teacher preparation requirements. After all, it does seem curious that anyone would seriously propose that teaching can be improved by increasing the professional ignorance of its practitioners. Cost/benefit analysis suggests some possibilities. One benefit for state and local education officials, for example, is that such reductions increase the pool of applicants for teaching positions at precisely the time when there is a growing shortage. Another benefit for these officials is that increased supplies of teachers depresses the market value of teacher certificates, thereby holding down salaries. Still another benefit is that educators who have weak preparation are more likely to participate in the mass processing of factory schooling without complaint. Cheapening the teacher certification process also enhances state and local authority by reducing the probability that teachers will have the knowledge necessary to determine what is best for their students. Of course, research suggests that one of the chief costs is less effective teachers.

State Certification

Teacher certification is the process of licensing teachers to teach in the public schools of a particular state. Teaching certificates are issued by state education authorities when candidates have met minimal standards established in state regulations.

The first teaching certificates were issued at the local or county level. They were usually obtained after a grueling all-day examination on a wide variety of school subjects. There was little or no attempt to determine the candidate's knowledge of pedagogy or children.[10] Young teachers began their careers without any technical level knowledge of their craft. They did not know how children develop and learn, and their methodology relied solely on tradition.

Teacher certification eventually became the exclusive function of state government, and it remains so today. When state certificates were first issued, regulations required only that the candidate pass exams in subjects like algebra, geometry, natural philosophy, physiology, drawing, civil government, general history and American literature. Sometimes they were also quizzed on didactics (pedagogy). However, the "correct" responses were rooted in the formal rather than the technical level of culture.

Presently, while the states differ as to details, they all require the same general procedure (Figure 21.1). In order to become a certified teacher the

---

[8]Ibid.
[9]Ibid., p. 4.
[10]Andrew Gulliford, *America's Country Schools* (Washington, D.C.: Preservation Press, 1984), p. 71.

Figure 21.1   **THE MAJOR COMPONENTS OF TEACHER CERTIFICATION PROGRAMS**

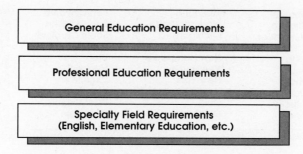

candidate must attend a college or university that has an appropriate teacher education program that has been approved by the state department of education in which the school is located. In order to gain this approval colleges and universities design their teacher preparation programs so that all of its major components meet or exceed state minimum standards. They then request that the state send a visiting committee to review the programs to make sure that they are in conformity. If the committee approves the programs, the college or university is then empowered to recommend candidates for the teaching credential to the state department of education.

In some states this recommendation results in the automatic issuance of a credential. Recently, however, most states have instituted examinations that certification candidates also must pass before the certificate is issued. The most common approach is to use the Educational Testing Service's National Teachers Examination. This test is now required in 30 states.[11]

Because of criticism that this test is an inadequate measure of teaching competence, E.T.S. has announced that beginning in 1992 they will replace it with two more sophisticated exams—one given during the sophomore year of college, and a second after teacher training—as well as an evaluation of classroom performance.

Many states have **reciprocity agreements** for honoring one another's certificates (Figure 21.2). However, teachers moving from state to state can sometimes experience difficulties reestablishing their teaching credentials. The following chart lists the states which have developed extensive reciprocity agreements. If a state is listed, it is probable that it honors the certificates of most of the other listed states.

Testing and Minority Teacher Candidates

State-mandated teacher testing seems to result in a shortage of minority teachers. According to a major research study jointly sponsored by the National

---

[11]Susan Tifft, "Who's Teaching Our Children?" *Time*, November 14, 1988, p. 63.

Figure 21.2 **STATES WITH EXTENSIVE RECIPROCITY AGREEMENTS**

Alabama	Maryland	Pennsylvania
California	Massachusetts	Rhode Island
Connecticut	Michigan	South Carolina
Delaware	Nebraska	South Dakota
Florida	New Hampshire	Utah
Hawaii	New Jersey	Vermont
Idaho	New York	Virginia
Indiana	North Carolina	Washington
Kentucky	Ohio	West Virginia
Maine	Oklahoma	Wisconsin

Source: Interstate Certification Contract Administrators Association

Education Association and the Council of Chief State School Officers, almost 38,000 minority candidates have been excluded from teaching because of their failure to pass such tests. "Almost without exception," the report concludes, "state-determined cutoff scores on paper-and-pencil tests have been set at a level that eliminates a majority of the minority candidates either from teacher-education programs or from certification upon graduation."[12]

The report notes that first-time pass rates on the tests range from 71 percent to 96 percent of white candidates but only 15 percent to 50 percent of black candidates. Pass rates for other minorities are 39 percent to 65 percent for Hispanics, 37 percent to 77 percent for Asian Americans, and 20 percent to 70 percent for native Americans.[13]

Gregory Anrig, President of ETS, challenged the report's findings, saying they were, "wrong, unfair and unsupported." He also stated, "one cannot assume that if a teacher fails a licensing test, it is the test that is at fault, since the test is supposed to measure the basic skills that a teacher is required to have."

Other experts caution that testing may only be the small end of things. For example, Linda Darling-Hammond of the Rand Corporation notes that the most academically talented blacks were opting for other careers even before teacher testing started. She also maintains that enhancing the inducements and rewards for teaching, not abandoning the tests, is the most promising approach to altering the situation.[14]

The large number of minorities leaving teaching seems to substantiate the claim that state teacher testing is far from the only factor contributing to a shortage of minority teachers. According to the *Metropolitan Life Survey of the American Teacher 1988*, 41 percent of minority teachers say they are

---

[12]Lynn Olson, "Tests Found Barring Thousands of Minority Teacher Candidates," *Education Week*, November 23, 1988, p. 1.
[13]Ibid.
[14]Ibid.

likely to leave teaching over the next five years compared to 25 percent of nonminority teachers. Fully 55 percent of minority teachers with less than five years experience say they are likely to leave the field. Even out of the minority teachers who are very satisfied with their careers, one out of five say they are likely to choose another career.[15]

Given the intensity of concern regarding this situation, it is interesting to note that minorities are fairly well represented in teaching when compared with many other skilled occupations. For example, African-Americans represent 9.5 percent of all elementary and secondary school teachers but only 6 percent of the nation's executives, 3.7 percent of all the engineers, 3.3 percent of the physicians, 3.2 percent of the architects, and only 2.5 percent of the nation's natural scientists.[16]

Board Certification

The **board certification** proposal sponsored by the Carnegie Task Force on Teaching as a Profession is altogether different from state certification. It is a nongovernmental initiative intended to certify the competence of professional educators rather than to license them.

To qualify for board certification the candidate must successfully complete a "national teacher entrance assessment process." At the time of writing this process is being established by a nongovernmental board of the teaching profession with a majority of practicing teachers.

Although Board Certification will be voluntary, the Carnegie Task Force is confident that local officials will recognize it for hiring. Indeed, they predict that board-certified teachers will be in great demand. As far as state officials are concerned, they are being encouraged to adopt the board's standards for state certification.[17]

Whether or not board certification works as planned remains to be seen. Certainly, it is an ambitious venture.

Current Teacher Preparation Reform Efforts

Despite the favorable research findings cited earlier that indicate that courses in pedagogy do lead to improved teaching, there is widespread belief that the nation's 1200 teacher preparation programs can and must be improved. Beginning with the federal government's landmark 1983 report *A Nation At Risk*, national attention has focused on upgrading the teacher preparation process.

The **Holmes Group**, a consortium of education deans from about 100 of the nation's major research universities, has agreed on one such improvement

---

[15]*Metropolitan Life Survey of the American Teacher 1988* (New York: Metropolitan Life Foundation, 1988).

[16]*Statistical Abstract of the United States* (Washington, D.C.: U.S. Government Printing Office, 1988), p. 377.

[17]*A Nation Prepared: Teachers for the 20th Century*, the Carnegie Task Force on Teaching as a Profession.

plan. They have begun to phase out baccalaureate degrees in education and require all prospective teacher to major in the academic subjects they intend to teach. After graduation they are to take a fifth year of graduate work focusing exclusively on pedagogy. The Holmes Group also proposes a new system of licensure, which would create three tiers of teachers, based on their training, performance, and experience. Thus far state authorities have been unenthusiastic regarding this recommendation.

The Holmes Group proposals immediately became a source of controversy and conflict. The education deans from many of the nation's state colleges and universities issued a statement praising the Holmes Group's intentions, but criticizing their proposals. Specifically, they cautioned that the proposal to eliminate undergraduate education majors in favor of graduate-level programs was "not sufficiently supported to warrant its being the only curricular model to be endorsed."[18]

Still another effort to upgrade teacher preparation has been launched by the **National Council for Accreditation of Teacher Education**, a private, nonprofit organization that accredits approximately 550 of the nation's 1,276 teacher-education programs. Beginning in the 1988–1989 school year NCATE will require students entering NCATE-approved programs to take a standardized basic-skills test and to have at least a 2.5 college grade point average. Tougher procedures by which schools are accredited were also adopted.[19]

The new NCATE standards have been criticized by some education-school deans as too demanding, too expensive, and unrealistic in view of an impending teacher shortage.[20] Nevertheless, the changes are being implemented. As a consequence twice as many institutions are now failing to win NCATE approval. However, because NCATE certification is voluntary, the programs will not necessarily be shut down. Improvements and a reexamination are far more likely.

A Fundamental Ambivalence

Disagreements about the preparation of teachers reflect a far more fundamental disagreement about teaching itself. There still is no clear consensus on the crucial question of whether teachers should be **semiskilled workers** who, under close supervision, implement standards set by others, or **skilled self-governing professionals** who apply specialized knowledge to meet the unique needs of individual students.

In a report released in 1988 by the Rand Corporation, Linda Darling-Hammond and Barnett Berry note that the first wave of educational reform, which stressed regulation and tighter control, reflects the semiskilled view. On the

---

[18]"State College Deans Rap Holmes Report as a 'Source of Conflict'," *Education Week*, May 7, 1986.

[19]Blake Rodman, "Accrediting Group Adopts Stiffer Standards for Education Schools," *Education Week,* June 19, 1985, p. 5.

[20]Ibid.

What kind of reform?

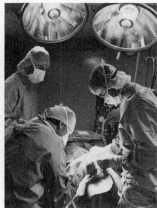

other hand, "second wave" reformers such as the Carnegie Task Force on Teaching as a Profession, the Holmes Group, and the National Governor's Association, maintain that teachers must be skilled professionals exercising far greater control over their own occupation and the process of schooling. These differences reflect, say the report's authors, "... the acute ambivalence that many policy-makers feel about the nature of teaching and the role of teachers."[21]

This ambivalence is perhaps best illustrated by the fact that at the same time that twenty-seven states adopted stiffer requirements for teacher preparation programs, twenty-three states were busy creating **alternative routes to certification** that allow teachers to bypass many of the weak requirements presently in force.[22]

Teaching as a Career

Despite this unresolved issue, teaching offers promising career opportunities. In many districts working conditions and pay have improved substantially. In addition, there are strong prospects for continuing improvement in the future.

Working Conditions

Although pay is obviously important, working conditions are critical to teacher satisfaction. If teachers are isolated from other educators, powerless in the face of legislative orders, frustrated with administrative practices, and forced to comply with standardized state and local controls that they had no role in shaping, we cannot expect many of the nation's best and brightest to seek out the field.

[21]Linda Darling-Hammond and Barnett Berry, *The Evolution of Teacher Policy* (Santa Monica, Calif.: The Rand Corporation, 1988).
[22]Ibid.

The mass-process factory school is perhaps the biggest obstacle to improving teacher's working conditions. There is no room for new relationships between students and teachers, no leeway in planning the year or the day.

But it does not have to be this way. Imaginative **restructuring**, as opposed to reform, of schools can facilitate moving teaching toward the skilled professional end of the continuum. In Indianapolis, for example, eight teachers have convinced school authorities to let them run their own elementary school based on the theories of Howard Gardner, the Harvard psychologist who convincingly argues that there are various forms of human intelligence. The teachers have restructured the curriculum so that although the children study traditional academic subjects, they also have opportunities to explore and develop their own special intelligence. The teachers use a schoolwide theme, such as people's relation to their environment, which is changed every nine weeks.[23]

In Miami the Dade County Public Schools have turned the running of thirty-two schools over to a variety of different management teams set up and run by a number of different combinations of administrators, parents, and classroom teachers. Joseph Fernandez, the Superintendent of Schools, is convinced that including the teachers is the right approach because, "It's the classroom teachers who know what the kids need."[24]

Most of the administrative and teaching functions of the experimental schools were blended. In some schools assistant principals were replaced with two faculty members who divide the day among teaching, discipline, and counseling. In others the teacher took over the responsibility for planning curriculum. With waivers granting relief from the teachers' contract, the teachers are free to make special efforts, like giving up their free class period each day in return for smaller classes.

The Dade County experiment is an outgrowth of Florida legislation that permits greater autonomy for individual schools. Similar projects are under way in smaller school systems like Rochester, New York, and Hammond, Indiana.[25]

Pay

Teaching as an occupation has seldom been as attractive as it is useful. The recurrent temptation is to rely on the teacher's realization of the moral importance of the work. This, it is hoped, will provide teachers with symbolic benefits that will sustain and animate them while more substantial benefits, like money, can be put to work elsewhere.

In the past several decades it has become evident that this approach has not been attracting enough able candidates. Increasing opportunities for

---

[23]Fred Hechinger, "About Education," *New York Times*, February 17, 1988, p. B 9.
[24]Edward Fiske, "Miami Schools: Laboratory for Major Changes," *New York Times*, January 10, 1988, p. 1.
[25]Ibid.

Figure 21.3

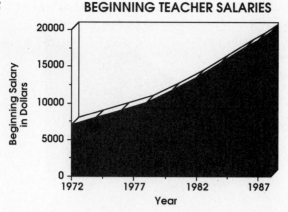

BEGINNING TEACHER SALARIES

Source: American Federation of Teachers

women have had a particularly negative effect on the supply of highly capable individuals interested in becoming teachers.

In order to deal with this situation, public officials have begun substantially improving pay for teachers. Figure 21.3 illustrates this improvement.

The average starting pay for teachers was about $19,000 nationally in 1988.[26] That is roughly comparable to what most liberal arts graduates make. We should note, however, that certain occupations, such as engineers, lawyers, physicians and computer experts, make considerably more money to start. This is illustrated in Figure 21.4.

---

[26]*Survey and Analysis of Salary Trends 1988* (Washington, D.C.; American Federation of Teachers, 1988), p. 42.

Figure 21.4

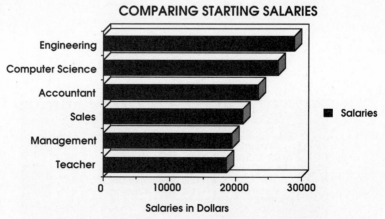

COMPARING STARTING SALARIES

Source: American Federation of Teachers

Figure 21.5

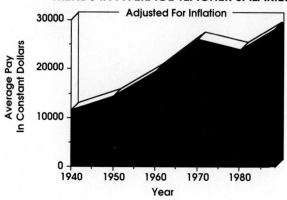

TRENDS IN AVERAGE TEACHER SALARIES

The average salary of the nation's 2.5 million public school teachers has also been climbing. In 1987–1988 it was $28,085, up more than 100 percent from 1976 and climbing twice as fast as inflation.[27] Figure 21.5 illustrates that trend.

Of course average teacher salaries vary from state to state. Figure 21.6 indicates the best and worst states for average teacher salaries over the decade 1976–1986. We should keep in mind that dramatic improvement, such as that shown by the states in the left column, is often a function of very poor past pay. After adjustments for cost of living differences, Michigan, Alaska, California, and Minnesota pay teachers the most. Louisiana, Arkansas, Hawaii and South Dakota have the nation's most poorly paid teachers.[28]

Figure 21.7 lists the highest and lowest paying states in terms of both starting pay and average pay. Cost of living factors were not considered. We

---

[27]Source: National Education Association Research: Estimates data bank.
[28]*Survey and Analysis of Salary Trends 1988*, op. cit., pp. 8–9.

Figure 21.6

**PERCENT INCREASE IN AVERAGE
PUBLIC SCHOOL TEACHER'S SALARIES**

1976–1977 to 1986–1987

Increase				
Highest		Lowest		
Alabama	124%	Hawaii	60%
South Carolina	121%	Iowa	80%
Rhode Island	120%	Louisiana	84%
Georgia	117%	South Dakota	84%
Wyoming	115%	Washington	84%

Source: National Education Association

Figure 21.7   **HIGHEST AND LOWEST PAY FOR TEACHING**

Starting Pay

Highest		Lowest	
Alaska	$26,880	Idaho	$14,793
California	$21,900	Vermont	$14,996
Connecticut	$20,703	Louisiana	$14,996
New York	$20,650	South Dakota	$15,020
New Jersey	$20,500	West Virginia	$15,055

Average Pay

Highest		Lowest	
Alaska	$40,424	South Dakota	$19,750
New York	$33,600	Arkansas	$20,340
Connecticut	$33,515	Mississippi	$20,669
California	$33,092	Louisiana	$20,885
Rhode Island	$32,926	North Dakota	$21,660

Source: *Newsweek*, October 17, 1988

might note that teachers in California, Connecticut, New York, and New Jersey make about 25 percent more than those in Idaho, Vermont, Louisiana, South Dakota, or West Virginia. The high starting pay for Alaska is a function of that state's higher cost of living and does not provide an accurate comparison. Note too that except for the substitution of Rhode Island for New Jersey, the same states have both the highest starting pay and the highest average pay for teachers. Only South Dakota is on both lowest pay lists.

Salary Schedules

A teacher's pay has traditionally been based on years of service and graduate degrees and/or graduate credits obtained. The precise formula is spelled out in the contract negotiated between the local board of education and the local teacher's organization. According to this pay arrangement teachers who are extraordinarily effective are paid the same salary as those who are ineffective.

Merit Pay and Career Ladders

Many public officials and school reformers favor efforts to link pay with competence. Some simply call for **merit pay**, that is, raises based solely on the quality of the teacher's performance. Others prefer a **career ladder** approach that permits promotion to higher rank as well as increased pay. The idea is to replace today's undifferentiated system with a differentiated one, in which it is possible for teachers to advance through different ranks, each having greater responsibilities. Substantial salary increases would be attached.

In *A Nation Prepared*, the Carnegie Forum provides an example career ladder plan that includes issuance of a national certificate. Their National Board of Professional Teaching Standards plans not only to issue a standard "Teacher's Certificate," but also to offer an "Advanced Teacher's Certificate." This would signify that the holder has demonstrated "the highest levels of competence as a teacher" and also is able to provide schoolwide leadership. Those holding the certificate would be eligible to become what the Carnegie Forum calls "Lead Teachers." Their distinctive mission will be to provide leadership in the redesign of schools and to help their colleagues maintain the highest standards of teaching.[29]

The Holmes Group calls for the creation of a comparable Career Professional Teacher who would assume schoolwide responsibility for curriculum development and teacher supervision. The Career Professional Teacher is distinct from the "Professional Teacher" who is certified for independent practice in his or her own classroom. The Holmes Group also envisions "Instructors" who are well trained in subject matter but lack pedagogic training. They would be closely supervised by Career Professionals.[30]

In addition to these private initiatives, many states have merit pay or career ladder programs that are either in place, being tried out in pilot form, or under consideration. Tennessee provides an example of the career ladder approach. In 1984, state officials launched a "Master Teacher" career program designed to reward outstanding classroom performance with both pay and promotion. Tennessee uses teams of teachers to evaluate those who want to qualify for the career ladder. The candidates are evaluated on the basis of three classroom observations; their lesson plans; an interview; questionnaires given to the principal; students and peers; and a professional skills test. Those judged to be superior are granted raises of up to $7,000 and promotion to Master Teacher status.

This Master Teacher Program was accomplished despite determined opposition. The Tennessee Education Association was a particularly active opponent. They argued that objective evaluations were impossible and that differential pay would ruin teacher morale. Many were also concerned that the plan challenged tenure and collective bargaining agreements.[31]

Paradoxically, just as schools are beginning to adopt merit pay plans, some human resource experts are beginning to question the traditional reliance on extrinsic rewards for motivating employees. They point out that merit pay, which is really designed to control behavior, can reduce intrinsic motivation and become self-defeating.[32]

Industrial experience and research also suggest that merit pay programs tend to be demeaning and paternalistic because they emphasize the employ-

---

[29]William R. Johnson, "Empowering Practitioners: Holmes, Carnegie, and the Lessons of History," *History of Education Quarterly*, Vol. 27, No. 2 (Summer 1987), p. 223.

[30]Ibid.

[31]Helen Pate-Bain, "A Teacher's Point of View on the Tennessee Master Teacher Plan," *Phi Delta Kappan*, Vol. 64, No. 10 (June 1983), pp. 722–726.

[32]Edward Deci, "The Hidden Cost of Rewards," *Organizational Dynamics*, Vol. 4, No. 3 (Winter 1976), pp. 61–72.

Some satisfactions of teaching.

ees' dependence on their supervisors. They also create competition that generates mutual hostility, distorts perceptions of self and others, and lessen interaction and communication.[33]

How merit pay or career ladders will work out is still unclear. A lot depends on how such programs are administered, what criteria are used, who judges competence, how much and how many are paid, and what opportunities and responsibilities are incorporated.

One alternative to merit pay plans are "merit **praise** plans." Here good performance is rewarded with recognition and positive feedback.[34] Praise and support can enhance intrinsic motivation while simultaneously encouraging competence and self-determination.[35] Figure 21.8 provides some recent data concerning the issue of teacher satisfaction.

Teacher Hiring Trends

There is considerable disagreement concerning whether the supply of new teachers will be able to meet the nation's growing demand. Many experts are concerned that the supply of new teachers will not grow rapidly enough to provide the 1.5 million new teachers that will be needed by the year 2000. However, Daniel Hecker of the U.S. Census Bureau is more optimistic. He maintains that rising enrollments in teacher preparation programs will create a supply of new teachers adequate for the demand. Emily Feistritzer of the National Center for Education Information agrees with Hecker, but only because of the surplus of teachers produced in the 1970s, who may still be looking for teaching jobs. She also thinks the supply of new teachers created

---

[33]Herbert Meyer, "The Pay-for-Performance Dilemma," *Organizational Dynamics*, Vol. 3, No. 3 (Winter 1975), pp. 39–50.
[34]ERIC Clearinghouse on Educational Management, "Merit Pay," Research Action Brief Number 15 (Eugene, Ore.: University of Oregon, 1981).
[35]Deci, op. cit.

Figure 21.8

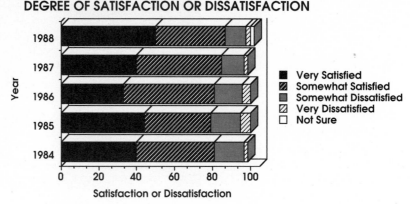

**TEACHING AS A CAREER (1984—1988)
DEGREE OF SATISFACTION OR DISSATISFACTION**

in the 23 states now offering alternative routes to certification may be an important factor.[36]

There is one other element to consider. The supply and demand of teachers are influenced by general labor market conditions. Shortages of teachers are far less likely to develop where there are few other jobs available. But where jobs are plentiful, as they are at this writing, and schools must compete with other attractive employers, it is a different story.[37]

Teacher Organizations

Eighty-five percent of all American public school teachers belong to one of the two main teacher organizations in the United States, the National Education Association or the American Federation of Teachers. Although these organizations have dissimilar histories, they now share similar goals and tactics. Nevertheless, they remain rivals, competing for members and often facing each other in school district elections that determine who will represent the teachers in collective bargaining sessions with the schoolboard.

National Education Association

Organized in 1857 as the National Teachers Association, the National Education Association has over 1.7 million members comprising elementary and secondary school teachers, college and university professors, administrators, principals, and counselors making it almost three times larger than the American Federation of Teachers.

---

[36]Sherwood and Lorna Harris (eds.), *The Teacher's Almanac 1988–89* (New York: Facts on File, 1988), p. 113.
[37]*Covering the Education Beat*, op. cit., pp. 86–87.

Unlike the AFT, it is **not** affiliated with organized labor. Instead, the NEA has a three-tiered organizational structure—national, state, and local—and is supported by a $75 million budget. Its national headquarters, in Washington, D.C., has about 600 staffers and both standing and special committees that deal with a wide variety of school-related issues.

Political action is one of the most important national activities. The NEA-sponsored **Political Action Committee for Education** has a budget of over $1 million—the fifth richest political action committee in the nation. This money is used to influence the outcomes of national elections through campaign contributions to candidates and to encourage political involvement on the part of the membership.

There are also statewide organizations headquartered in the respective state capitals. One of their most critical functions is to influence state education policy through lobbying. They also promote sympathetic candidates for state office with campaign contributions.

The 10,000 front-line locals are the third tier of the NEA organizational structure. They operate at the school district level where they represent teachers in collective bargaining with schoolboards, maintain liaison with the board and school administration, and monitor compliance with the collective bargaining agreement.

The NEA restricts its membership to educators rather than all school employees. To this end it permits school administrator membership, but does not seek to organize school secretaries, custodians, bus drivers, and the like. This policy distinguishes it from the AFT, which does **not** permit school administrators to join, on the grounds that there is a conflict of interest, but does actively recruit noneducators.

American Federation of Teachers

The 660,000-member American Federation of Teachers was established in 1916. It is affiliated with the 15 million member AFL-CIO—the nation's largest union.

The AFT is supported by a $40 million budget and has a three-tiered organizational structure similar to that of the NEA. The national headquarters in Washington, D.C., employs about 200 who perform a variety of tasks similar to those addressed by NEA staffers.

Like the NEA, the national AFT maintains a political action committee. Called the **Committee on Political Education (COPE)**, it too lobbies, gives campaign contributions to sympathetic candidates, and encourages its membership's political activities.

Unlike the NEA, the AFT is actively broadening its membership to include professionals "with concerns similar to those of teachers." Targets for recruitment include civil service employees, through the AFT-sponsored Federation of State Employees, and health care workers through the Federation of Nurses and Health Care Workers Division.

At the local level the AFT engages in collective bargaining negotiations.

The 2,200 local affiliates represent their members in working out detailed agreements with local schoolboards.[38]

Obstacles to Reform?

William J. Bennett, the Reagan administration's Secretary of Education, repeatedly blasted both the NEA and the AFT as "obstacles to reform." In his report, "American Education: Making It Work," for example, he charged that, "sound educational reforms are threatened by the determined opposition they elicit" from those who argue that fixing the schools, "will require a fortune in new funding." "Almost without fail, wherever a worthwhile school proposal or legislative initiative is under consideration, those with a vested interest in the educational status quo will use political muscle to block reform."

Bennett raises a critical point. Teachers' organizations do sometimes oppose actions touted as school reforms. But is there evidence that teacher unions block reforms in Bennett's words "with no good reason but only the flex of political muscle"? A study commissioned by Bennett's own Department of Education says **no.** The Rand Corporation study, which analyzed 151 teacher contracts reached between 1970 and 1985, and studied reforms enacted in six states, found that: "Despite charges to the contrary, teachers unions have not been a major obstacle to educational reform." Instead they have tried to accommodate demands for reform, "even in those instances where a specific reform initiative has run counter to their organizational interests or has been at odds with the professional judgment of their members."[39]

Mary Futrell, president of the NEA, answered Bennett's charges with countercharges of her own. She claimed that the administration "frustrated" reform by failing to "recognize that excellence costs, and failing to become an active partner in the reform movement."[40]

Despite Bennett's denunciation, Albert Shanker, president of the AFT, has been a particularly aggressive advocate of basic reform of the nation's public schools. Shanker advocates a radical restructuring intended to make teaching a self-governing profession. He criticizes many state-imposed school reforms as attempts to "teacher proof" the schools through more and more ill-considered external controls. Shanker warns that public schools will collapse unless **teachers** find new and better ways to educate children. He also calls for experiments in a thousand or more school districts where groups of six or more teachers would be allowed to set up schools within schools, run by teams of teachers without interference from central office bureaucracies. In such a setting they could use team teaching and technology to free themselves from lecturing and permit children to advance at their own pace.[41]

---

[38]*Encyclopedia of Associations* (Detroit, Mich.: Gale Research, 1989), pp. 1,876–1,877.
[39]Christopher Connell, "Teachers Union Backs Reforms," *Philadelphia Inquirer*, July 4, 1988, p. 8.
[40]Barbara Vobejda, "Bennett Spars With Educators," *Philadelphia Inquirer*, April 27, 1988, p. 4.
[41]Christopher Connell, op. cit., p. 8.

Teacher Strikes

Although the first recorded teachers' strike was in 1902, teachers began to really use that weapon following the success of an independent teacher organization-led strike in Buffalo, New York, in 1947. This caused AFT officials to abandon their no-strike policy. In 1961 the AFT won a crucial victory over the New York City Board of Education when after a strike that board agreed to bargain collectively. The tendency to use the strike grew rapidly following its success in the nation's largest school system.

Historically, the NEA took the stance that it was a "professional" organization rather than a union. For this reason it did not endorse strikes. The growing success of the more militant AFT and the discontent fostered by Factory-type schooling forced a change in that policy in the 1960s.

At that time the NEA leadership adopted **professional sanctions** as a weapon they hoped would prevent the need for strikes. Professional sanctions involved publishing lists identifying school districts that refused to reach agreements with NEA locals as unprofessional places to work. The hope was that teachers would not seek employment there. It did not work out that way. Many aspiring teachers ignored the lists. Because boards of education found the costs of professional sanctions did not equal the benefits of ignoring NEA locals, schoolboards shrugged off the efforts of NEA locals and went about their business. Ultimately, this forced NEA officials to adopt the strike.

While teachers have the legal right to belong to unions, only a few states (Hawaii, Montana, Maine, New Hampshire, Oregon, Pennsylvania, and Vermont) permit teachers to strike. Over half the states have a variety of legal prohibitions against such job actions. In some states very specific penalties for striking are spelled out.[42]

Still, teachers do strike. And when school district officials seek legal relief, judges sometimes order the jailing of union officials and/or they impose heavy fines on the teachers' organization if they have issued an injunction and the strike still goes on. True to the functions of conflict outlined in Chapter 4, these often serve to revitalize the teachers' determination and strengthen the underlying value of union membership.

In most cases teacher strikes are eventually settled with compromise rather than legal penalties. But in many cases they result in loss of pay for striking teachers, and in a few cases they ultimately lead to their dismissal. When, for example, the Hortonville, Wisconsin, Education Association struck the Hortonville Joint School District No. 1 in 1974, the school district fired all striking teachers because they were violating Wisconsin law. The Supreme Court of the United States upheld the constitutionality of this firing.[43]

Teacher strikes are far less frequent today than they were in the 1960s and 1970s. Figure 21.9 illustrates the trend since 1971.

---

[42]Michael La Morte, *School Law* (New York: Prentice-Hall, 1987) p. 273.
[43]*Hortonville Joint School District No. 1 v. Hortonville Education Association*, 1976 (486 U.S. 482).

Figure 21.9

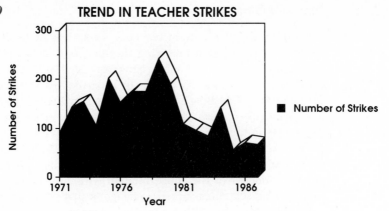

Collective Bargaining

Collective bargaining, also known as collective negotiations, involves the negotiation of wages and other conditions of employment for employees on a combined basis. In the case of schools, these negotiations are carried out by the schoolboard and authorized representatives of whichever teacher organization has been elected by the secret ballot of those represented.

Approximately half the states provide good-faith bargaining between school districts and teachers' organizations. A few require that schoolboards "meet and confer" with teachers. North Carolina and Virginia actually prohibit negotiations between teachers and schoolboards.[44]

Terms and Conditions of Employment

The topics of collective bargaining can be divided into two broad areas of concern. The first concern is the **terms and conditions of employment**. Wages, extra pay, benefit packages, teaching rosters, hours of work, class size, holidays, and sick leave are all typical topics for collective bargaining. Matters relating to promotions, termination of contracts, disciplinary rules governing teachers, and settlement of individual disputes are also covered.

As noted earlier, barring merit pay or career ladders, the wage package is typically negotiated in a series of steps relating to years of service and degrees obtained. The School District of Philadelphia's salary schedule for 1990 is in Figure 21.10. In this fairly typical example there are four salary categories based on degrees obtained. Within those categories there are eleven steps.

Collective Relations

The second main topic of collective bargaining concerns the **collective relations** between the parties. Here, enforcement of agreements, establishment

---

[44]La Morte, op. cit., p. 272.

Figure 21.10

**SCHOOL DISTRICT OF PHILADELPHIA SALARY SCHEDULE
1990**

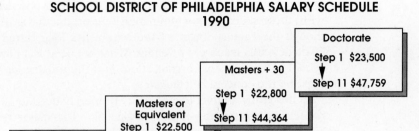

of fair practices, resolution of differences, and similar matters are spelled out. The agreement between the Board of Education of the School District of Philadelphia and the Philadelphia Federation of Teachers, for example, stipulates:

> The principal of a school who may be accompanied by one (1) vice principal of his choice shall meet at least once a month with the Federation Building Committee at its request to discuss school operations and questions relating to the implementation of this Agreement. The Federation Building Committee shall consist of not more than five (5) teachers from that school and may include, in addition, not more than one (1) member from that school of each of the other bargaining units represented by the Federation. Proposed changes in existing policies and procedures and new policies and procedures for that school shall be the subjects for discussion at such meetings.

REORGANIZING FOR PRODUCTION

Almost everyone is in favor of reform. The idea of restructuring the school appeals to many. But what do reform and restructuring mean practically? In this section we will look at some specific ways in which substantial reforms can be achieved.

One of the most important changes in our society is that abilities and attitudes that were at best symbolic, valued in rather small communities, have become substantial, that is, valued widely across society. These abilities are literacy, critical thinking, and basic knowledge of mathematics. We do not imagine that such skills are valued by everyone in every circumstance, but there is substantial recognition that not only our political but our economic structure depends heavily upon the widespread possession of these abilities.

Unfortunately, schools are often structured to obscure, even to interfere with, these skills as the culmination of a productive process of teaching. Although the Factory image of the school has long rested on the rhetoric of efficiency, this is merely a veneer. What we need is a new conception of the school as a productive organization. And the touchstone of this organization must be the concept of efficiency.

Is this really a novel idea? Aren't we merely dusting off a tired old Factory model and pretending it still works? No. The major reason efficiency has become a caricature of itself is that the school has become institutionalized. And the reason for this institutionalization is that schools have been allowed to grow to such a size that the proper recognition of its stakeholders requires that it work as a political instrument, rather than as a productive organization.

A Productive Organization: Not a Factory

We will explore here a concept of efficiency that gives room to professional expertise on the part of teachers and principals. This concept recognizes the claims of stakeholders on the schools and adjusts itself in accord with them. **Efficiency** means achieving goals selected by **both immediate and relevant stakeholders** in a manner that **minimizes costs and maximizes benefits to those stakeholders**. This is an old concept that has seldom been tried because the Factory model of the school preaching it had no place for the voices of immediate and relevant stakeholders.

Schools have always been for salvation, or uplift, or Americanization, or social reform or economic development. But the people who chose these goals were not immediate or relevant stakeholders. Indeed, the immediate and relevant stakeholders often resisted. Even so, when the goals appeared to have been achieved, the schools were celebrated as the means of their achievement. There is ample reason to believe that they seldom were.

What is needed is a new model. A model where knowledge, not hyperbole, is the essential factor in production. A model scaled down, perhaps, to that level where their support can be assured by the constituencies they benefit.

Options For Productivity

In 1966 organizational sociologist Joan Woodward published a seminal book about industrial organization.[45] Industrial organizations, wrote Woodward, fell into three classes depending upon their goals, that is, the kind of product they made, and the kind of technology they used to produce it. Most important for those of us who contemplate restructuring the schools is that the variables of goal and technology structure both the productive and social relationships between workers in the organization. What we try to do and how we go about doing it affect the way we work together.

---

[45]Joan Woodward, *Industrial Organization. Theory and Practice* (London: Oxford U. Press, 1966).

Large-batch and mass production industries provide us the traditional Factory image of the school. Their goal is to produce uniform items for a pre-existent mass market. Their technology, although complex, can be made piecemeal. Causal connections are generally clear. Uniform inputs produce uniform outputs. This structure diminishes the need for research and development. Management isolates itself as it controls low-skilled workers through a variety of highly elaborate sanctions. Communication occurs only to exchange information of interest to management. The technical rationality of the workplace tends to fragment social relationships as these tend to undermine efficiency.

Process industries such as oil refineries, chemical plants, and pharmaceutical companies are technology-rich. They produce specialized products for hard-to-identify specialty markets. Complex though well-defined causal processes are built into plant equipment so as to minimize the need for workers. Those few workers who are needed tend to be highly skilled technicians who can maintain and troubleshoot the production process. Control by management is of little concern since both the equipment and the technical orientation of the workers assure success. As in the mass production industries, communication is necessary only for exchange of information. The technical rationality of the process does not support—though it need not undermine—the social relationships of organization members.

Unit and small-batch industries produce custom-designed specialty items, such as locomotive engines and custom cars. Specialty demands provide the impetus for the research and development of processes and methods that take the very specific characteristics of inputted material and, with much skilled worker attention, transform it into unique outputs. Management-worker relationships tend to be nonhierarchical and communication occurs on an operational basis as the process requires it. Since teaming and mutual support are often necessary, social relationships are as important as technical ones.

If we consider now that schooling has the following characteristics, it becomes abundantly clear which industrial model can inform and legitimate the restructuring we are after. In general, it is well recognized that:

- schools do not process uniform inputs. Students vary greatly and teachers are expected to make adjustments for these variations.
- there is no well-established, cut-and-dried set of causal processes by which to transform input students into skilled graduate outputs.
- there is no mass market for many of the forms of schooling as they presently exist. Even with compulsory education laws and much exaggeration about college and job requirements, school attendance has been dropping drastically, especially for those thought to have most need of it.

We need to retire the Factory image of the school as a large-batch and mass production unit. In its place we might consider the unit and small-batch process model. Chart 21.1 summarizes and compares the characteristics of

Chart 21.1   **TYPES OF PRODUCTIVE ORGANIZATION**

type / dimension	Large Batch & Mass	Process	Unit & Small Batch	Present Schools
Inputs	Uniform	Uniform	Not Uniform	Not Uniform
Processes	Well Defined	Well Defined	Not Well Defined	Not Well Defined
Outputs	Well Defined Uniform	Well Defined	Not Uniform	Not Well Defined Not Uniform
Control	Top-Down Nonconsultative	Top-Down Nonconsultative	Front Line Consultative	Top-Down Front Line Nonconsultative
Social Relations	Unimportant to Production	Unimportant to Production	Important to Production	Important to Production

industrial organizations and compares them to present schools. We should note the conflict in the present school organization and how the switch to unit and small-batch organization might reduce it.

Any proposal for change is a proposal to change the distribution of costs and benefits as they now stand. What would be the cost and benefits of changing to a unit and small-batch model of the school?

Scaling Down: Costs and Benefits

School consolidation after World War II was sold to the public by the promise of outcomes that were seldom realized. (See Chapter 8, footnote 11, for references.) Bigger, more comprehensive schools did not clearly produce bigger benefits. The former product orientation of the schools was transformed into a process orientation, and economies of scale were realized at the cost of reduced product quality. A major problem in the scaling up was that the market became ill-defined. It was no longer clear who wanted what. Earlier criteria of success, as vague as they were, were replaced with rhetoric and slogan.

The present state of the schools is much a consequence of perception. Many, if not most, people still see their local school in the image of the Temple. They work to influence it through the processes of the Town Meeting. Yet they expect it to produce like the Factory. These are, as we have seen time and time again throughout this text, conflicting perspectives. If we add to them the mechanics of running massive, ever-growing school organizations, we can be almost thankful that institutionalization is the most common pathology we encounter.

We also know by now that there are no such animals as costs and benefits per se. This is ceremonial rhetoric. The question is not, What are the costs and benefits of restructuring the schools? but Who benefits and for whom does it cost if we restructure the schools? Lacking specific research, we must defer detailed answers to other authors. For the moment, however, it seems reasonable in the light of the information and theory we have covered in this text to venture the following assessments.

Costs

Governmental units, large teachers' and administrators' organizations, and corporations may find it more costly to deal with a scaled-down, locally controlled school. By "locally controlled" we do not merely mean local political control as it is now practiced, but on-site control in partnership with technical and political school people. This kind of control may also be seen as costly to local powerholders, who prefer a top-down orientation to what goes on in the schools.

Teacher accreditation and licensing might be made more difficult for state agencies, although board licensure procedures would fit in well with scaled-down school systems. One fear about scaling down is that some of the political influence of large organizations would be lost, since they can usually afford to support greater lobbying effort in federal and state legislatures.

Wealthy districts would no doubt have the lesser burden in restructuring because they can support their own schools. Poor communities would face real problems. If public monies are to be used to support the variety of school types likely to be desired, then a voucher system of some sort may be worth looking at. Of course, the costs of safeguards to assure that such a system is not being abused has to be reckoned into the change.

Benefits

What would be some benefits of restructuring the schools? And to whom? A clear benefit across the board will be a slowing down, perhaps a reversal of institutionalization. There could also be a change from grandiose yet haphazard school outcomes adorned with celebratory slogans to perhaps more humble goals actually achieved. And while there might not be so many schools in pursuit of excellence, a good many more may achieve adequacy.

Clearly, restructuring for on-site control will benefit both teachers and school-site administrators—not with an easier workload or a less demanding school experience, but with a sense of having some control over what may happen to themselves and to the students in their charge.

Finally, those most important stakeholders least likely to be powerholders, the students, would benefit. Scaled-down schools would more likely be in touch with their needs and aspirations.

PURSUING CONSENSUS

Knowing it is time for a change is one thing. Finding the people who agree and agree deeply enough to support change is another. Public schools serve communities deeply divided on issues such as religion in the schools, evolution, and sex education.

Marketing the School

Is it possible to run a school within the confines of small community values and still serve interests desired across society as a whole? Perhaps it is, but only if educators pay more attention to marketing. Educators, encased in the image of the Temple or the Factory, their jobs protected by tenure and compulsory schooling laws, have shown little interest in marketing. Marketing sounds so . . . unacademic. But, like that other much maligned American activity, politics, marketing is a central, if not the central activity of our society.

Marketing, from an educator's perspective, should not be dismissed as an attempt to foist off goods of questionable value on a confused public. This way of looking at marketing makes the extreme the norm; it is more caricature than characterization. Rather, marketing should be looked at as trying to discover what people perceive to be benefits and costs with an eye to offering them benefits.

In the second chapter of this book we looked at one measure of the pluralism of values that constitutes American society. The Gallup poll identified eleven groups clustered about nine value orientations. Michael J. Weiss, in his book, *The Clustering of America*, presents a picture of American pluralism quite different from that of the Gallup poll.[46] The basis of the Gallup poll was professed commitments to values. But Weiss' polls—conducted by the Claritas Corporation—are based on data about how money was actually spent and on what items. The results he presents indicate an even greater variety of life styles and positions on school-related issues than the Gallup poll did. And it makes the case even more strongly that educators do themselves a disservice when they overlook marketing as a tool.

The Pluralism of American Lifestyles

What the Claritas Corporation has done, reports Weiss, is to analyze patterns of buying below the level of ZIP coded areas. Then, for ease of use, all the ZIP coded areas of the United States were grouped into forty neighborhood types, each with a suggestive name, for example, Pools & Patios, Towns and Gowns, Hard Scrabble. Here is a sample description:

> Once the nation's child-rearing suburbs, Pools & Patios has come of age—old age. Built during the postwar surburban boom, Pools

---

[46]Michael J. Weiss, *The Clustering of America* (New York: Harper & Row, 1988).

& Patios communities have since been swallowed by metropolitan sprawl, making their spacious split-levels and ranch houses often too costly for younger families. Older couples now reside in these stable, prosperous and empty-nested subdivisions. With their double incomes, and white-collar jobs, these residents enjoy laid-back-yard comfort—a place for Saturday night cocktail parties.[47]

Weiss provides us with a variety of suggestive demographic data on the people who live in Pools & Patios:

   a.   they comprise 3.4 percent of U.S. households;
   b.   they are more concerned about fiscal conservatism than about the plight of the poor and unemployed;
   c.   they read the *Wall Street Journal* and the *New Yorker* more than twice as frequently as the Average American;
   d.   they tend to be politically indifferent and, within the GOP, more tolerant of the Moral Majority.

If, by way of contrast we look at Young Suburbia, another ZIP-code neighborhood-type, we find that:

   a.   it comprises 5.3 percent of U.S. households, the biggest group next to the childless golden-agers of Golden Ponds (5.2 percent);
   b.   it has growing families and it supports modern schools but
   c.   is solidly Republican and is conservative on fiscal matters and laissez-faire on government activism;
   d.   it reads *World Tennis* twice as frequently and *True Story* half as much as the Average American.

For a group with a different agenda consider the Urban Gold Coast. This group is so named for the fact that its highest concentrations are on the East Coast and West Coast and around Chicago. The **mostly childless** Urban Gold Coast:

   a.   comprises 0.5 percent of U.S. households;
   b.   espouses a liberal or moderate ideology (60 percent voted for Mondale);
   c.   supports civil liberties, liberal foreign policy, and religious pluralism, yet is fiscally conservative;
   d.   reads the *New York Times* fifty times as frequently as the Average American; and *Hunting* not at all.

Remember, there are thirty-seven more of these groups. Here is pluralism with a vengeance! Should we imagine that these forty neighborhood types

---

[47]Weiss, op. cit., pp. 281–284.

would be more similar in their preferences for schooling than they are, for example, in the selection of their reading matter? This seems highly unlikely. Yet educators often go about their business as if they need not take any trouble to find out what neighborhood types such as these expect from their schools.

There is work to be done. Educators must recognize that theirs is a discipline of inquiry. There are no longer, if there ever were, any pat answers to major questions about the schools. What are schools for? What should be taught? Who should teach? What is teaching? What is learning? How can we come to some kind of consensus on these issues? What will be the form of the school that survives such a consensus?

It would be comforting to read in a text such as this that the answers to these problems are being worked on by reliable authorities and we are momentarily awaiting their definitive answers. All that can truthfully be said is that some of these questions are being given honest consideration by fallible human beings who find them perplexing. Who supports what kind of school? This is a question of central importance. We invite those of you who have come with us through this text, our own journey of inquiry, to continue the quest.

SUMMARY

1.   Pay and working conditions for teachers has been improving, kindling a new interest in teaching as a career.

2.   Teacher education, which struggles to balance subject matter knowledge, training in the liberal arts, and knowledge about teaching, is currently undergoing a number of reforms including state-mandated testing prior to certification, a new emphasis on graduate level training, and the inauguration of a national board certification process.

3.   There is still a fundamental ambivalence regarding whether teachers should be skilled, self-governing professionals or semiskilled workers.

4.   In some districts working conditions have been changing as teachers there become more and more involved in policy making and school administration.

5.   Both starting and average teacher salaries have improved in the past several years.

6.   Many favor efforts to link teacher's pay with competence. Some simply call for **merit pay**, that is, raises based solely on the quality of the teacher's performance. Others prefer a **career ladder** approach that permits promotion to higher rank as well as increased pay.

7.   Teacher career satisfaction is clearly on the rise.

8. There is considerable disagreement on whether the supply of new teachers will be able to meet the nation's growing demand.

9. Eighty-five percent of all American public school teachers belong to one of the two main teacher organizations in the United States, the National Education Association or the American Federation of Teachers. Although these organizations have dissimilar histories, they now share similar goals and tactics.

10. Approximately half the states provide good-faith bargaining between school districts and teacher's organizations. The bargaining concerns wages and conditions of employment.

11. Woodward's investigation of different industrial models of productive organizations suggests that the restructuring of the schools might proceed on the model of the Unit & Small-Batch factory.

12. Weiss' presentation of American pluralism based on buying habits indicates an even greater variety of life styles and positions on school-related issues than the *Times Mirror* poll did.

QUESTIONS

1. How has teacher preparation changed over the past century?
2. Identify at least two new additions to state teacher certification requirements.
3. What effect do state requirements seem to have on minority candidates? Can you suggest alternative explanations?
4. Distinguish board certification from state certification.
5. Discuss the fundamental ambivalence in current teacher preparation reform efforts.
6. Compare and contrast merit pay and career ladders for teachers.
7. What factors influence teacher job satisfaction? How does the Dade County experiment relate to this?
8. Compare and contrast the NEA with the AFT.
9. How do Woodward's classification compare with Elmore's implementation models? With the original expectation models of the school?
10. What kind of appeal do you imagine you would have to make to each of the neighborhood groups sketched from Weiss' book?

TECHNICAL APPENDICES

TECHNICAL APPENDIX TO CHAPTER 2

More About School Images

From the perspective of the school administrator facing the task of retrenchment, Deal and Wiske offer additional contrasts and comparisons, which are given in Chart TA 2.1.[1] In the Temple image of the school, the administrator plays a role aimed at maintaining faith in the institution as pursuing a bigger purpose. Research findings, if used at all, are part of the ritual of legitimation used to justify reorganization with all its attendant unhappiness. In the Factory, unquestioned goals provide the rationale for technical inquiries into the most efficient means of retrenchment and reorganization. Problem solving is the metaphor this image supports. In the Jungle, which Deal and Wiske give as the administrator's perception of the Town Meeting, reorganization and retrenchment are a matter of playing interests against each other to achieve a win for one's own position. Research is used as ammunition against one's opponents.

Although the purpose of Deal and Wiske's research was to point up organizational problems for administrators, their classifications fairly resound with long-standing complaints and slogans about American public schooling. For example, the row of key problems reiterates the cries, "Can we have faith

Chart TA 2.1

MORE ABOUT SCHOOL IMAGES adapted from Deal and Wiske, 1983			
Item ⟍ **Image**	**Temple**	**Factory**	**The Jungle**
Emphasis	Ritual and Ceremony	Goals	Power
Primary Focus	Performing	Exploring	Winning
Process	Role Playing	Problem Solving	Game Playing
Key Problem	Faith, Meaning	Quality	Interest Groups vs. General Welfare
Research Metaphor	Scriptural Exegesis	Getting Information	Getting Ammunition
Basis of Effectiveness	Faith, Meaning	Quality	Dealing with Conflict

[1] Deal and Wiske, pp. 455, 457, 460.

in the schools?" "Are kids getting a quality education?" "Are some kids getting things at the expense of others?"

The bases of effectiveness are particularly poignant. In the first two columns we find faith, meaning, and quality. It is the lack of these that people decry when they question the effectiveness of the schools. But in the political dimension, Chart TA 2.1 indicates a third basis of effectiveness: dealing with conflict. Educators have heretofore been ill-prepared to deal with conflict. Locked into the Temple and Factory images they have been taught to discount its importance.

TECHNICAL APPENDIX FOR CHAPTER 9

A Model of the Institutionalized School

The institutionalization of the school has come about because there are two kinds of schooling tasks:

- **certain tasks** that reliably produce **substantial** benefits and costs, and
- **uncertain tasks** that irregularly produce celebrated **symbolic** benefits and costs.

Activities that produce substantial benefits tend to receive the most influential if not the largest share of resources. Figure TA 9.1 depicts these distinctions in a bureaucratic model of the school. The varying thickness of the flowchart arrows is intended to suggest relative amounts of control and support. We should notice that Uncertain Tasks support Symbolic Benefits and Costs, which are evaluated irregularly to see if Goals and Related Policies have been met.

Figure TA 9.1

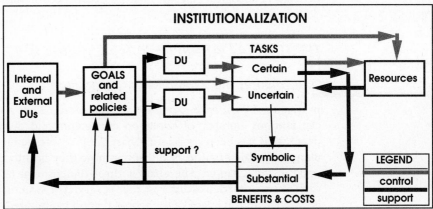

Figure TA 9.2

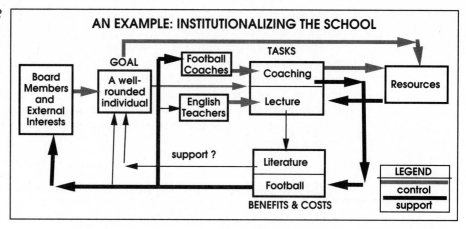

The discretionary units are supported by substantial products and services.

Figure TA 9.2 illustrates a specific example of Institutionalization from within the school.

The relationship between teacher lecturing and knowledge of literature is uncertain. That between coaching and fielding a team to play football is certain. The goals of the school may include literature, but football is generally justified as contributing symbolic benefits such as school spirit. The substantial benefits of football coaching support a variety of discretionary units within the school organization including the coaches, the board of education and external interests such as equipment suppliers, newspaper editors, alumni associations, professional scouts, and so forth. The public impact of the football coach is generally greater than that of a good lecturer. Thus, the football coach is more likely to be evaluated more rigorously than the literature teacher.

Institutionalization tends to sacrifice academic outcomes for substantial benefits. Pedagogical efficiency takes a distant second place to public relations.

TECHNICAL APPENDIX TO CHAPTER 17

Determining the Specifics of Curriculum

In Chapter 17 we have examined the question, "What should be taught?" We can find any number of books on curriculum and discover in bewildering detail what has been proposed. Chart TA 17.1 cites some well-known curriculum proposals or authors and shows how they fit into the categories developed in this chapter. The chart is three-dimensional in that it indicates for each entry a curricular interest that is served, a structure of knowledge that is assumed and an image of the school that is championed. Items in the margins should be read across the row or down the column.

Chart TA 17.1

A TYPOLOGY OF CURRICULUM AUTHORS AND PROPOSALS
Marginal entries hold for entire column or row

INTEREST / STRUCTURE	STATUS	VOCATIONAL	SOCIAL CONTROL
	Cardinal Principles		Tyler
LOGICAL Plato Dewey Bloom	**A.S. Neill** Illich Piaget Industrial Ed.	**A.S. Neill** Illich Piaget Industrial Ed.	**A.S. Neill** Illich Vocational Ed.
PEDAGOGICAL Dewey **A.S. Neill** **Kilpatrick** Bloom **Rousseau** Piaget	Illich Piaget **Maslow** Humanistic Ed.	Illich Piaget	Illich Skinner
DISCIPLINARY Conant **A.S. Neill** **Back-to-Basics** Environmentalism	**Hutchins** Sex Education New Math **Great Books**		Sex Education New Math
INSTITUTIONAL Conant Environmentalism Life Adjustment Tracked Curricula	Sex Education Ethnic Studies Drug Education	Vocational Ed.	Sex Education Snedden Bobbit Vocational Ed.

Typeface indicates image of school:

Bold face (Dewey, Skinner) = Temple Image
Light face (Dewey, Skinner) = Factory Image

The usefulness of the chart will depend upon some acquaintance with the authors and cited works.[2] The categorizations that are given are certainly not uncontroversial, but only better acquaintance with the relevant works will help you to achieve a better understanding of the overall curricular picture. However, we should expect that the tone of the original presentations will be persuasive rather than analytic. Generally missing from such presentations is an indication of the interests underlying the proposals. The rationales offered for curriculum proposals are intended to persuade the reader to adopt

---

[2]Previously uncited authors listed in Figure 17.9 include: B. Bloom et al., *Taxonomy of Educational Objectives* (New York: Longman, 1956); James Bryant Conant, *American High School Today* (New York: 1959); William A. Kilpatrick, *The Project Method* (New York: Columbia U. Press, 1918); Ivan Illich, *Deschooling Society* (New York: Harper & Row, 1971); Abraham Maslow, *Motivation and Personality* (New York: Harper & Row, 1954); *Cardinal Principles of Secondary Education,* National Education Association, 1918; A. S. Neill, *Summerhill: A Radical Approach to Child-rearing* (New York: Hart, 1960); Jean Piaget, *The Origins of Intelligence in Children* (New York: Norton, 1952); Jean Jacques Rousseau, *Emile*: see William Boyd (ed.), *The Emile of Jean Jacques Rousseau* (New York: Teachers' College Press, 1956); B. F. Skinner, *Science and Human Behavior* (New York: Free Press, 1953); Ralph W. Tyler, *Basic Principles of Curriculum and Instruction* (Chicago: U. of Chicago Press, 1949).

them, not to examine their costs and benefits. Thus, curriculum proposals, like reform proposals—which are a subtype of them—tend to make recommendations arguing their wisdom in terms of slogans, "literary style" as Travers calls it.

TECHNICAL APPENDIX TO CHAPTER 18

Item A: Summative and Ascriptive Learning

Ascriptions tend to be **defeasible**,[3] that is, subject to "defeat" (withdrawal) if knowledge of certain invalidating conditions is found. Much that occurs in schooling is a matter of social ascription, rather than a summative description of achievement. For example, a student receives a Ph.D. from a university. This degree is a recognition rather than an achievement, even though it may be based on achievements. The diploma might be rendered worthless or revoked if any of the following conditions is later discovered:

    a. the student cheated on his comprehensives;
    b. his major professors had falsified their credentials and were not eligible to examine him;
    c. the college had lost its accreditation;
    d. a mistake had been made in computing his credit hours.

These conditions are not normally reviewed for each and every student—a good reason for introducing the term **defeasible** to identify such conditions rather than merely generalizing that all descriptions are conditional upon satisfying certain criteria. Defeasible conditions are **normally assumed rather than investigated** and **judgmentally critical**. They are a matter of social convention rather than summative procedure. And they play a large part in evaluating schooling outcomes.

But, to be bestowed, even descriptive judgments require a decision. And someone must be recognized as having the authority to make such a bestowal. How many quadratic equations must a student do before the teacher will certify him or her as knowing how to do quadratics? Two? A thousand?[4] Consider what might happen if we discovered that the judge were a music teacher, or a relative. This single point of evidence might **defeat** the characterization of the student as competent. If we were concerned, we would have to correct and repeat the testing process. But why should a test be relevant?

For example, we might agree among ourselves to have a computer designate the student as "competent in quadratics" if the student interacted with the computer by solving problems of different sorts. We could decide in advance of all such testing that such outcomes indicated competence. But this

---

[3]See H. L. A. Hart on "defeasible concepts" in "The Ascriptions of Responsibility and Rights."
[4]Cf. Ludwig Wittgenstein, *Philosophische Untersuchungen* (Frankfurt-am-Main: Suhrkamp, 1967), Sections 151, 152.

is still **our decision**! And the computer has no authority over and above those who programmed it to render that decision in specific cases! These considerations indicate the considerable complexity underlying judgments of competence. Let's see if we can illustrate it simply.

Item B: Authority and Defeasibility

There are two main factors to consider: **authority** and **defeasibility**. Let's first distinguish between authorities who use **public criteria** of judgment and those who use **private criteria**. Public criteria are those that can be articulated and presented for anyone's inspection, whether or not they understand or are interested in the judgmental process to be undertaken. Private criteria are those a person conceded authority uses in making a judgment, even if he or she is unable to articulate them for public presentation.

A characterization is **defeasible** to the extent that specific defeating conditions are normally assumed to be absent. The greater the number of such conditions, the higher the defeasibility. Consider, for example, the following judgments made after some reasonable procedures, for example, measuring with a tape measure, giving a math test, and inquiring of the neighbors:

a. John is five feet tall.
b. John can do quadratic equations.
c. John is honest.

What could defeat these judgments? A variety of things, but they would have to be more bizarre for **a** than for **b** and **c**: for example, the tape measure was misprinted; Harry was mistaken for John or John was wearing lifts in his heels. Much more pedestrian are the defeating conditions for **b**: for example, John cheated; the problems were too easy; he has forgotten how or he took the test on drugs by mistake. **c** might be defeated if John had stolen something, told a lie, or committed a hundred other peccadilloes.

We began Chapter 18 by considering the various conceptions of cause used to explain the connections people see between things. A technical concept of cause was given with the warning that it is disputable whether our traditional notions of cause are illumined by it. Now, people tend to believe that the relationship between teaching and learning is causal. Again, it is not clear that they believe that the relationship between teaching and learning is causal in the technical sense. This technical sense of cause is summative. The reason for identifying defeasible learnings is that they cannot be summative, because the conditions that bring us to concede or bestow the judgment of learning hold only so long as they are not overridden. Summative judgments cannot be overridden. What does this mean?

A startling conclusion we can draw is that some kinds of learning are not caused in any scientific sense of cause. Should we give up, then, on trying to develop a scientific pedagogy? No. What we might give up on is accepting traditional defeasible ascriptions of learning as anything more than rough approximations of what we are looking for. If we really want to do a summative causal analysis, we may have to rely on a newly developed language of learning. This task has yet to be seriously undertaken. Teaching is truly an enterprise of inquiry.

We should note here that the less explicit the procedures for rendering the judgments of learning, the more defeasible such judgments likely are. Certainly, there will be more consensus on what it means to be five feet tall than on what it means to be able to do quadratics or to be honest. What defeasibility seems to point out is that while we may not easily agree on what something is, we tend to agree on what it is not. Perhaps this dichotomy demonstrates why criticism is more likely than praise in the political environment of the school.

Figure TA 18.1 schematizes a range of learning outcomes as they depend on authority and defeasibility. In Figure TA 18.1 both "John is five feet tall" and "John is honest" are in parentheses because it is controversial that they are learnings. We might include them as learnings if our conceptions of physical and developmental possibility were to change. They are included on the chart merely to indicate the endpoints of the range of items.

An interesting point is illustrated by Figure TA 18.1. To claim that John speaks some Spanish is a different kind of claim from saying unconditionally that he can speak Spanish. A few, finite tests can determine that he speaks some Spanish. What justifies the claim that he speaks Spanish, not just some Spanish? One way such decisions are made is to have authorities (experts) recognized as being able to speak Spanish make the decision. We can see that unless we are willing to acknowledge some people as authorities on Spanish, the argument leads infinitely backward. (For example, "On what basis do we determine someone is an authority?" is like asking how much power it takes to give authority.) The general point is that important judgments about learning depend upon established social practices of recognizing some people to be authorities.

If the argument of this section is correct then rehabilitation is not merely

Figure TA 18.1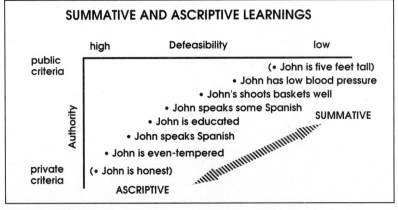

a matter of learning to refrain from dishonesty, but of acceptance into a community willing to bestow trust.

TECHNICAL APPENDIX TO CHAPTER 20

Item A: What Does A Test Test For?

We should not overlook the fact that student goals and motives can have a great influence on test results. Figure TA 20.1 illustrates how independent student goals can be. It also shows how test outcomes may not support student goals. Under such conditions we should expect difficulty in trying to determine the relationship between student knowledge and outcomes.

Figure TA 20.1

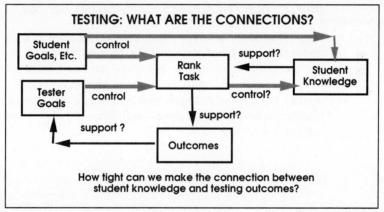

Item B: Reasoning with Formulas

School people walk around with mathematics-like "equations" in their heads. Such informal equations control to some extent the way students are evaluated and the "treatments" believed to be appropriate to them. They represent slogans that structure our thought about human abilities. These equations rest on vague generalizations and "teacher lore" but lack the consensus to enable their use as actual measurement models. The difficulty with such formulas is that the terms are not clear and that the consensus about them is often shallow. Examples of such slogan-formulas are:

1. Potential + Learning = Ability
2. Ability + Motivation = Performance
3. Achievement = Σ(Performances)
4. Ability − Achievement = Need

---

[5]For simplicity's sake only "+" and "−" have been used in the formulas. But something like "opportunity" is clearly a multiplier since, without opportunity, no amount of ability and motivation will yield performance. A formula relating these notions might be **opportunity (ability + motivation) = performance**.

Each of these "formulas" captures a general belief about learners.[5] For example, **Potential + Learning = Ability** expresses the general belief that the actual ability of a student depends upon his or her "potential" together with the amount of learning he or she has experienced which has actualized that potential.

Teachers often account for poor performance by explaining that although a student has the ability, he or she is poorly motivated in a given situation. Thus we have **Ability + Motivation = Performance.**

Because luck can enhance or foul up any individual performance, achievement is generally thought of as an averaging or "summation" of many performances. Thus **Achievement = Σ(Performances)** the "summation" of performances.

Item C. Two Dimensions of Schooling Benefit

Figure TA 20.2 identifies commonly recognized school benefits in the two dimensions we have discussed. As with other charts and figures in this text, the locations of particular items are intended to provoke discussion. They have placed according to the authors' own insights that further inquiry might modify. Notice, for example, that Excellence is located as an absolute benefit. Couldn't it be positional just as well? After all, excellence means ranking very high, if not highest.

Figure TA 20.2

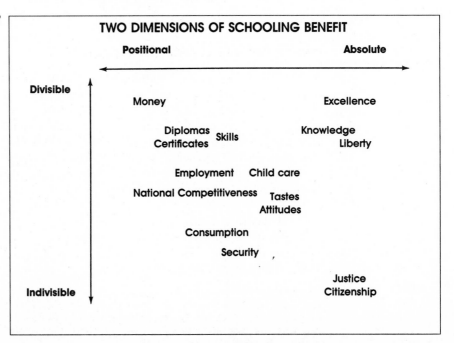

There are several considerations here. The first is that excellence may be determined by means of a standard rather than by a choice of who is best in the group. It is possible in that case for a whole school to have excellent students. But excellent students may enjoy no more positional benefits than a student judged to be good or passing, just as an excellent doctor may earn no more than a good or mediocre one. Excellence that is valued intrinsically tends to be absolute rather than positional.

The practical upshot of distinguishing between divisible and indivisible, or absolute and positional benefits is to realize that certain goals compete and in that competition use up more resources than do compatible goals. It is easier for a school system to pursue increased achievement scores for some, together with better supervision (child care), than to seek diplomas for all as well as increased achievement scores. We should take with more than a grain of salt rationales given to justify competing goals. When goals compete, their pursuit tends to become the main justification for the expenditure of resources.

The problem of dealing with conflicting goals is a burden the Fair Share conception of justice must face and the Fair Play conception of justice can avoid. Assuring a proportional distribution of positional benefits in order to fulfill a Fair Share conception of justice is likely to run afoul of a Fair Play conception of justice. For example, the 3 percent of the Cajun recipients of high school diplomas might in fact have lower grade point averages than do members of another group denied the diploma. Such concerns motivate much of today's actual controversy in the schools over equal educational opportunity.

Item D. More on Psychological Differentiation

Of the many tests that have been devised to identify school-relevant characteristics, Field Dependence-Independence has been found to relate to a wide variety of them. Figure TA 20.3 indicates a number of related traits.[6] A review of the characteristics correlating with high field independence suggest that students with such characteristics will do well in a traditional school setting. However, high field independence correlates with low levels of interpersonal skills. But interpersonal skills are certainly valued highly in our culture. Furthermore, high level functioning as a clinical diagnostician seems to require a balancing of factors associated with both high and low field independence.[7]

These findings seem to suggest that the ideal of the "well-rounded" individual, one who by himself or herself demonstrates a wide range of excellence, lures us to frustration. Perhaps a well-functioning society requires a pluralism of interests and talents among people rather than within individuals.

---

[6]Herman A. Witkin, Donald R. Goodenough, and Philip K. Oltman, "Psychological Differentiation: Current Status," *The Journal of Personality and Social Psychology*, Vol. 37, No. 7 (July 1979), pp. 1,127–1,145.
[7]Cf. Christopher E. Bork, *The Influence of Cognitive Style upon Clinical Evaluation*. Ph.D. Dissertation, SUNY at Buffalo, 1980. Unpublished.

Figure TA 20.3

PSYCHOLOGICAL DIFFERENTIATION: PARALLELS ACROSS DOMAINS

A person who is

field dependent   field dependent

measures in this trait

Restructuring Skills	LOW sees simple figures in complex gestalts achieves alternate perspectives shows Piagetian conservation	HIGH
Interpersonal Relations	LOW is autonomous in interpersonal relations has an impersonal, non-social orientation has a lack of interpersonal skills	HIGH
Control Functions	LOW has impulse control and deliberateness has motoric inhibition skills retains stressfully learned material	HIGH
Defenses	Uses denial, repression ←→ Uses intellectualization, projection	
Brain Dominance	LOW Has this kind of Bilateral Differentiation	HIGH
Dominant Type in	Societies stressing conformity Societies stressing autonomy	

(adapted from Witkin, Goodenough and Oltman 1979)

Item E. Another Dimension of "Human Nature"

Individual vs. social definition indicates the degree to which our conceptions of personhood are thought to depend upon individual characteristics or upon socially defined characteristics.[8] At one extreme of this dimension are the irreducibly individual traditional Christian conception of soul and similar conceptions of self that transcends circumstances: "individuality that overrides racial and ethnic identities and differences."[9] At the other extreme is a conception of the individual as a "coreless" conglomeration of roles[10]:

> Some time in the future, a long, long time from now, when culture is more completely explored, there will be the equivalent of musical scores that can be learned, each for a different type of man or

---

[8]See, for example these distinctions expounded in Tzvetan Todorov, *Mikhail Bakhtin: The Dialogical Principle*, trans. Wlad Godzich (Minneapolis, Minn.: U. of Minnesota Press, 1984), pp. 29–34.

[9]Anita M. Rogers and Diane Guerin, *Conflict Resolution: A Facilitator's Guide* (Philadelphia: The Consortium, 1984), p. 5.

[10]Cf. Erving Goffman, *Relations in Public* (New York: Basic Books, 1971), p. 27, "If we look closely at the concept of territoriality . . . the notion of the individual ceases to have an analytically coherent, single meaning, and several different terms have to be employed in its stead."

Figure TA 20.4

INDIVIDUAL VS. SOCIAL DEFINITION		
THEORY	The Transcendent Self	The Person as a Locus of Roles
CONTENT OF THEORY	The individual exists independently of what society makes him or her out to be.	The individual is nothing more than what social practices recognize him or her to be.
CONCEPTS IN USE	individual **Responsibility, Guilt**	social **Culture, Ethnicity, Class**
SCHOOLING PRACTICE	Moral Education	Citizenship Education

woman in different types of jobs or relationships, for time, space, work, or play.[11]

Some schooling concepts that fit into this dimension are: personality, responsibility, and fairness, that is, equitable practices based on group characteristics. Practices that assume its validity are tracking, individualization, and moral education. Figure TA 20.4 illustrates this last dimension.

Our traditions that hold that each person is responsible for what he or she does and that upbringing and circumstance do not excuse one from such responsibility, rest on some conception that individuals have a personal "core," a soul, a unique executive function,[12] an ego. In contrast, the concepts of culture, ethnicity, and class are thought to offer other explanations for human behavior. Similarly, moral education is aimed at the "inner core" personhood whereas citizenship education emphasizes social norms. These two extremes of the spectrum often conflict. It is not clear how they can be reconciled.

The possibility that human nature may to some extent be socially defined brings up a point made in Chapter 18 about what can be influenced by some direct, summative action. Many schooling outcomes are socially defined and changing them depends upon reconceptualizing them. This would be very much like transforming the school culture. Socially defined attributes are changed not by changing nature but by changing social criteria.

---

[11]*Culture 20-2* of the Multicultural Educational Resource Information and Training Center (Philadelphia: Temple University, 1978). Mimeographed pamphlet, p. 6.

[12]Cf. Ernest R. Hilgard, "Neodissociation Theory of Multiple Cognitive Control Systems," in Gary E. Schwartz and David Shapiro (eds.), *Consciousness and Self-Regulation*, Vol. 1 (New York: Plenum, 1976), pp. 137–173.

PHOTO CREDITS

REFERENCES

Acker, Joan, and Donald R. Van Houten. "Differential Recruitment and Control: The Sex Structuring of Organizations," *Administrative Science Quarterly* Vol. 19, No. 12 (June 1974).

Acton, H.B. "Berkeley, George," Vol.1, pp. 295–304, and "Idealism," in Edwards, Vol.4.

Adams, G. B. *Civilization During the Middle Ages.* New York: Scribner, 1932.

Adler, Nancy J. *International Dimensions of Organizational Behavior.* Boston: Kent Publ. Co., 1986.

The Age of Enlightenment: The 18th Century Philosophers. Selected and with Introduction and interpretive commentary by Isaiah Berlin. New York: Mentor, 1956.

Aiken, Henry D. *The Age of Ideology.* New York: Mentor, 1956.

Allen, Dwight W., and Jeffrey C. Hecht (eds.) *Controversies in Education.* Philadelphia: W. B. Saunders, 1974.

Allison, Graham. *Essence of Decision: Explaining the Cuban Missile Crisis.* Boston: Little, Brown, 1971.

Alschuler, Alfred S., *School Discipline: A Socially Literate Solution.* New York: McGraw-Hill, 1980.

American Federation of Teachers. *Survey and Analysis of Salary Trends 1988.* Washington, D.C.: American Federation of Teachers, 1988.

Anderson, Barry F. *The Psychology Experiment.* Belmont, Calif.: Brooks-Cole, 1971.

Andrews, William. *Old Time Punishments.* London: Tabbard Press, 1890.

Appel, Karen. *America's Changing Families: A Guide for Educators.* Washington, D.C.: Phi Delta Kappa, 1985.

Apple, Michael W. (ed.). *Cultural and Economic Reproduction in Education: Essays on Class, Ideology and the State.* Boston: Routledge & Kegan Paul, 1982.

———. "The Political Economy of Text Publishing," *Educational Theory*, Vol. 34, No. 4 (Fall 1984).

Applegate, Arthur, et al. "Learning to Be Literate in America," *The National Assessment of Educational Progress, The Nation's Report Card.* Educational Testing Service, Princeton, N.J.: 1987.

Aries, Philippe. *Centuries of Childhood.* London: Jonathan Cape, 1962.

Arnove, Robert, and Harvey Graff. "National Literacy Campaigns: Historical and Comparative Lessons," *Phi Delta Kappan*, Vol. 69, No. 3 (November 1987).

Asher, S. R., P. D. Renshaw, and S. Hymel. "Peer Relations and the Development of Social Skills," *The Young Child: Reviews of Research*, Vol. 3. S. G. Moore and C. R. Cooper, eds. Washington, D.C.: National Association for the Education of Young Children, 1982.

———., R. S. Hymel, and P. D. Renshaw. "Loneliness in Children," *Child Development*, No. 55, 1984; *Avery v. Homewood City Board of Education*, U. S. Court of Appeals (5th Circuit, 1982).

Ausubel, David P., "Crucial Psychological Issues in the Objectives, Organization and Evaluation of Curriculum Reform Movements," in Taylor and Cowley.

Bacharach, Samuel B. (ed.). *Perspectives in Organizational Sociology: Theory and Research.* Greenwich, Conn.: JAI Press, 1981.

Bailyn, Bernard. *Education in the Forming of American Society.* New York: W. W. Norton, 1972.

Baldridge, Victor, and Terrence Deal (eds.). *The Dynamics of Organizational Change in Education.* Berkeley, Calif.: McCutchan, 1983.

Baltzell, E. Digby *The Protestant Establishment.* New York: Random House, 1964.

Bannister v. Paradis, 316 F. Supp. 185. (D.N.H. 1970).

Barker, Roger G., and Paul V. Gump. *Big School, Small School: High School Size and Student Behavior*. Stanford, Calif.: Stanford U. Press, 1964.

Barnard, Chester I. *The Functions of the Executive*. Cambridge, Mass.: Harvard U. Press, 1938.

Barr, Rebecca, and Robert Dreeben. *How Schools Work*. Chicago: U. of Chicago Press, 1983.

Barrow, Robin, "Teacher Education and Research: The Place of Philosophy," *Philosophy of Education 1984*.

Battersby, W. J. *De La Salle, A Pioneer in Modern Education*. New York: Longmans, 1949.

Bauman, R. "Ethnography of Children's Folklore," in P. Gilmore and A. A. Glatthorn (eds.), *Children in and Out of School: Ethnography and Education*. Washington, D.C.: Center for Applied Linguistics, 1982.

Bax, E. Belfort. *The Peasant War in Germany*. New York: Russell and Russell, 1899, reissued 1968.

Baynes, Kenneth, James Bohman, and Thomas McCarthy (eds.). *After Philosophy: End or Transformation?* Cambridge, Mass.: MIT Press, 1987.

Beard, Charles and Mary. *Rise of American Civilization*, Vol. I. New York: Macmillan, 1927.

Beck, F. A. G. *Greek Education 450–350 B.C.* London: Methuen, 1964.

Bell, Wendell. "Comparative Research on Ethnicity: A Conference Report," *Social Science Research Council Items*, Vol. 28 (December 1974).

Benedict, Ruth. *Chrysanthemum and the Sword: Patterns of Japanese Culture*. New York: Meridian Books, 1974.

Benn, S. I. and R. S. Peters. *The Principles of Political Thought: Social Foundations of the Democratic State*. New York: Free Press, 1965.

Benn, Stanley I. "Nature of Political Philosophy" in Edwards, Vol. 6.

Berger, Peter L., and Thomas Luckmann. *The Social Construction of Reality*. Garden City, N.Y.: Anchor Books, 1967.

Berman, Paul, and Milbrey Wallin, in McLaughlin, *Federal Programs Supporting Educational Change*. Vol. VIII, Implementing and Sustaining Innovations. R-1589/8-HEW. Santa Monica, Calif.: Rand Corp., 1978.

Bestor, Arthur. *Educational Wastelands*. 2nd Ed. Urbana, Ill.: U. of Illinois Press, 1985.

Beyer, Landon, and Kenneth Zeichner. "Teacher Training and Educational Foundations: A Plea for Discontent," *Journal of Teacher Education*, Vol. XXXIII, No. 3 (May–June 1982).

Bhagavad-Gita, or "Song Celestial," Sir Edward Arnold (trans.), in Charles W. Eliot (ed.). *The Harvard Classics*, Vol. 43. New York: Collier, 1910.

Birch, Jack W. *Mainstreaming: Educable Mentally Retarded Children in Regular Classes*. Monograph. University of Minnesota Leadership Training Institute/Special Eduction. Undated. Available from The Council for Exceptional Children, 1920 Association Drive, Reston, VA 22091.

Bloom, B., et al., *Taxonomy of Educational Objectives*. New York: Longman, 1956.

Blum, Jerome, Rondo Cameron, and Thomas Barnes. *A History of the European World*. New York: Little, Brown, 1966.

Blumberg, Arthur. *The School Superintendent: Dealing With Conflict*. New York: Teachers College Press, 1985.

Bobbitt, John Franklin. "The Supervision of City Schools: Some General Principles of Management Applied to the Problems of City School Systems," *Twelfth Yearbook of the National Society for the Study of Education*, Part 1. Bloomington, Ill.: 1913.

Boike, Mary, et al. "Relationships Between Family Background Problems and School Problems and Competencies of Normal Young Children," *Psychology in the Schools*, Vol. 15, No. 2 (April 1978).

Bolger, R. R. "Education and Learning," in *The New Cambridge Modern History*, R. B. Wernham (ed.). Cambridge, England: Cambridge U. Press, 1968.

Bonner, Stanley J. *Education in Ancient Rome*. Berkeley: U. of California Press, 1977.

Boorstin, Daniel. *The Americans: The National Experience*. New York: Random House, 1967.

Bork, Christopher E. *The Influence of Cognitive Style upon Clinical Evaluation*. Ph.D. Dissertation. S.U.N.Y at Buffalo, 1980. Unpublished.

Boudon, Raymond. *Education, Opportunity, and Social Inequality*. New York: Wiley, 1973.

Boulding, Kenneth E. *Conflict and Defense: A General Theory*. New York: Harper Torchbooks, 1963.

Bowen, James. *A History of Western Education*, Vol. I, New York: St. Martin's Press, 1972.

————, and Peter R. Hobson. *Theories of Education*. New York: Wiley, 1974.

Bowles, Samuel and Herbert Gintis. *Schooling in Capitalist America*. New York: Basic Books, 1976.

Boyd, William (ed.). *The Emile of Jean Jacques Rousseau*. New York: Teachers' College Press, 1956.

————. "The Politics of Curriculum Change and Stability," *Educational Research*, Vol. 8, No. 2 (February 1979).

Boydston, Jo Ann (ed.). *John Dewey: The Middle Works, 1899–1924*. 15 vols. Carbondale: Southern Illinois U. Press, 1976–1983.

Boyer, Ernest L. *High School*. New York: Harper & Row, 1983.

Brady, John Paul, Lester Luborsky, and Reuben E. Kron. "Blood Pressure Reduction in Patients with Essential Hypertension Through Metronome-Conditioned Relaxation: A Preliminary Report" in Dicara et al.

Breasted, James. *A History of Egypt From the Earliest Times to the Persian Conflict*. New York: Scribner, 1937.

————. *The Conquest of Civilization*. New York: Harper & Row, 1926.

Broderick v. Oklahoma, Supreme Court of the United States, 1973, 413 U.S. 601.

Brody, Herb. "RISC-y Business," *High Technology Business*, August 1988.

Brodzinsky, Ben. *How A School Board Operates*. Bloomington, Ind.: Phi Delta Kappa, 1977.

Bronfenbrenner, Urie. *Two Worlds of Childhood*. New York: Pocket Books, 1973.

Bronowski, Jacob. "The Creative Aspects of Science," in Louise Young (ed.), *Exploring the Universe*. New York: McGraw-Hill, 1963.

Broudy, Harry S. "Can We Define Good Teaching?" *The Record—Teachers' College*, Vol. 70, No. 7 (April 1969).

————. *The Real World of the Public Schools*. New York: Harcourt Brace Jovanovich, 1972.

————. *Truth and Credibility. The Citizen's Dilemma.* New York: Longman, 1981.

Brown v. Board of Education, Supreme Court of the United States, 1954, 347 U.S. 483.

Bruner, Jerome. *The Process of Education*. Cambridge, Mass.: Harvard U. Press, 1960.

Buetow, Harold. *Of Singular Benefit, The Story of Catholic Education in the United States*. New York: Macmillan, 1970.

Bunge, Mario. *Causality*. Cleveland: World Publishing, 1963.

Bureau of the Census. *Statistical Abstract of the United States.* Washington, D.C.: U.S. Government Printing Office, 1988.

——. *Statistical Abstract of the United States, 10th Edition*, 1987. Washington, D.C.: U.S. Department of Commerce, Bureau of the Census.

Burke, James. *The Day the Universe Changed.* Boston: Little, Brown, 1985.

Burns, Edward, and Philip Ralph. *World Civilizations from Ancient to Contemporary*, Vol. II. New York: Norton, 1958.

Burton, Christine. "Children's Peer Relationships," *ERIC Digest*, ERIC Clearinghouse on Elementary and Early Childhood Education. Urbana, Ill.: U. of Illinois, 1980.

Button, H. Warren, and Eugene F. Provenzo, Jr. *History of Education and Culture in America.* Englewood Cliffs, N.J.: Prentice-Hall, 1989.

Bylinsky, Gene. "Here Come the Bionic Piglets," *Fortune*, Vol. 116 (October 1987).

Byrns, Ralph, and Gerald Stone. *Economics.* Glenview, Ill.: Scott-Foresman, 1987.

Cahn, Steven M. *The Philosophical Foundations of Education.* New York: Harper & Row, 1970.

Callahan, Raymond E. *Education and the Cult of Efficiency.* Chicago: U. of Chicago Press, 1962.

Campbell, Bernard. *"The Roots of Language,"* in John Morton, ed., Biological and Social Factors in Psycholinguistics. Urbana, Ill.: U. of Illinois Press, 1970.

Campbell, Donald T., and Julian C. Stanley. *Experimental and Quasi-experimental Designs for Research.* Chicago: Rand-McNally, 1963.

Cantor, Norman F. *Medieval History.* New York: Macmillan, 1963.

The Carnegie Forum on Education and the Economy. *A Nation Prepared: Teachers for the 21st Century.* Washington, D.C.: The Carnegie Forum on Education and the Economy, 1986.

Carrol, Steven J. "The Search for Equity in School Finance," in McMahon and Geske.

Center for Educational Statistics. *The Condition of Education: A Statistical Report, 1987 Edition.* Washington, D.C.: Office of Educational Research and Improvement, U.S. Department of Education.

Chambliss, J. J. "Reason, Conduct and Revelation in the Educational Theory of Locke, Watts and Burgh," *Educational Theory*, Fall 1976.

Charters, W. W., Jr. "The Social Background of Teaching," in N. L. Gage (ed.), *Handbook of Research on Teaching.* Chicago: Rand McNally, 1963.

Childe, V. Gordon. *Social Evolution.* New York: Henry Schuman, 1951.

Chinitz, Benjamin (ed.). *City and Suburb.* Englewood Cliffs, N.J.: Prentice-Hall, 1964.

Chomsky, Noam. "Review of B.F. Skinner, *Verbal Behavior*," *Language*, Vol. 35, 1959.

Christensen, Carol A., Michael M. Gerber, and Robert B. Everhart. "Toward a Sociological Perspective on Learning Disabilities," *Educational Theory*, Vol. 36, No. 4 (Fall 1986).

Clabaugh, Gary. "A History of Male Attitudes Toward the Education of Women," *Educational Horizons*, Vol. 64, No. 3.

Cobban, A. B. *The Medieval Universities: Their Development and Organization.* London: Methuen, 1975.

Cohen, Rosalie. "Conceptual Styles, Culture Conflict and Non-Verbal Tests of Intelligence," *American Anthropologist*, Vol. 71, No. 5 (1969).

Cole, Bob. "Teaching in a Time Machine: The 'Make-Do' Mentality in Small-Town Schools," *Phi Delta Kappan*, October 1988.

Coleman, James. *The Adolescent Society.* New York: Free Press, 1961.

————. "Rawls, Nozick, and Educational Equality" Reflections. *The Public Interest*, No. 44 (Summer 1976).

Coleman, J. S., et al. *Equality of Educational Opportunity*. Washington, D.C.: U.S. Government Printing Office, 1966.

Collins, Randall. *The Credential Society*. New York: Academic Press, 1979.

————. "Some Comparative Principles of Educational Stratification," *Harvard Educational Review*, Vol. 47, No. 1 (February 1977).

Comer, James. "Is 'Parenting' Essential to Good Teaching?" *NEA Today Special Edition*, January 1988.

Commission on the Reorganization of Secondary Education. *Cardinal Principles of Secondary Education*, Bull. 35. Washington, D.C: Government Printing Office, 1918.

Compact Edition of The Oxford English Dictionary. New York: Oxford University Press, 1971.

Comstock, George, et al. *Television and Human Behavior*. New York: Columbia U. Press, 1978.

Conant, James Bryant. *American High School Today*. New York: 1959.

Condition of Education, The. Washington, D.C.: Center for Education Statistics, 1987.

Confucius, c. 550–478 B.C. Book XVI, *HSIO KI (Record on the Subject of Education)*.

Connors, Dennis A., and Donald B. Reed. "The Turbulent Field of Public School Administration," *The Executive Review*, Vol. 3, No. 4 (Ames: Institute for School Executives, The University of Iowa, January 1983).

Cookson, Peter, Jr., and Caroline Persell. *Preparing for Power: America's Elite Boarding Schools*. New York: Basic Books, 1985.

Coser, Lewis. *The Functions of Social Conflict*. New York: Free Press, 1956.

Council of Chief State School Officers. Position Paper and Recommendations for Action, "Education and the Economy," November 1986, Washington, D.C.

————. *Staffing the Nation's Schools: A National Emergency*. A report of the Council of Chief State School Officers Ad Hoc Committee on Teacher Certification, Preparation and Accreditation. (Washington, D.C.: Council of Chief State School Officers, January 1984.)

Council of Learned Societies in Education. "Standards for Academic and Professional Instruction in Foundations of Education," *Educational Studies and Educational Policy Studies*. Ann Arbor, Mich.: Prakken Publication, 1986.

Cremin, Lawrence A. *American Education: The Colonial Experience 1607–1783*. New York: Harper & Row, 1970.

————. *American Education: The National Experience, 1783–1876*. New York: Harper & Row, 1980.

————. *Traditions of American Education*. New York: Basic Books, 1977.

————. *The Transformation of the School*. New York: Vintage, 1961.

Cronbach, L. J., G. C. Gileser, H. Nanda, and N. Rajaratnam. *The Dependability of Behavioral Measurements: Theory of Generalizability for Scores and Profiles*. New York: Wiley, 1972.

Cubberly, Ellwood P. *A Brief History of Education*. New York: Houghton Mifflin, 1922.

————. *The History of Education*. Boston: Houghton Mifflin, 1920.

Culture 20–2. Pamphlet of the Multicultural Educational Resource Information and Training Center. Philadelphia: Temple University, 1978. Mimeograph.

Cumming v. Board of Education, Supreme Court of the United States, 1899, 175 U.S. 528.

Current, Richard N., et al. *A Survey of American History*, Vol. I. *Since 1865*. New York: Alfred Knopf, 1983.

Cutler, Paul. *Problem Solving in Clinical Medicine: From Data to Diagnosis*. Baltimore, Md.: Wilkins & Wilkins, 1979.

Cutler, William W., III. "Cathedral of Culture: The Schoolhouse in American Educational Thought and Practice since 1820," *History of Education Quarterly*, Vol. 29, No. 1 (Spring 1989).

Darling-Hammond, Linda, and Barnett Berry. *The Evolution of Teacher Policy*. Santa Monica, Calif.: The Rand Corporation, 1988.

Dawe, H. "Teaching: a performing art, *Phi Delta Kappan*, Vol. 66, No. 3 (1984).

Deal, Terrence E., and Allen A. Kennedy, *Corporate Cultures: The Rites and Rituals of Corporate Life*. Reading, Mass.: Addison-Wesley, 1982.

Deal, Terrence, and Martha Stone Wiske. "Planning, Plotting and Playing in Education's Era of Decline," in Baldridge and Deal.

Deci, Edward., "The Hidden Cost of Rewards," *Organizational Dynamics*, Vol. 4, No. 3 (Winter 1976).

Degler, Carl N. *At Odds*. New York: Oxford U. Press, 1980.

———. *Out of Our Past: The Forces That Shaped Modern America*. New York: Harper & Row, 1984.

Degler, Maxine. *The Public School and the Private Vision: A Search for America in Education and Literature*. New York: Random House, 1965.

Derr, Richard L. *A Taxonomy of Social Purposes of Public Schools*. New York: McKay, 1973.

Dewan, E. M. "Consciousness as an Emergent Causal Agent in the Context of Control System Theory," in Globus, et al.,

Dewey, John. *Democracy and Education*. New York: Macmillan, 1916.

———. *How We Think*. Boston: D. C. Heath, 1933.

———. *The School and Society*. (1899), in Boydston (ed.),

DeYoung, Alan. *Economics and American Education*. White Plains, N.Y.: Longman, 1989.

Dicara, Leo V., et al. *Bio-Feedback and Self-Control 1974*. Chicago: Aldine, 1975.

Dickinson, G. Lowes. *The Greek View of Life*. New York: Collier, 1961.

DiNicola, Daniel R. "The Education of the Emotions," *Philosophy of Education* 19.

———. *Evaluation and Grading: A Philosophical Analysis*. Ph.D. dissertation. Unpublished. Harvard University, 1973.

Dobson, J. F. *Ancient Education and Its Meaning To Us*. New York: Cooper Square, 1963.

Dobzhansky, Theodosius. "On Species and Races of Living and Fossil Man," *American Journal of Physical Anthropology*, Vol. 2, 1944.

Domhof, G. William. *Who Rules America?* Englewood Cliffs, N.J.: Prentice-Hall, 1967.

Dornbusch, Sandy. "Helping Your Kid Make the Grade." Reston, Va.: National Association of Secondary School Principals, 1987.

Due, John F. "Shifting Sources of Financing Education and the Taxpayer Revolt," in McMahon and Geske.

Duggan, Stephen. *A Student's Textbook in the History of Education*. New York: Appleton-Century, 1927.

Dunnigan, James F. *How to Make War*. New York: Quill, 1983.

Durant, Will. *The Story of Philosophy*. New York: Pocket Books, 1960.

Durant, Will and Ariel, "Kant," Chapter XXI in Durant, Book 10, *Rousseau and Revolution*, pp. 531–551; and "Hegel" in Chapter XXXII, "German Philosophy," in Durant, Book 11, *The Age of Napoleon*.

————. *The Story of Civilization*. Eleven Volumes. New York: Simon & Schuster, 1967.

Durkheim, Emile. *Education and Sociology*, trans. Sherwood Fox. Glencoe, Ill.: The Free Press, 1956.

Dykhuizen, George. *The Life and Mind of John Dewey*. Carbondale, Ill.: Southern Illinois U. Press, 1973.

Easton, Loyd D. "Harris, William Torey" in Edwards, Vol. 3.

Edelman, Marian Wright. "Children's Time." The 1988 Martin Buskin Memorial Lecture, delivered at the National Seminar of the Education Writers Association, New Orleans, April 16, 1988.

Education Writers Association. *Covering the Education Beat: A Current Guide for Editors and Writers*. Washington, D.C.: Education Writers Association, 1987.

————. "Illiteracy: Chicken or Egg?" *The Literacy Beat: A Special Newsletter of the Education Writers Association*, Vol. 1 (August 1987).

————. "Myth #1: There Is an Epidemic of Illiteracy in American Society," *The Literacy Beat*, Vol. 1, No. 3 (September 1987).

Edward, Burns. *Western Civilizations: Their History and Culture*. New York: W.W. Norton, 1968.

Edwards, Paul (ed.). *The Encyclopedia of Philosophy*. Eight Volumes. New York: Collier-Macmillan, 1967.

Egan, Kieran. "The Necessary Role of Myths in Education," *Philosophy of Education 1972*.

Eisner, Elliot W. "Can Educational Research Inform Educational Practice?" *Phi Delta Kappan*, March 1984.

————. *The Educational Imagination: On the Design and Evaluation of School Programs*. New York: Macmillan, 1979.

Elam, Stanley M. "Differences Between Educators and the Public on Questions of Education Policy," *Phi Delta Kappan*, December 1987.

Elmore, Richard F. "Organizational Models of Social Program Implementation," *Public Policy*, Vol. 26, No. 2 (Spring 1978).

Elmore, Richard F., and Milbrey Wallin McLaughlin. *Steady Work. Policy, Practice and the Reform of American Education*. RAND/R-3574-NIE/RC. Santa Monica, Calif.: Rand Corp., 1988.

Emery, F. E., and E. L. Trist. "The Causal Texture of Organizational Environments," *Human Relations* Vol. 18, No. 1 (February 1965).

Encyclopedia of Associations. Detroit, Mich.: Gale Research, 1989.

Engle v. Vitale, Supreme Court of the United States, 1962, 370 U.S. 421.

Ennis, Robert H. "Is Answering Questions Teaching?" *Educational Theory*, Vol. 36, No. 4 (Fall 1986).

ERIC. "A Closer Look at Children in Single-Parent Families," ERIC/Clearinghouse on Urban Education Digest No. 23 (June 1984).

ERIC Clearinghouse on Educational Management. "Merit Pay," Research Action Brief Number 15. Eugene, Ore.: U. of Oregon, 1981.

ERIC Document ED262028, William Shreeve et al. (eds.). "Single Parents and Student Achievement—A National Tragedy," 1985.

Evertson, Carolyn, Willis Hawley, and Marilyn Zlotnik. "Making a Difference in Educational Quality Through Teacher Education," *Journal of Teacher Education*, May-June 1985.

Fairbank, Reischauer, and Craig. *East Asia: Tradition and Transformation*. Boston: Houghton Mifflin, 1973.

Farrington v. Tokushige, 1926, 273 U.S. 284.

Feden, Preston D., and Gary K. Clabaugh. "Developmental Education: LaSalle's Rationale and Program for Integrative Teacher Education," *Teacher Education and Special Education*, Vol. 9, 1987.

Fennell, Jon M. B. *Rousseau, the Curriculum, and the Standard of Nature*. Unpublished dissertation. Champaign, Ill.: U. of Illinois, 1976.

Fine, M. A., et al. "Long-term Effects of Divorce on Parent-Child Relationships," *Developmental Psychology*, Vol. 19, No. 5.

Finklestein, Barbara. "Technicians, Mandarins, and Winesses: Searching for Professional Understanding," *Journal of Teacher Education*, Vol. XXXIII, No. 3 (May-June 1982).

Fisher, Berenice M. *Industrial Education: American Ideals and Institutions*. Madison: U. of Wisconsin Press, 1967.

Fisher, Roger, and William Ury. *Getting to YES. Negotiating Agreement Without Giving In*. New York: Penguin, 1987.

Fleming, Standord. *Children and Puritanism: The Place of Children in the Life and Thought of the New England Churches, 1620–1847*. New Haven, Conn.: Yale University Press, 1933.

Flew, Anthony (ed.). *Logic and Language*. Garden City, N.Y.: Doubleday Anchor, 1965.

Flygare, Thomas. *The Legal Rights of Teachers*. Bloomington, Ind.: The Phi Delta Kappa Foundation, 1976.

Fodor, Jerry. *Psychological Explanation: An Introduction to the Philosophy of Psychology*. New York: Random House, 1968.

Freeman, R. "Search For Freedom—the Story of American Education," *NEA Journal*, March 1960.

Friedman, Milton. "The Role of Government in Education," in Robert A. Solo (ed.), *Economics and the Public Interest*. New Brunswick, N.J.: Rutgers U. Press, 1955.

Friesen, John W., Evelina Ortega y Miranda, and Henry C. Lu. "Philosophy of Education: A Description of the Field," *Philosophy of Education 1972*.

Froomkin, J., D. Jamison, and R. Radner (eds.). *Education as an Industry*. Cambridge, Mass.: Ballinger, 1976.

Frost, S. E. *Essentials of History of Education*. New York: Barrons, 1947.

———. *Historical and Philosophical Foundations of Western Civilization*. Columbus, Ohio: Merrill, 1966.

Gallup, Alec M., and David I. Clark. "The 19th Annual Gallup Poll of the Public's Attitudes Toward the Public Schools," *Phi Delta Kappan*, Vol. 69, No. 1 (September 1987).

———. "The 20th Annual Gallup Poll of the Public's Attitudes Toward the Public Schools," *Phi Delta Kappan*, Vol. 70, No. 1 (September 1988).

Gannes, Stuart. "Back to the Basics: Computers With Sportscar Speed," *Fortune*, Vol. 112 (September 30, 1985).

Gardiner, H. Norman (ed.). *Selected Sermons of Jonathan Edwards*. New York: Macmillan, 1904.

Gardner, Howard. *Frames of Mind: The Theory of Multiple Intelligence*. New York: Basic Books, 1983.

Garvin, James P. "What Do Parents Expect from Middle Level Schools?" *Middle School Journal*, November 1987.

Gatti, Daniel, and Richard Gatti. *The Teacher and the Law*. West Nyack, N.Y.: Parker, 1972.

George, Paul S., and Lynn I. Oldaker. "A National Survey of Middle School Effectiveness," *Educational Leadership*, December 1985/January 1986.

Geske, M. Terry. "Educational Finance: Research Findings and Policy Implications," in Walter McMahon and Terry Geske (eds.), *Financing Education: Overcoming Inefficiency and Inequity*. Urbana, Ill.: U. of Illinois Press, 1982.

Getzels, Jacob W., James M. Lipham, and Roald F. Campbell. *Educational Administration as a Social Process. Theory, Research, Practice*. New York: Harper & Row, 1968.

Giarelli, James M. "Philosophy, Education and Public Practice," Presidential Address, Middle Atlantic States Philosophy of Education Society. Manuscript. New Brunswick, N.J.: Rutgers Graduate School of Education, unpublished, May 2, 1987.

Gibboney, Richard A. *Toward Intellectual Excellence: Some Things to Look for in Classrooms and Schools*. Manuscript. Philadelphia: U. of Pennsylvania Graduate School of Education.

Gies, Frances and Joseph. *Marriage and the Family in the Middle Ages*. New York: Harper & Row, 1987.

Glazer, Nathan. "IQ on Trial," *Commentary*, June 1981.

Globus, Gordon G., Grover Maxwell, and Irwin Savodnik (eds.). *Consciousness and the Brain. A Scientific and Philosophical Inquiry*. New York: Plenum, 1976.

Goffman, Erving. "On Cooling the Mark Out. Some Aspects of Adaptation to Failure," *Psychiatry: Journal for the Study of Interpersonal Processes*, Vol. 15, No. 4 (November 1952).

———. *Relations in Public*, New York: Basic Books, 1971.

Gonzalez, Justo. *The Story of Christianity*, Vol. 1. San Francisco: Harper & Row, 1984.

Good, H. G. *A History of Western Education*. New York: Macmillan, 1960.

Good, Thomas, and Jere Brophy. *Educational Psychology. 3rd ed*. New York: Longman, 1986.

Goode, William. *The Family*. Englewood Cliffs, N.J.: Prentice-Hall, 1964.

Goodlad, John. "Studying the Education of Educators: Values-Driven Inquiry," *Phi Delta Kappan*, October 1988.

———. *A Place Called School*. New York: McGraw-Hill, 1984.

Goodson, Ivor. *School Subjects and Curriculum Change*. Philadelphia: Falmer Press, 1987.

Goody, Jack, and I. P. Watts. "The Consequences of Literacy," in Jack Goody (ed.), *Literacy in Traditional Societies*. Cambridge: Harvard U. Press, 1968.

Goss v. Lopez, United States Supreme Court, 1975, 419 U.S. 565

Gould, Stephen Jay. *The Mismeasure of Man*. New York: Norton, 1981.

Gouldner, Alvin W. "Cosmopolitans and Locals: Toward an Analysis of Latent Social Roles," *Administrative Science Quarterly*, Vol. 2, No. 3 (December 1957).

———. *Patterns of Industrial Bureaucracy*. Glencoe, Ill.: Free Press of Glencoe, 1954.

Green v. County School Board of New Kent County, Supreme Court of the United States, 1968, 391 U.S. 430.

Green, Thomas F. *Predicting the Behavior of the Educational System*. Syracuse, N.Y.: Syracuse U. Press, 1980.

————. "Weighing the Justice of Inequality," *Change*, Vol. 12, No. 5 (July/August 1980).

Greene, Maxine. *Landscapes of Learning*. New York: Teachers College Press, 1979.

Greer, Colin *The Great School Legend*. New York: Basic Books, 1972.

Grubb, W. Norton, and Marvin Lazerson. "Rally 'Round the Workplace: Continuities and Fallacies in Career Education," *Harvard Educational Review*, Vol. 45, No. 4 (November 1975).

Guilford, J. P. *The Nature of Human Intelligence*. New York: McGraw-Hill, 1967.

Gulick, Luther. "Notes on the Theory of Organization," in Shafritz and Hyde (eds.)

Gulliford, Andrew. *America's Country Schools*. Washington, D.C.: Preservation Press, 1984.

Gutek, Gerald. *Education and Schooling in America*. Englewood Cliffs, N.J.: Prentice-Hall, 1988.

————. *Education in the United States: An Historical Perspective*. Englewood Cliffs, N.J.: Prentice-Hall, 1986.

————. *Philosophical and Ideological Perspectives on Education*. Englewood Cliffs, N.J.: Prentice-Hall, 1988.

Guthrie, James, Walter Garms, and Lawrence Pierce. *School Finance and Education Policy*. 2nd Ed. Englewood Cliffs, N.J.: Prentice-Hall, 1988.

————. *School Finance and Education Policy: Enhancing Educational Efficiency, Equality and Choice*. Englewood Cliffs, N.J.: Prentice-Hall, 1988.

Haberman, Martin. "Recruiting and Selecting Teachers for Urban Schools." New York: ERIC Clearinghouse for Urban Education, Teachers College, Columbia University, 1987.

Hahn, Hans. "The Crisis in Intuition," pp. 1956–1976, in Newman (ed.).

Hall, E. "Bad Education—A Conversation with Jerome Bruner," *Psychology Today*, No. 4, 1970.

Hall, Edward T. *The Silent Language*. Greenwich, Conn.: Fawcett, 1959.

Hallinan, Maureen, and Stevens Smith. "Classroom Characteristics and Student Friendship Cliques." Paper presented at the Annual Meeting of the American Educational Research Association. Washington, D.C.: April 20–24, 1987.

Harrington, Michael. *The Other America: Poverty in the United States*. Baltimore: Penguin Books, 1963.

Harrington, Michael. *The Politics at God's Funeral*. New York: Penguin, 1983.

Harris, Marvin. *Cannibals and Kings, The Origins of Culture*. New York: Vintage, 1977.

Harris, Sherwood and Lorna Harris (eds.). *The Teacher's Almanac 1988–89*. New York: Facts on File, 1988.

————. *The Teacher's Almanac, 1987–88*. New York: Facts on File, 1987.

Hart, H. L. A., "The Ascription of Responsibility and Rights" in Flew (ed.), pp. 151–174.

Harvard Business Review. *On Human Relations*. New York: Harper & Row, 1979.

Haskins, C. *The Rise of the Universities*. New York: Holt, 1923.

Hayes, Carlton. *The Historical Evolution of Modern Nationalism*. New York: Macmillan, 1950.

————, Marshall Baldwin, and Charles Cole. *History of Western Civilization*. Vol. II. New York: Macmillan, 1967.

Heatherington, E., et al. "Cognitive Performance, School Behavior and Achievement of Children from One-Parent Households." Prepared for the Families as Educators Team of the National Institute of Education, 1981.

Hersey, Paul, and Kenneth H. Blanchard. *Management of Organizational Behavior.* Englewood Cliffs, N.J.: Prentice-Hall, 1988.

Hessong, Robert F., and Thomas H. Weeks. *Introduction to Education.* New York: Macmillan, 1987.

Hilgard, Ernest R. *Introduction to Psychology.* 3rd Ed. New York: Harcourt, Brace & World, 1962.

————. "Neodissociation Theory of Multiple Cognitive Control Systems," in Schwartz and Shapiro (eds.),

Hill, Christopher. *Society and Puritanism in Pre-Revolutionary England.* New York: Schocken, 1967.

Hill, Paul, Arthur Wise, and Leslie Shapiro. "Educational Progress: Cities Mobilizing To Improve Their Schools." Santa Monica, Calif.: Rand Corporation Center for the Study of the Teaching Profession, 1989.

Hirsch, Fred. *The Social Limits to Growth.* Cambridge: Harvard U. Press, 1976.

Hodgson, Godfrey. "Do Schools Make A Difference?" in Holger Stubb (ed.), *The Sociology of Education: A Sourcebook.* Homewood, Ill.: Dorsey Press, 1975.

Hofstede, Geert. "Motivation, Leadership and Organization: Do American Theories Apply Abroad," *Organizational Dynamics* (Summer 1980), cited in Adler (ed.).

Hogan, David. "Education and Class Formation: the Peculiarities of the Americans," in Apple (ed.), *Cultural and Economic Reproduction in Education,*

Hogan, M. J., R. A. Sirotkin, and R. E. Gallagher. "Clinical Problem Solving: The Relationship of Cognitive Abilities to PMP Performance," *Proceedings of the 16th Annual Conference on Research in Medical Education, 1977.*

Holt, David R. "Sensitizing New Teachers about Father-absent Boys," *Action in Teacher Education,* Vol. VIII, No. 3 (Fall 1986).

Honey, H. deS. *Tom Brown's Universe: The Development of the English Public School in the Nineteenth Century.* New York: Quadrangle, 1977.

Hopper, Earl. "Stratification, Education and Mobility In Industrial Societies," in Earl Hopper (ed.), *Readings in the Theory of Educational Systems.* London: Hutchison, 1971.

Hortonville Joint School District No. 1 v. Hortonville Education Association, Supreme Court of the United States, 1976 (486 U.S. 482).

Howe, Louise. *The Future of the Family.* New York: Simon & Schuster, 1972.

Hoy, Wayne K., and Cecil G. Miskel. *Educational Administration.* New York: Random House, 1982.

Hullett, J. "Which Structure?" *Educational Theory,* Vol. 24, No. 1 (Winter 1974).

Hummel, John F. *A Study of Selected Personality Characteristics and Science Related Attitudes of Ninth Grade, Female Students in Urban, Parochial High Schools.* Unpublished Ed.D. Dissertation. Temple University, 1981.

Hurn, Christopher J. *The Limits and Possibilities of Schooling.* Boston: Allyn & Bacon, 1978.

Hutchins, Robert M. "The Basis of Education," reprinted in Noll,

Illich, Ivan. *Deschooling Society.* New York: Harper & Row, 1971.

Ingraham v. Wright, United States Supreme Court, 1977, 430 U.S. 651.

Isaac, Rhys. *The Transformation of Virginia.* Chapel Hill, N.C.: The U. of North Carolina Press, 1982.

Jacobs, Roderick A., and Peter S. Rosenbaum. *English Transformational Grammar.* Waltham, Mass.: Blaisdell, 1968.

Jencks, Christopher. *Inequality: A Re-assessment of the Effect of Family and Schooling in America*. New York: Harper, 1972.

Jensen, Arthur R. "How Much Can We Boost I.Q. and Scholastic Achievement?" *Harvard Educational Review*, Winter 1969.

Johnson, Harry. *Sociology: A Systematic Introduction*. New York: Harcourt, Brace & World, 1960.

Johnson, James A., Harold W. Collins, Victor L. Dupuis, and John H. Johansen. *Introduction to the Foundations of American Education*. Sixth Ed. Boston: Allyn & Bacon, 1985.

Johnson, William R. "Empowering Practitioners: Holmes, Carnegie, and the Lessons of History," *History of Education Quarterly*, Vol. 27, No. 2 (Summer 1987).

Joncich, Geraldine M. *Psychology and the Science of Education: Selected Writings of Edward L. Thorndike*. New York: Teachers' College Press, 1962.

Kadrmas v. Dickenson Public Schools, United States Supreme Court 1988, 108 S.Ct. 2481.

Kaestle, Carl, and Maris Vinovskis. *Education and Social Change in Nineteenth-Century Massachusetts*. Cambridge, England: Cambridge U. Press, 1980.

Kaestle, Carl F. *Pillars of the Republic: Common Schools and American Society, 1780–1860*. New York: Hill & Wang, 1983, quoted in Andrew Gulliford. *American Country Schools*. Washington, D.C.: Preservation Press, 1984.

Kahneman, Daniel, Paul Slovic, Amos Tversky (eds.). *Judgment under Uncertainty: Heuristics and Biases*. Cambridge, England: Cambridge U. Press, 1982.

Kane, S. J. *History of Education*. Chicago: Loyola U. Press, 1954.

Karass, Chester L. *Give & Take. The Complete Guide to Negotiating Strategies and Tactics*. New York: Crowell, 1974.

Karier, Clarence J. "Retrospective One" in Bestor

———. "Testing for Order and Control in the Corporate Liberal State," *Educational Theory*, Vol. 22 (Spring 1972).

Katz, Michael B. "Connections Between the Origins of Public Education and the Major Themes in American Social History," unpublished paper distributed at the University of Pennsylvania.

Katznelson, Ira, and Margaret Weir. *Schooling for All*. New York: Basic Books, 1985.

Kaufman, Bel. *Up the Down Staircase*. New York: Avon, 1964.

Kaufman, Polly Welts. "A Wider Field of Usefulness: Pioneer Women Teachers in the West, 1848–1854," quoted in Andrew Gulliford. *American Country Schools*. Washington, D.C.: Preservation Press, 1984.

Kaye, Evelyn. *The Family Guide to Children's Television*. New York: Pantheon, 1974.

Kean, Thomas. "Partners for Today and Tomorrow," *Education and Society*, Vol. 1, No. 3 (Fall 1988).

Keegan, John. *The Mask of Command*. New York: Viking, 1987.

Kentucky State Board of Elementary and Secondary Education v. Rudasill, 589 S.W. 2d 877 (Ky. 1979)., cert. denied, 1000 S.Ct. 2158 (1980).

Ker, William. *The Dark Ages*. New York: Mentor 1958, original publication 1904.

Kilpatrick, William A. *The Project Method*. New York: Columbia U., 1918.

Kindsvatter, Richard, William Wilen, and Margaret Ishler. *The Dynamics of Effective Teaching*. New York: Longman, 1988.

Kirst, Michael. "Who Should Control Our Schools?" *NEA Today: Special Edition*, January 1988.

Kliebard, Herbert M. "The Rise of the Scientific Curriculum and its Aftermath," *Curriculum Theory Network*, Vol. 5, No. 1 (1975).

Knape, Carl, and Paul T. Rosewell. "The Philosophically Discerning Classroom Teacher," *Educational Studies,* Vol. 2, 1980.

Kneller, George F. *Movements of Thought in Modern Education*. New York: Wiley, 1984.

Knight, Edgar, *Twenty Centuries of Education*. Boston: Ginn, 1940.

————. *Education in the United States*. Boston: Ginn, 1941.

Koerner, Stephen. *The Philosophy of Mathematics: An Introduction*. New York: Harper & Row, 1960.

Kohl, Herbert. *The Open Classroom*. New York: Vintage, 1969.

Komisar, B. Paul, "Conceptual Analysis of Teaching" *The High School Journal*, Vol. 50, No. 1 (October 1966).

————. "The Language of Education" in Leighton, Vol. 5.

————. "More on the Concept of Learning," *Educational Theory*, Vol. XV, No. 3 (July 1965).

————. "The Paradox of Equality in Schooling" *Teachers' College Record*, Vol. 68, No. 3 (December 1966).

————. and C. B. J. MacMillan (eds.). *Psychological Concepts in Education*. Chicago: Rand McNally, 1967.

The Koran. 65 in Thomas Tripp (ed.), Chaps. 6 and 7.

Kotter, John P., and Leonard A. Schlesinger. "Choosing Strategies for Change," *Harvard Business Review*, March-April 1979.

Kozol, Jonathan. *The Night is Dark and I am Far From Home*. New York: Bantam, 1973.

Krajewski, Robert T. "Secondary Principals Want to Be Instructional Leaders," *Phi Delta Kappan*, September 1978.

Kramer, S. M. *History Begins at Sumer*. London: Thames and Hudson, 1976.

Krohne, P. W. *An Analysis of the State Board of Education in Indiana - Its Composition, Organization, Operation and Areas of Jurisdiction* (Bloomington, Indiana: Indiana University unpublished doctoral dissertation, 1982).

Kupersmidt, J. B. "Predicting Delinquency and Academic Problems from Childhood Peer Status." Paper presented at the biennial meeting of the Society for Research in Child Development, Detroit, Mich.: April 21–24, 1983.

La Morte, Michael. *School Law: Cases and Concepts*. Englewood Cliffs, N.J.: Prentice-Hall, 1987.

Langer, Ellen J. "The Illusion of Control," in Kahneman, Slovic, and Tversky (eds.).

Language, Literacy, and Instruction in Bilingual Settings: A K-4 Longitudinal Study. Austin, Texas: Southwest Educational Development Laboratory, 1987.

Larkin, Jack. *The Reshaping of Everday Life*. New York: Harper & Row, 1988.

Lau v. Nichols, Supreme Court of the United States, 1974, 414 U.S. 563.

Layton, D. "Science as General Education," *Trends in Education*, January 1972, cited in Goodson.

Leary, James. *Education on Trial*. Pymouth, Mich.: Teachers Central Clearing House, 1981.

Leighton, L. C. (ed.). *The Encyclopedia of Education*. New York: Macmillan, 1971.

Lemon v. Kurtzman, Supreme Court of the United States, 1971, 403 U.S. 602.

Lepper, M. R., D. Greene, and R. E. Nisbett. "Undermining children's intrinsic interest with extrinsic rewards: a test of the overjustification hypothesis," *Journal of Personality and Social Psychology*, Vol. 28, 1973.

Levin, Henry D. "Concepts of Economic Efficiency and Educational Production," in Froomkin (ed.).

Levin, Michael. "Why Not Pragmatism?" *Commentary*, January 1983, pp. 43–47.

Lewis, C. I. *An Analysis of Knowledge and Valuation*. LaSalle, Ill.: Open Court, 1946.

Lieberman, Myron. *Education as a Profession*. Englewood Cliffs, N.J.: Prentice-Hall, 1956.

Lindblom, Charles E. "The Science of 'Muddling Through,'" *Public Administration Review*, Vol. 19 (Spring 1959).

Lipman, Matthew, Ann Margaret Sharp, and Frederick S. Oscanyan. *Philosophy in the Classroom*. Upper Montclair, N.J.: Institute for the Advancement of Philosophy for Children, 1977.

Lutz, Frank W. "Tightening up Loose Coupling in Organizations of Higher Education," *Administrative Science Quarterly*. Vol. 27, 1982.

————, and Aaron Gresson III. "Local School Boards as Political Councils," in *Educational Studies*. Vol. 11, 1980.

Macaulay, Thomas Babington. "Machiavelli," in Charles W. Eliot (ed.) *The Harvard Classics*, Vol. 27. New York: Collier, 1910.

Machiavelli, Niccolo. *Discourses on the First Ten Books of Titus Livius*, Book 1. Trans. Christian E. Detmold. New York: Carlton House, undated, Chap. IV.

Machlup, Fritz. *The Production and Distribution of Knowledge in the United States*. Princeton, N.J.: Princeton U. Press, 1972.

MacIntyre, Alasdair. *After Virtue*. Notre Dame, Ind.: Notre Dame U. Press, 1981.

MacKinney, Loren C. *The Medieval World*. New York: Farrar & Rinehart, 1938.

MacMillan, C. J. B., and James W. Garrison. "An Erotetic Concept of Teaching," *Educational Theory*, Vol. 33, Nos. 3 and 4 (Summer-Fall 1983).

————. "Erotetics Revisited," *Educational Theory*, Vol. 36, No. 4 (Fall 1986).

MacNeill, W. H. *The Rise of the West: A History of the Human Community*. New York: Mentor, 1963.

Mansbridge, Jane J. *Beyond Adversary Democracy*. New York: Basic Books, 1980.

March, James G. *How We Talk and How We Act: Administrative Theory and Administrative Life*. 7th ed. David D. Henry Lecture. Urbana-Champaign: U. of Illinois, 1980.

————, and Johan P. Olsen. *Ambiguity and Choice*. Bergen, Norway: Universitetsforlaget, 1976.

————, and Herbert A. Simon. *Organizations*. New York: Wiley, 1958.

Marvin L. Pickering v. Board of Education of Township High School District 205, Supreme Court of the United States, 1968, 391 U.S. 563.

Marx, Karl. *Criticism of the Gotha Programme*, 1875. In Tucker, Robert C. (ed.), *The Marx-Engels Reader*. 2nd. ed. New York: Norton, 1978, pp. 528–541.

Maslow, Abraham. *Motivation and Personality*. New York: Harper & Row, 1954.

Masnick, George, and Mary Jo Bane. "The Nation's Families: 1960–1990." Cambridge, Mass.: Joint Center for Urban Studies, M.I.T and Harvard U., 1980.

Maynard, Theodore. *The Story of American Catholicism*. New York: Macmillan, 1941.

McCarthy, Mary, and Nelda Cambron. *Public School Law: Teachers' and Students' Rights*. Boston: Allyn & Bacon, 1981.

McClellan, James E. *Toward an Effective Critique of American Education*. Philadelphia: Lippincott, 1968.

McGregor, Douglas M. *The Human Side of the Enterprise*. New York: McGraw-Hill, 1960.

McKeatchie, Wilbert J. "The Decline and Fall of the Laws of Learning," *Educational Researcher*, March 1974.

McKeown, Richard. *Introduction to Aristotle*. New York: Modern Library, 1947.

McMahon, Walter, and Terry Geske, eds. *Financing Education: Overcoming Inefficiency and Inequity*. Urbana, Ill.: U. of Illinois Press, 1982.

McMurray, Foster. "Concepts of Mind and Intelligence in Educational Theory," *Educational Theory*, Vol. 25, No. 3 (Summer 1975).

————. "Retrospective Two," in Bestor (ed.)

McNeil, Linda M. "The Contradictions of Control, Part 1: Administrators and Teachers," *Phi Delta Kappan*, January 1988.

McNeill, W. H. *The Rise of the West: A History of the Human Community*. New York: Mentor, 1965.

Melvin, A. Gordon. *Education: A History*. New York: John Day, 1946.

Mendenhall, Thomas, et al. *Ideas and Institutions in European History*. New York: Holt, 1948.

Merton, Robert K. *Social Theory and Social Structure*. New York: Harcourt, 1976.

————. *Sociological Ambivalence and Other Essays*. New York: Free Press, 1976.

Messick, Samuel. "The Criterion Problem in the Evaluation of Instruction: Assessing Possible, Not Just Intended Outcomes," in Taylor and Cowley (eds.).

Metropolitan Life Foundation. *Metropolitan Life Survey of the American Teacher 1988*. New York: Metropolitan Life Foundation, 1988.

The Metropolitan Life Insurance Company. *The Metropolitan Life Survey of the American Teacher, 1987*. New York: The Metropolitan Life Insurance Company.

Meyer, Herbert. "The Pay-for-Performance Dilemma," *Organizational Dynamics*, Vol. 3, No. 3 (Winter 1975).

Meyer, John W., and Brian Rowan. "Institutionalized Organizations: Formal Structure as Myth and Ceremony," *American Journal of Sociology*, Vol. 83, No. 2 (1977).

————. "The Structure of Educational Organizations," in Baldridge and Deal (eds.).

Michelson, Steven. "The Political Economy of Public School Finance," in Martin Carnoy (ed.). *Schooling in a Corporate Society*. New York: David McKay, 1972.

Middle States Association of Colleges and Schools. *Preferred Wisdom of Elementary Schools: An Anthology of School Philosophies*. Middle States Association of Colleges and Schools, 3624 Market Street, Philadelphia, Pa. 19104.

Mill, John Stuart. *Logic*, in Morton White (ed.).

Milliken v. Bradley, Supreme Court of the United States, 1977, 433 U.S. 267. (Milliken II).

Mischel, Theodore (ed.). *Human Action: Conceptual and Empirical Issues*. New York: Academic Press, 1969.

Moles, O. C. "Trends in Divorce and Effects on Children." Presented at the meeting of the American Academy for the Advancement of Science, Washington, D.C., January 1982.

Monell v. Department of Social Services of City of New York, Supreme Court of the United States, 1978, 436 U.S. 658.

Monks, Robert, and Ernest Prouix. *Legal Basics for Teachers*. Bloomington, Ind.: Phi Delta Kappa Educational Foundation, 1986.

Monroe, Paul. *Source Book of the History of Education for the Greek and Roman Period*. New York: Macmillan, 1939.

Monroe, Will. *Comenius and the Beginning of Educational Reform*. New York: Scribner, 1900.

Moon, Bob. *The "New Math's" Curriculum Controversy: An International Story*. Philadelphia: Falmer Press, 1986.

Moorhead, Paul. *A Short History of the Ancient World*. New York: Appleton-Century-Crofts, 1939.

Morris, Richard, William Greenleaf, and Robert Farrell. *America: A History of the People*. New York: Rand McNally, 1971.

Nagel, Ernest, and James R. Newman. "Goedel's Proof," in Newman (ed.), pp. 1668–1695.

Nasaw, David. *Schooled to Order: A Social History of Public Schooling in the United States*. Oxford, England: Oxford U. Press, 1979.

Nash, Robert, and Russell Agne. "Beyond Marginality: A New Role for Foundations of Education," *Journal of Teacher Education*, Vol. XXXIII, No. 3 (May-June 1982).

National Assessment of Educational Progress, 1984. Princeton, N.J.: Educational Testing Service, under a grant from the Department of Education.

National Center for Education Statistics. *The Conditions of Education*. Washington, D.C.: Government Printing Office, 1985.

The National Commission on Excellence in Education. *A Nation At Risk: The Imperative for Educational Reform*. Washington, D.C.: Superintendent of Documents, U.S. Government Printing Office, 1985.

National Education Association, *Cardinal Principles of Secondary Education*. Washington, D.C.: National Education Association, 1918.

National Governor's Association. *Time for Results: The Governor's 1991 Report on Education*. Washington, D.C.: National Governor's Association, 1986.

Neill, A. S. *Summerhill: A Radical Approach to Child-rearing*. New York: Hart, 1960.

New Jersey v. T.L.O., United States Supreme Court, 1985, 105 S.Ct 733.

Newberg, Norman, and Richard H. DeLone. "Bureaucracy as the Milieu for Educational Change," *Education and Urban Society*, Vol. 13, No. 4 (August 1981).

Newman, James R. (ed.). *The World of Mathematics*. 4 vols. New York: Simon & Schuster, 1956.

Nietzsche, Friedrich. *Beyond Good and Evil*. Trans. Marianne Cowan. Chicago: Gateway, 1955.

Nine-Curt, Judith. "Non-Verbal Communication and English as a Second Language," *B.E.S.L. Reporter*, Vol. 1, No. 1 (January 1975).

Noll, James W. (ed.). *TAKING SIDES: Clashing Views on Controversial Educational Issues*. Guilford, Conn.: Dushkin, 1987.

Nozick, Robert. *Anarchy, State and Utopia*. New York: Basic Books, 1974.

Nunnaly, Jum C. *Psychometric Theory*. New York: McGraw-Hill, 1967.

O'Conner, D. J. *An Introduction to the Philosophy of Education*. London: Routledge & Kegan Paul, 1967.

O'Sullivan, J., and J. Burns. *Medieval Europe*. New York: Crofts, 1946.

Odden, Allen. "State and Federal Pressures for Equity and Efficiency in Education Financing," in McMahon (ed.).

Oklahoma Laws, 1987, Chapter 46 (Oklahoma State title 70, 11–103.3).

Oliker, Michael A. "Review of *Predicting the Behavior of the Educational System*," by Thomas F. Green, *Journal of Thought*, Vol. 18 (Spring 1983).

Oliker, Michael A. "Douglas McGregor's Theory Y and the Structure of Educational Institutions," *Dissertation Abstracts International*, Vol. 37, No. 10, pp. 6158A–6159A.

O'Neil, Robert. *Classrooms in the Crossfire*. Bloomington: Indiana U. Press, 1981.

Ornstein, Allan C., and Daniel U. Levine. *An Introduction to the Foundations of Education*. 3rd ed. Boston: Houghton Mifflin, 1984.

Orth, J., and S.B. Zacariya. "The School and the Single-Parent Student: What Can Schools Do to Help," *Principal*, Vol. 62, No. 1 (1982).

Osterloh, Karl-Heinz. "Intercultural Differences and Communicative Approaches to Foreign Language Teaching in the Third World," *Studies in Second Language Acquisition*, Vol. 3, No. 1 (Fall 1980).

Ostrander, Susan. *Women of the Upper Class*. Philadelphia: Temple U. Press, 1984.

Ouchi, William. *Theory Z: How American Business Can Meet the Japanese Challenge*. Reading, Mass.: Addison-Wesley, 1981.

"Our Eleventh Annual Survey," *The American School Board Journal*, Vol. 176, No. 1 (January 1989), pp. 19–24.

Owen, David. *None of the Above. Behind the Myth of Scholastic Aptitude*. Boston: Houghton Mifflin, 1985.

———. "Recent Textbook Cases and Children's Rights," *Religion and Public Education*, Vol. 15, No. 3 (Summer 1988).

Owens, Robert G. *Organizational Behavior in Education*. Englewood Cliffs, N.J.: Prentice-Hall, 1970.

Ozmon, Howard A., and Samuel M. Craver. *Philosophical Foundations of Education*. Columbus, Ohio: Merrill, 1981.

Page, Ralph C. "Educational Inquiry Supports Its Own Foundations," *Philosophy of Education 1978*. Champaign, Ill.: Philosophy of Education Society, 1978.

Pajak, Edward F. "Schools as Loosely Coupled Organizations," *Educational Forum*, Vol. 44 (November 1979), pp. 83–95.

Parrillo, Vincent. *Strangers to These Shores*. New York: Macmillan, 1985.

Parsons, Talcott. "The School Class as a Social System," *Harvard Educational Review*, Vol. 29 (Fall 1959).

Pascal, R. *The Social Basis of the German Reformation*. London: Watts, 1933.

Passmore, John. "Philosophy," in Edwards (ed.).

———. "Sex Education," *The New Republic*, October 4, 1980.

Pate-Bain, Helen. "A Teacher's Point of View on the Tennessee Master Teacher Plan," *Phi Delta Kappan*, Vol. 64, No. 10 (June 1983).

Patterson, Jerry L., and Theodore J. Czajkowski, "District Needs Assessment: One Avenue to Program Improvement" *Phi Delta Kappan*, Vol. 58, No. 4 (December 1976), pp. 327–329.

Payzant, Thomas. "Making a Difference in the Lives of Children: Educational Leadership in the Year 2000," *Basic Education: Issues, Answers and Facts*, Vol. 2, No. 3 (Spring 1987).

Pendlebury, Shirley. "Teaching: Response and Responsibility," *Educational Theory*, Vol. 36, No. 4 (Fall 1986).

Percell, Caroline. *Understanding Society: An Introduction to Sociology*. New York: Harper & Row, 1987.

Perrow, Charles. *Complex Organizations*. Oakland, N.J.: Scott-Foresman, 1979.

———. "A Short and Glorious History of Organizational Theory," in Shafritz and Whitbeck (eds.),

Peters, R. S. (ed.). *The Concept of Education*. London: Routledge & Kegan Paul, 1967.

——— (ed.). *John Dewey Reconsidered*. London: Routledge & Kegan Paul, 1977.

———, and C. A. Mace. "Psychology," in Edwards (ed.), Vol. 7.

Petrie, Hugh G. "Can Education Find Its Lost Objectives Under the Street Lamp of Behaviorism?" in Ralph A. Smith (ed.).

Pfeffer, Jeffrey, "Management as Symbolic Action: The Creation and Maintainance of Organizational Paradigms" *Research in Organizational Behavior*, Vol. 35. JAI Press, 1981.

———. *Organizations and Organization Theory*. Boston: Pitman, 1982.

———, and Gerald R. Salancik, "Organizational Decision Making as a Political Process: The Case of a University Budget." *Administrative Science Quarterly*, Vol. 19, 1974.

Phillips, Linda M., and Laurence Walker. "Three Views of Language and Their Influence on Instruction in Reading and Writing," *Educational Theory* Vol. 37, No. 2, 1987.

Piaget, Jean. *The Origins of Intelligence in Children*. New York: Norton, 1952.

Pierce v. Society of Sisters, Supreme Court of the United States, 1925 268 U.S. 510.

Pierce, Charles Sanders. "How to Make Our Ideas Clear," in Morton White (ed.).

Pincoffs, Edmund L. "What Can Be Taught?" *Philosophy of Education* 1967.

Plato's Meno, Alexander Sesonske and Noel Fleming (eds.). Belmont, Calif.: Wadsworth, 1965.

Plessy v. Ferguson, Supreme Court of the United States, 1896, 168 U.S. 537.

Polya, George. "How to Solve It," in Newman (ed.), pp. 1980–1992.

Popkewitz, Thomas S. (ed.). *Critical Studies in Teacher Education*. Philadelphia: The Falmer Press, 1987.

———. "The Formation of School Subjects and the Political Context of Schooling" in Popkewitz.

———. "Knowledge and Interest in Curriculum Studies" in Popkewitz.

Popp, Jerome A. "Philosophy of Education and the Education of Teachers," *Philosophy of Education* 1972, pp. 222–229.

Popp, Jerome A. "Practice and Malpractice in Philosophy of Education," *Educational Studies*, Vol. 9, 1978, p. 290.

Power, Edward. *Main Currents in the History of Education*. New York: McGraw-Hill, 1970.

Prakash, Madhu Suri, and Mark Weinstein. "After Virtue: A Quest for Moral Objectivity." Book review. *Educational Theory*, Vol. 32, No. 1 (Winter 1982).

Pratte, Richard. "Public Education and Its Public: The Changing Relationship," *Philosophy of Education*, 1976.

Price, Kingsley. "Philosophy of Education, History of," in Edwards (ed.), Vol. 6.

Proceedings of the American Psychological Association for the Year 1975. *American Psychologist*, Vol. 30, No. 620.

Pruit, Dean G., and Jeffry Z. Rubin. *Social Conflict. Escalation, Stalemate and Settlement*. New York: Random House, 1986.

Putnam, John J. "The Search for Modern Humans," *National Geographic*, Vol. 174, No. 4 (October 1988).

Quinton, Anthony. "Inquiry, Thought and Action: John Dewey's Theory of Knowledge," pp. 1–17, in Peters (ed.), *John Dewey Reconsidered*.

Raiffa, Howard. *The Art and Science of Negotiation*. Cambridge, Mass.: Belknap Press, 1982.

Rankin, J. H., and L. E. Wells. "The Preventive Effects of the Family on Delinquency," in Elmer Johnson (ed.), *Handbook on Crime and Delinquency Prevention*. New York: Greenwood, 1987.

Raup, R. Bruce, George Axtelle, Kenneth Benne, and B. Othaniel Smith. *The Improvement of Practical Intelligence*. New York: Harper, 1950.

Ravitch, Diane. *The Great School Wars: New York City, 1805–1973*. New York: Basic Books, 1974.

Rawls, John. *A Theory of Justice*.

Reagan, Gerald M. "Do Institutions Teach?" *Philosophy of Education 1965*.

Reeves, J. Don. "Toward an Understanding of Schooling: A Model for Teaching Foundations of Education, *Educational Foundations*, No. 1 (Fall 1986).

Reeves, Richard, *American Journey*. New York: Simon & Schuster, 1982.

Resnick, Lauren B. "Learning in School and Out," *Educational Researcher*, December 1987.

Rich, John Martin. "The Role of Philosophy of Education in Educational Policy Studies," *Philosophy of Education 1973*.

Rieff, Phillip. *The Triumph of the Therapeutic. Uses of Faith After Freud*. New York: Harper & Row, 1966.

Robertson, Ian. *Sociology*. 3rd ed. New York: Worth, 1987.

Robinson, Adam, and John Katzman. *Cracking the System: the SAT. The Princeton Review* (New York: Villard Books, 1986).

Roebuck, Janet. *The Shaping of Urban Society*. New York: Scribners, 1947.

Rogers, Anita M., and Diane Guerin. *Conflict Resolution: A Facilitator's Guide* (Philadelphia: The Consortium, 1984).

Rorty, Richard. "Pragmatism and Philosophy," in Baynes et al. (eds.).

Rossow, Lawrence. "Conflicting Directives From Congress and the Courts Put You In the Hot Seat," *American School Board Journal*, Vol. 174, No. 2 (February 1987).

Rothblatt, S. *The Revolution of the Dons*. London: Faber & Faber, 1969.

Rozycki, Edward. G. "The Functional Analysis of Behavior," *Educational Theory*, Vol. 26, No. 3 (Summer 1975).

———. "Hope as Educational Theory: Rejoinder to Wain," *Educational Theory*, Vol. 39, No. 2 (Spring 1989).

———. *Human Behavior: Measurement and Cause. Can there be a science of education?* Ed.D. dissertation, Temple University. Ann Arbor: Xerox University Microfilms, 1974.

———. "Measurability and Educational Concerns," *Educational Theory*, Winter 74.

———. "More on Rewards and Reinforcers," *Ethics*, July 74.

———. "Pain and Anguish: The Need for Corporal Punishment," *Philosophy of Education 1978*.

———. "Policy and Social Contradiction: The Case of Lifelong Learning," *Educational Theory*, Vol. 37, No. 4 (Fall 1987).

———. "Review of *Teaching with Charisma* by Lloyd Duck." *Educational Studies*, Vol. 13, No. 1 (Spring 1982).

———. "Rewards, Reinforcers and Voluntary Behavior," *Ethics*.

———. "From Test to Treatment: Rationales for Intervention," *Foundational Studies*, Vol. 9, No. 1 and 2. Cortland, N.Y.: New York State Foundations of Education Association, 1981.

———. "Values, Rationality and Pluralism: A Plea for Intolerance," *Philosophy of Education 1979*. Proceedings of the Thirty-fifth Annual Meeting of the Philosophy of Education Society. Champaign, Ill.: McKee, 1980.

Rubin, Lillian Breslow. *Worlds of Pain: Life in the Working Class Family*. New York: Basic Books, 1976.

Russell, Bertrand. *A History of Western Philosophy*. New York: Simon & Schuster, 1945.

Rutter, Michael, et al. *Fifteen Thousand Hours*. Cambridge, Mass.: Harvard U. Press, 1979.

Ryan, Kevin, and James M. Cooper. *Those Who Can, Teach*. 4th Ed. Boston: Houghton Mifflin, 1984.

Ryan, William. *Equality*. New York: Vintage, 1982.

Sadker, Myra Pollack, and David Miller Sadker. *Teachers, Schools, and Society*. New York: Random House, 1988.

Saily, Mary. "Learning Remains Elusive for Handicapped Children," *Educational R&D Report*, Vol. 4, No. 4 (Winter 1981–1982).

Samuelson, Paul A., and William D. Nordhaus. *Economics*. New York: McGraw-Hill, 1989.

San Antonio I.S.D. v. Rodriguez, United States Supreme Court, 1973, 411 U.S. I.

Sarason, Seymour B. *The Culture of the School and the Problem of Change*. Boston: Allyn & Bacon, 1971.

Scandura, J. M. *Problem Solving: A Structural/Process Approach with Instructional Implications*. New York: Academic Press, 1977.

Schelling, Thomas C. *The Strategy of Conflict*. Cambridge, Mass.: Harvard U. Press, 1960.

Schleffler, Israel. *The Language of Education*. Springfield, Ill.: Charles C. Thomas, 1960.

Schneider, Frank, and Larry Coutts. "Person Orientation of Male and Female High School Students: To the Personal Educational Disadvantage of Males?" *Sex Roles*, Vol. 13, No. 2 (July 1985).

School Committee of the Town of Boston. *Proceedings of the School Committee of the Town of Boston, Respecting an English Classical School*, June 17, 1820.

School District of Abington Township v. Schempp, United States Supreme Court, 1963, 374 U.S., 203.

Schumacher, E. F. *Small is Beautiful. Economics as if People Mattered*. New York: Harper & Row, 1975.

Schuman, Marvin E. "A letter of thanks to the PFT rank and file," *The PFT Reporter*. Philadelphia: Philadelphia Federation of Teachers, June 1988.

Schwab, Joseph J. "Problems, Topics and Issues," in B. O. Smith (ed.).

Schwartz, Gary E., and David Shapiro (eds.). *Consciousness and Self-Regulation*. Vol. 1. New York: Plenum, 1976.

Scriven, Michael. "The Methodology of Evaluation," Chap. 5 in Taylor and Cowley (eds.).

Selden, Steven. "Curricular Metaphors: From Scientism to Symbolism" *Educational Theory*, Vol. 25, No. 3 (Summer 1975).

Selznick, Philip. "Foundations of the Theory of Organization," in Shafritz and Whitbeck (eds.).

————. *Leadership in Administration: A Sociological Interpretation*. Evanston, Ill.: Row, Peterson, 1957.

Sennett, Richard. *Authority*. New York: Vintage, 1981.

Sergiovanni, John, Martin Burlingame, Fred S. Coombs, and Paul W. Thurston. *Educational Governance and Administration*. Englewood Cliffs, N.J.: Prentice-Hall, 1987.

Shafritz, Jay M., and Albert C. Hyde (eds.). *Classics of Public Administration*. Oak Park, Ill.: Moore, 1978.

Shafritz, Jay M., and Philip H. Whitbeck (eds.). *Classics of Organization Theory*. Oak Park, Ill.: Moore, 1978.

Shalaway, Linda. "For High Scores, Test What You Teach" *Educational R&D Report*, Vol. 5, No. 3. Washington, D.C.: Council for Educational Development and Research, 1982.

Siegel, Harvey. "How 'Practical' Should Philosophy of Education Be," *Educational Studies*, Vol. 12, 1981.

Skinner, B.F. "The Genetic Nature of the Concepts of Stimulus and Response," *The Journal of General Psychology*, Vol. 12, 1935.

————. *Science and Human Behavior*. New York: Free Press, 1953.

Smiles, Samuel. *Happy Homes and the Hearts That Make Them*. Chicago: U.S. Publishing House, 1882.

Smith, B. Othaniel. "Introduction" to *Education and the Structure of Knowledge*. Fifth Annual Phi Delta Kappa Symposium on Educational Research. Chicago: Rand McNally, 1964.

————, and Robert Ennis (eds.). *Language and Concepts in Education*. Chicago: Rand McNally, 1961.

Smith, Charles, and Grady Moorhead. *A Short History of the Ancient World*. New York: Appleton-Century-Crofts, 1939.

Smith, Frank. *Understanding Reading*. New York: Holt, Rinehart & Winston, 1971.

Smith, Kenwyn K. *Groups in Conflict: Prisons in Disguise*. Dubuque, Ia: Kendall/Hunt, 1982.

Smith, Ralph A. (ed.). *Regaining Educational Leadership*. New York: Wiley, 1975.

Snodin, David. *A Mighty Ferment: Britain in the Age of Revolution*. New York: Seabury, 1978.

Soltis, Jonas F. "Philosophy of Education: Retrospect and Prospect," *Philosophy of Education 1975*. Champaign, Ill.: Philosophy of Education Society, 1975.

Sowards, J. Kelley. *Western Civilization to 1660*. New York: St. Martin's Press, 1964.

Sowell, Thomas. *A Conflict of Visions*. New York: Morrow, 1987.

————. *The Economics and Politics of Race: An International Perspective*. New York: William Morrow, 1983.

————. *Ethnic America*. New York: Basic Books, 1981.

————. *Race and Economics*. New York: Longman, 1975.

Spencer, Herbert. *Essays on Education*. New York: Dutton, Everyman's Library, 1963.

Spring, Joel. *American Education: An Introduction to Social and Political Aspects*. New York: Longman, 1985.

————. *The American School 1642–1985*. White Plains, N.Y.: Longman, 1986.

Stake, Robert E. "The Countenance of Educational Evaluation," in Taylor and Cowley (eds.)

Stalker, Douglas Frank. *Deep Structure*. Philadelphia: Philosophical Monographs, 1976.

Stallings, Jane A. "Are We Evaluating What We Value?" *Action in Teacher Education*, Vol. IX, No. 3 (Fall 1987).

Standing Committee on Instruction and Professional Development of the National Education Association. "Teachers for Tomorrow," Washington, D.C., July 1987.

Starr, Kathleen, and Bertram C. Bruce. "Reading Comprehension: More Emphasis Needed," *ASCD Curriculum Update*. Washington, D.C.: Association for Supervision and Curriculum Development, March 1983.

State of North Carolina v. Columbus Christian Academy, C.A. No. 78. Clearinghouse #26 481 A, 5 September 1978.

Steinbeck, John. *East of Eden*. New York: Viking Press, 1952.

Steinmetz, Suzanne, and Murray Strauss. *Violence in the Family*. New York: Harper & Row, 1974.

Stephens, W. Richard, and William Van Til. *Education in American Life*. Boston: Houghton Mifflin, 1972.

Stern, Joyce D. (ed.). *The Condition of Education 1987 Edition*. Statistical Report, Center for Education Statistics. Washington, D.C.: Office of Educational Research and Improvement, U.S. Dept. of Education, 1987.

Stinchcombe, Arthur L. *Constructing Social Theories*. New York: Harcourt, Brace & World, 1968.

Stinchcombe, Arthur L. *Rebellion in a High School*. Chicago: Quandrangle Books, 1964.

Stone, Lawrence. *The Family, Sex, and Marriage in England 1500–1800*. New York: Harper & Row, 1977.

Strahan, Richard, and L. Charles Turner. *The Courts and the Schools*. New York: Longman, 1987.

Strain, John Paul. "Idealism: Clarification of an Educational Philosophy," *Educational Theory*, Vol. 25, No. 3.

Strickland, Charles, and Charles Burgess (ed.). *Health Growth and Heredity: G. Stanley Hall on Natural Education*. New York: Teachers College Press, Columbia U., 1965.

Sullivan v. Meade Independent School District No. 101, U.S. Court of Appeals (8th Cir. 1976).

Susskind, Lawrence, and Jeffrey Cruikshank. *Breaking the Impasse. Consensual Approaches to Resolving Public Disputes*. New York: Basic Books, 1987.

Swann v. Charlotte-Mecklenberg Board of Education, United States Supreme Court, 1971, 402 U.S. 1.

Szasz, Thomas S. *The Manufacture of Madness*. New York: Delta Books, Dell, 1970.

Tanner, Danniel. "Are Reforms Like Swinging Pendulums?" in Herbert Walberg and James Keefe, (eds.), *Rethinking Reform: A Principal's Dilemma*. Reston, Va.: National Association of Secondary School Principals, 1986.

Tanner, Nancy. *On Becoming Human*. New York: Cambridge U. Press, 1981.

Taylor, Charles. *The Explanation of Behavior*. London: Routledge & Kegan Paul, 1964.

Taylor, Peter A., and Doris M. Cowley. *Readings in Curriculum Evaluation*. Dubuque, Ia.: Brown, 1972.

Taylor, Richard. *The Empiricists Locke, Berkeley, Hume*. Garden City, N.Y.: Doubleday, undated.

Teague Ashton, Patricia. "Cross-Cultural Piagetian Research: An experimental perspective," *Harvard Educational Review*, Vol. 45, No. 4 (November 1975).

Thomas Tripp, Rhoda (compiler). *The International Thesaurus of Quotations*. New York: Harper & Row, 1987.

Thomas, M. Donald. "What Is an Effective School?" *The Effective School Report*, Vol. 17, No. 1 (January-February 1989). New York: Kelwyn Press, 1989.

Thomas, William. "To Solve 'The Discipline Problem', Mix Clear Rules with Consistent Consequences," *The American School Boards Journal*, June 1988.

Thompson, John B. *Studies in the Theory of Ideology*. Berkeley: U. of California Press, 1984.

Thorndike Barnhart Junior Dictionary. 7th Ed. New York: Scott-Foresman, 1968.

Thurow, Lester. *Generating Inequality*. New York: Basic Books, 1975.

————. "Education and Economic Equality," *The Public Interest*, No. 28 (Summer 1972).

Times-Mirror. *The People, Press & Politics*. Washington, D.C.: Times-Mirror, 1987.

Tinker v. DesMoines Independent Community School District, United States Supreme Court, 1969, 393 U.S. 503.

Todorov, Tzvetan. *Mikhail Bakhtin. The Dialogical Principle*. Trans. Wlad Godzich. Minneapolis: U. of Minnesota Press, 1984.

Townsend, Robert. *Up the Organization*. New York: Fawcett, 1971.

Tozer, Steven, and Stuart McAninch. "Social Foundations of Education in Historical Perspective," *Educational Foundations*, No. 1 (Fall 1986).

Trammel, Niles. "Radio and Television Broadcasting," *The Encyclopedia Americana*, Vol 23. New York: Americana Corporation, 1962.

Travers, Robert M. W. "Unresolved Issues in Defining Educational Goals," *Educational Theory*, Vol. 37, No. 1 (Winter 1987).

Turner, Frederick Jackson. *The Frontier in American History*. New York: H. Holt, 1920.

Tyack, David (ed.). *Turning Points in American Educational History*. Waltham, Mass.: Blaisdell, 1967.

Tyler, Ralph W. *Basic Principles of Curriculum and Instruction*. Chicago: U. of Chicago Press, 1949.

Tyson-Bernstein, Harriet. *Improving the Quality of Textbooks*. Secaucus, N.J.: Matsushita Foundation, 1987.

U.S. Department of Labor, Bureau of the Census. *Statistical Abstract of the United States: 1988*. Washington, D.C.: U.S. Government Printing Office, 1987.

U.S. Department of Commerce, Bureau of the Census. *Statistical Abstract of the United States 1988*. Washington, D.C.: U.S. Government Printing Office, 1988.

U.S. Department of Labor. *International Comparisons of Manufacturing Productivity and Labor Cost Trends, Preliminary Measures for 1984*. Revised tables, June 10, 1985.

————. "Survey of Current Business," July 1986.

Unitarian Universalist Association of Congregations. "Against Censorship in Public Schools." Boston: Unitarian/Universalist Association, 1988.

United Nations. OECD *National Accounts 1951–80*, Vol. 1, 1982.

————. *National Accounts Statistics: Main Aggregates and Detailed Tables, 1984*.

United States Department of Education. *What Works: Research About Teaching and Learning*. Washington, D.C.: U.S. Government Printing Office, 1986.

Vaughan, William. "Fundamental Value Conflicts in Education: Towards Reconciliation," *Philosophy of Education 1974*, pp. 127–136.

Vellutino, Frank R. "Dyslexia," *Scientific American*, Vol. 256, No. 3 (March 1987).

Veyne, Paul. *A History of Private Life from Pagan Rome to Byzantium*. Cambridge, Mass.: The Belknap Press of Harvard U. Press, 1987.

Von Bertalanffy, Ludwig. *General System Theory*. New York: George Braziller, 1968.

Wachtel, Paul L. "Field Dependence and Psychological Differentiation: Reexamination," *Perceptual and Motor Skills*, Vol. 35 (1972).

Waks, Leonard. *Needs and Needs Assessment: A Conceptual Framework*. Monograph. Philadelphia: Research for Better Schools, 1979.

Wallace v. Jaffree, United States Supreme Court, 1985, 472 U.S. 105 S.Ct, 2479.

Wallerstein, J. S., and J. B. Kelly. "The Effects of Parental Divorce: Experiences of the Child in Later Latency," *American Journal of Orthopsychiatry*, Vol. 46, No. 2 (1982).

Wayson, William W. "The Politics of Violence in School: Doublespeak and Disruptions in Public Confidence," *Phi Delta Kappan*, October 1985.

Weatherley, Richard, and Michael Lipsky. "Street-Level Bureaucrats and Institutional Innovation: Implementing Special Education Reform," *Harvard Educational Review*, Vol. 47, No. 2 (May 1977).

Weaver, Kenneth F. "The Search for Our Ancestors," *National Geographic*, Vol. 168, No. 5 (November 1985).

Webster, Noah. *A Collection of Essays and Fugitive Writings on Moral, Historical and Political Subjects*. Boston: Thomas & Andrews, 1790.

Weick, Karl. "Educational Organizations as Loosely Coupled Systems," *Administrative Science Quarterly*, Vol. 23 (December 1978).

Weimer, Walter B. "Psycholinguistics and Plato's Paradoxes of the *Meno*," *American Psychologist*, January 1973.

———. "Science as Rhetorical Transaction: Toward a Nonjustificational Conception of Rhetoric," *Philosophy and Rhetoric*, Vol. 10, No. 1 (Winter 1977).

Weiss, Michael J. *The Clustering of America*. New York: Harper & Row, 1988.

Westby-Gibson, Dorothy. "Unity and Diversity of our Educational Goals," in *Social Perspectives on Education*. New York: Wiley, 1965, Chap. 5.

Westie, Frank R., and Richard Hummel. "Normative Absolutism vs. Sociological Relativism: An Investigation of Two World Views," *Educational Studies*, Vol. 11 (1980).

Wexler, Philip. *The Sociology of Education: Beyond Equality*. Indianapolis: Bobbs-Merrill, 1976.

White, Karl. "Socioeconomic Status and Academic Achievement." Logan: Exceptional Child Center, UMC 68, Utah State University, undated.

White, Morton. *The Age of Analysis*. New York: Mentor, 1955.

Wiggin, Gladys. *Education and Nationalism*. New York: McGraw-Hill, 1962.

Wiggins, Grant. "11 Suggestions for Reform That Are Radical But Shouldn't Be." Providence, R.I.: Coalition of Essential Schools, Brown U., 1988.

Wilson, Dave. "The Risc Race Is On," *ESD: The Electronic System Design Magazine*, Vol. 18, No. 5 (May 1988).

Wilson, James. *American Government: Institutions and Policies*. Lexington, Mass.: D.C. Heath, 1986.

Wilson, Ron. "Motorola Unveils New Risc Microprocessor Flagship," *Computer Design*, Vol. 27, No. 9 (May 1, 1988).

Wilson, William. *The Declining Significance of Race*. Chicago: U. of Chicago Press, 1978.

———. *The Truly Disadvantaged*. Chicago: U. of Chicago Press, 1988.

Winn, Marie. *The Plug-in Drug: Television, Children and the Family*. New York: Viking, 1977.

Wirth, Louis. "Observations delivered at the World Congress of Sociology, Zurich, Switzerland," September 1950.

Wisconsin v. Yoder, United States Supreme Court, 1972, 406 U.S. 205.

Wise, Arthur. "Why Educational Policies Often Fail: the hyperrationalization hypothesis," *Journal of Curriculum Studies*, Vol. 9, No. 1 (1977).

Witkin, H. A. "Individual Differences in Ease of Perception of Embedded Figures," *Journal of Personality*, Vol. 19 (1950).

————, Donald R. Goodenough, and Philip K. Oltman. "Psychological Differentiation: Current Status," *The Journal of Personality and Social Psychology*, Vol. 37, No. 7 (July 1979).

Wittgenstein, Ludwig. *Philosophische Untersuchungen*. Frankfurt-am-Main: Suhrkamp, 1967.

Wolters, Raymond. *The Burden of Brown*. Knoxville, Tenn.: The U. of Tennessee Press, 1984.

Wood v. Strickland, United States Supreme Court, 1975, 420 U.S. 308.

Woodward, Joan. *Industrial Organization: Theory and Practice*. Reprint. London: Oxford U. Press, 1966.

Wygant v. Jackson Board of Education, United States Supreme Court, 1986, 106 S.Ct. 1842.

Zaleznik, Abraham. "Power and Politics in Organizational Life," in *Harvard Business Review. On Human Relations*.

Zinn, Maxine, and D. Stanley Eitzen. *Diversity in American Families*. New York: Harper & Row, 1987.

Zucker, Lynne G. "Organizations as Institutions," in Bacharach, Samuel B. (ed.).

GLOSSARY

ability - to - pay principle the idea that one's tax burden should be based on ability to support government activities.

absolute benefits benefits that retain their value even as they become commonplace; opposite of positional benefits. Example: knowledge, or anything intrinsically valued.

academies a distinctively American style secondary school chiefly serving the middle class. Most retained Latin in their curriculum, but they also emphasized useful studies such as English, geography, drawing, writing, arithmetic, algebra, and science.

accreditation the recognition that a school meets certain standards. It is done by boards of accreditation who, through tradition or assertion, claim such authority.

affirmative action actions intended to redress the consequences of past discrimination by using sex, race, ethnic background, or national origin as a criteria for hiring, promotion, and so forth.

alternative schooling schooling restructured to adapt to various kinds of at-risk students.

American Federation of Teachers the nation's second largest teacher's union. Established in 1916, the AFT is affiliated with the AFL-CIO—the largest union in the United States.

apprentice historically, an unpaid novice living as a surrogate member of a household where he learned trade or merchant skills from a master craftsman or merchant who provided supervision, training, room, and board.

assault an overt attempt to put another in fear of bodily harm.

assimilation the process of taking in and incorporating as one's own; as in absorbing another population.

at risk a slogan referring to children who are likely to become dropouts or school failures without some sort of special attention.

attractive nuisance the sort of hazard created when, for example, a teacher fails to lock up hazardous chemicals, leaves climbing ropes dangling in the gym, or fails to safeguard children from any similar inducement to harm.

Australopithecus   afarensis (Southern ape of Africa) the oldest hominids yet discovered, dating back 4 million years.

authority the right to make decisions; someone conceded to have such a right.

battery actual physical contact with intent to inflict bodily harm.

behavioral objectives curricular objectives specified in terms of "behavioral" outcomes as these are generally understood within a Behaviorist philosophy.

Behaviorism a philosophy of psychology that holds that only behavior considered to be "directly observable" may be investigated and that theories may use explanations that involve only "directly observable" physical phenomena.

benefit principle of taxation the principle that holds that taxes should be in proportion to the benefits people receive from government.

bioengineering biotechnological research concerned with advances in plant tissue culture, genetic alteration, recombinant DNA techniques—splicing genes from foreign organisms into a plant's genetic material—and similar techniques.

block grants intergovernmental fund transfers that can be used for broadly defined.

board certification a voluntary, privately   sponsored   process through which it is proposed teachers will be "certified." To qualify, candidates must successfully complete a "national teacher entrance assessment process" currently being designed.

board of education an elected or appointed state or local governmental body with specific powers and duties respecting the operation of the public schools.

breadth of consensus a measure of consensus determined by the number of people who agree on an issue.

Broca's area the brain region essential to speech.

career ladder a plan that permits a teacher to be promoted to higher rank as well as to receive increased pay.

Carnegie Forum on Education and the Economy a broad group of business executives, educators, and politicians who are attempting to bring about major reforms of the nation's schools. At present, their major goal is professionalizing teaching.

case law principles of law established by court decisions.

categorical grants intergovernmental fund transfers designated for specific purposes.

Cathedral   Schools schools sponsored by the Bishop and customarily located in or near his palace. By the 1200s they had replaced monasteries as the chief educational institution during the Age of Faith.

chief state school officer the chief executive officer of a state department of education.

choice plans school reform plans permitting parents to select their child's school from the public schools of their district or state. The idea is to apply the principles of the marketplace to public elementary and secondary schools.

citharist Greek specialist teacher who taught music.

collective bargaining a process involving the negotiation of wages and other conditions of employment. Also known as collective negotiations.

collective bargaining the negotiating process that develops the content of school district/teacher contracts. It usually governs wages, hours, and conditions of employment.

College the name given to the hospices, halls, or residences endowed by wealthy individuals for poor scholars. In time, particularly in England, these colleges became centers of university life and teaching.

Committee on Political Education (COPE) The American Federation of Teachers' political action arm. It lobbies, gives campaign contributions to sympathetic candidates, and encourages its membership's political activities.

commodity any item treated as divisible and exchangeable.

competencies movement a curricular philosophy that allows statements about what a person should be able to do to serve as curricular objectives.

conflict a situation arising when one action, or one plan of action, impedes another.

conflict model a model of society which asserts that societies are political arenas in which various groups seek antagonistic goals, and which contends that antagonisms

and conflicts between social institutions and groups are fundamental and unavoidable.

consensus general agreement.

consensus model a model of society that emphasizes the forces and mechanisms that keep societies stable, and that stresses the central importance of common perceptions, values, and morality.

consolidation the merger of school districts.

contributory negligence circumstance in which a victim has contributed to his or her own injury by ignoring instructions or failing to use the safety equipment provided.

corporal punishment the use of physical contact, such as paddling or spanking, for disciplinary purposes.

counterculture affiliations based upon norms and values that contradict the norms and values of the broader culture.

Court Schools schools available to a very limited number of upper class children, that addressed the status and, to some extent, the vocational concerns of aristocratic families during the Age of Faith.

cryptia a sort of war declared on helots by the Spartans once a year.

cultural capital interests and values considered as commodities.

cultural lag a clinging to customs or educational practices that no longer serve the functions that gave them birth.

culture a system of shared meanings, language, customs, values, ideas, and material goods.

DU (discretionary unit) a person or group that controls organizational goals, tasks, or resources.

de facto segregation segregation that results from customs, housing patterns, and racial atti-

tudes rather than segregationist legislation.

de jure segregation segregation that results from legislation or other government action.

defeasible characteristic a characteristic that can be denied even if a normal, practical set (logical sum) of conditions is not denied; for example, honesty.

defensive utility the value of a diploma as a defense against "dropout" status rather than as an instrument to attain a good job.

demography the science of vital and social statistics such as births and deaths in a population.

depth of consensus a measure of consensus determined by the number of additional agreements believed to follow from agreement on an initial issue.

didaskalos the Greek word for teacher.

discriminant a test item by which group differences can be identified.

dissensus lack of agreement; opposite of consensus.

District Power Equalizing Plan state funding equalization scheme designed to ensure that each district has an equal opportunity to obtain funds for schooling provided they make the same effort.

divisible benefits (costs) benefits (costs) that some can have while others can't; opposite of indivisible benefits (costs). Examples are skills, money, taxes.

ESOL (English for Speakers of Other Languages) instruction emphasizing the practical aspects of English usage.

educatio the Latin root of the English word "education." It did not refer to schooling, but to a child's upbringing.

education   deliberate and systematic teaching over a sustained period of time.

effectiveness   a measure of ability to achieve a pursued goal.

efficiency   a measure of the costs of effectiveness, for example, the lower the costs of a given output, the higher the measure of efficiency.

efficiency criteria   efforts to link state aid to greater school efficiency through provisions for tax and expenditure limitation.

elastic   describes a tax base that provides ever-increasing revenues without increasing taxes.

encasement   habits of perception and attitude toward others determined by the power relationships one has with them.

English-First   political enthusiasm that pursues the goal of making English the official language of the United States.

equality of opportunity   the situation in which everyone is *not* guaranteed equal pay or equal status, but does have an equal chance to compete for them.

equifinality   the principle that there are many ways of producing the same results within a system.

equilibrium   a situation in which systemic powers and influences are in a balanced state.

eruditus   the term used to describe a well-schooled Roman child.

ethnic group   a group distinguished by common cultural traditions and a mutual sense of identity, language, religion, and distinctive customs.

exegetical curriculum   curriculum items selected on the basis of an "interpretation" of goal statements.

expectation models   organizational models developed from analysis of expectations of the school.

extrinsic   treated as a means; instrumental. Opposite of intrinsic or final.

Factory image   the school considered as a kind of productive organization.

family   a social organization in which members communicate with one another in terms of their roles as mother, father, husband, wife, grandfather, grandmother, daughter, son, brother, or sister.

Flat Grant Plan   the simplest and most equitable of state fund distribution plans. Here state aid is simply based on the number of students in attendance in each local school district.

formal culture   that level of culture, taught by precept and admonition, which, while explicit, is taken at face value and simply understood to be true, proper or right. It includes both manners and morality.

Foundation Plan   state funding equalization scheme intended to guarantee each district a minimum amount of funding per pupil (the foundation level) based on the local district's property tax rate.

functional prerequisites   the social functions that must be accomplished if a society is to survive. They include subsistence, distribution, reproduction, protection, communication, and socialization.

gender   chromosomally defined differences between males and females.

generic process   of a single type; not involving substantially different processes.

grammatist   Greek specialist teacher who taught reading and writing.

guilds   groups of merchants and craftsmen who carefully regulated commerce and industry. Created for mutual assistance, the defense of free citizens against the nobility, and the furtherance of trade monopoly, guilds came to dominate city life during the Age of Faith.

helots   the serfs who were owned by the government of Sparta and allotted to local landowners.

High Schools   a type of secondary school that developed in the late nineteenth century, the curriculum of which emphasizes "useful and practical studies" such as English composition, the study of "the best" English authors, mathematics, natural philosophy (science), geography, and history.

Holmes Group   a consortium of education deans from about 100 of the nation's major research universities.

Hominid   the human family.

Homo erectus (upright man) dating back about 1.6 million years, the first hominids to walk fully upright.

Homo habilis (man the handy) dating back 2 million years, the earliest known members of our own genus.

Homo sapiens (man the thinker) dating back 300,000 years, modern humans and the archaic forebears who shared their complex brain structure.

horizontal equity   the principle requiring that equals be treated equally. For example, two individuals who live in homes of equal value should pay equal property tax.

human capital human abilities considered as commodities.

humanism a term derived from *studia humanitatis*, the Latin term for studies that empower a human being to express individuality in conduct, speech, and writing.

immersion program type of ESOL program featuring massive doses of English on a nearly continuous basis.

implementation the process of translating directives and policies into specific actions.

implementation models organizational models developed from concerns about implementing policy.

in loco parentis a legal term literally meaning "in place of the parent."

income tax a tax on income.

individualistic model a model of society which states that all of its attributes are ultimately reducible to the relations and actions of particular individuals.

indivisible benefits benefits that no one has if some don't have; opposite of divisible benefits. An example is justice.

informal culture that level of culture, caught rather than taught, which is transparent, is unquestioned, and requires no justification. It includes "correct" postures, tone of voice, and sexual mannerisms.

institution a system of formalized statuses, roles, and norms centered on an important social need.

institutionalization change in organizations from production of celebrated symbolic outcomes to uncelebrated substantial outcomes. *See* Symbolic benefit, or Substantial benefit.

intentional tort action the type of suit based on the allegation that one person has intentionally impaired the rights of another. It usually involves the charge of assault and battery.

internalized socially derived knowledge, values, and behaviors that operate in the background, below the level of conscious awareness.

intrinsic treated as an end in itself; final. The opposite of extrinsic or instrumental.

journeyman the status to which an apprentice was promoted after a number of years of training, typically seven.

Junior High School a secondary school type, developed in the early 1900s for grades 7 and 8 or 7, 8, and 9, which evolved from criticism of the academic inefficiency of the seventh- and eighth-grade classes in traditional elementary schools. In many ways Junior High Schools were virtually indistinguishable from high schools as students moved from class to class and teacher to teacher every period.

Kindergarten (child's garden) schools for young children first developed in the nineteenth century by Friedrich Froebel. They have become increasingly popular in our present century.

latent functions functions that are not intended, or at least not recognized openly.

Latin Grammar School the Roman equivalent of our secondary schools. Schools of the same name were developed during the Renaissance. Devoted to humanistic studies, as well as to the status con-

cerns of a new mercantile elite, these schools remained popular for more than 300 years.

ludus the Roman primary school.

maintenance program type of ESOL program intended to maintain the child's original language and culture while simultaneously introducing English.

manifest functions those functions that are intended and stated openly.

master the status to which a journeyman could be promoted if his masterwork were judged satisfactory in an examination.

merit goods services, like low income housing, considered so socially desirable that the government intervenes in the marketplace to make a certain amount of it available, passing the costs on to taxpayers.

merit pay a system of raises based solely on the quality of a teacher's performance.

merit praise plan a plan that emphasizes rewarding effective teaching with recognition and positive feedback.

Middle Schools secondary schools developed during the 1960s that usually contain grades 6, 7, and 8. Middle schools are tailored to the needs of early adolescents by often including teachers with either elementary or secondary certification on the staff and by being broken down into managerial units of less than a hundred students each. The units are led by a team of teachers who share a common planning time. In some schools they also teach together.

model a metaphor or image together with a theory that carefully lays out the relationships of part to whole, or subprocess to process.

Monastery Schools schools maintained by monasteries which were operating in the Benedictine tradition during the Age of Faith.

Monitorial Schools charity schools initiated by the Englishman Andrew Bell (1753–1832), and further developed by Joseph Lancaster (1778–1838). They made use of a hierarchy of pupil "monitors" to teach large numbers of less advanced students. This was accomplished through a systematic mass process based on the division of labor characteristic of factories.

monochronism dealing with people one at a time in social situations.

monocratic controlled by one person or one group of people.

Municipal or Town Schools Age of Faith schools sponsored by municipal authorities rather than the Church. They were originally concerned with providing the children of the town's upper classes with a status-related, Latin Grammar type of literary education similar to that offered in Cathedral and Monastery Schools.

National Council for Accreditation of Teacher Education a private, nonprofit organization that accredits approximately 550 of the nation's 1,276 teacher-education programs.

National Education Association the nation's largest teacher's union. Founded in 1857, the NEA has over 1.7 million members comprising elementary and secondary school teachers, colleges and university professors, administrators, principals, and counselors, making it almost three times larger than the American Federation of Teachers.

negligence conduct that falls below an acceptable standard of care and results in an injury.

normal school type of teacher training school first developed in the nineteenth century.

open system a system influenced by changes in its basic environment, or in other systems.

overhead organizational costs of coordination and support not directly varying with product outcomes.

paedotribe Greek specialist teacher who taught gymnastics.

pedagogue commonly a slave, though sometimes a freedman, entrusted with a child's physical safety and moral development in ancient Greece and, later, Rome.

pluralism the recognition of more than one ultimate principle.

Political Action Committee for Education (PACE) the National Education Association's political action arm. It seeks to influence the outcomes of national elections through campaign contributions to candidates and to encourage political involvement on the part of the membership.

polychronism simultaneously dealing with as many as five persons at a time in social situations.

positional benefits benefits whose value increases with their scarcity; opposite of absolute benefits. An example is wealth.

power the control of resources.

powerholder someone who controls resources.

premise-setting the formation, generally unconscious, of informal cultural norms for rationales.

principle of correspondence the principle stating that schooling conforms to the social structure, social values, and norms of the host society.

professional sanctions a tactic once used by the NEA in hopes that it would prevent the need for strikes. It involved publishing lists identifying as unprofessional places to work school districts that refused to reach agreements with NEA locals.

progressive education a school reform movement, greatly influenced by John Dewey, that placed great value on scientific knowledge, technological expertise, and well-designed bureaucracies. The movement encompassed two contradictory elements—one promoting the dignity of the individual and the other embracing social efficiency.

progressive era a late nineteenth- and early twentieth-century period of multifaceted reform sparked by a diverse coalition of social reformers who were convinced that American society could be improved, though they disagreed on how that could be accomplished.

progressive tax a tax based on one's ability to pay.

property tax a tax on real estate.

proximate cause concept regarding alleged negligent conduct necessitating a causal connection to the injury incurred. In addition, an actual loss or injury must have been sustained.

pure accidents the sort of incidents that can occur with the best of supervision.

race a conceptual device used to classify local variations of a single species into subdivisions based on genetically inherited physical features. In human beings, skin color, eye color, hair type, the shape of facial features, the roundness of the skull, blood type, and the measurement of various body parts have all been considerations.

rank a sorting of items into lesser, equal, and greater in some respect.

Ratio Studiorum issued in final form by the Jesuits in 1599, this program of study spelled out a standardized curriculum as well as classroom methods and management. The curriculum defined included the classics, math, cosmology, geography, rhetoric, good manners, and Holy Scripture.

rationale a narrative accepted as a justification for decisions.

reciprocity agreements interstate agreements for honoring one another's teaching certificates.

regional school agencies the intermediate level of school governance that functions between the state department of education and the local school districts and whose scope of authority is defined by state law.

regressive tax any tax by which the wealthy pay a smaller percentage of their income in taxes than those who can least afford it. *See* Ability-to-pay principle.

resources skills, attitudes, wealth, charisma, influence, knowledge, and so forth; in general, any item that can support a task.

revenue resilience economic state in which taxes are elastic in periods of prosperity, increasing in yield faster than the economy, but also inelastic during a recession, decreasing in yield little if at all even if the recession is severe.

RISC Reduced Instruction Set Computing

Scholasticism the term applied to a wide variety of philosophical studies guided by Aristotelian logic, but dominated by theology.

school code the common name for the body of state legislation affecting schools.

school district the basic administrative unit of American public schooling which is directed by an elected or appointed board and functions within a scope of authority defined by state law.

schooling formalized education usually accomplished by specialists, and commonly taking place in buildings specifically set aside for instruction.

Schools of Rhetoric the Roman equivalent of modern higher education.

seven liberal arts derived from the Greeks and further defined by the Romans, a program of study divided into the Trivium, composed of grammar, rhetoric and logic, and the Quadrivium, consisting of arithmetic, music, geometry, and astronomy.

sexuality the cultural expression of gender consisting of social roles, man or woman, boy or girl, that are learned rather than biologically inherited.

social class a category of people with roughly equal social status.

social constructionist theory the theory that knowledge is constructed from the concerns and activities of humans and not a matter of some abstract relation between language and an extrahuman reality.

social control the patterned and systematic ways in which members of a society are guided and restrained so that they act in predictable and desired ways.

social status rank or social position.

socialization the process of cultural transmission.

society a group of humans occupying a common territory and accepting common political authority, sharing language, customs, values, ideas, and material goods that reflect a way of life.

socioeducational system the interrelated, interdependent relationship of the family, peers, the school, and socioeconomic factors, as well as ethnic, sexual, and racial factors which educate all of us.

Sophists private teachers who went from city to city in ancient Greece selling a form of higher education.

sovereign immunity a legal precedent based on the ancient common law legal notion that "the King can do no wrong." It is used to grant immunity to government agencies from tort liability.

spurious correlation mistaken belief that two things occurring together indicates that one causes the other.

stakeholder someone who receives benefits or suffers costs in a situation.

state certification a process of teacher licensure set up and administered by state education authorities. Not to be confused with board certification.

statute law law established through legislation.

Studium Generale the term used to describe the first universities of Western Europe which evolved from Cathedral or Town Schools beginning in the 1100s.

subculture social not differentiated enough to constitute a separate culture. Subcultures possess their own common traditions, mutual sense of identity, and distinctive customs that often reflect age groups, occupational specializations, religious affiliations, social stratification, ethnicity, and race.

substantial benefit (or cost) something recognized as a benefit (or cost) across many communities.

summative causation a technical conception of causation on the basis of which cause can be denied only if the combination (the logical sum) of defining conditions is denied.

superintendent of schools the chief executive officer of a school district. He or she advises the school board, acts on their behalf, and is responsible for the day-to-day functioning of the district.

symbolic benefit (or cost) something recognized as a benefit (or cost) only within a specific community.

system a set of mutually interdependent items.

taxonomy a system of classification.

technical culture that level of culture, taught systematically by experts, which is explicit, logically developed, and justified in terms of effectiveness. It includes activities like designing satellites, solving equations, or building a car.

Temple image the school considered as a kind of moral community.

tenure established by legislation to protect teachers from yielding to political preferences and to guarantee to each teacher employment after a long period of satisfactory service regardless of politics or the likes or dislikes of those charged with the administration of school affairs.

tort liability laws providing that an individual is entitled to compensation for harm caused them by the unreasonable conduct of another.

Town Meeting image the school considered as a kind of political arena.

transitional program type of ESOL program providing non-English speaking students with the opportunity to study basic subjects in their native language while they learn English through special instruction.

tuition tax credits the idea that parents should be given a tuition tax credit equal to either all or a portion of their children's private school tuition.

tutor teachers privately employed by upper class Roman families.

underclass a group occupying an inferior position within a culture, isolated from the social mainstream and confined by custom and prejudice to very limited opportunities. This status is usually assigned on the basis of ethnicity, race, or religion.

Universitas Latin term, meaning "corporation," which became the popular name for the *Studium Generale*.

value-added tax (VAT) a tax similar to the retail sales tax. It is applied only to the difference between a firm's sales and the cost of material and supplies used to produce the item.

vertical equity principle that a wealthy individual should pay more taxes than a poor one for each to bear a fair portion of public costs. Taxes of this type are called "progressive."

voucher plans school reform plans that permit the inclusion of private schools in the choice pool. In their purest form, voucher plans would completely dismantle the present system of publicly operated schools. Instead, governments would require a minimum level of schooling that would be financed by providing parents with vouchers redeemable for a specific sum at any "approved" school.

wealth the total value of what is owned.

Weighted Student Plan a common method of distributing state funds to local districts based on the special characteristics of the children attending school in that district. Children from impoverished homes, those with handicaps, those who require bilingual services, or those enrolled in vocational education programs, for example, are worth more in state funds.

zero correlation, law of the instrumental value of a commodity, for example, a diploma, is zero when no one has it, or when everyone has it. At these extremes, it can correlate with nothing.